bubble

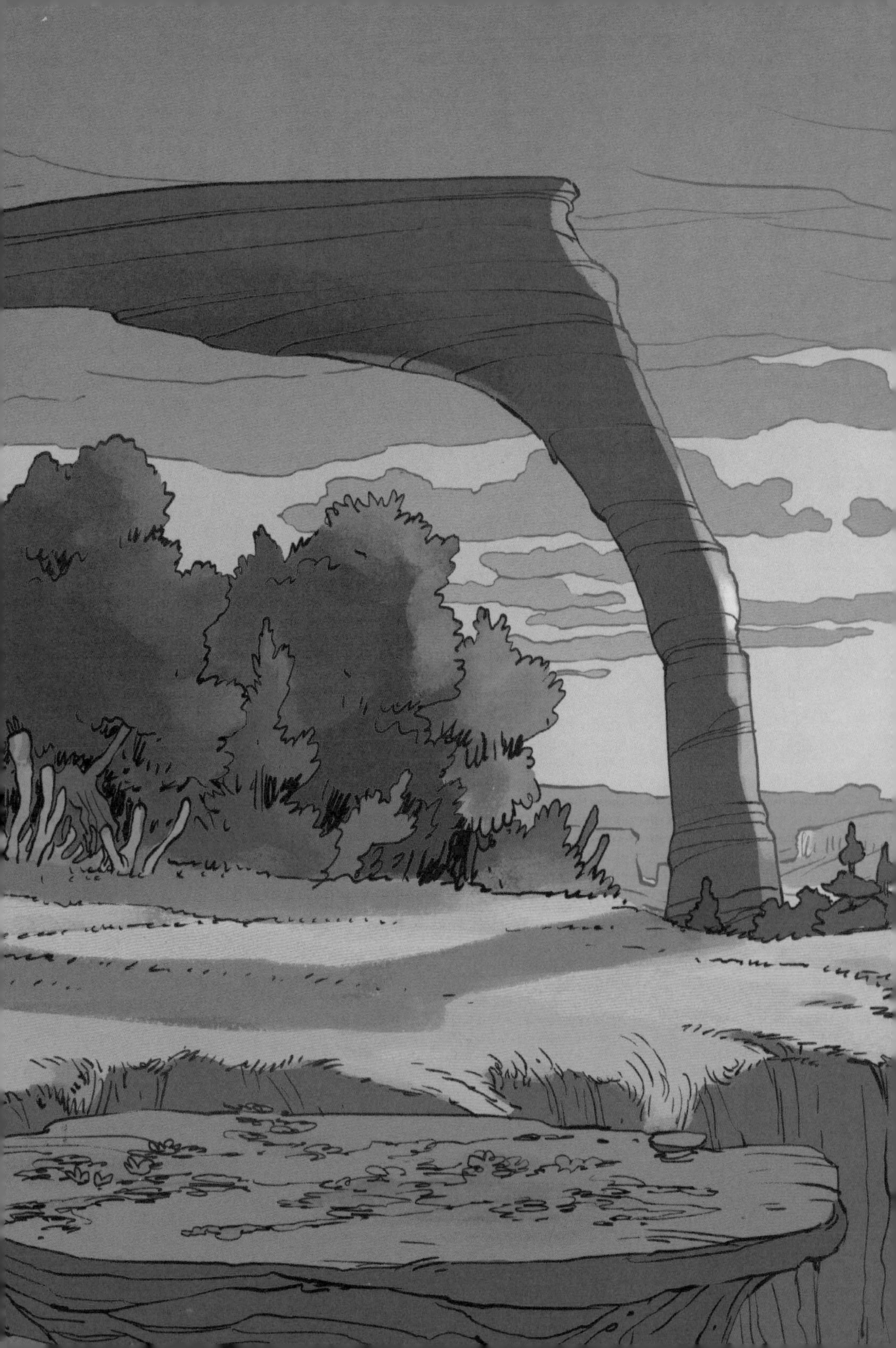

bubble

created by **JORDAN MORRIS**
written by **JORDAN MORRIS** and **SARAH MORGAN**
adapted by **TONY CLIFF, JORDAN MORRIS,**
and **SARAH MORGAN**
color by **NATALIE RIESS**

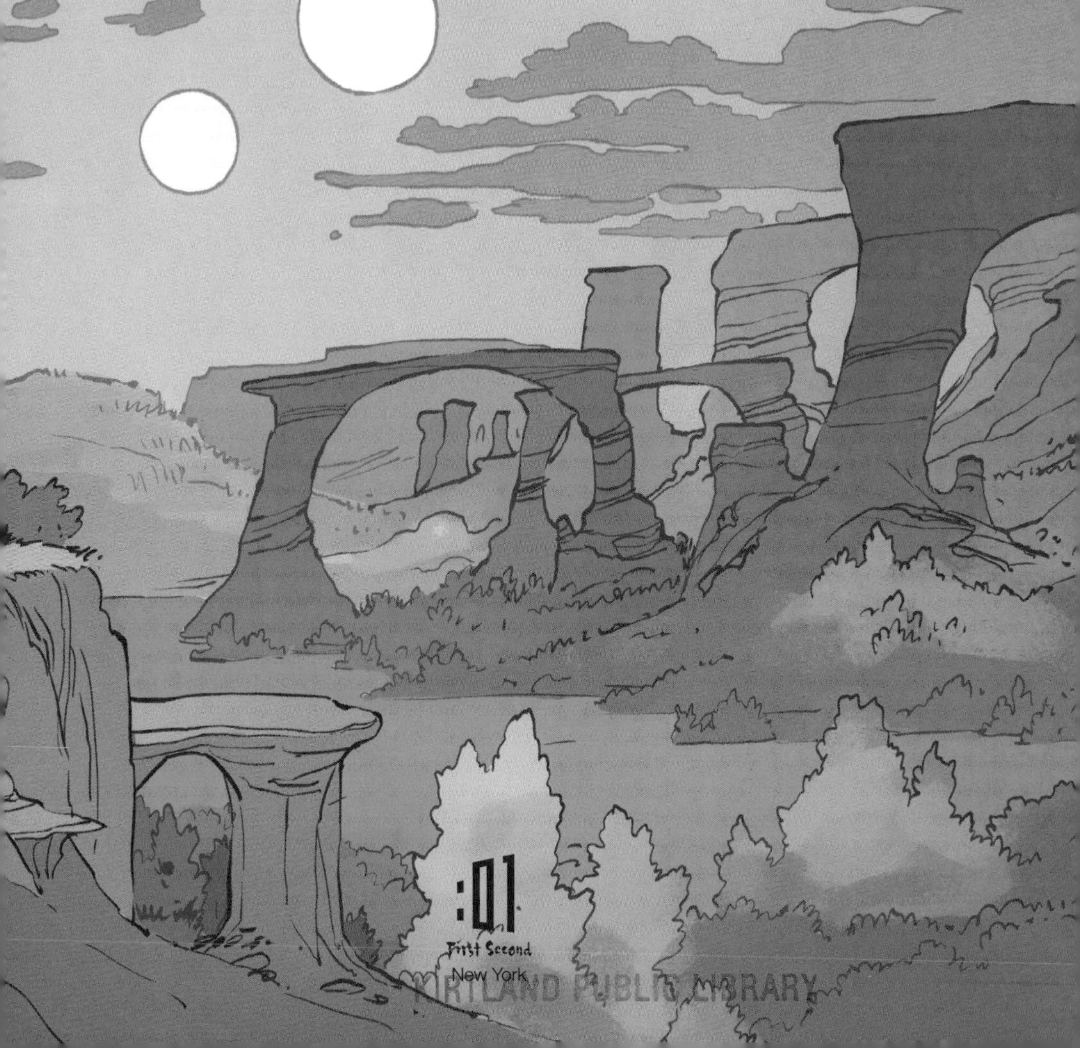

:01
First Second
New York

:01

First Second

Published by First Second • First Second is an imprint of Roaring Brook Press, a division of Holtzbrinck Publishing Holdings Limited Partnership • 120 Broadway, New York, NY 10271 • firstsecondbooks.com Text © 2021 by Jordan Morris and Maximum Fun, Inc. • Illustrations © 2021 by Tony Cliff • All rights reserved • Library of Congress Control Number: 2020919578 • Our books may be purchased in bulk for promotional, educational, or business use. Please contact your local bookseller or the Macmillan Corporate and Premium Sales Department at (800) 221-7945 ext. 5442 or by email at MacmillanSpecialMarkets@ macmillan.com. ⓒ First edition, 2021 • Edited by Calista Brill and Alison Wilgus • Cover design by Kirk Benshoff • Interior book design by Sunny Lee • Color by Natalie Riess • Printed in China • Illustrated using a combination of traditional and digital techniques. • ISBN 978-1-250-24556-4 (paperback) • 10 9 8 7 6 5 4 3 2 1 • ISBN 978-1-250-24555-7 (hardcover) • 10 9 8 7 6 5 4 3 2 1 • Don't miss your next favorite book from First Second! For the latest updates go to firstsecondnewsletter.com and sign up for our enewsletter.

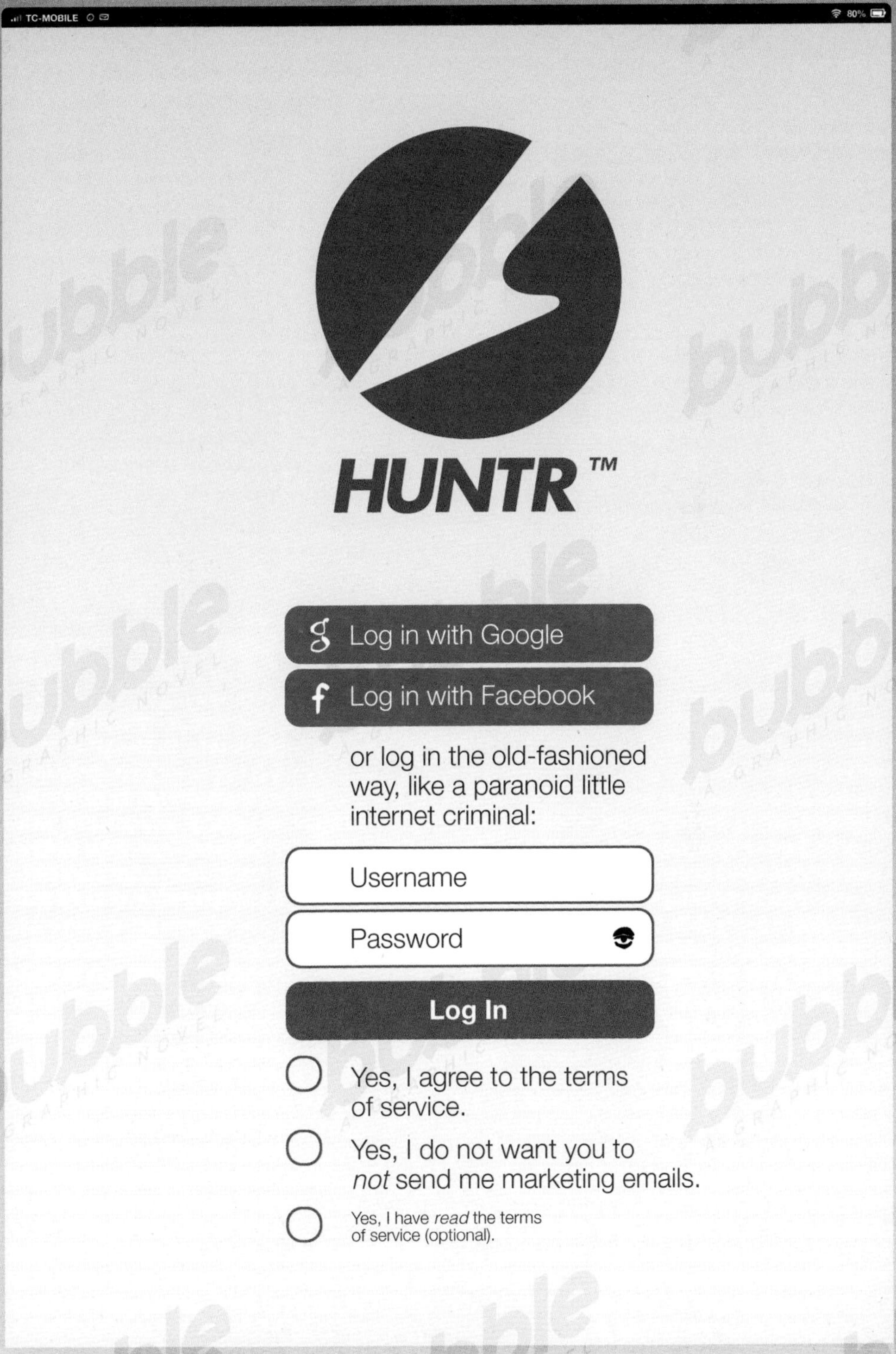
TC-MOBILE
80%
HUNTR ™
Log in with Google
Log in with Facebook
or log in the old-fashioned way, like a paranoid little internet criminal:
Username
Password
Log In
Yes, I agree to the terms of service.
Yes, I do not want you to *not* send me marketing emails.
Yes, I have *read* the terms of service (optional).

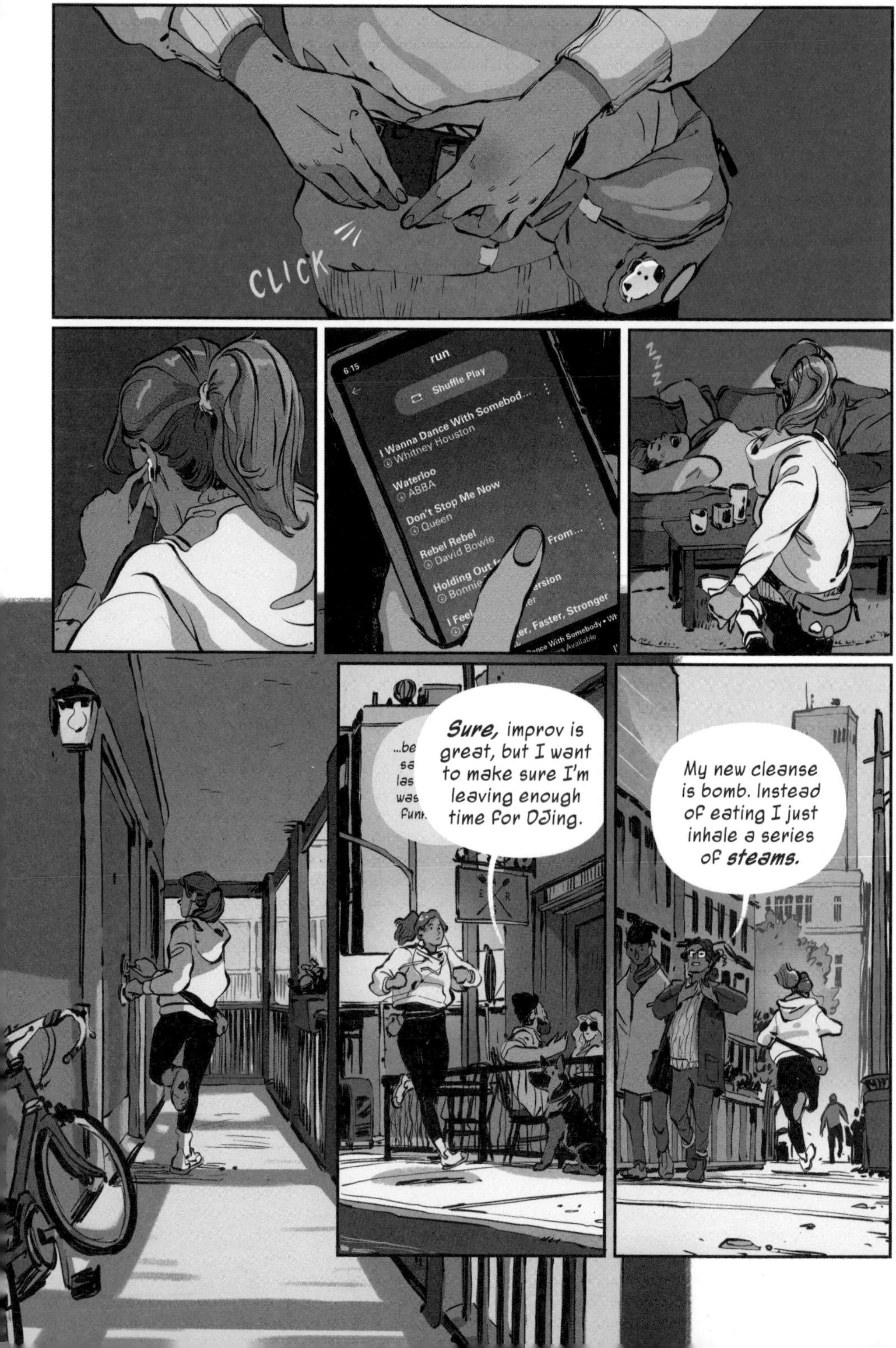
CLICK
6:15
run
Shuffle Play
I Wanna Dance With Somebod...
Whitney Houston
Waterloo
ABBA
Don't Stop Me Now
Queen
Rebel Rebel
David Bowie
ZZZ
Sure, improv is great, but I want to make sure I'm leaving enough time for DJing.
My new cleanse is bomb. Instead of eating I just inhale a series of steams.

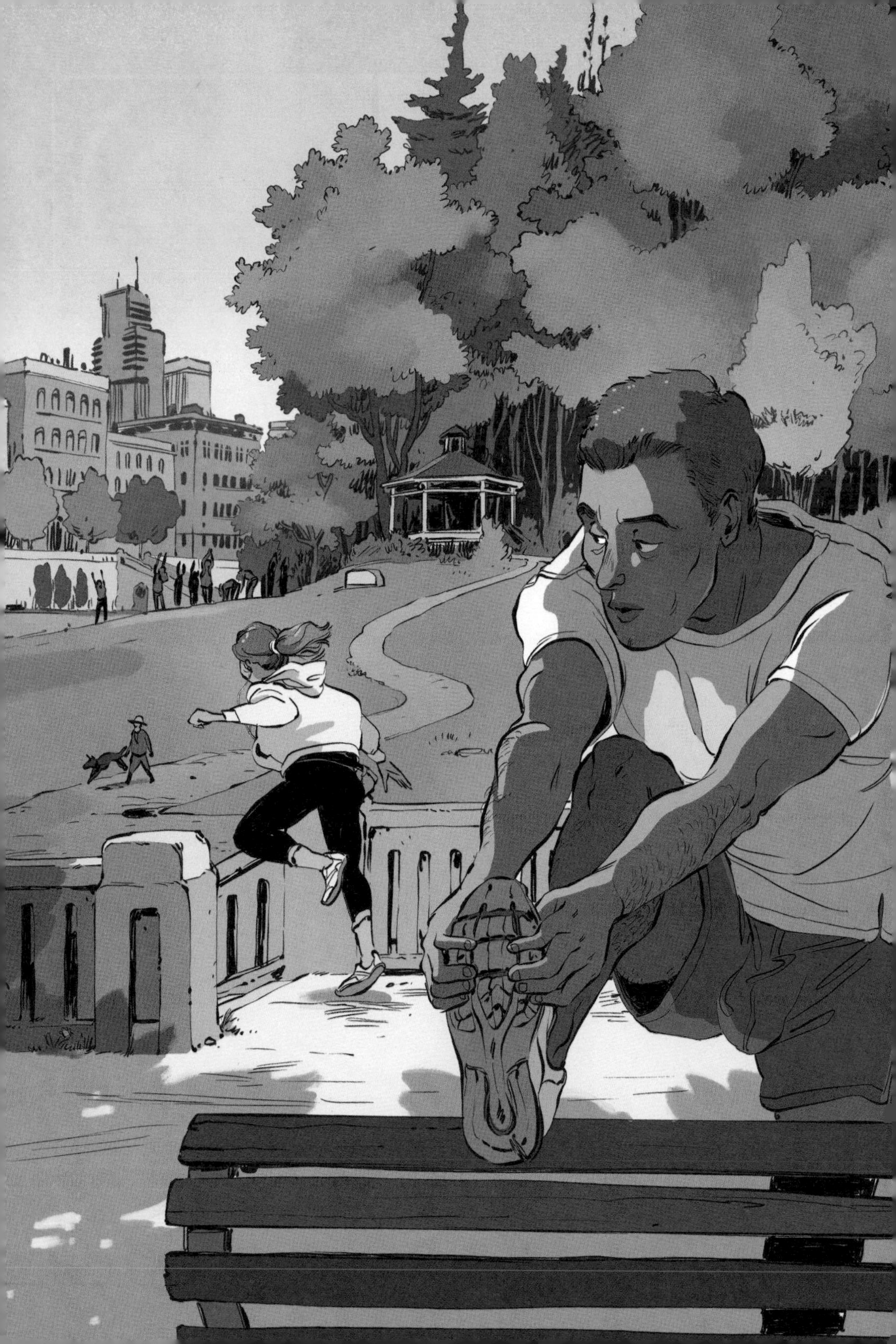

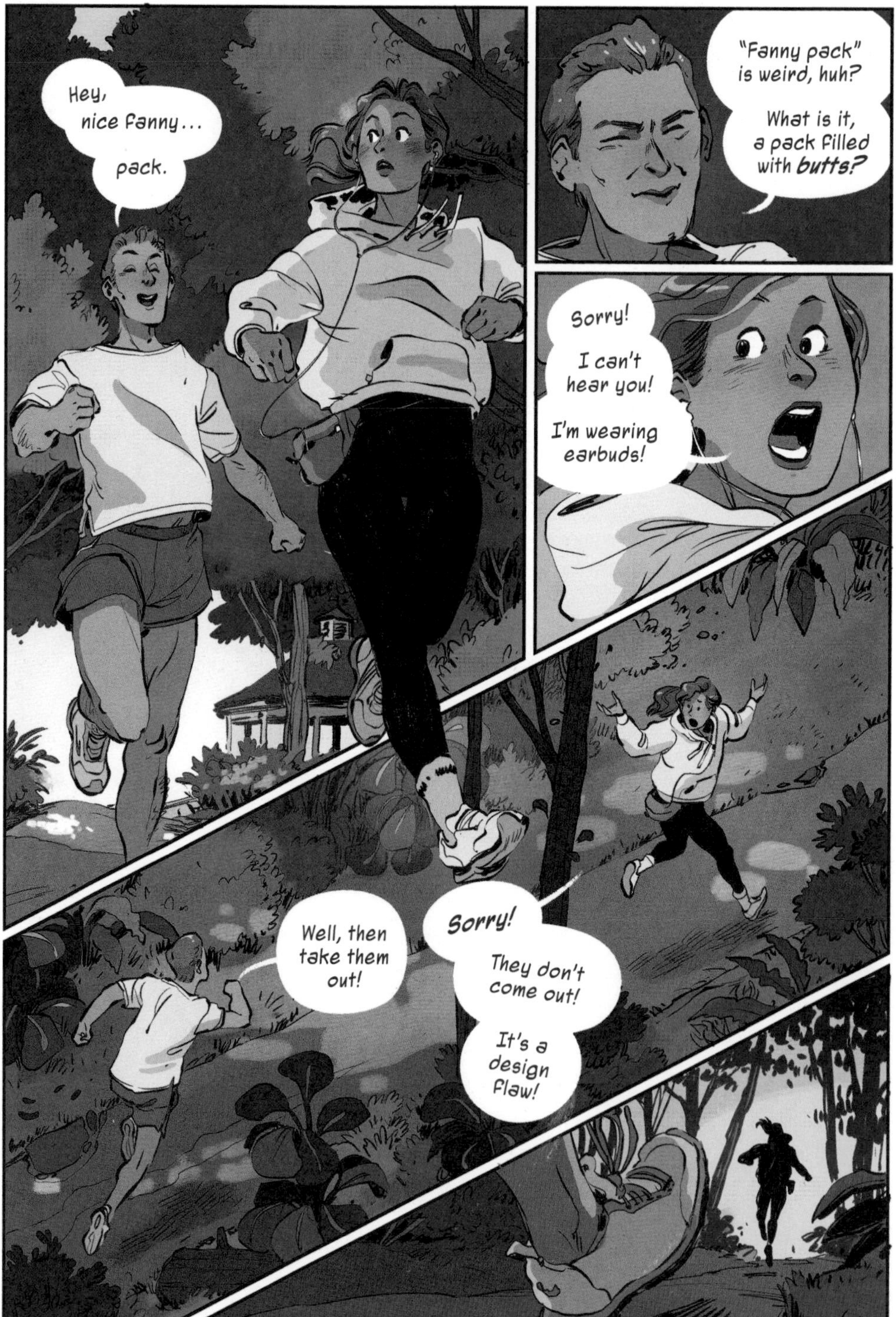

Hey, nice fanny... pack.
"Fanny pack" is weird, huh?
What is it, a pack filled with ***butts?***
Sorry!
I can't hear you!
I'm wearing earbuds!
Well, then take them out!
Sorry!
They don't come out!
It's a design flaw!

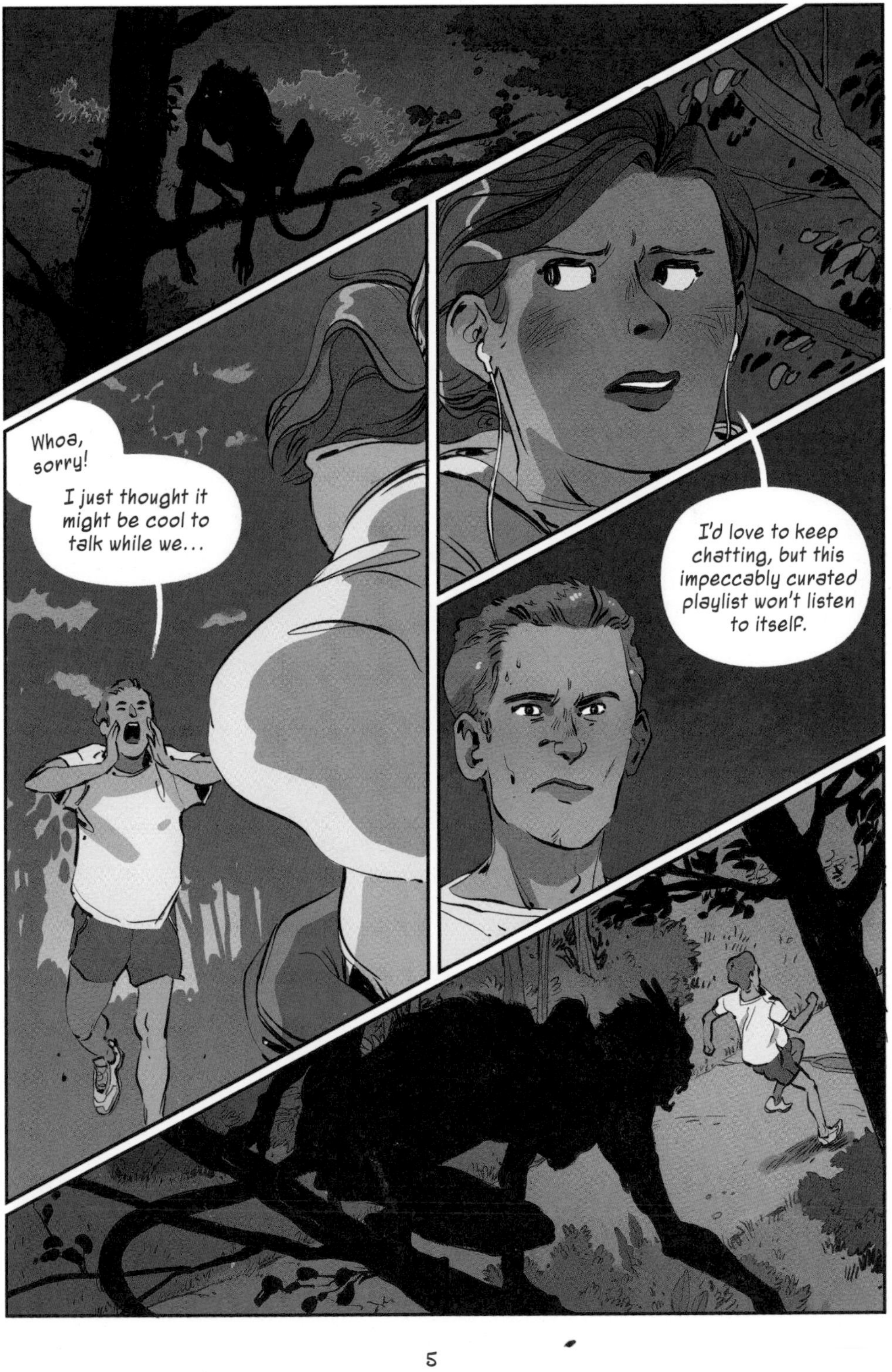
Whoa, sorry!
I just thought it might be cool to talk while we…
I'd love to keep chatting, but this impeccably curated playlist won't listen to itself.

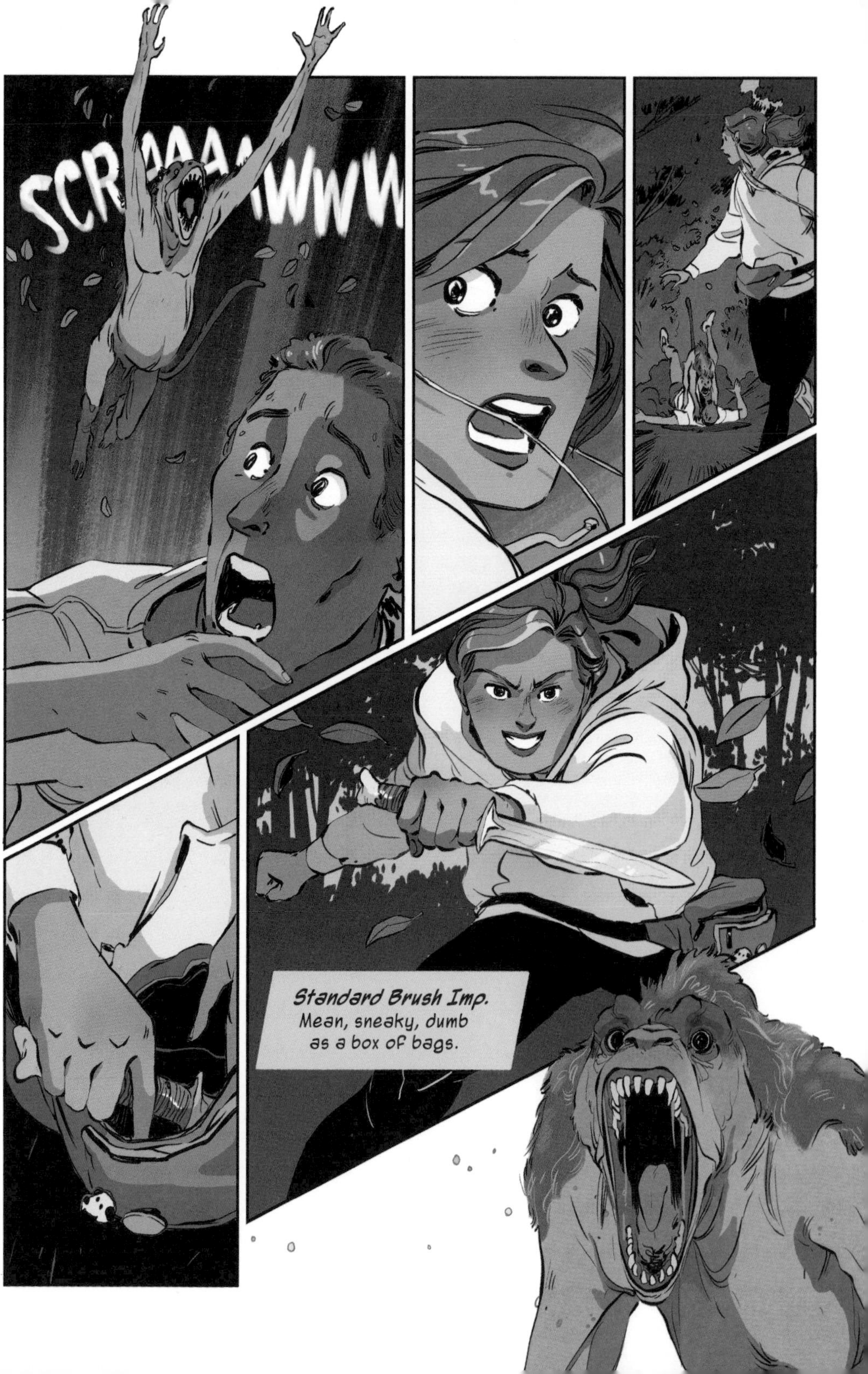
SCRAAAAWWWW
Standard Brush Imp.
Mean, sneaky, dumb
as a box of bags.

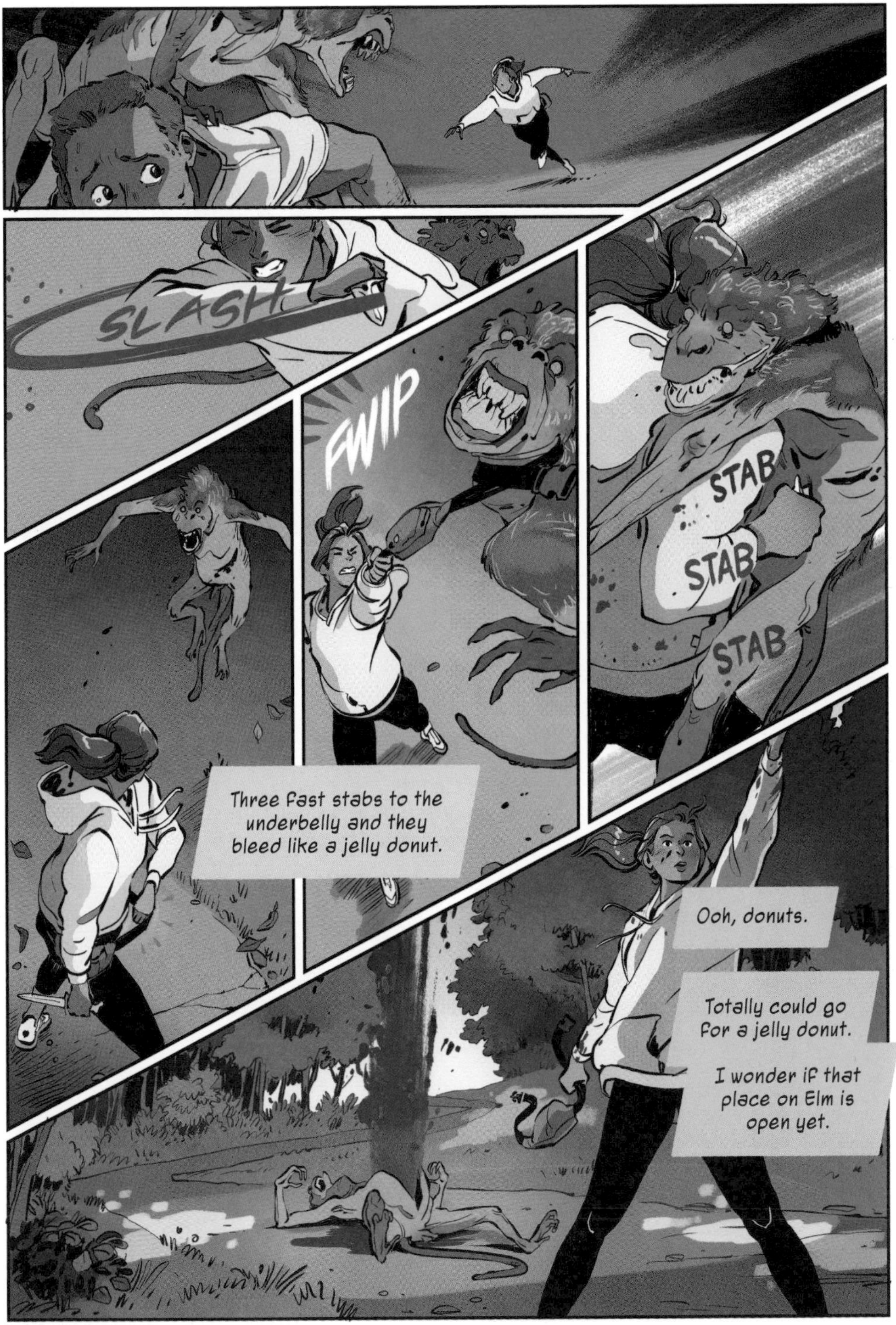
SLASH
FWIP
STAB
STAB
STAB
Three fast stabs to the underbelly and they bleed like a jelly donut.
Ooh, donuts.
Totally could go for a jelly donut.
I wonder if that place on Elm is open yet.

Wow! *Thanks!*

Hey, if you want to keep chillin' I know a *great* little brunch plac—

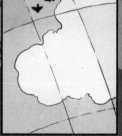

BZZT

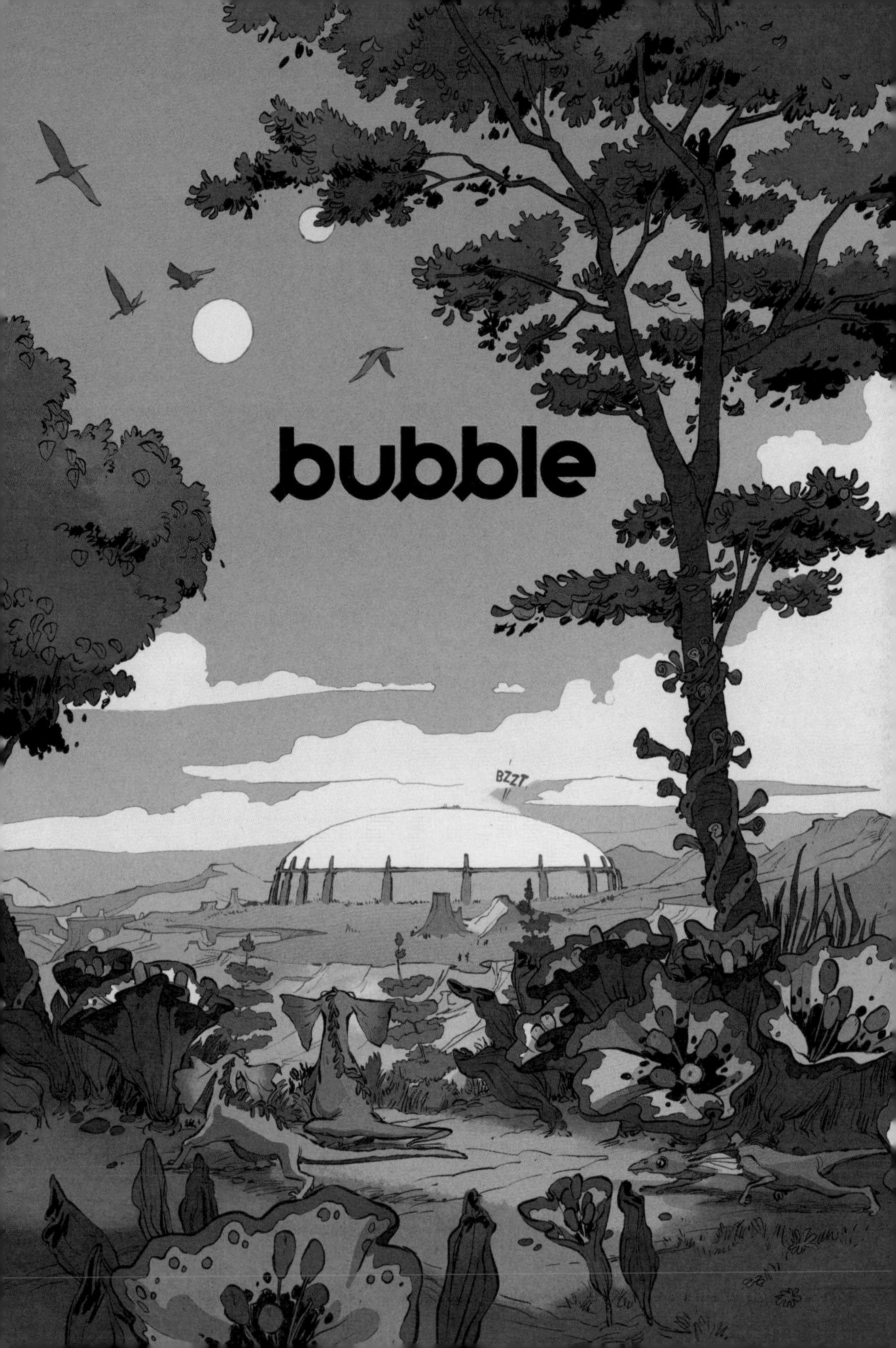
bubble
BZZT

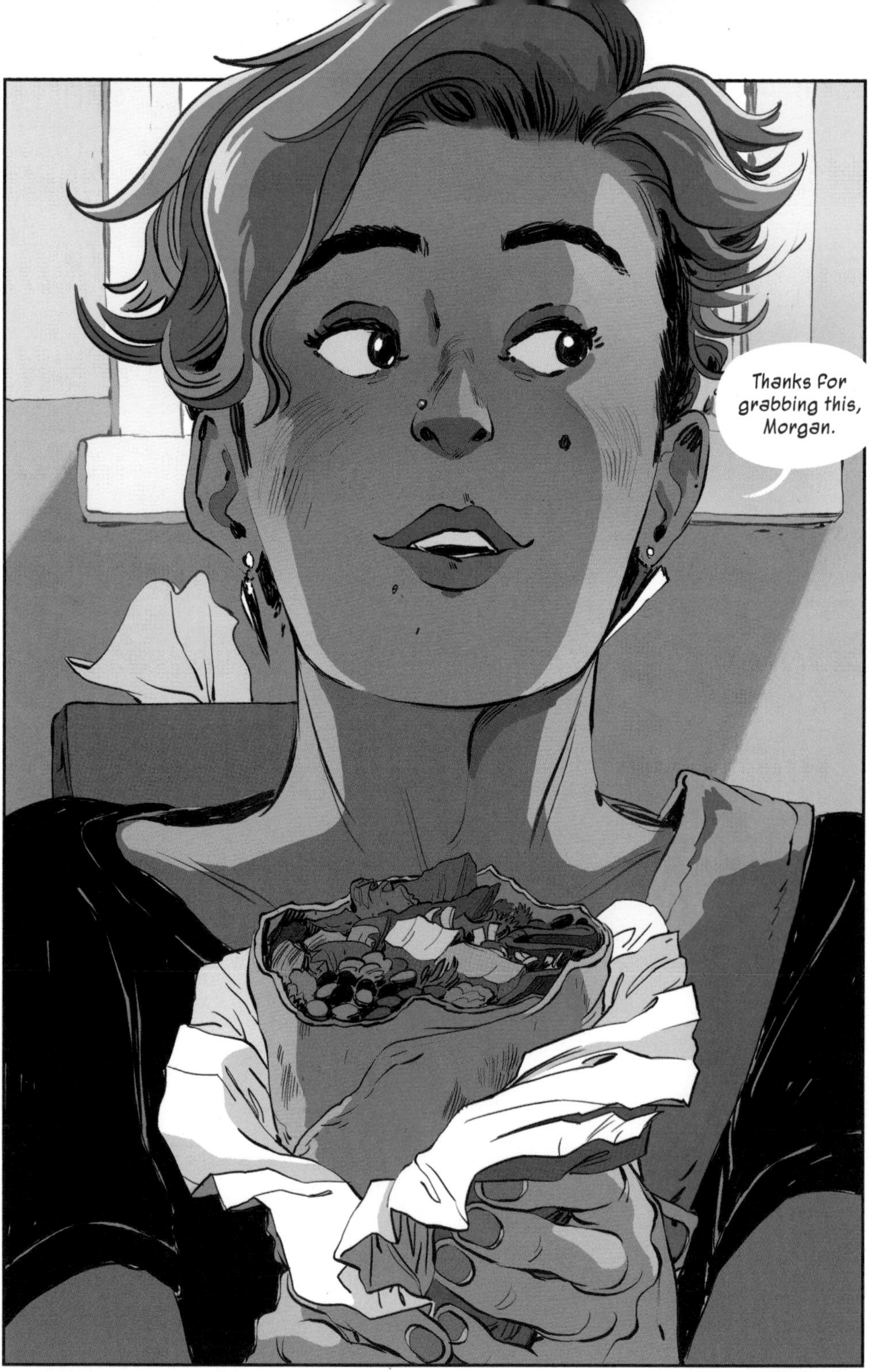
Thanks for grabbing this, Morgan.

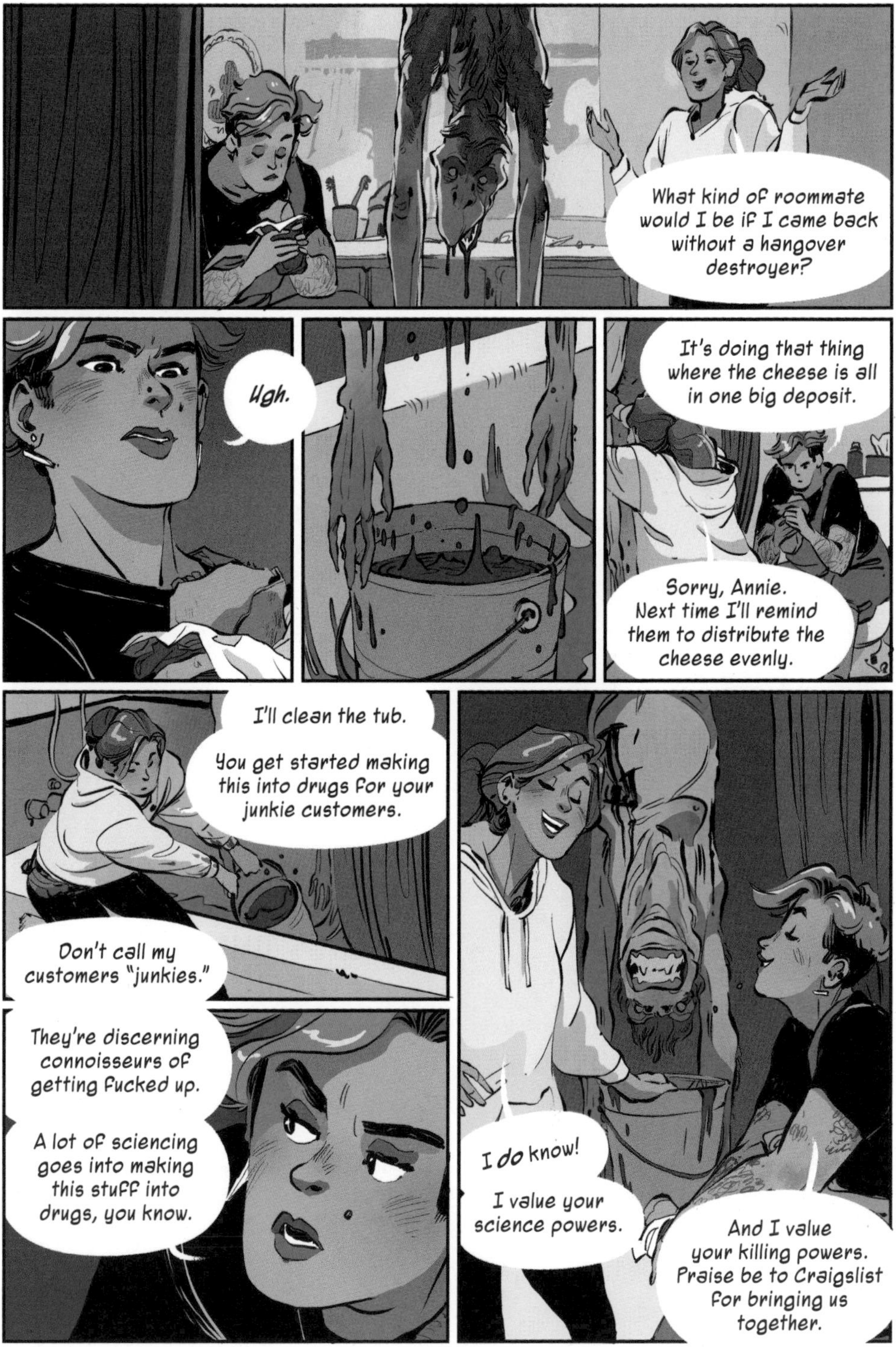
What kind of roommate would I be if I came back without a hangover destroyer?
Ugh.
It's doing that thing where the cheese is all in one big deposit.
Sorry, Annie. Next time I'll remind them to distribute the cheese evenly.
I'll clean the tub.
You get started making this into drugs for your junkie customers.
Don't call my customers "junkies."
They're discerning connoisseurs of getting fucked up.
A lot of sciencing goes into making this stuff into drugs, you know.
I *do* know!
I value your science powers.
And I value your killing powers. Praise be to Craigslist for bringing us together.

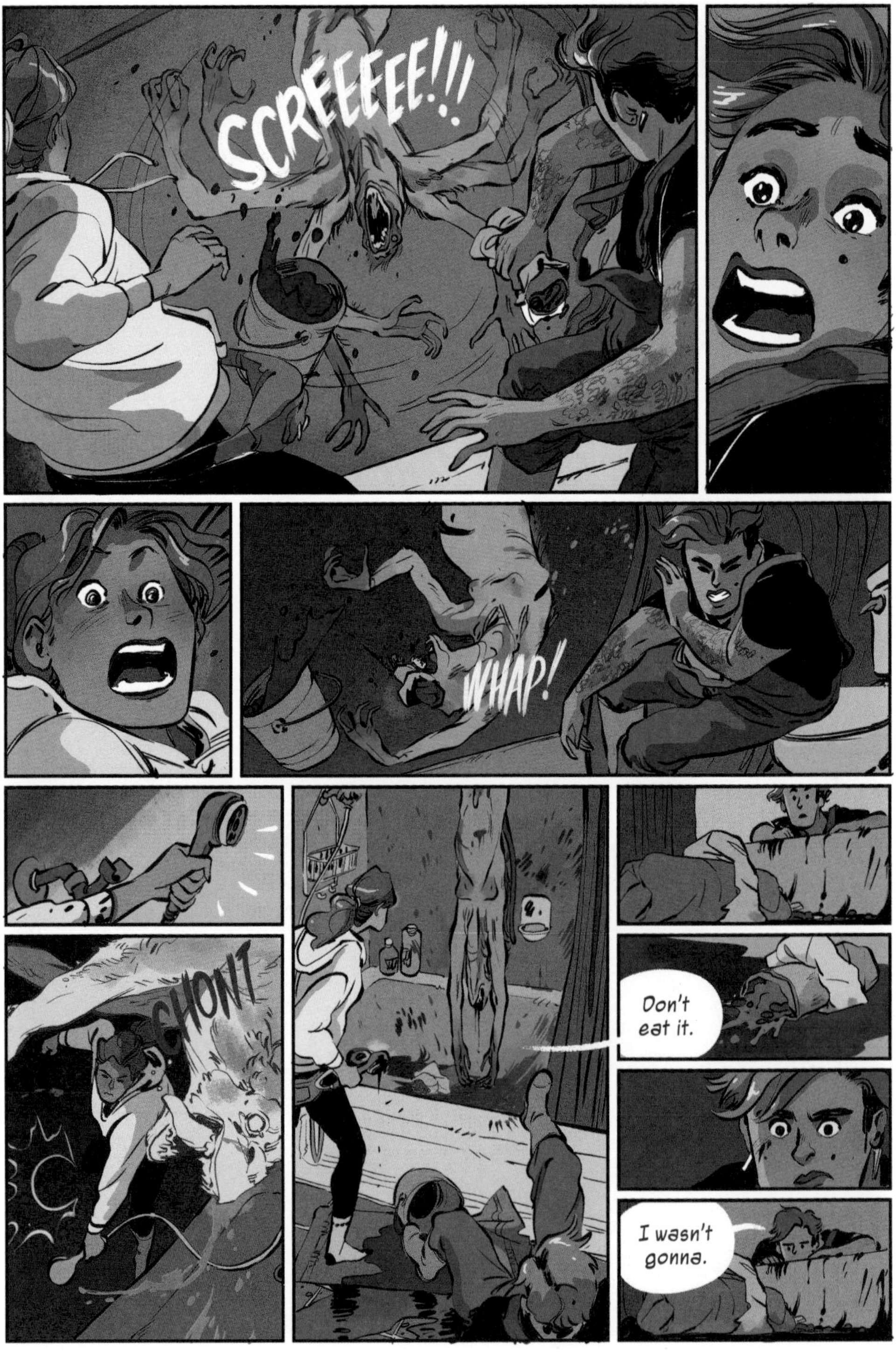
SCREEEEEE!!!
WHAP!
CHONT
Don't eat it.
I wasn't gonna.

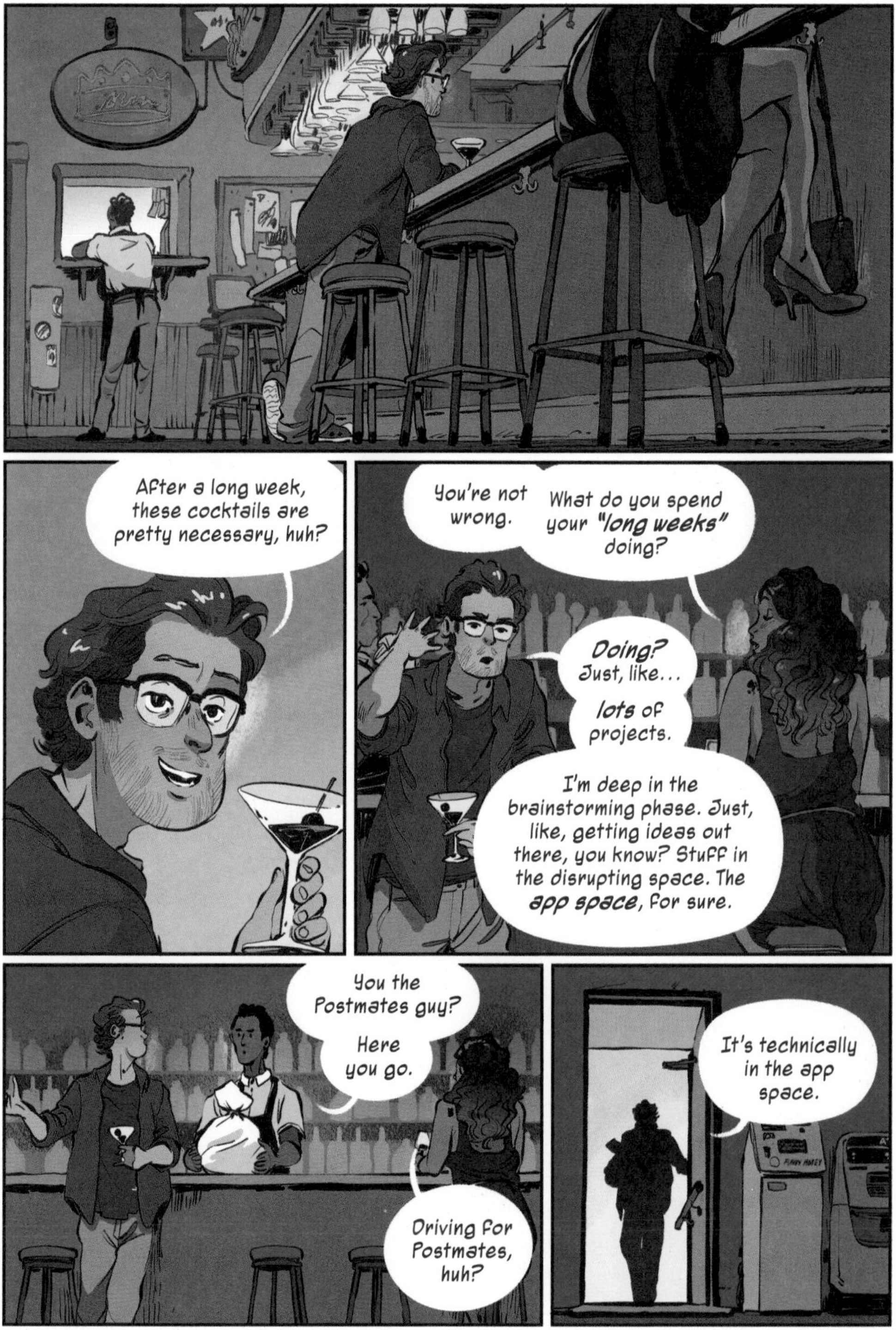
After a long week, these cocktails are pretty necessary, huh?
You're not wrong.
What do you spend your *"long weeks"* doing?
Doing? Just, like...
lots of projects.
I'm deep in the brainstorming phase. Just, like, getting ideas out there, you know? Stuff in the disrupting space. The *app space*, for sure.
You the Postmates guy?
Here you go.
Driving for Postmates, huh?
It's technically in the app space.

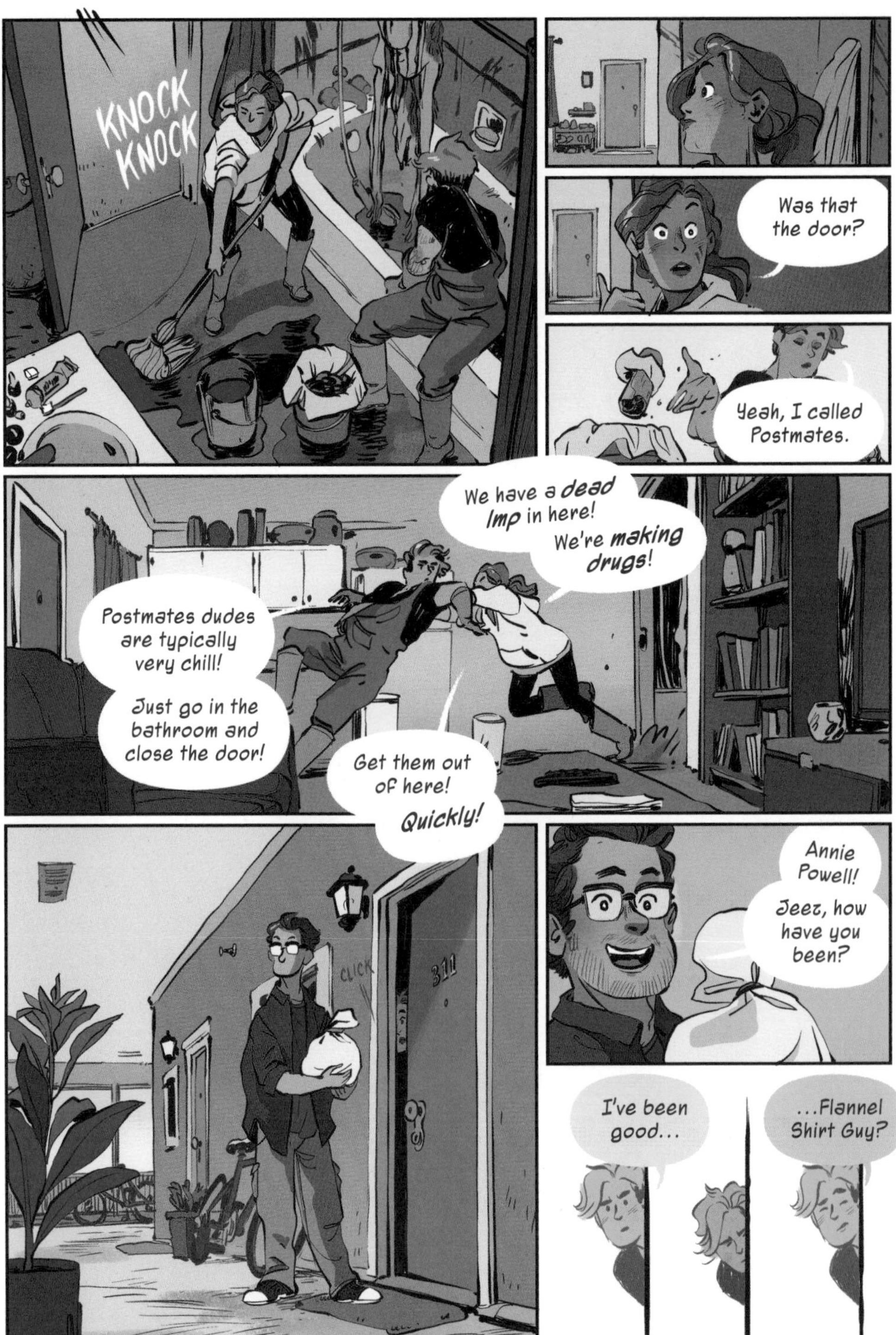
KNOCK KNOCK
Was that the door?
Yeah, I called Postmates.
We have a *dead Imp* in here!
We're *making drugs*!
Postmates dudes are typically very chill!
Just go in the bathroom and close the door!
Get them out of here!
Quickly!
CLICK
311
Annie Powell!
Jeez, how have you been?
I've been good...
...Flannel Shirt Guy?

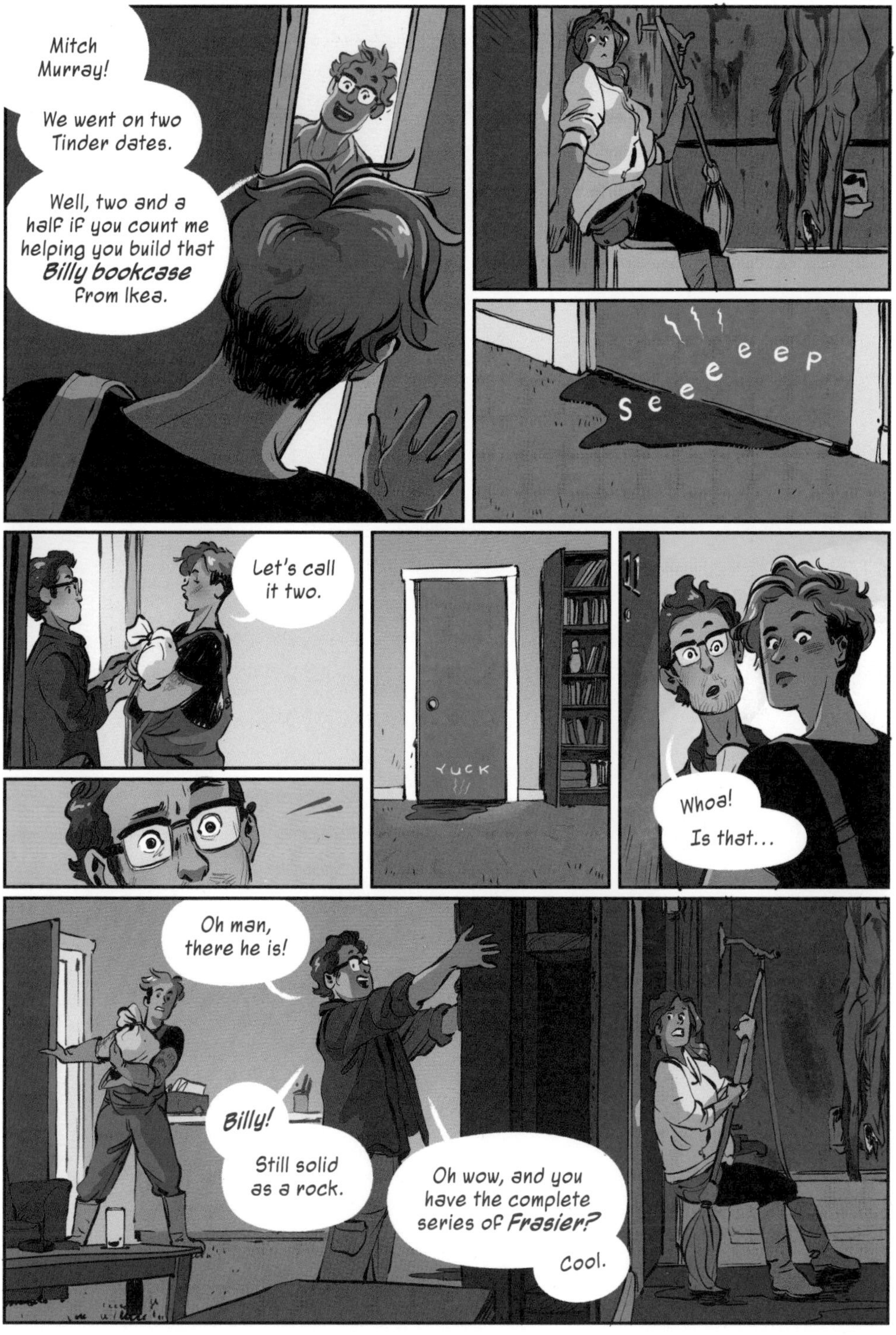
Mitch Murray!
We went on two Tinder dates.
Well, two and a half if you count me helping you build that *Billy bookcase* from Ikea.
seeeeeep
Let's call it two.
YUCK
Whoa! Is that...
Oh man, there he is!
Billy!
Still solid as a rock.
Oh wow, and you have the complete series of *Frasier?*
Cool.

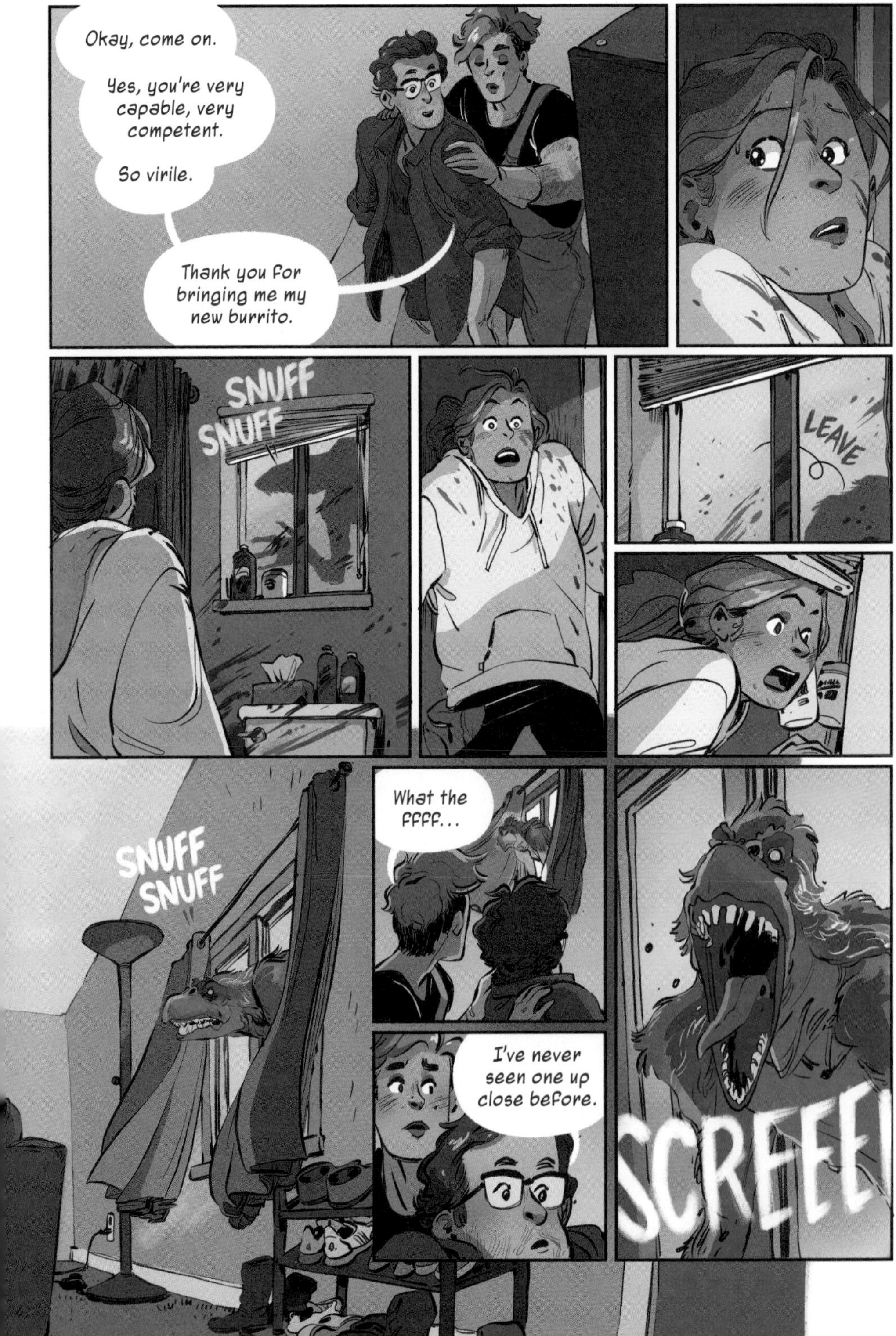
Okay, come on.
Yes, you're very capable, very competent.
So virile.
Thank you for bringing me my new burrito.
SNUFF
SNUFF
LEAVE
SNUFF
SNUFF
What the FFFF...
I've never seen one up close before.
SCREEE

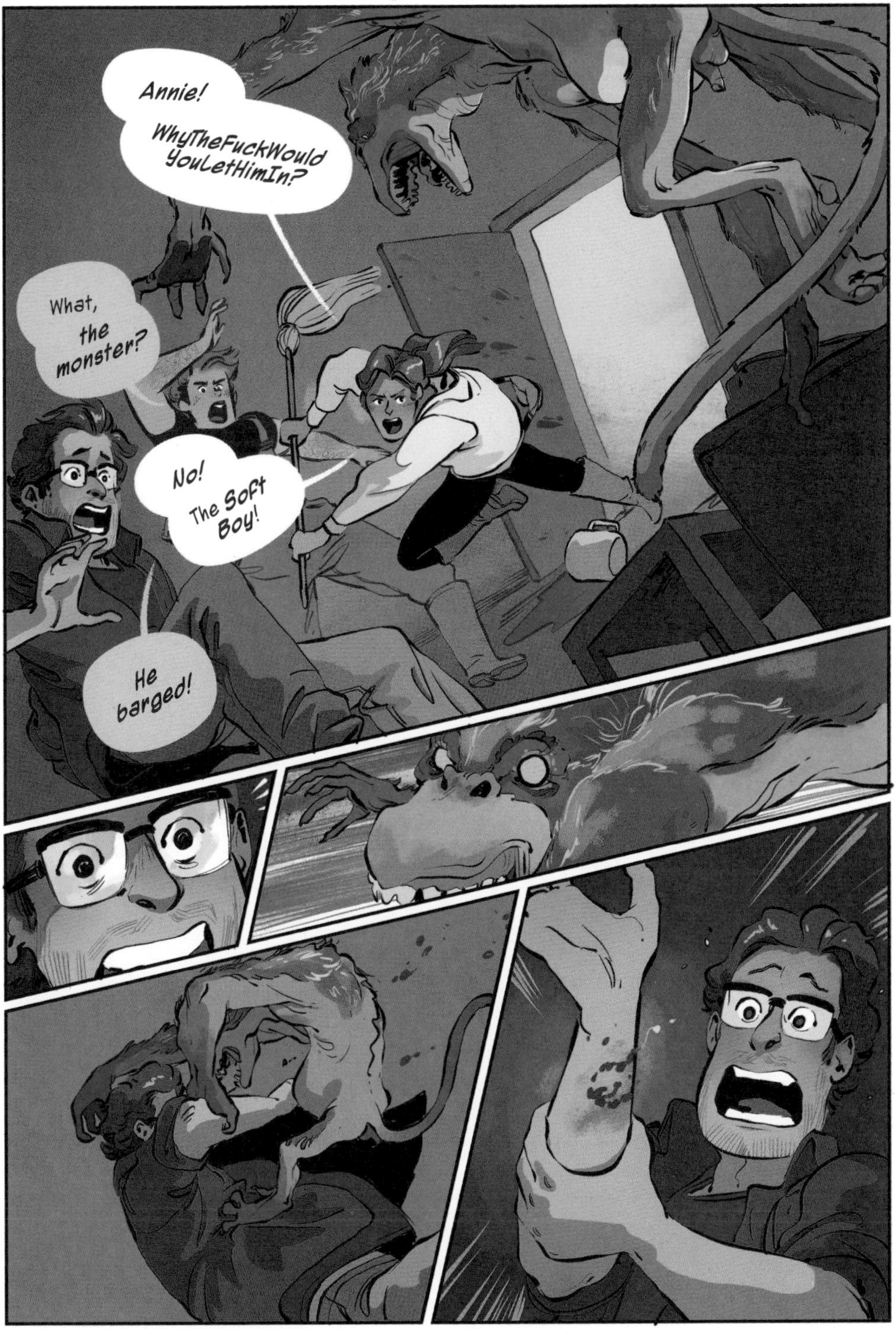
Annie!
WhyTheFuckWould YouLetHimIn?
What, the monster?
No! The Soft Boy!
He barged!

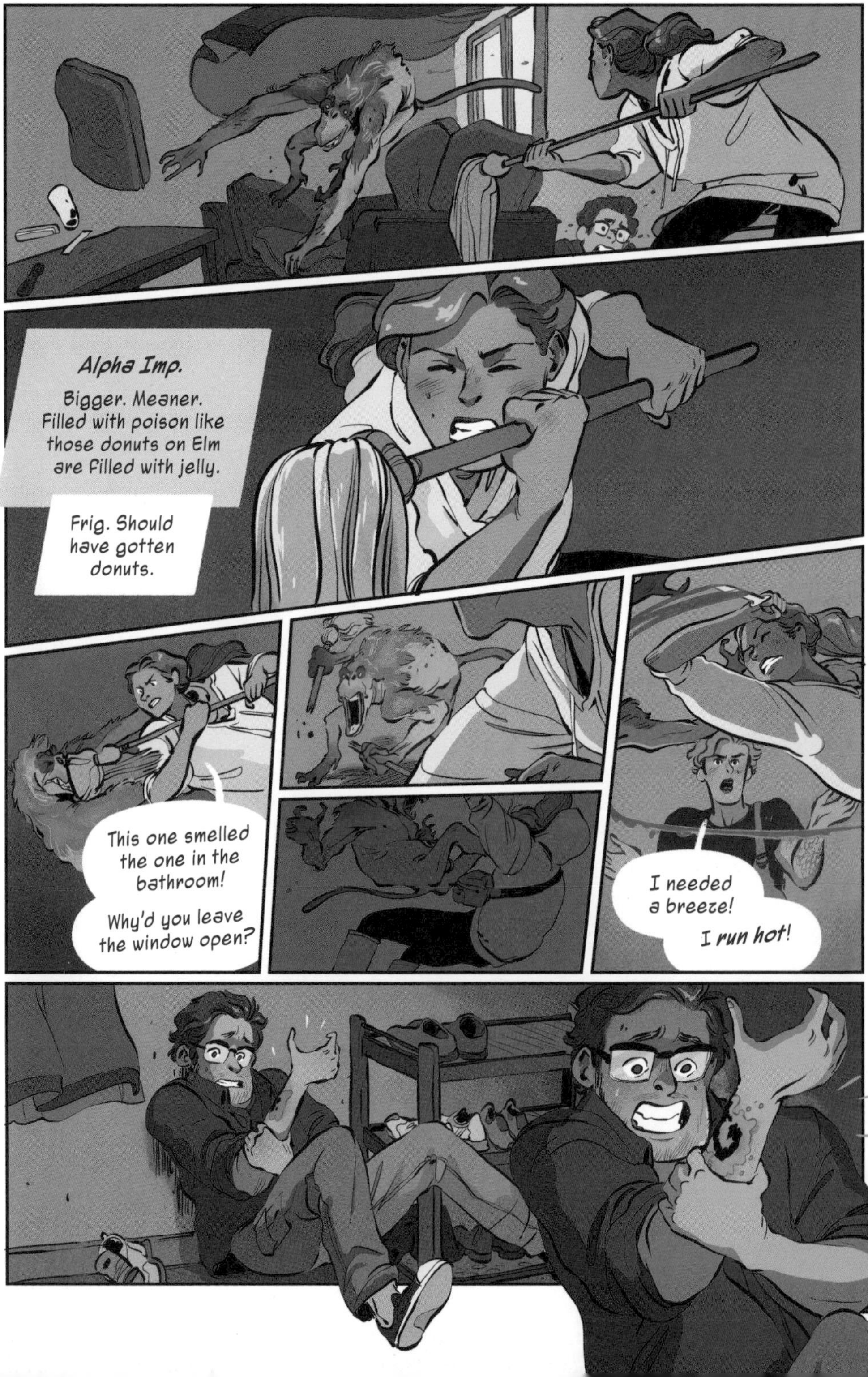

Alpha Imp.
Bigger. Meaner. Filled with poison like those donuts on Elm are filled with jelly.
Frig. Should have gotten donuts.
This one smelled the one in the bathroom!
Why'd you leave the window open?
I needed a breeze!
I *run hot*!

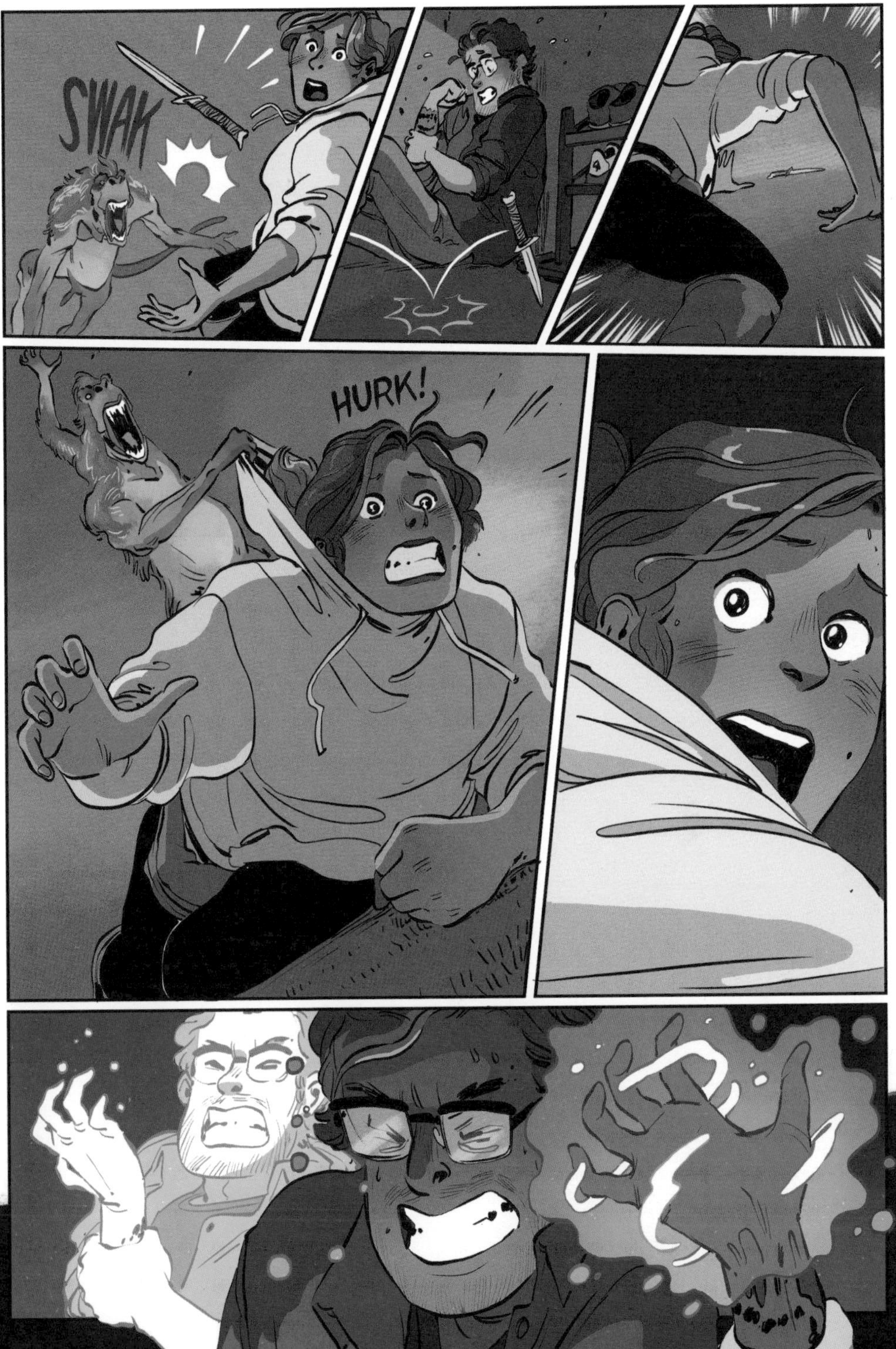
SWAK
HURK!

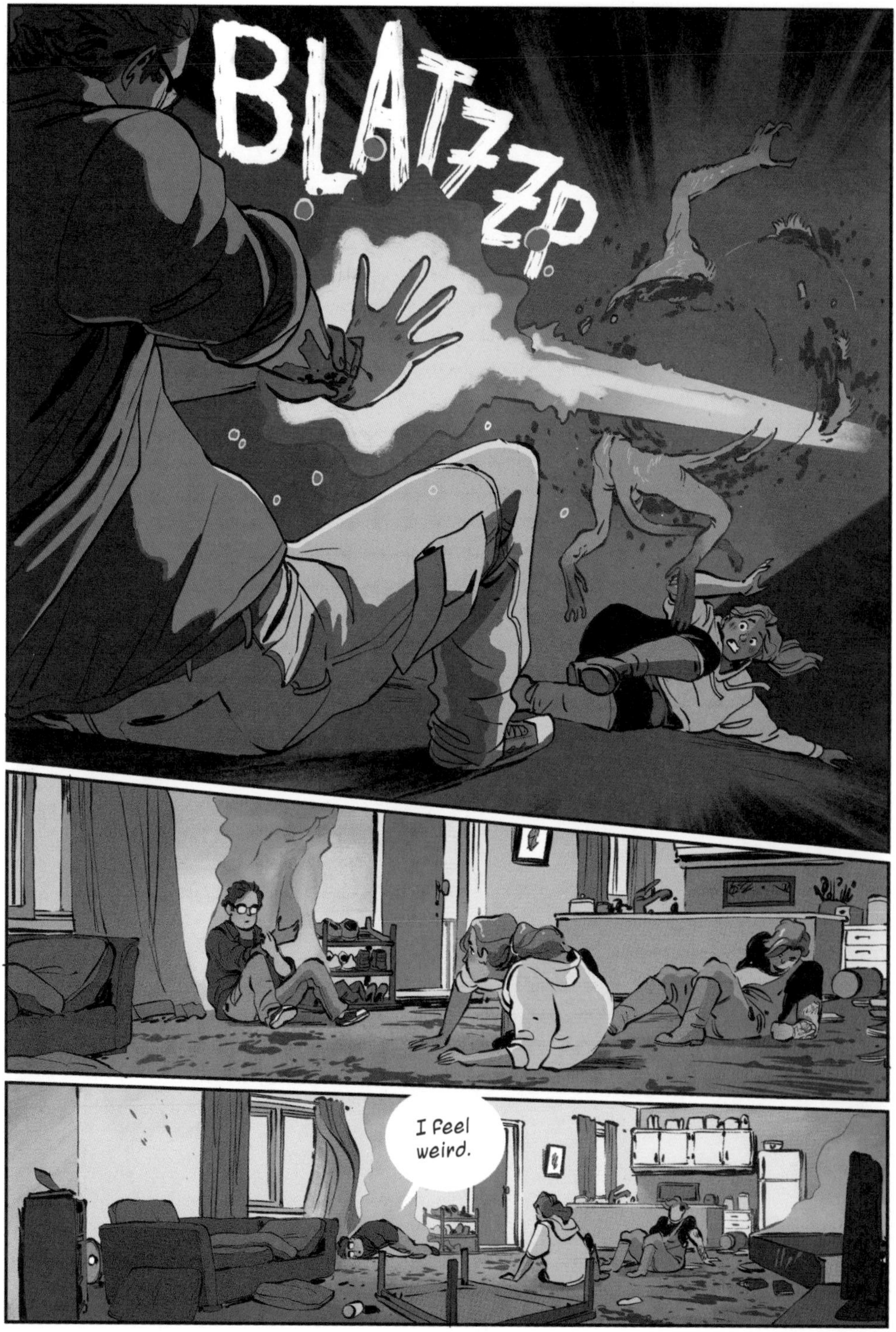
BLATZZP
I feel weird.

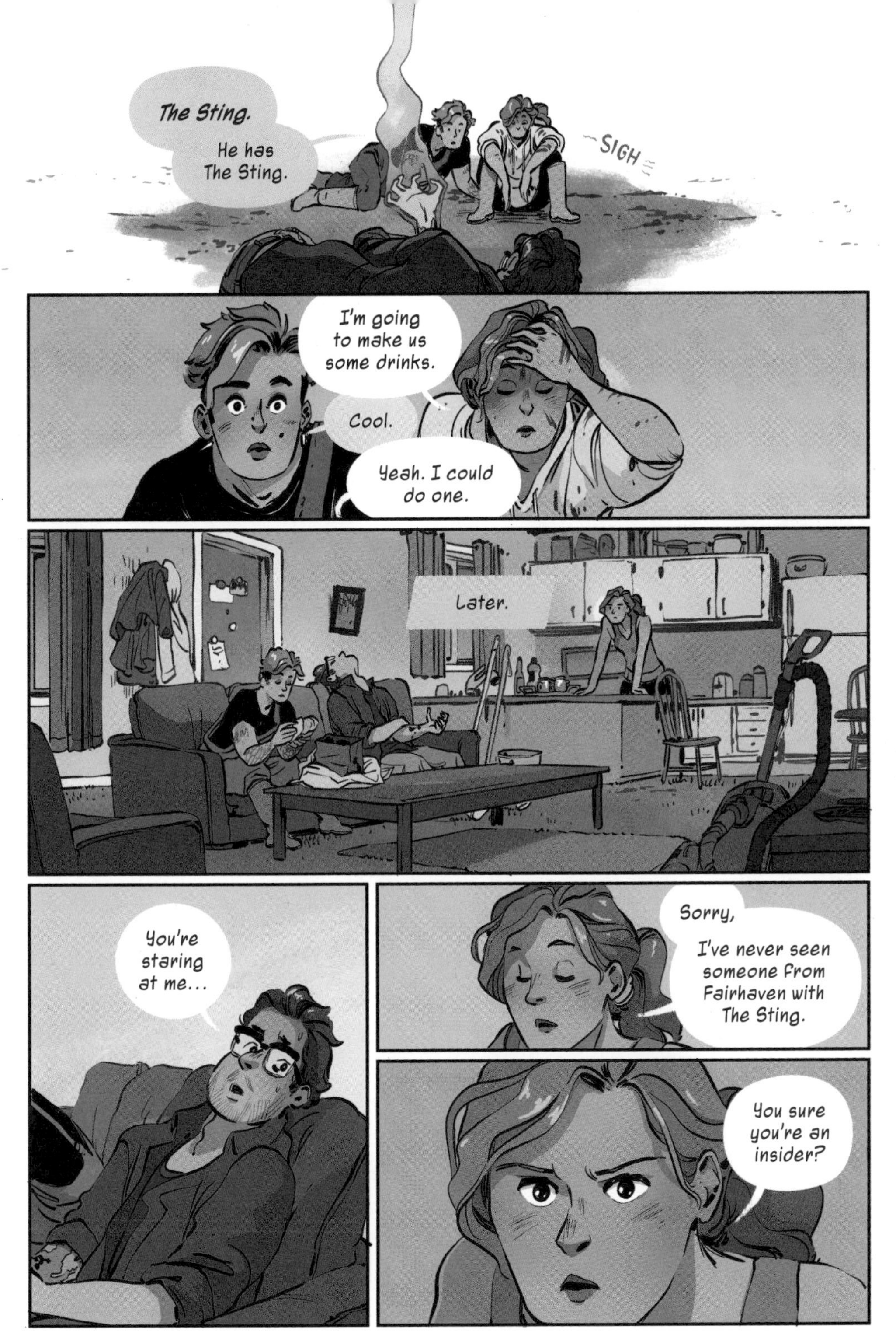
The Sting.
He has The Sting.
SIGH
I'm going to make us some drinks.
Cool.
Yeah. I could do one.
Later.
You're staring at me...
Sorry,
I've never seen someone from Fairhaven with The Sting.
You sure you're an insider?

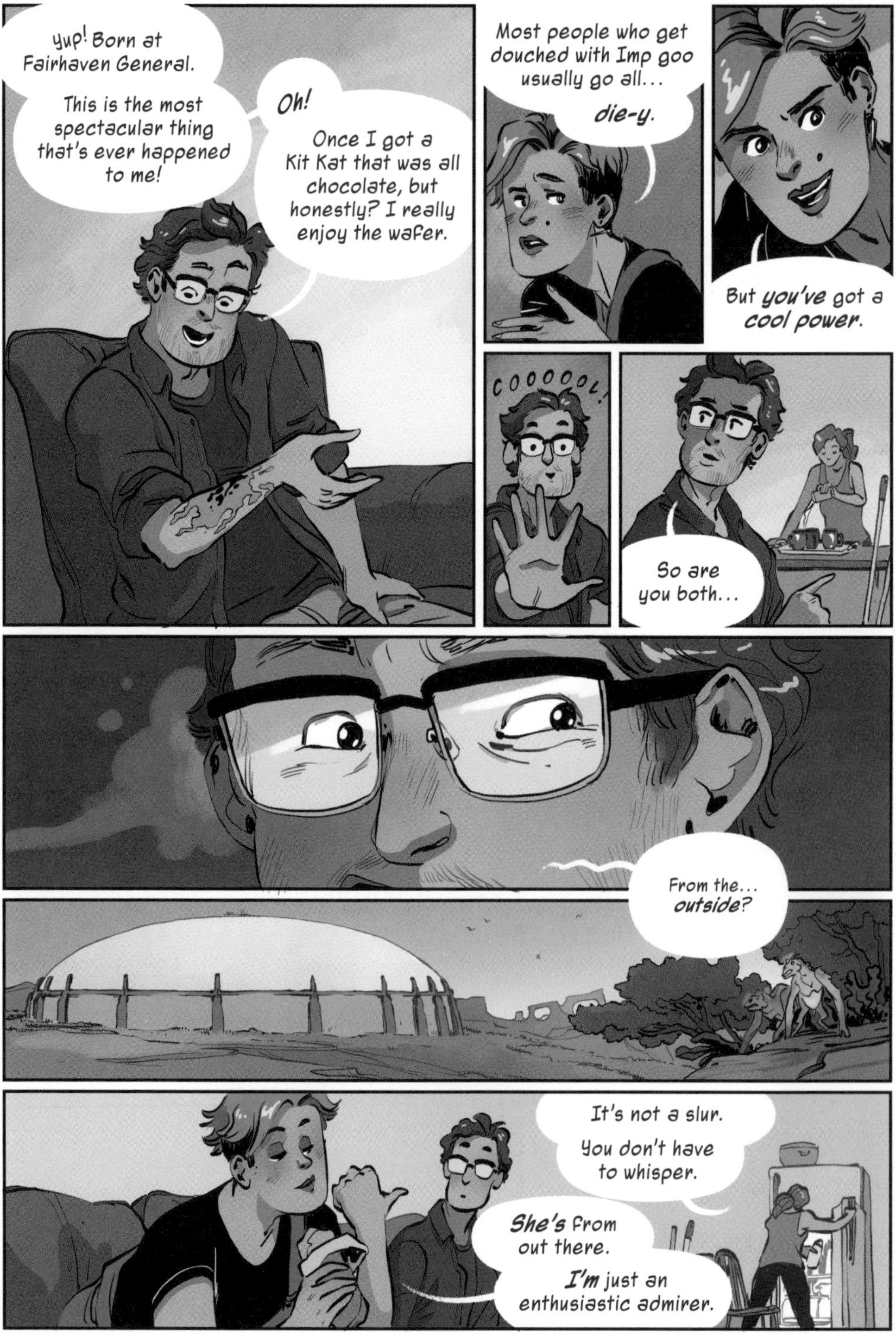
Yup! Born at Fairhaven General.
This is the most spectacular thing that's ever happened to me!
Oh!
Once I got a Kit Kat that was all chocolate, but honestly? I really enjoy the wafer.
Most people who get douched with Imp goo usually go all...
die-y.
But you've got a cool power.
COOOOOOL!
So are you both...
From the... outside?
It's not a slur.
You don't have to whisper.
She's from out there.
I'm just an enthusiastic admirer.

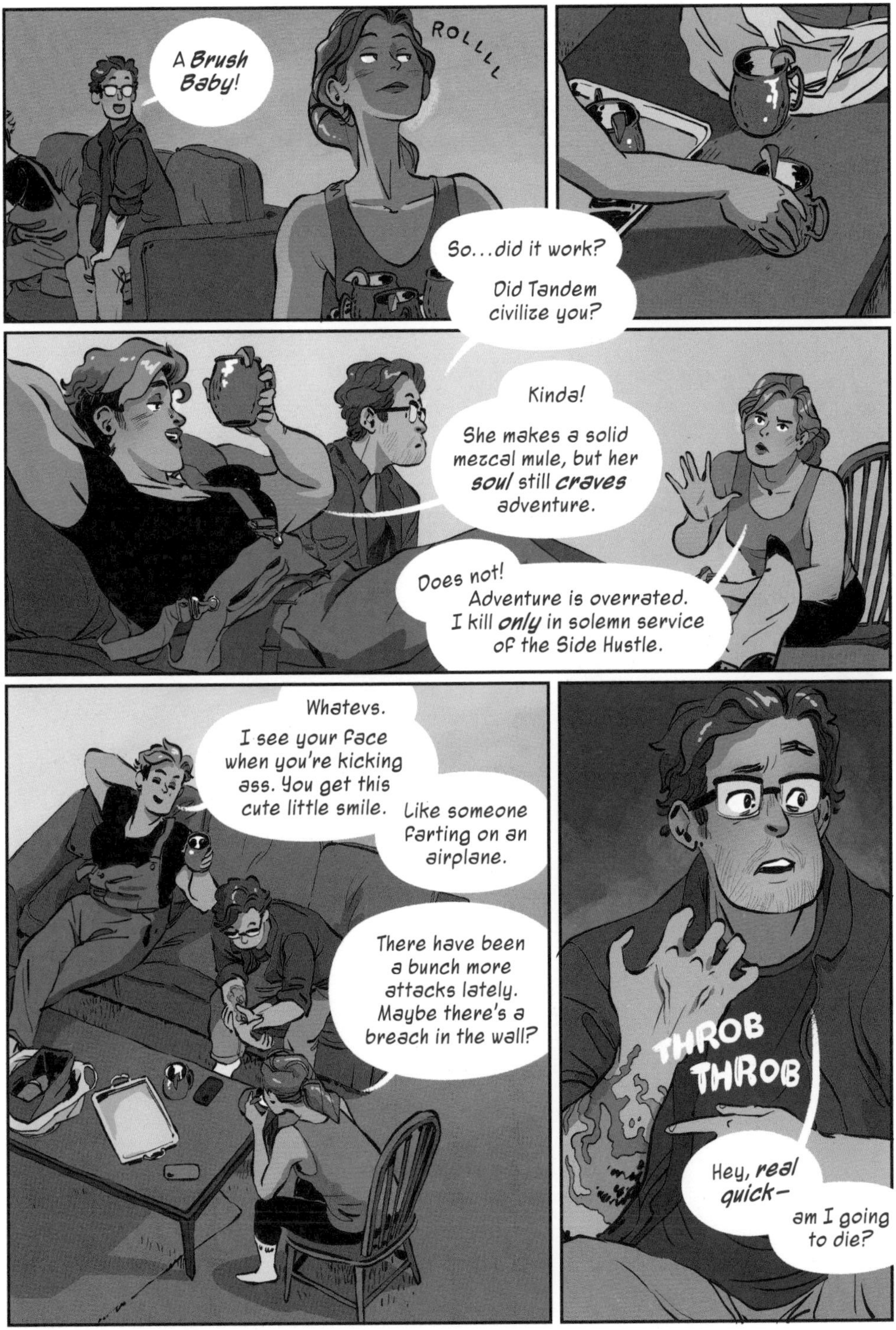

A Brush Baby!
ROLLLLL
So...did it work?
Did Tandem civilize you?
Kinda!
She makes a solid mezcal mule, but her soul still craves adventure.
Does not!
Adventure is overrated. I kill only in solemn service of the Side Hustle.
Whatevs.
I see your face when you're kicking ass. You get this cute little smile.
Like someone farting on an airplane.
There have been a bunch more attacks lately. Maybe there's a breach in the wall?
THROB THROB
Hey, real quick—
am I going to die?

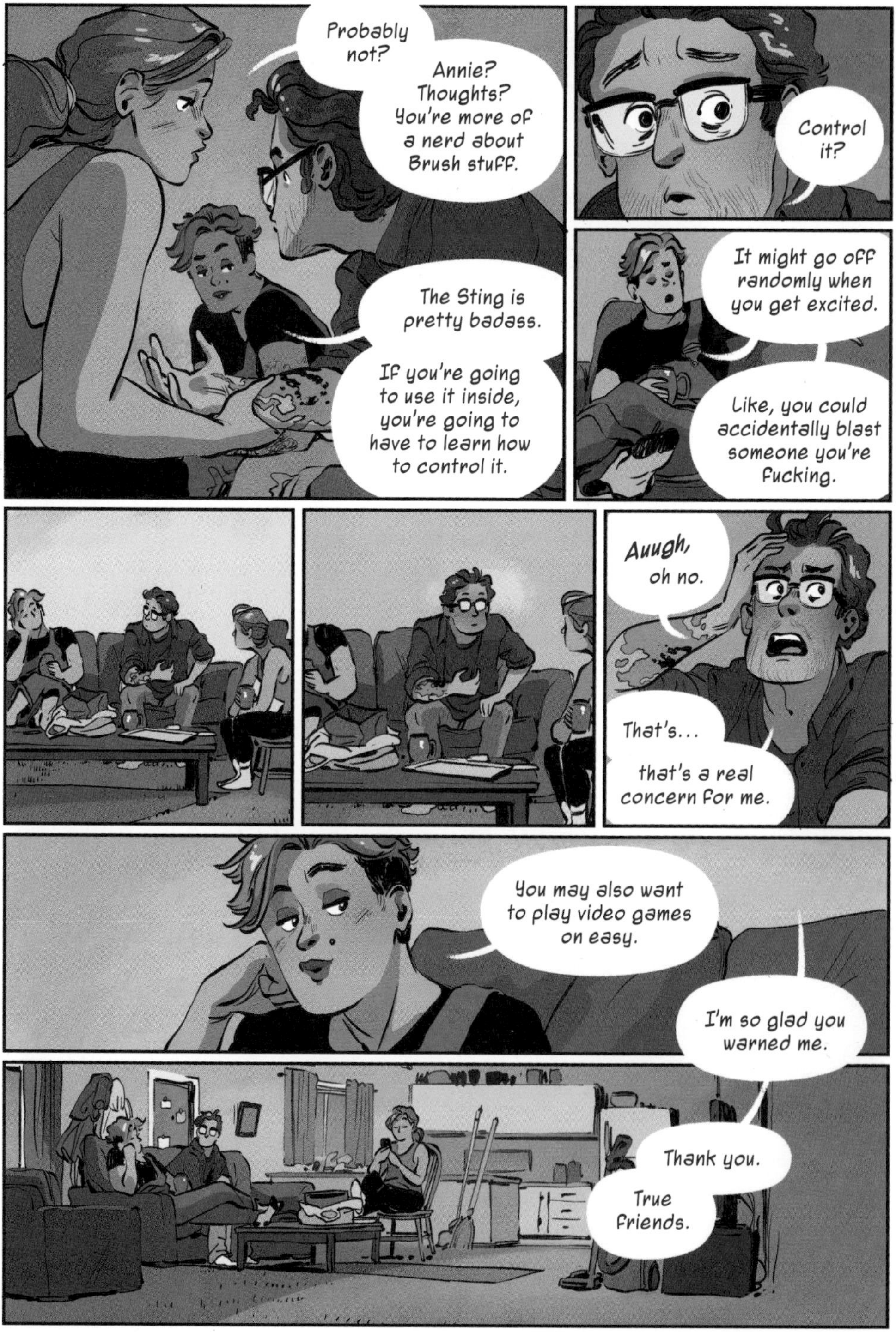
Probably not?
Annie? Thoughts? You're more of a nerd about Brush stuff.
The Sting is pretty badass.
If you're going to use it inside, you're going to have to learn how to control it.
Control it?
It might go off randomly when you get excited.
Like, you could accidentally blast someone you're fucking.
Auugh, oh no.
That's...
that's a real concern for me.
You may also want to play video games on easy.
I'm so glad you warned me.
Thank you.
True friends.

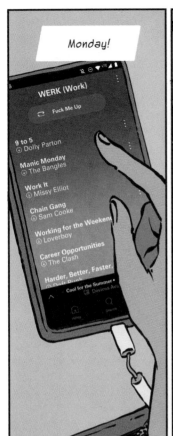

Monday!

WERK (Work)

Fuck Me Up

9 to 5
Dolly Parton

Manic Monday
The Bangles

Work It
Missy Elliot

Chain Gang
Sam Cooke

Working for the Weekend
Loverboy

Career Opportunities
The Clash

Harder, Better, Faster,

Cool for the Summer

GRUNT BOX meal plans are 50% off RIGHT MEOW for when you feel like you want to

Schedule Tweet   Tweet

TIK
TAP
TAK
T

KIK
TAK
PIK
TEK
TAP

Bonnie Ramos

BING!

Now

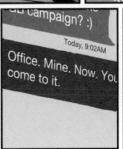

GB campaign? :)

Today, 9:02AM

Office. Mine. Now. You come to it.

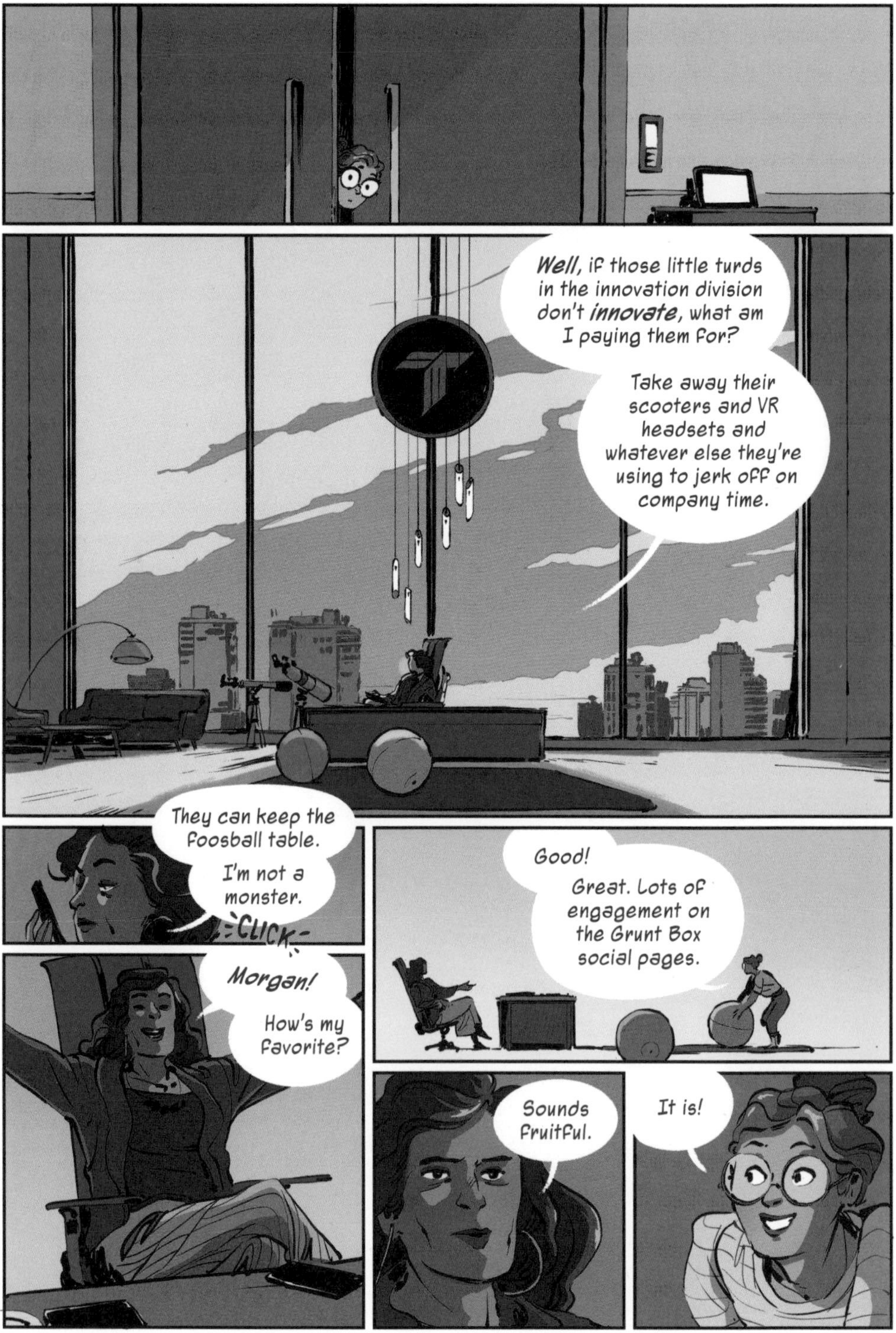

Well, if those little turds in the innovation division don't *innovate*, what am I paying them for?
Take away their scooters and VR headsets and whatever else they're using to jerk off on company time.
They can keep the foosball table.
I'm not a monster.
CLICK
Morgan!
How's my favorite?
Good!
Great. Lots of engagement on the Grunt Box social pages.
Sounds fruitful.
It is!

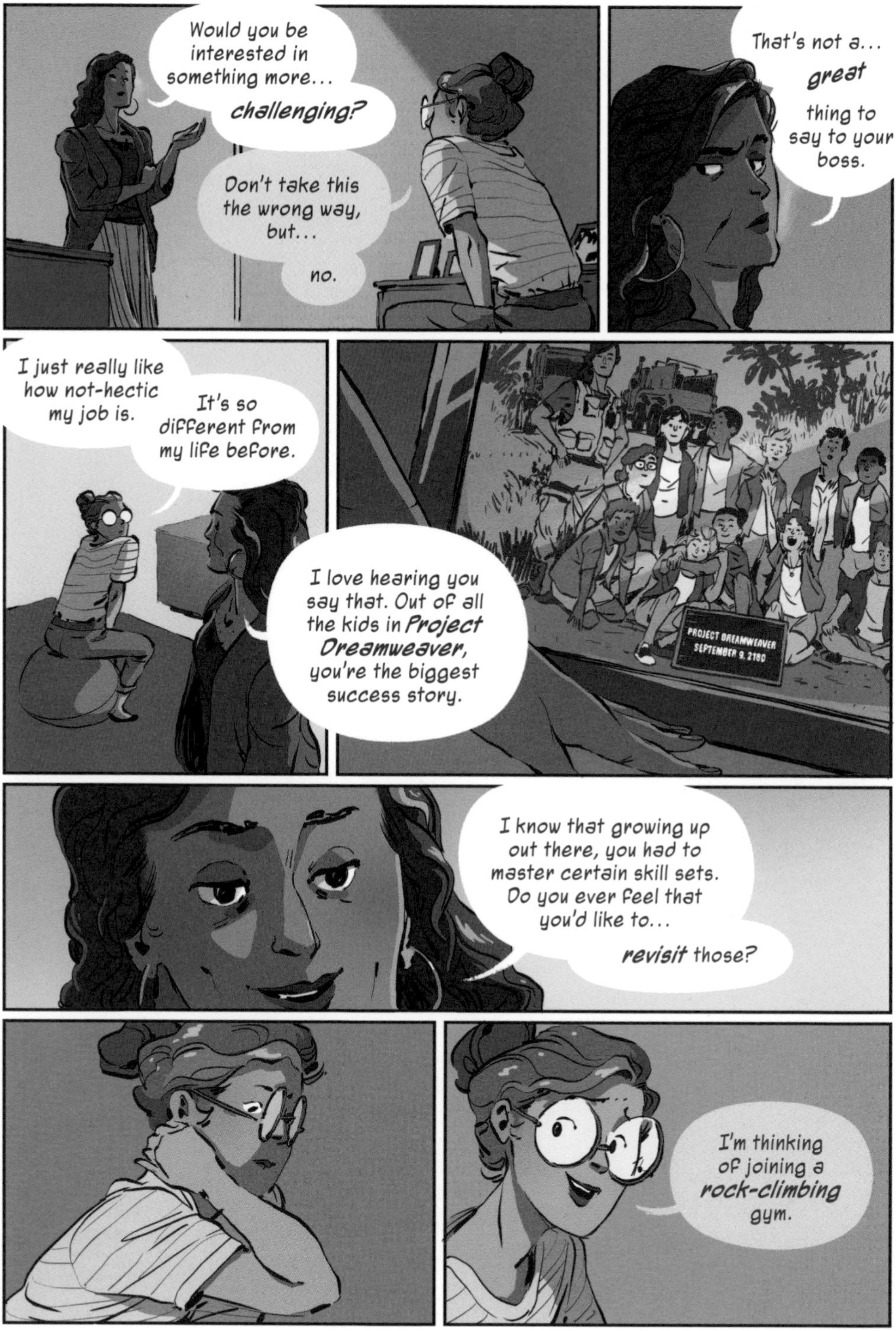
Would you be interested in something more... *challenging?*
Don't take this the wrong way, but...
no.
That's not a... *great* thing to say to your boss.
I just really like how not-hectic my job is.
It's so different from my life before.
PROJECT DREAMWEAVER SEPTEMBER 9, 2180
I love hearing you say that. Out of all the kids in *Project Dreamweaver*, you're the biggest success story.
I know that growing up out there, you had to master certain skill sets. Do you ever feel that you'd like to...
revisit those?
I'm thinking of joining a *rock-climbing* gym.

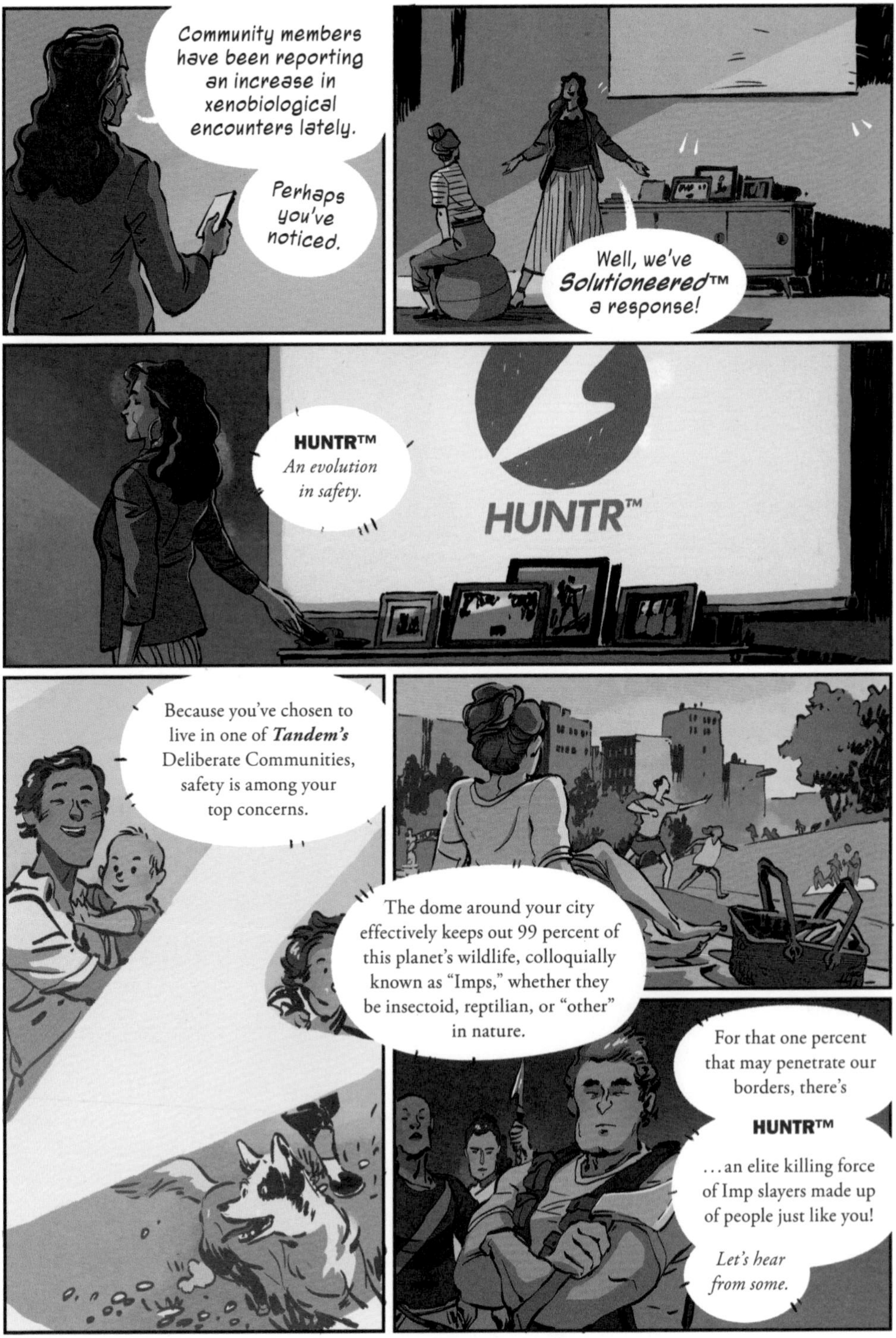
Community members have been reporting an increase in xenobiological encounters lately.
Perhaps you've noticed.
Well, we've Solutioneered™ a response!
HUNTR™
An evolution in safety.
HUNTR™
Because you've chosen to live in one of Tandem's Deliberate Communities, safety is among your top concerns.
The dome around your city effectively keeps out 99 percent of this planet's wildlife, colloquially known as "Imps," whether they be insectoid, reptilian, or "other" in nature.
For that one percent that may penetrate our borders, there's
HUNTR™
...an elite killing force of Imp slayers made up of people just like you!
Let's hear from some.

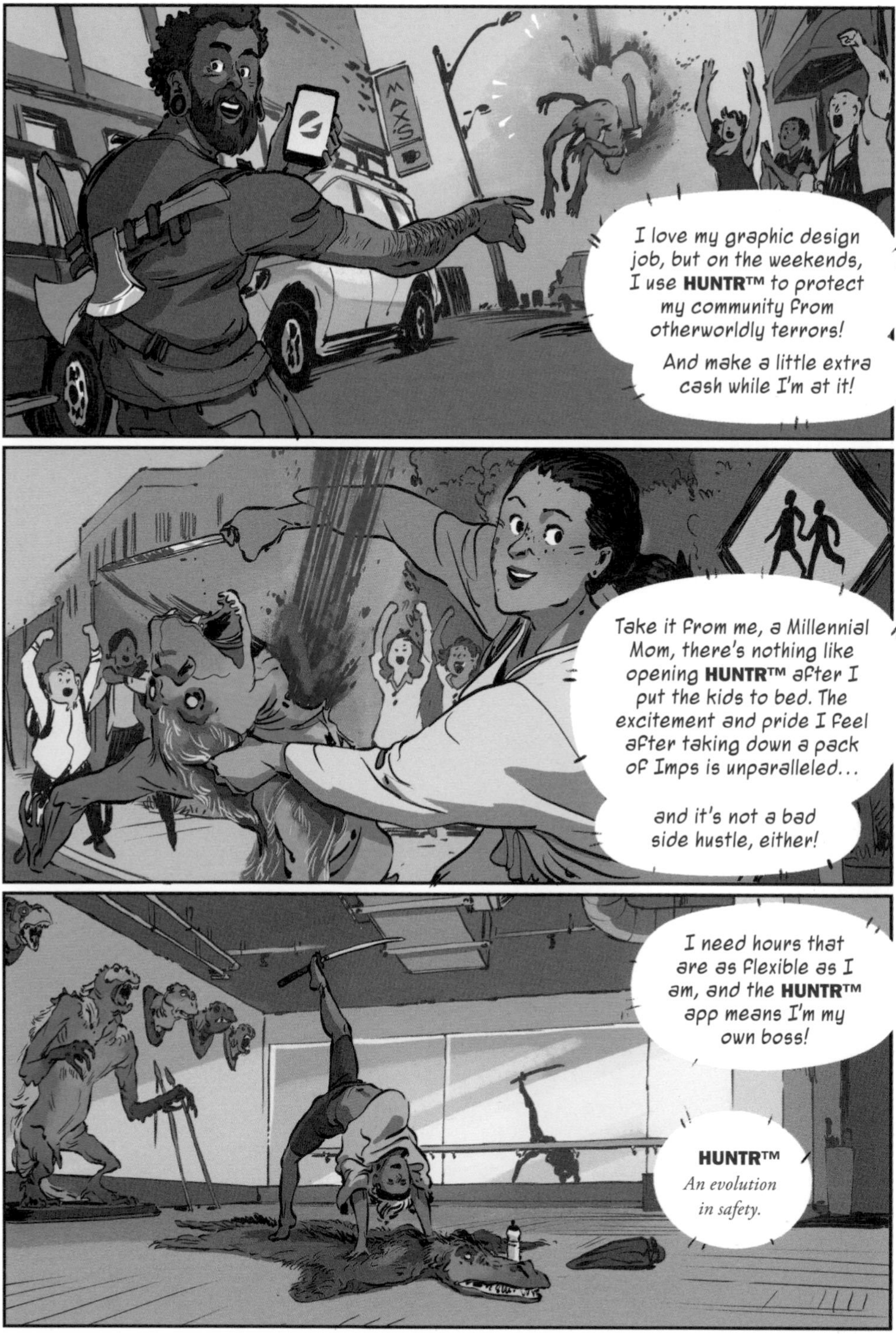
MAX'S
I love my graphic design job, but on the weekends, I use **HUNTR™** to protect my community from otherworldly terrors!
And make a little extra cash while I'm at it!
Take it from me, a Millennial Mom, there's nothing like opening **HUNTR™** after I put the kids to bed. The excitement and pride I feel after taking down a pack of Imps is unparalleled...
and it's not a bad side hustle, either!
I need hours that are as flexible as I am, and the **HUNTR™** app means I'm my own boss!
HUNTR™
An evolution in safety.

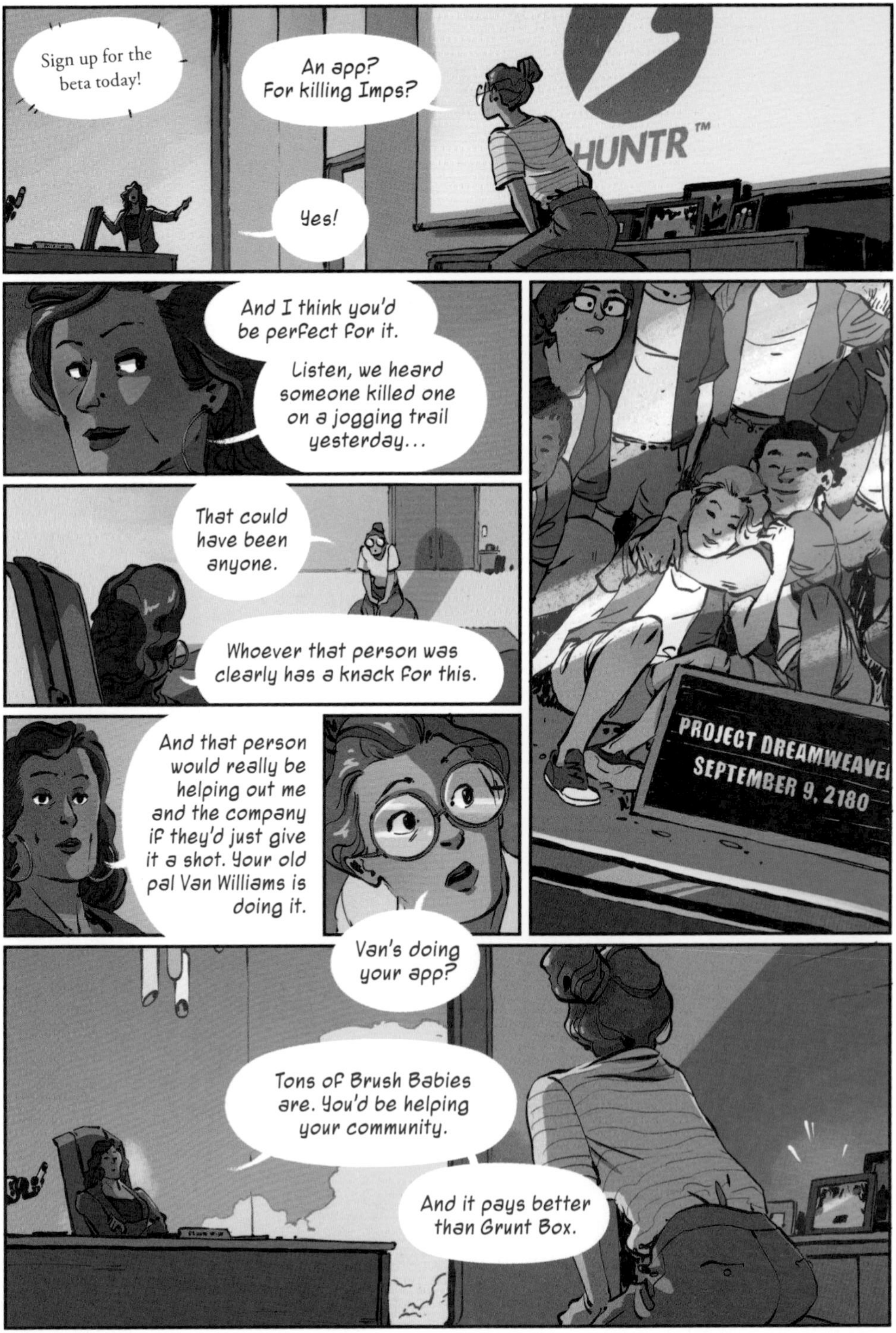
Sign up for the beta today!
An app? For killing Imps?
HUNTR™
Yes!
And I think you'd be perfect for it.
Listen, we heard someone killed one on a jogging trail yesterday...
That could have been anyone.
Whoever that person was clearly has a knack for this.
PROJECT DREAMWEAVE
SEPTEMBER 9, 2180
And that person would really be helping out me and the company if they'd just give it a shot. Your old pal Van Williams is doing it.
Van's doing your app?
Tons of Brush Babies are. You'd be helping your community.
And it pays better than Grunt Box.

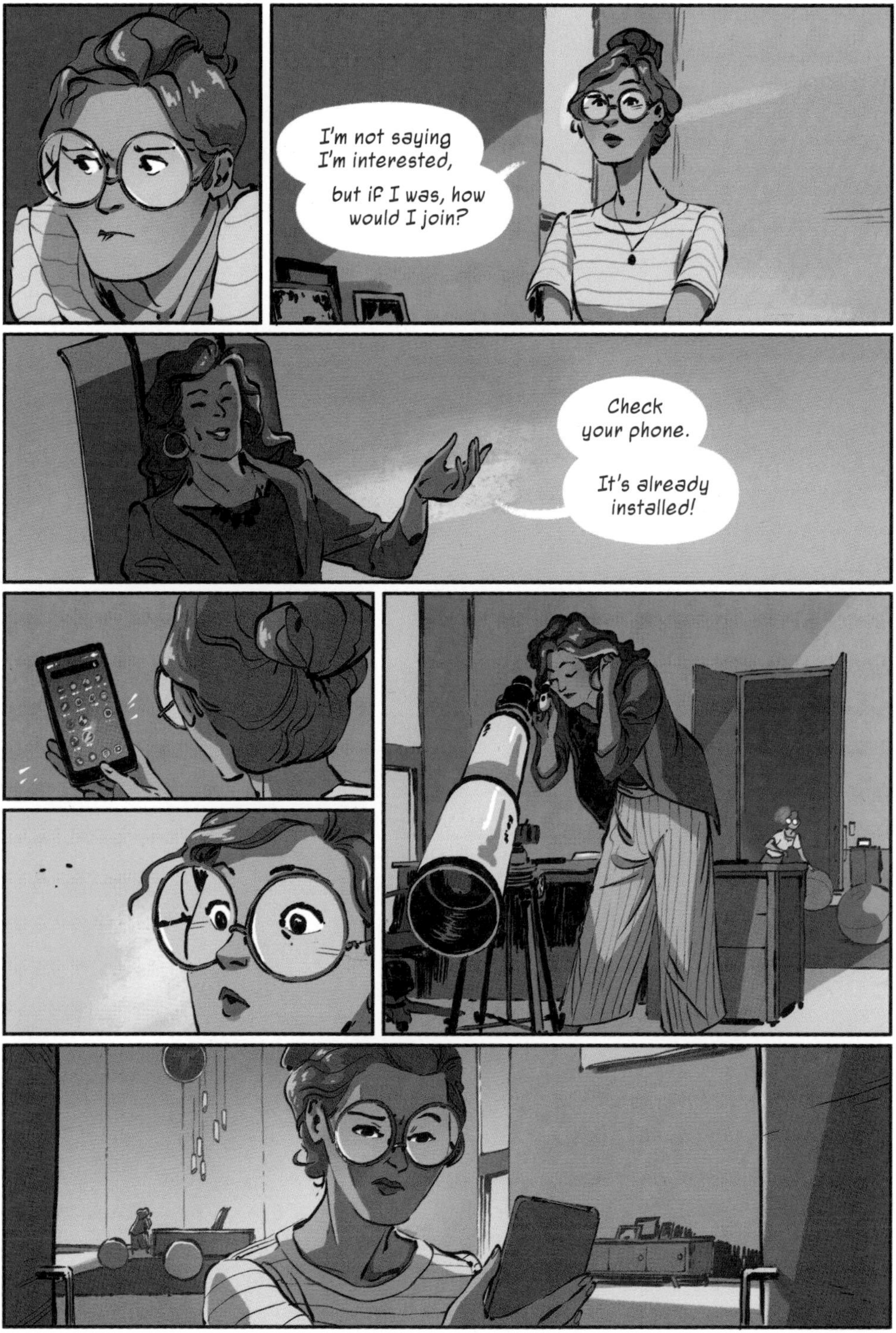
I'm not saying I'm interested,
but if I was, how would I join?
Check your phone.
It's already installed!

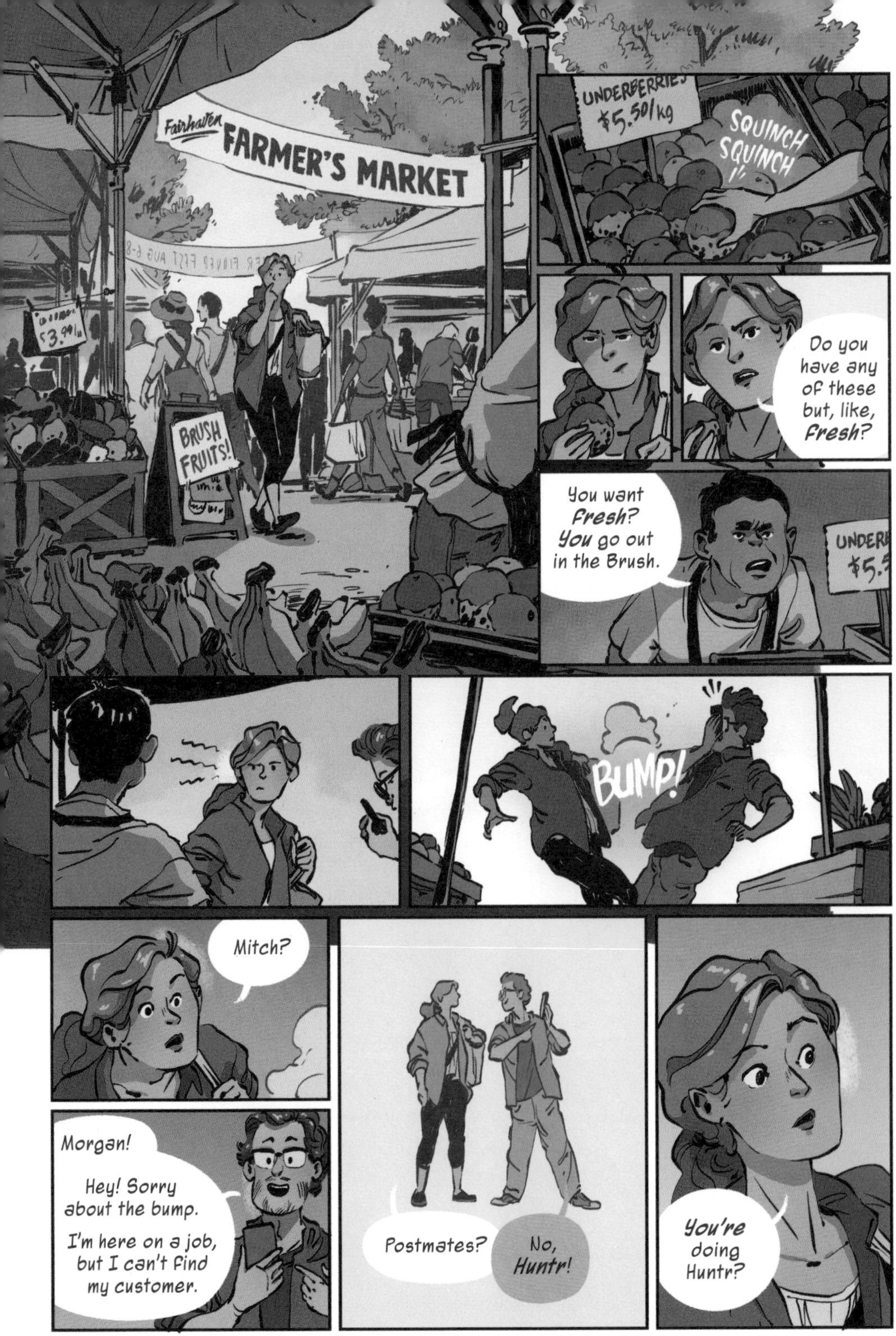
Fairhaven FARMER'S MARKET
BRUSH FRUITS!
UNDERBERRIES $5.50/kg
SQUINCH SQUINCH
Do you have any of these but, like, *fresh*?
You want *fresh*? *You* go out in the Brush.
BUMP!
Mitch?
Morgan!
Hey! Sorry about the bump.
I'm here on a job, but I can't find my customer.
Postmates?
No, *Huntr*!
You're doing Huntr?

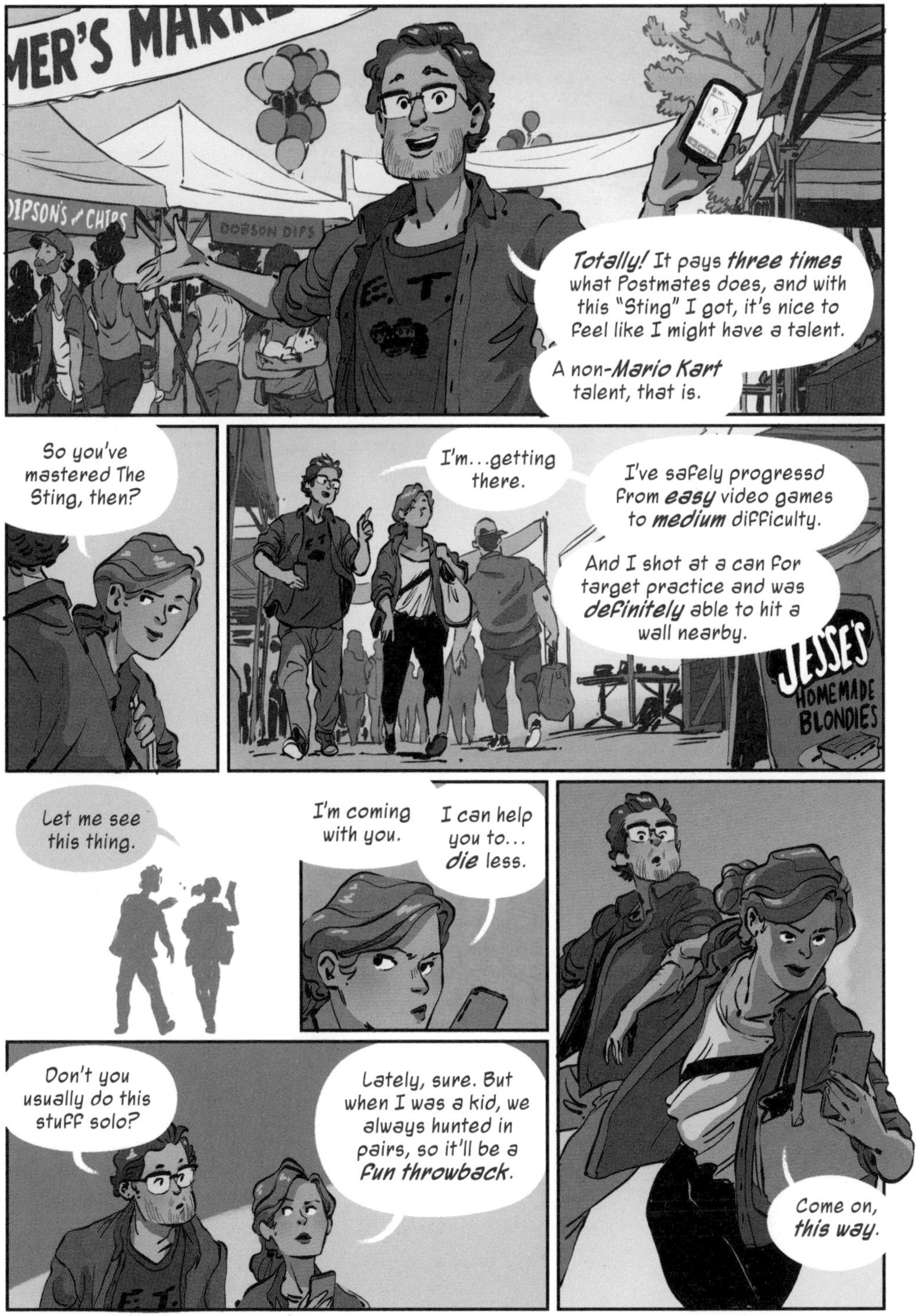
MER'S MARK
DIPSON'S CHIPS
DOBSON DIPS
Totally! It pays three times what Postmates does, and with this "Sting" I got, it's nice to feel like I might have a talent.
A non-Mario Kart talent, that is.
So you've mastered The Sting, then?
I'm...getting there.
I've safely progressd from easy video games to medium difficulty.
And I shot at a can for target practice and was definitely able to hit a wall nearby.
JESSE'S HOMEMADE BLONDIES
Let me see this thing.
I'm coming with you.
I can help you to... die less.
Don't you usually do this stuff solo?
Lately, sure. But when I was a kid, we always hunted in pairs, so it'll be a fun throwback.
Come on, this way.

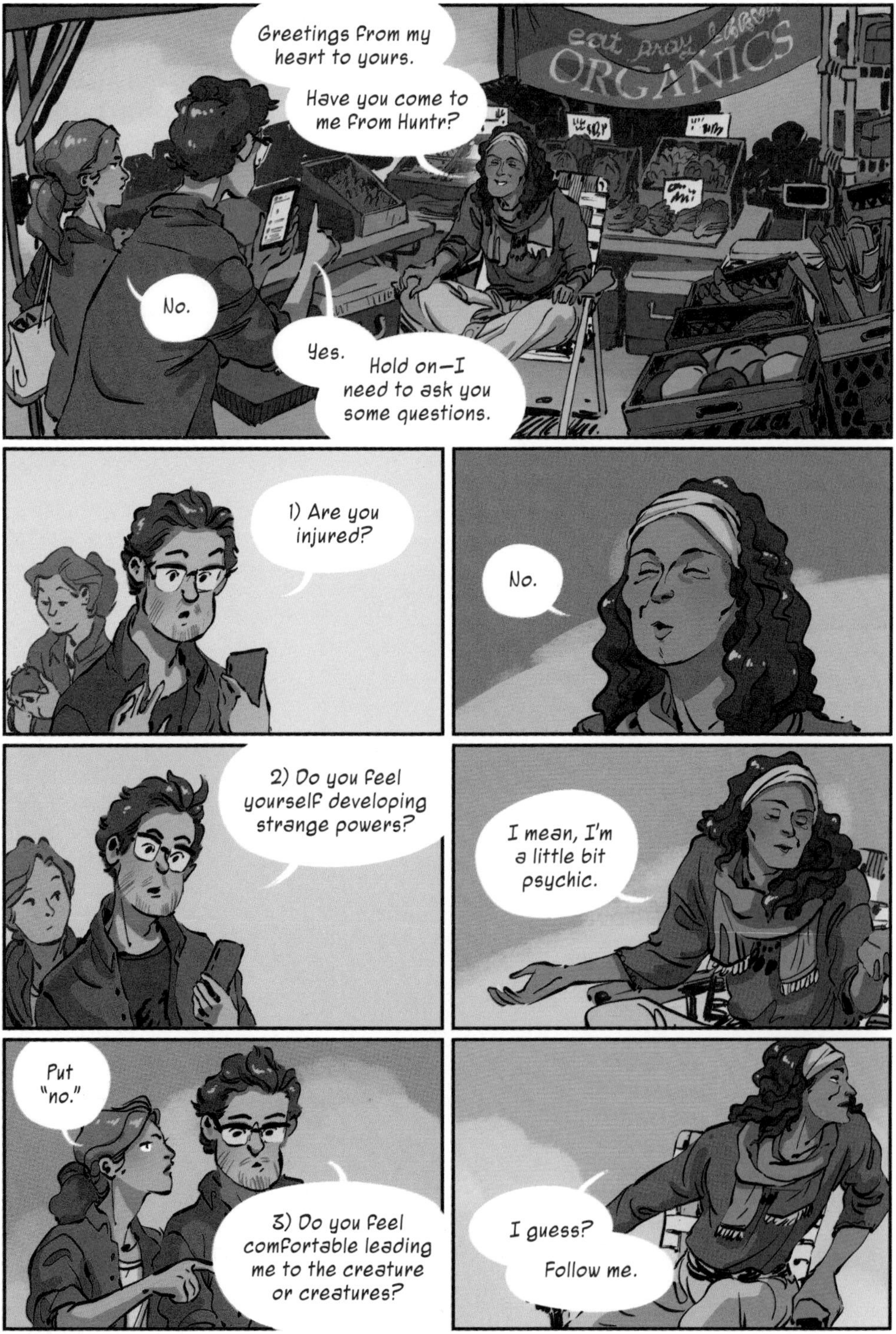
Greetings from my heart to yours.
Have you come to me from Huntr?
No.
Yes.
Hold on—I need to ask you some questions.
ORGANICS
1) Are you injured?
No.
2) Do you feel yourself developing strange powers?
I mean, I'm a little bit psychic.
Put "no."
3) Do you feel comfortable leading me to the creature or creatures?
I guess?
Follow me.

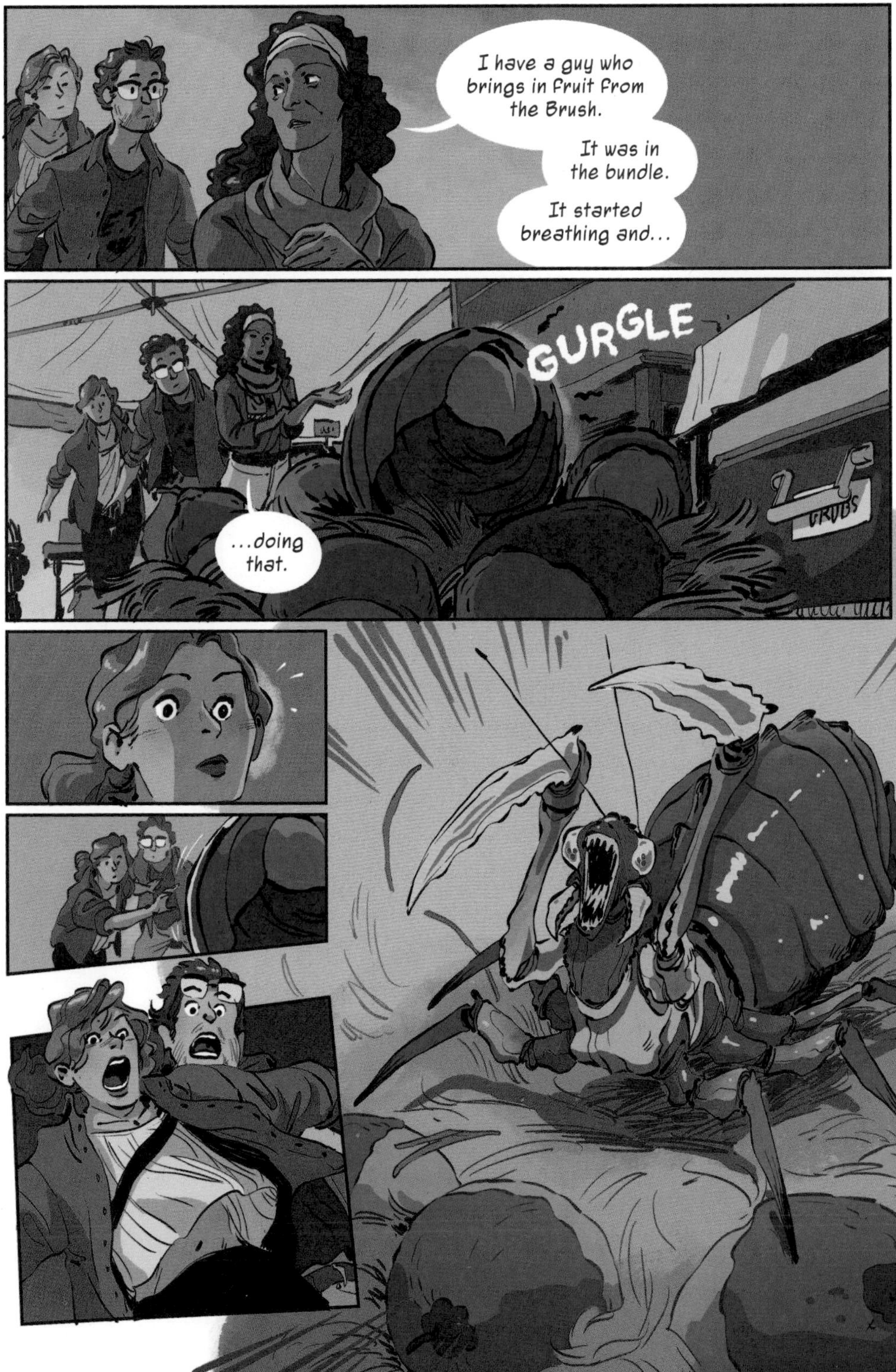
I have a guy who brings in fruit from the Brush.
It was in the bundle.
It started breathing and...
GURGLE
...doing that.
GRUBS

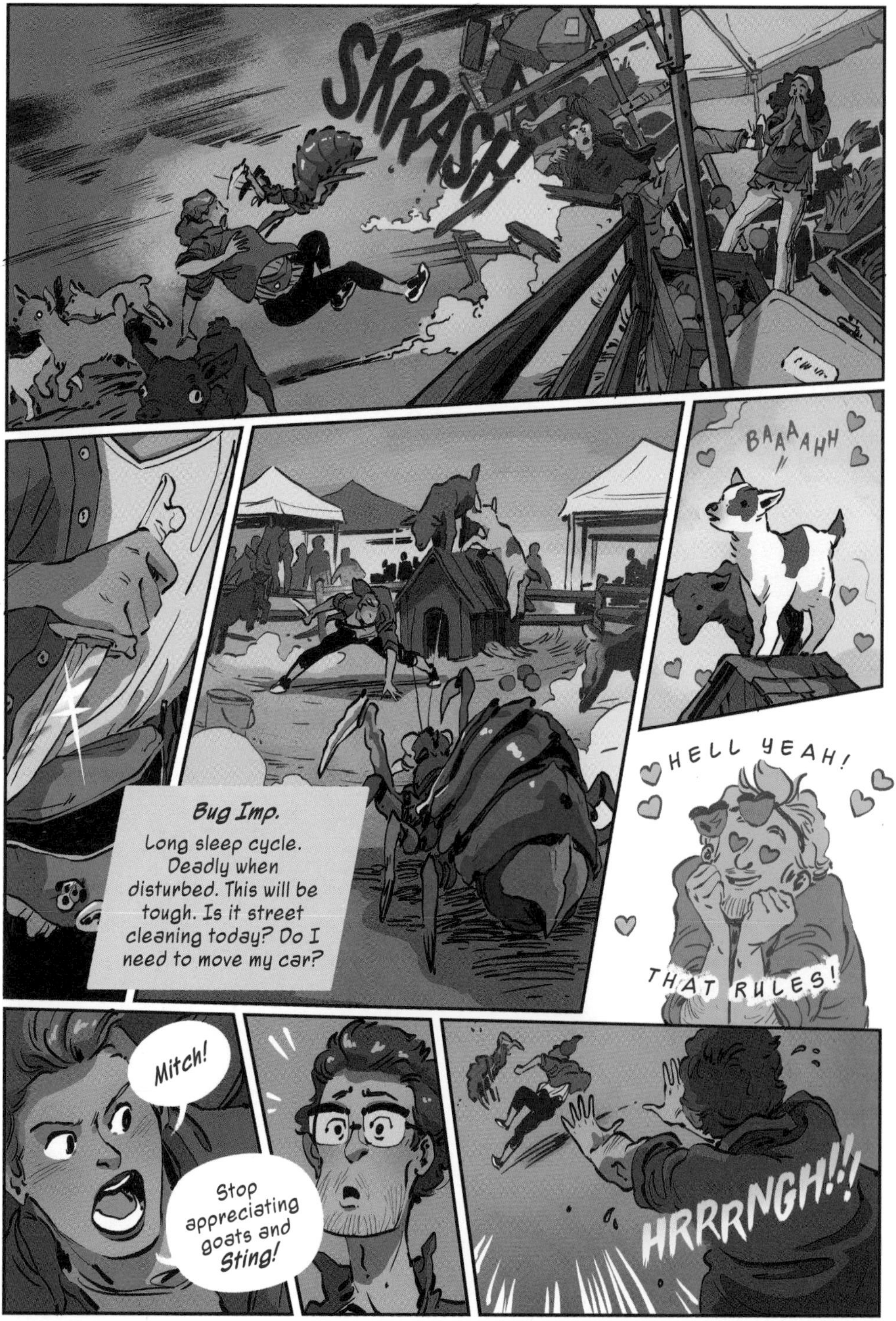
SKRASH
BAAAAHH
Bug Imp.
Long sleep cycle. Deadly when disturbed. This will be tough. Is it street cleaning today? Do I need to move my car?
HELL YEAH!
THAT RULES!
Mitch!
Stop appreciating goats and Sting!
HRRRNGH!!!

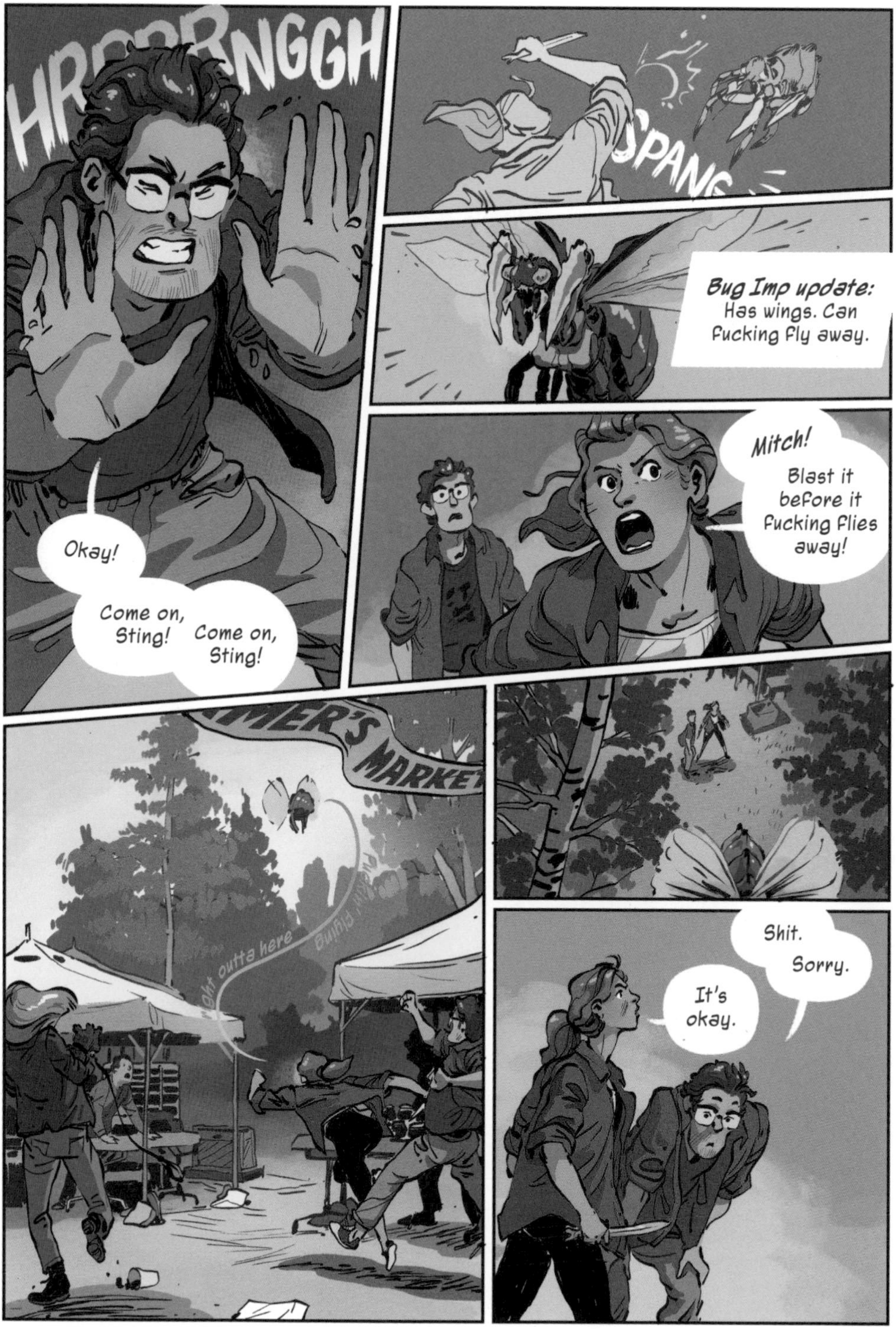
HRRRRNGGH
SPANG
Bug Imp update:
Has wings. Can fucking fly away.
Mitch!
Blast it before it fucking flies away!
Okay!
Come on, Sting!
Come on, Sting!
MER'S MARKET
ght outta here
thing
Shit.
Sorry.
It's okay.

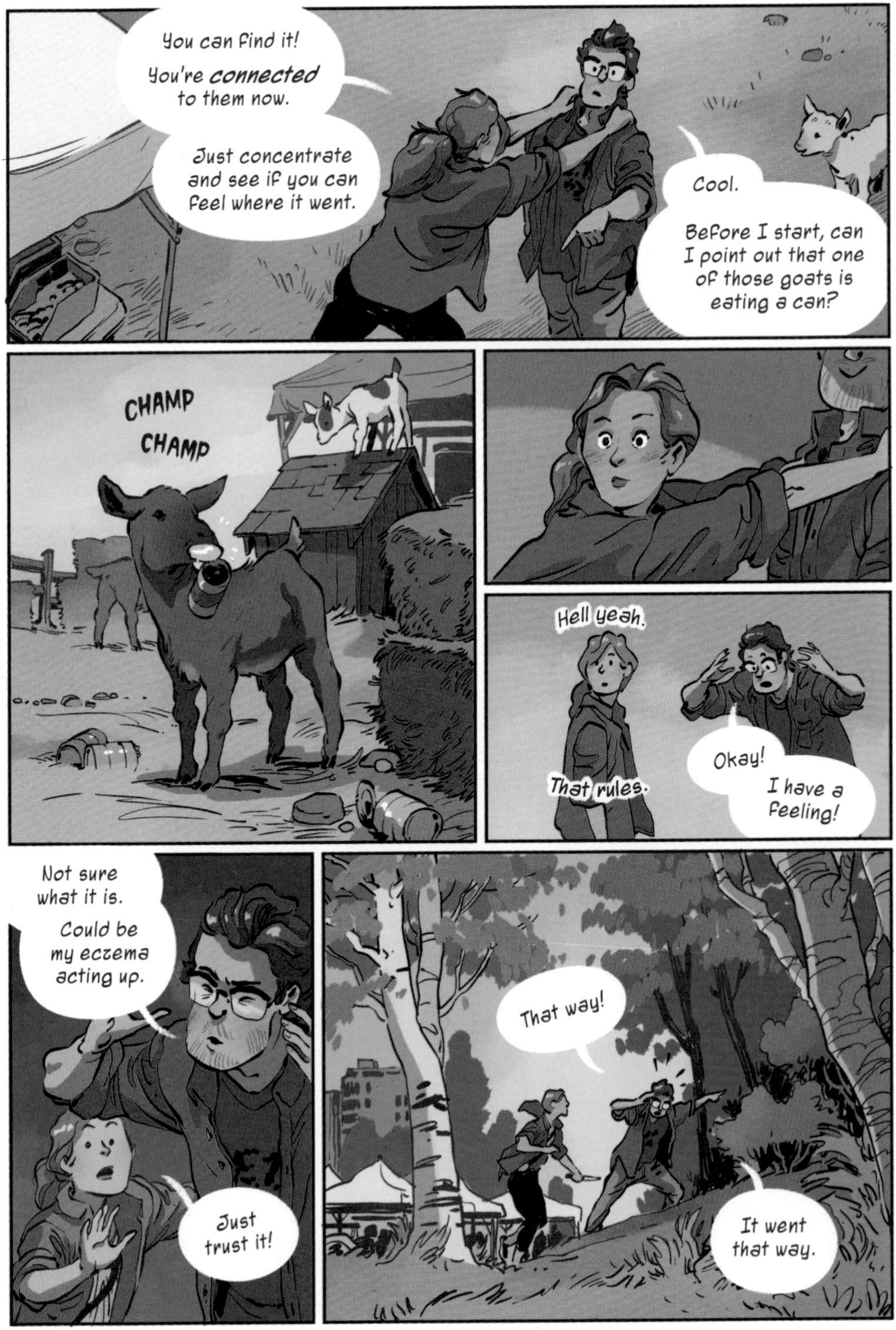
You can find it!
You're **connected** to them now.
Just concentrate and see if you can feel where it went.
Cool.
Before I start, can I point out that one of those goats is eating a can?
CHAMP
CHAMP
Hell yeah.
That rules.
Okay!
I have a feeling!
Not sure what it is.
Could be my eczema acting up.
Just trust it!
That way!
It went that way.

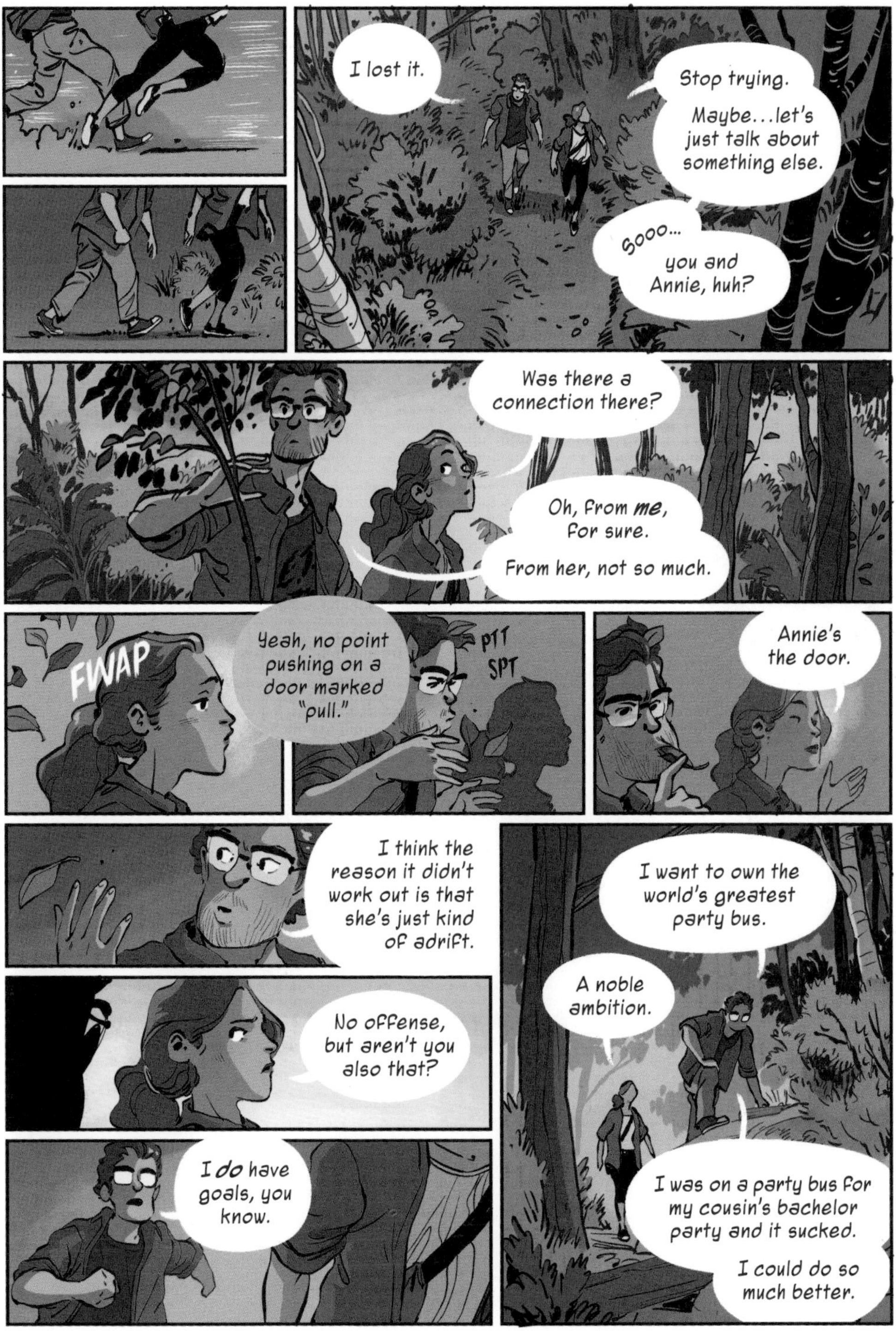
I lost it.
Stop trying.
Maybe...let's just talk about something else.
Sooo...
you and Annie, huh?
Was there a connection there?
Oh, from *me*, for sure.
From her, not so much.
FWAP
Yeah, no point pushing on a door marked "pull."
PTT
SPT
Annie's the door.
I think the reason it didn't work out is that she's just kind of adrift.
No offense, but aren't you also that?
I *do* have goals, you know.
I want to own the world's greatest party bus.
A noble ambition.
I was on a party bus for my cousin's bachelor party and it sucked.
I could do so much better.

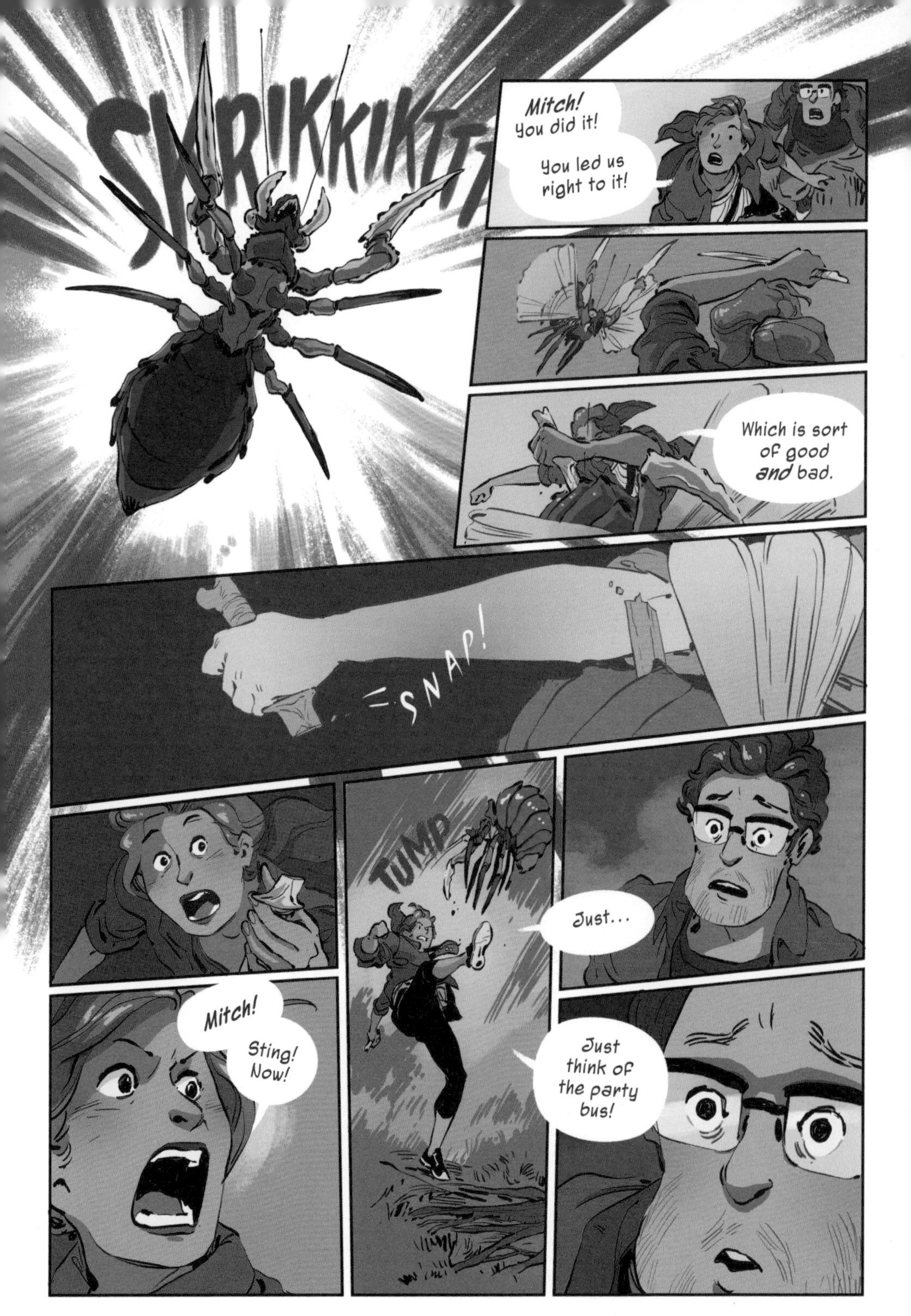
SKRIKKIKITT
Mitch!
You did it!
You led us right to it!
Which is sort of good *and* bad.
SNAP!
TUMP
Just...
Mitch!
Sting! Now!
Just think of the party bus!

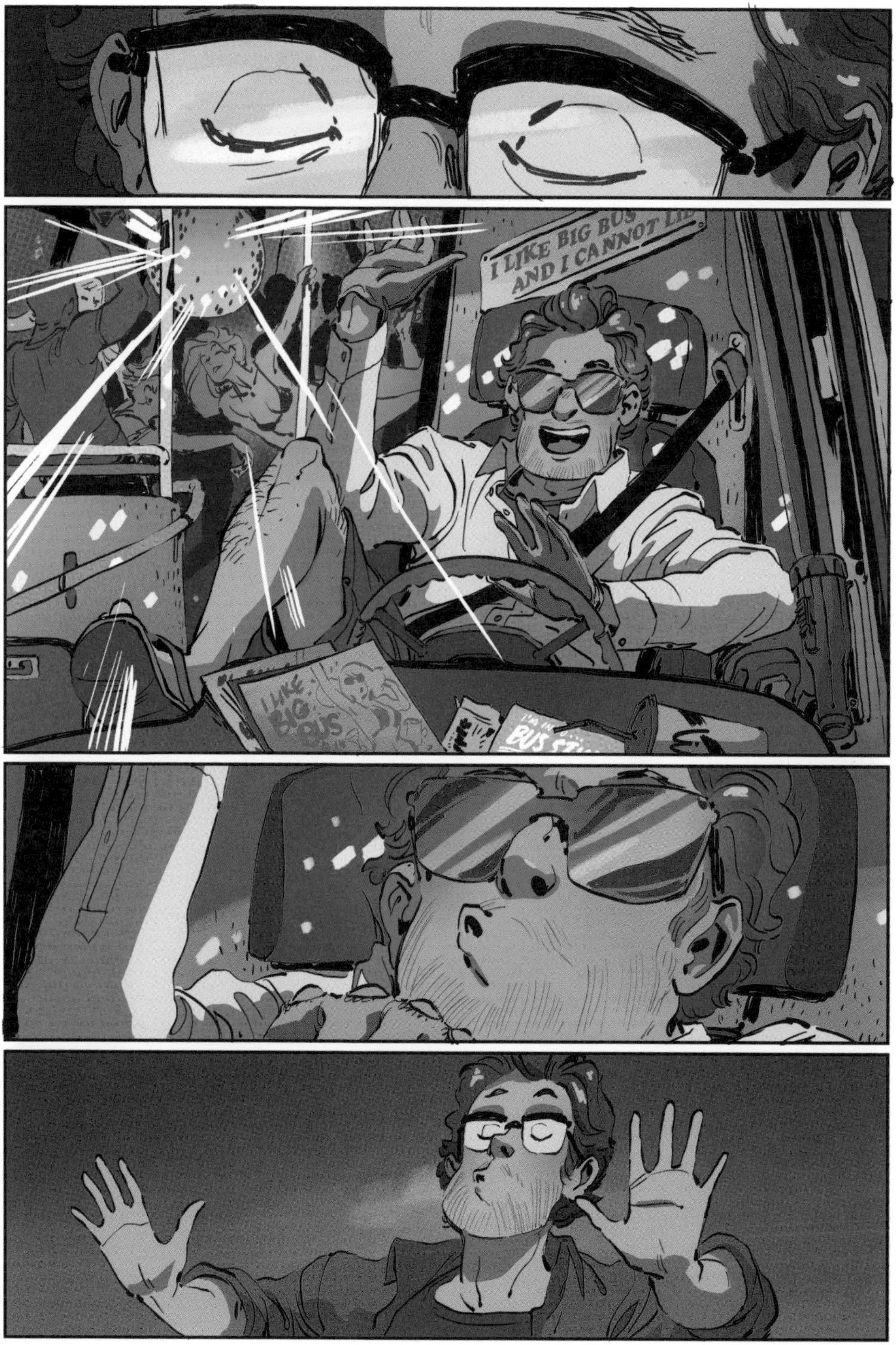
I LIKE BIG BUS
AND I CANNOT LIE
I LIKE BIG BUS

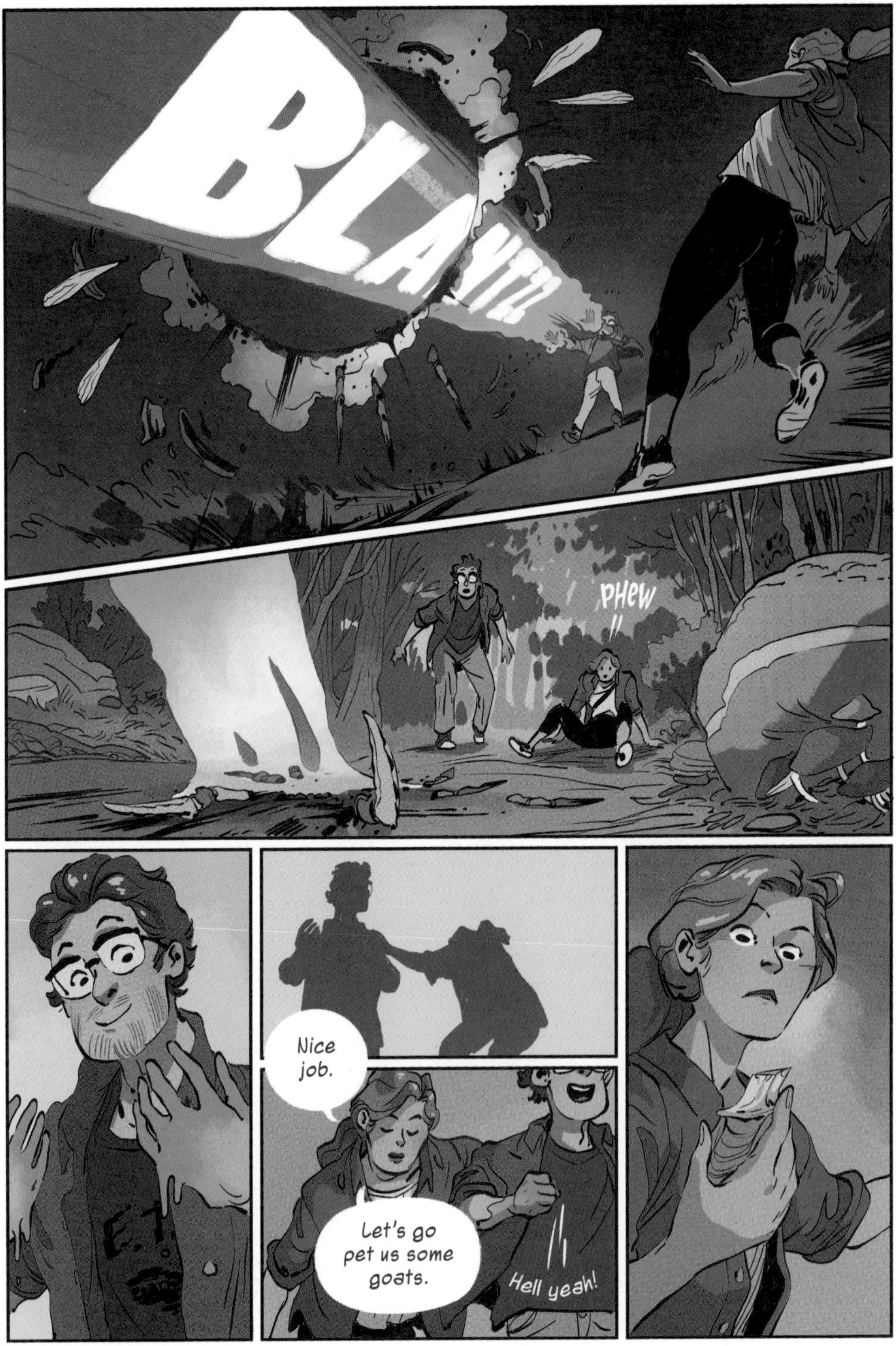
BLAMM
PHEW
Nice job.
Let's go pet us some goats.
Hell yeah!

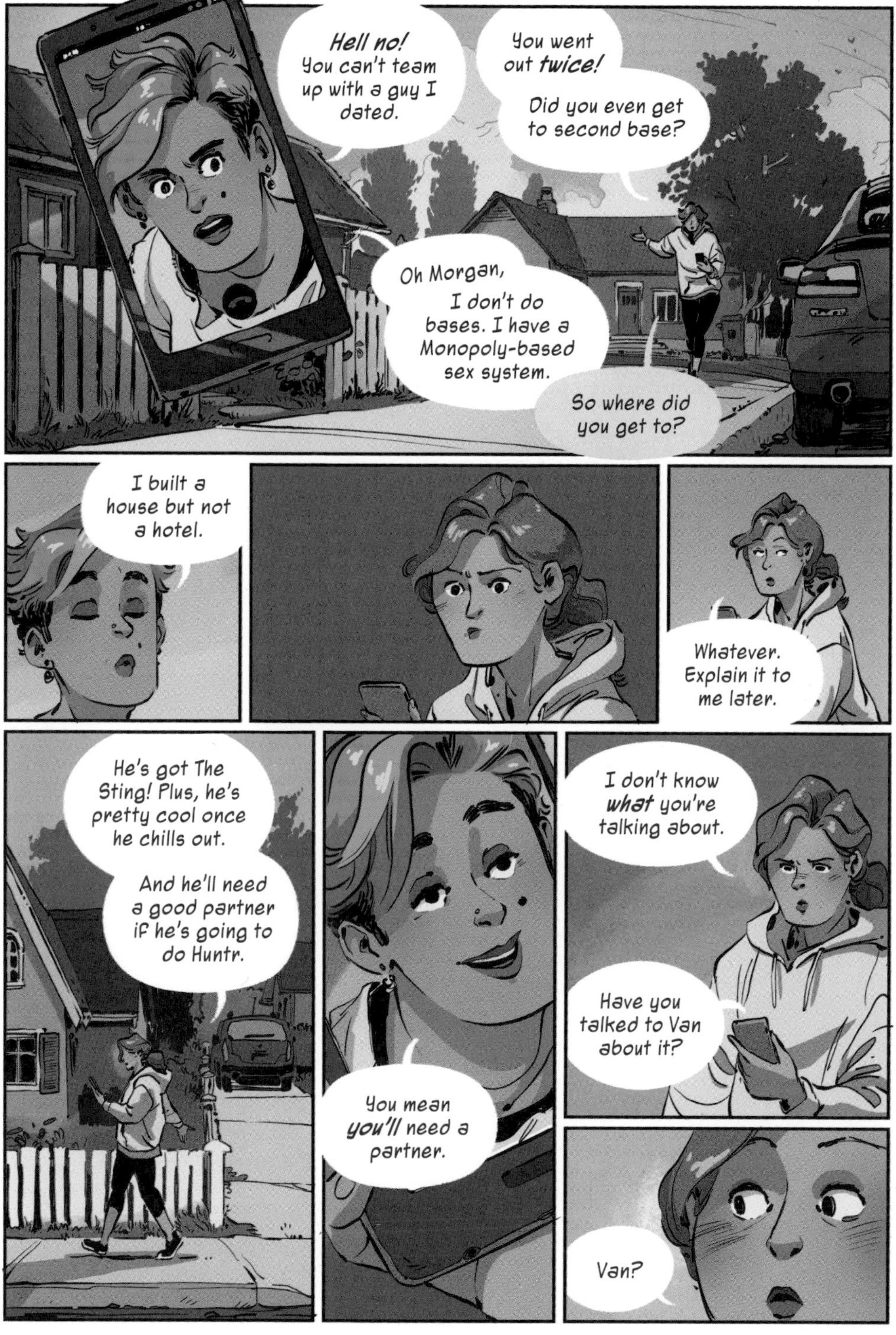
Hell no! You can't team up with a guy I dated.
You went out twice!
Did you even get to second base?
Oh Morgan, I don't do bases. I have a Monopoly-based sex system.
So where did you get to?
I built a house but not a hotel.
Whatever. Explain it to me later.
He's got The Sting! Plus, he's pretty cool once he chills out.
And he'll need a good partner if he's going to do Huntr.
You mean you'll need a partner.
I don't know what you're talking about.
Have you talked to Van about it?
Van?

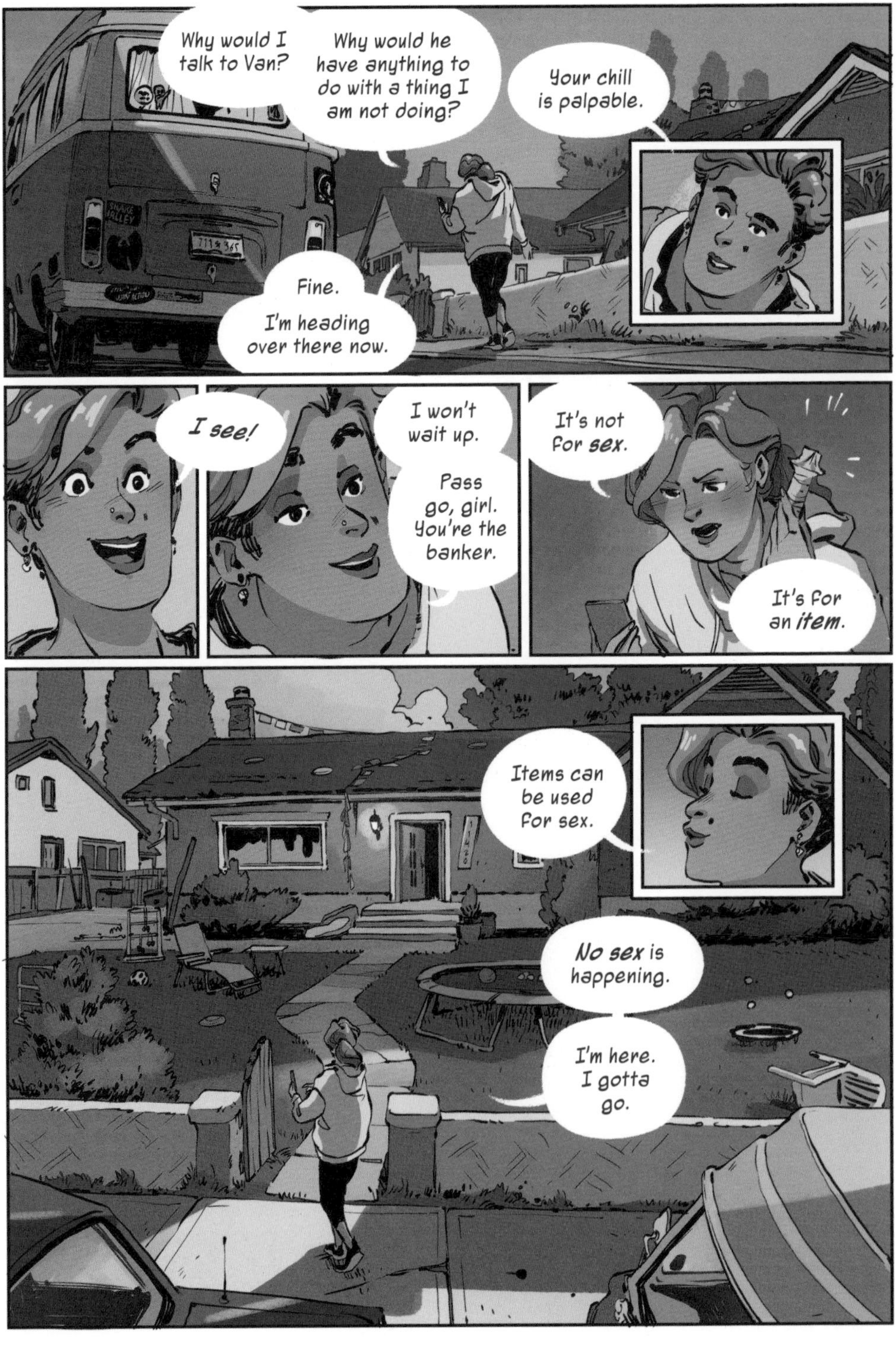
Why would I talk to Van?
Why would he have anything to do with a thing I am not doing?
Your chill is palpable.
Fine. I'm heading over there now.
I see!
I won't wait up.
Pass go, girl. You're the banker.
It's not for sex.
It's for an item.
Items can be used for sex.
No sex is happening.
I'm here. I gotta go.

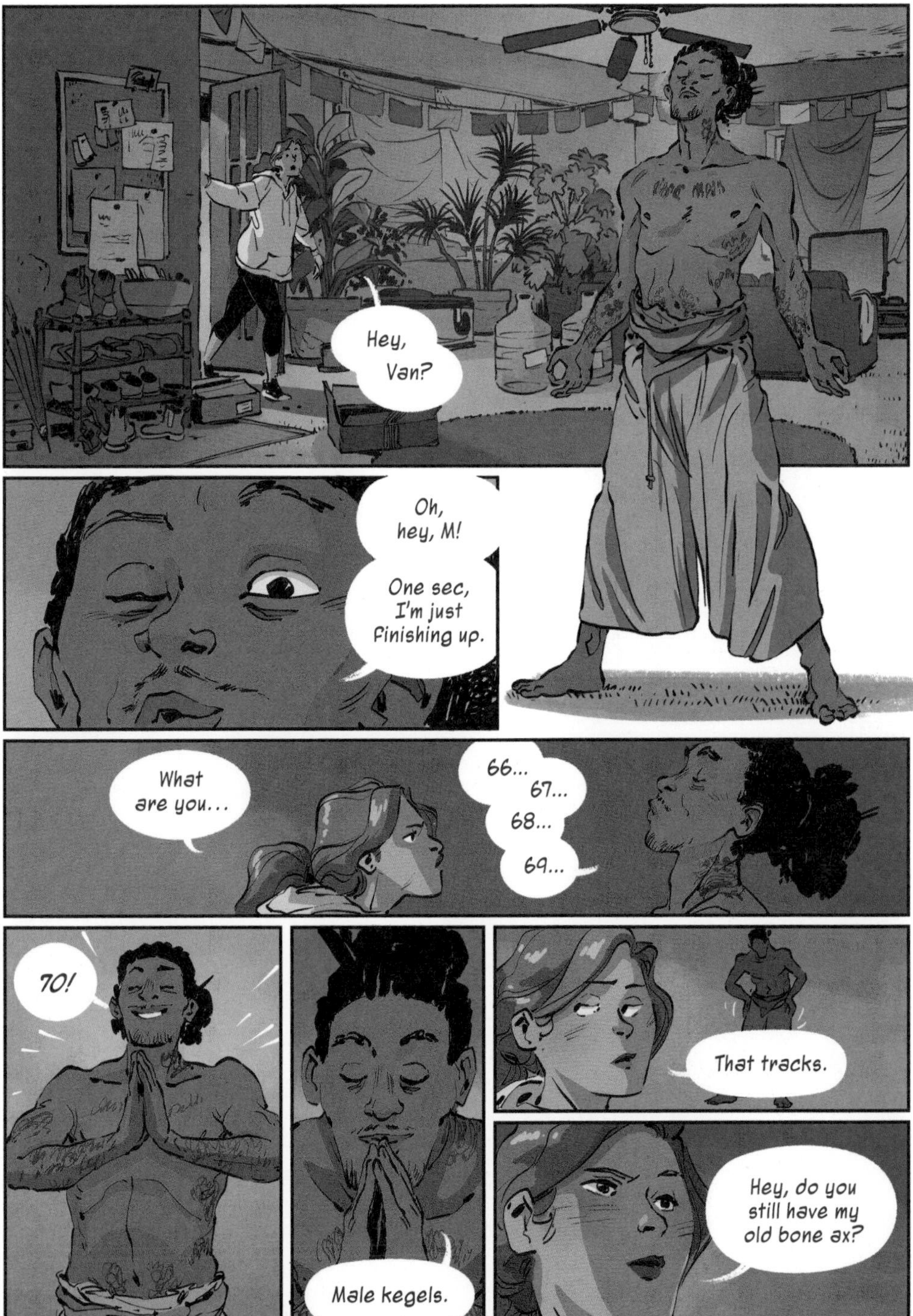
Hey,
Van?
Oh,
hey, M!
One sec,
I'm just
finishing up.
What
are you...
66...
67...
68...
69...
70!
Male kegels.
That tracks.
Hey, do you
still have my
old bone ax?

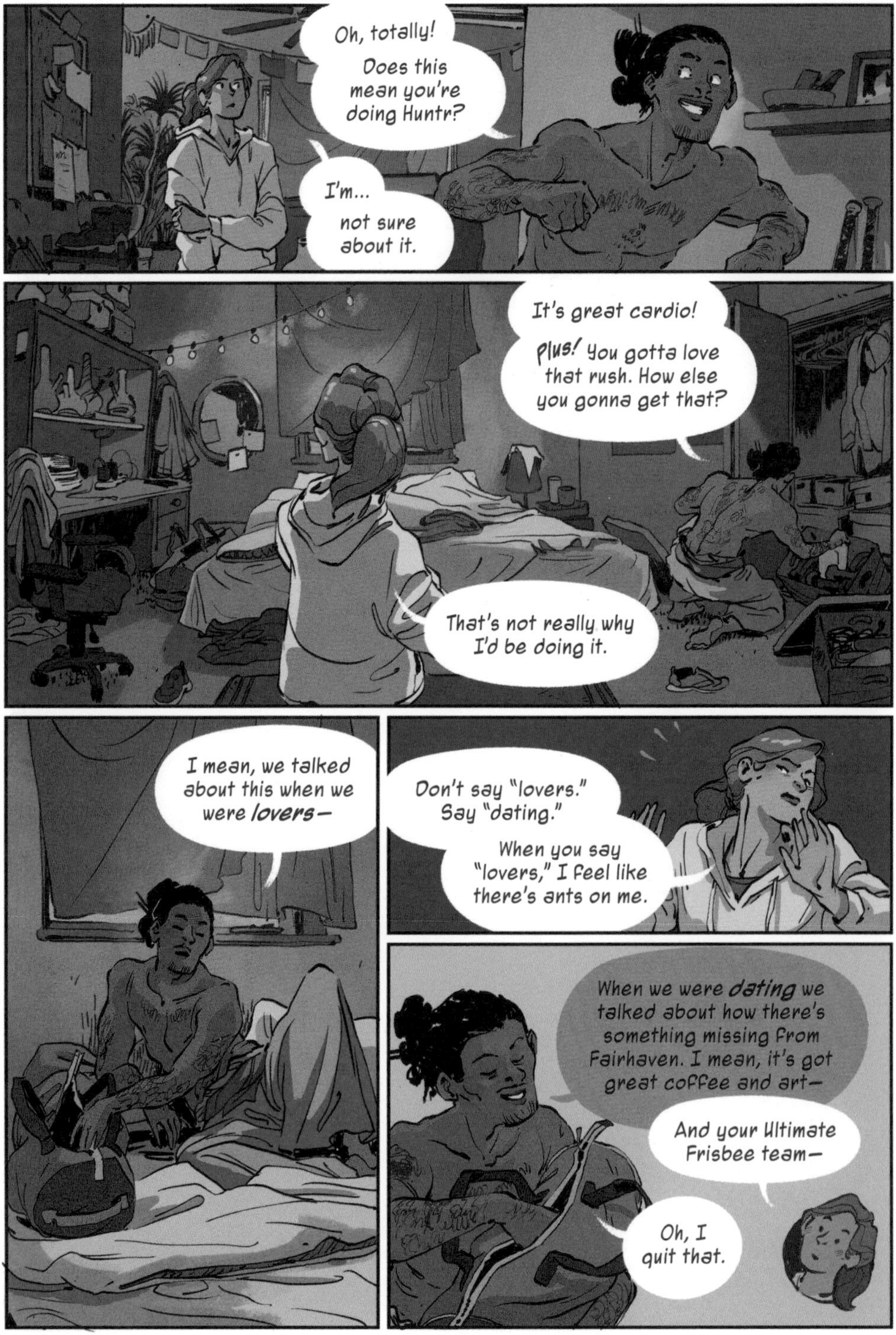
Oh, totally!
Does this mean you're doing Huntr?
I'm... not sure about it.
It's great cardio!
PLUS! You gotta love that rush. How else you gonna get that?
That's not really why I'd be doing it.
I mean, we talked about this when we were lovers—
Don't say "lovers." Say "dating."
When you say "lovers," I feel like there's ants on me.
When we were dating we talked about how there's something missing from Fairhaven. I mean, it's got great coffee and art—
And your Ultimate Frisbee team—
Oh, I quit that.

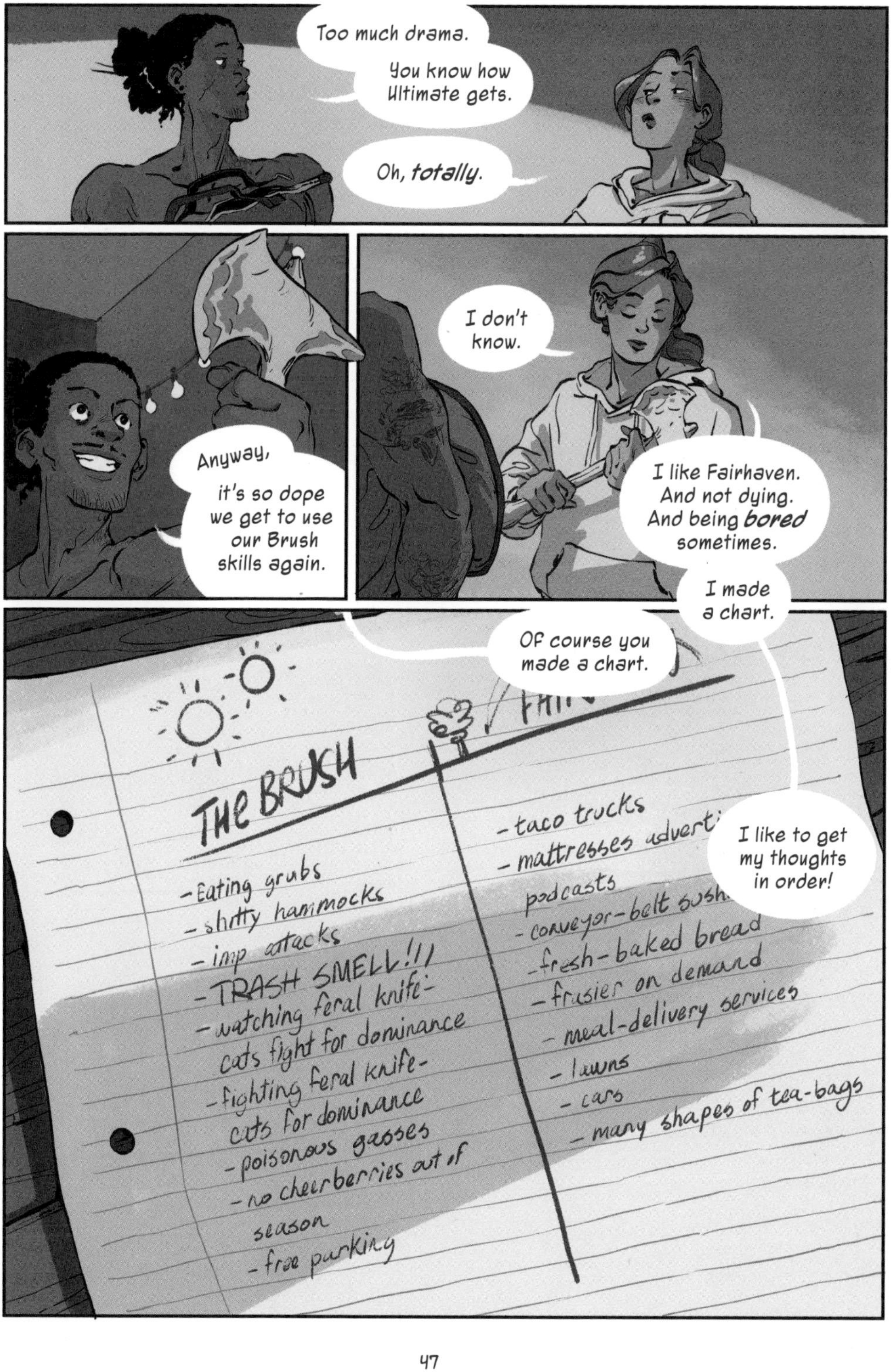
Too much drama.
You know how Ultimate gets.
Oh, *totally*.
Anyway,
it's so dope we get to use our Brush skills again.
I don't know.
I like Fairhaven. And not dying. And being *bored* sometimes.
I made a chart.
Of course you made a chart.
I like to get my thoughts in order!
THE BRUSH
-Eating grubs
-shitty hammocks
-imp attacks
-TRASH SMELL!!!
-watching feral knife-cats fight for dominance
-fighting feral knife-cats for dominance
-poisonous gasses
-no cheerberries out of season
-free parking
-taco trucks
-mattresses
podcasts
-conveyor-belt
-fresh-baked bread
-frasier on demand
-meal-delivery services
-lawns
-cars
-many shapes of tea-bags

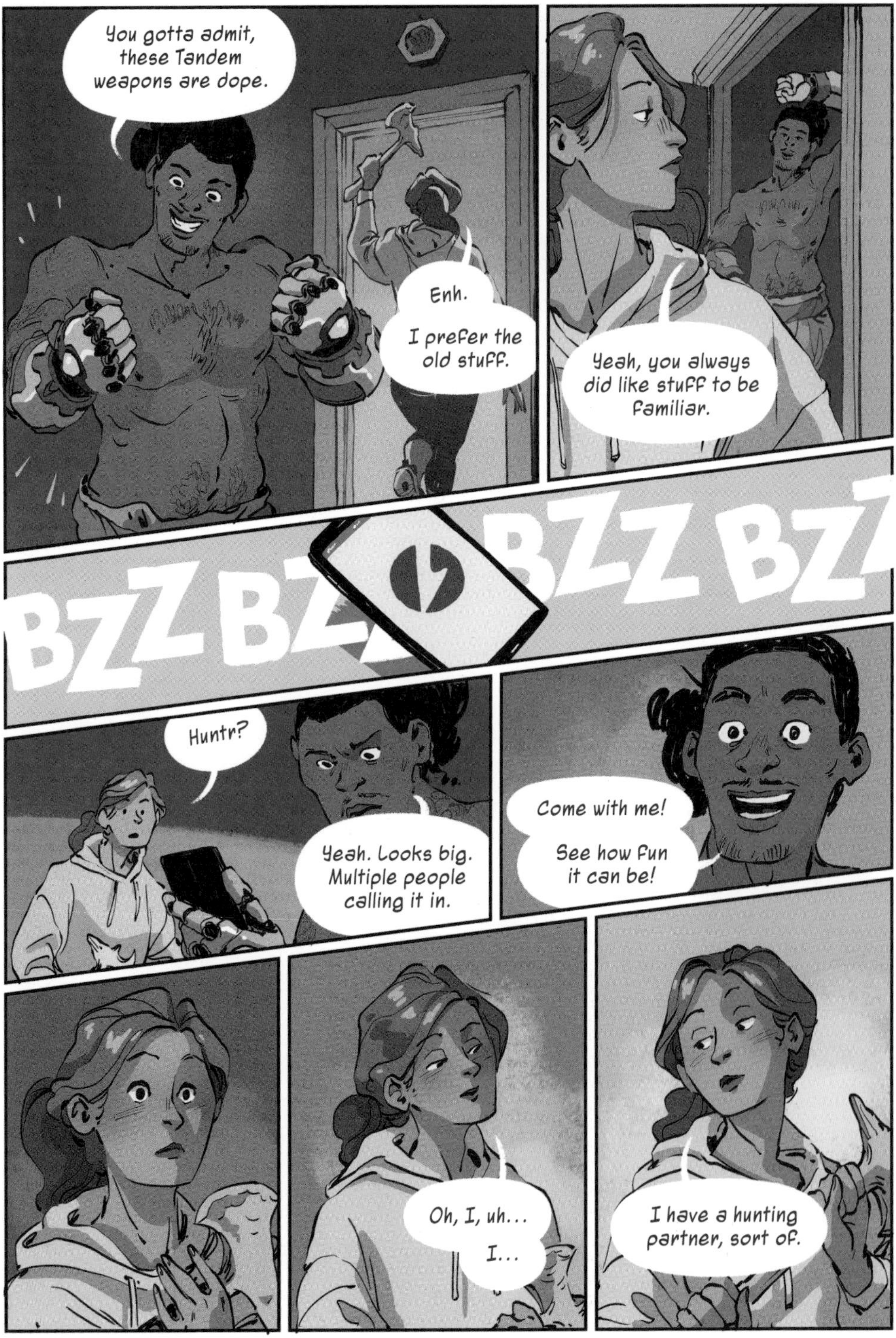
You gotta admit, these Tandem weapons are dope.
Enh.
I prefer the old stuff.
Yeah, you always did like stuff to be familiar.
BZZ BZZ BZZ BZ
Huntr?
Yeah. Looks big. Multiple people calling it in.
Come with me!
See how fun it can be!
Oh, I, uh...
I...
I have a hunting partner, sort of.

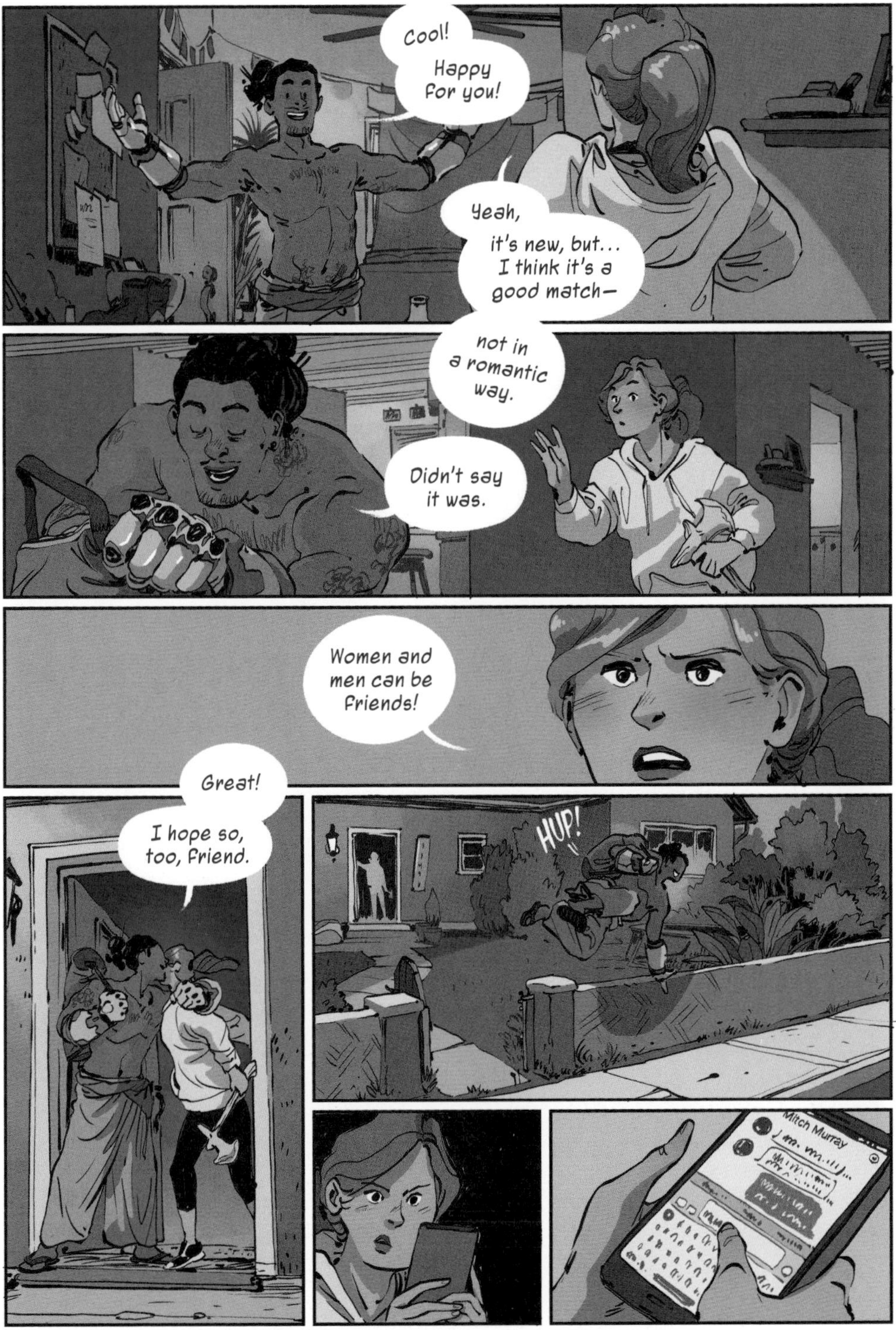
Cool!
Happy for you!
Yeah,
it's new, but... I think it's a good match—
not in a romantic way.
Didn't say it was.
Women and men can be friends!
Great!
I hope so, too, friend.
HUP!
Mitch Murray

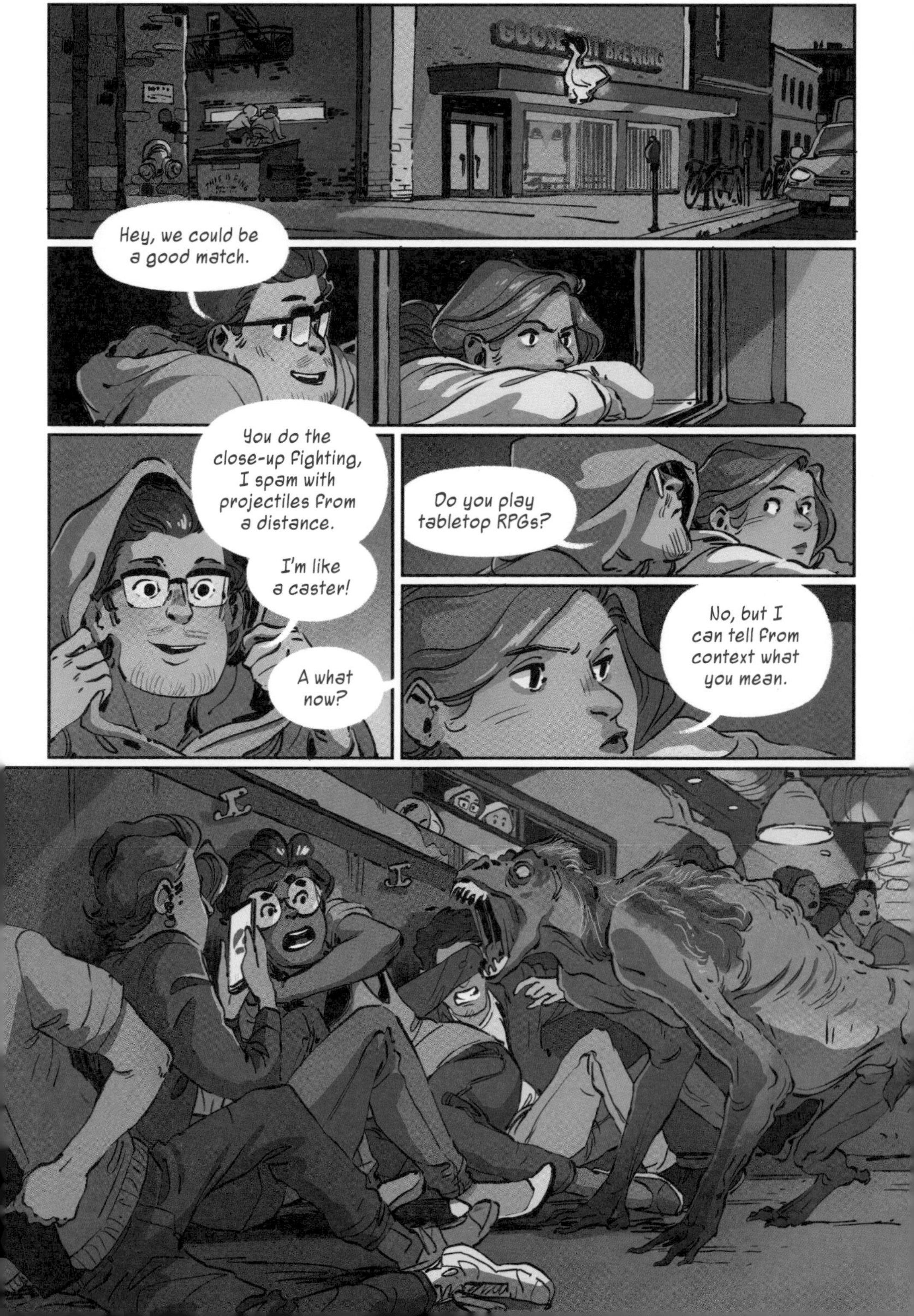
Hey, we could be a good match.
You do the close-up fighting, I spam with projectiles from a distance.
I'm like a caster!
A what now?
Do you play tabletop RPGs?
No, but I can tell from context what you mean.

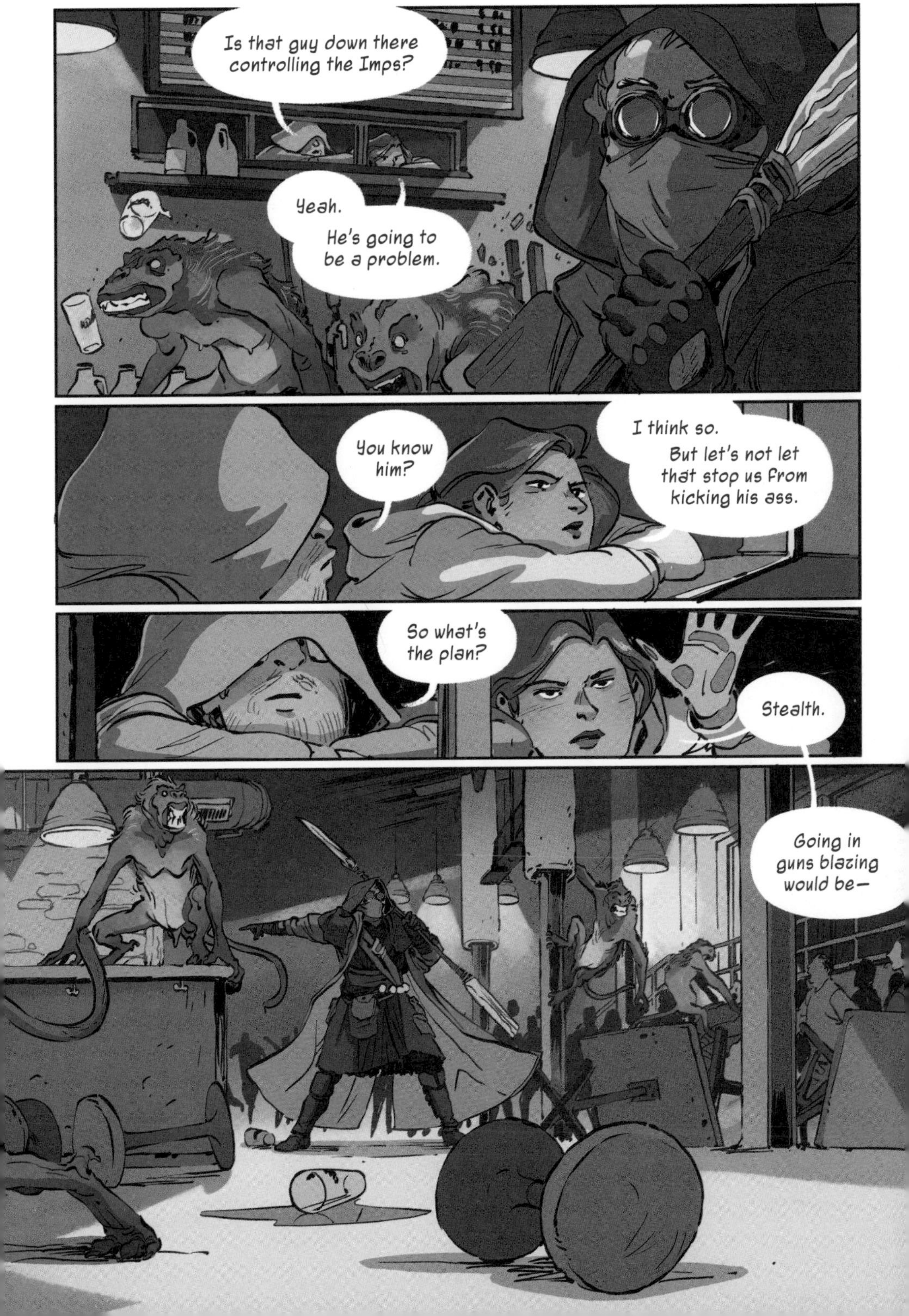

Is that guy down there controlling the Imps?
Yeah.
He's going to be a problem.
You know him?
I think so.
But let's not let that stop us from kicking his ass.
So what's the plan?
Stealth.
Going in guns blazing would be—

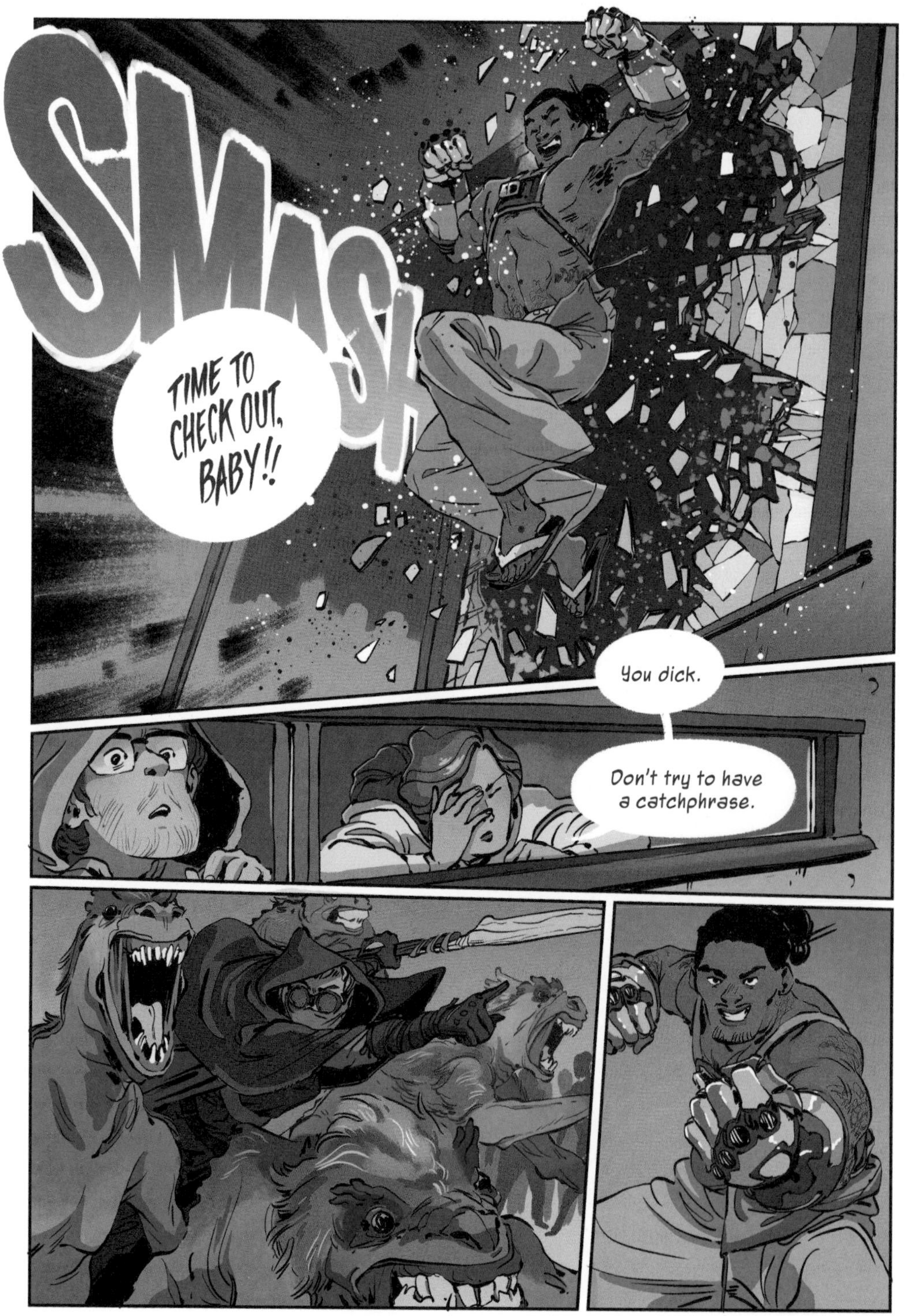
SMASH
TIME TO CHECK OUT, BABY!!
You dick.
Don't try to have a catchphrase.

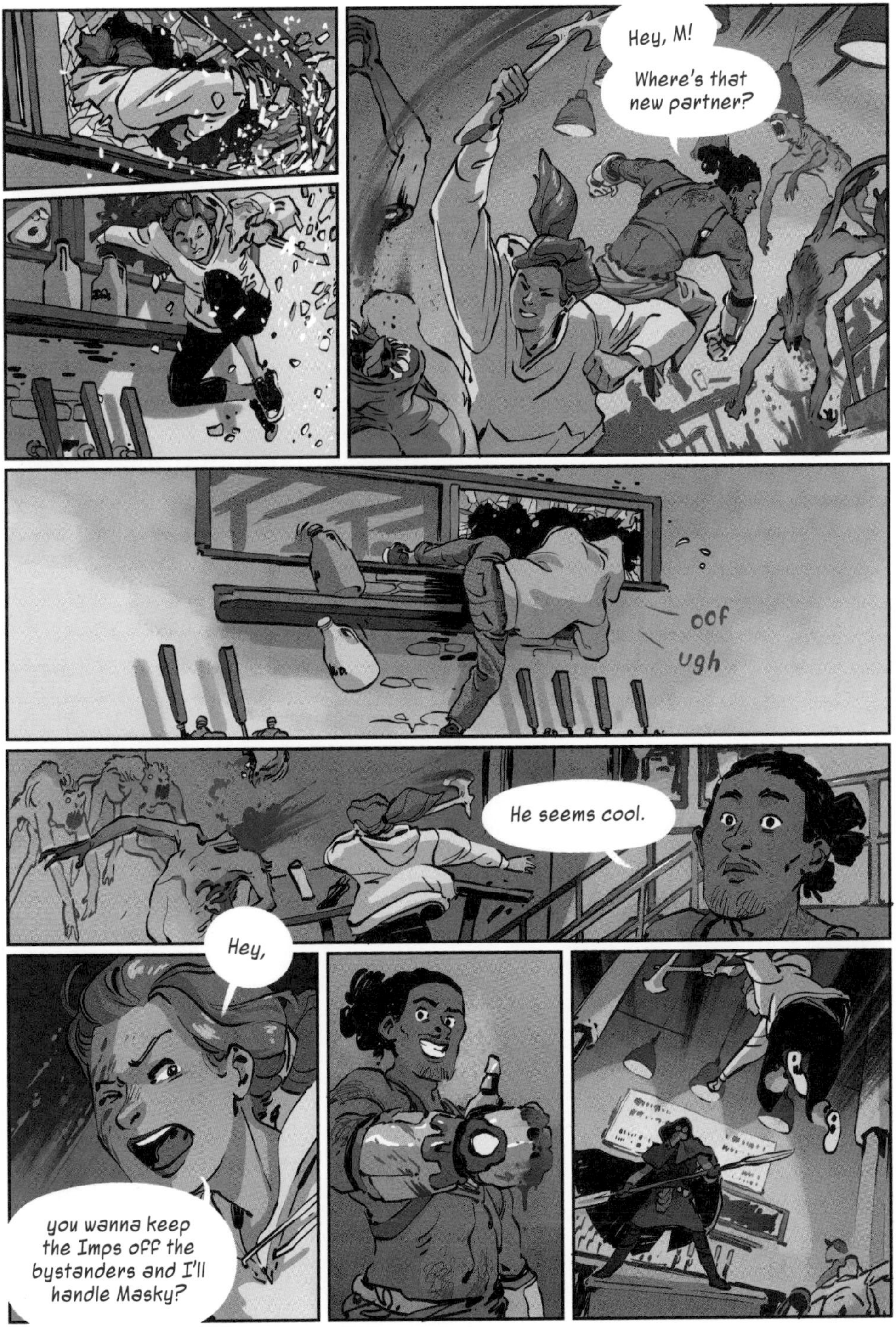
Hey, M!
Where's that new partner?
oof
ugh
He seems cool.
Hey,
you wanna keep the Imps off the bystanders and I'll handle Masky?

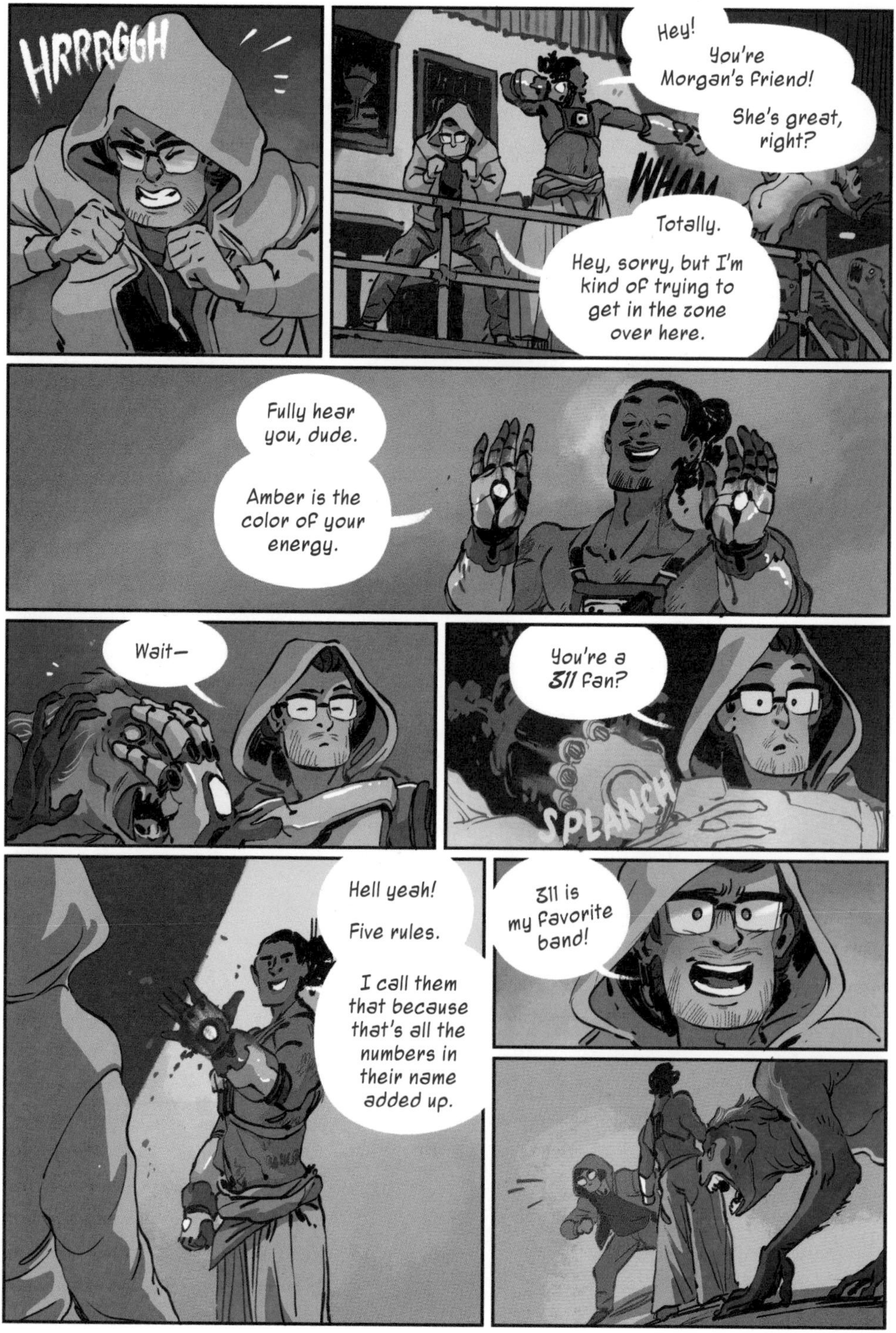
HRRRGGH
Hey!
You're Morgan's friend!
She's great, right?
WHAM
Totally.
Hey, sorry, but I'm kind of trying to get in the zone over here.
Fully hear you, dude.
Amber is the color of your energy.
Wait—
You're a 311 fan?
SPLANCH
Hell yeah!
Five rules.
I call them that because that's all the numbers in their name added up.
311 is my favorite band!

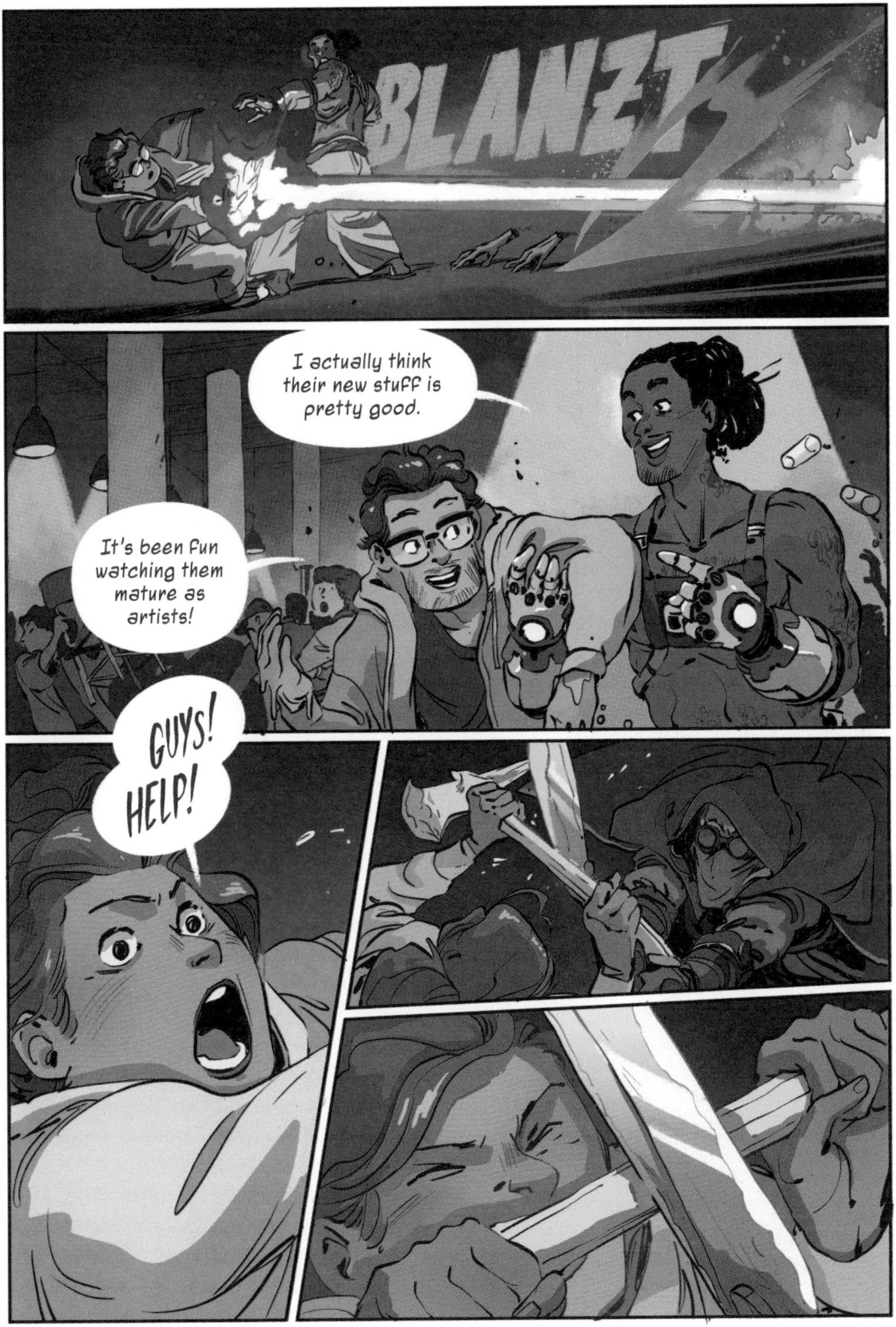
BLANZT
I actually think their new stuff is pretty good.
It's been fun watching them mature as artists!
GUYS! HELP!

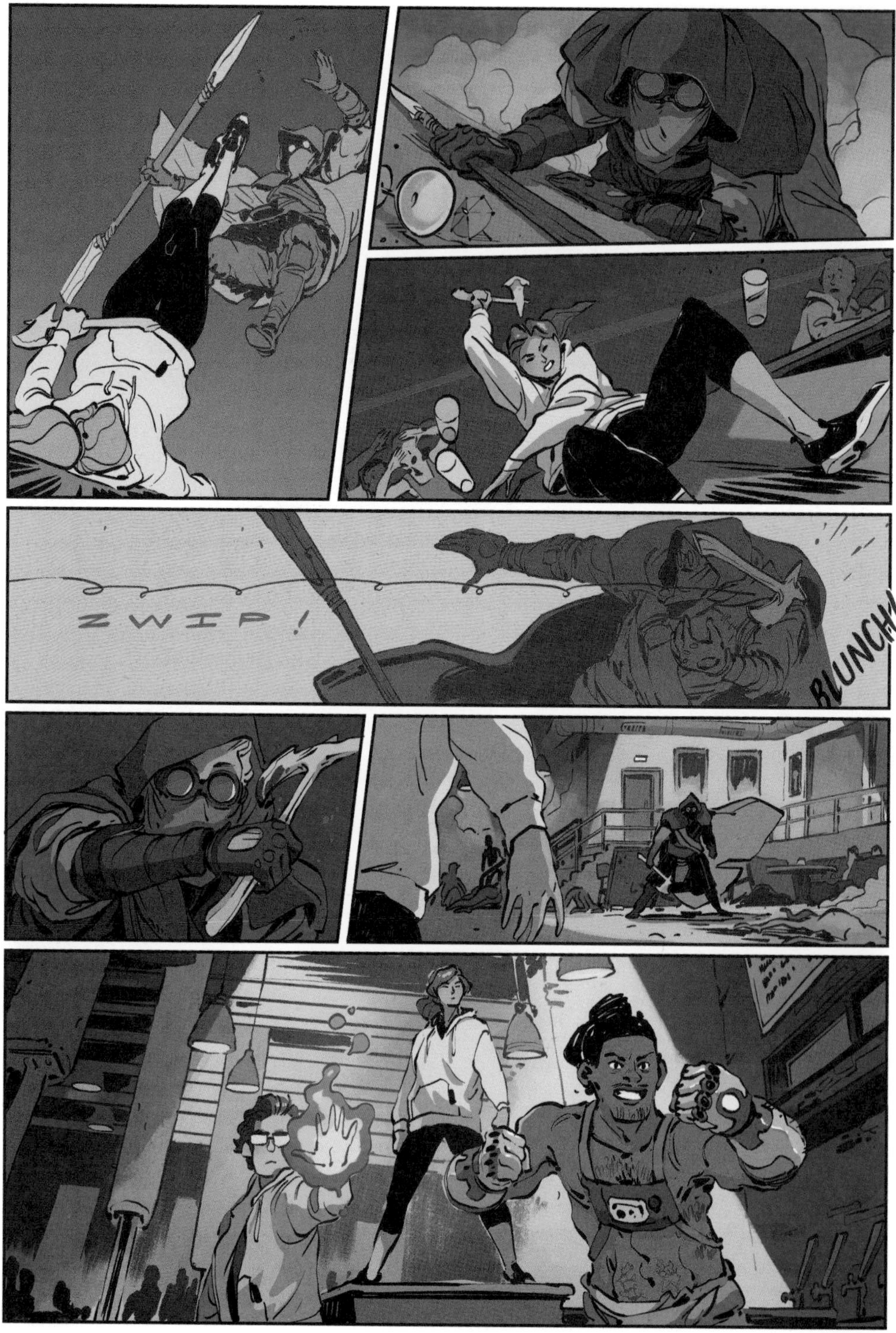
ZWIP!
BLUNCH!

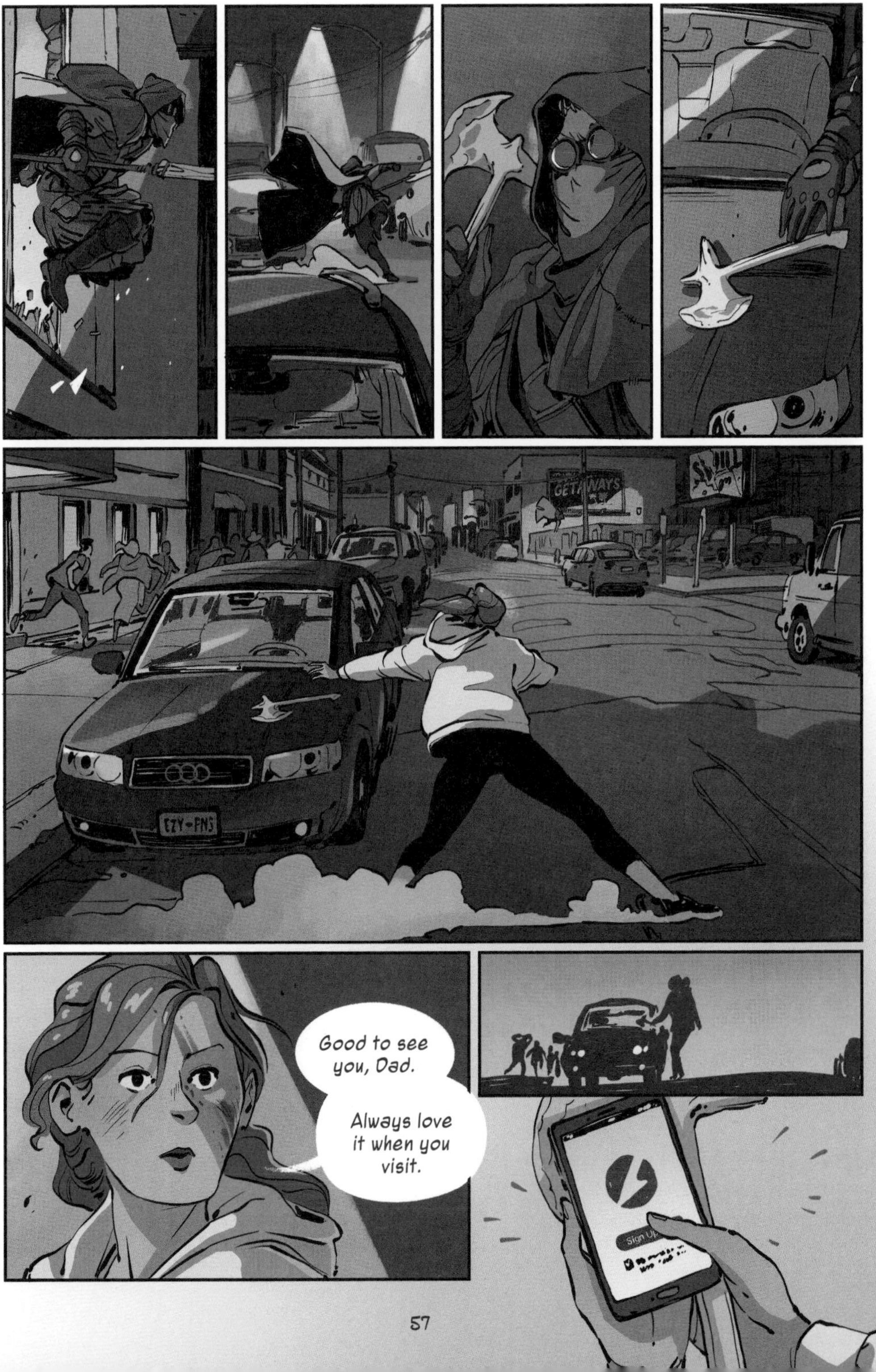
GETAWAYS
EZY-PNS
Good to see you, Dad.
Always love it when you visit.
Sign Up

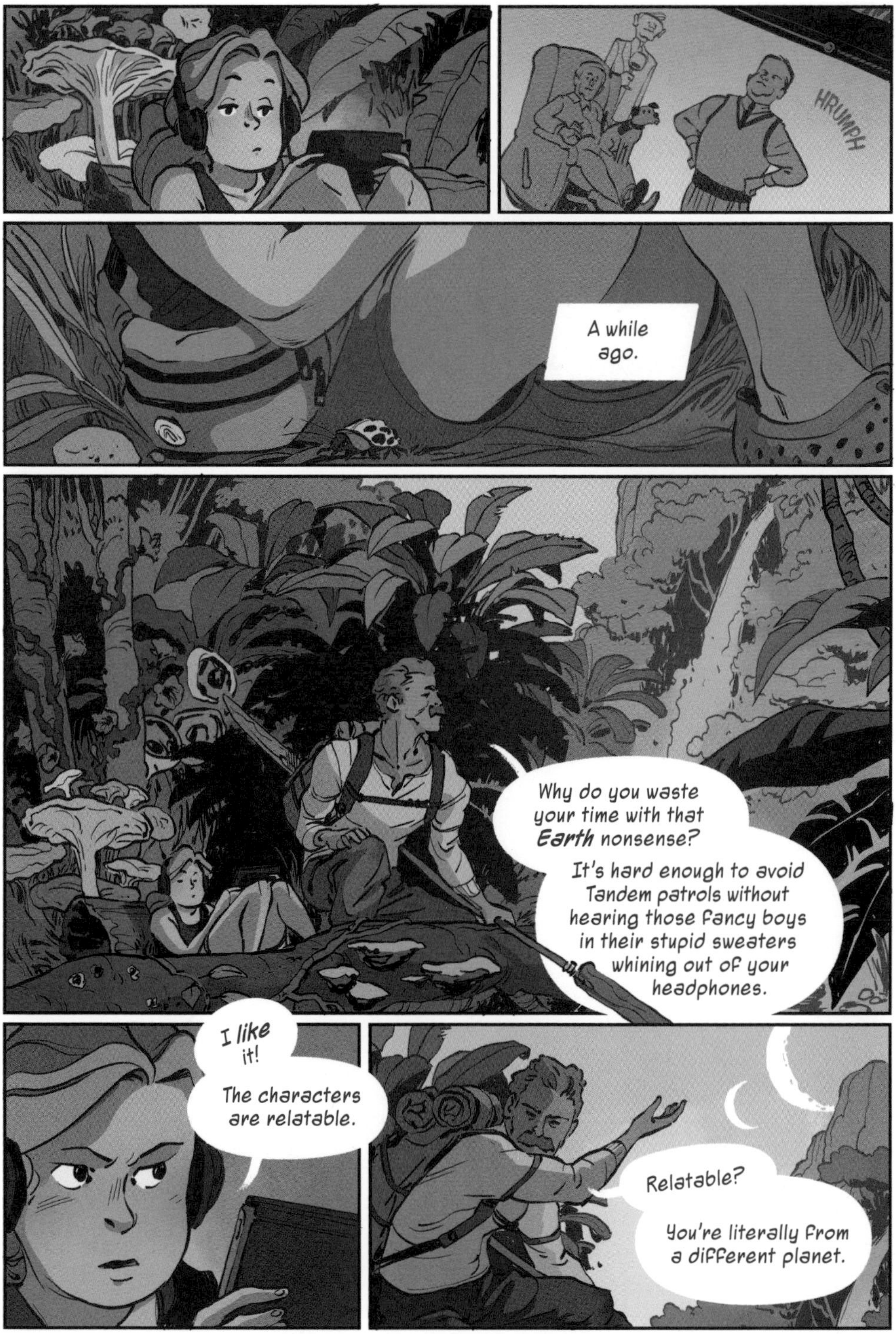
HRUMPH
A while ago.
Why do you waste your time with that Earth nonsense?
It's hard enough to avoid Tandem patrols without hearing those fancy boys in their stupid sweaters whining out of your headphones.
I like it!
The characters are relatable.
Relatable?
You're literally from a different planet.

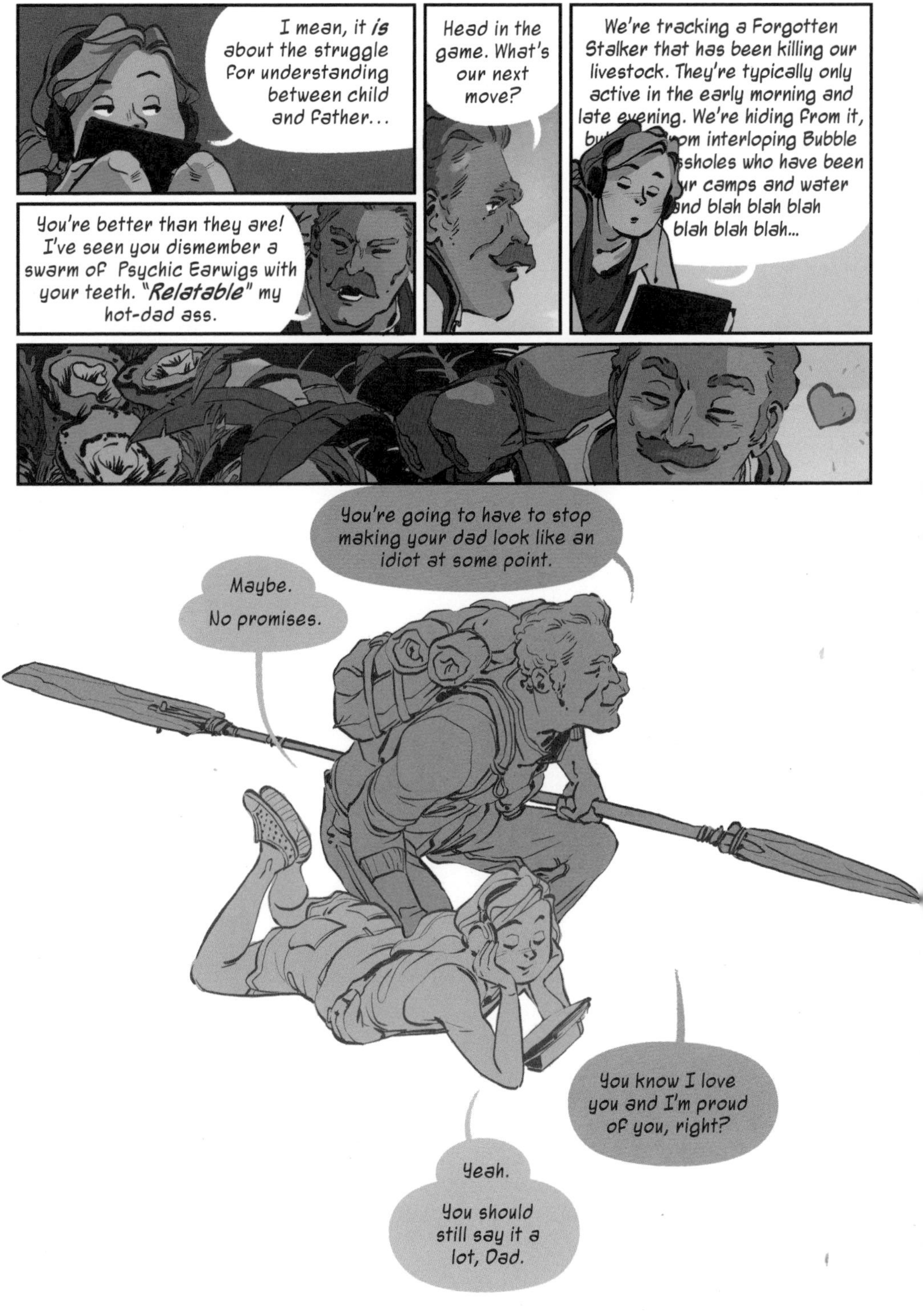
I mean, it *is* about the struggle for understanding between child and father...
You're better than they are! I've seen you dismember a swarm of Psychic Earwigs with your teeth. "*Relatable*" my hot-dad ass.
Head in the game. What's our next move?
We're tracking a Forgotten Stalker that has been killing our livestock. They're typically only active in the early morning and late evening. We're hiding from it,
om interloping Bubble
sholes who have been
r camps and water
nd blah blah blah
blah blah blah...
You're going to have to stop making your dad look like an idiot at some point.
Maybe.
No promises.
You know I love you and I'm proud of you, right?
Yeah.
You should still say it a lot, Dad.

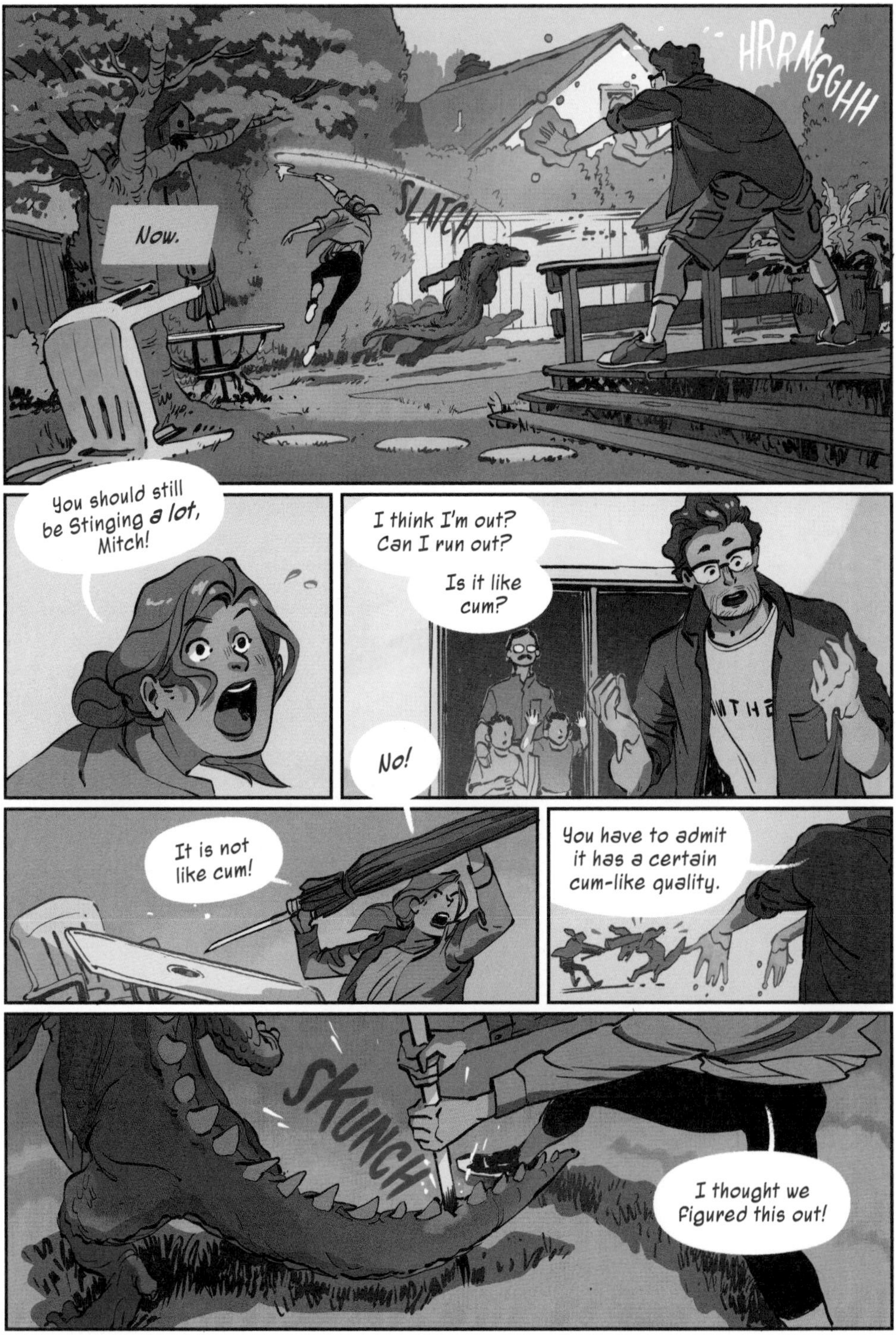
HRRNGGHH
Now.
SLATCH
You should still be Stinging *a lot*, Mitch!
I think I'm out? Can I run out?
Is it like cum?
No!
It is not like cum!
You have to admit it has a certain cum-like quality.
SKUNCH
I thought we figured this out!

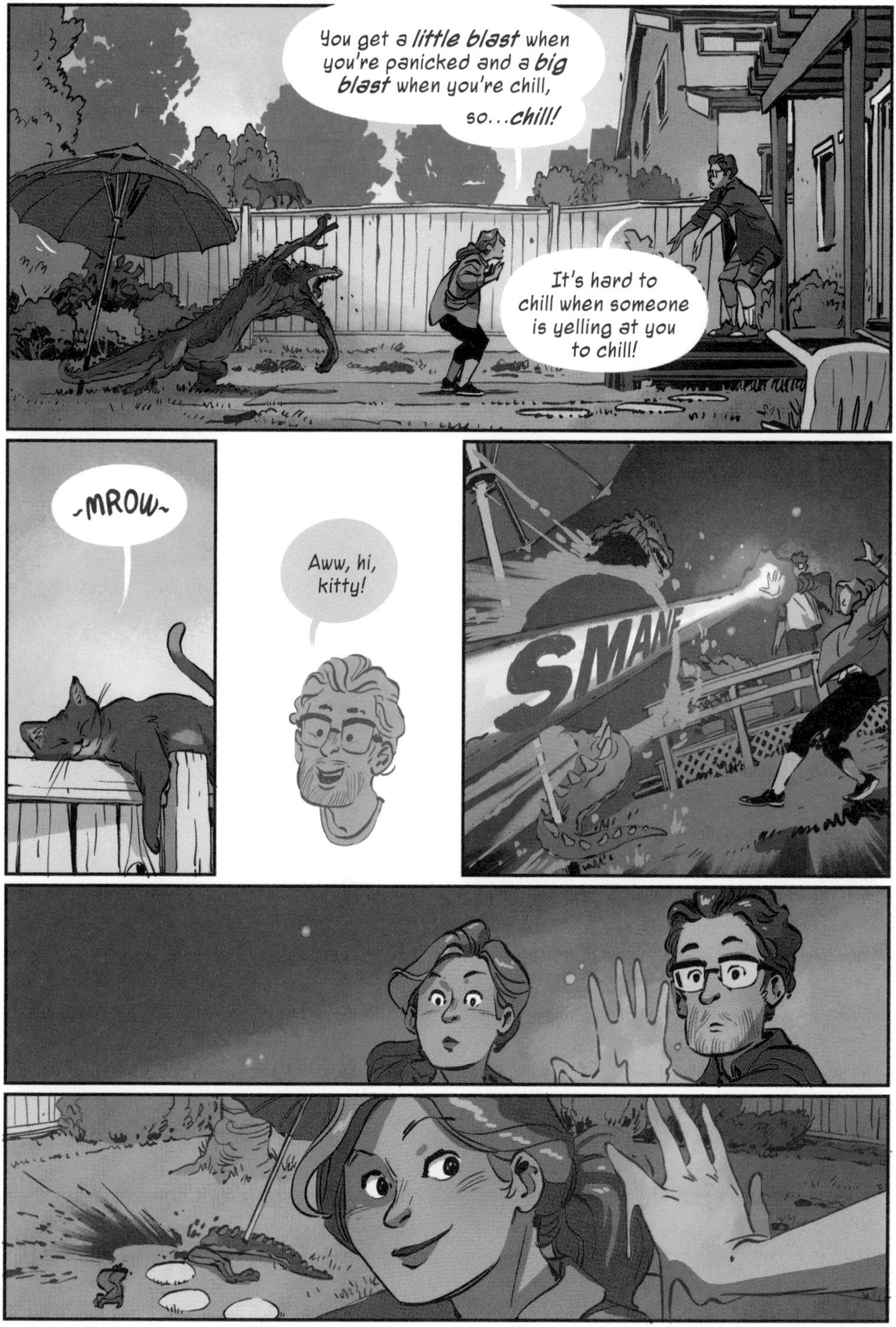
You get a *little blast* when you're panicked and a *big blast* when you're chill, so...*chill!*
It's hard to chill when someone is yelling at you to chill!
-MROW-
Aww, hi, kitty!
SMANF

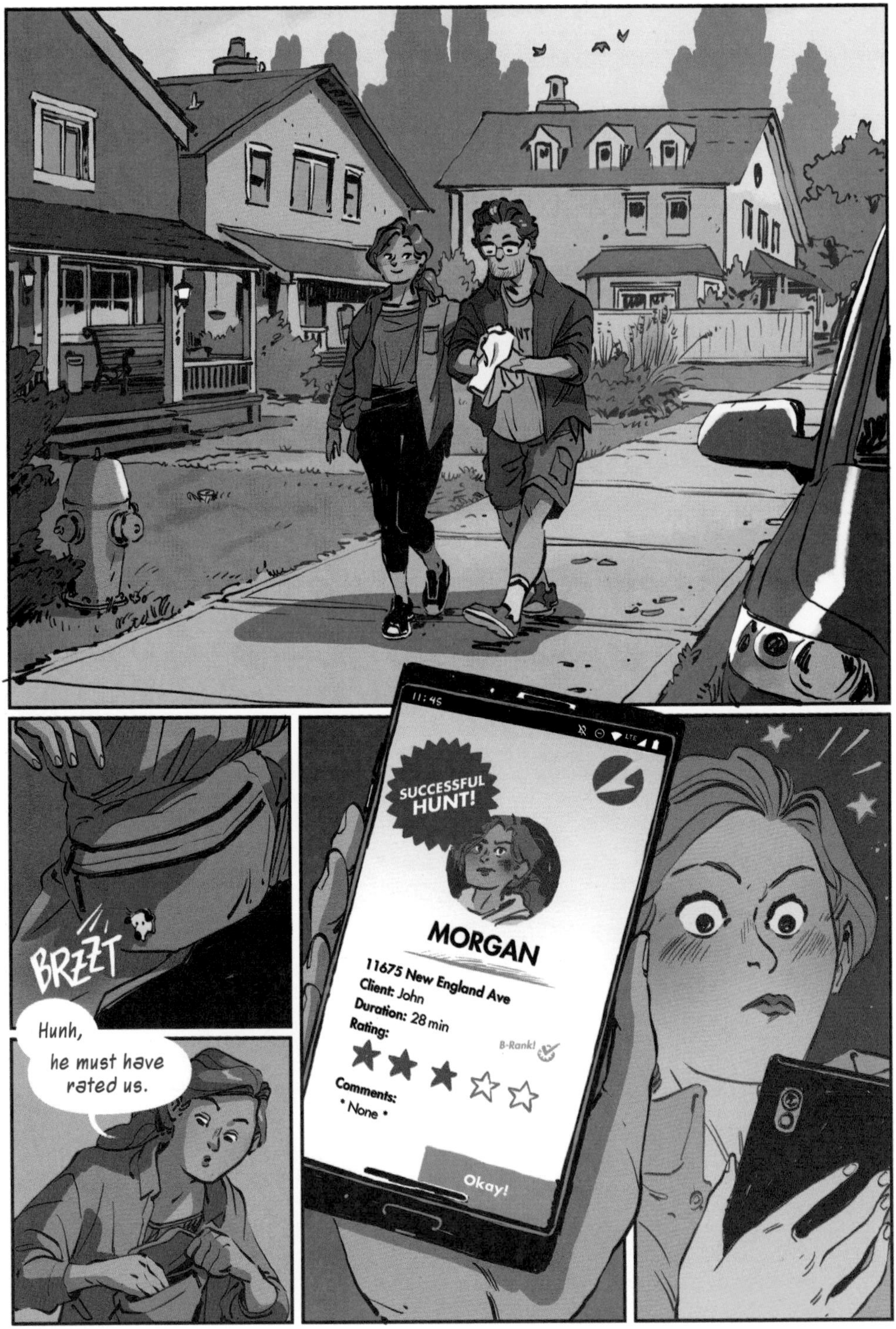
BRZZT
Hunh, he must have rated us.
11:45
SUCCESSFUL HUNT!
MORGAN
11675 New England Ave
Client: John
Duration: 28 min
Rating:
B-Rank!
Comments:
* None *
Okay!

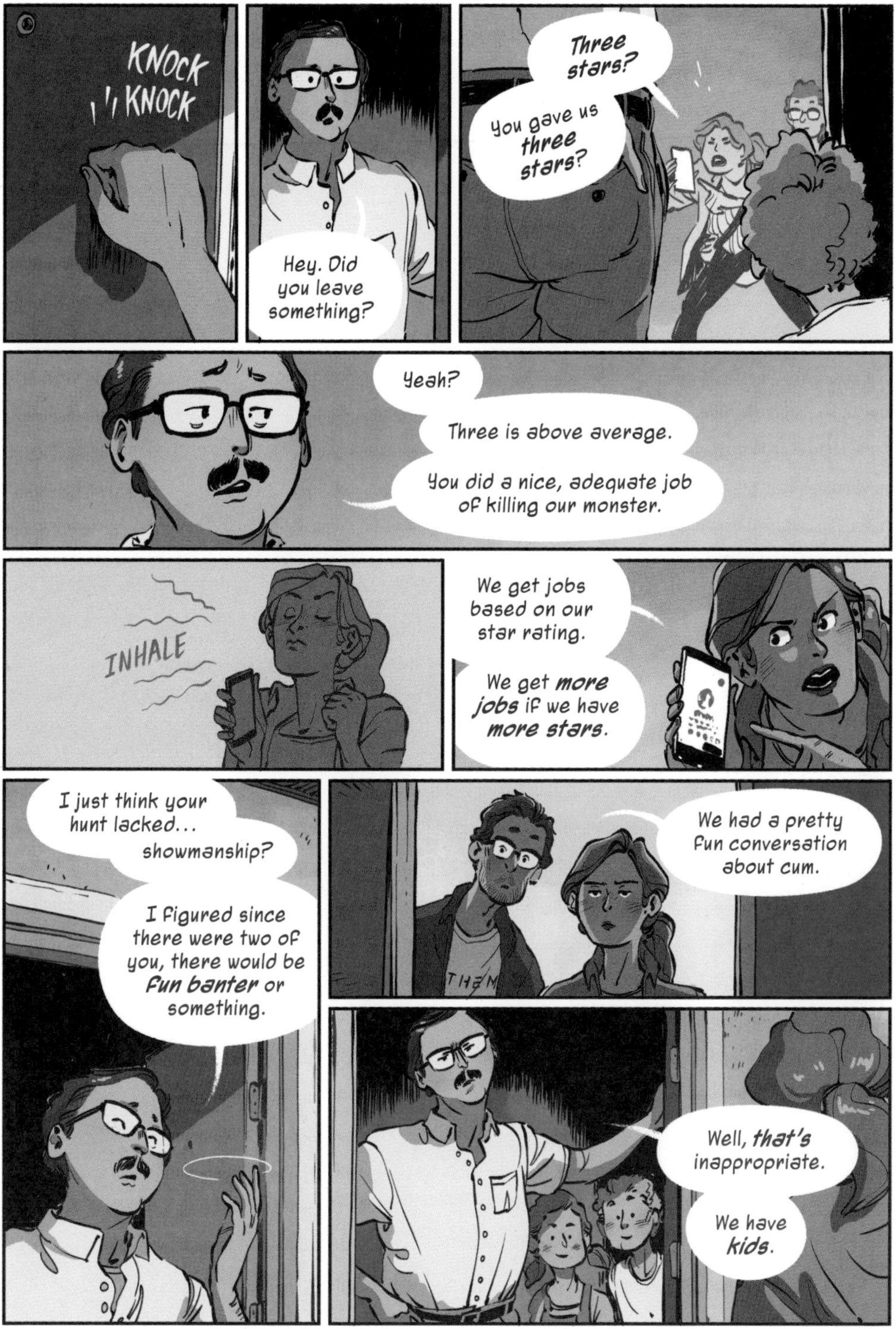
KNOCK KNOCK
Hey. Did you leave something?
Three stars?
You gave us three stars?
Yeah?
Three is above average.
You did a nice, adequate job of killing our monster.
INHALE
We get jobs based on our star rating.
We get more jobs if we have more stars.
I just think your hunt lacked... showmanship?
I figured since there were two of you, there would be fun banter or something.
We had a pretty fun conversation about cum.
Well, that's inappropriate.
We have kids.

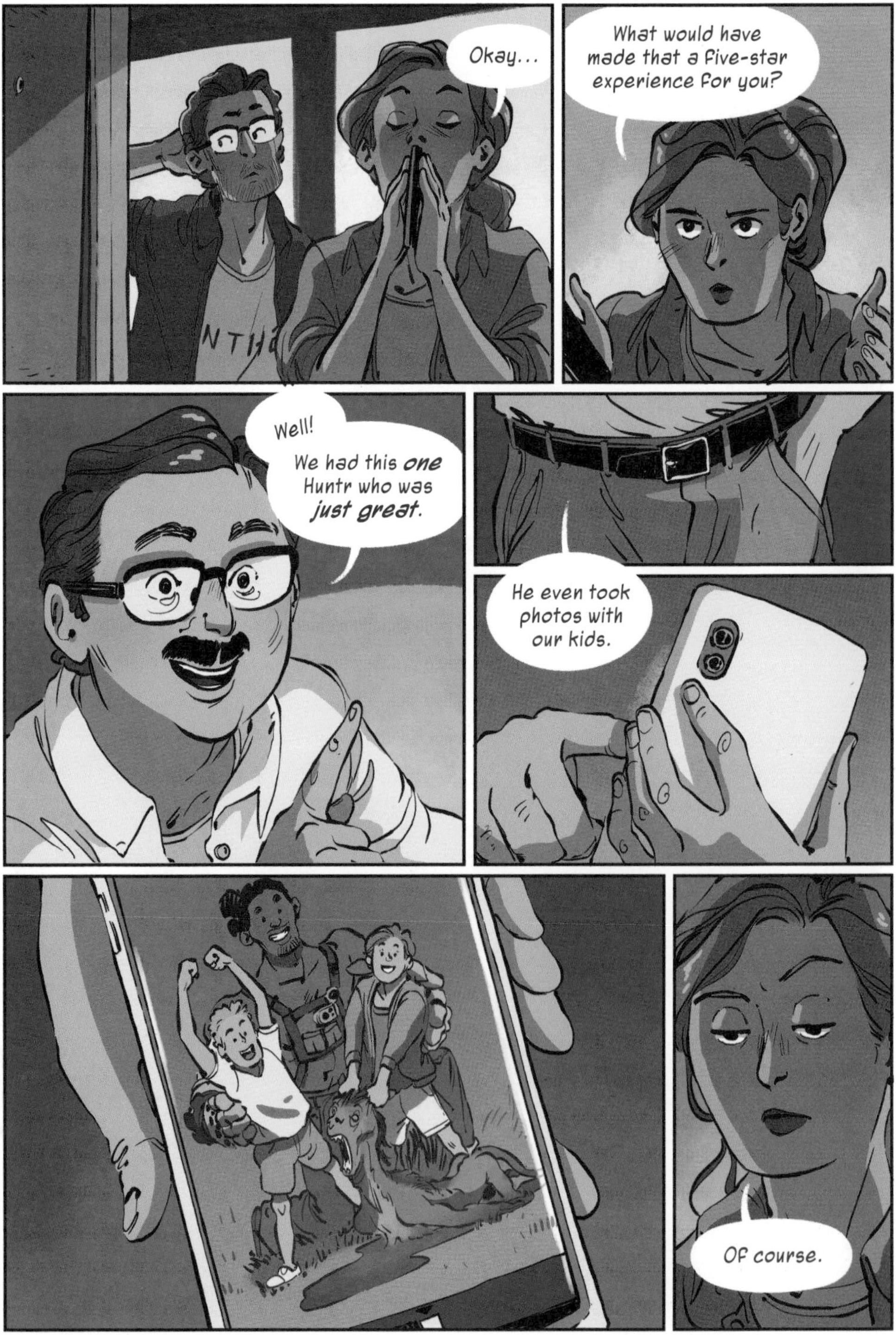
Okay...
What would have made that a five-star experience for you?
Well!
We had this *one* Huntr who was ***just great***.
He even took photos with our kids.
Of course.

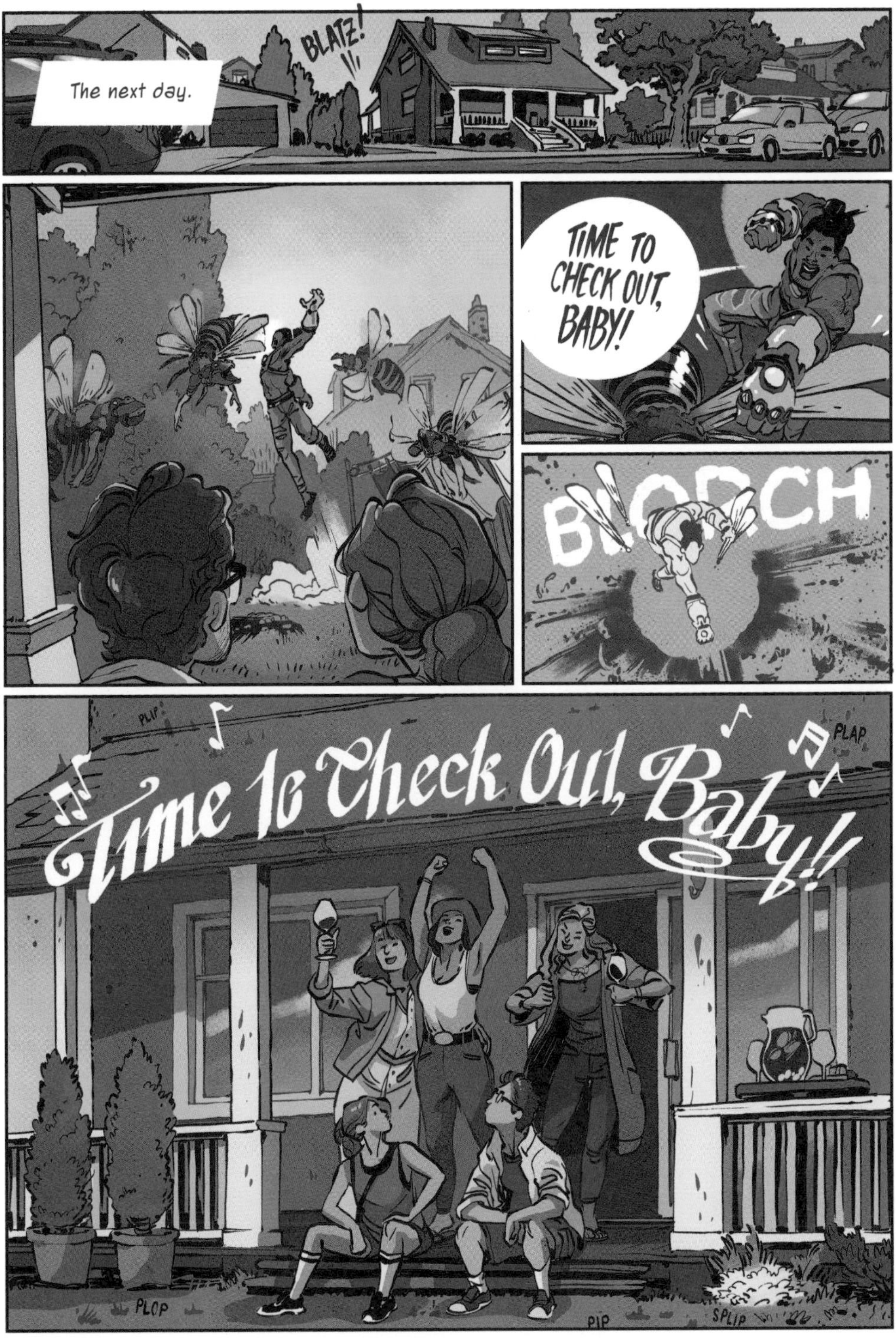
The next day.
BLATZ!
TIME TO CHECK OUT, BABY!
BLORCH
PLIP
PLAP
Time to Check Out, Baby!!
PLOP
PIP
SPLIP

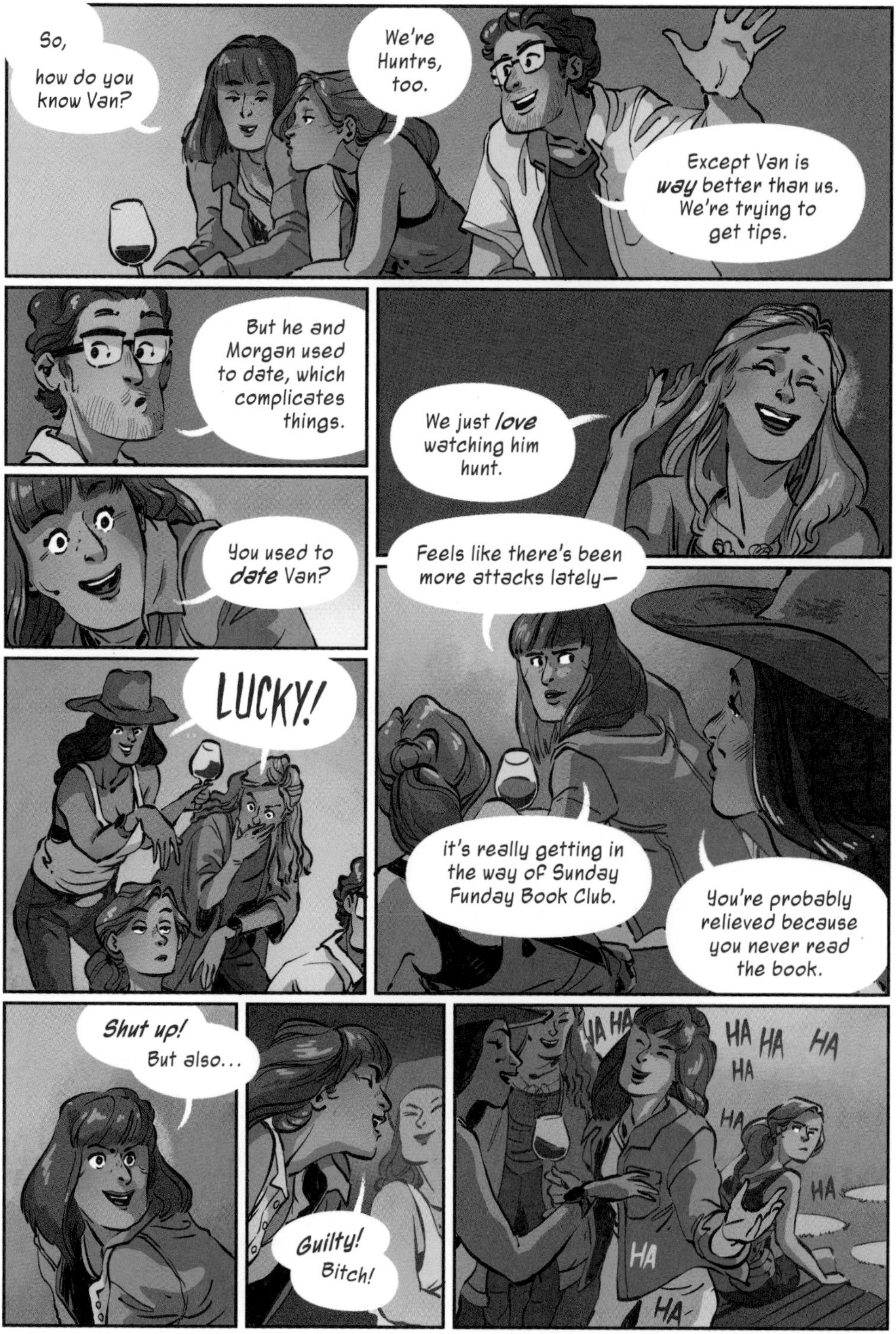
So,
how do you know Van?
We're Huntrs, too.
Except Van is *way* better than us. We're trying to get tips.
But he and Morgan used to date, which complicates things.
We just *love* watching him hunt.
You used to *date* Van?
LUCKY!
Feels like there's been more attacks lately—
it's really getting in the way of Sunday Funday Book Club.
You're probably relieved because you never read the book.
Shut up!
But also...
Guilty!
Bitch!
HA HA
HA HA HA
HA
HA
HA
HA
HA

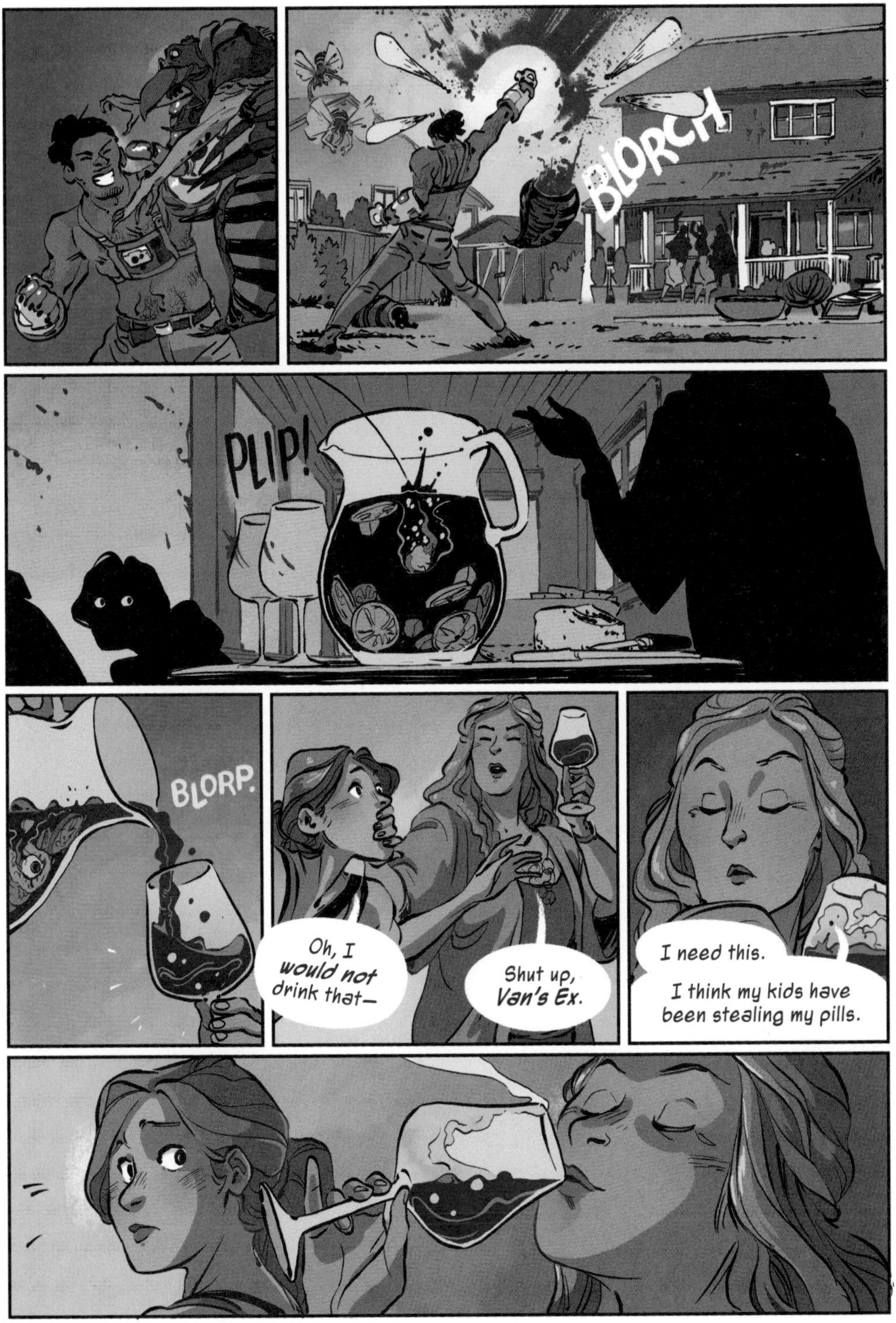
BLORCH
PLIP!
BLORP.
Oh, I *would not* drink that—
Shut up, *Van's Ex.*
I need this.
I think my kids have been stealing my pills.

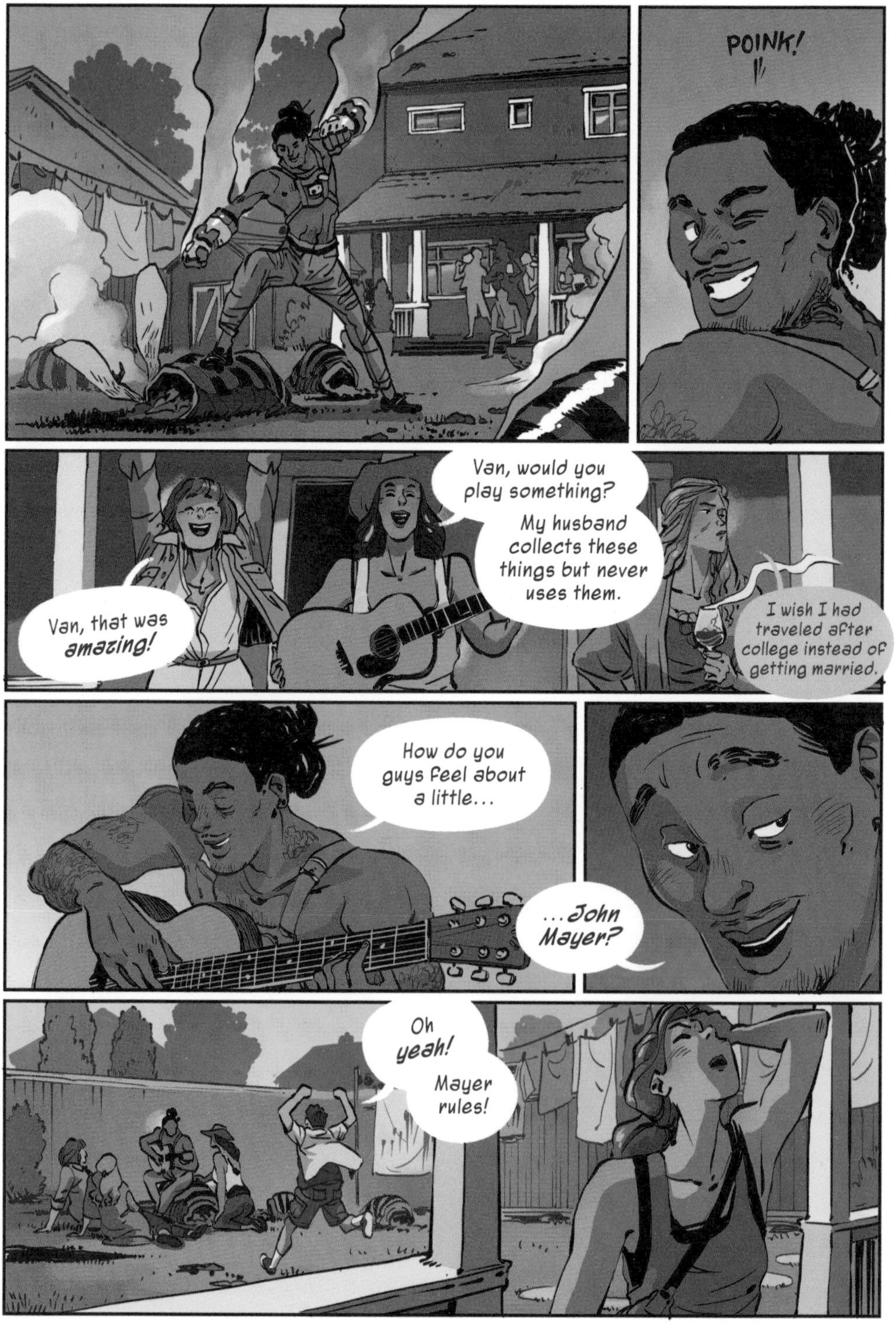
POINK!
Van, would you play something?
My husband collects these things but never uses them.
Van, that was *amazing!*
I wish I had traveled after college instead of getting married.
How do you guys feel about a little...
...John Mayer?
Oh *yeah!*
Mayer rules!

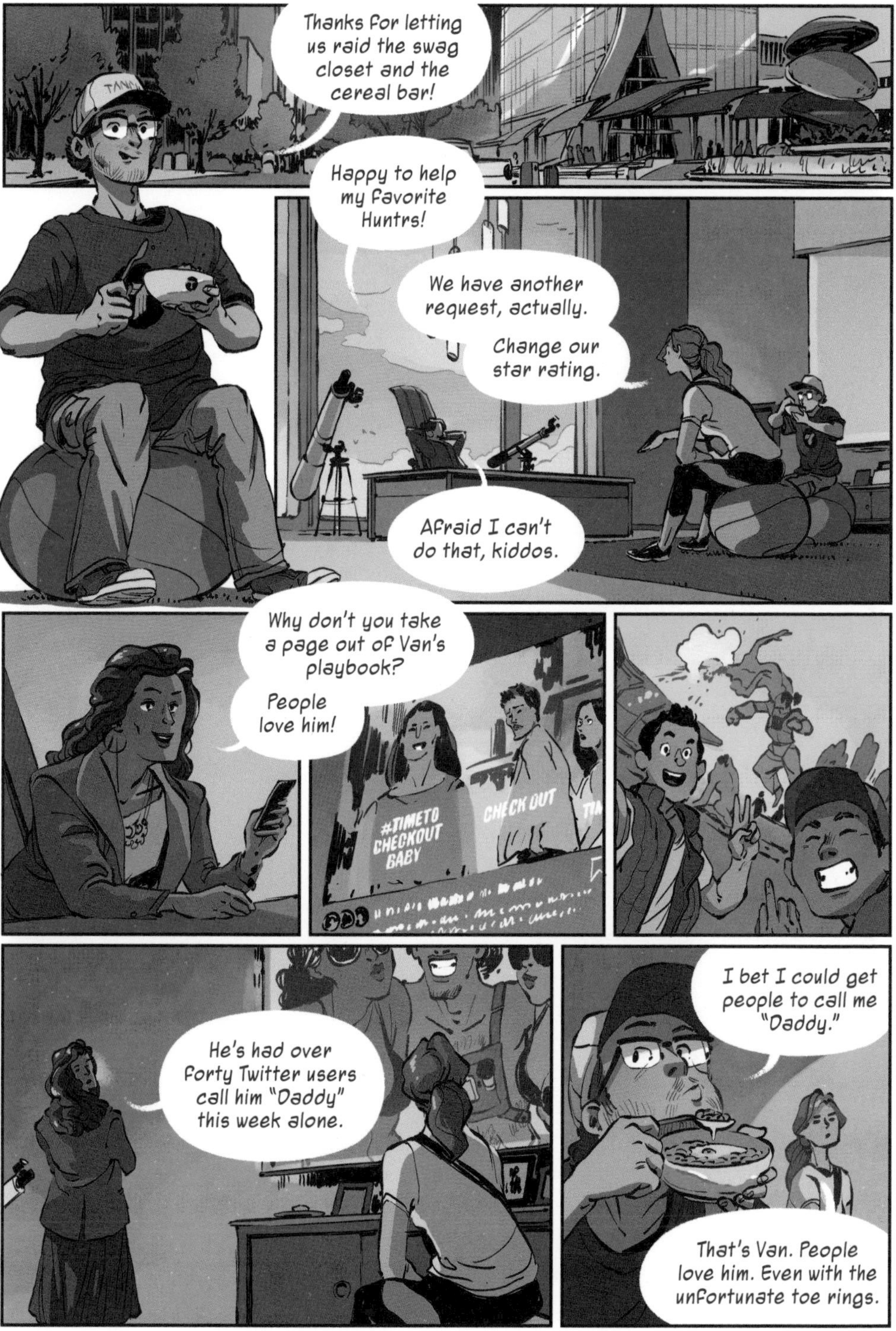
Thanks for letting us raid the swag closet and the cereal bar!
Happy to help my favorite Huntrs!
We have another request, actually.
Change our star rating.
Afraid I can't do that, kiddos.
Why don't you take a page out of Van's playbook?
People love him!
#TIMETO CHECKOUT BABY
CHECK OUT
He's had over forty Twitter users call him "Daddy" this week alone.
I bet I could get people to call me "Daddy."
That's Van. People love him. Even with the unfortunate toe rings.

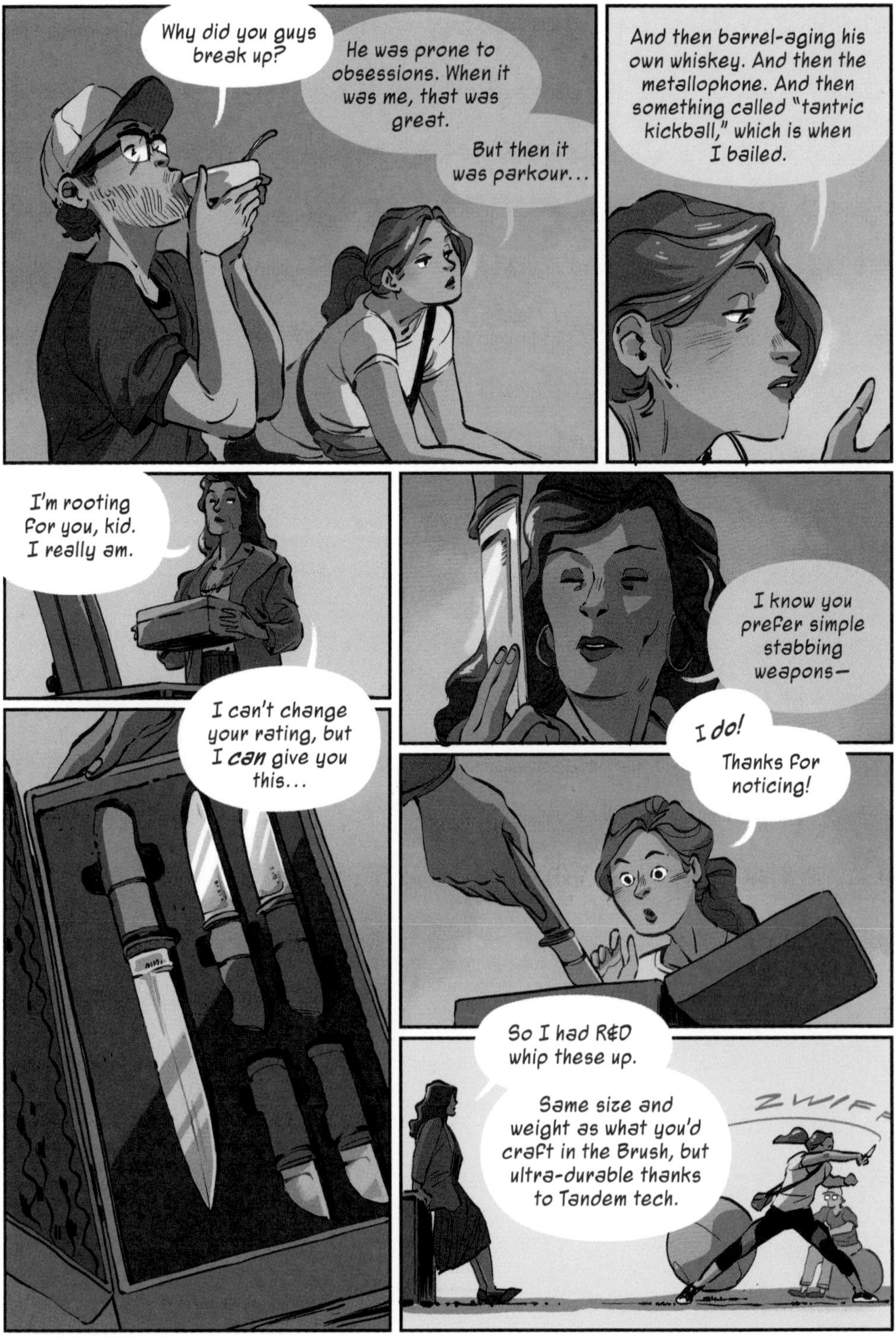
Why did you guys break up?
He was prone to obsessions. When it was me, that was great.
But then it was parkour...
And then barrel-aging his own whiskey. And then the metallophone. And then something called "tantric kickball," which is when I bailed.
I'm rooting for you, kid. I really am.
I can't change your rating, but I *can* give you this...
I know you prefer simple stabbing weapons—
I *do!*
Thanks for noticing!
So I had R&D whip these up.
Same size and weight as what you'd craft in the Brush, but ultra-durable thanks to Tandem tech.
ZWIFF

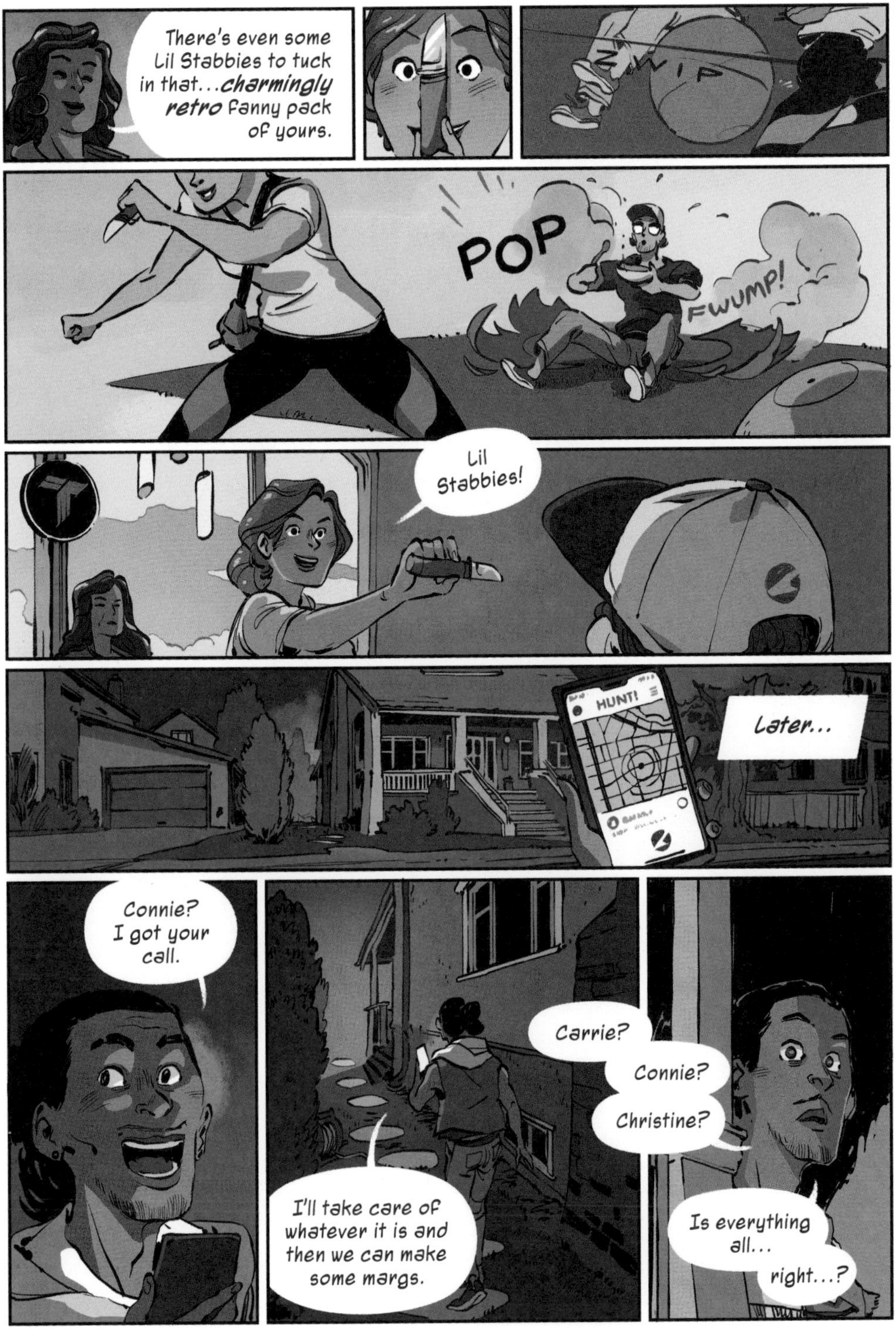
There's even some Lil Stabbies to tuck in that... ***charmingly retro*** fanny pack of yours.
ZWIP
POP
FWUMP!
Lil Stabbies!
HUNT!
Later...
Connie? I got your call.
I'll take care of whatever it is and then we can make some margs.
Carrie?
Connie?
Christine?
Is everything all... right...?

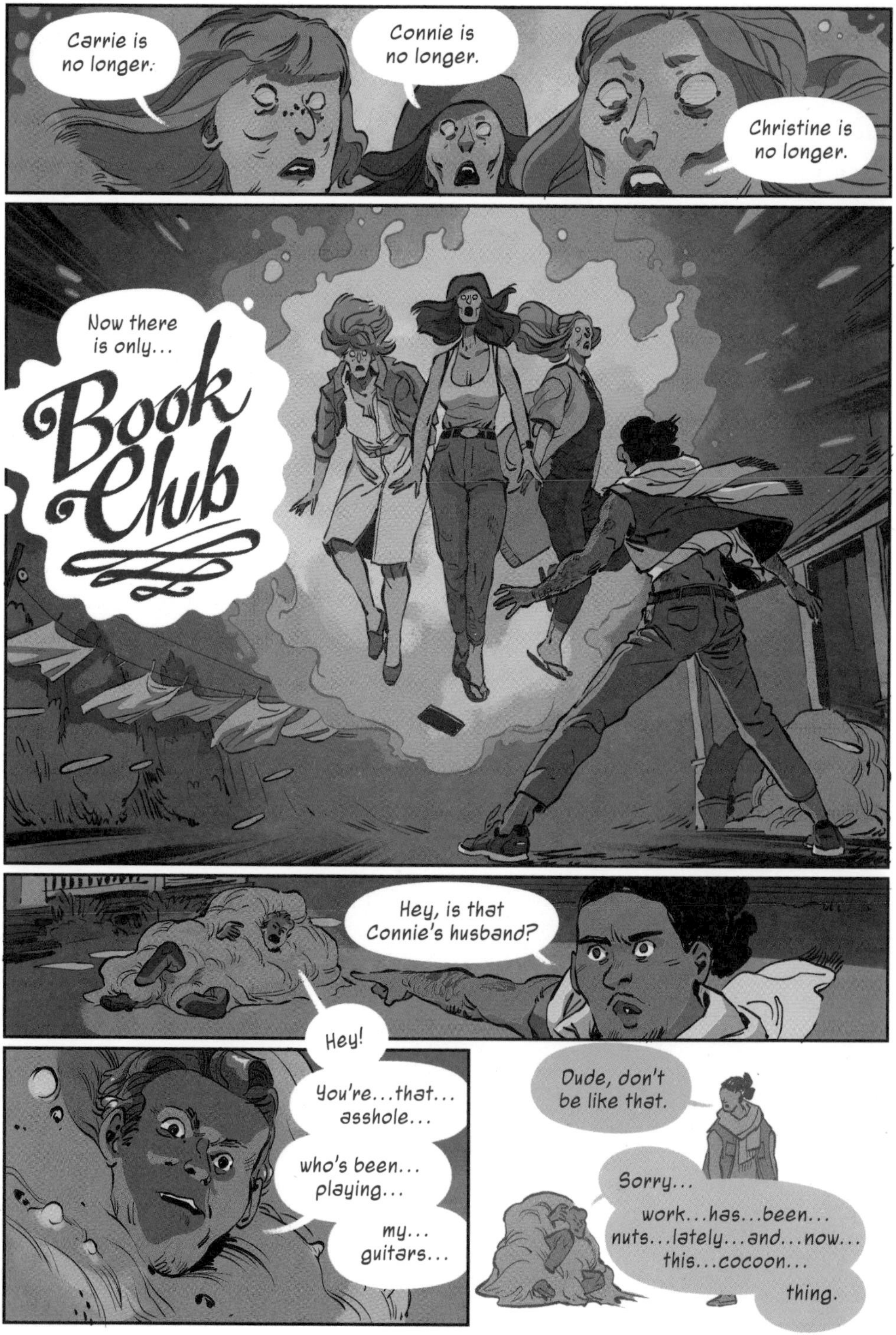
Carrie is no longer.
Connie is no longer.
Christine is no longer.
Now there is only...
Book Club
Hey, is that Connie's husband?
Hey!
You're...that... asshole...
who's been... playing...
my... guitars...
Dude, don't be like that.
Sorry...
work...has...been... nuts...lately...and...now... this...cocoon...
thing.

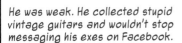

He was weak. He collected stupid vintage guitars and wouldn't stop messaging his exes on Facebook.

He will now be *nutrients* for *Book Club*.

Whoa, whoa, whoa,

why don't we all chill and go inside?

I can whip us up some guac—

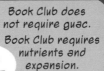

Book Club does not require guac.

Book Club requires nutrients and expansion.

You are strong. You will join Book Club.

Thanks for the invite,

but I'll pass.

You are Book Club.

You are **Book Club**

You are Book Club

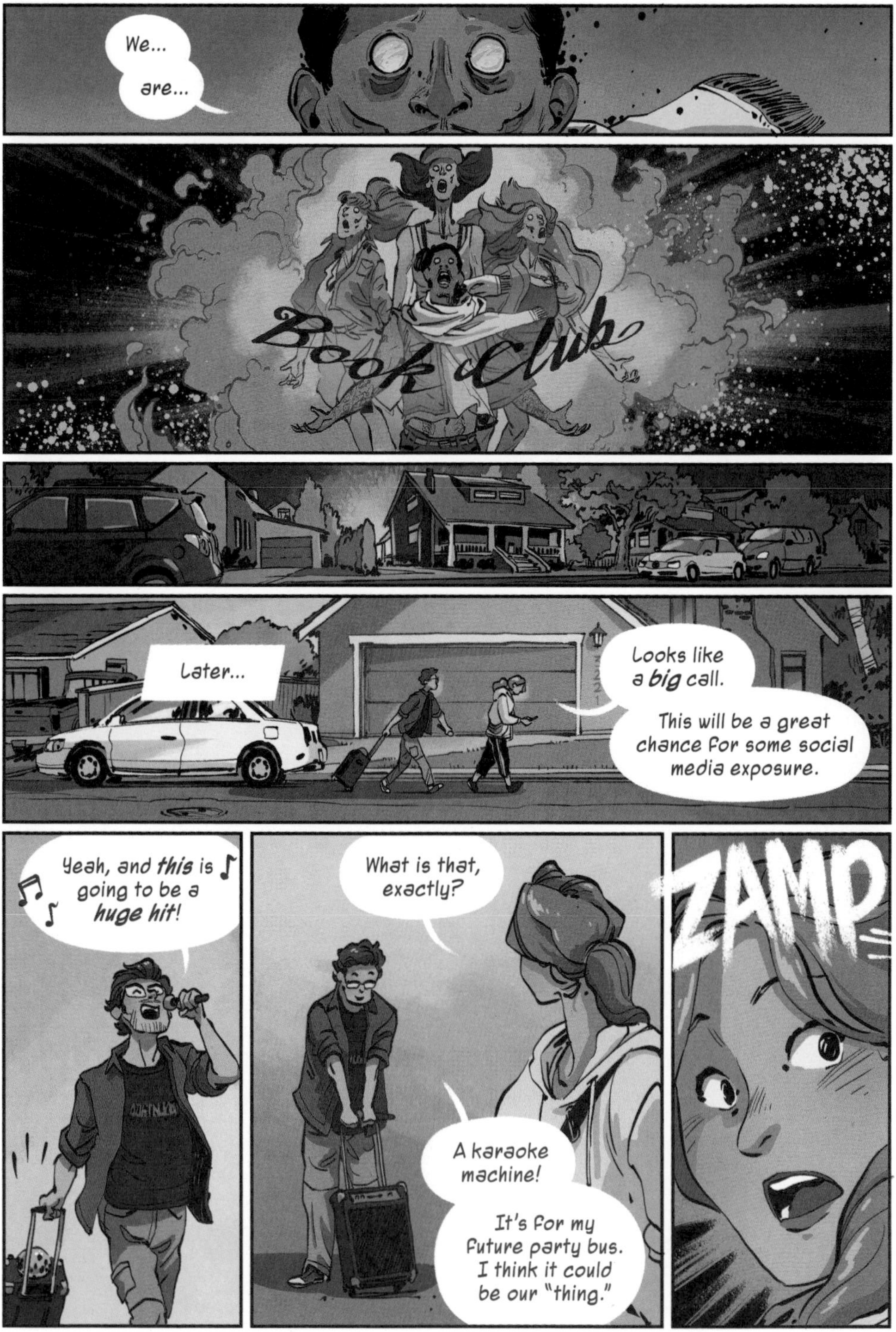
We...
are...
Book Club
Later...
Looks like a **big** call.
This will be a great chance for some social media exposure.
Yeah, and **this** is going to be a **huge hit**!
What is that, exactly?
A karaoke machine!
It's for my future party bus. I think it could be our "thing."
ZAMP

ZAMP

Humans with a bad case of *Hive Poisoning*.

Operating as a collective. Driven by a need to expand. Corral them and hit them all with one Sting. Three women and one...

Crap.

BLURDDTZZ

It got Van.

What *happened?*

The Imp blood that fell in the book club's drinks made them into a unified *hive mind.*

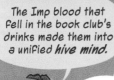

Oh, that's a thing?

It's happened in the Brush. The hive mind part, not the book club. We don't have those.

Are you wondering if people in the Brush can read?

No.

We *read.*

We just don't make a big thing of it.

Jeez.

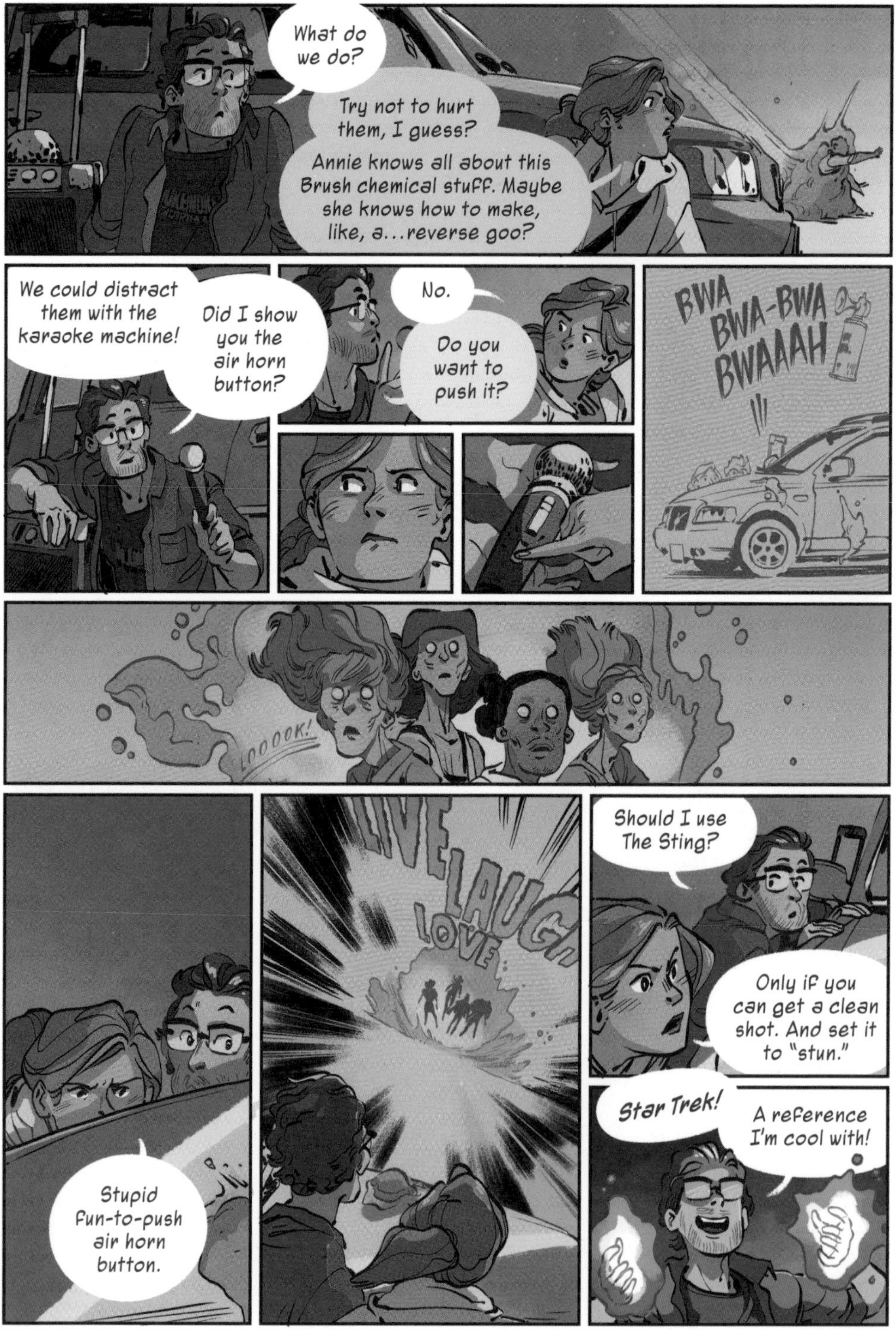
What do we do?
Try not to hurt them, I guess?
Annie knows all about this Brush chemical stuff. Maybe she knows how to make, like, a...reverse goo?
We could distract them with the karaoke machine!
Did I show you the air horn button?
No.
Do you want to push it?
BWA BWA-BWA BWAAAH
LOOOOK!
LIVE LAUGH LOVE
Stupid fun-to-push air horn button.
Should I use The Sting?
Only if you can get a clean shot. And set it to "stun."
Star Trek!
A reference I'm cool with!

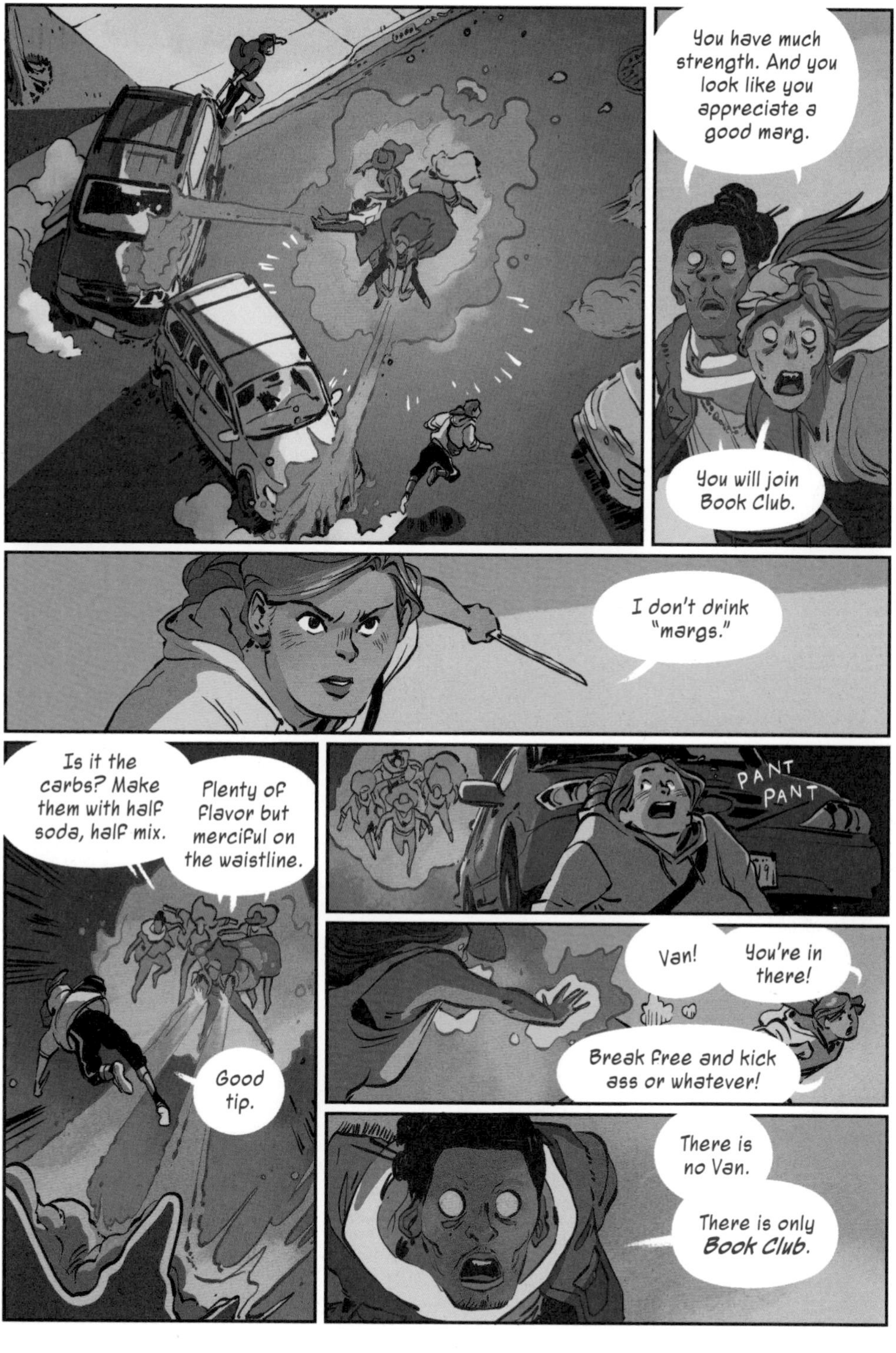
You have much strength. And you look like you appreciate a good marg.
You will join Book Club.
I don't drink "margs."
Is it the carbs? Make them with half soda, half mix.
Plenty of flavor but merciful on the waistline.
Good tip.
PANT PANT
Van!
You're in there!
Break free and kick ass or whatever!
There is no Van.
There is only *Book Club*.

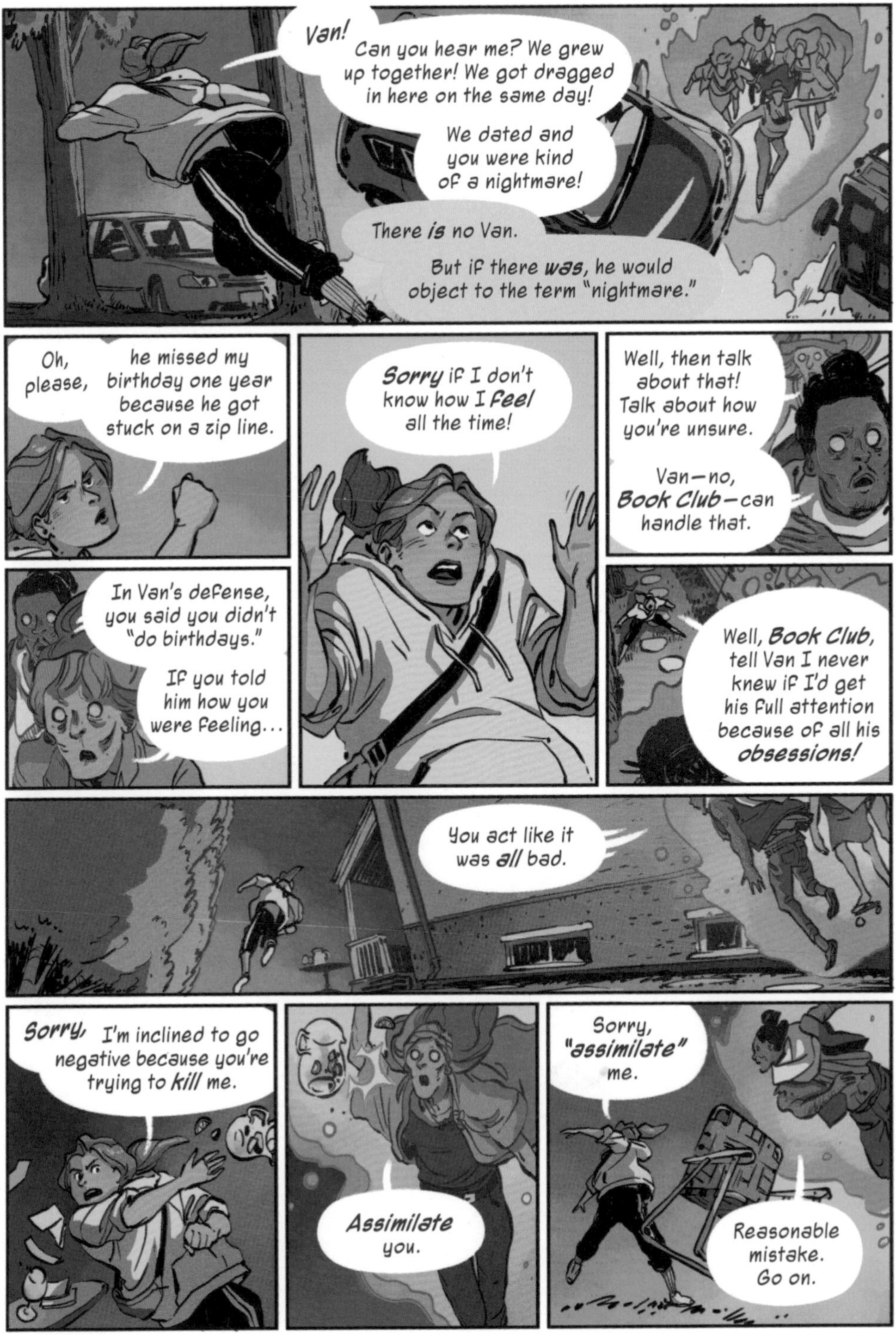
Van!
Can you hear me? We grew up together! We got dragged in here on the same day!
We dated and you were kind of a nightmare!
There *is* no Van.
But if there **was**, he would object to the term "nightmare."
Oh, please,
he missed my birthday one year because he got stuck on a zip line.
Sorry if I don't know how I **feel** all the time!
Well, then talk about that! Talk about how you're unsure.
Van—no, **Book Club**—can handle that.
In Van's defense, you said you didn't "do birthdays."
If you told him how you were feeling...
Well, **Book Club**, tell Van I never knew if I'd get his full attention because of all his **obsessions!**
You act like it was **all** bad.
Sorry,
I'm inclined to go negative because you're trying to **kill** me.
Assimilate you.
Sorry, **"assimilate"** me.
Reasonable mistake. Go on.

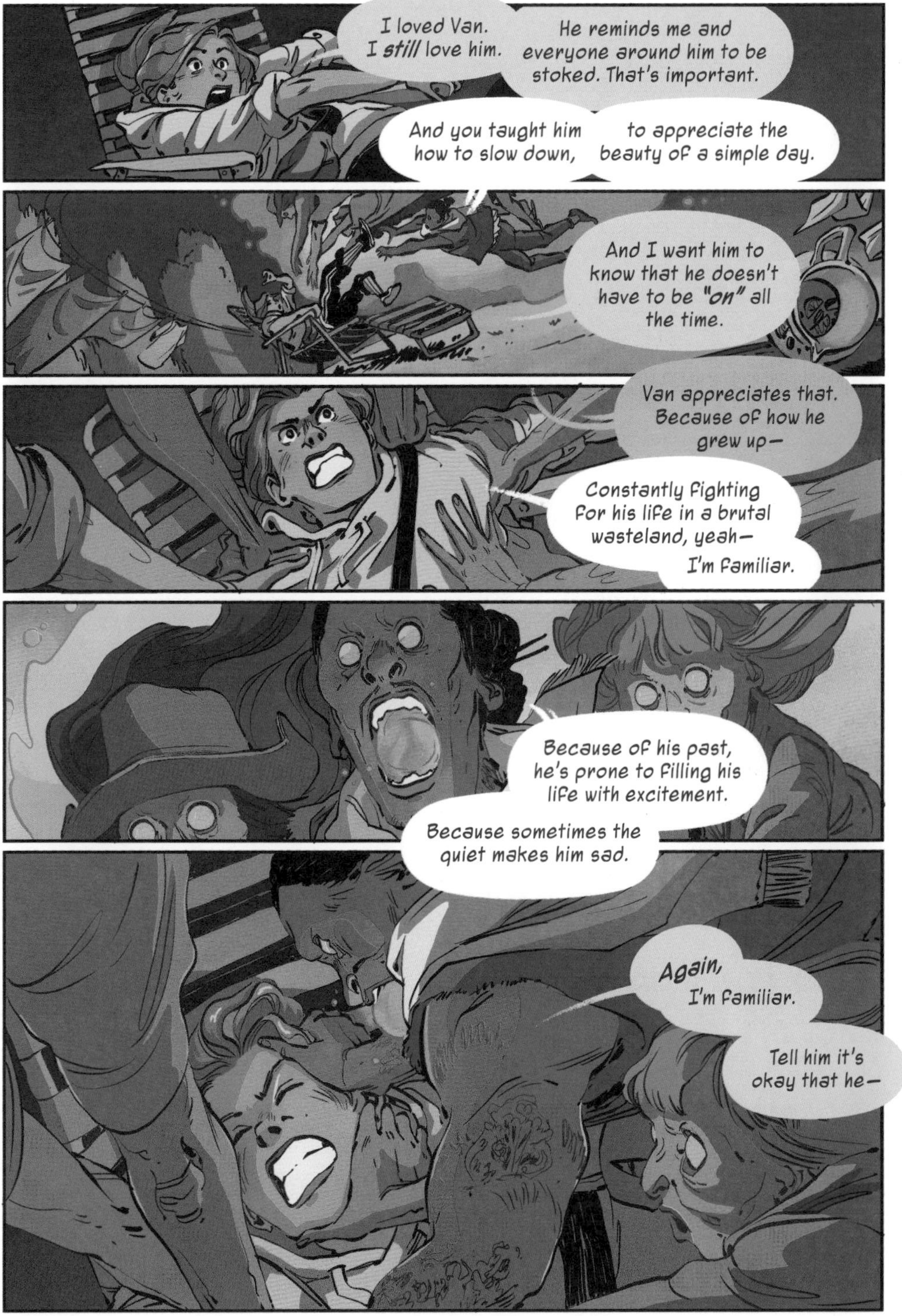

I loved Van. I *still* love him.
He reminds me and everyone around him to be stoked. That's important.
And you taught him how to slow down,
to appreciate the beauty of a simple day.
And I want him to know that he doesn't have to be *"on"* all the time.
Van appreciates that. Because of how he grew up—
Constantly fighting for his life in a brutal wasteland, yeah—
I'm familiar.
Because of his past, he's prone to filling his life with excitement.
Because sometimes the quiet makes him sad.
Again, I'm familiar.
Tell him it's okay that he—

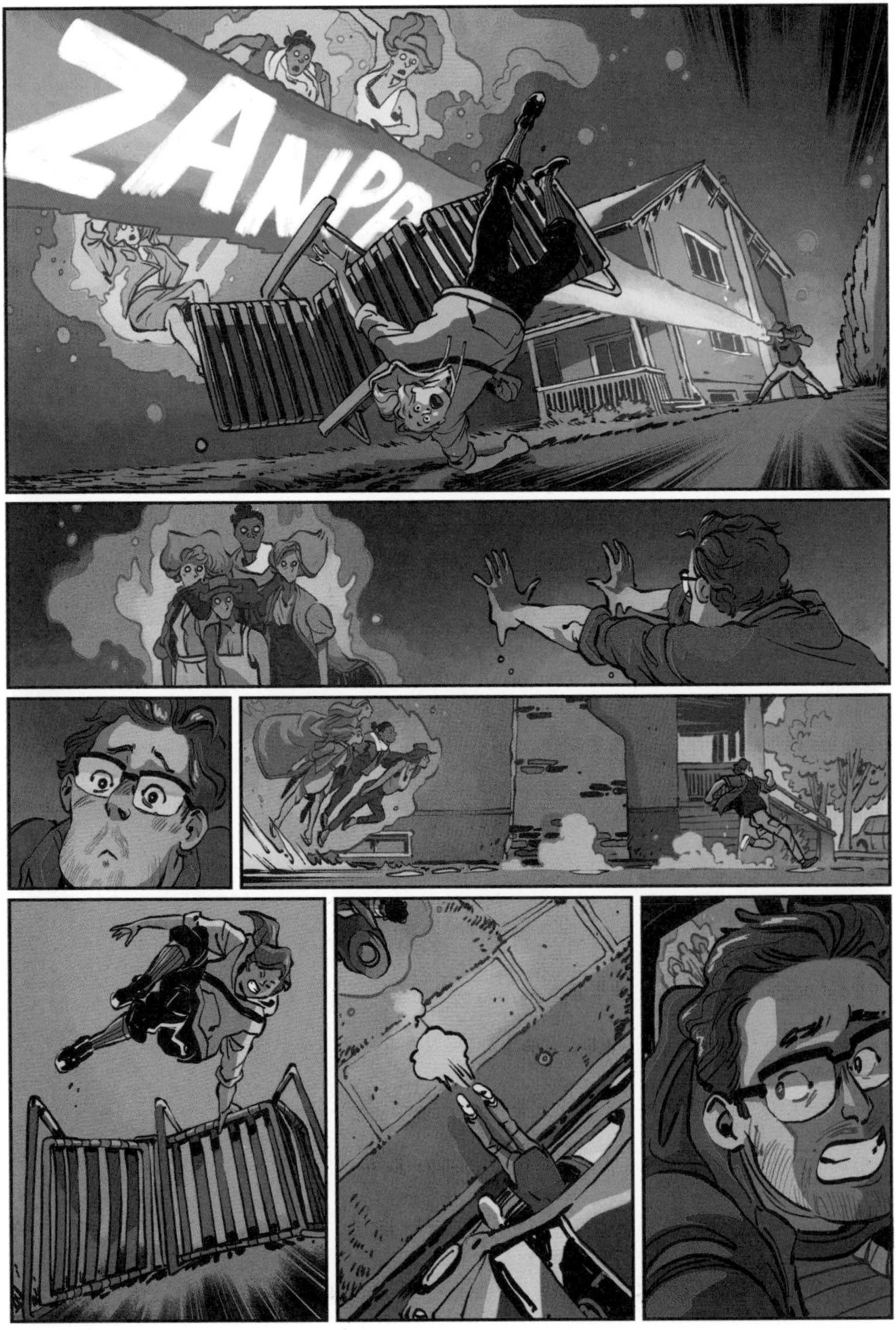
ZANPP

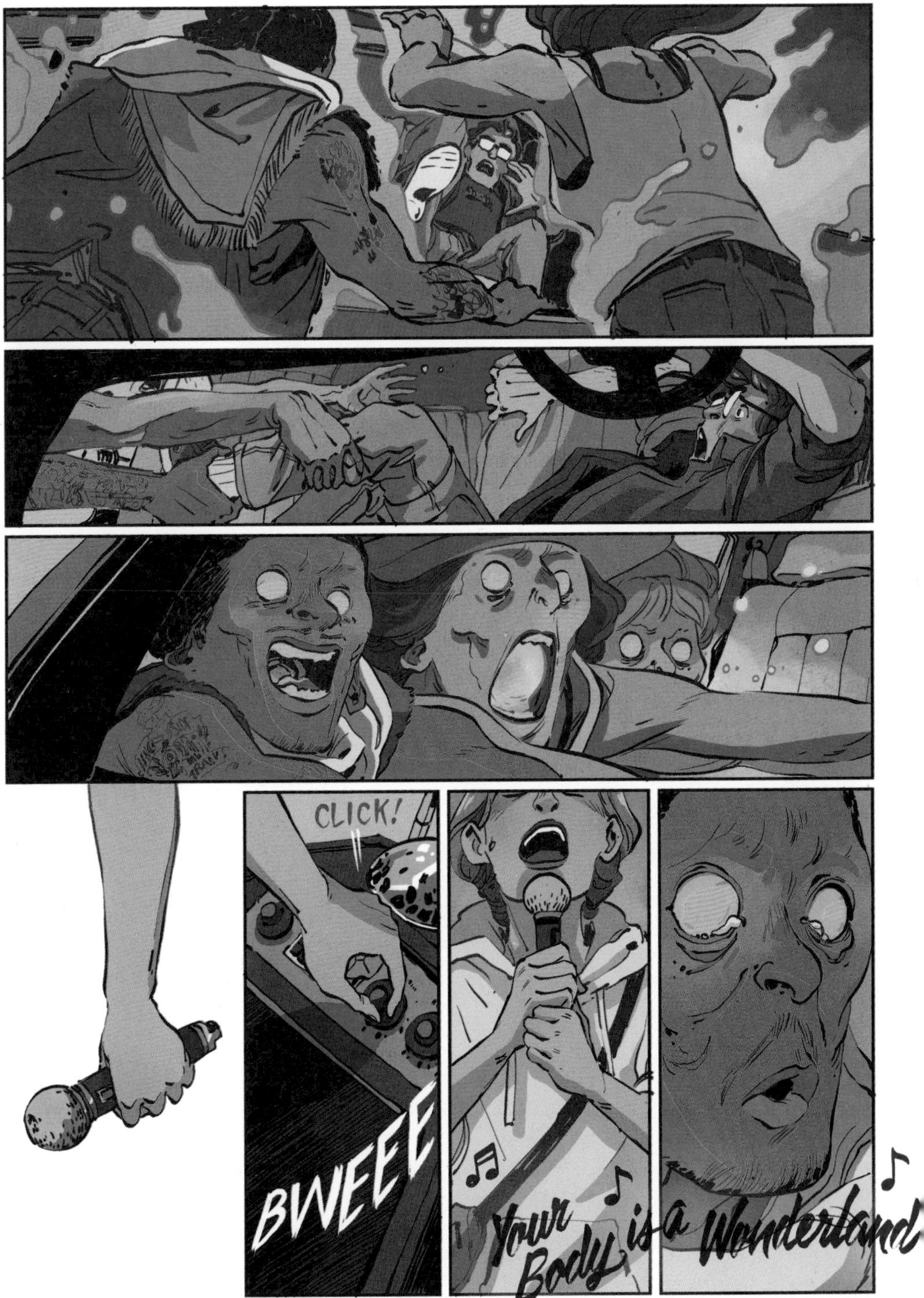
CLICK!
BWEEE
Your Body is a Wonderland

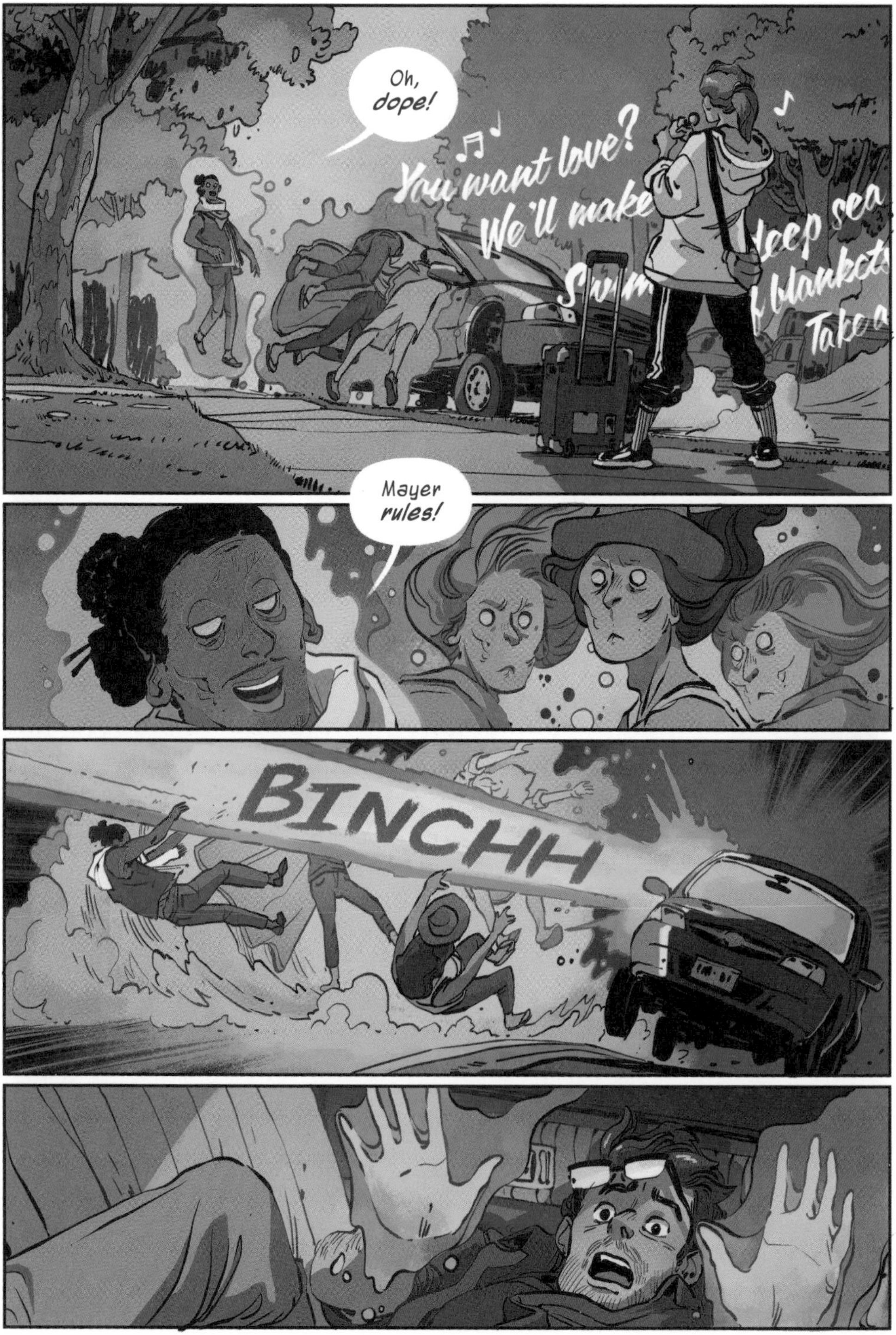

Oh, dope!
You want love?
We'll make
deep sea
blankets
Take a
Mayer rules!
BINCHH

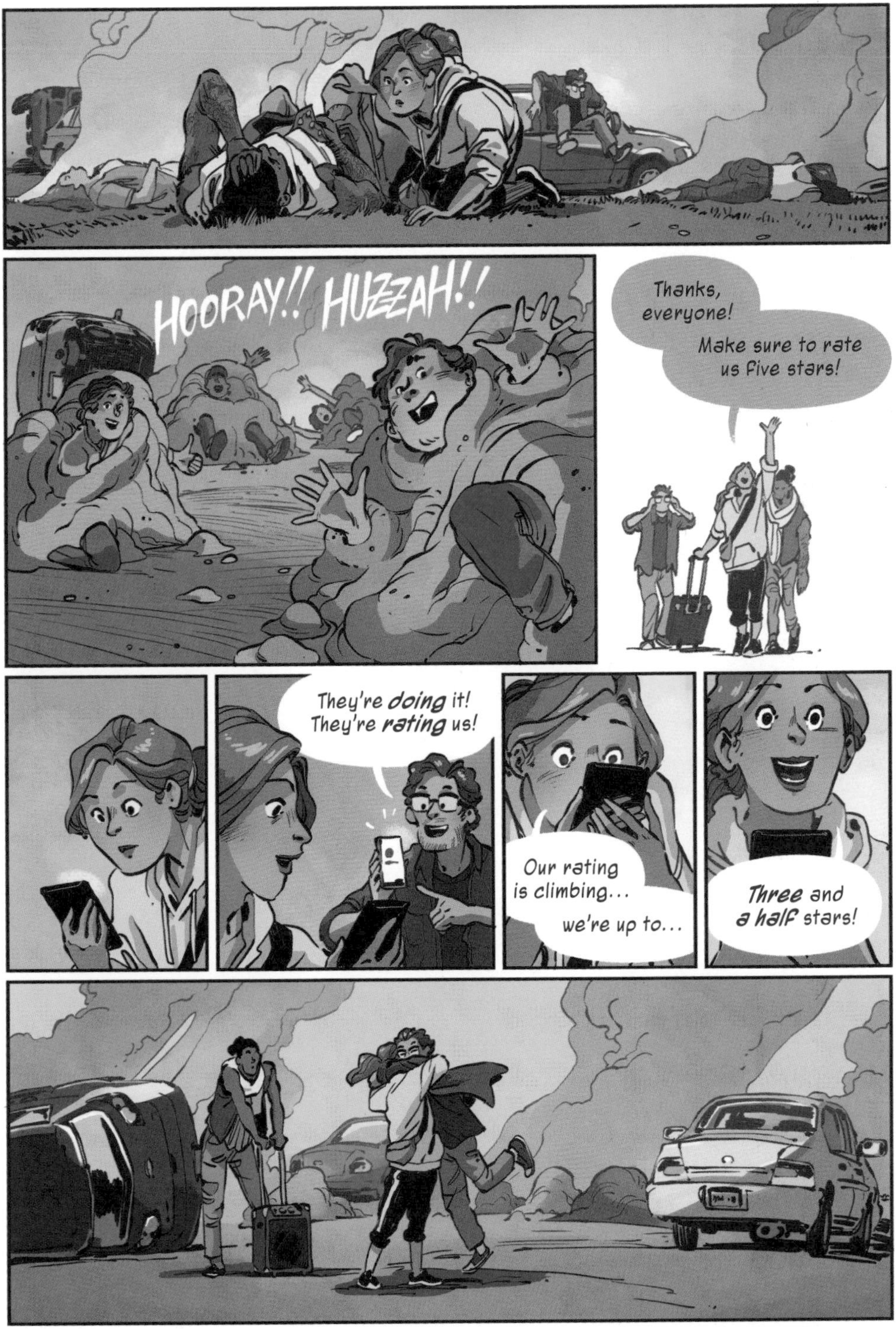
HOORAY!! HUZZAH!!
Thanks, everyone!
Make sure to rate us five stars!
They're *doing* it! They're *rating* us!
Our rating is climbing...
we're up to...
Three and *a half* stars!

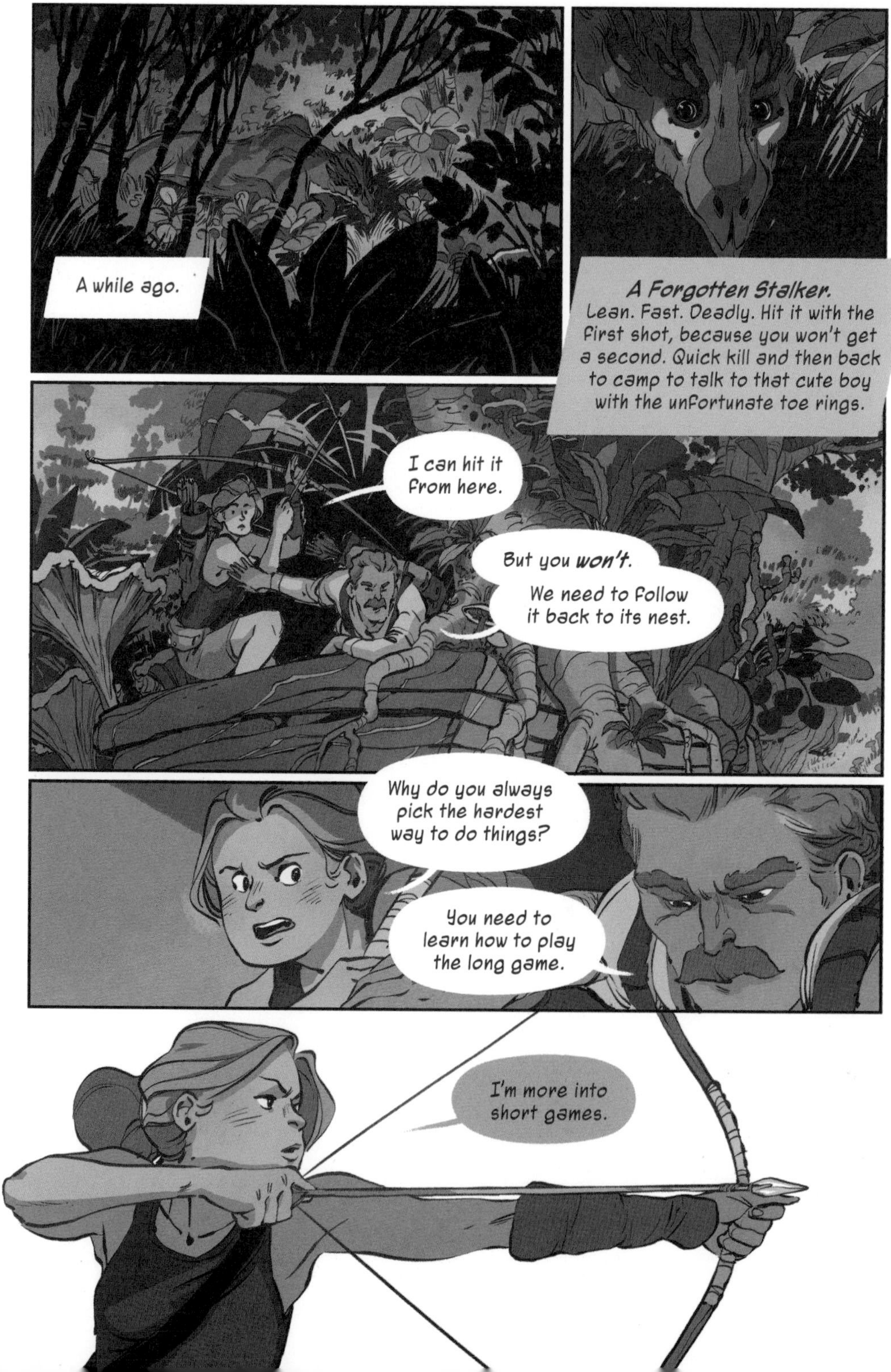

A while ago.
A Forgotten Stalker.
Lean. Fast. Deadly. Hit it with the first shot, because you won't get a second. Quick kill and then back to camp to talk to that cute boy with the unfortunate toe rings.
I can hit it from here.
But you *won't*.
We need to follow it back to its nest.
Why do you always pick the hardest way to do things?
You need to learn how to play the long game.
I'm more into short games.

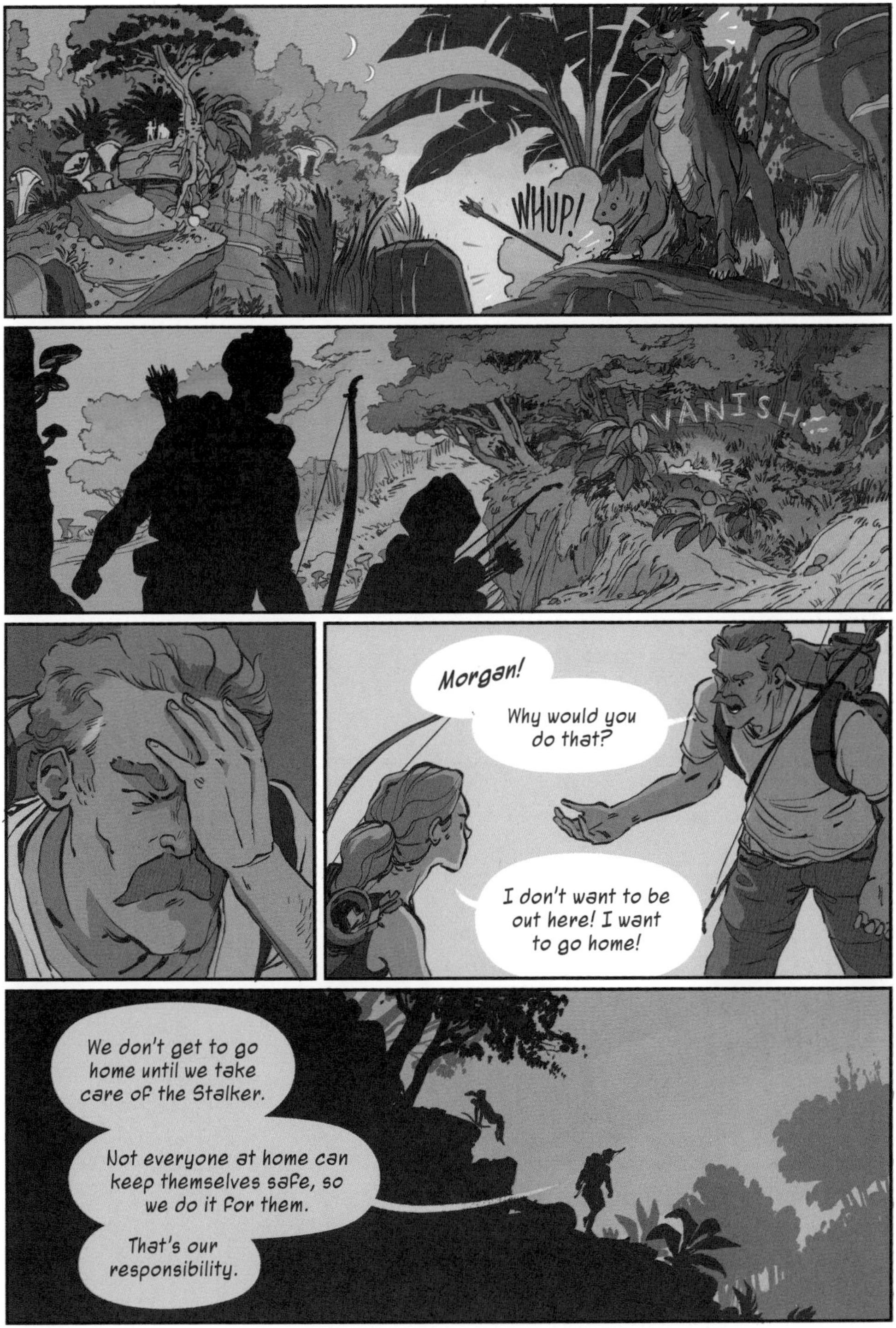
WHUP!
VANISH
Morgan!
Why would you do that?
I don't want to be out here! I want to go home!
We don't get to go home until we take care of the Stalker.
Not everyone at home can keep themselves safe, so we do it for them.
That's our responsibility.

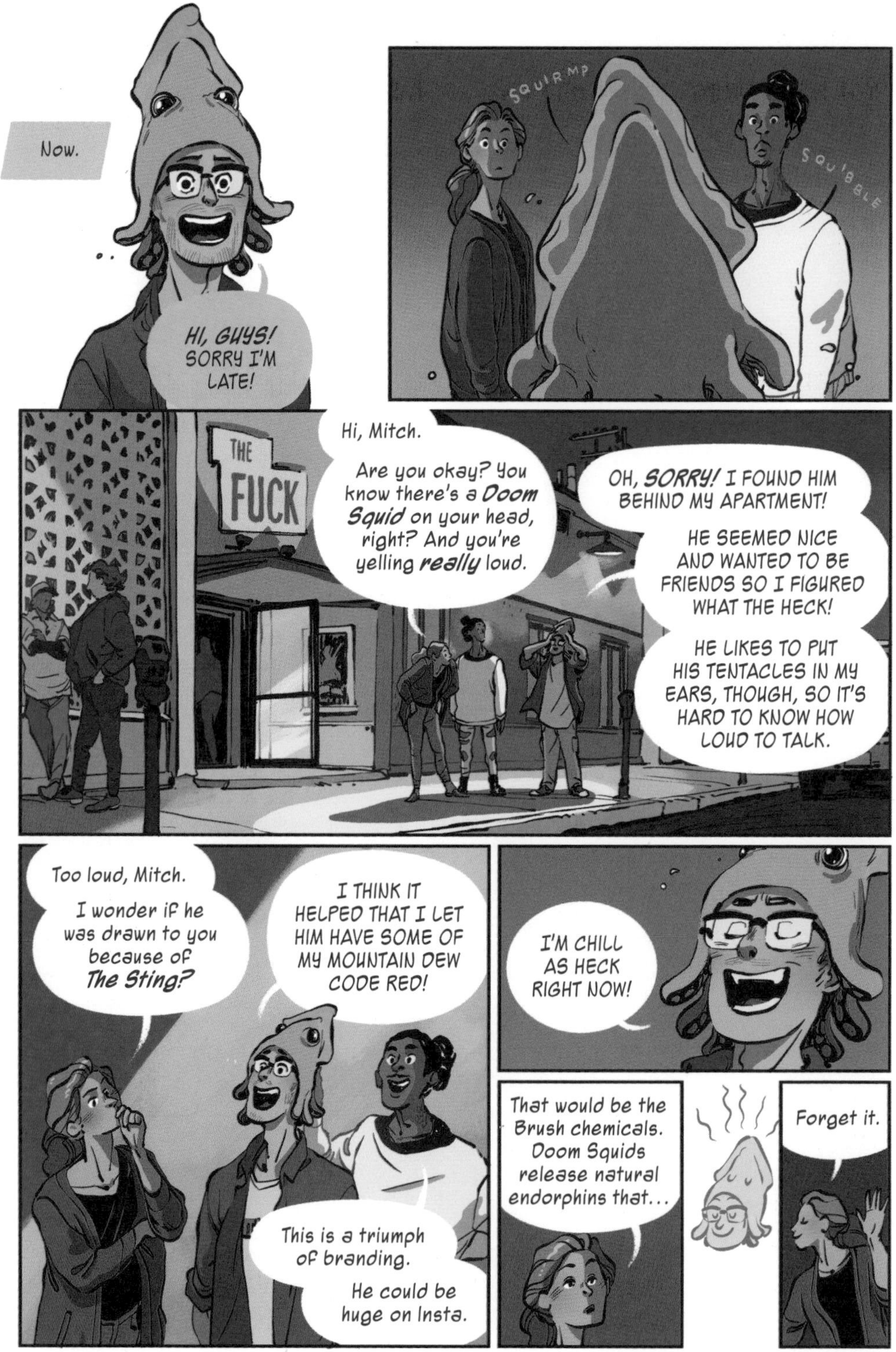
Now.
HI, GUYS! SORRY I'M LATE!
SQUIRMP
SQUIBBLE
THE FUCK
Hi, Mitch.
Are you okay? You know there's a Doom Squid on your head, right? And you're yelling really loud.
OH, SORRY! I FOUND HIM BEHIND MY APARTMENT!
HE SEEMED NICE AND WANTED TO BE FRIENDS SO I FIGURED WHAT THE HECK!
HE LIKES TO PUT HIS TENTACLES IN MY EARS, THOUGH, SO IT'S HARD TO KNOW HOW LOUD TO TALK.
Too loud, Mitch.
I wonder if he was drawn to you because of The Sting?
I THINK IT HELPED THAT I LET HIM HAVE SOME OF MY MOUNTAIN DEW CODE RED!
This is a triumph of branding.
He could be huge on Insta.
I'M CHILL AS HECK RIGHT NOW!
That would be the Brush chemicals. Doom Squids release natural endorphins that...
Forget it.

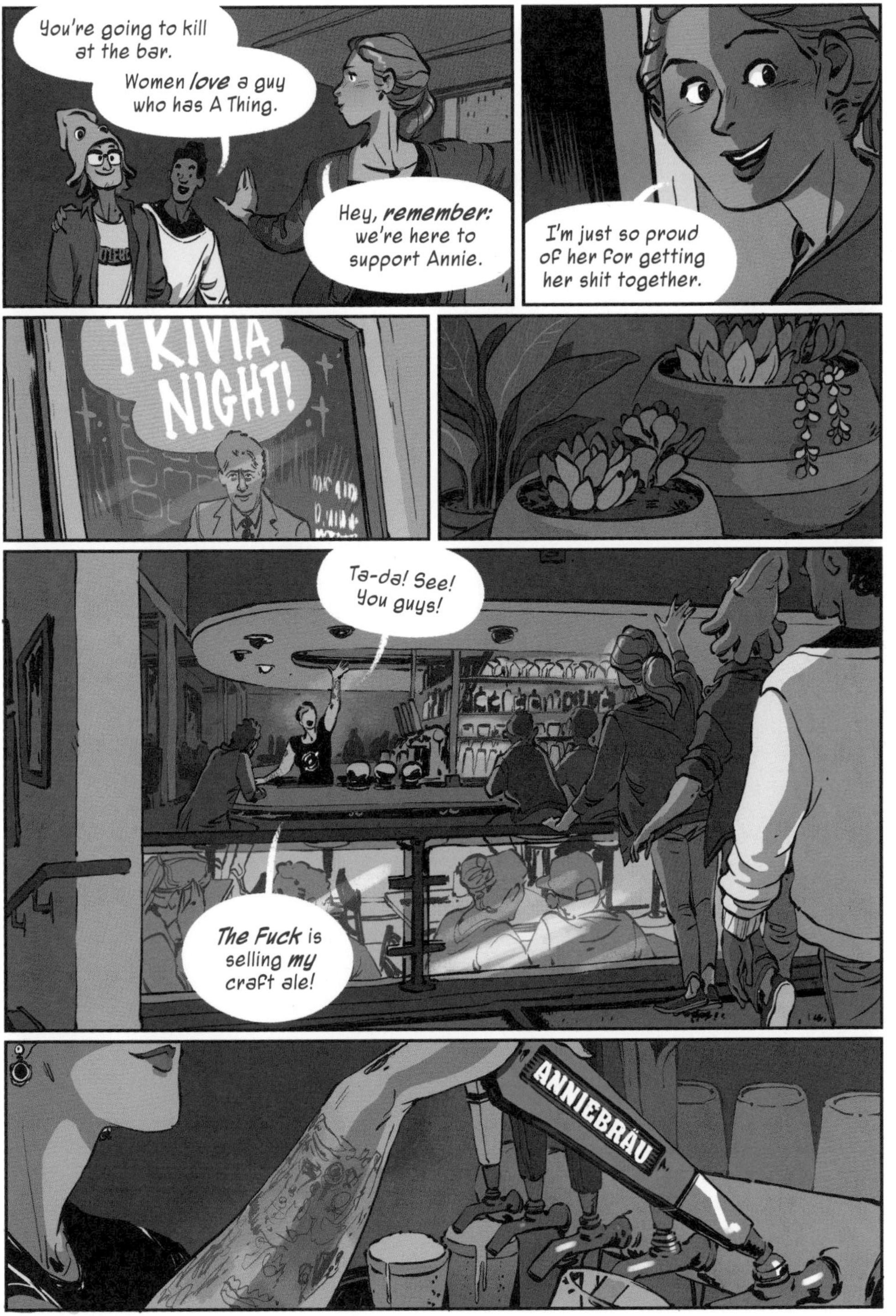
You're going to kill at the bar.
Women *love* a guy who has A Thing.
Hey, ***remember:*** we're here to support Annie.
I'm just so proud of her for getting her shit together.
TRIVIA NIGHT!
Ta-da! See! You guys!
The Fuck is selling ***my*** craft ale!
ANNIEBRÄU

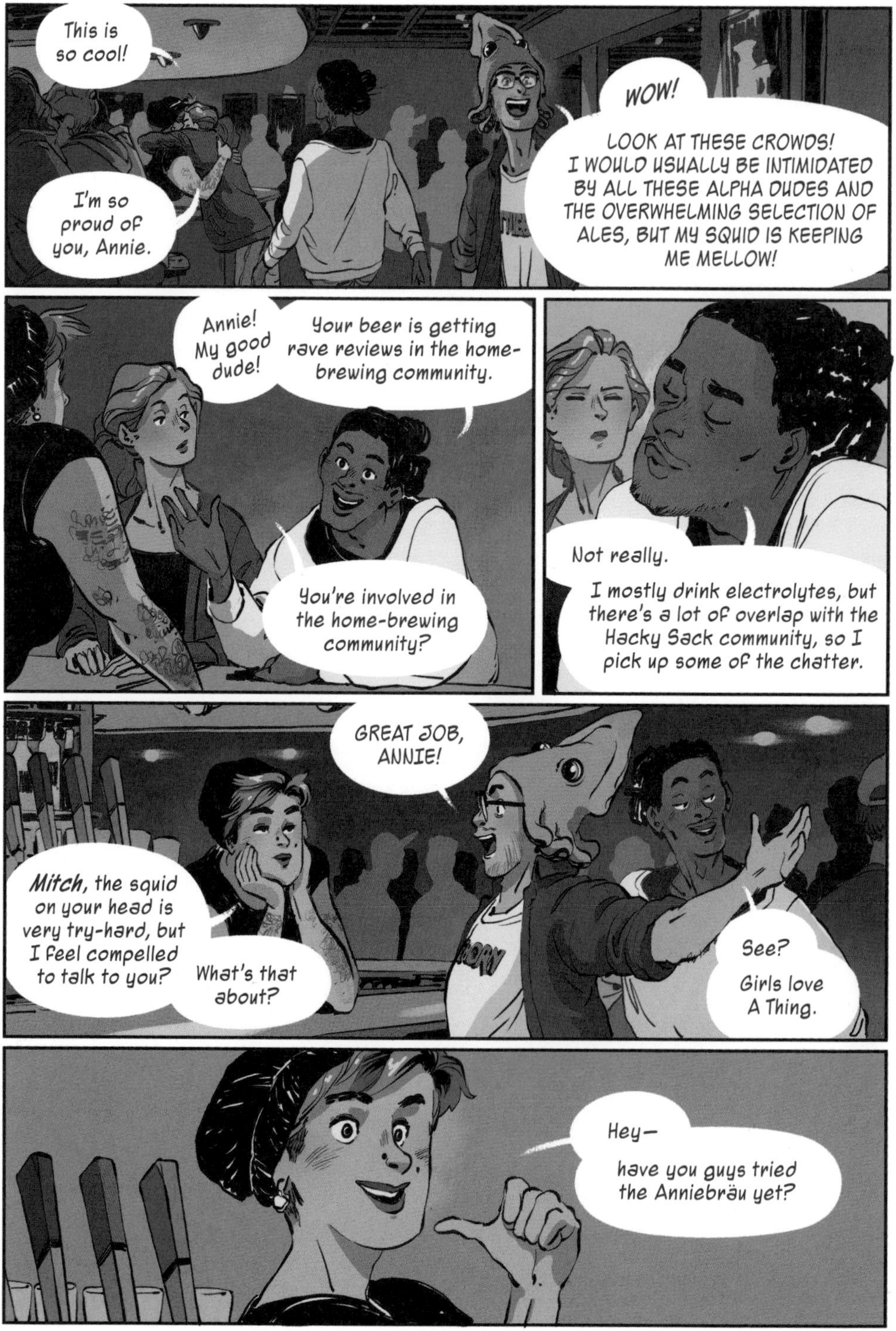
This is so cool!
I'm so proud of you, Annie.
WOW!
LOOK AT THESE CROWDS! I WOULD USUALLY BE INTIMIDATED BY ALL THESE ALPHA DUDES AND THE OVERWHELMING SELECTION OF ALES, BUT MY SQUID IS KEEPING ME MELLOW!
Annie! My good dude!
Your beer is getting rave reviews in the home-brewing community.
You're involved in the home-brewing community?
Not really.
I mostly drink electrolytes, but there's a lot of overlap with the Hacky Sack community, so I pick up some of the chatter.
GREAT JOB, ANNIE!
Mitch, the squid on your head is very try-hard, but I feel compelled to talk to you?
What's that about?
See?
Girls love A Thing.
Hey—
have you guys tried the Anniebräu yet?

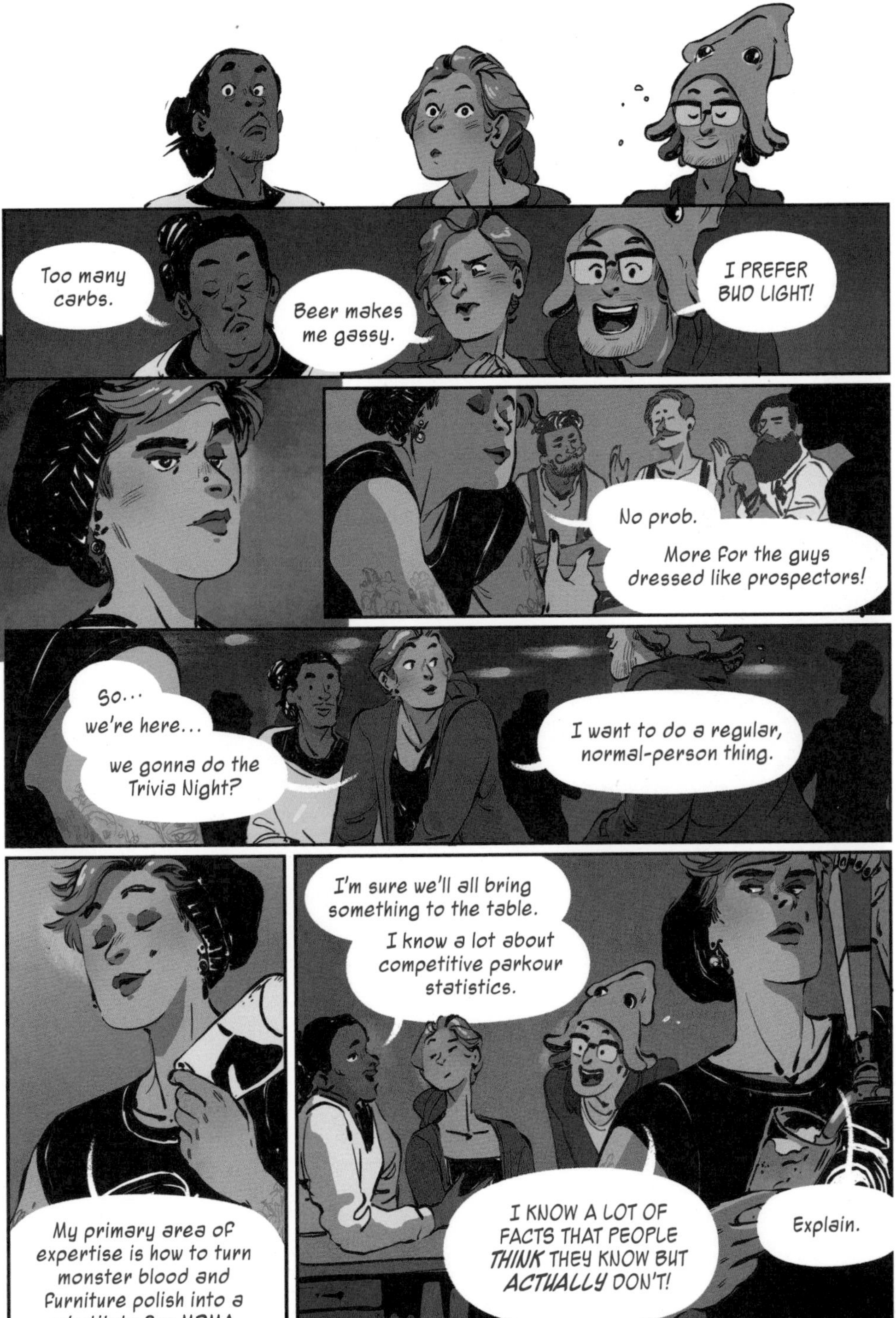

Too many carbs.
Beer makes me gassy.
I PREFER BUD LIGHT!
No prob.
More for the guys dressed like prospectors!
So...
we're here...
we gonna do the Trivia Night?
I want to do a regular, normal-person thing.
My primary area of expertise is how to turn monster blood and furniture polish into a substitute for MOMA.
I'm sure we'll all bring something to the table.
I know a lot about competitive parkour statistics.
I KNOW A LOT OF FACTS THAT PEOPLE *THINK* THEY KNOW BUT *ACTUALLY* DON'T!
Explain.

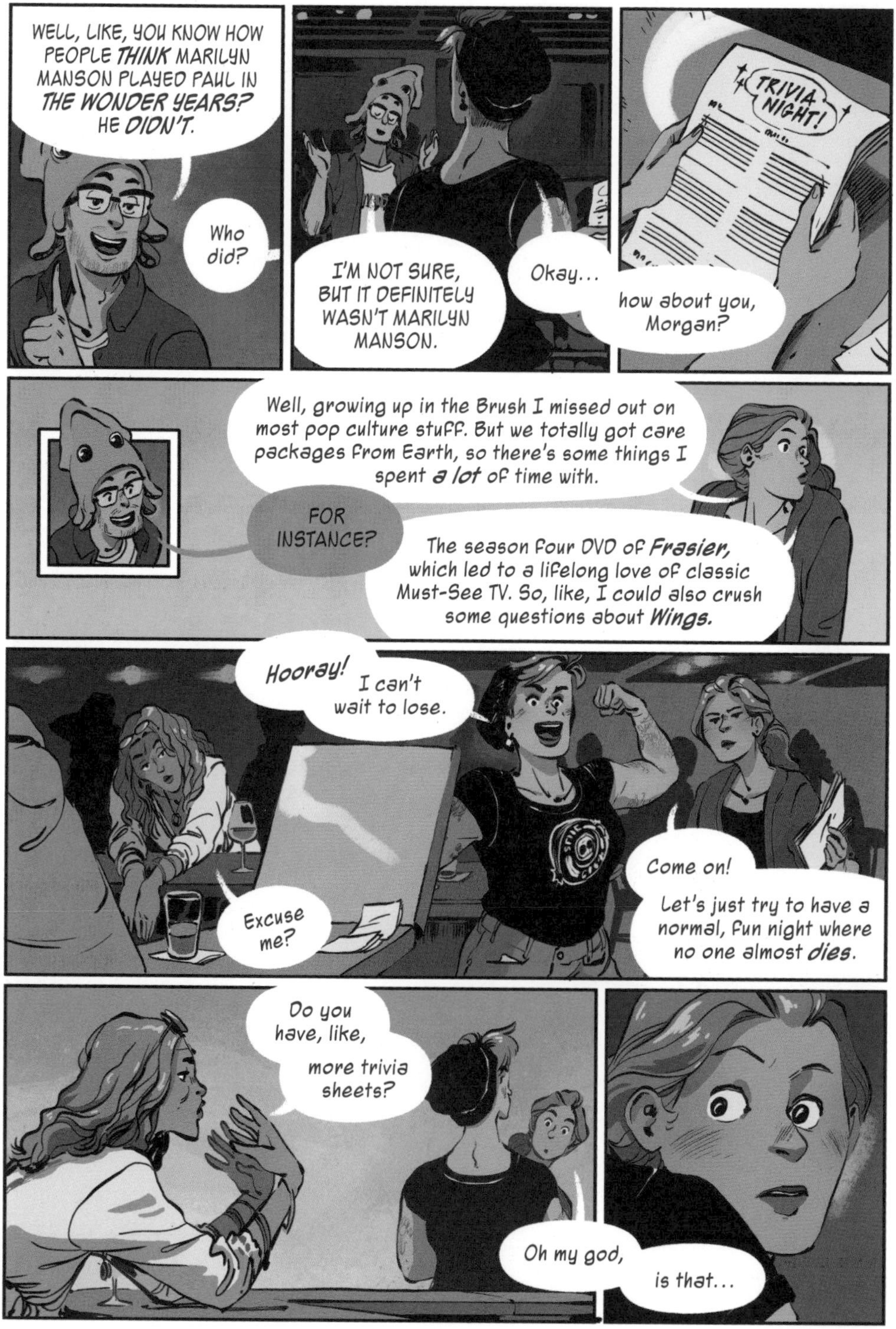
WELL, LIKE, YOU KNOW HOW PEOPLE THINK MARILYN MANSON PLAYED PAUL IN THE WONDER YEARS? HE DIDN'T.
Who did?
I'M NOT SURE, BUT IT DEFINITELY WASN'T MARILYN MANSON.
TRIVIA NIGHT!
Okay...
how about you, Morgan?
Well, growing up in the Brush I missed out on most pop culture stuff. But we totally got care packages from Earth, so there's some things I spent a lot of time with.
FOR INSTANCE?
The season four DVD of Frasier, which led to a lifelong love of classic Must-See TV. So, like, I could also crush some questions about Wings.
Hooray! I can't wait to lose.
Excuse me?
Come on!
Let's just try to have a normal, fun night where no one almost dies.
Do you have, like,
more trivia sheets?
Oh my god,
is that...

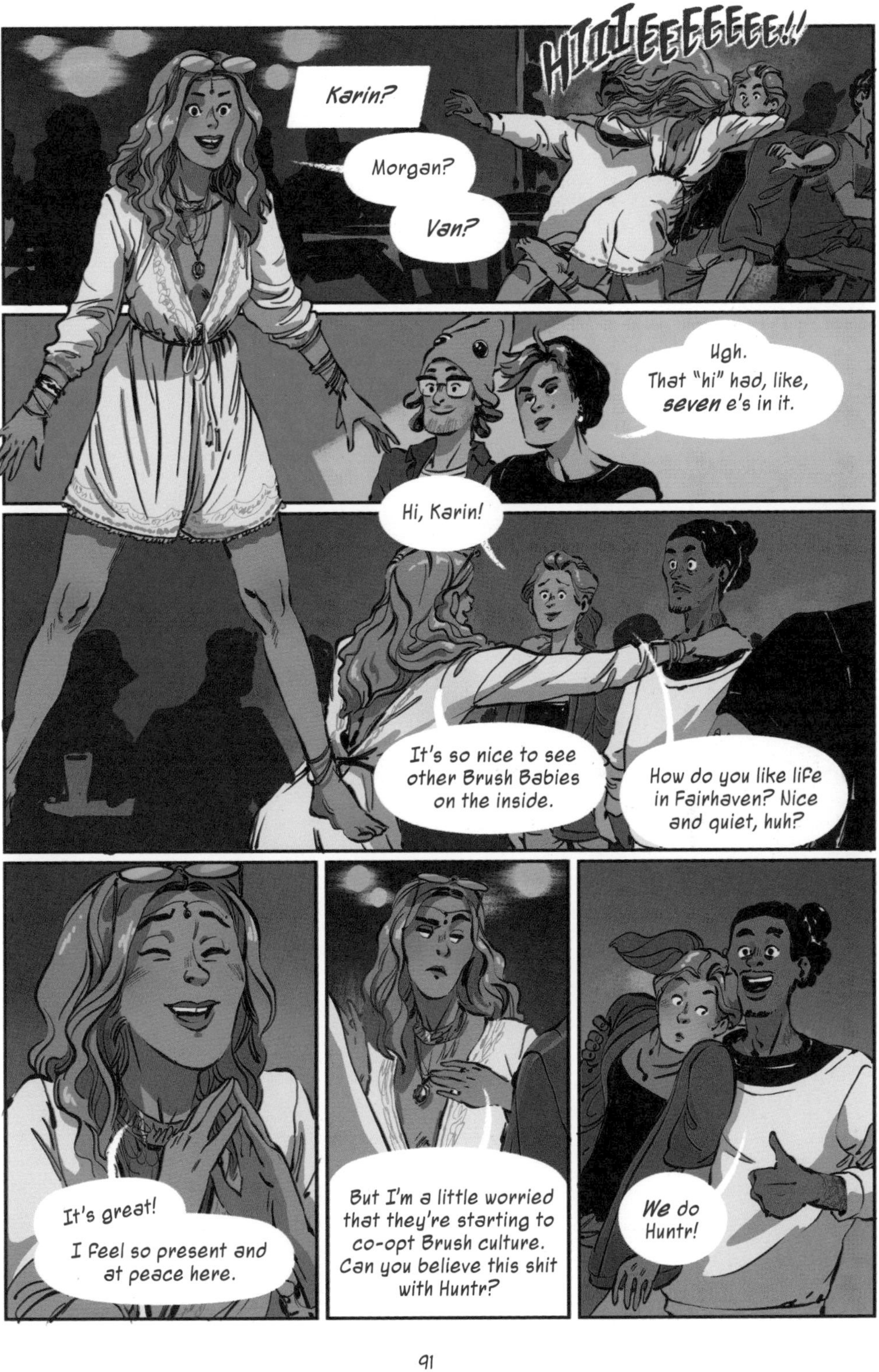
HIIIIEEEEEEE!!
Karin?
Morgan?
Van?
Ugh. That "hi" had, like, *seven* e's in it.
Hi, Karin!
It's so nice to see other Brush Babies on the inside.
How do you like life in Fairhaven? Nice and quiet, huh?
It's great!
I feel so present and at peace here.
But I'm a little worried that they're starting to co-opt Brush culture. Can you believe this shit with Huntr?
We do Huntr!

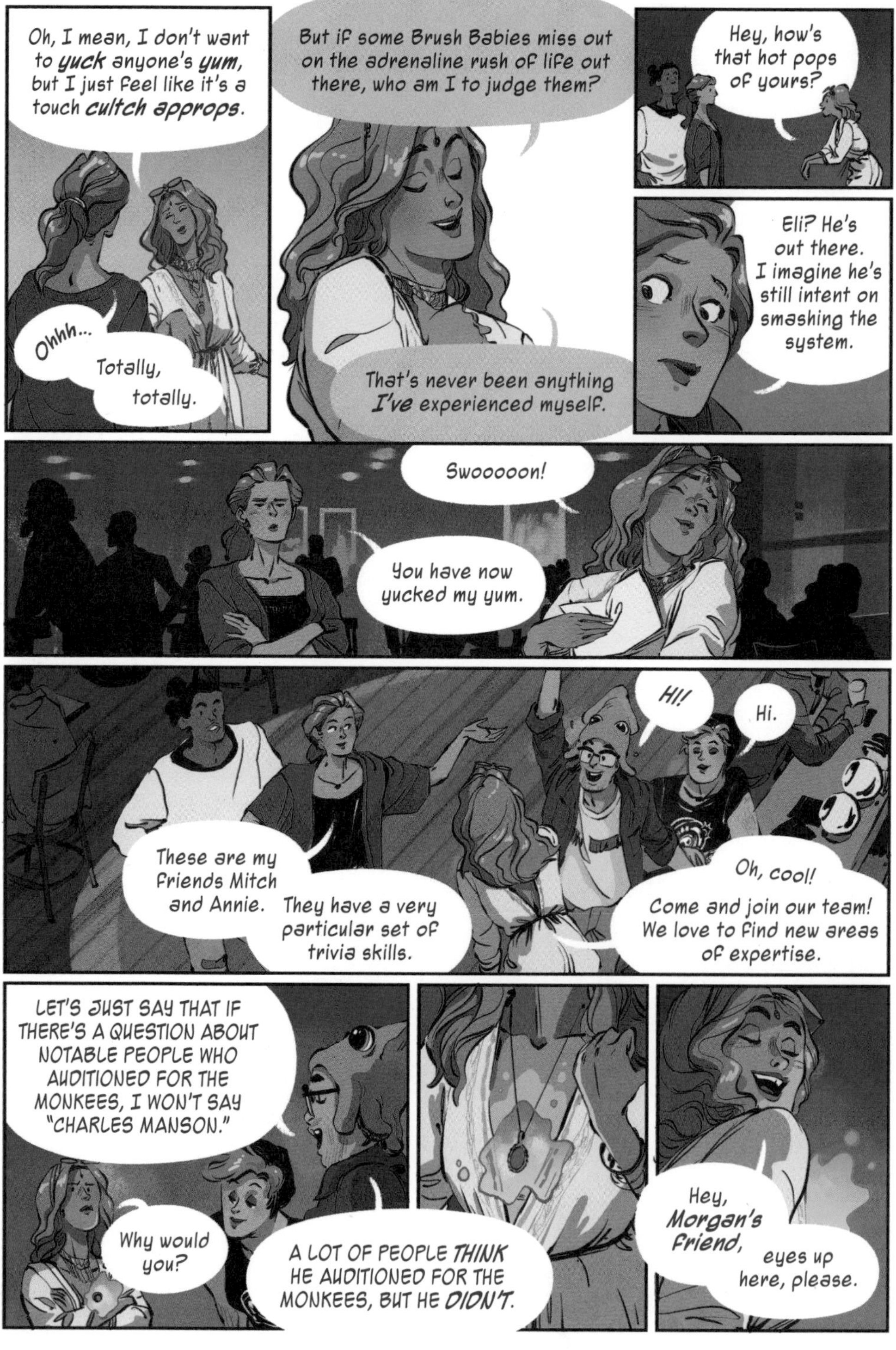
Oh, I mean, I don't want to yuck anyone's yum, but I just feel like it's a touch cultch approps.
Ohhh...
Totally, totally.
But if some Brush Babies miss out on the adrenaline rush of life out there, who am I to judge them?
That's never been anything I've experienced myself.
Hey, how's that hot pops of yours?
Eli? He's out there. I imagine he's still intent on smashing the system.
Swoooooon!
You have now yucked my yum.
HI!
Hi.
These are my friends Mitch and Annie.
They have a very particular set of trivia skills.
Oh, cool!
Come and join our team! We love to find new areas of expertise.
LET'S JUST SAY THAT IF THERE'S A QUESTION ABOUT NOTABLE PEOPLE WHO AUDITIONED FOR THE MONKEES, I WON'T SAY "CHARLES MANSON."
Why would you?
A LOT OF PEOPLE THINK HE AUDITIONED FOR THE MONKEES, BUT HE DIDN'T.
Hey, Morgan's Friend,
eyes up here, please.

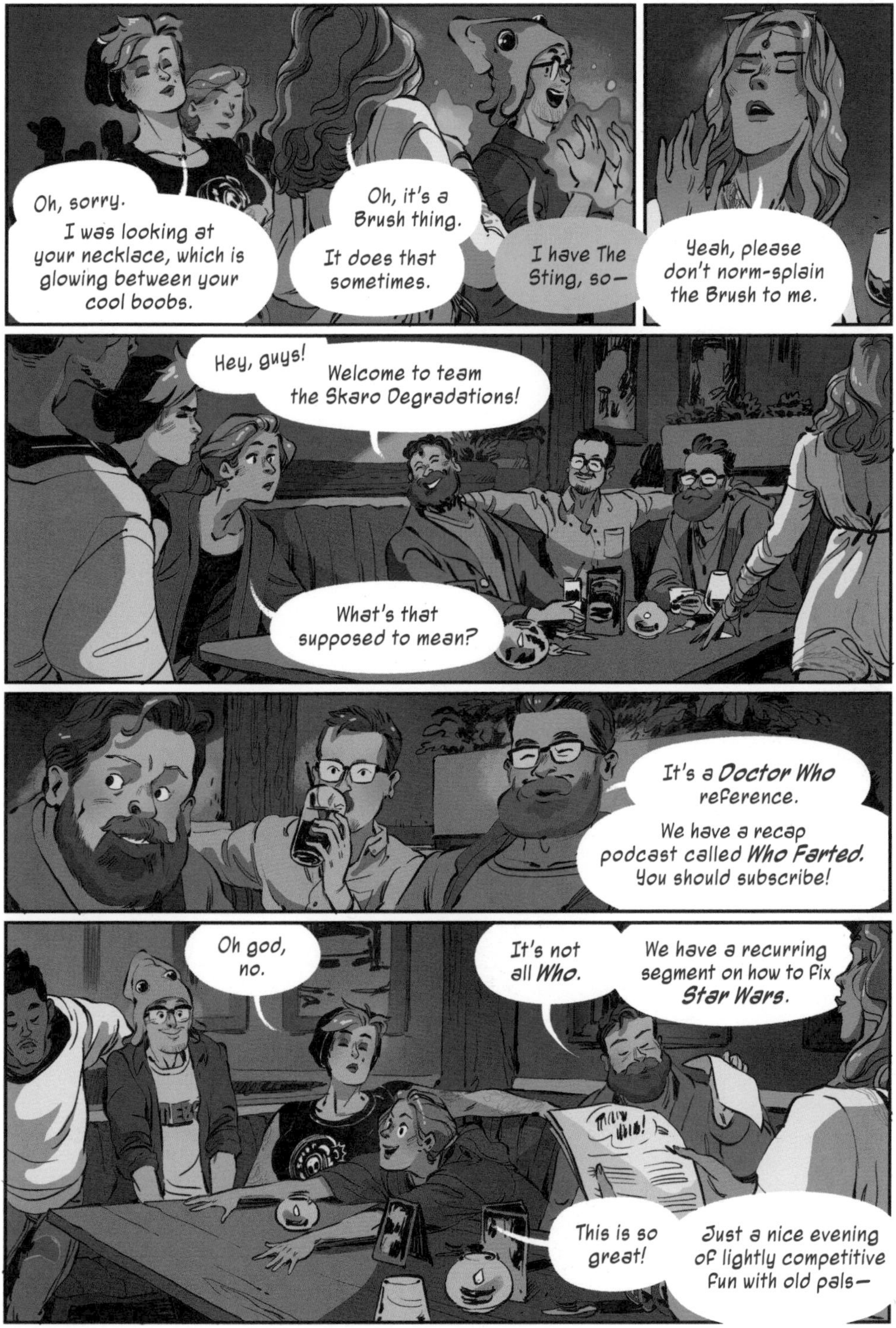
Oh, sorry.
I was looking at your necklace, which is glowing between your cool boobs.
Oh, it's a Brush thing.
It does that sometimes.
I have The Sting, so—
Yeah, please don't norm-splain the Brush to me.
Hey, guys!
Welcome to team the Skaro Degradations!
What's that supposed to mean?
It's a *Doctor Who* reference.
We have a recap podcast called *Who Farted.* You should subscribe!
Oh god, no.
It's not all *Who*.
We have a recurring segment on how to fix *Star Wars*.
This is so great!
Just a nice evening of lightly competitive fun with old pals—

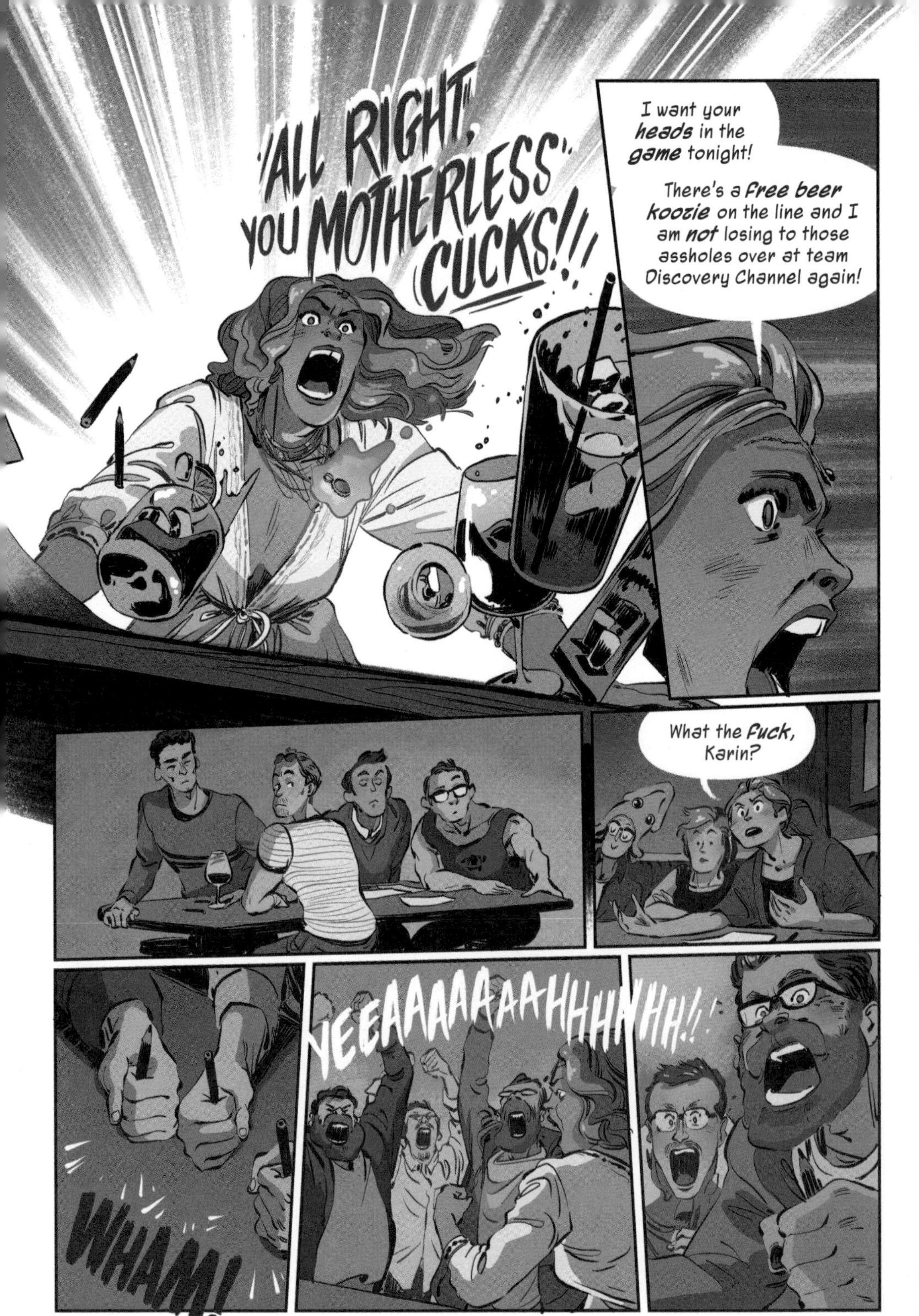
"ALL RIGHT," YOU MOTHERLESS" CUCKS!!!
I want your heads in the game tonight!
There's a free beer koozie on the line and I am not losing to those assholes over at team Discovery Channel again!
What the fuck, Karin?
WHAM!
YEEAAAAAAAAHHHHHH!!

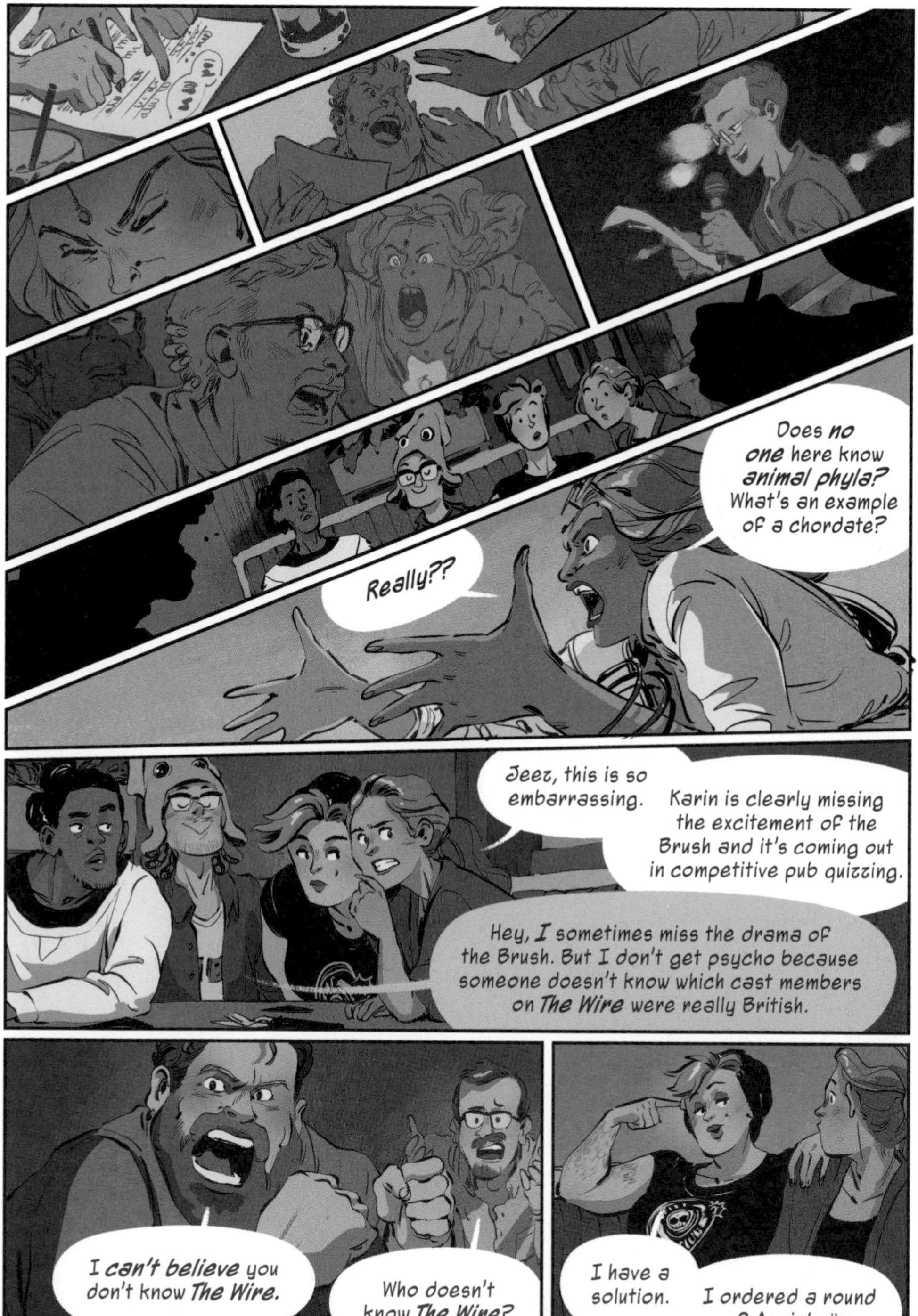
Does no one here know animal phyla? What's an example of a chordate?
Really??
Jeez, this is so embarrassing.
Karin is clearly missing the excitement of the Brush and it's coming out in competitive pub quizzing.
Hey, I sometimes miss the drama of the Brush. But I don't get psycho because someone doesn't know which cast members on The Wire were really British.
I can't believe you don't know The Wire.
Who doesn't know The Wire?
I have a solution.
I ordered a round of Anniebräu.

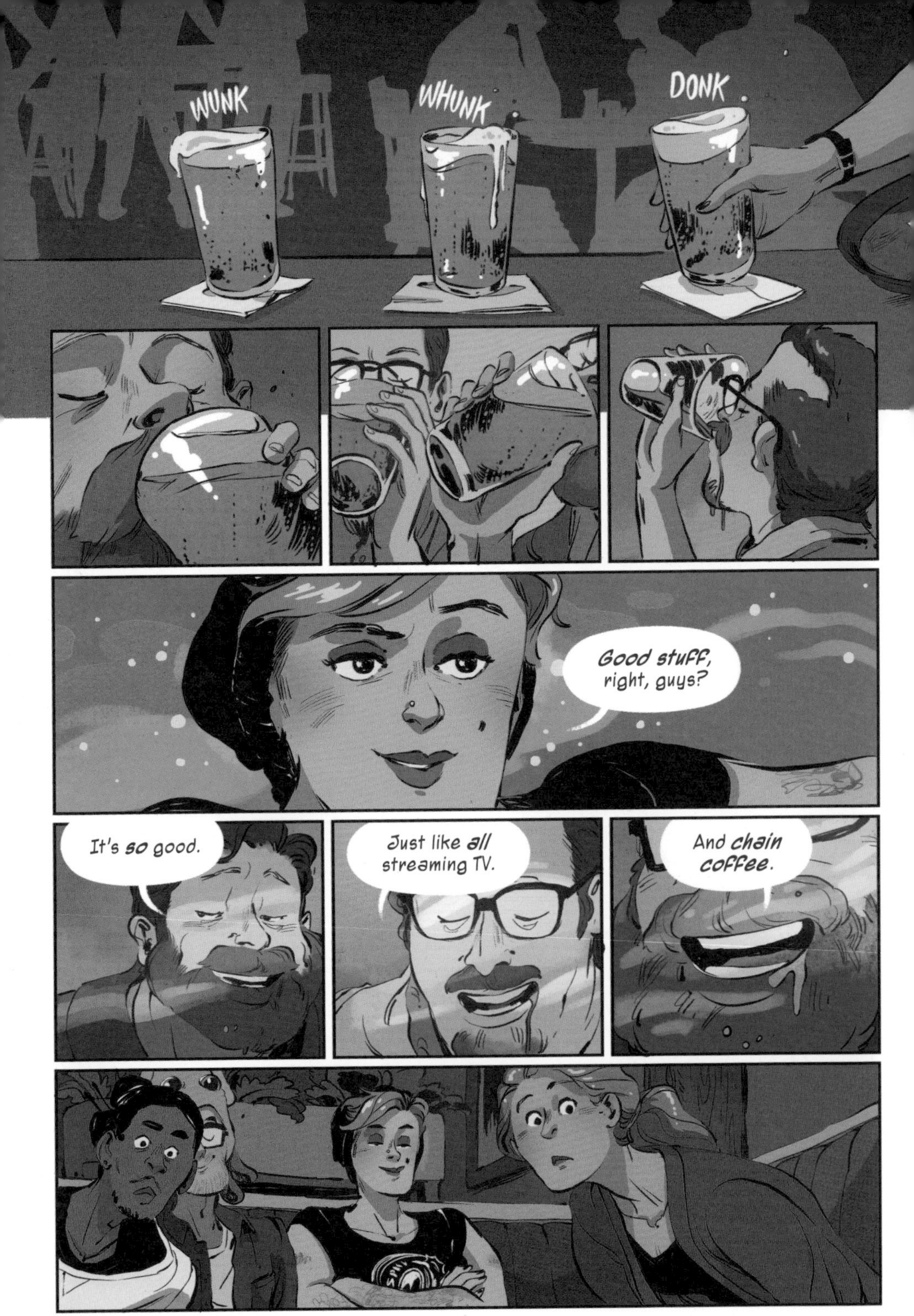
WUNK
WHUNK
DONK
Good stuff, right, guys?
It's so good.
Just like all streaming TV.
And chain coffee.

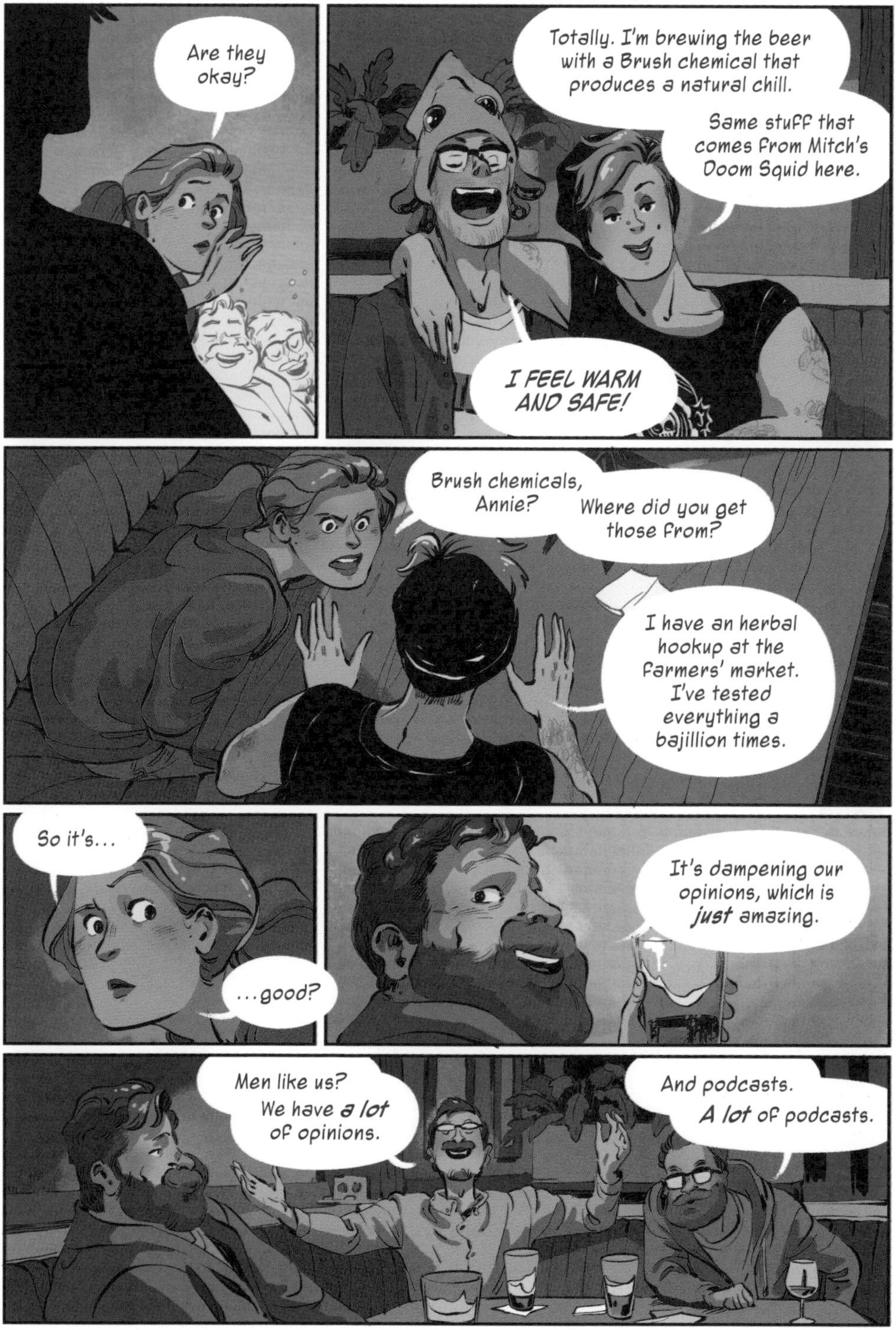
Are they okay?
Totally. I'm brewing the beer with a Brush chemical that produces a natural chill.
Same stuff that comes from Mitch's Doom Squid here.
I FEEL WARM AND SAFE!
Brush chemicals, Annie?
Where did you get those from?
I have an herbal hookup at the farmers' market. I've tested everything a bajillion times.
So it's...
...good?
It's dampening our opinions, which is *just* amazing.
Men like us? We have *a lot* of opinions.
And podcasts. *A lot* of podcasts.

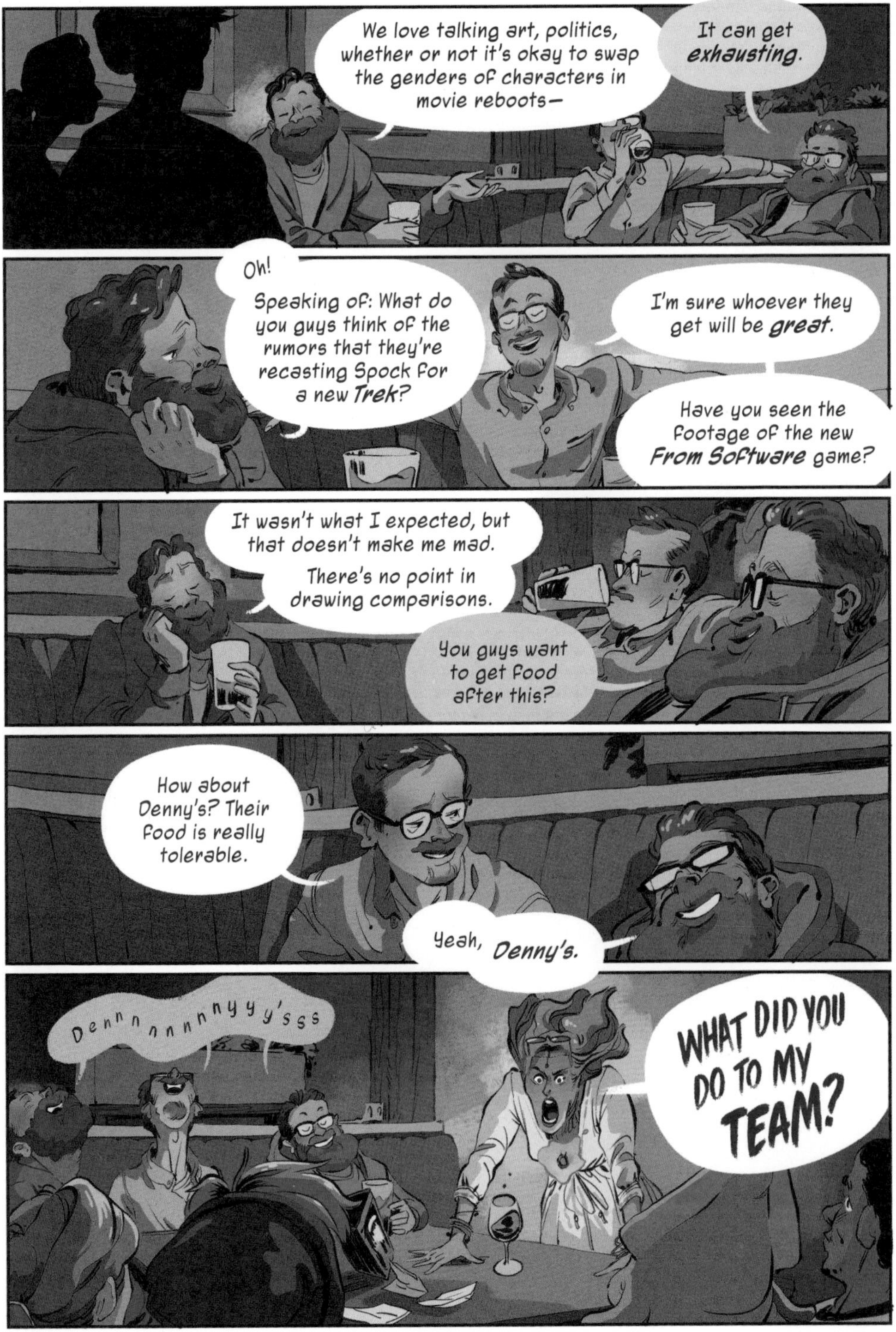
We love talking art, politics, whether or not it's okay to swap the genders of characters in movie reboots—
It can get *exhausting*.
Oh!
Speaking of: What do you guys think of the rumors that they're recasting Spock for a new *Trek*?
I'm sure whoever they get will be *great*.
Have you seen the footage of the new *From Software* game?
It wasn't what I expected, but that doesn't make me mad.
There's no point in drawing comparisons.
You guys want to get food after this?
How about Denny's? Their food is really tolerable.
Yeah, *Denny's*.
Dennnnnnnnyyyy'sss
WHAT DID YOU DO TO MY TEAM?

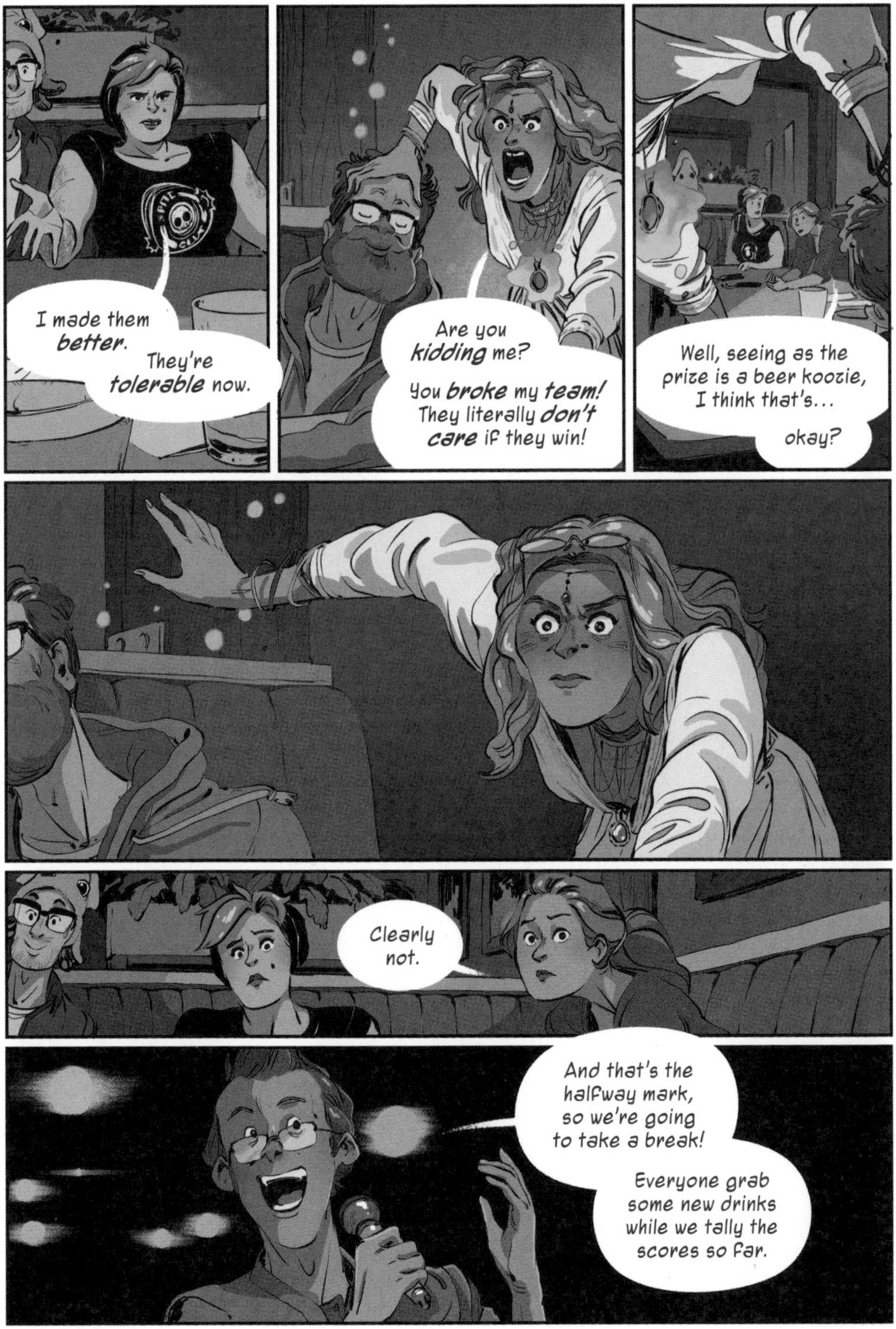
I made them **better**. They're **tolerable** now.
Are you **kidding** me?
You **broke** my **team!** They literally **don't care** if they win!
Well, seeing as the prize is a beer koozie, I think that's...
okay?
Clearly not.
And that's the halfway mark, so we're going to take a break!
Everyone grab some new drinks while we tally the scores so far.

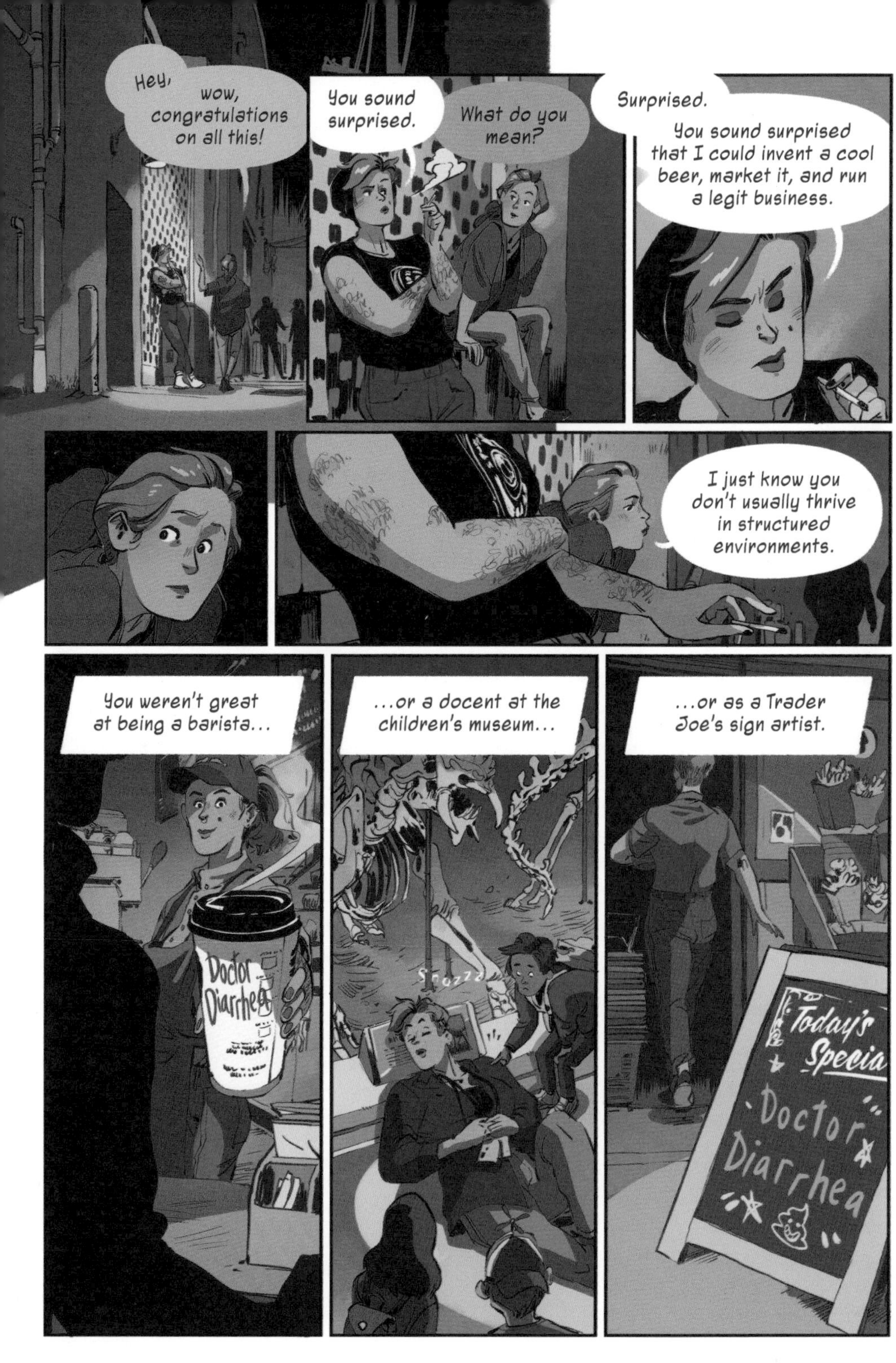
Hey, wow, congratulations on all this!
You sound surprised.
What do you mean?
Surprised.
You sound surprised that I could invent a cool beer, market it, and run a legit business.
I just know you don't usually thrive in structured environments.
You weren't great at being a barista...
Doctor Diarrhea
...or a docent at the children's museum...
...or as a Trader Joe's sign artist.
Today's Specia
Doctor Diarrhea

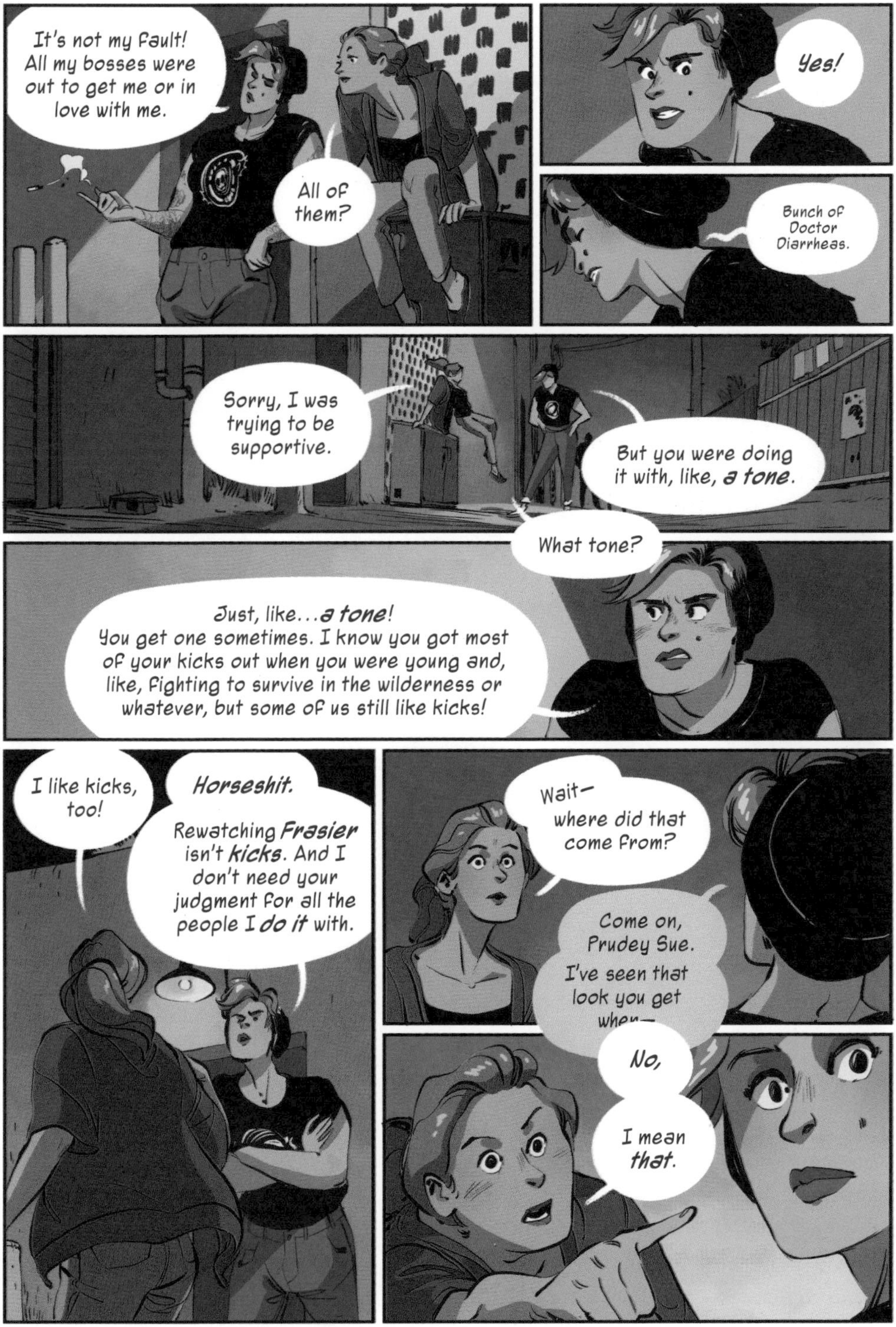

It's not my fault! All my bosses were out to get me or in love with me.
All of them?
Yes!
Bunch of Doctor Diarrheas.
Sorry, I was trying to be supportive.
But you were doing it with, like, *a tone*.
What tone?
Just, like... *a tone*! You get one sometimes. I know you got most of your kicks out when you were young and, like, fighting to survive in the wilderness or whatever, but some of us still like kicks!
I like kicks, too!
Horseshit.
Rewatching ***Frasier*** isn't ***kicks***. And I don't need your judgment for all the people I *do it* with.
Wait— where did that come from?
Come on, Prudey Sue.
I've seen that look you get when—
No,
I mean *that*.

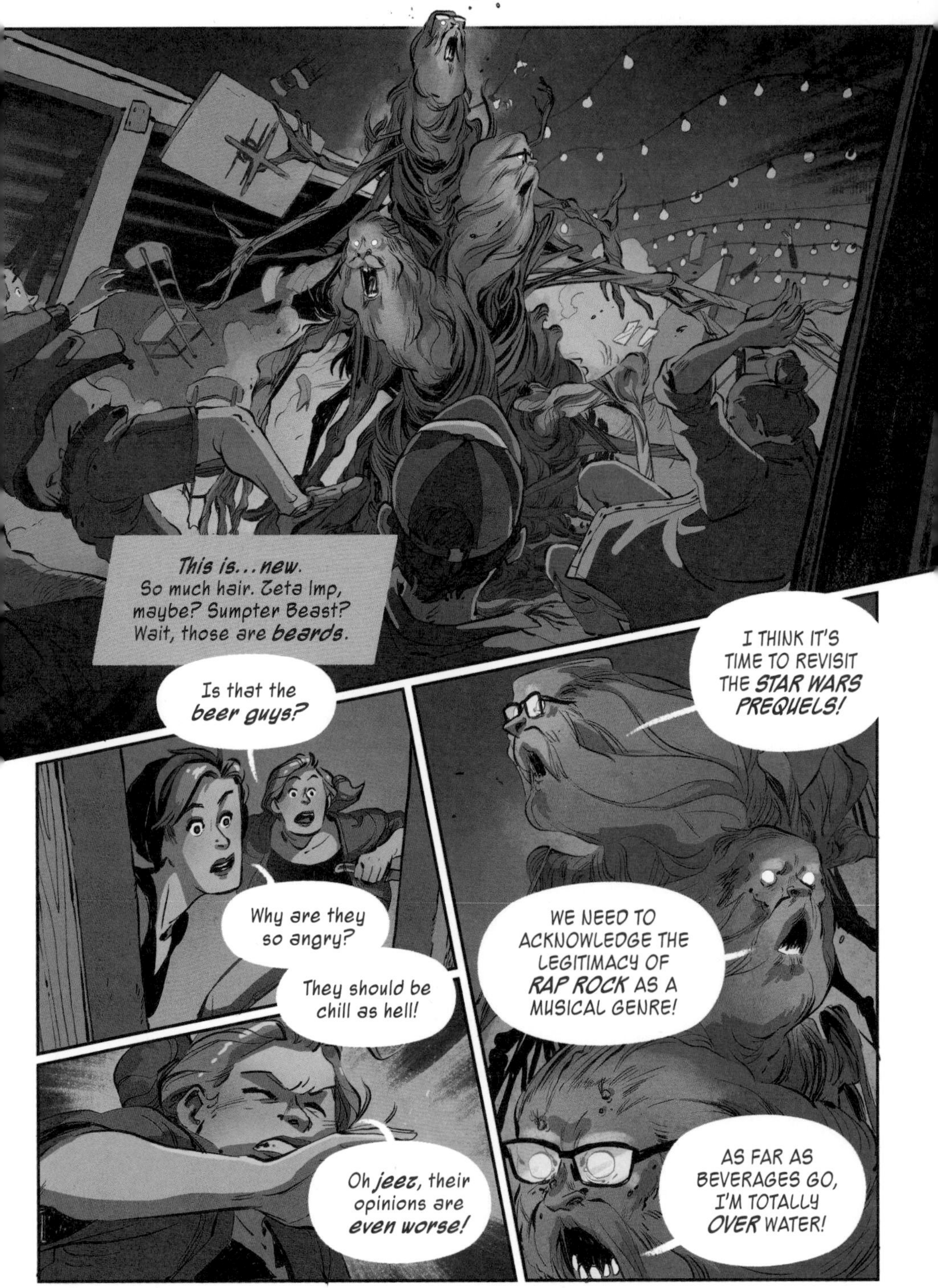
This is...new.
So much hair. Zeta Imp, maybe? Sumpter Beast? Wait, those are beards.
Is that the beer guys?
I THINK IT'S TIME TO REVISIT THE STAR WARS PREQUELS!
Why are they so angry?
They should be chill as hell!
WE NEED TO ACKNOWLEDGE THE LEGITIMACY OF RAP ROCK AS A MUSICAL GENRE!
Oh jeez, their opinions are even worse!
AS FAR AS BEVERAGES GO, I'M TOTALLY OVER WATER!

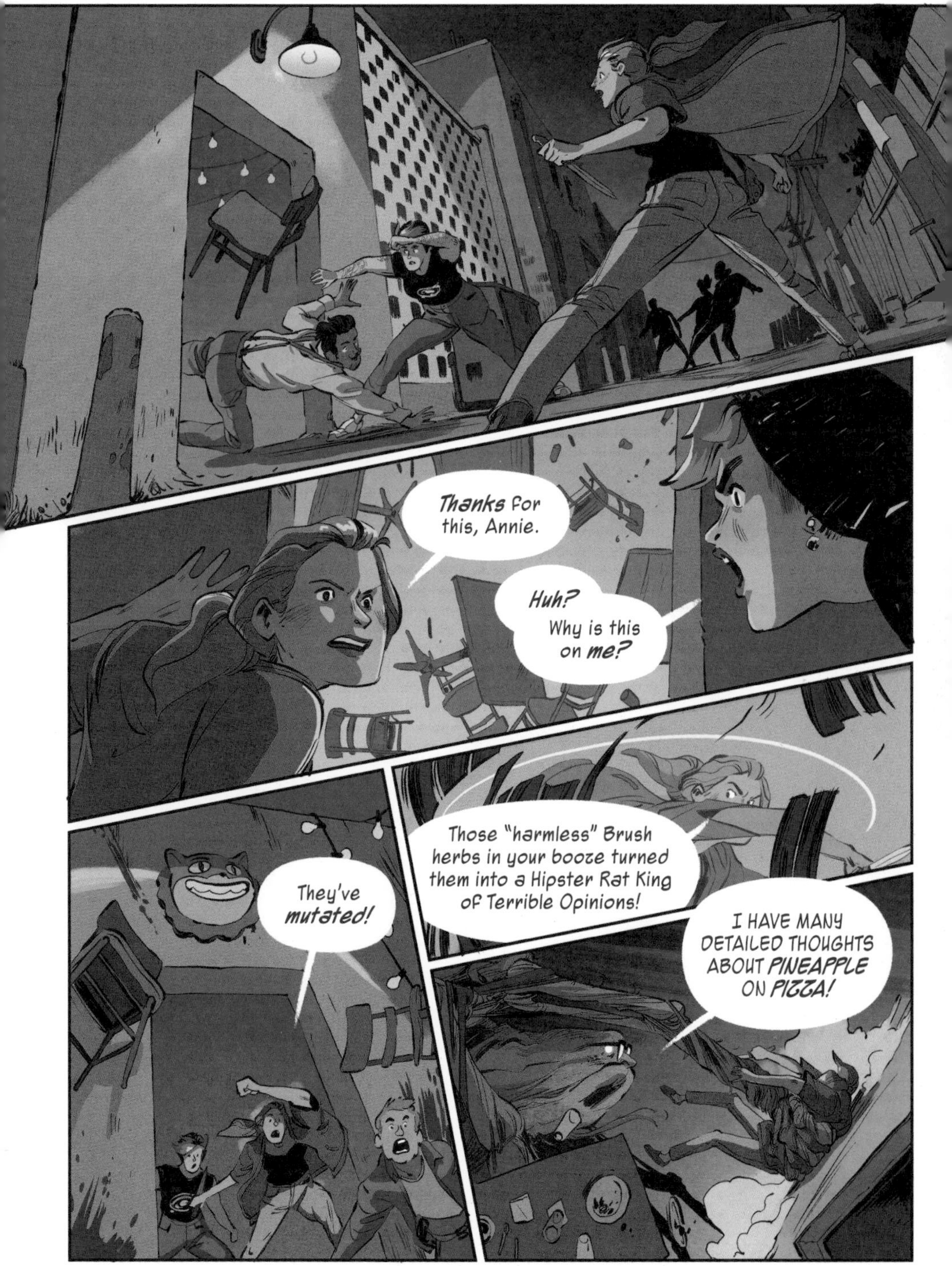

Thanks for this, Annie.
Huh? Why is this on *me?*
Those "harmless" Brush herbs in your booze turned them into a Hipster Rat King of Terrible Opinions!
They've *mutated!*
I HAVE MANY DETAILED THOUGHTS ABOUT *PINEAPPLE* ON *PIZZA!*

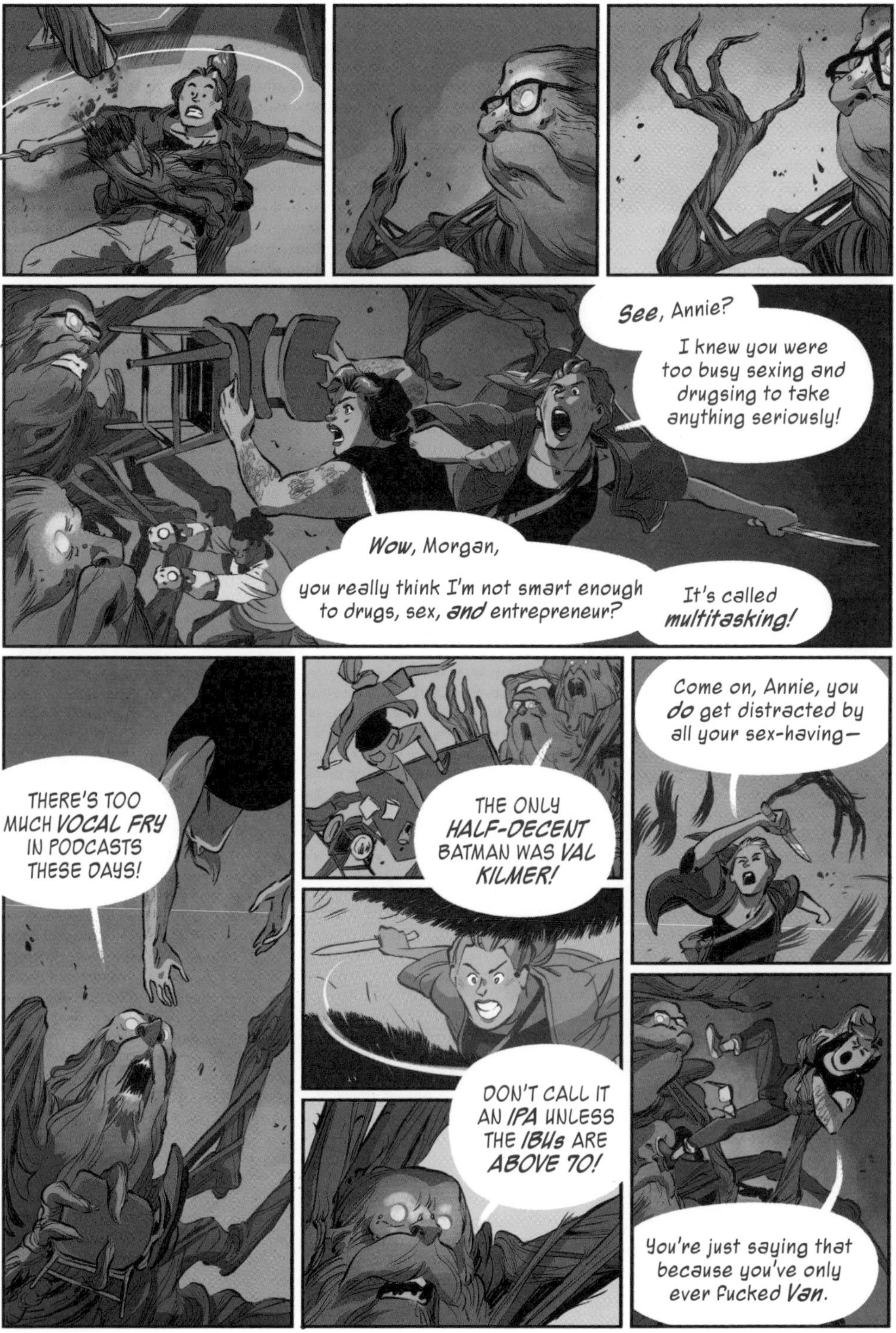

See, Annie?
I knew you were too busy sexing and drugsing to take anything seriously!
Wow, Morgan,
you really think I'm not smart enough to drugs, sex, and entrepreneur?
It's called multitasking!
THERE'S TOO MUCH VOCAL FRY IN PODCASTS THESE DAYS!
THE ONLY HALF-DECENT BATMAN WAS VAL KILMER!
Come on, Annie, you do get distracted by all your sex-having—
DON'T CALL IT AN IPA UNLESS THE IBUs ARE ABOVE 70!
You're just saying that because you've only ever fucked Van.

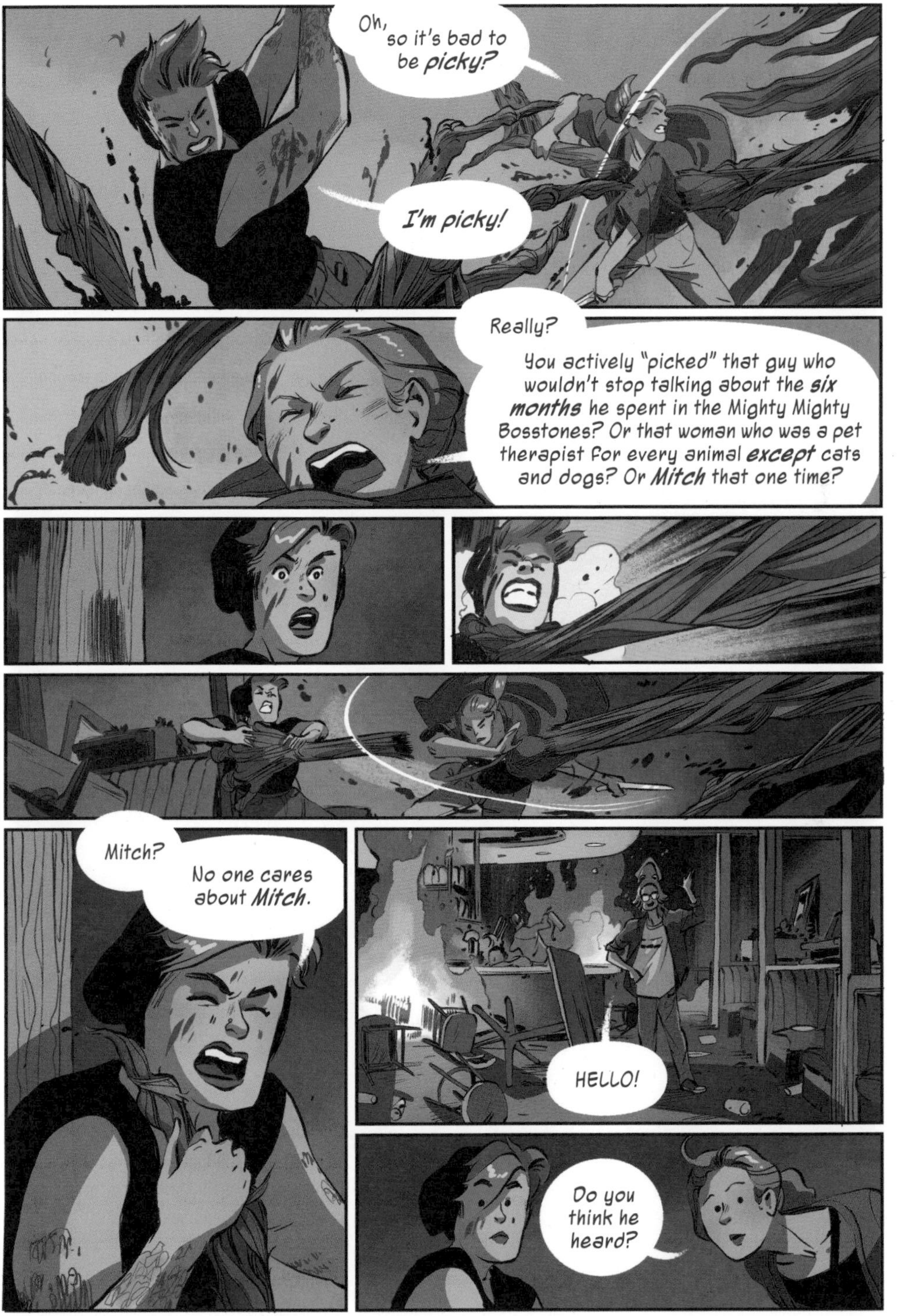
Oh, so it's bad to be *picky?*
I'm picky!
Really?
You actively "picked" that guy who wouldn't stop talking about the ***six months*** he spent in the Mighty Mighty Bosstones? Or that woman who was a pet therapist for every animal ***except*** cats and dogs? Or ***Mitch*** that one time?
Mitch?
No one cares about *Mitch*.
HELLO!
Do you think he heard?

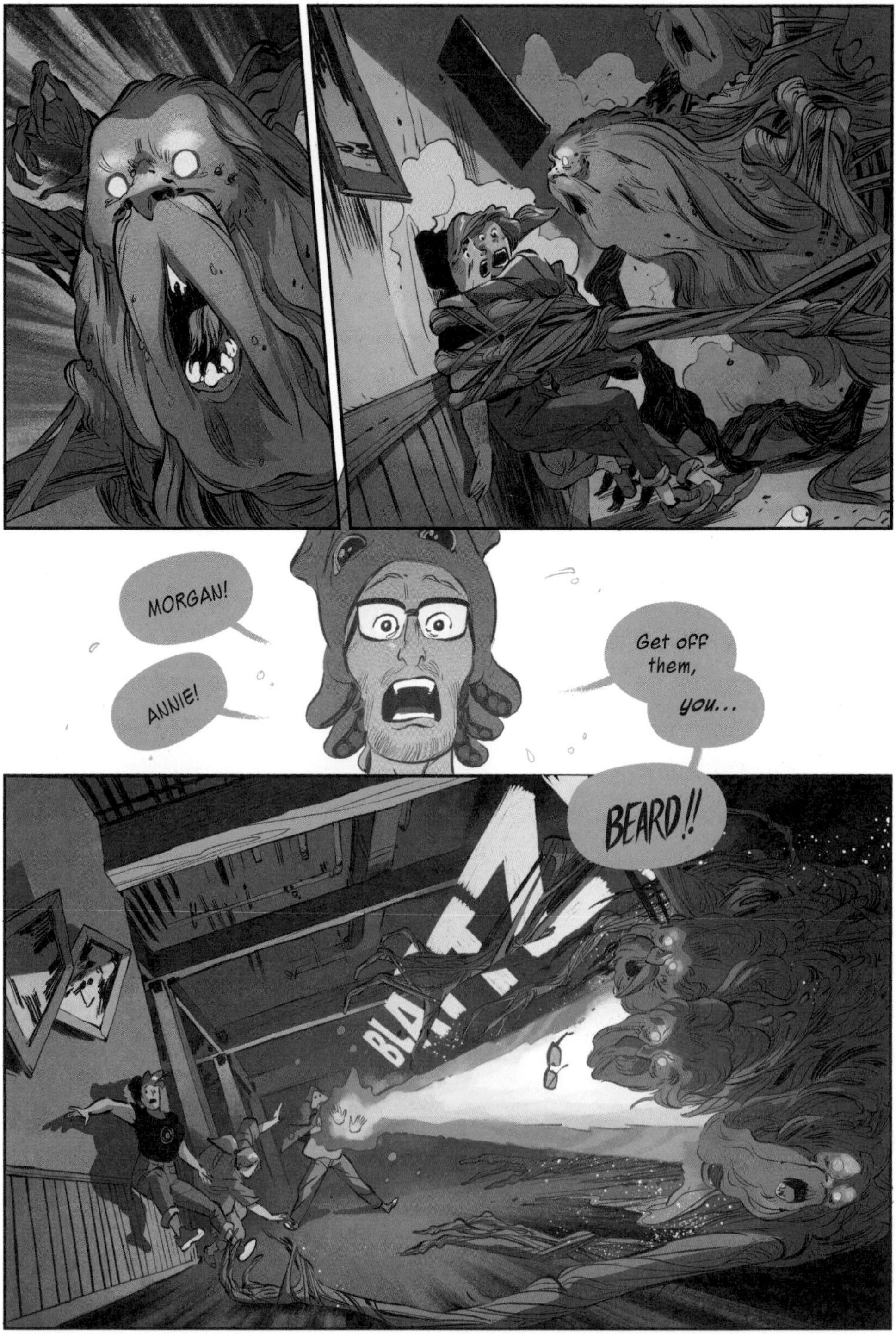
MORGAN!
ANNIE!
Get off them, you...
BEARD!!

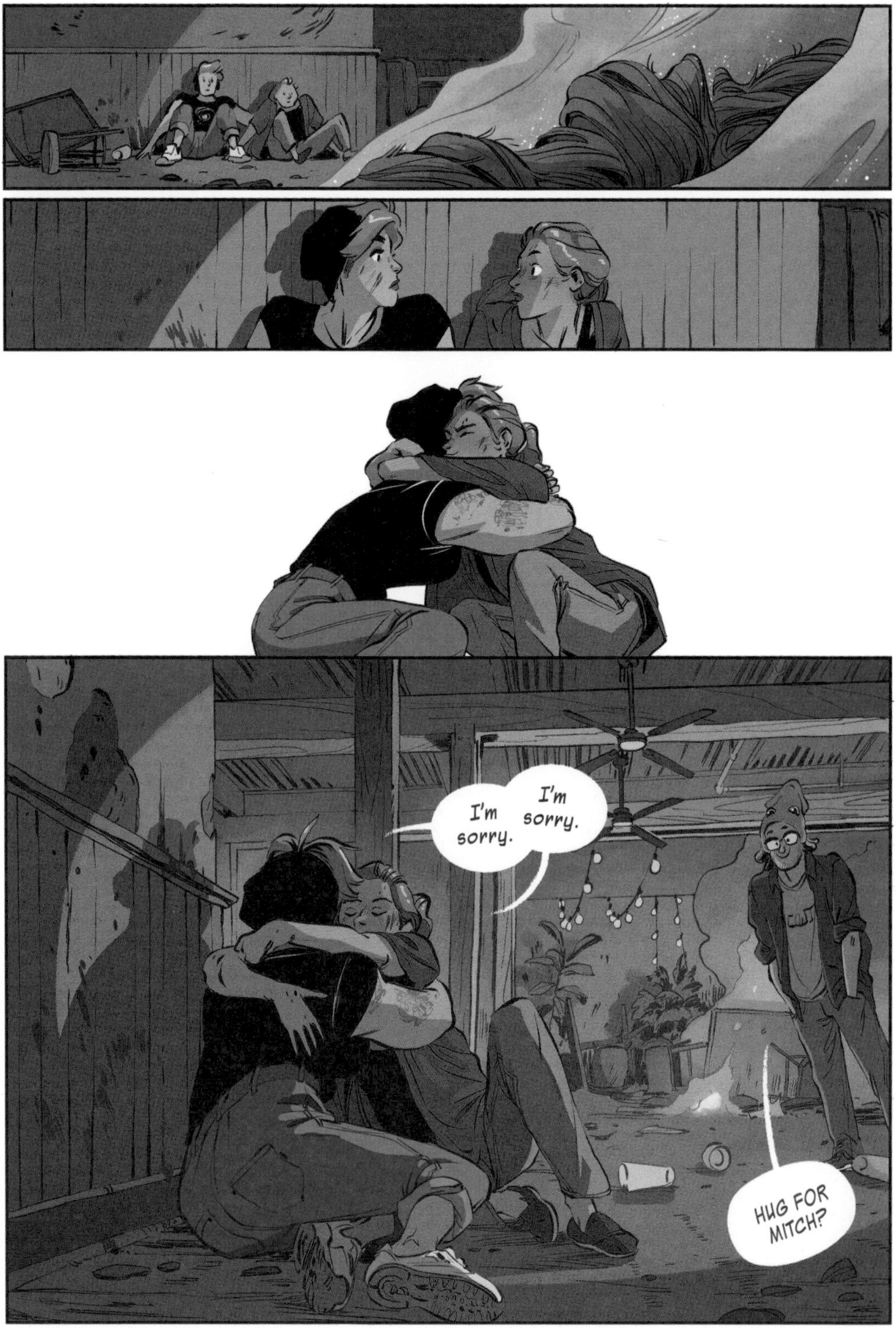
I'm sorry.
I'm sorry.
HUG FOR MITCH?

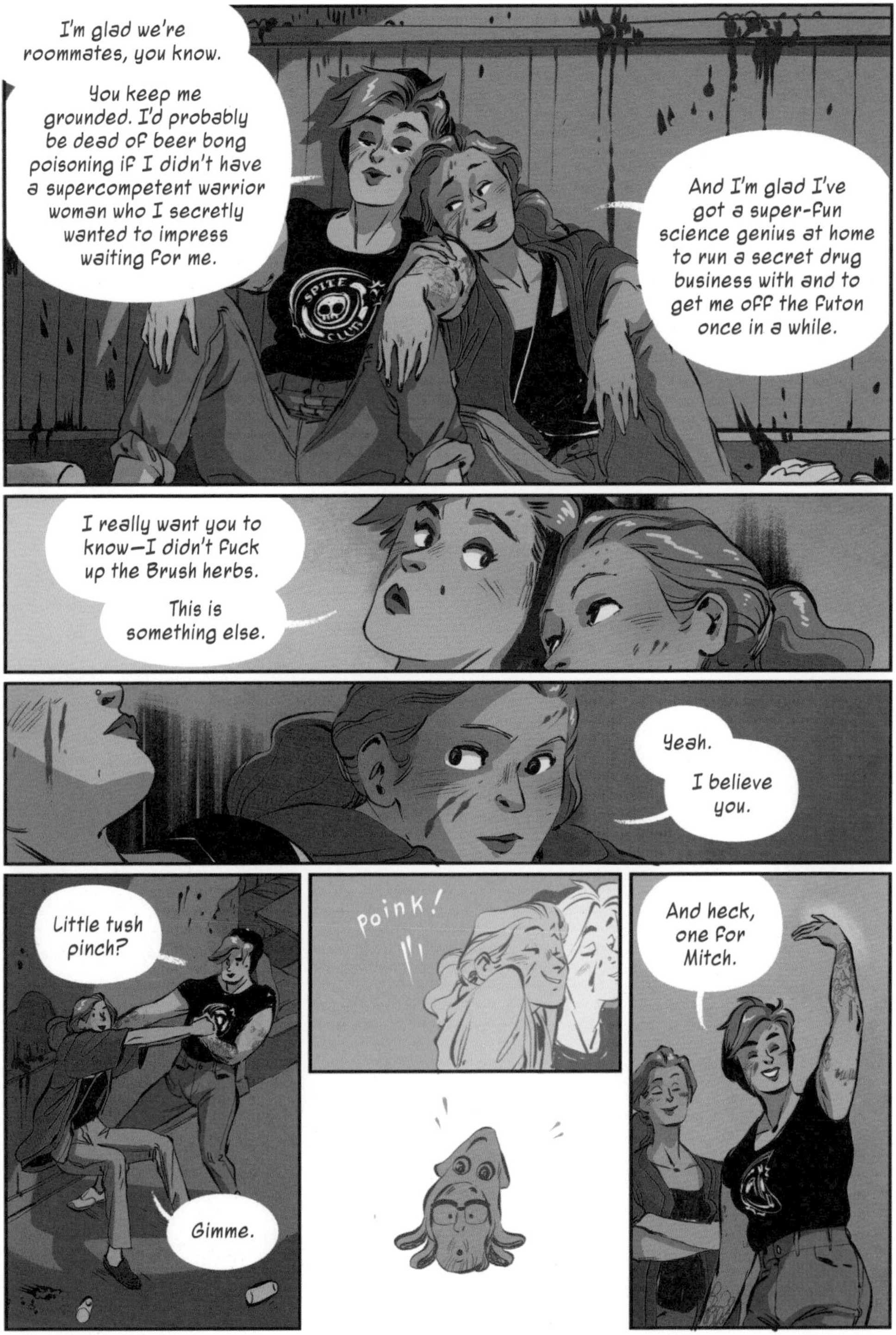
I'm glad we're roommates, you know.
You keep me grounded. I'd probably be dead of beer bong poisoning if I didn't have a supercompetent warrior woman who I secretly wanted to impress waiting for me.
And I'm glad I've got a super-fun science genius at home to run a secret drug business with and to get me off the futon once in a while.
SPITE CLUB
I really want you to know—I didn't fuck up the Brush herbs.
This is something else.
Yeah.
I believe you.
Little tush pinch?
Gimme.
poink!
And heck, one for Mitch.

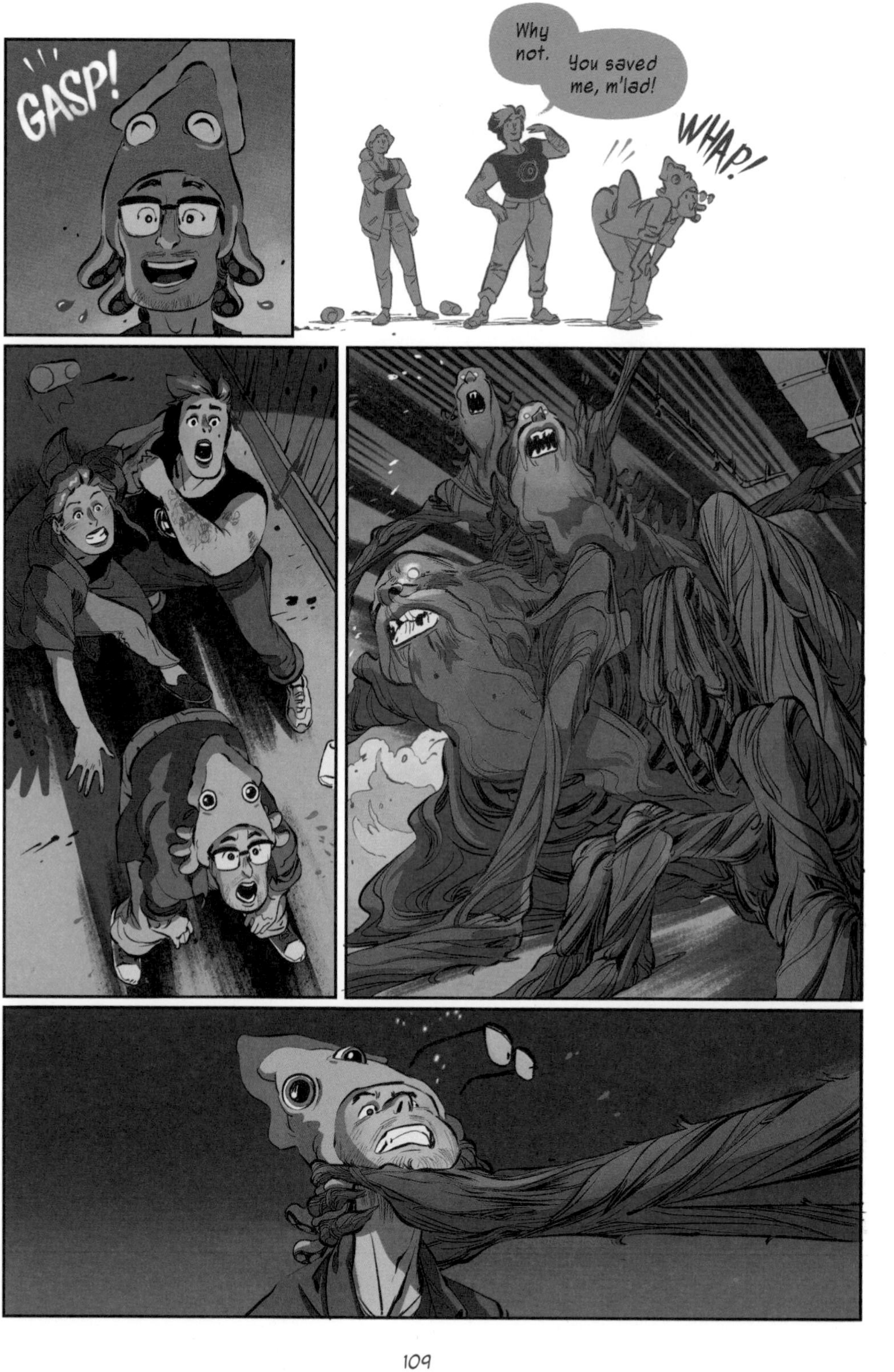
GASP!
Why not.
You saved me, m'lad!
WHAP!

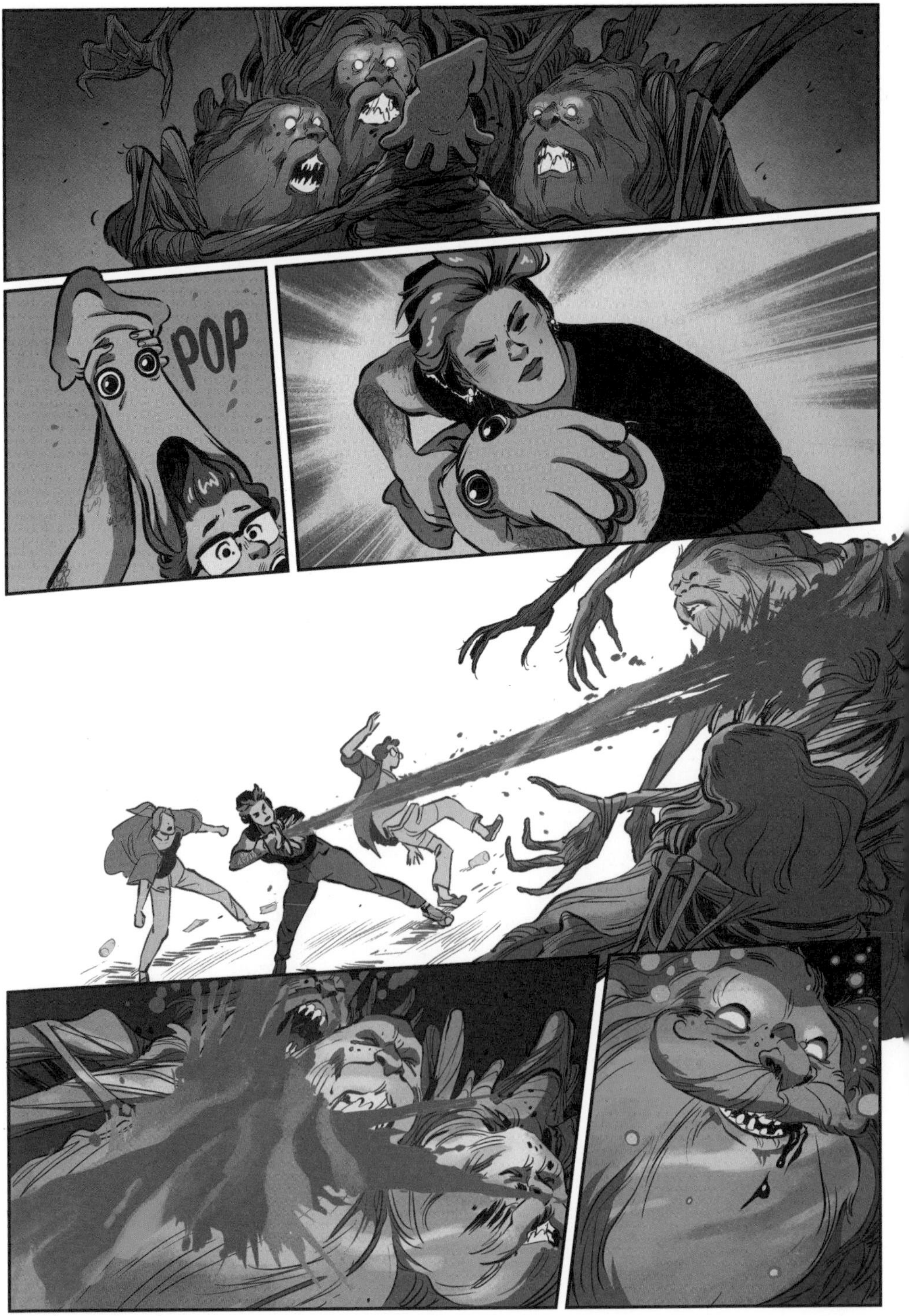
POP

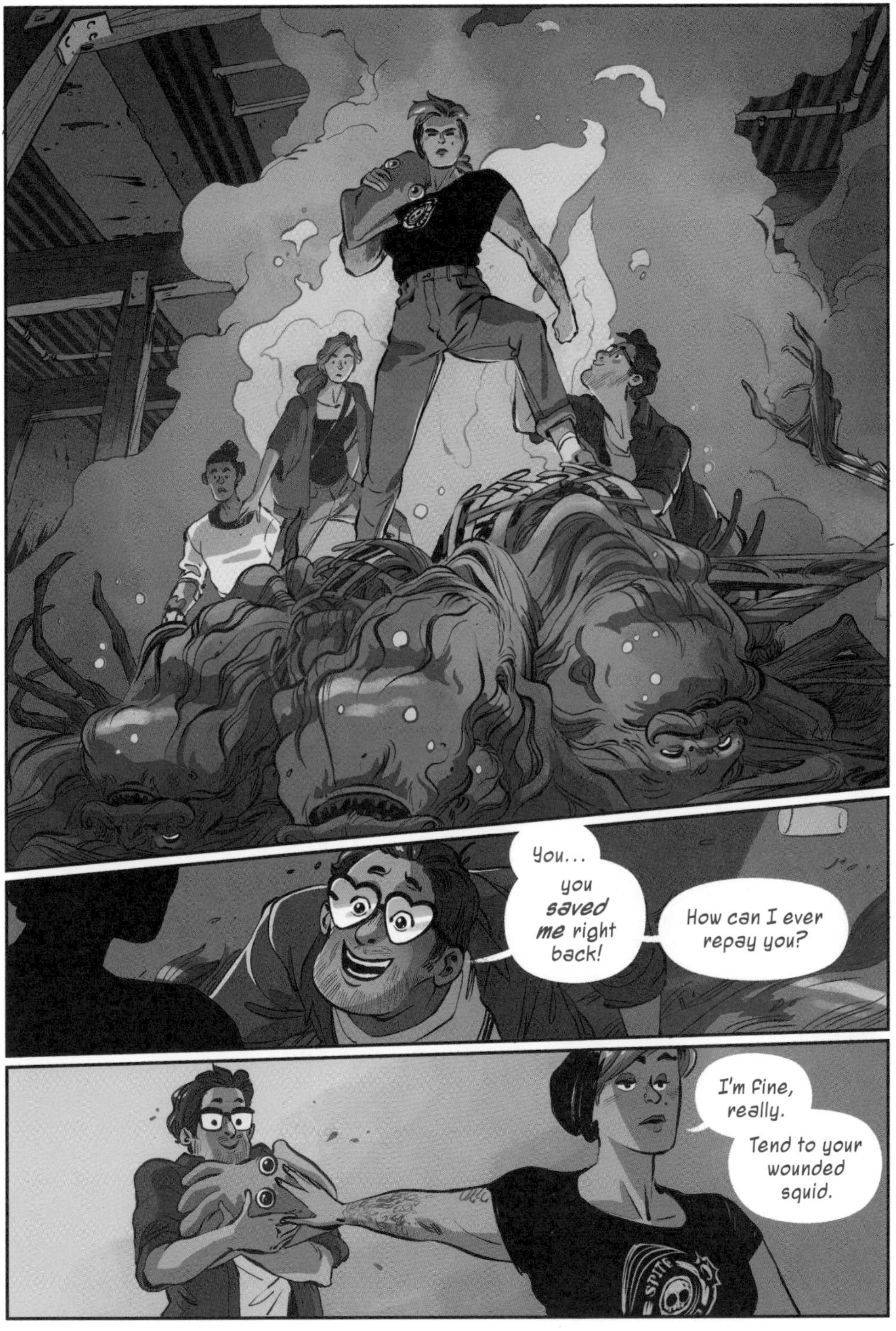
You... you saved me right back!
How can I ever repay you?
I'm fine, really.
Tend to your wounded squid.

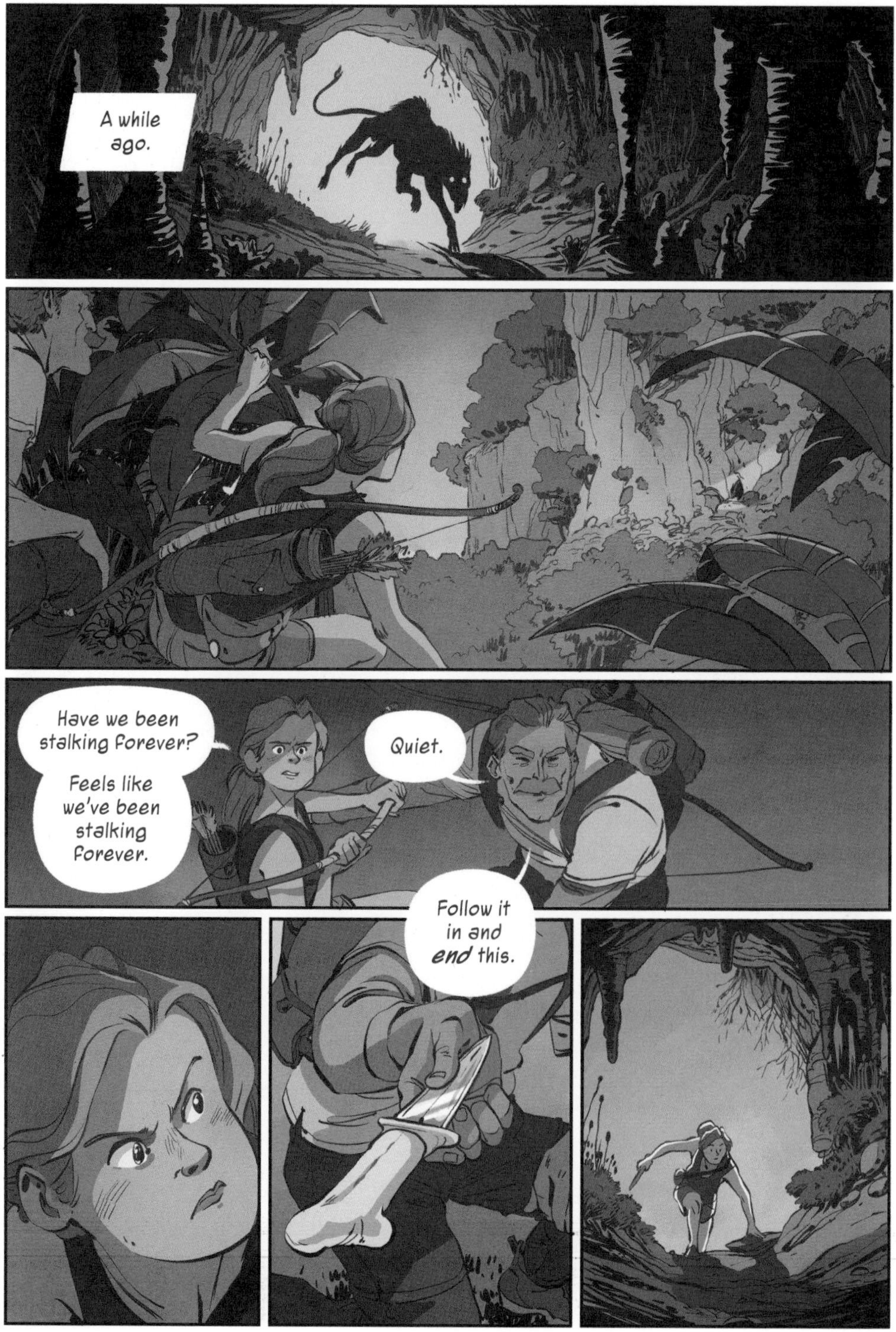
A while ago.
Have we been stalking forever?
Feels like we've been stalking forever.
Quiet.
Follow it in and *end* this.

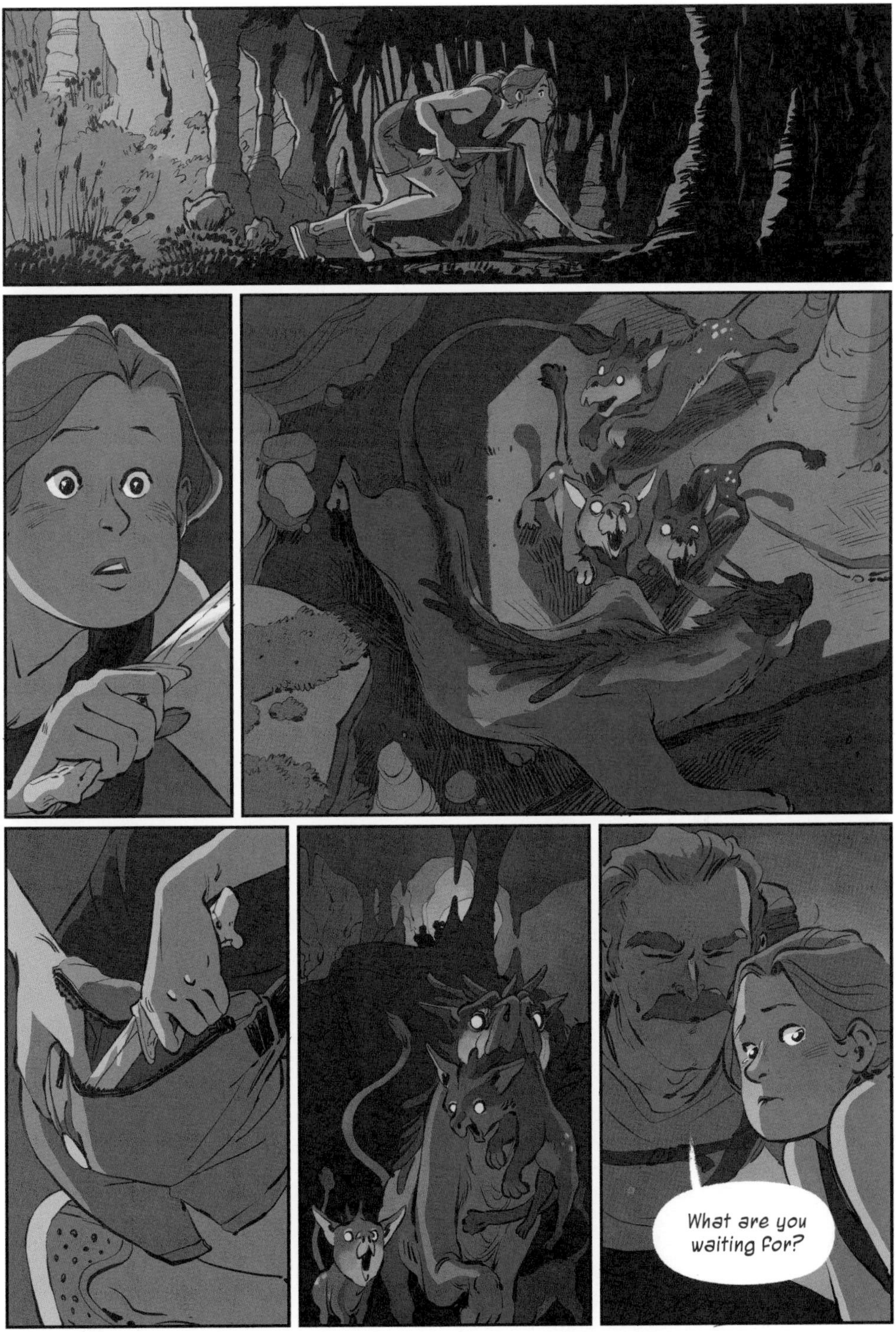
What are you
waiting for?

I *can't!*

They're *babies!*

That's why we followed it! If we killed it out there, we never would have found the nest and these things would grow up to become pains in our asses!

I won't do this!

It's not survival. It's just *mean.*

There's a *difference.*

Not a huge one.

And don't talk to me about survival.

I had to build a life out here before there was any infrastructure to care for you or your mom—

But Mom *left!*

Because she was tired of how freaking dramatic everything has to be with you!

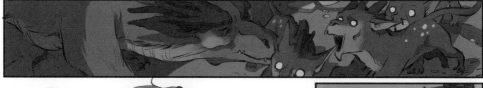

And I *get it* now!

I'm leaving, too.

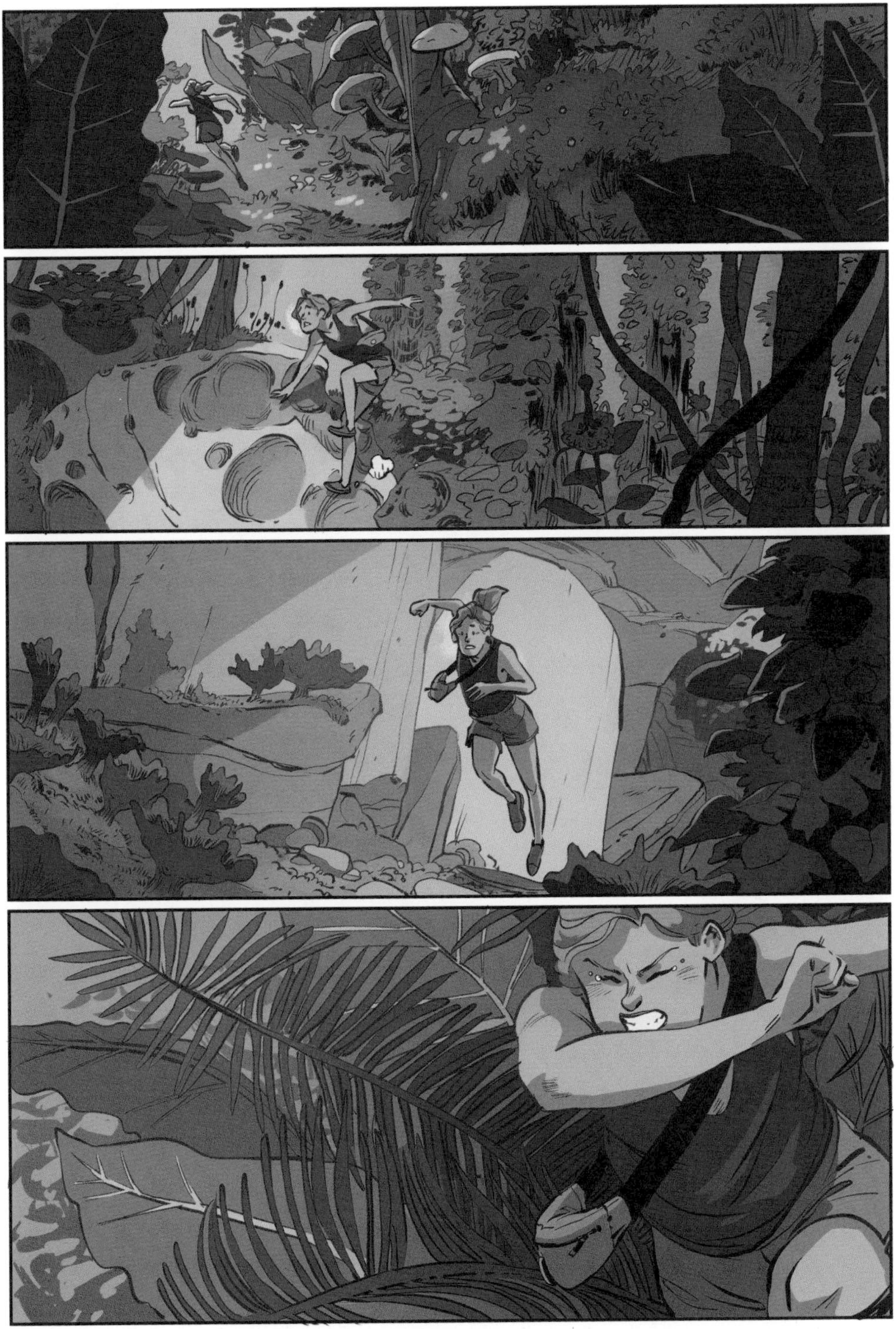

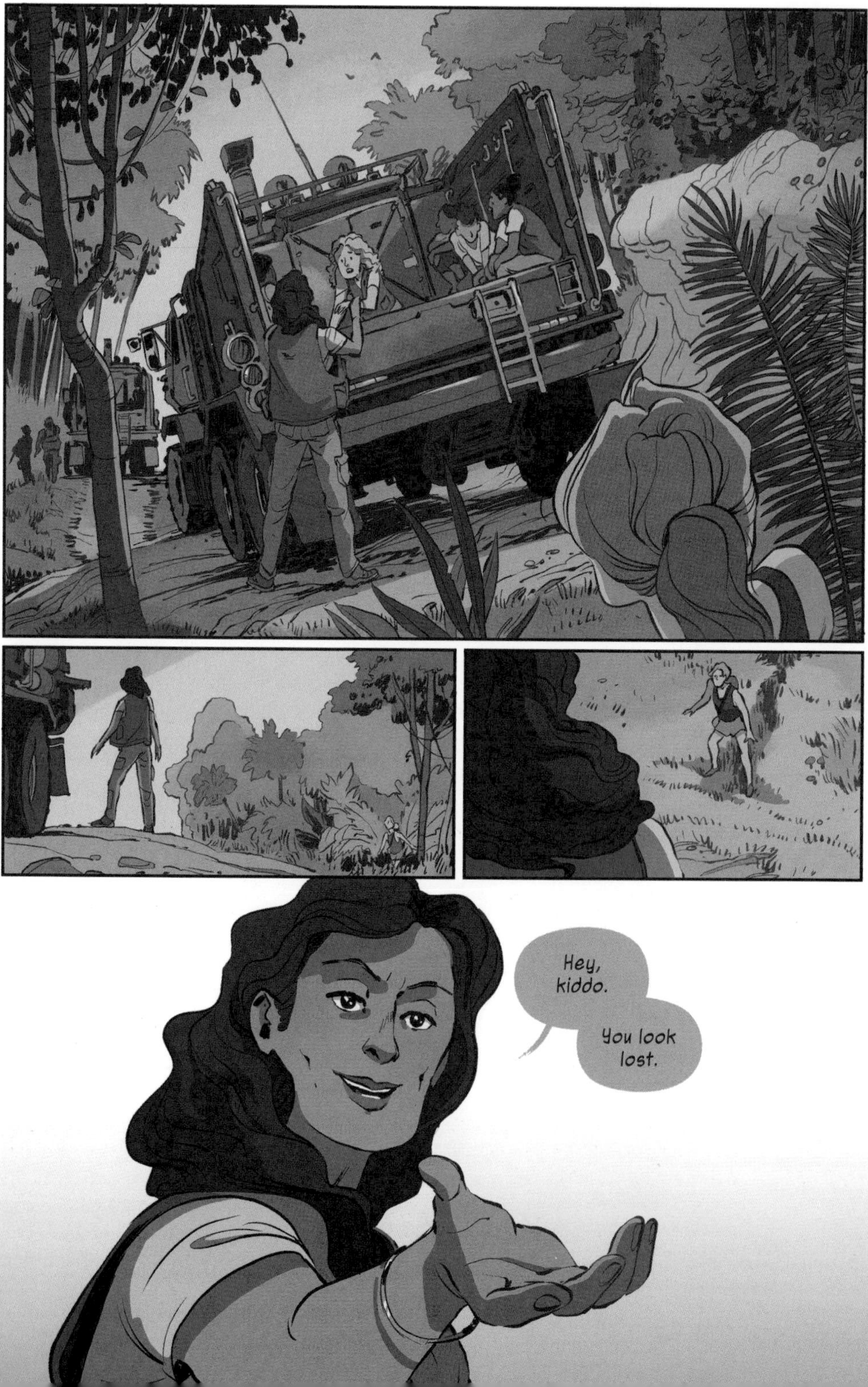

Hey, kiddo.
You look lost.

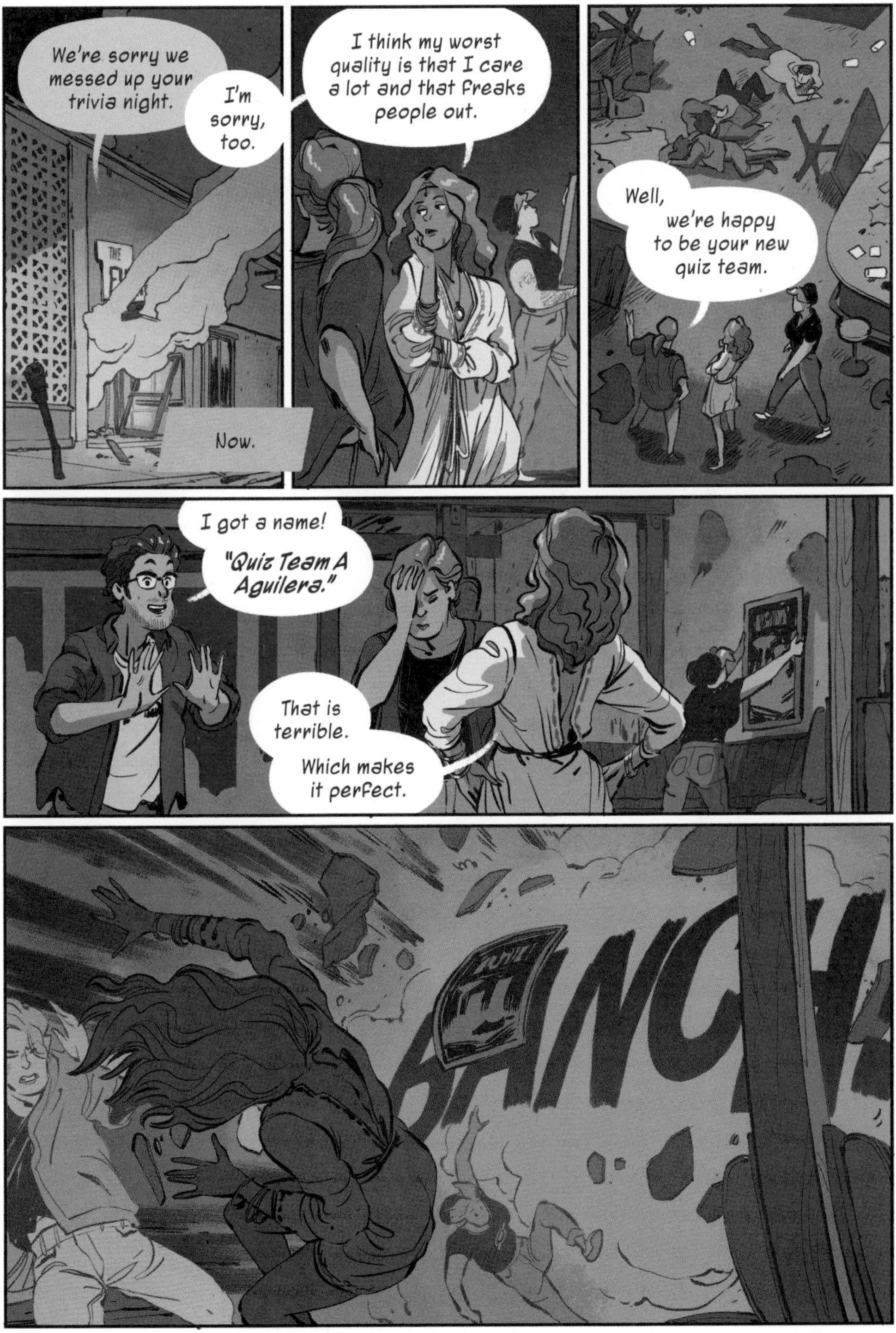

We're sorry we messed up your trivia night.
I'm sorry, too.
Now.
I think my worst quality is that I care a lot and that freaks people out.
Well, we're happy to be your new quiz team.
I got a name!
"Quiz Team A Aguilera."
That is terrible.
Which makes it perfect.

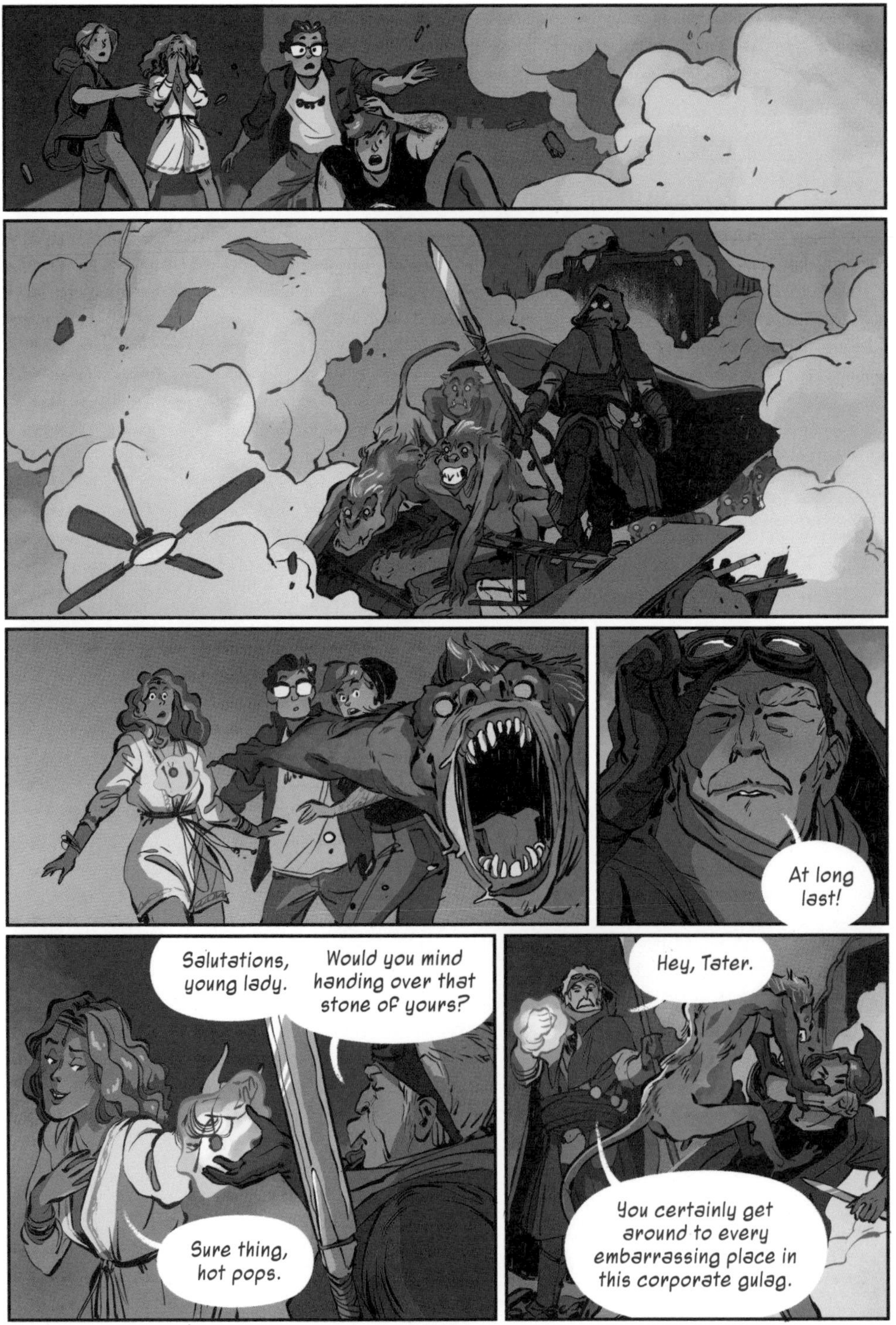
At long last!
Salutations, young lady.
Would you mind handing over that stone of yours?
Sure thing, hot pops.
Hey, Tater.
You certainly get around to every embarrassing place in this corporate gulag.

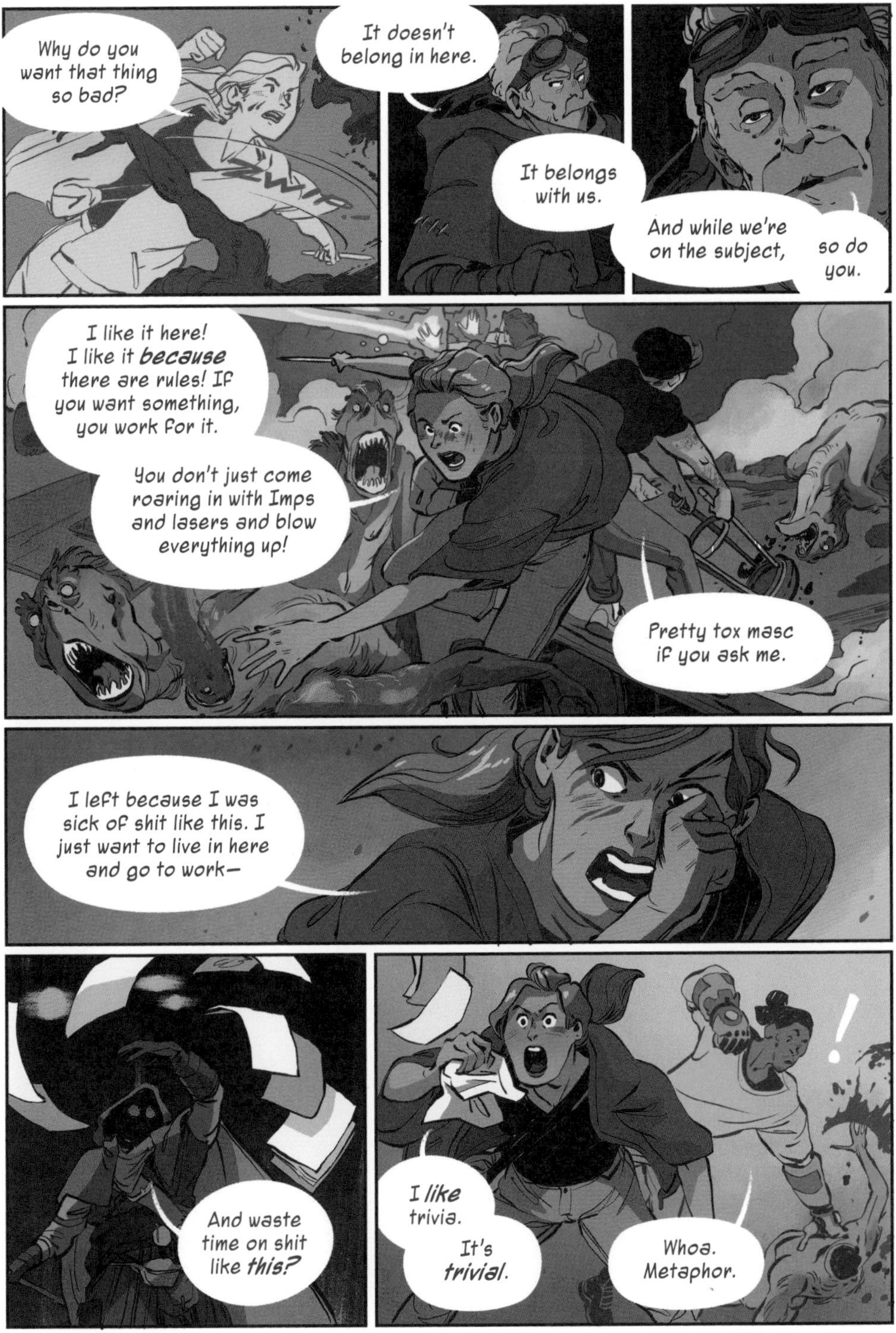
Why do you want that thing so bad?
ZWIP
It doesn't belong in here.
It belongs with us.
And while we're on the subject,
so do you.
I like it here! I like it *because* there are rules! If you want something, you work for it.
You don't just come roaring in with Imps and lasers and blow everything up!
Pretty tox masc if you ask me.
I left because I was sick of shit like this. I just want to live in here and go to work—
And waste time on shit like *this?*
I *like* trivia.
It's *trivial*.
Whoa. Metaphor.
!

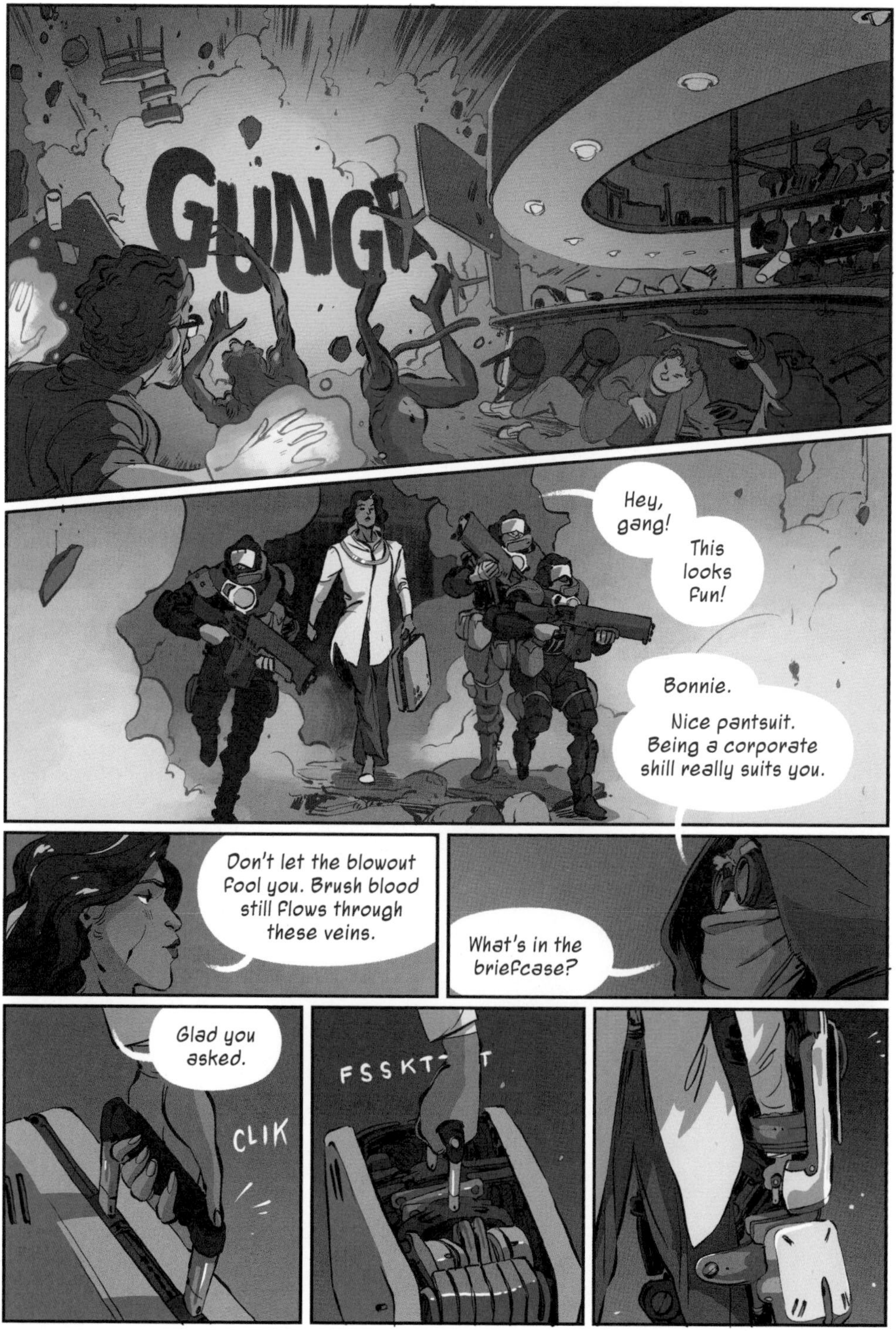
GUNGA
Hey, gang!
This looks fun!
Bonnie.
Nice pantsuit. Being a corporate shill really suits you.
Don't let the blowout fool you. Brush blood still flows through these veins.
What's in the briefcase?
Glad you asked.
CLIK
FSSKT-
T

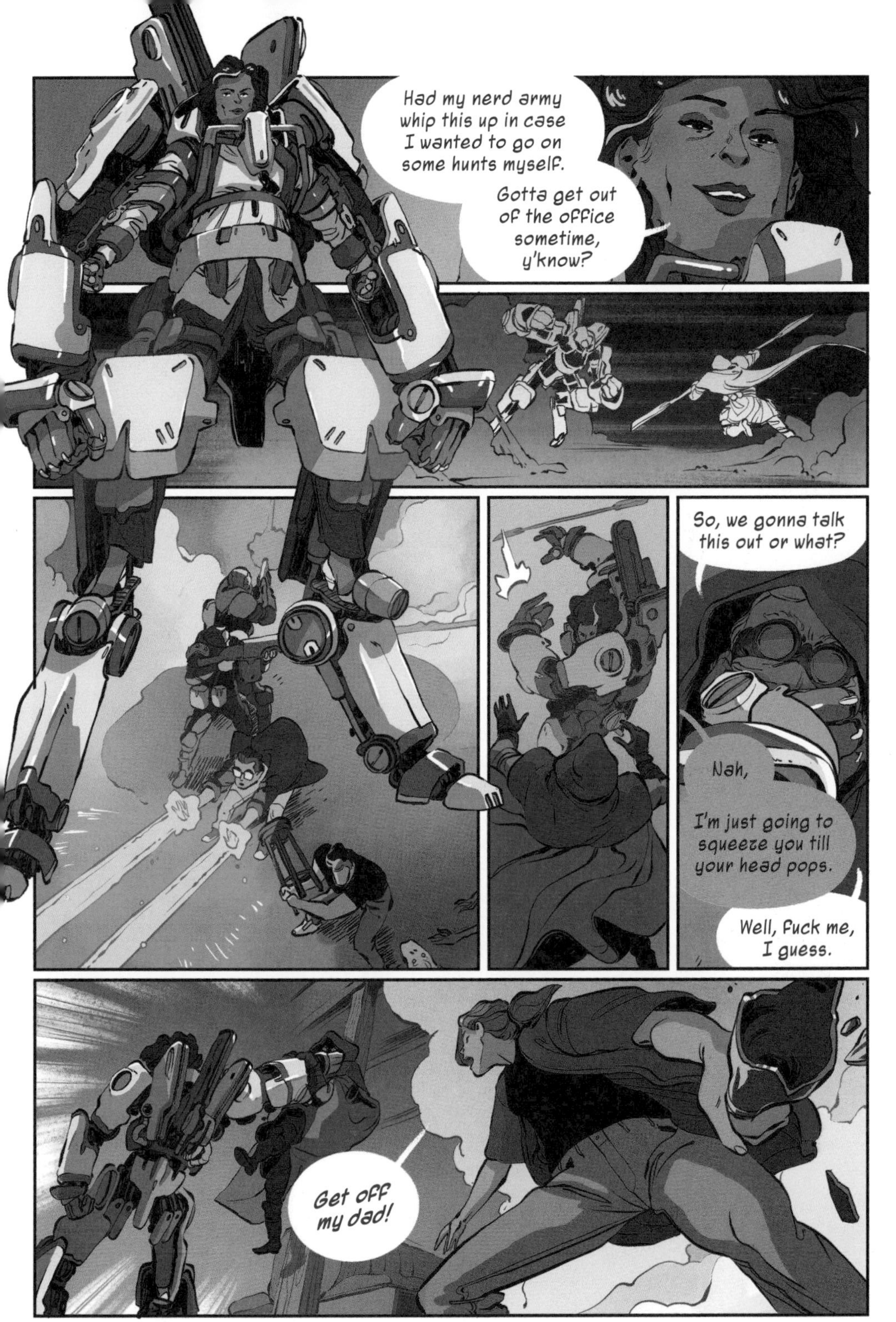
Had my nerd army whip this up in case I wanted to go on some hunts myself.
Gotta get out of the office sometime, y'know?
So, we gonna talk this out or what?
Nah,
I'm just going to squeeze you till your head pops.
Well, fuck me, I guess.
Get off my dad!

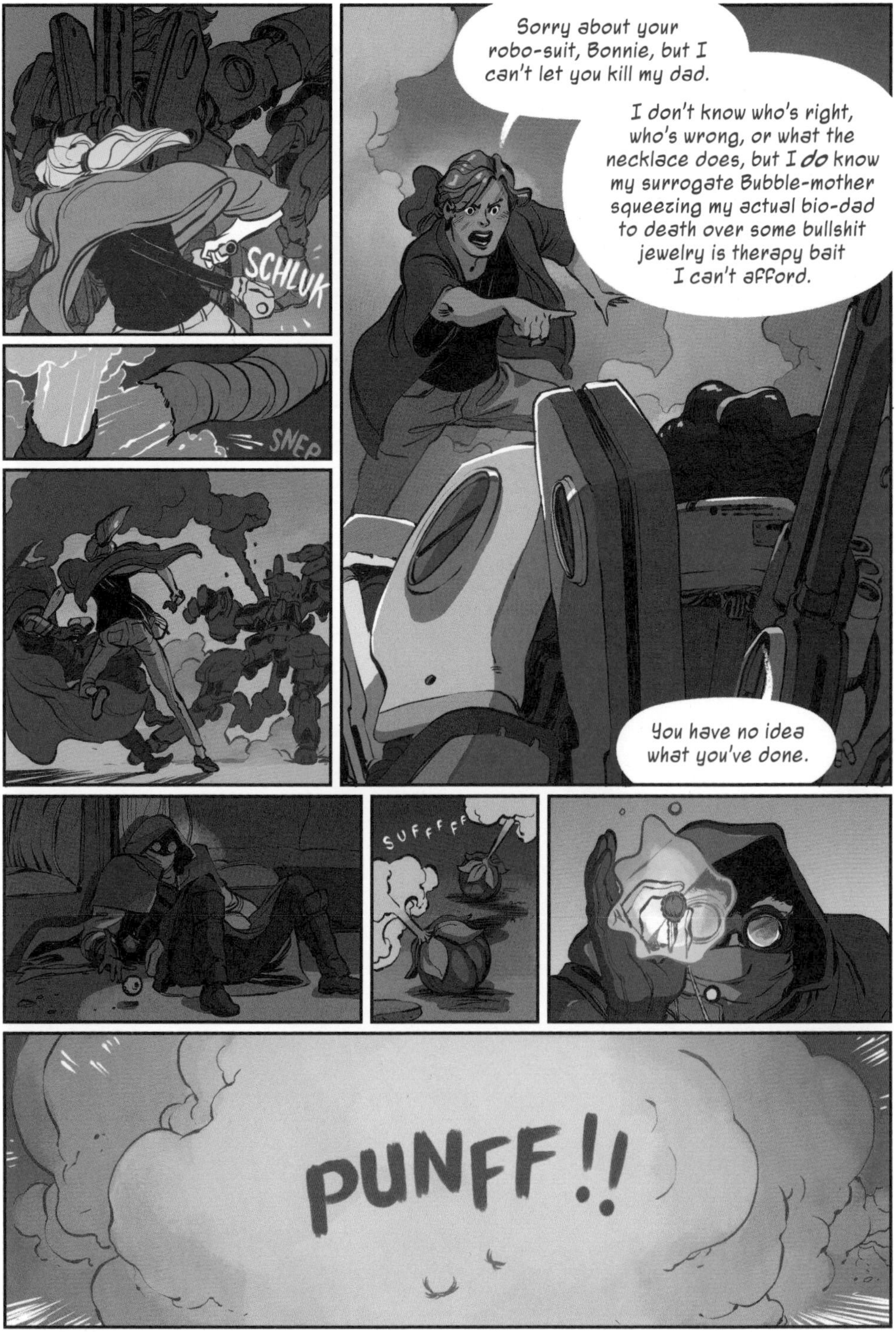
SCHLUK
SNEP
Sorry about your robo-suit, Bonnie, but I can't let you kill my dad.
I don't know who's right, who's wrong, or what the necklace does, but I *do* know my surrogate Bubble-mother squeezing my actual bio-dad to death over some bullshit jewelry is therapy bait I can't afford.
You have no idea what you've done.
SUFFFFF
PUNFF!!

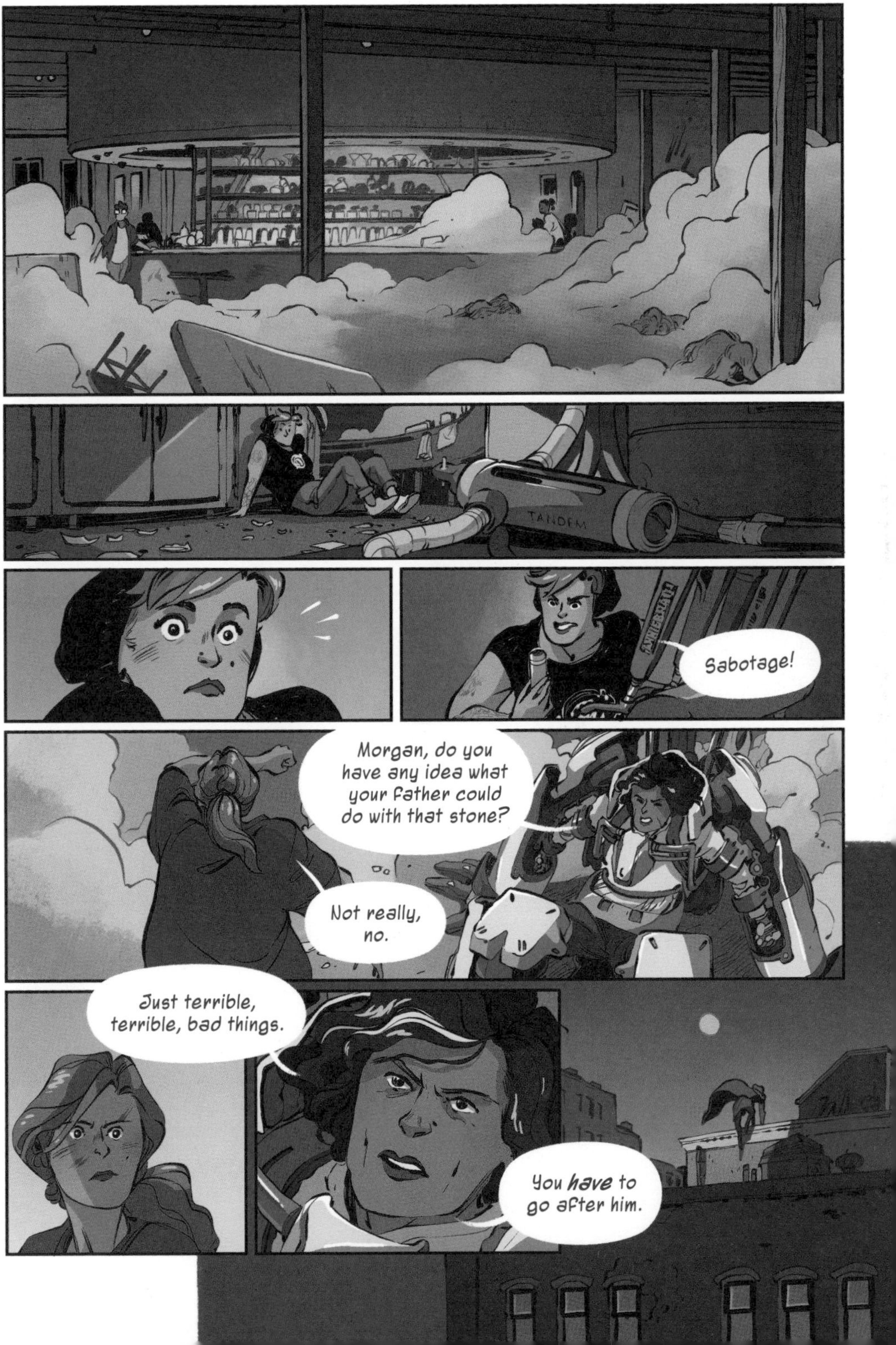
Sabotage!
Morgan, do you have any idea what your father could do with that stone?
Not really, no.
Just terrible, terrible, bad things.
You *have* to go after him.

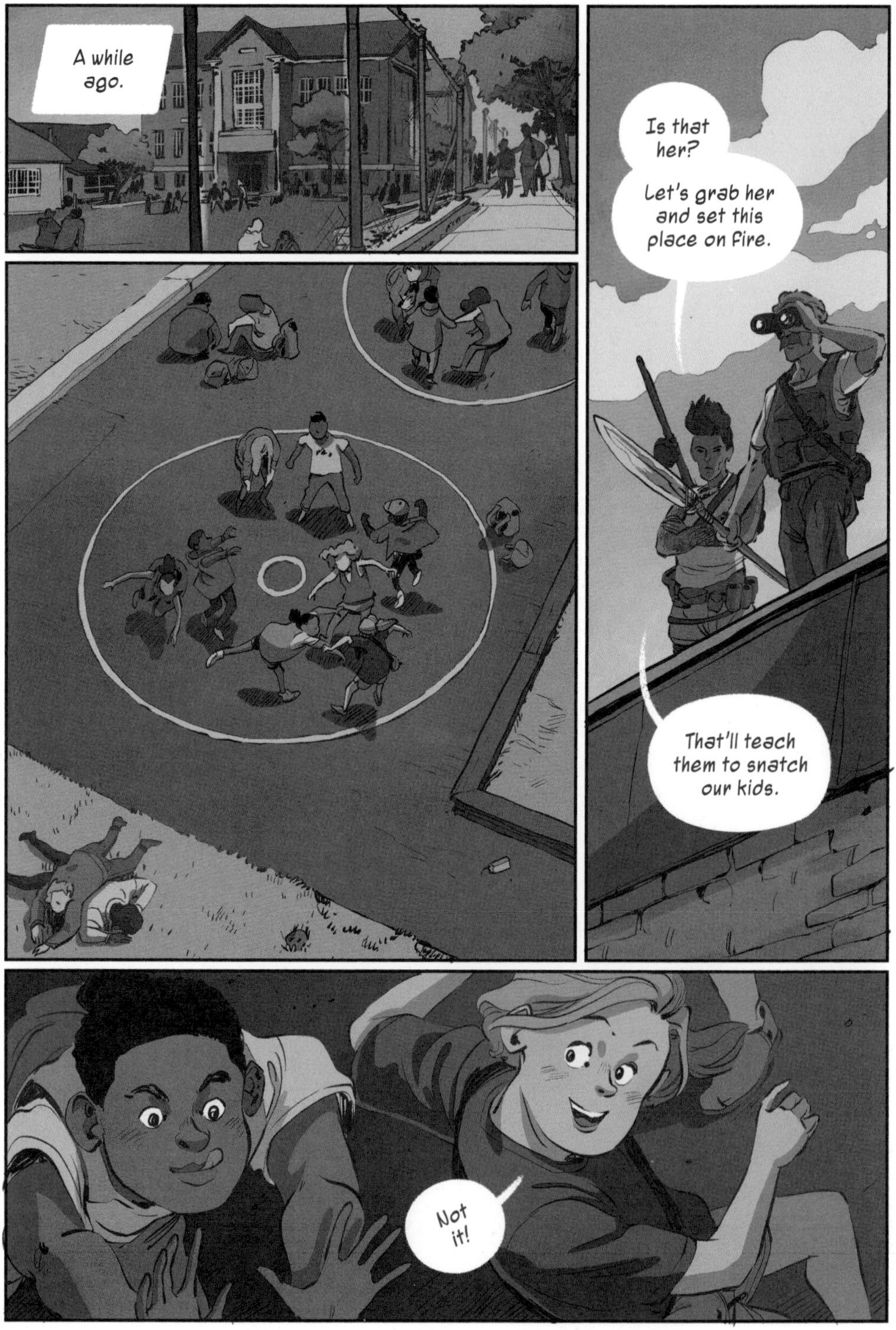
A while ago.
Is that her?
Let's grab her and set this place on fire.
That'll teach them to snatch our kids.
Not it!

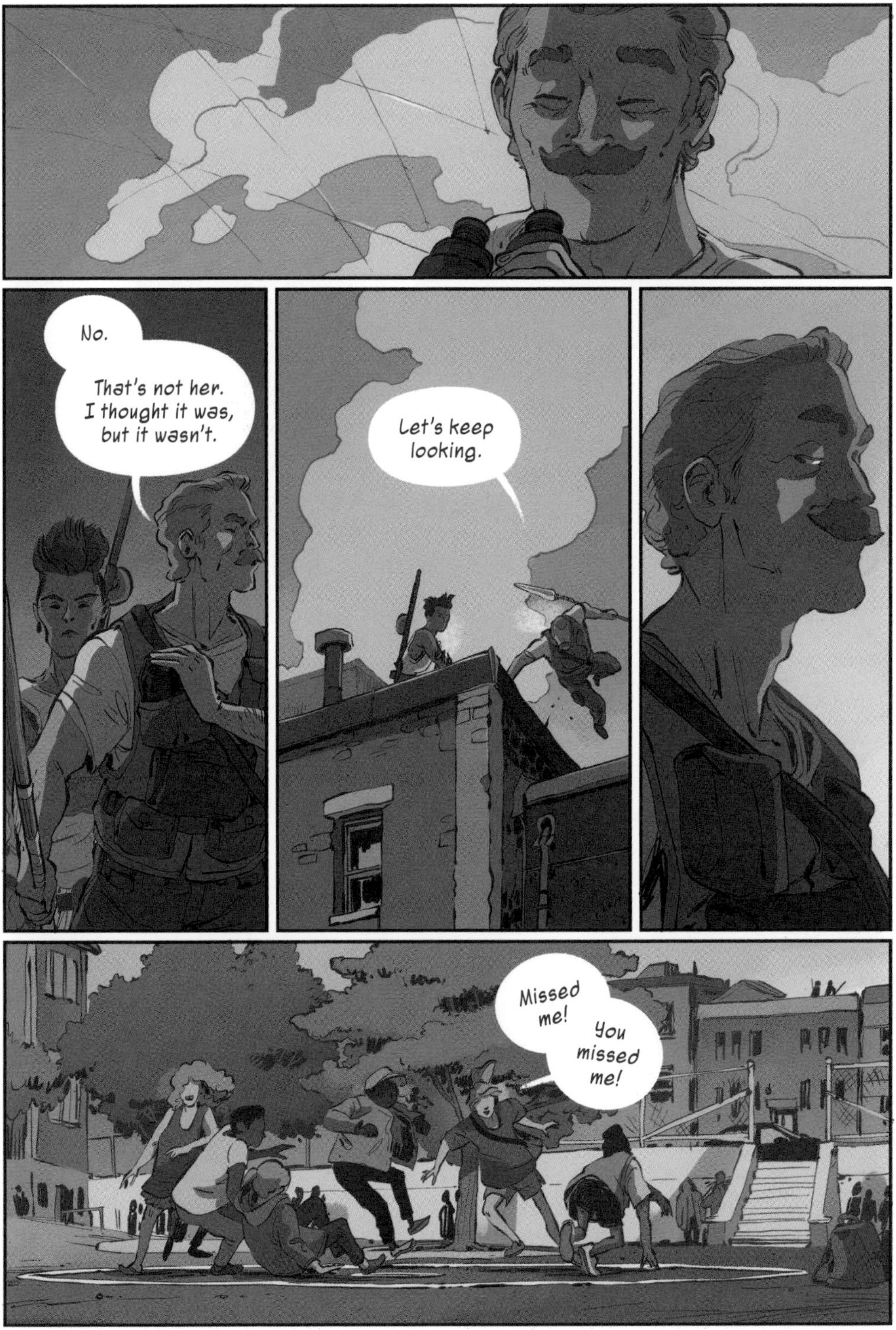
No.
That's not her. I thought it was, but it wasn't.
Let's keep looking.
Missed me!
You missed me!

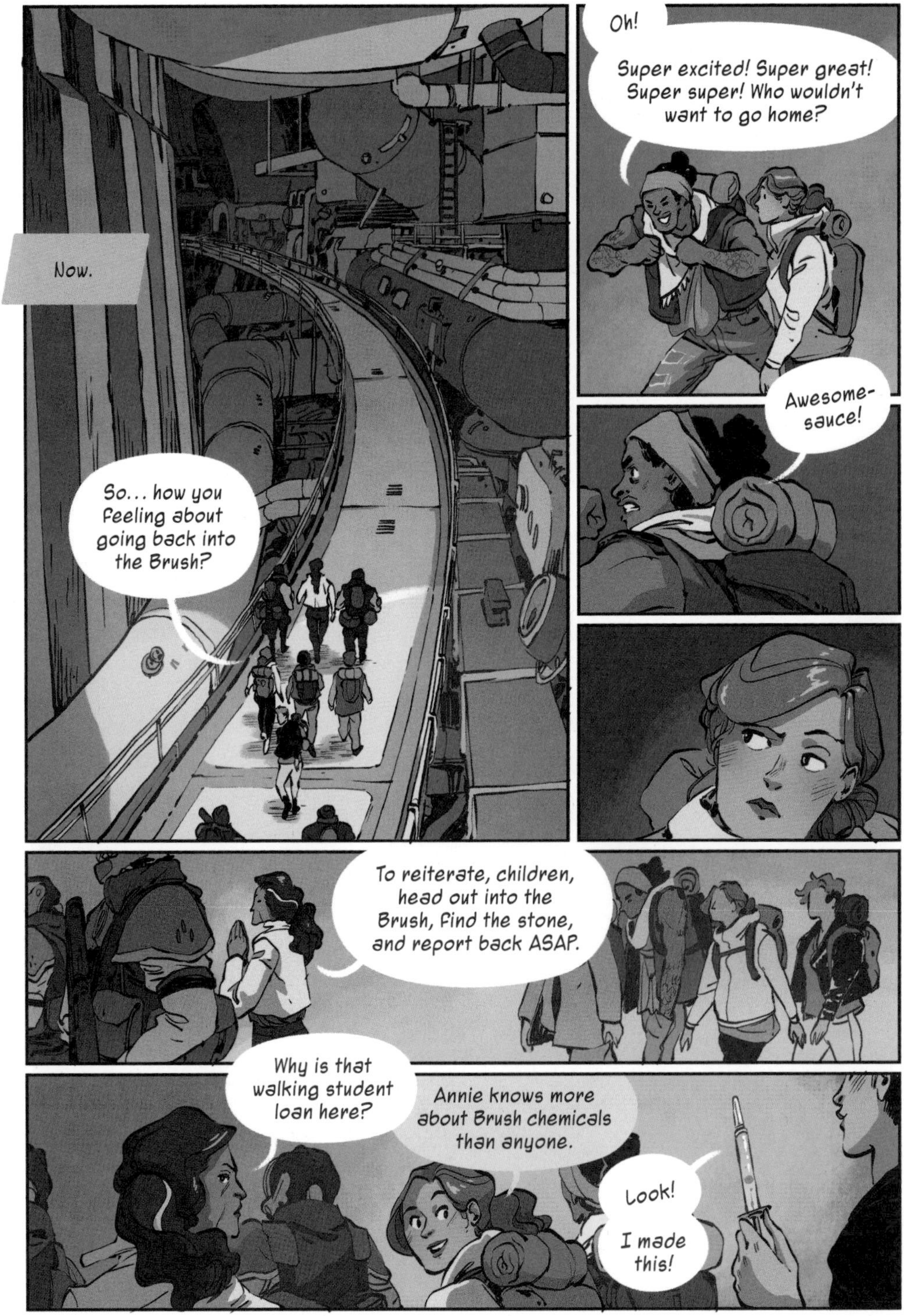
Now.
So... how you feeling about going back into the Brush?
Oh!
Super excited! Super great! Super super! Who wouldn't want to go home?
Awesome-sauce!
To reiterate, children, head out into the Brush, find the stone, and report back ASAP.
Why is that walking student loan here?
Annie knows more about Brush chemicals than anyone.
Look!
I made this!

Relax.

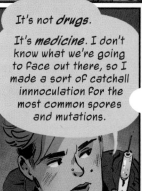

It's not *drugs*.

It's *medicine*. I don't know what we're going to face out there, so I made a sort of catchall innoculation for the most common spores and mutations.

I dunno.

Oh, come on.

What's in it?

This is safer than most major-label energy drinks.

It's all-natural.

Heroin is all-natural.

It's not heroin!

I know how to get people fucked up, but I also know how to make them *not die*.

You're being a bit reckless with Brush chemicals. We know about the fiasco at that filthy little bar.

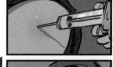

Yeah, about that...

Yes, the brew *did* have *some* Brush chemicals in it that I... obtained *legally*.

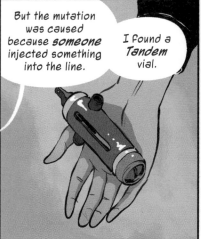

But the mutation was caused because *someone* injected something into the line.

I found a *Tandem* vial.

What?

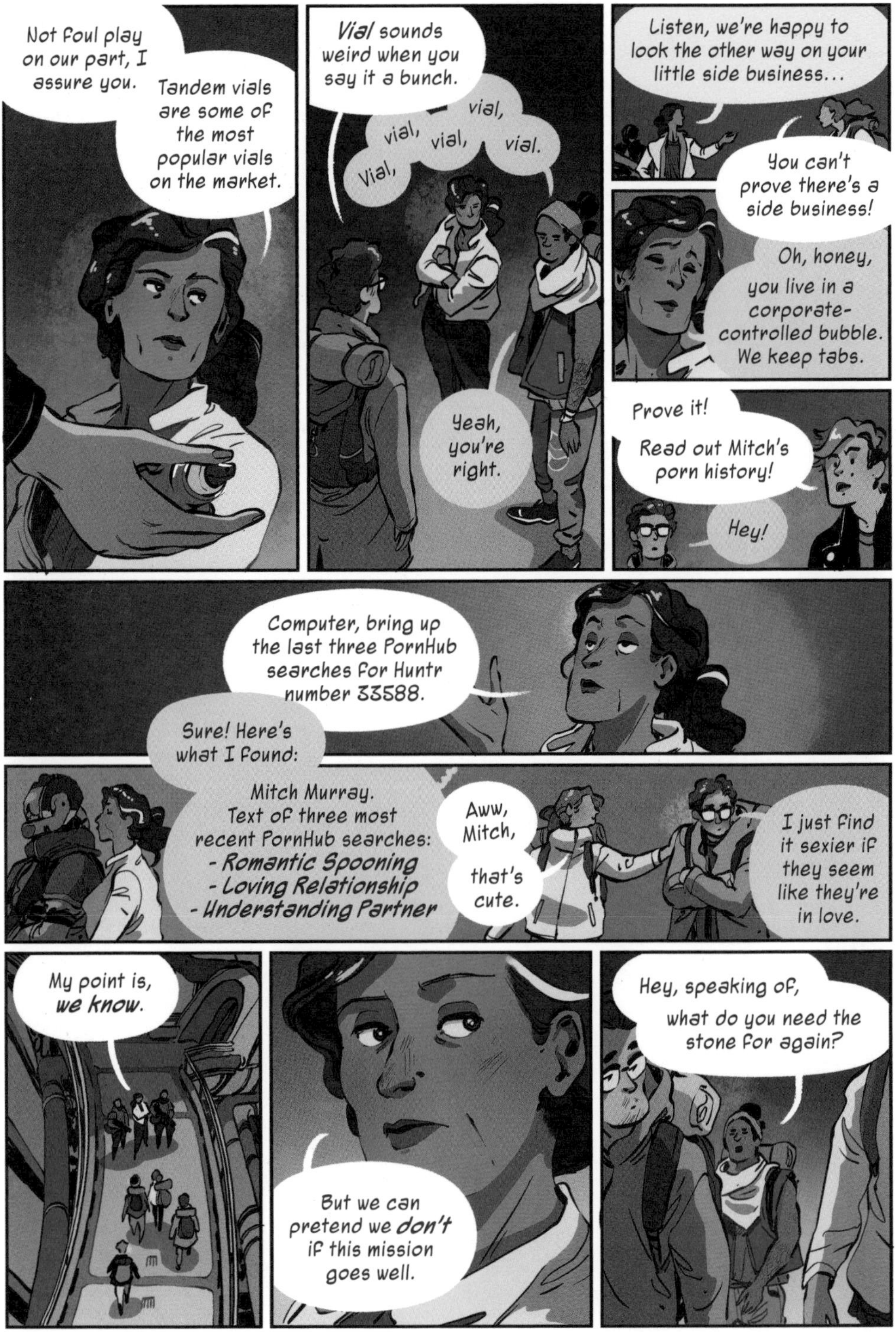

Not foul play on our part, I assure you.
Tandem vials are some of the most popular vials on the market.
Vial sounds weird when you say it a bunch.
Vial, vial, vial, vial, vial.
Yeah, you're right.
Listen, we're happy to look the other way on your little side business...
You can't prove there's a side business!
Oh, honey, you live in a corporate-controlled bubble. We keep tabs.
Prove it!
Read out Mitch's porn history!
Hey!
Computer, bring up the last three PornHub searches for Huntr number 33588.
Sure! Here's what I found:
Mitch Murray. Text of three most recent PornHub searches:
- *Romantic Spooning*
- *Loving Relationship*
- *Understanding Partner*
Aww, Mitch,
that's cute.
I just find it sexier if they seem like they're in love.
My point is, ***we know***.
But we can pretend we ***don't*** if this mission goes well.
Hey, speaking of,
what do you need the stone for again?

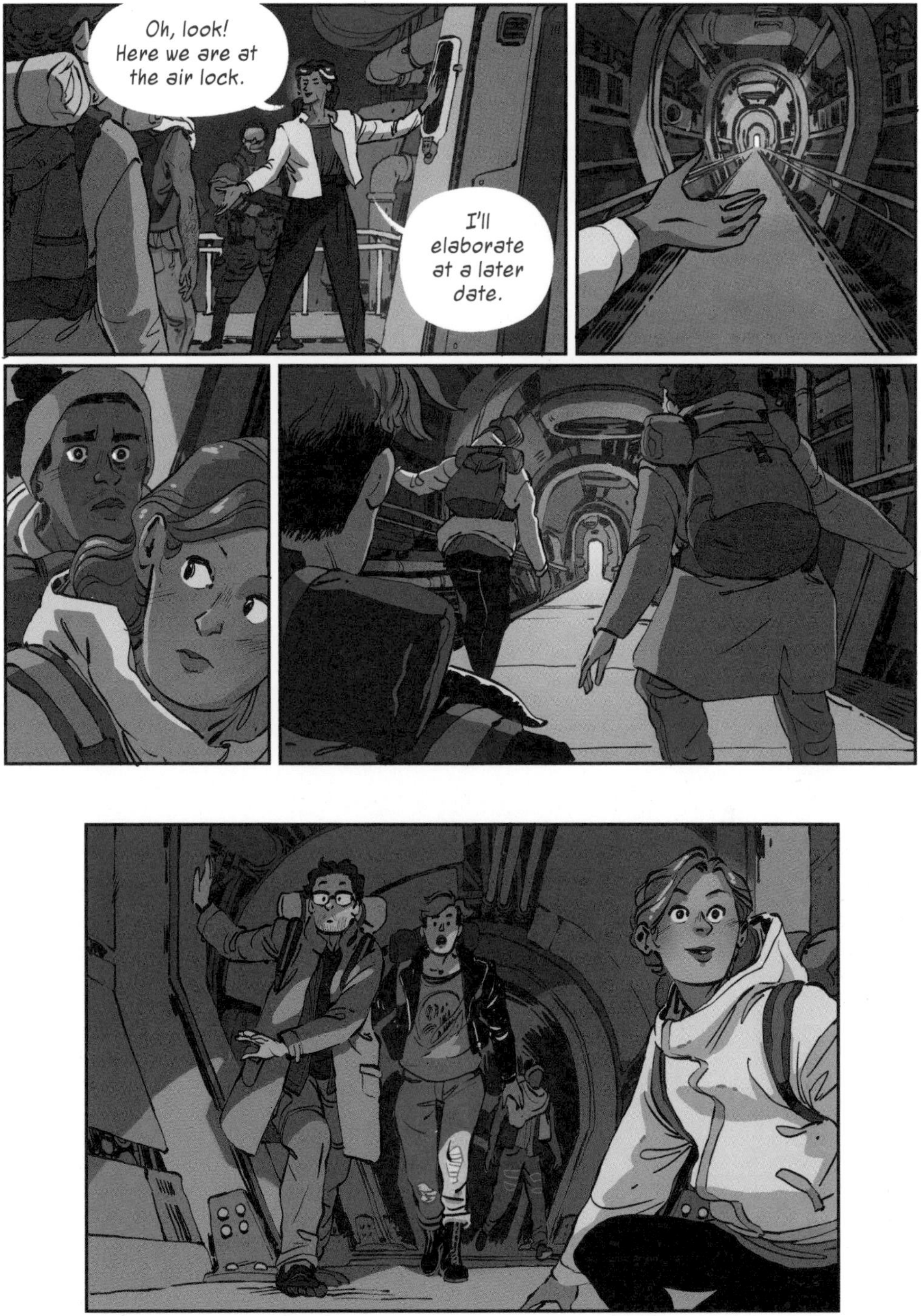
Oh, look! Here we are at the air lock.
I'll elaborate at a later date.

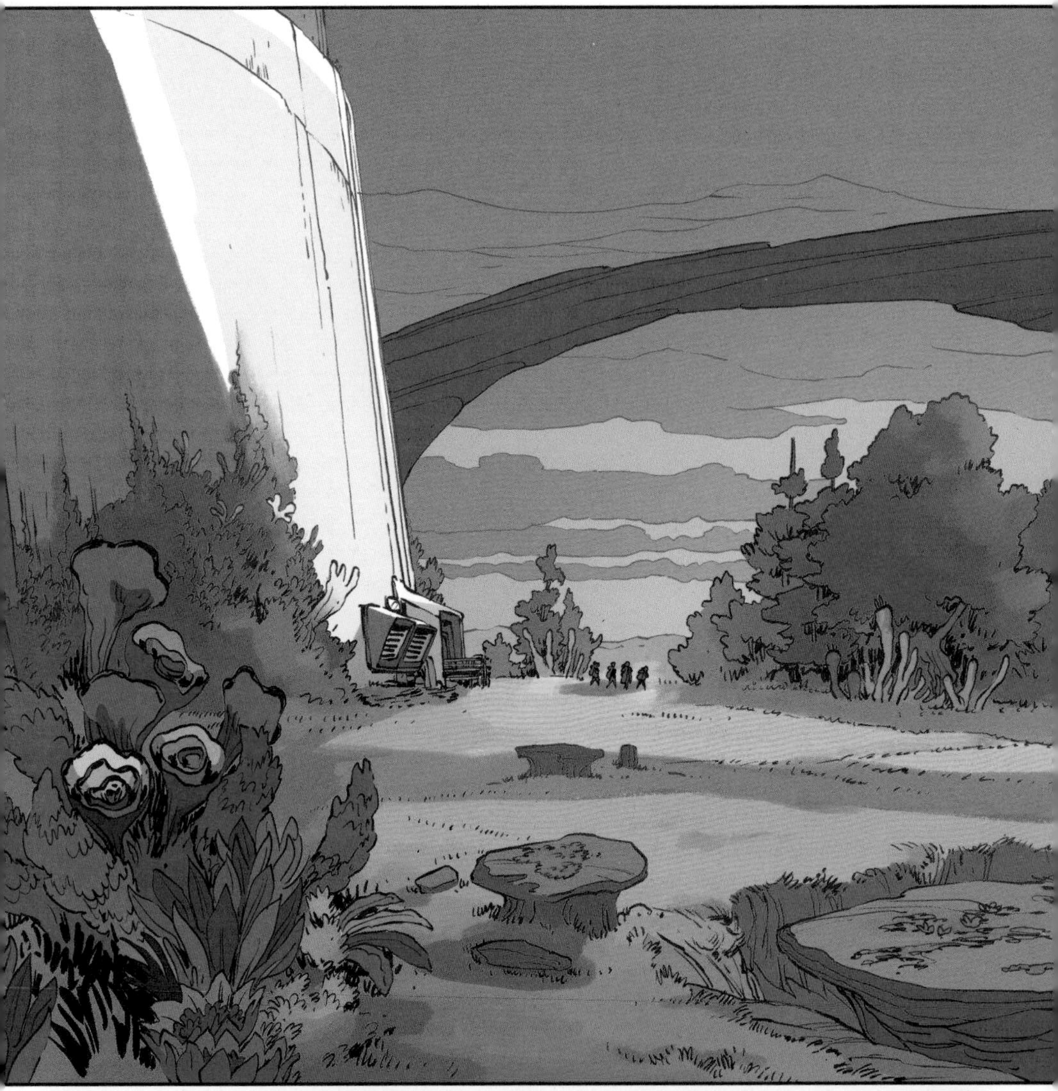

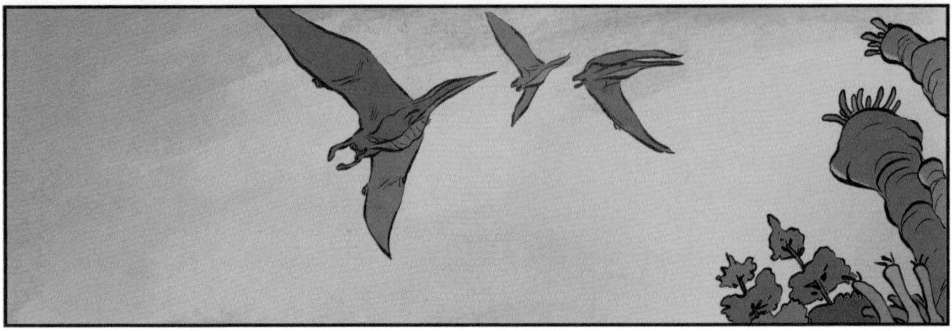

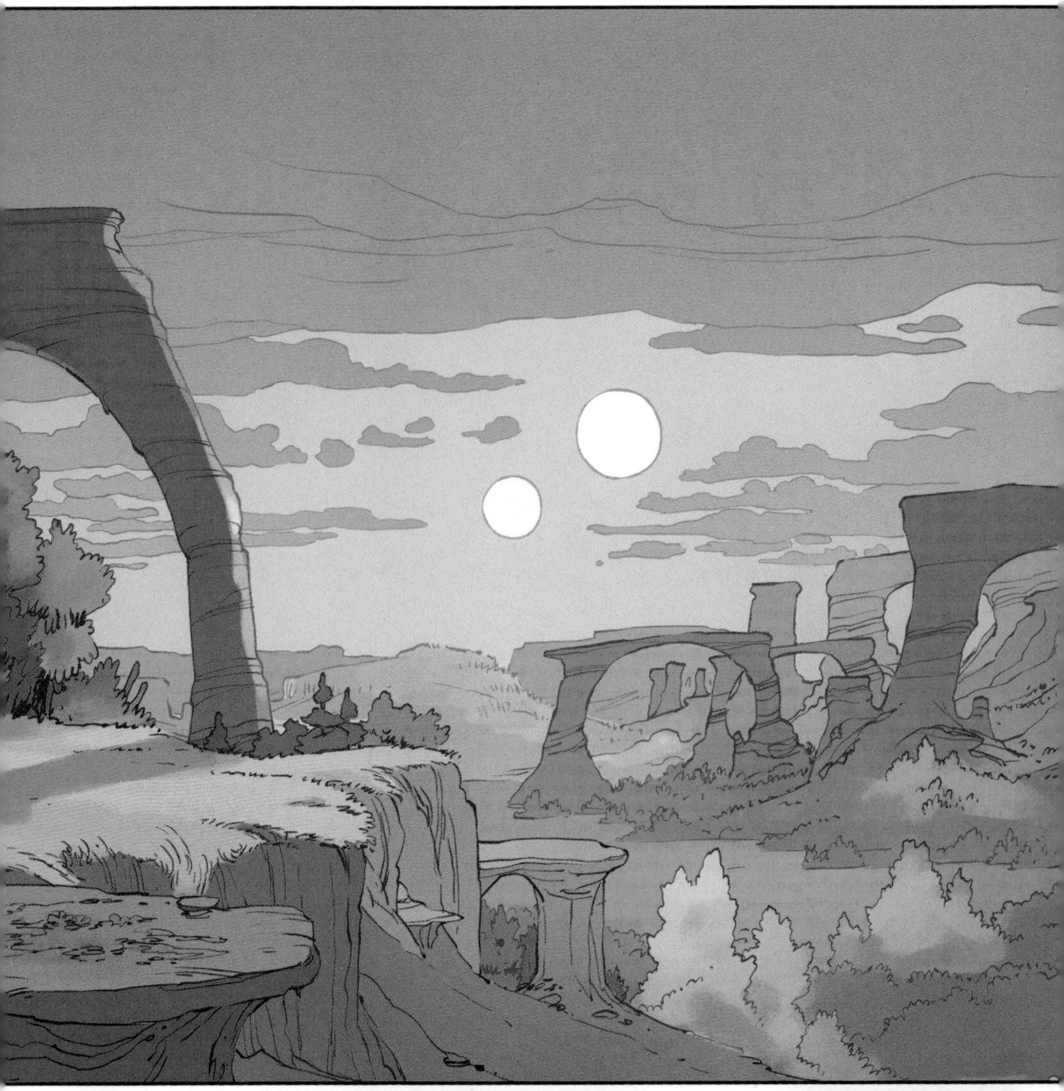

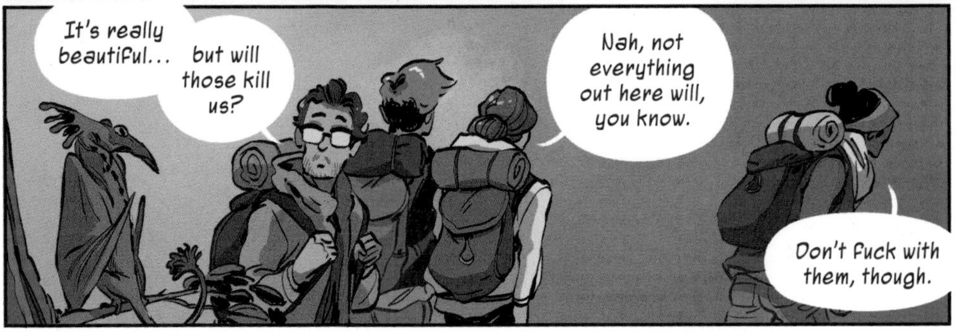
It's really beautiful...
but will those kill us?
Nah, not everything out here will, you know.
Don't fuck with them, though.

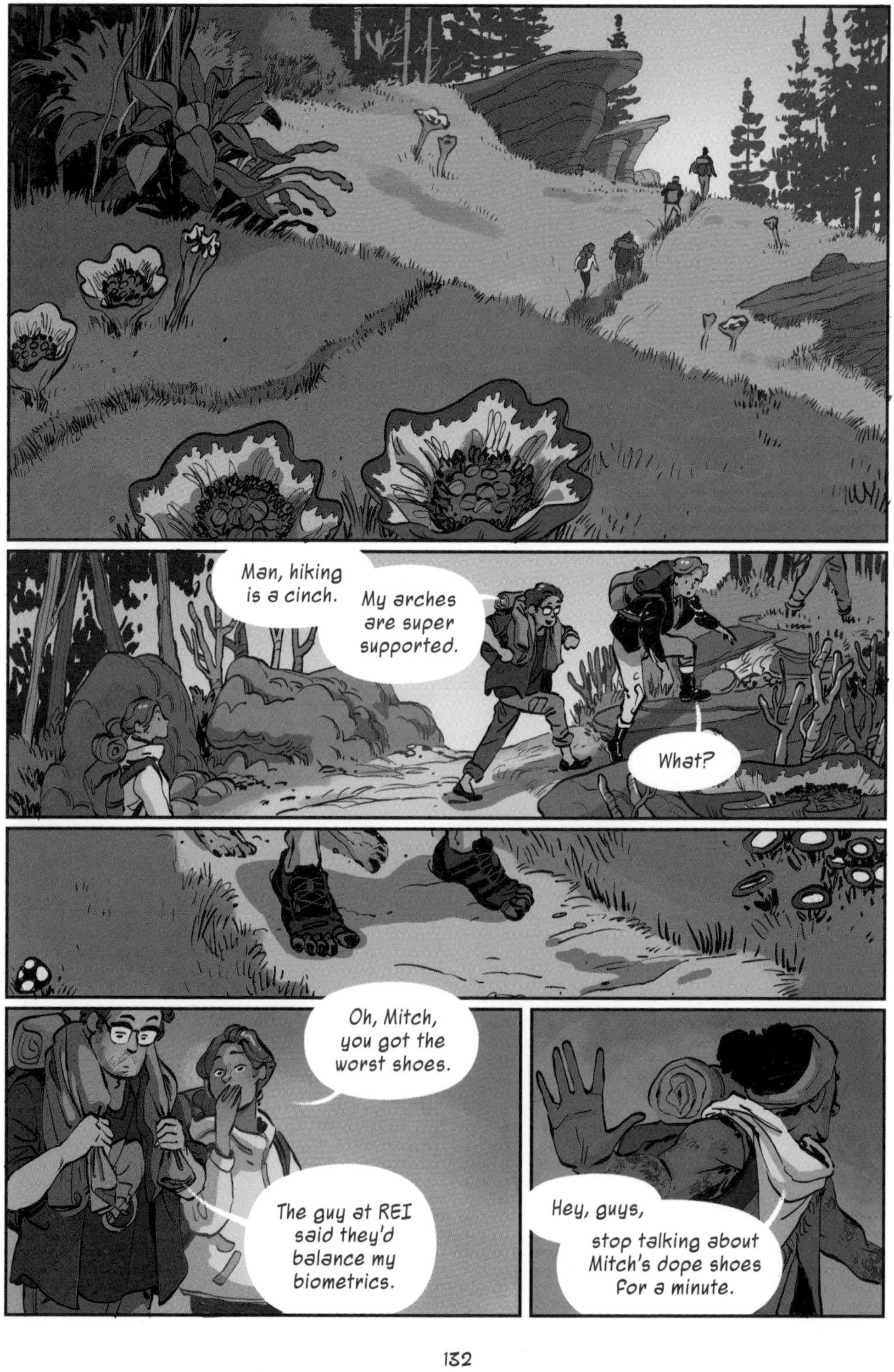
Man, hiking is a cinch.
My arches are super supported.
What?
Oh, Mitch, you got the worst shoes.
The guy at REI said they'd balance my biometrics.
Hey, guys,
stop talking about Mitch's dope shoes for a minute.

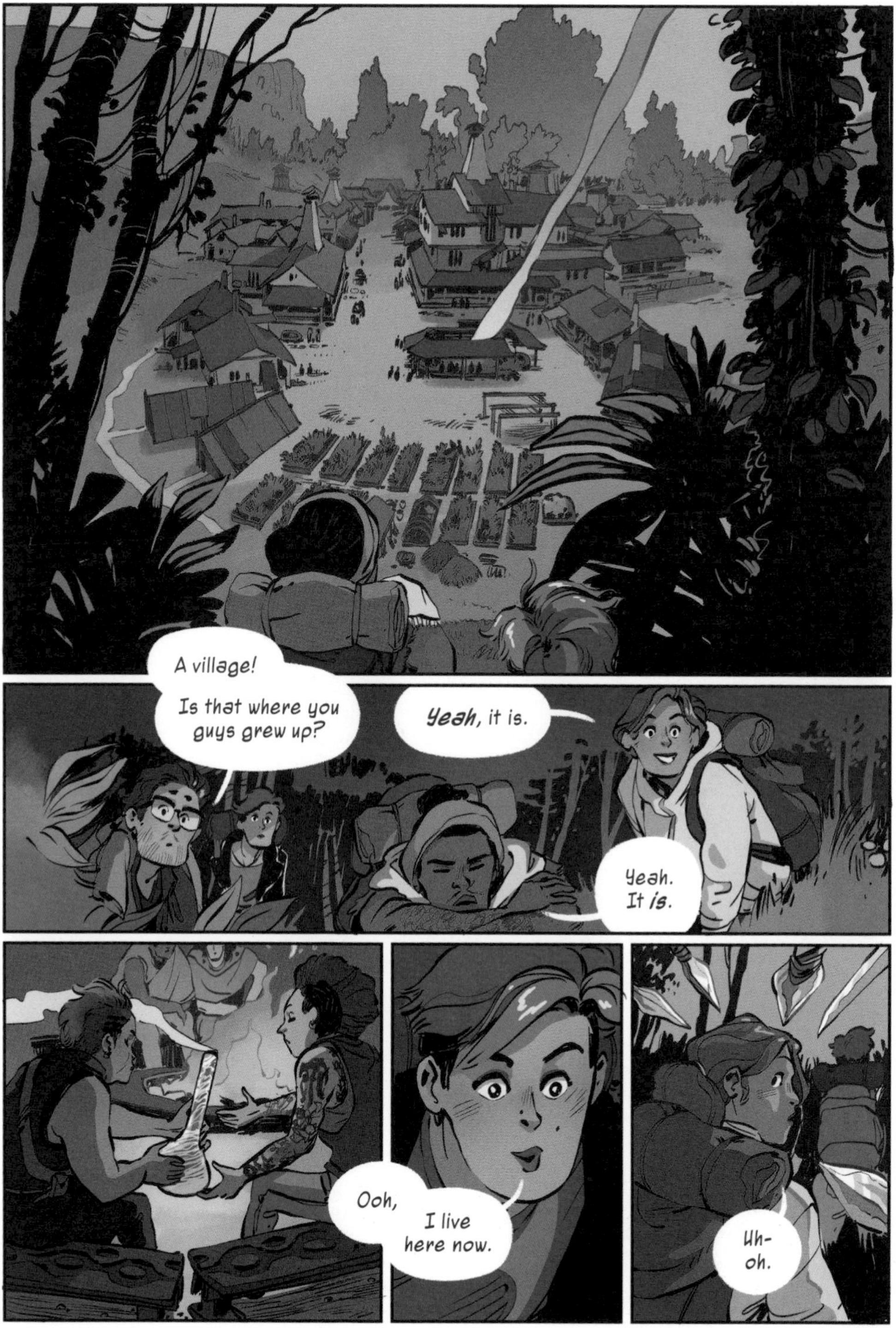
A village!
Is that where you guys grew up?
Yeah, it is.
Yeah. It *is*.
Ooh, I live here now.
Uh-oh.

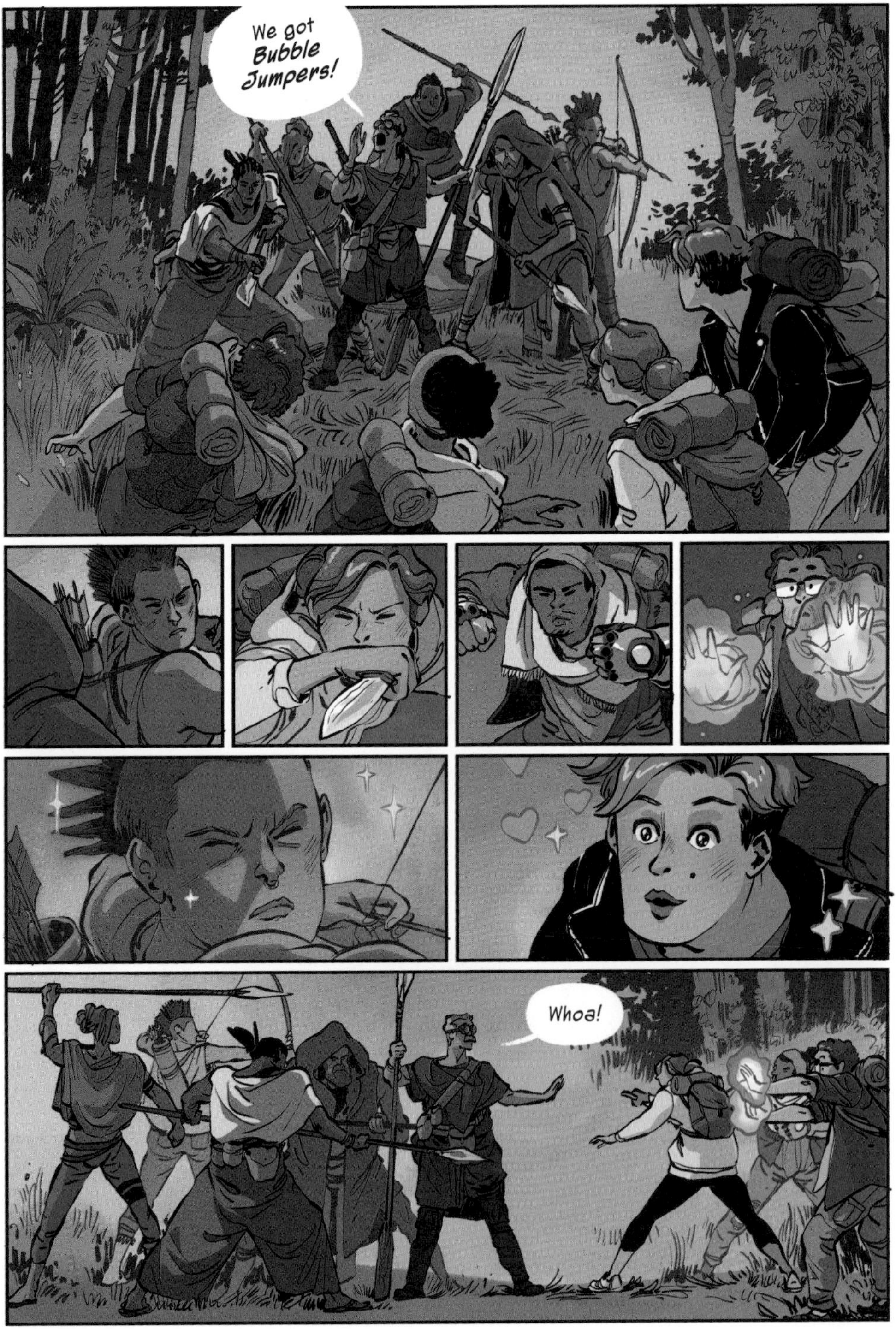
We got Bubble Jumpers!
Whoa!

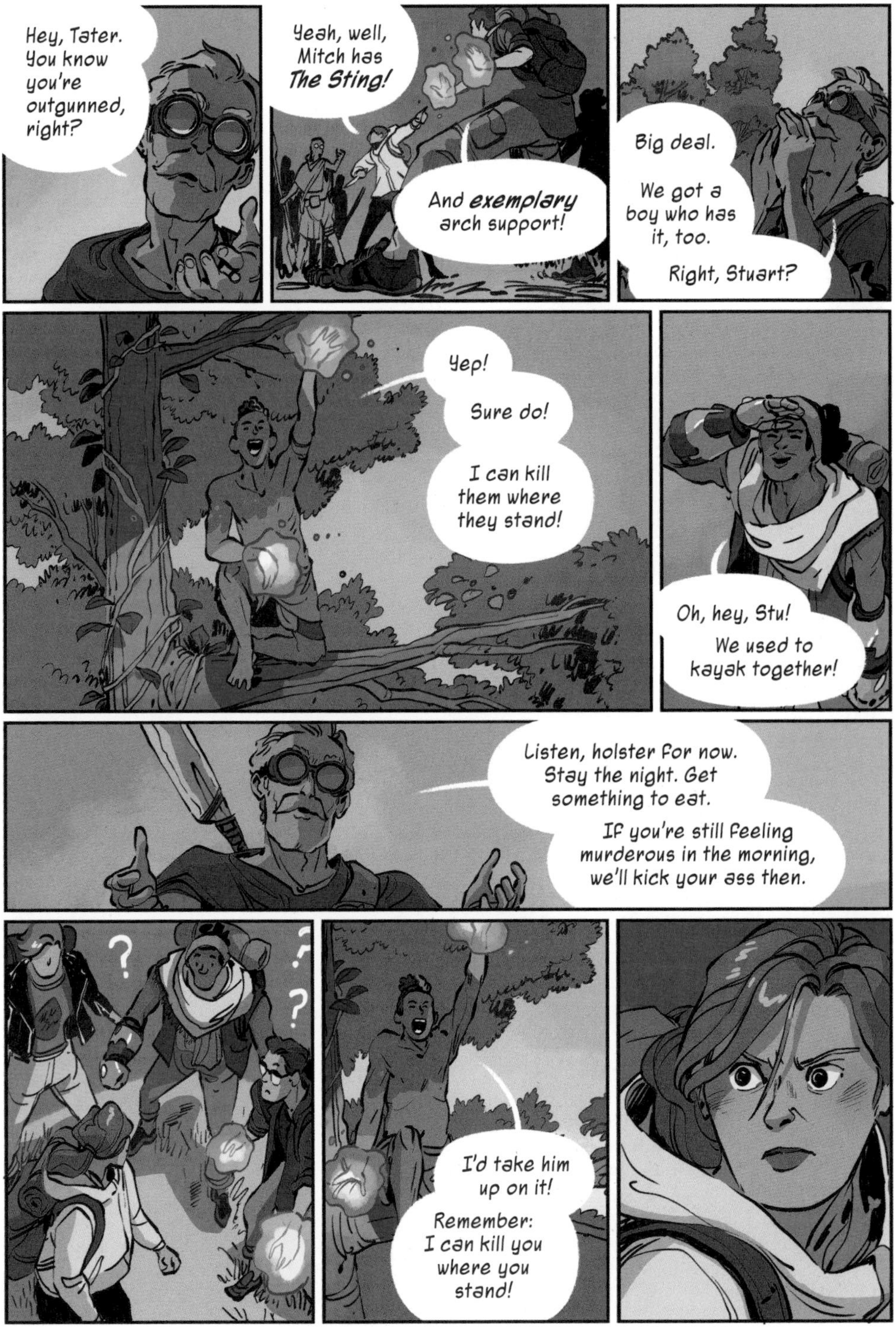
Hey, Tater. You know you're outgunned, right?
Yeah, well, Mitch has *The Sting!*
And ***exemplary*** arch support!
Big deal.
We got a boy who has it, too.
Right, Stuart?
Yep!
Sure do!
I can kill them where they stand!
Oh, hey, Stu!
We used to kayak together!
Listen, holster for now. Stay the night. Get something to eat.
If you're still feeling murderous in the morning, we'll kick your ass then.
?
?
?
I'd take him up on it!
Remember: I can kill you where you stand!

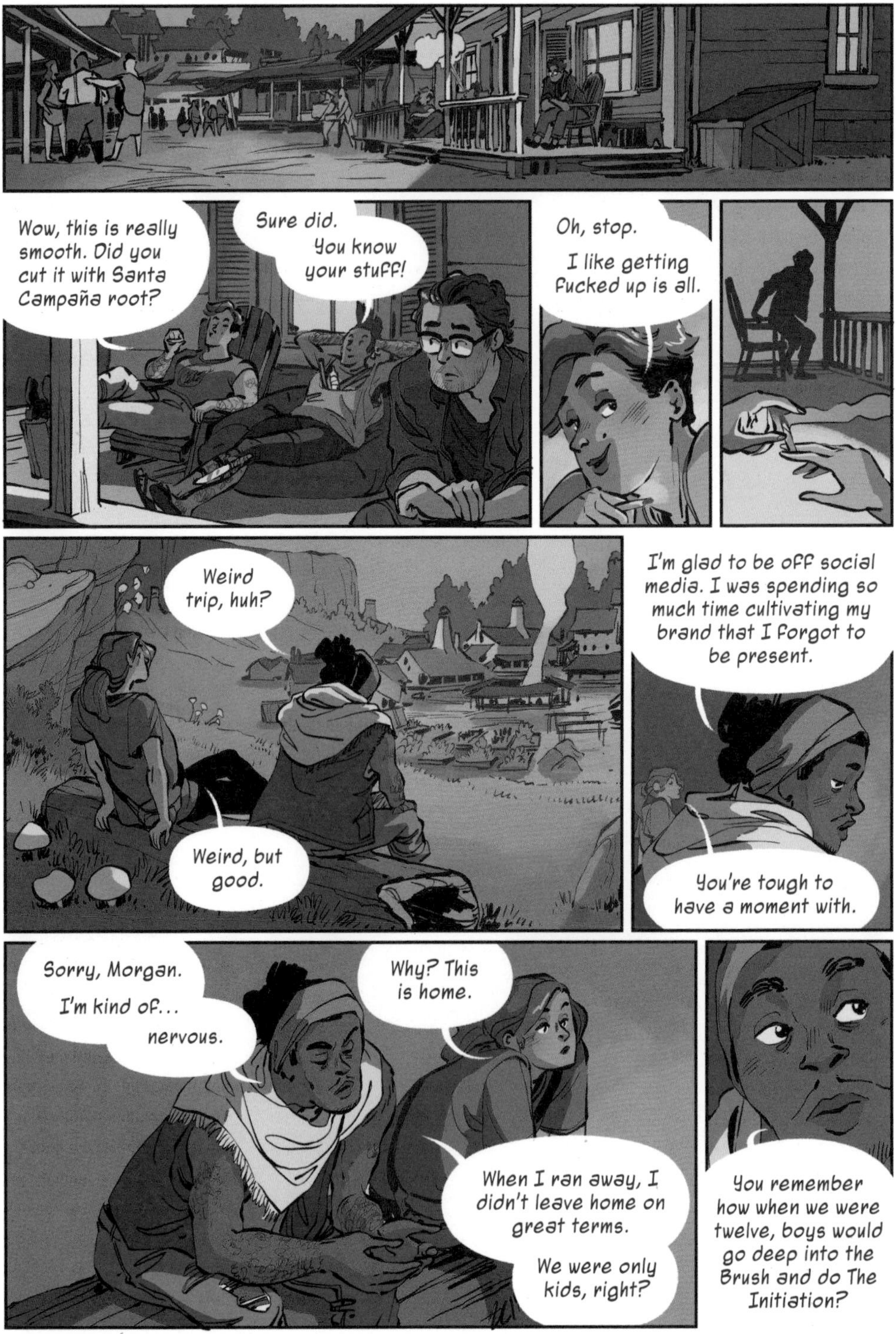

Wow, this is really smooth. Did you cut it with Santa Campaña root?
Sure did.
You know your stuff!
Oh, stop.
I like getting fucked up is all.
Weird trip, huh?
Weird, but good.
I'm glad to be off social media. I was spending so much time cultivating my brand that I forgot to be present.
You're tough to have a moment with.
Sorry, Morgan.
I'm kind of...
nervous.
Why? This is home.
When I ran away, I didn't leave home on great terms.
We were only kids, right?
You remember how when we were twelve, boys would go deep into the Brush and do The Initiation?

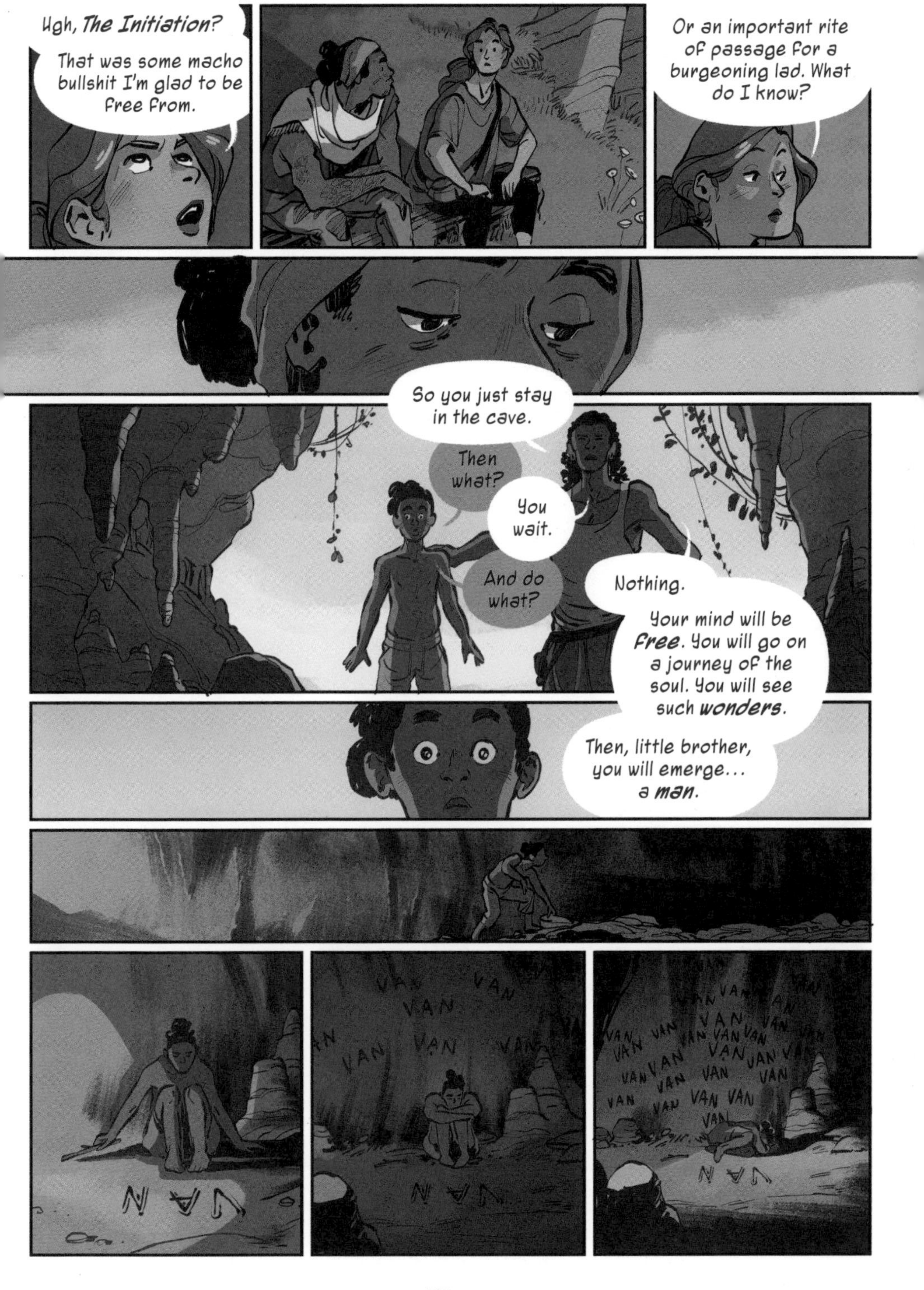

Ugh, *The Initiation*?
That was some macho bullshit I'm glad to be free from.
Or an important rite of passage for a burgeoning lad. What do I know?
So you just stay in the cave.
Then what?
You wait.
And do what?
Nothing.
Your mind will be ***free***. You will go on a journey of the soul. You will see such ***wonders***.
Then, little brother, you will emerge... a ***man***.
VAN
VAN VAN VAN VAN VAN VAN
VAN
VAN VAN VAN VAN VAN VAN VAN VAN VAN VAN VAN VAN VAN VAN VAN VAN VAN VAN VAN VAN
VAN

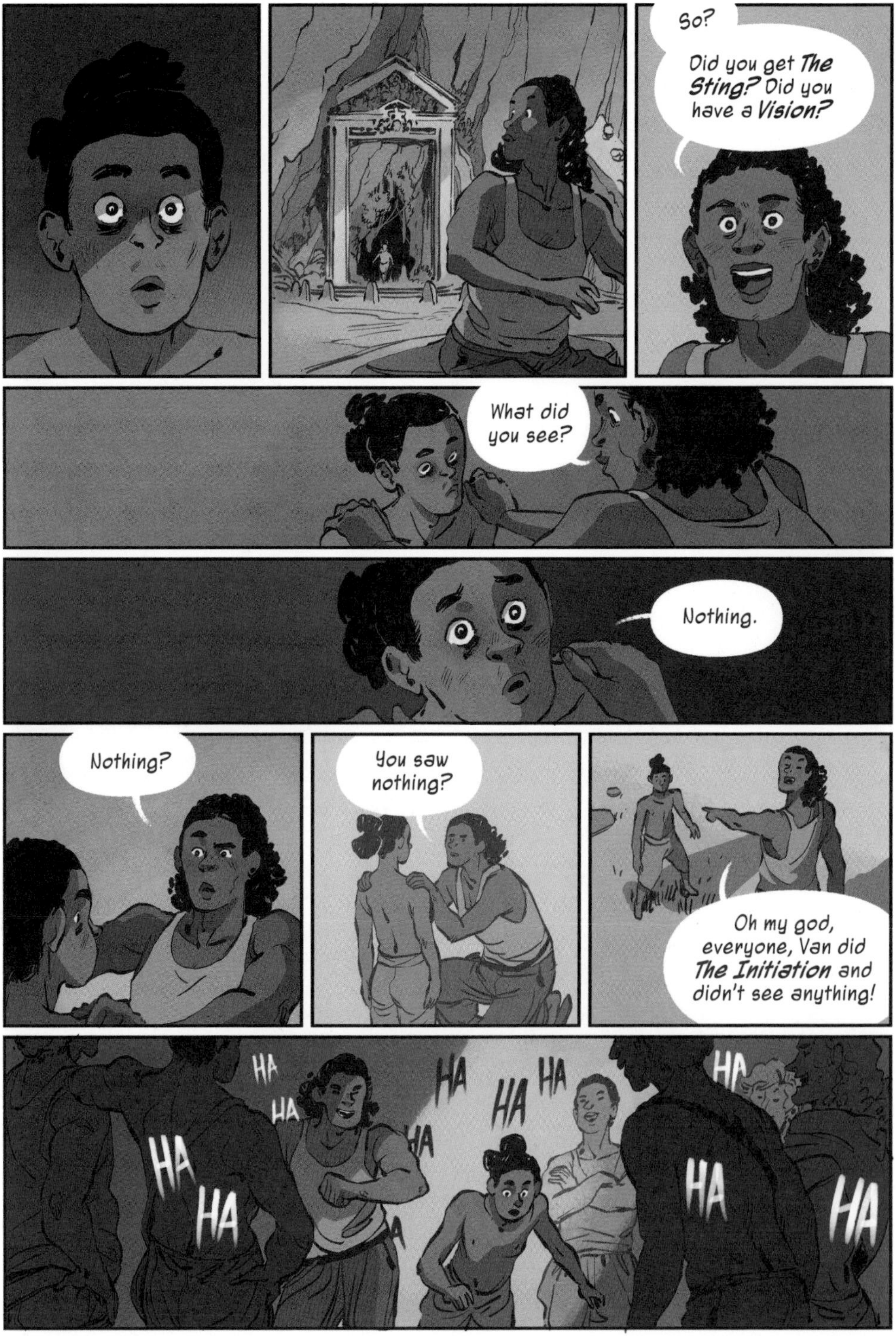
So?
Did you get The Sting? Did you have a Vision?
What did you see?
Nothing.
Nothing?
You saw nothing?
Oh my god, everyone, Van did The Initiation and didn't see anything!
HA HA HA HA HA HA HA HA HA HA HA

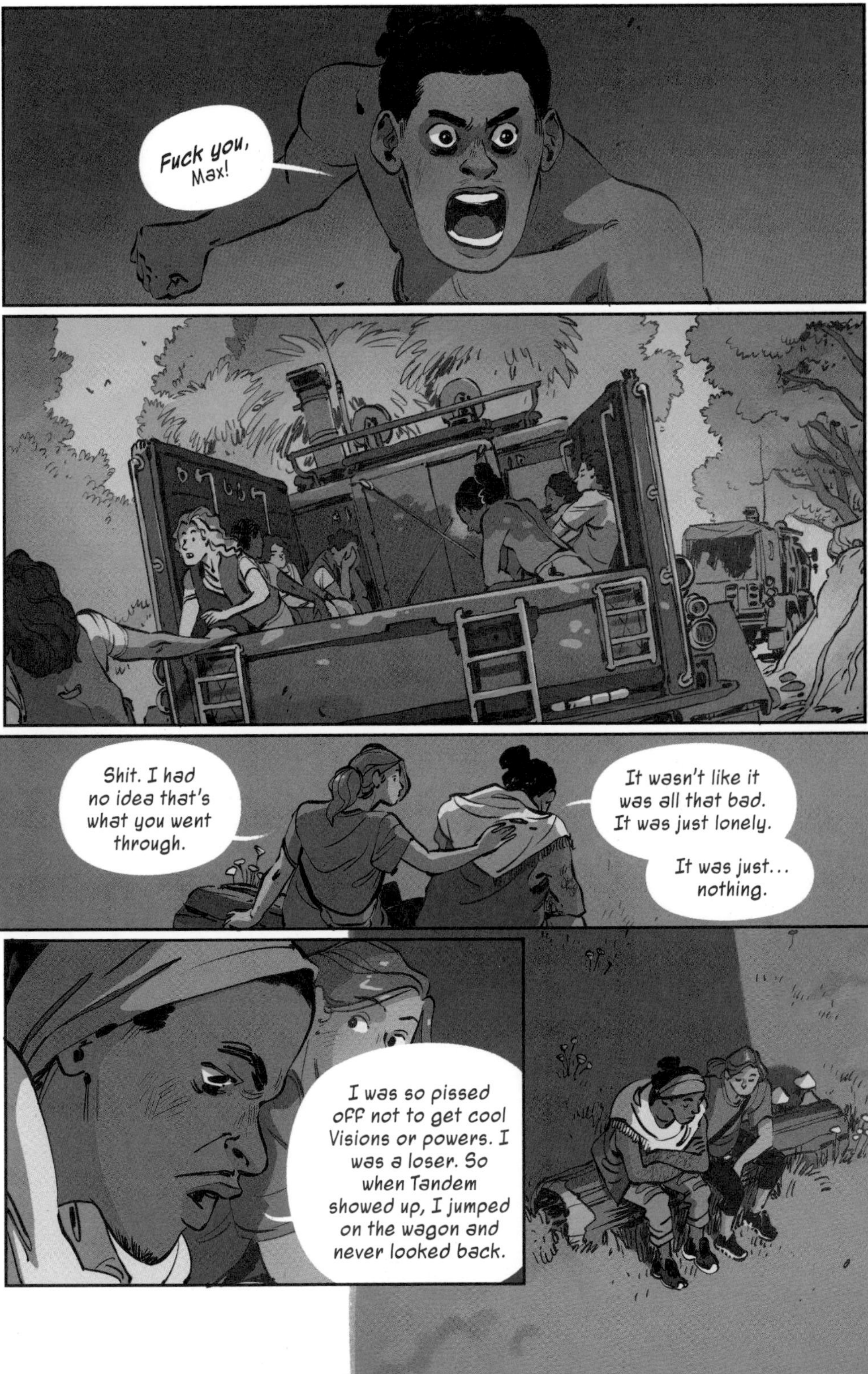
Fuck you, Max!
Shit. I had no idea that's what you went through.
It wasn't like it was all that bad. It was just lonely.
It was just... nothing.
I was so pissed off not to get cool Visions or powers. I was a loser. So when Tandem showed up, I jumped on the wagon and never looked back.

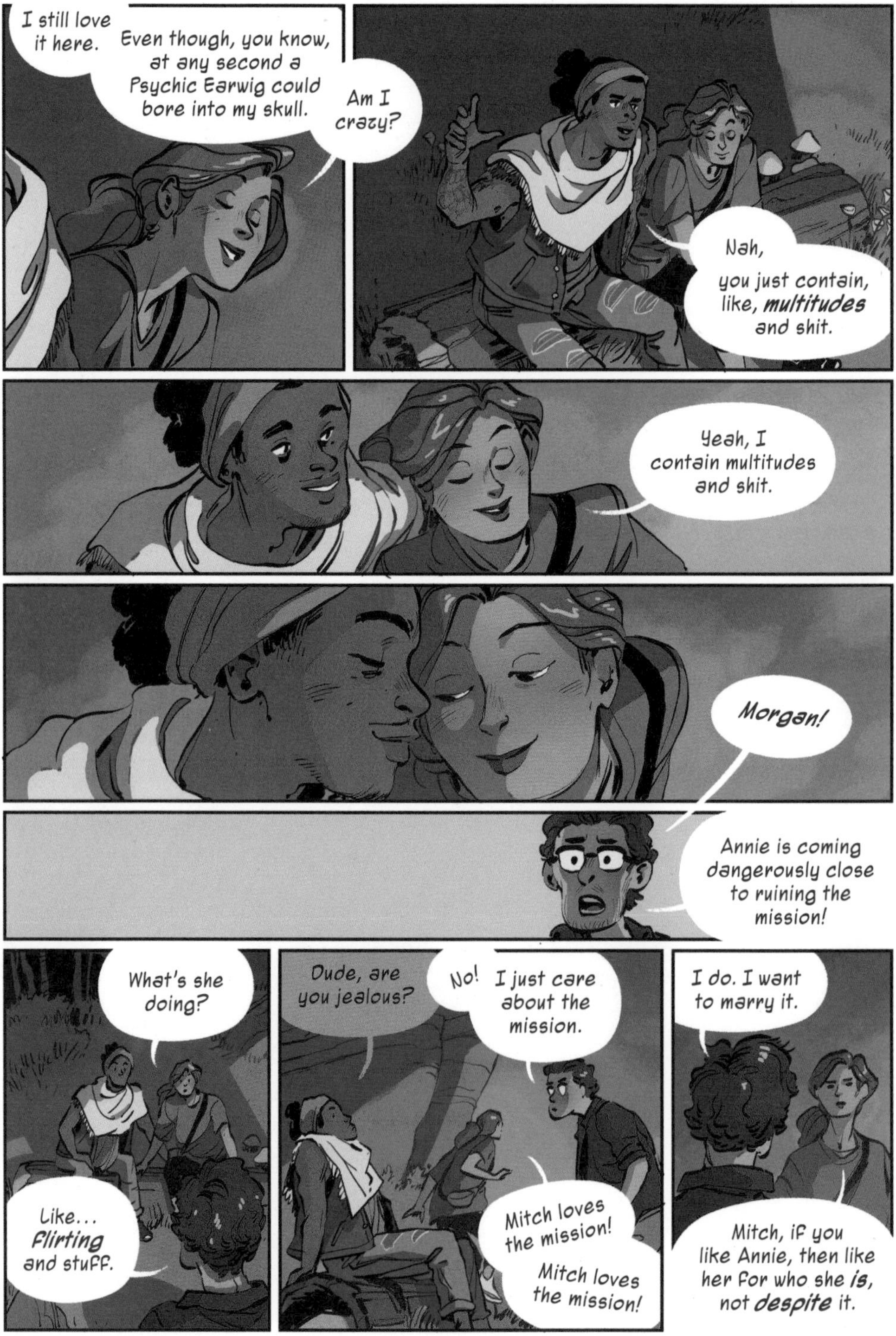
I still love it here.
Even though, you know, at any second a Psychic Earwig could bore into my skull.
Am I crazy?
Nah, you just contain, like, *multitudes* and shit.
Yeah, I contain multitudes and shit.
Morgan!
Annie is coming dangerously close to ruining the mission!
What's she doing?
Like... *flirting* and stuff.
Dude, are you jealous?
No!
I just care about the mission.
Mitch loves the mission!
Mitch loves the mission!
I do. I want to marry it.
Mitch, if you like Annie, then like her for who she *is*, not *despite* it.

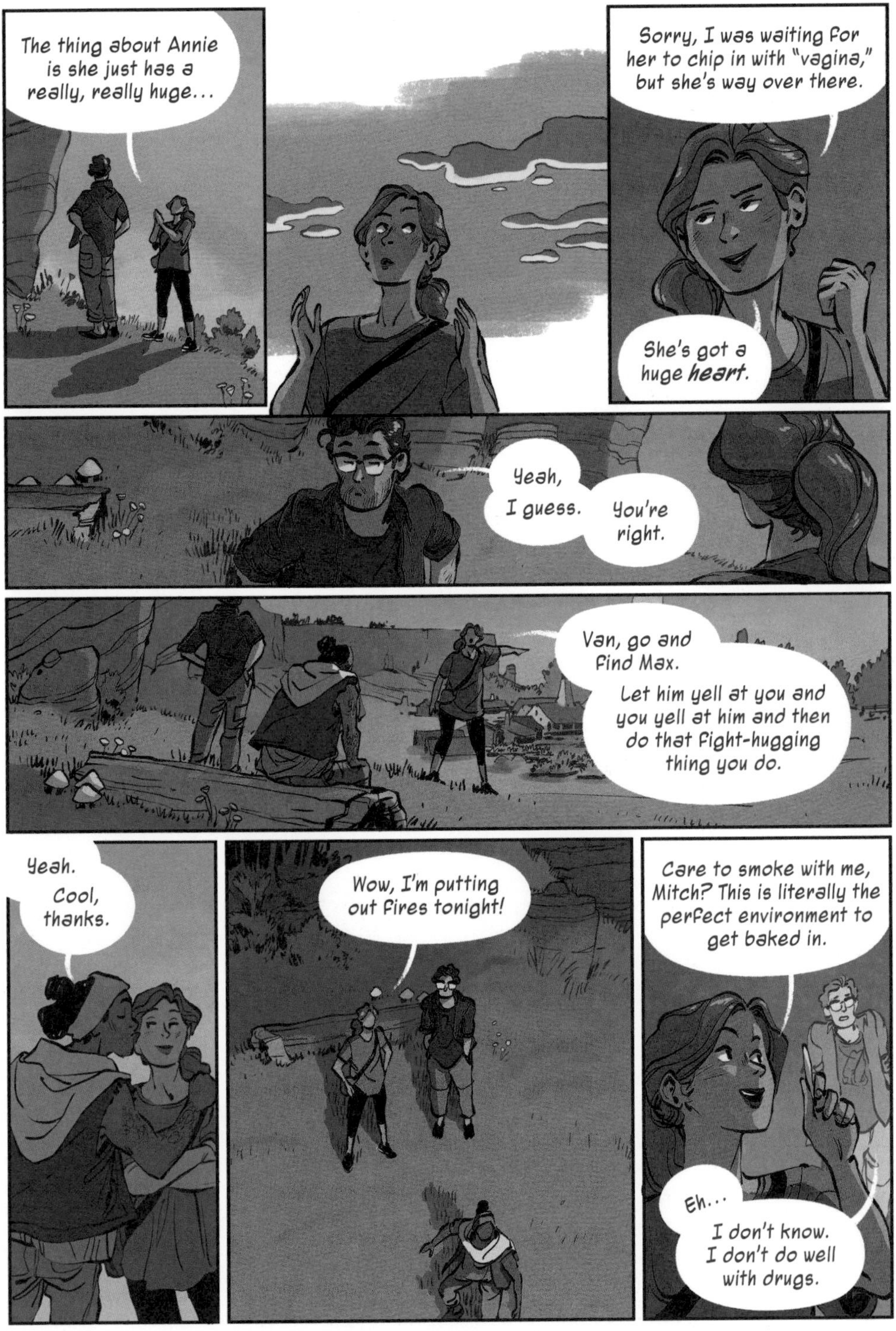

The thing about Annie is she just has a really, really huge...
Sorry, I was waiting for her to chip in with "vagina," but she's way over there.
She's got a huge **heart**.
Yeah,
I guess.
You're right.
Van, go and find Max.
Let him yell at you and you yell at him and then do that fight-hugging thing you do.
Yeah.
Cool, thanks.
Wow, I'm putting out fires tonight!
Care to smoke with me, Mitch? This is literally the perfect environment to get baked in.
Eh...
I don't know. I don't do well with drugs.

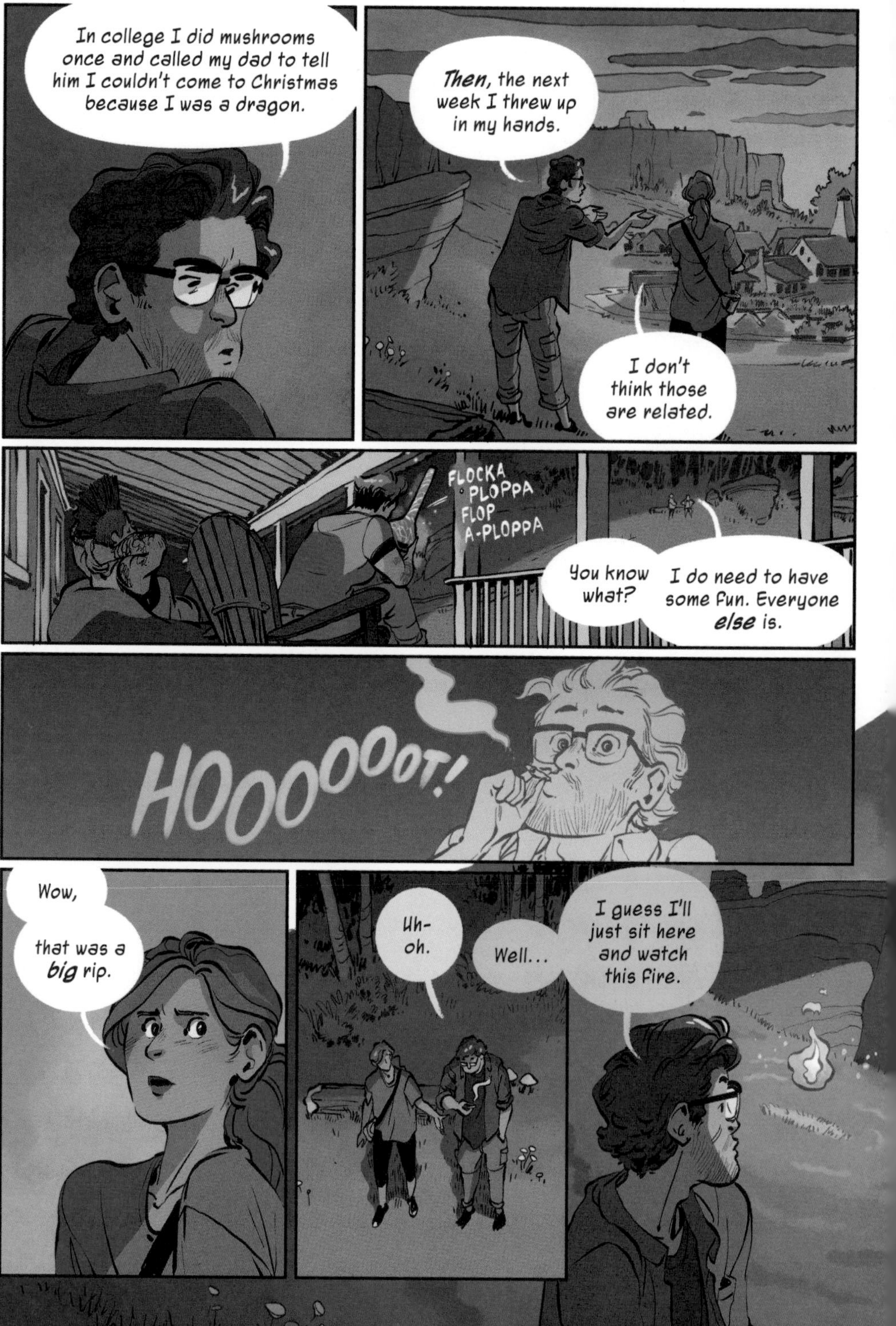
In college I did mushrooms once and called my dad to tell him I couldn't come to Christmas because I was a dragon.
Then, the next week I threw up in my hands.
I don't think those are related.
FLOCKA PLOPPA FLOP A-PLOPPA
You know what?
I do need to have some fun. Everyone *else* is.
HOOOOOOT!
Wow,
that was a *big* rip.
Uh-oh.
Well...
I guess I'll just sit here and watch this fire.

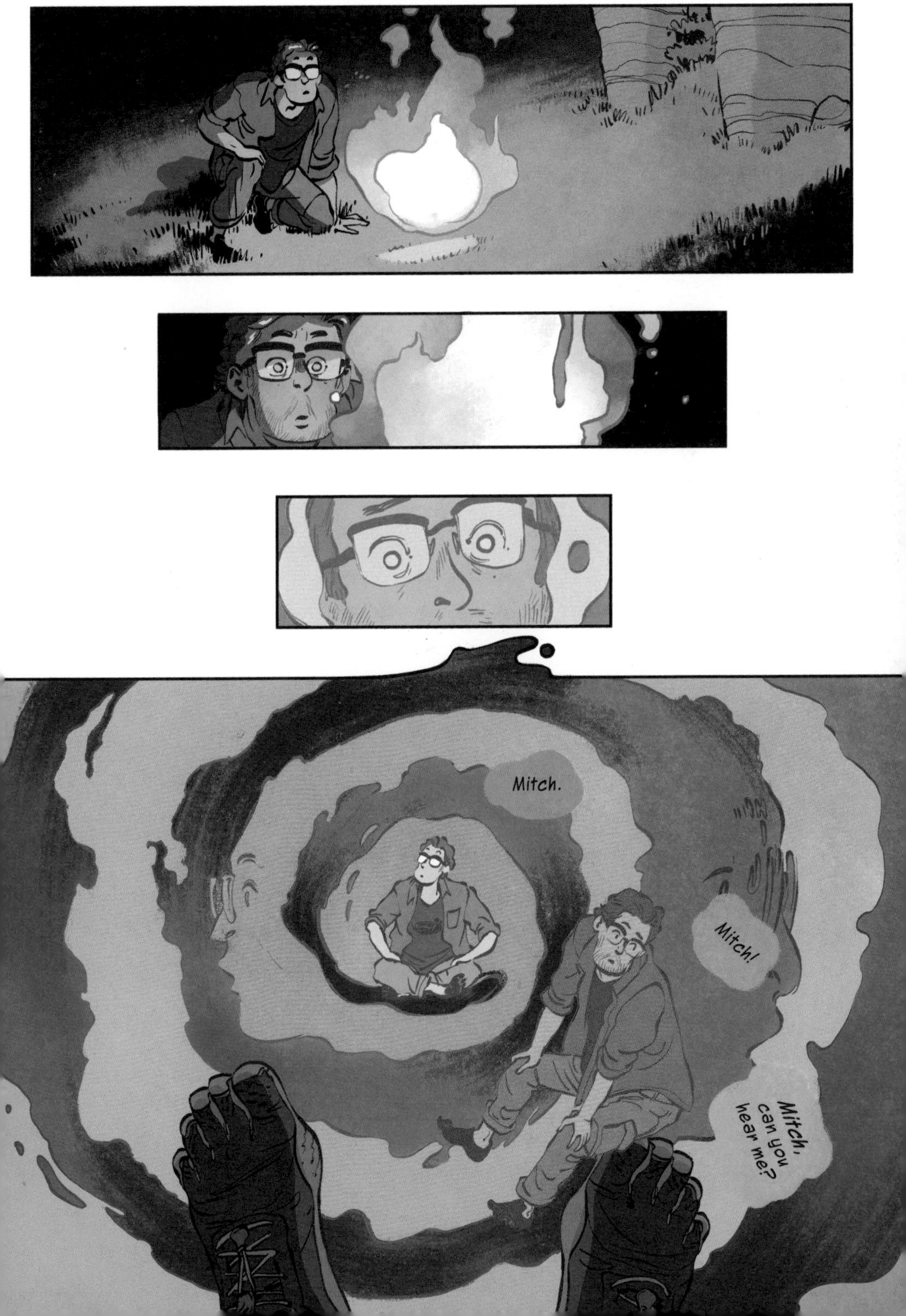
Mitch.
Mitch!
Mitch, can you hear me?

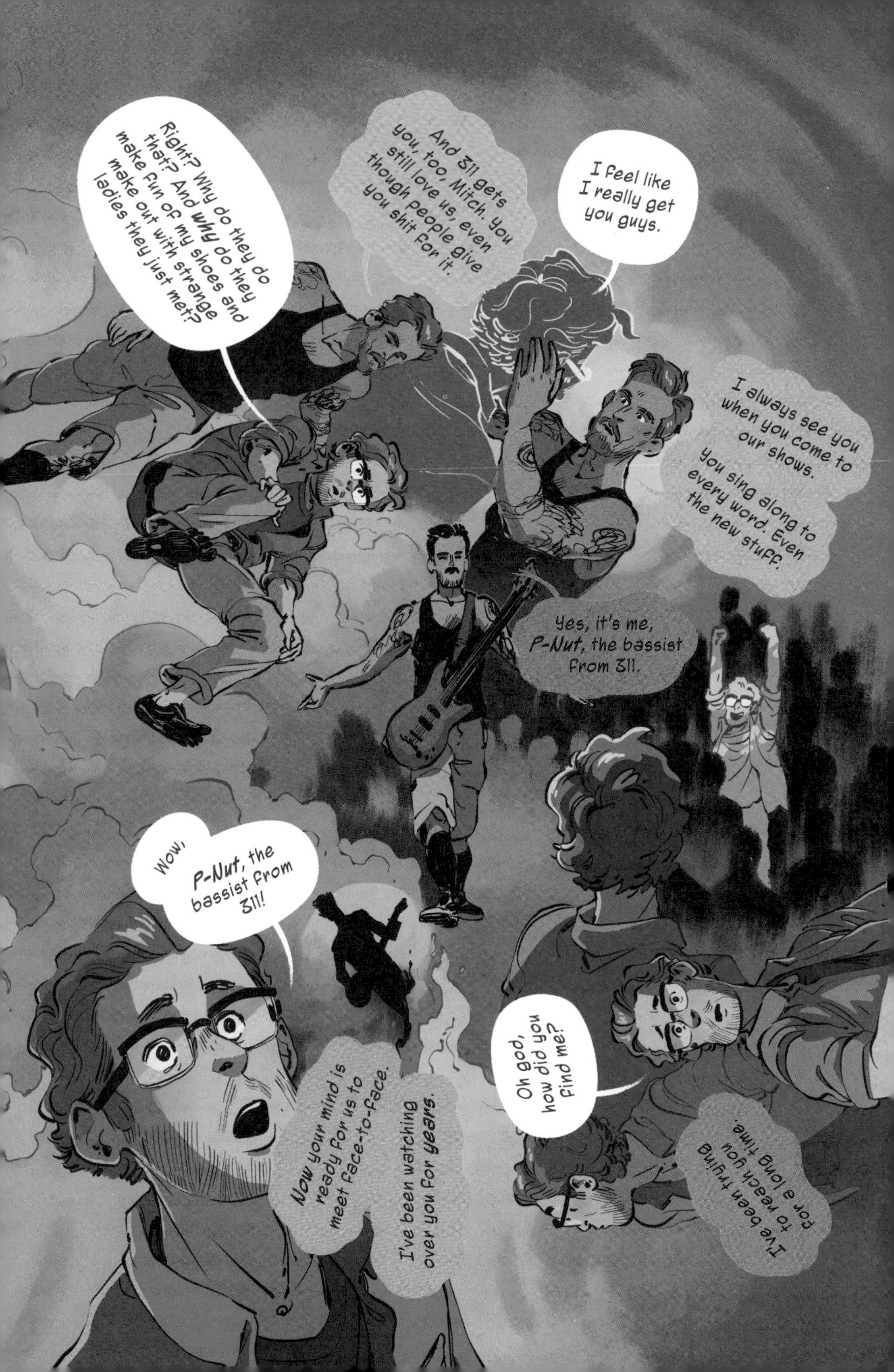
I always see you when you come to our shows.
You sing along to every word. Even the new stuff.
Yes, it's me, *P-Nut*, the bassist from 311.
I feel like I really get you guys.
And 311 gets you, too, Mitch. You still love us, even though people give you shit for it.
Right? Why do they do that? And *why* do they make fun of my shoes and make out with strange ladies they just met?
Wow, *P-Nut*, the bassist from 311!
Now your mind is ready for us to meet face-to-face.
I've been watching over you for *years*.
Oh god, how did you find me?
I've been trying to reach you for a long time.

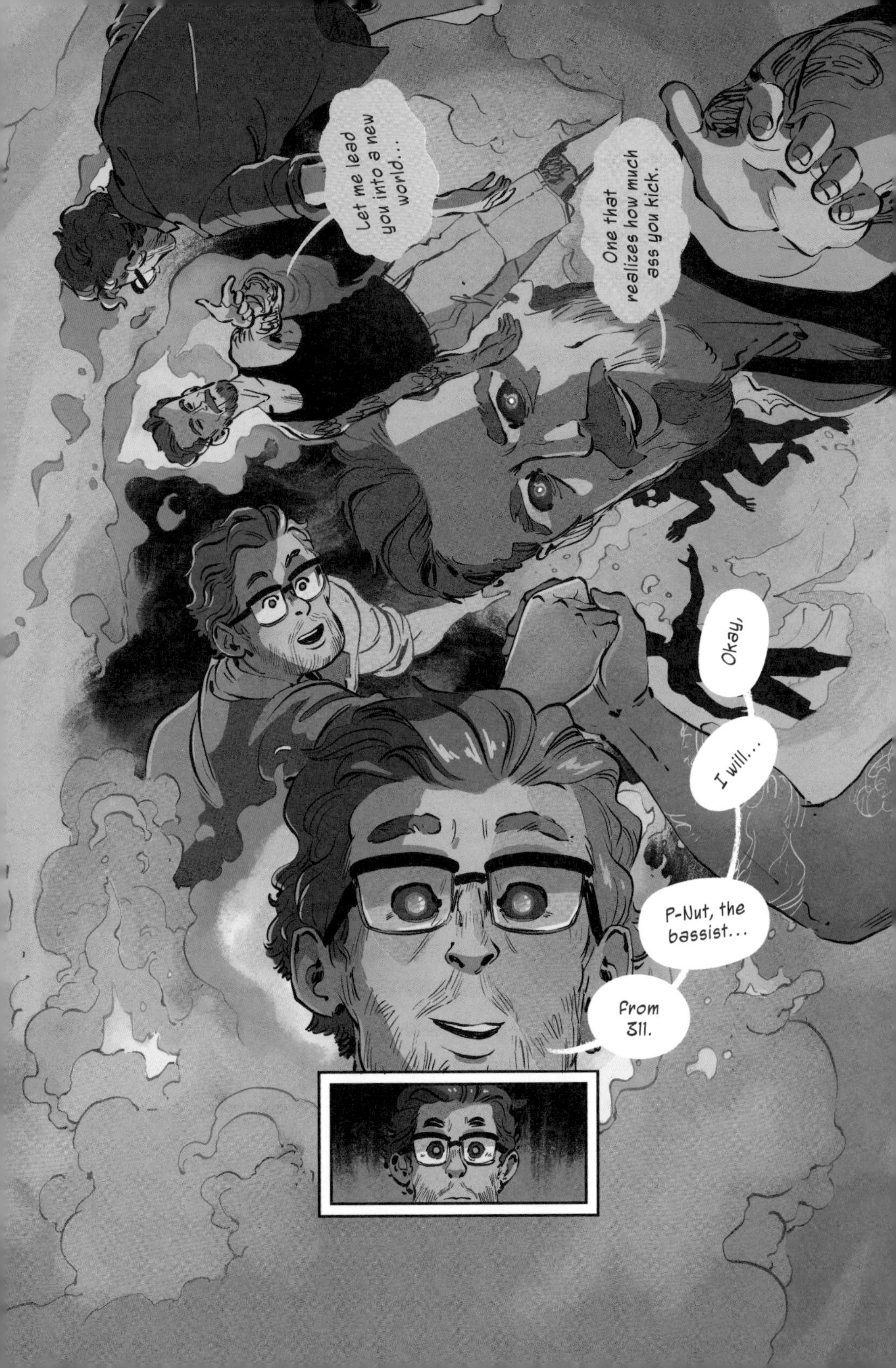
Let me lead you into a new world...
One that realizes how much ass you kick.
Okay,
I will...
P-Nut, the bassist...
From 311.

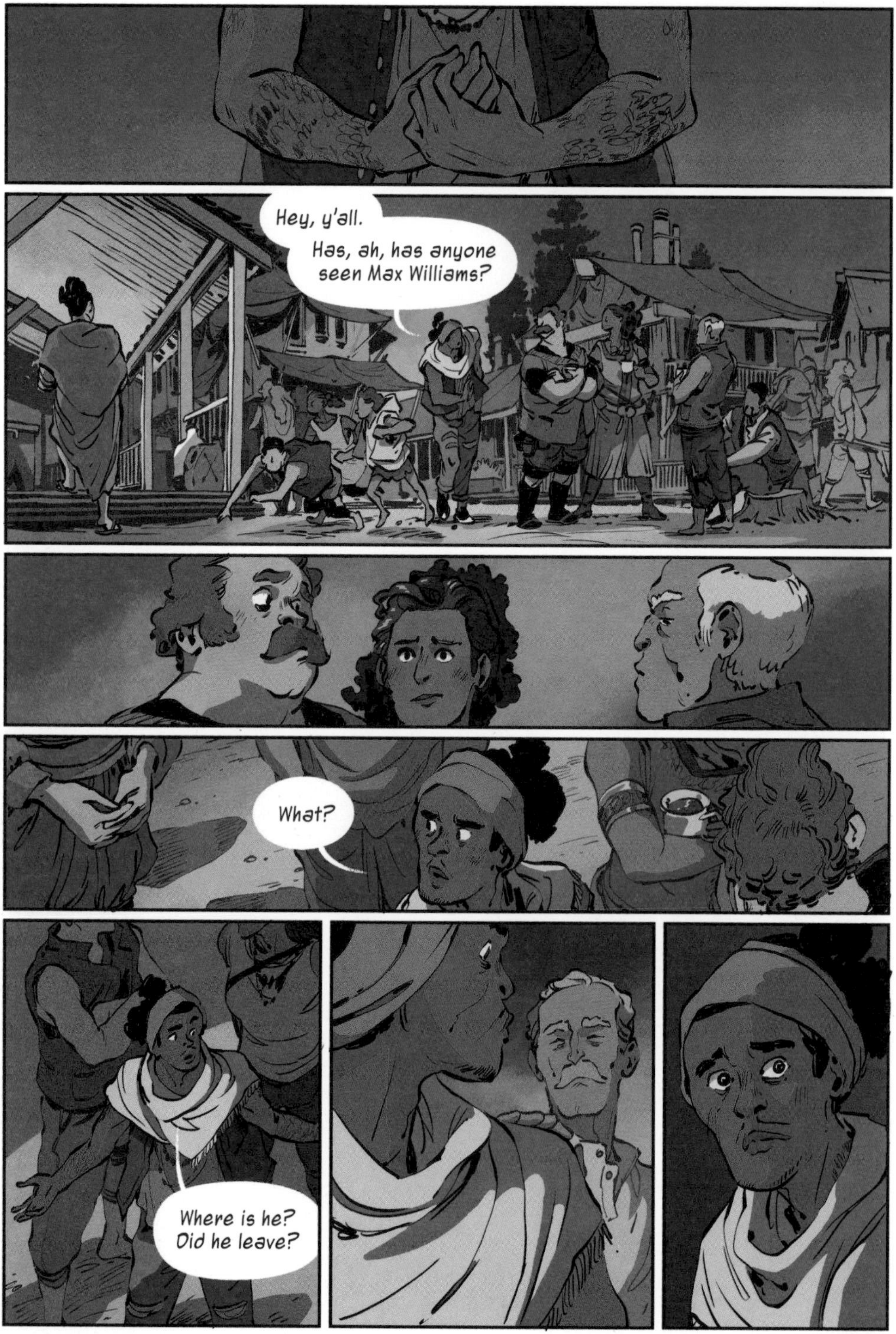
Hey, y'all.
Has, ah, has anyone seen Max Williams?
What?
Where is he? Did he leave?

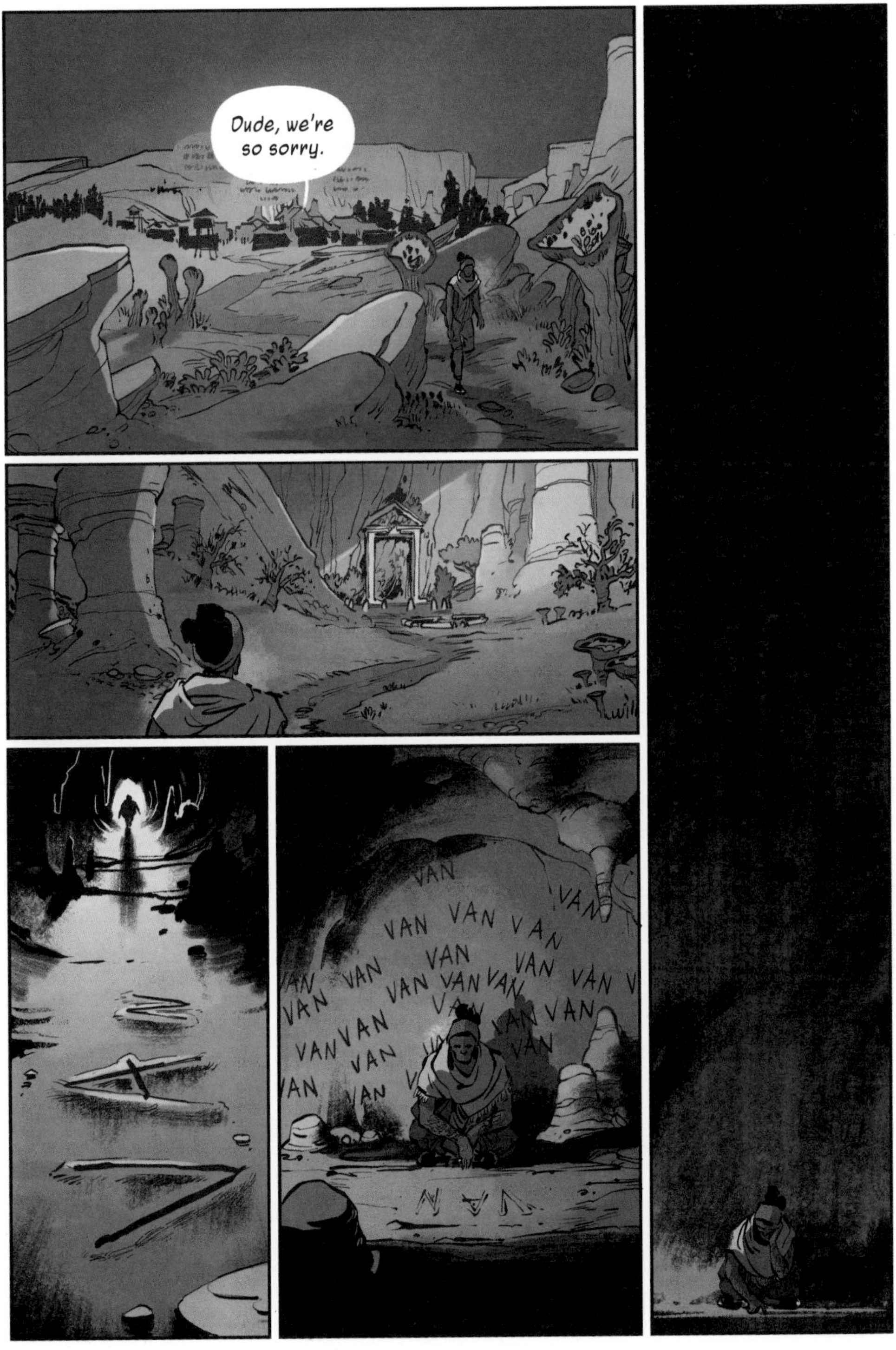
Dude, we're so sorry.
VAN
VAN
VAN VAN VAN
VAN VAN
VAN VAN VAN VAN VAN VAN
VAN VAN VAN
VAN VAN VAN
VAN VAN VAN
VAN VAN
VAN

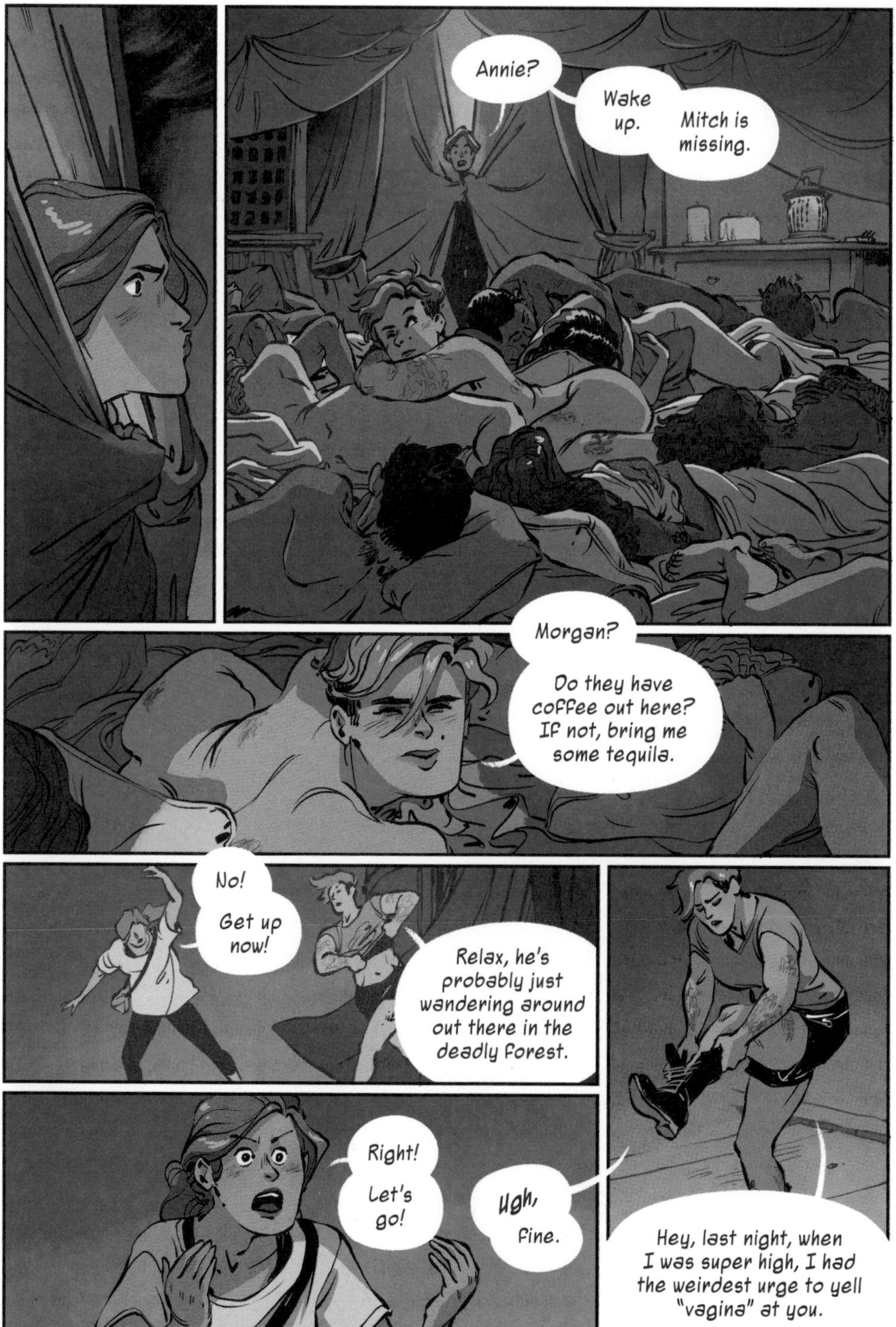
Annie?
Wake up.
Mitch is missing.
Morgan?
Do they have coffee out here? If not, bring me some tequila.
No!
Get up now!
Relax, he's probably just wandering around out there in the deadly forest.
Right!
Let's go!
Ugh,
fine.
Hey, last night, when I was super high, I had the weirdest urge to yell "vagina" at you.

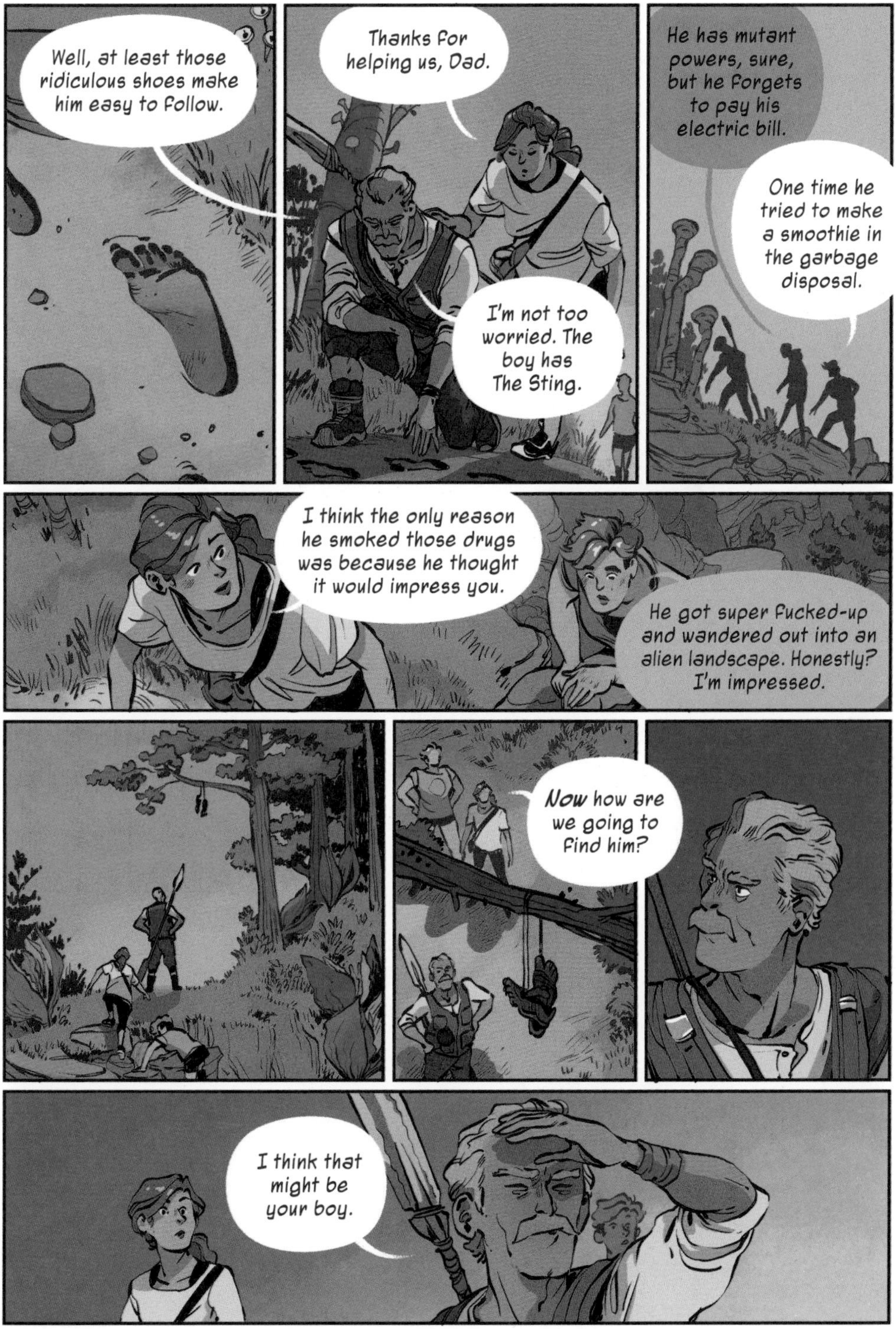
Well, at least those ridiculous shoes make him easy to follow.
Thanks for helping us, Dad.
I'm not too worried. The boy has The Sting.
He has mutant powers, sure, but he forgets to pay his electric bill.
One time he tried to make a smoothie in the garbage disposal.
I think the only reason he smoked those drugs was because he thought it would impress you.
He got super fucked-up and wandered out into an alien landscape. Honestly? I'm impressed.
Now how are we going to find him?
I think that might be your boy.

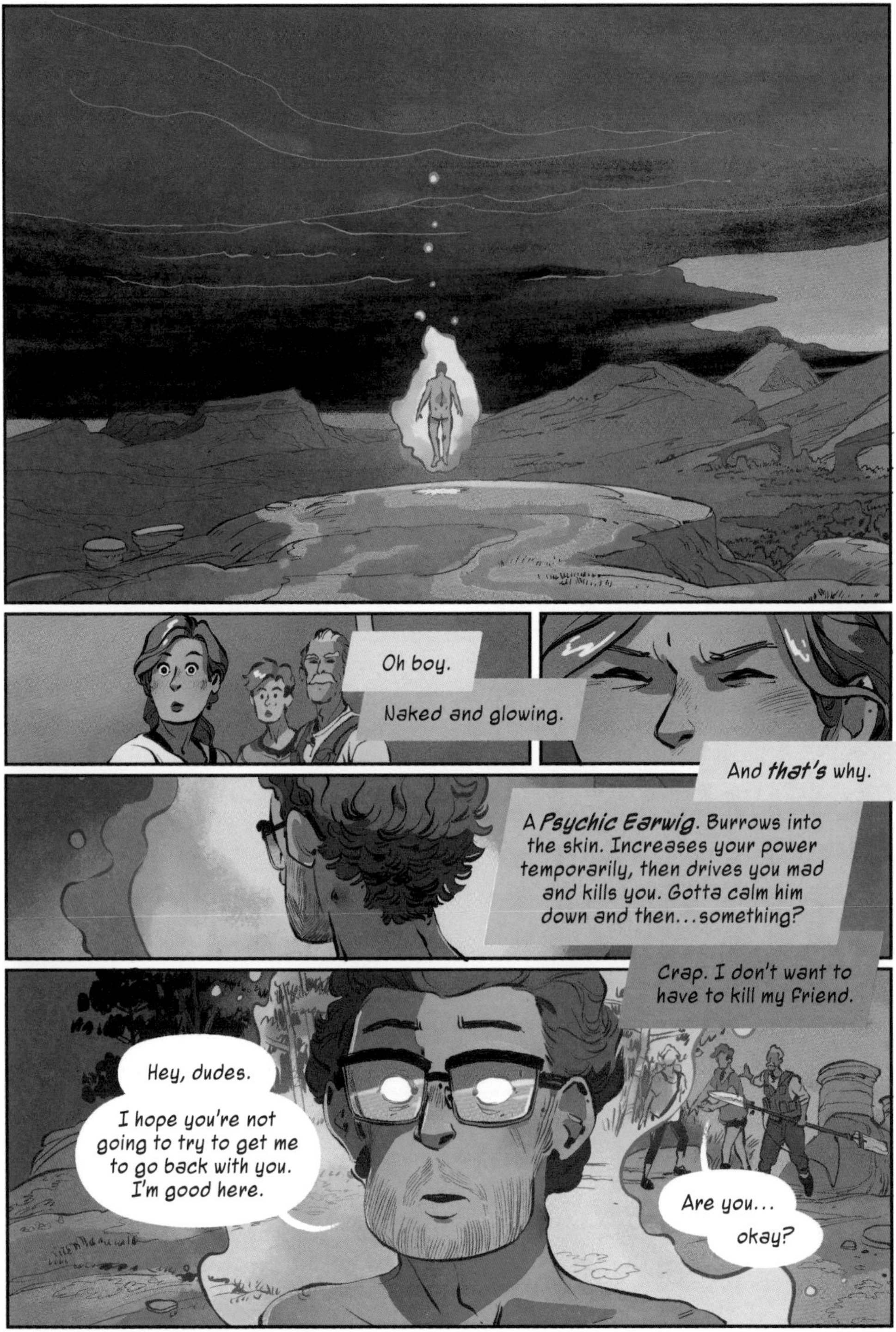
Oh boy.
Naked and glowing.
And that's why.
A Psychic Earwig. Burrows into the skin. Increases your power temporarily, then drives you mad and kills you. Gotta calm him down and then...something?
Crap. I don't want to have to kill my friend.
Hey, dudes.
I hope you're not going to try to get me to go back with you. I'm good here.
Are you... okay?

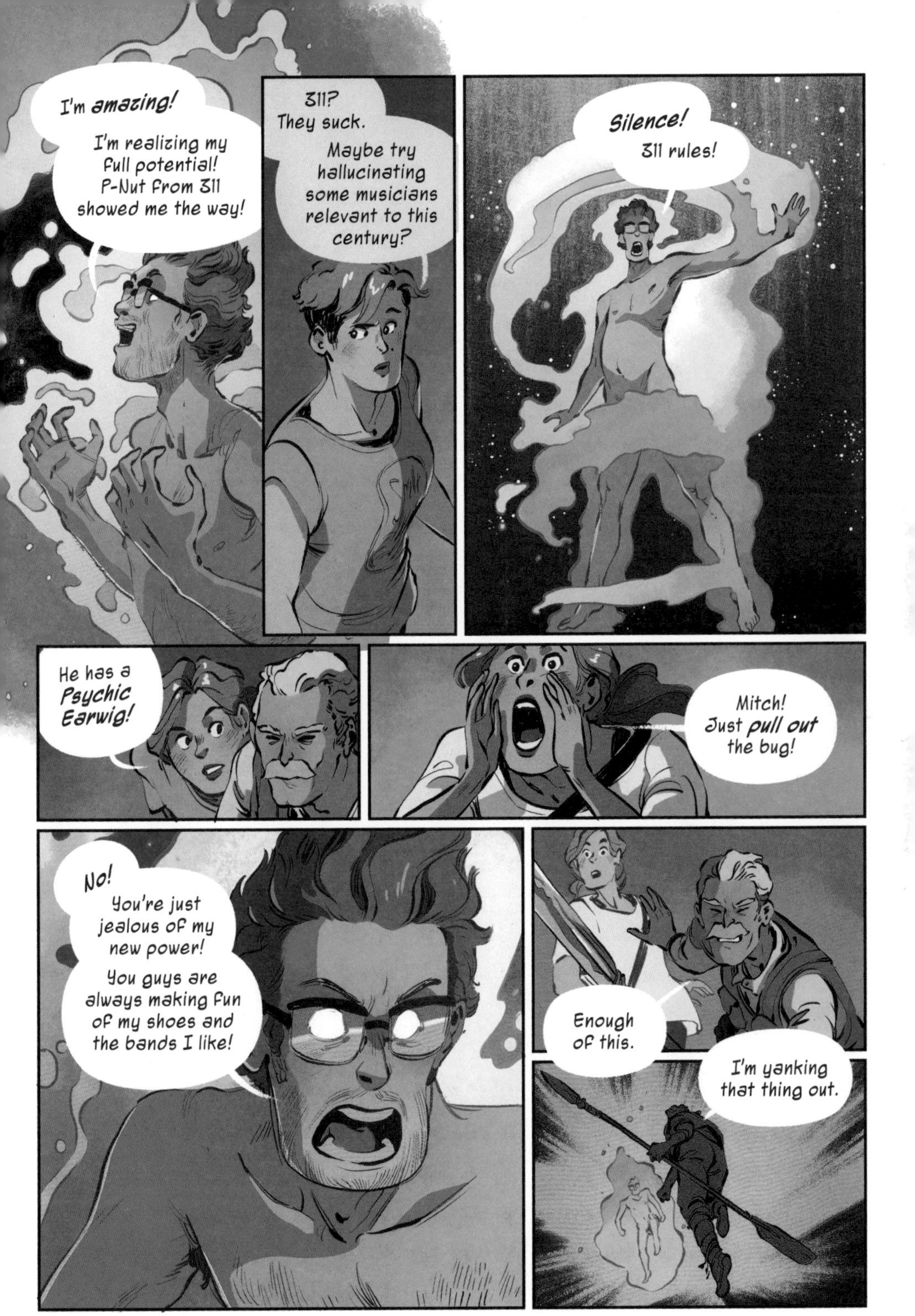
I'm amazing!
I'm realizing my full potential! P-Nut from 311 showed me the way!
311? They suck.
Maybe try hallucinating some musicians relevant to this century?
Silence!
311 rules!
He has a Psychic Earwig!
Mitch! Just pull out the bug!
No!
You're just jealous of my new power!
You guys are always making fun of my shoes and the bands I like!
Enough of this.
I'm yanking that thing out.

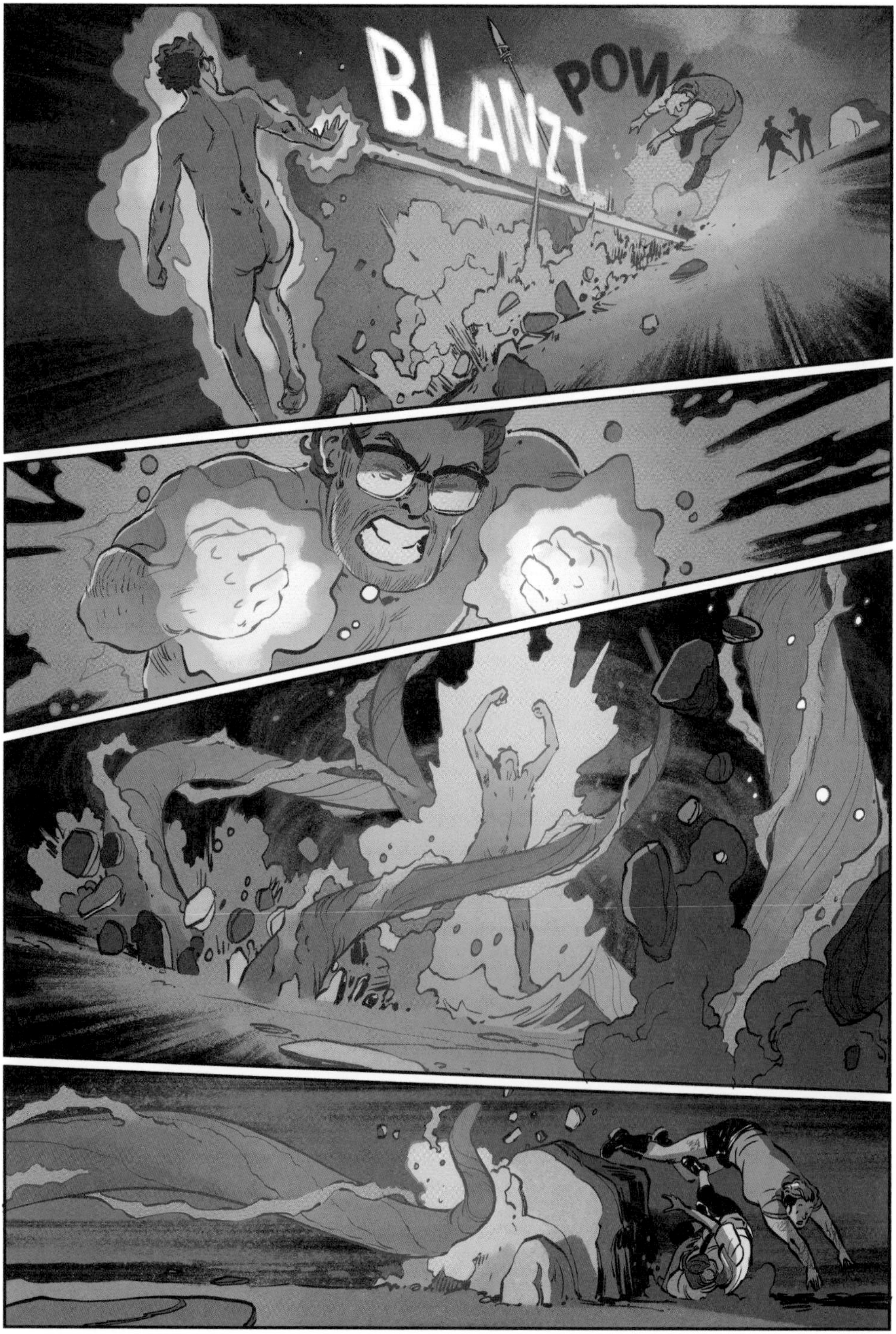
BLANZT
POW

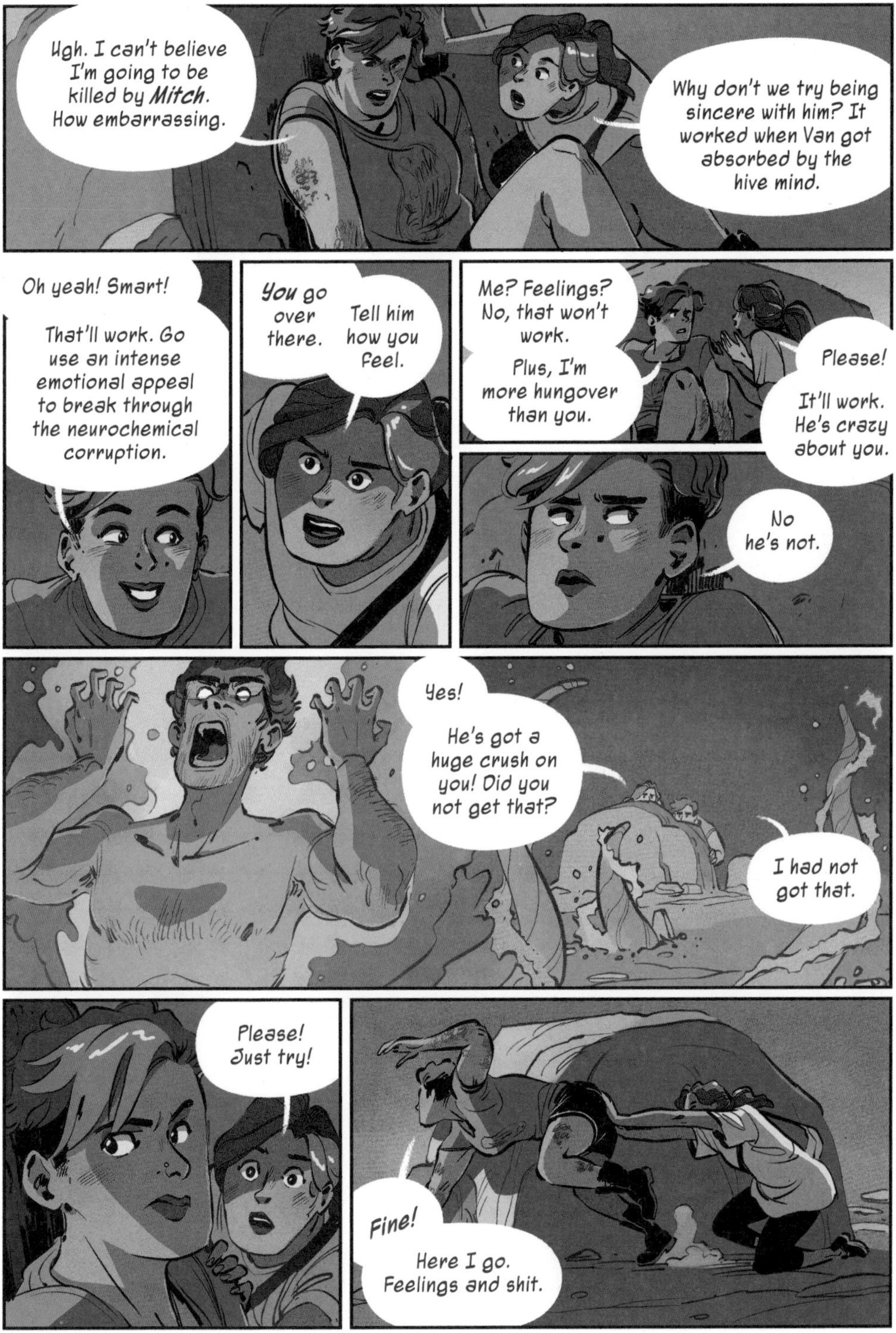
Ugh. I can't believe I'm going to be killed by *Mitch*. How embarrassing.
Why don't we try being sincere with him? It worked when Van got absorbed by the hive mind.
Oh yeah! Smart!
That'll work. Go use an intense emotional appeal to break through the neurochemical corruption.
You go over there.
Tell him how you feel.
Me? Feelings? No, that won't work.
Plus, I'm more hungover than you.
Please!
It'll work. He's crazy about you.
No he's not.
Yes!
He's got a huge crush on you! Did you not get that?
I had not got that.
Please! Just try!
Fine!
Here I go. Feelings and shit.

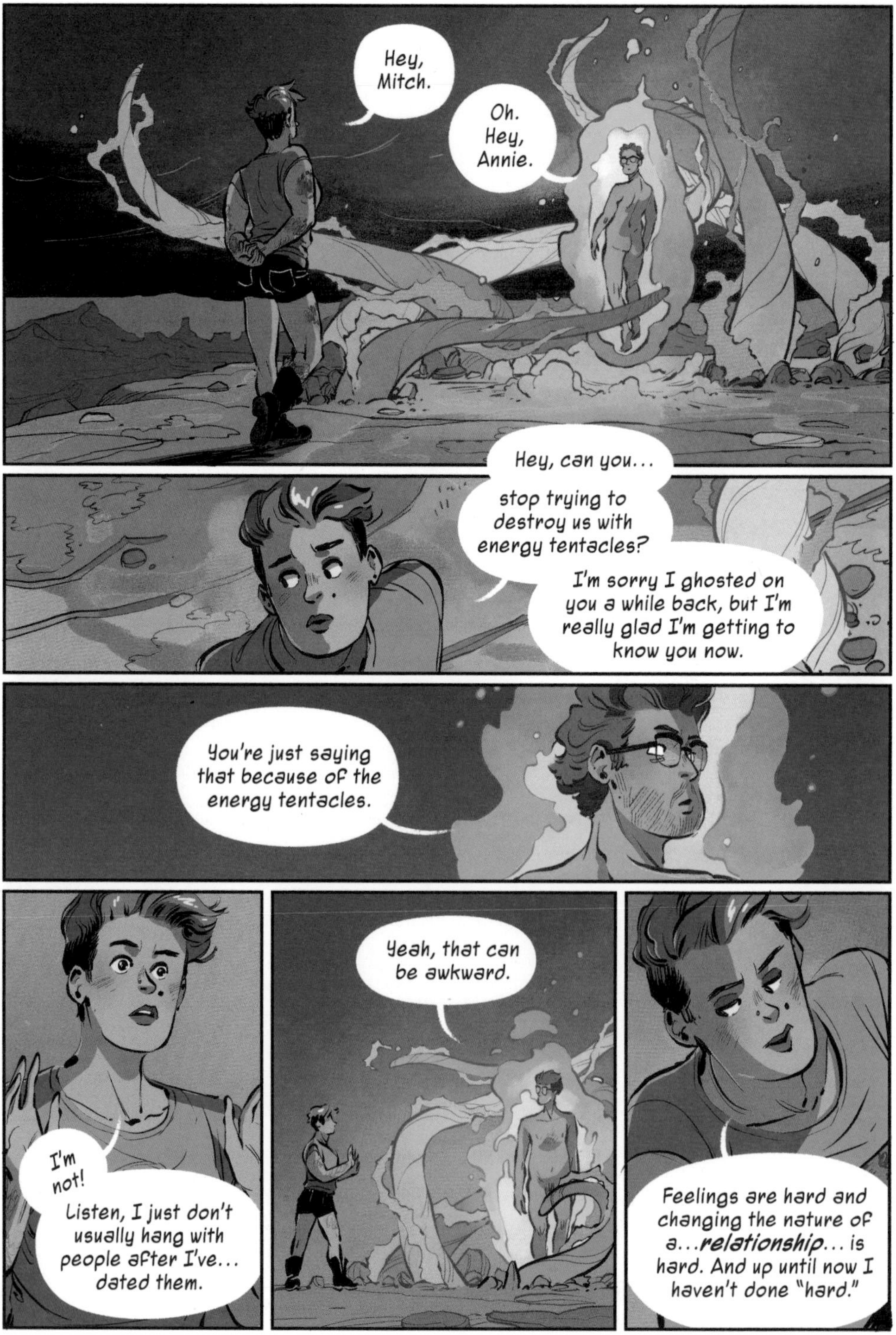
Hey, Mitch.
Oh. Hey, Annie.
Hey, can you...
stop trying to destroy us with energy tentacles?
I'm sorry I ghosted on you a while back, but I'm really glad I'm getting to know you now.
You're just saying that because of the energy tentacles.
I'm not!
Listen, I just don't usually hang with people after I've... dated them.
Yeah, that can be awkward.
Feelings are hard and changing the nature of a...*relationship*... is hard. And up until now I haven't done "hard."

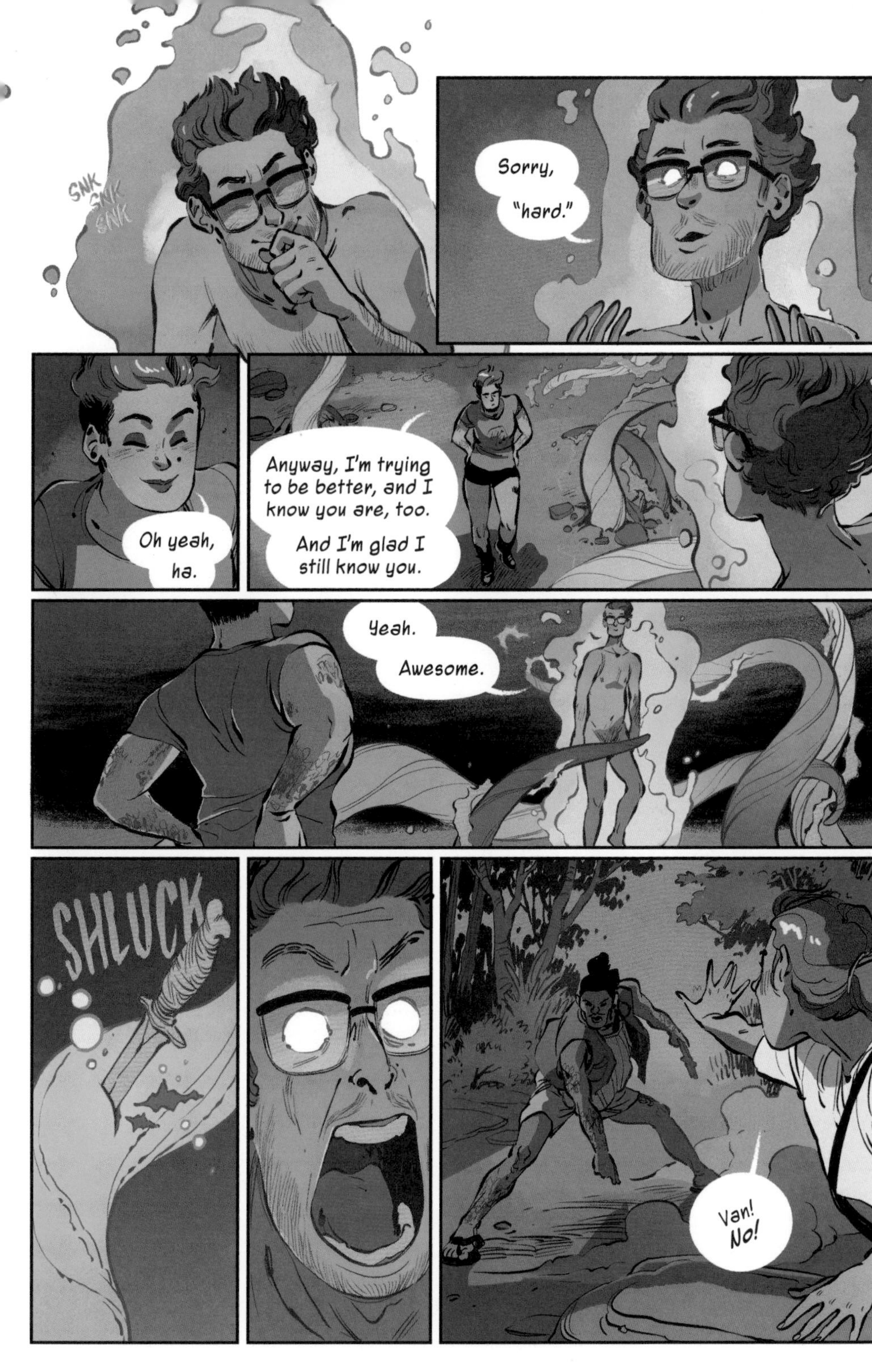
SNK SNK SNK
Sorry,
"hard."
Oh yeah, ha.
Anyway, I'm trying to be better, and I know you are, too.
And I'm glad I still know you.
Yeah.
Awesome.
SHLUCK
Van! No!

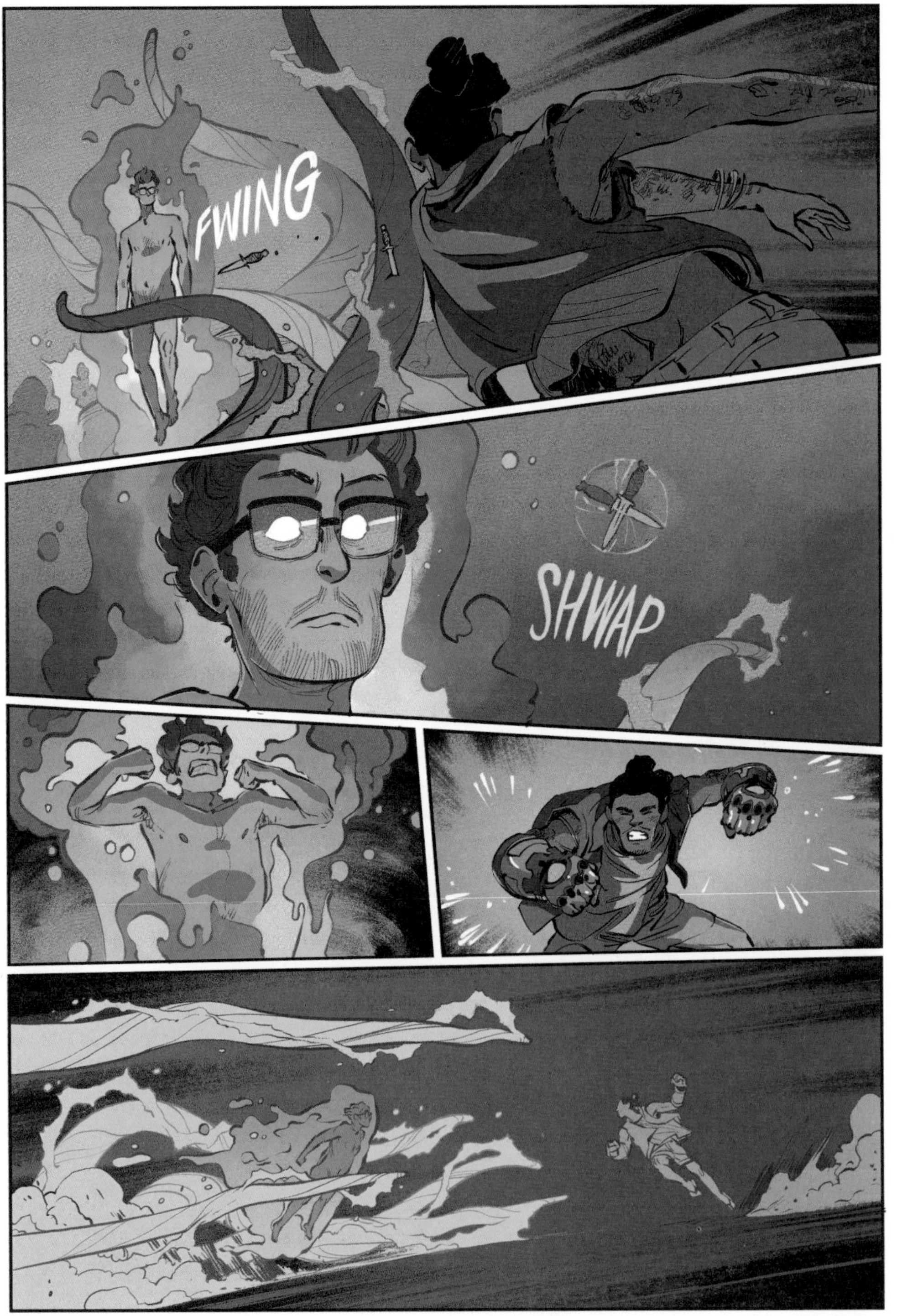
FWING
SHWAP

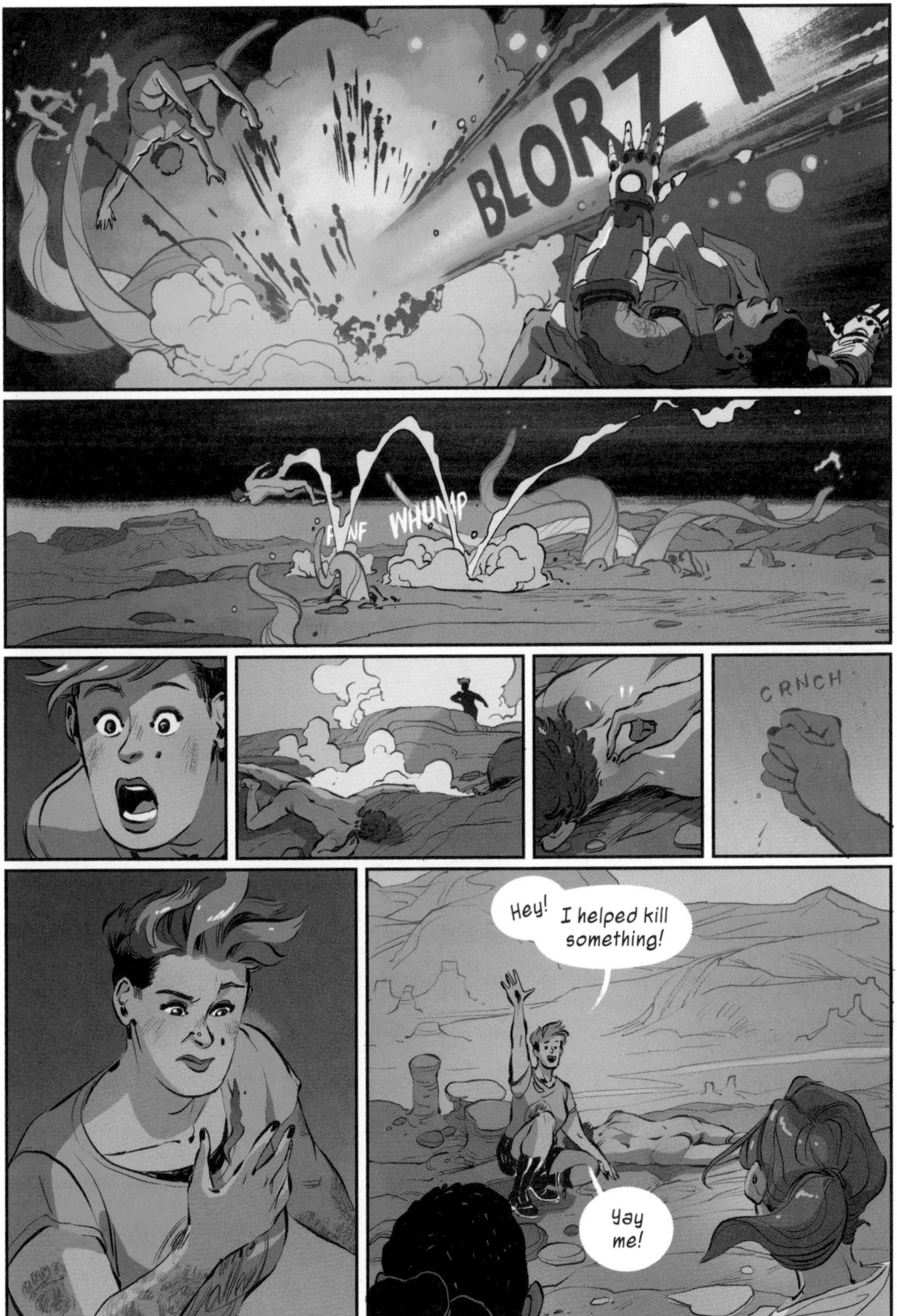
BLORZT
WHUMP
CRNCH
Hey!
I helped kill something!
Yay me!

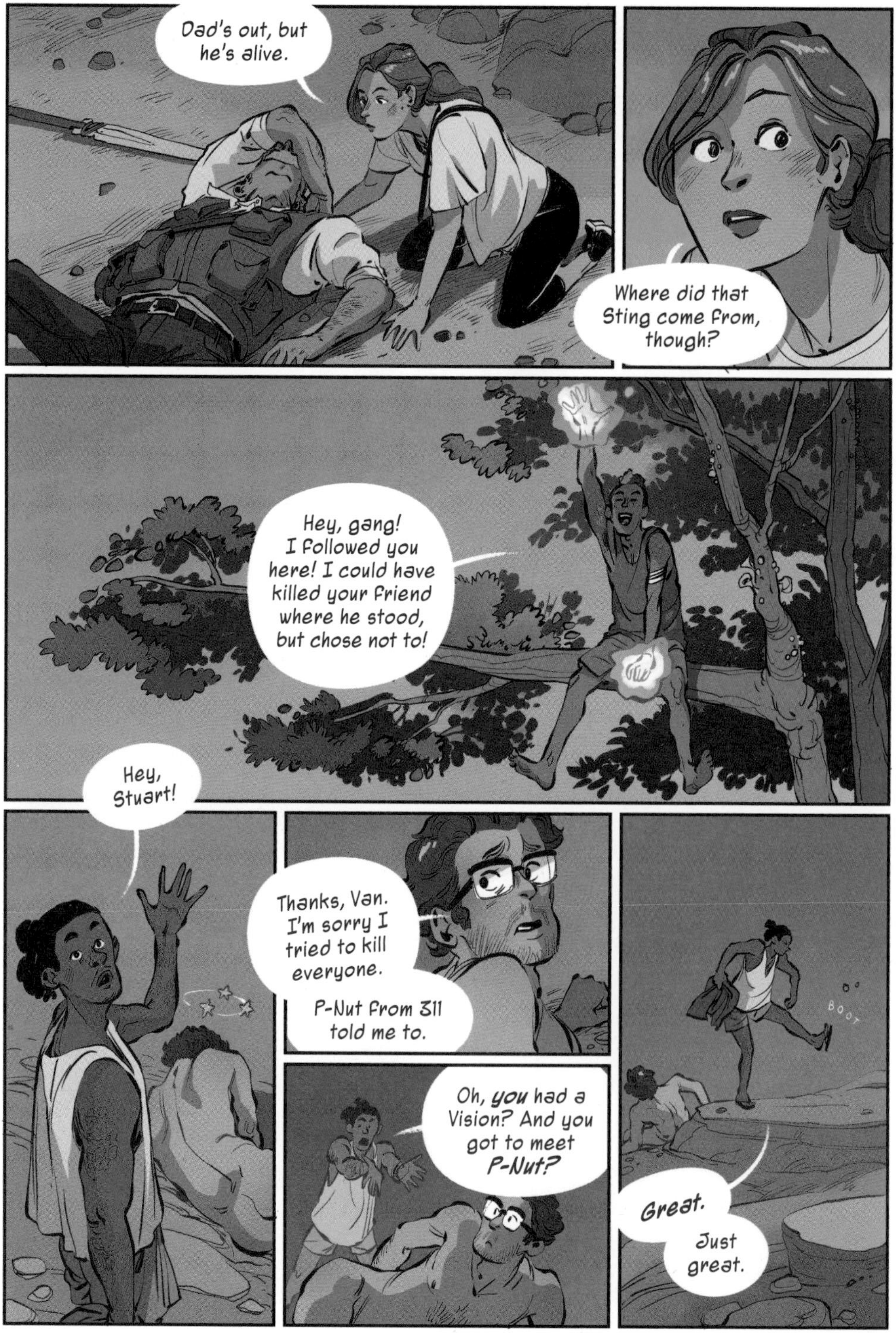
Dad's out, but he's alive.
Where did that Sting come from, though?
Hey, gang! I followed you here! I could have killed your friend where he stood, but chose not to!
Hey, Stuart!
Thanks, Van. I'm sorry I tried to kill everyone.
P-Nut from 311 told me to.
Oh, *you* had a Vision? And you got to meet *P-Nut?*
BOOT
Great.
Just great.

Hey, sorry.

No apologies necessary. Those Psychic Earwigs are tough. Looks like you're tougher.

Did I kill your dad?

Naw, he's fine.

Most people out here have built up a resistance to Brush attacks. You walloped him pretty good, though, which I am in favor of.

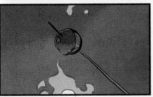

TIKKA TIKKA TIKI TIKKA

PO DONF

Hey, kids. Big day, huh?

Sorry about The Sting, Mr. Kay.

Water under the bridge.

Hey, Dad, we talked it over and decided that we're leaving.

Seems like everyone's a little suspicious about why Tandem wants that stone, so we're not about to deliver it to them.

That was in your boot the whole time?

Yeah. Anticlimactic, huh?

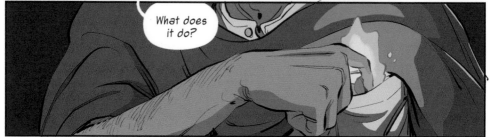

What does it do?

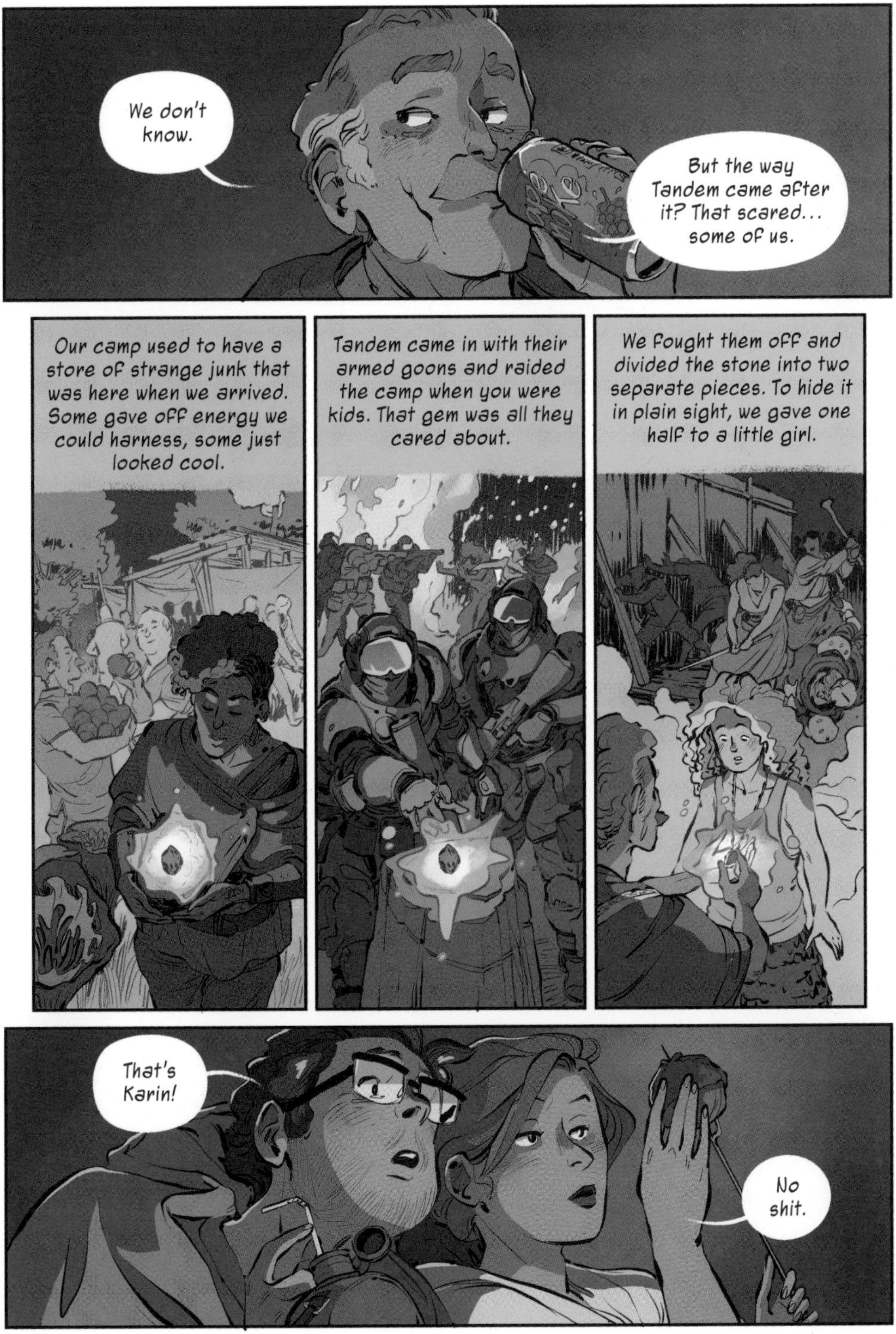
We don't know.
But the way Tandem came after it? That scared... some of us.
Our camp used to have a store of strange junk that was here when we arrived. Some gave off energy we could harness, some just looked cool.
Tandem came in with their armed goons and raided the camp when you were kids. That gem was all they cared about.
We fought them off and divided the stone into two separate pieces. To hide it in plain sight, we gave one half to a little girl.
That's Karin!
No shit.

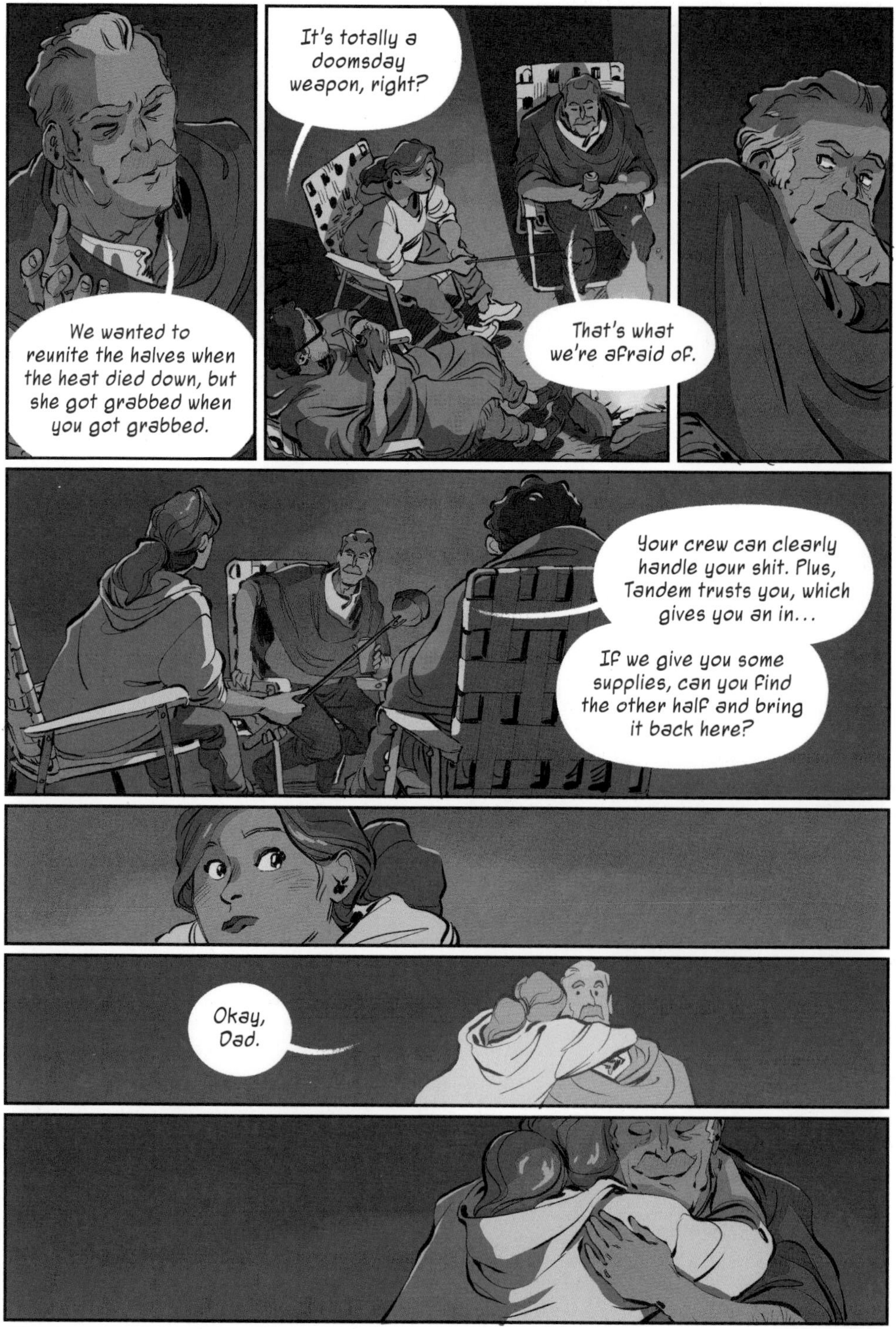
We wanted to reunite the halves when the heat died down, but she got grabbed when you got grabbed.
It's totally a doomsday weapon, right?
That's what we're afraid of.
Your crew can clearly handle your shit. Plus, Tandem trusts you, which gives you an in...
If we give you some supplies, can you find the other half and bring it back here?
Okay, Dad.

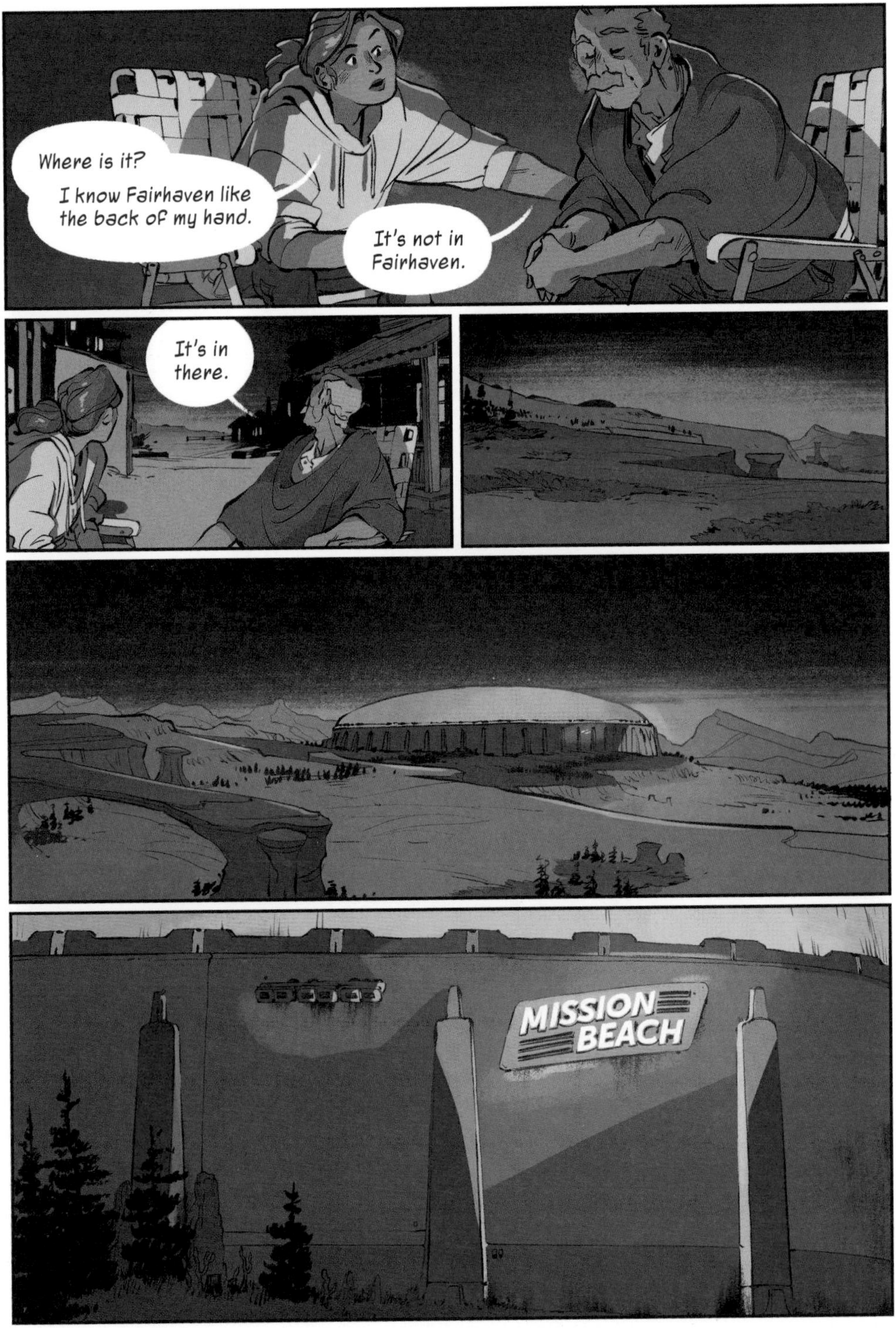
Where is it?
I know Fairhaven like the back of my hand.
It's not in Fairhaven.
It's in there.
MISSION BEACH

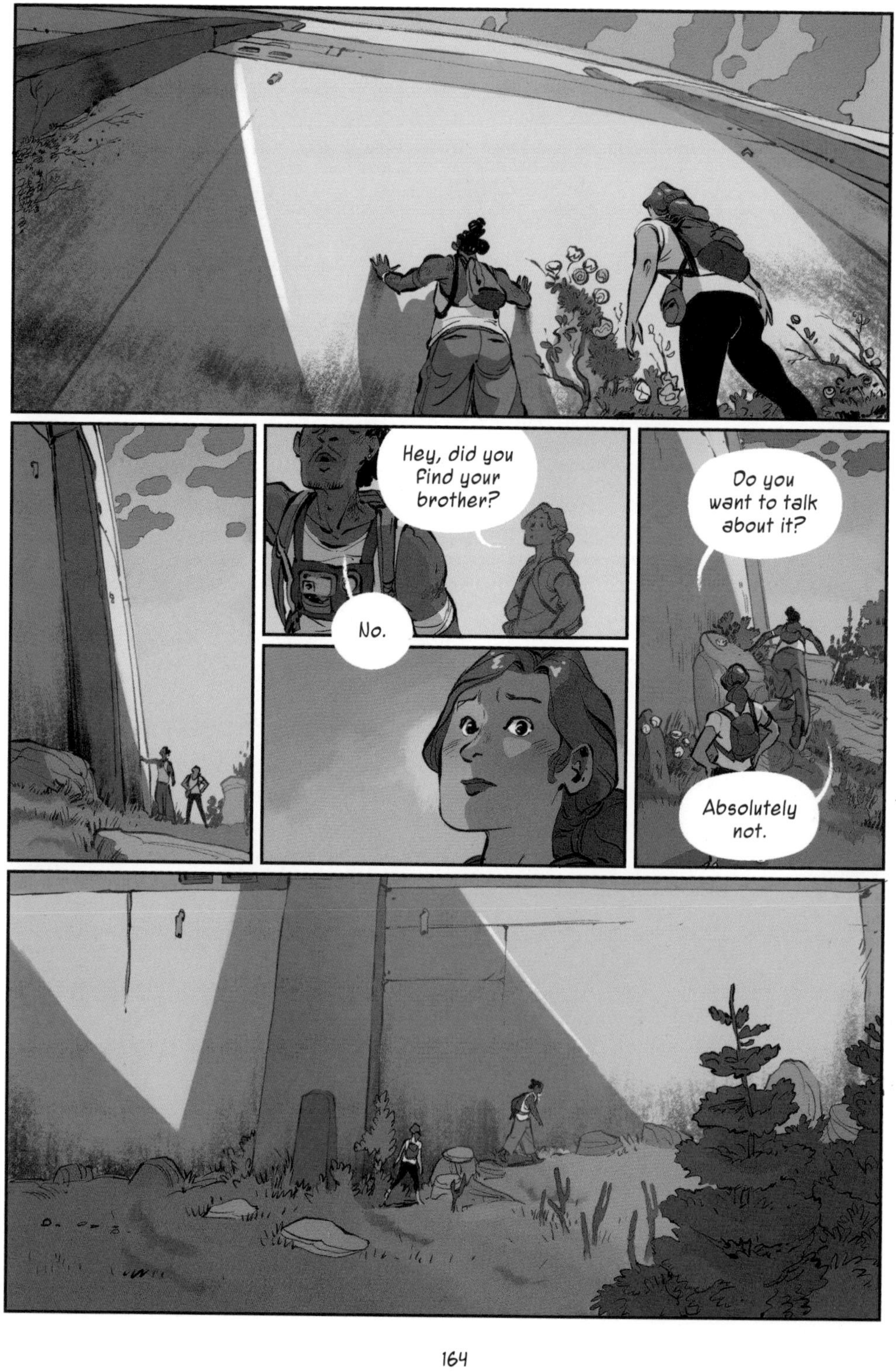
Hey, did you find your brother?
No.
Do you want to talk about it?
Absolutely not.

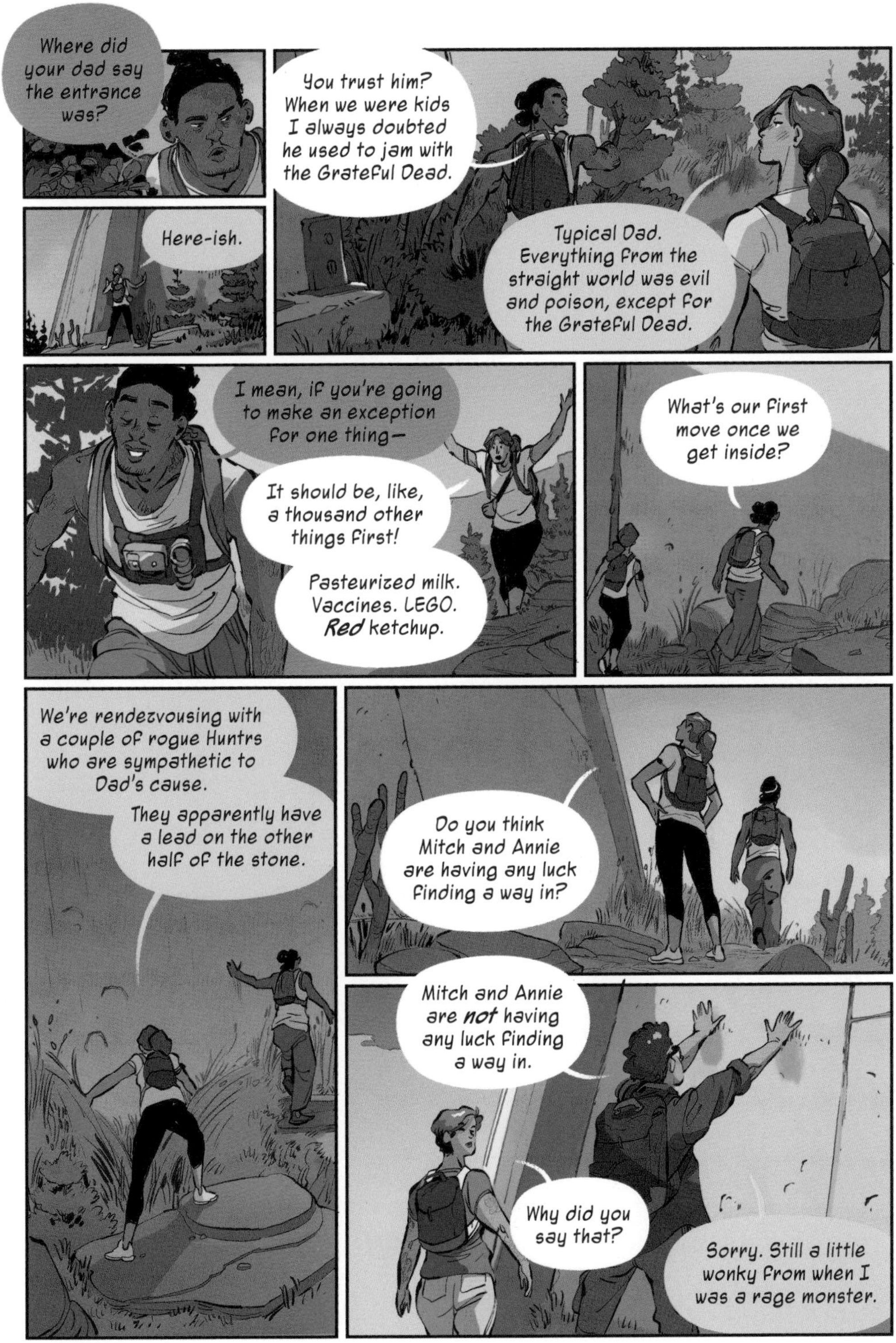
Where did your dad say the entrance was?
You trust him? When we were kids I always doubted he used to jam with the Grateful Dead.
Here-ish.
Typical Dad. Everything from the straight world was evil and poison, except for the Grateful Dead.
I mean, if you're going to make an exception for one thing—
It should be, like, a thousand other things first!
Pasteurized milk. Vaccines. LEGO. *Red* ketchup.
What's our first move once we get inside?
We're rendezvousing with a couple of rogue Huntrs who are sympathetic to Dad's cause.
They apparently have a lead on the other half of the stone.
Do you think Mitch and Annie are having any luck finding a way in?
Mitch and Annie are **not** having any luck finding a way in.
Why did you say that?
Sorry. Still a little wonky from when I was a rage monster.

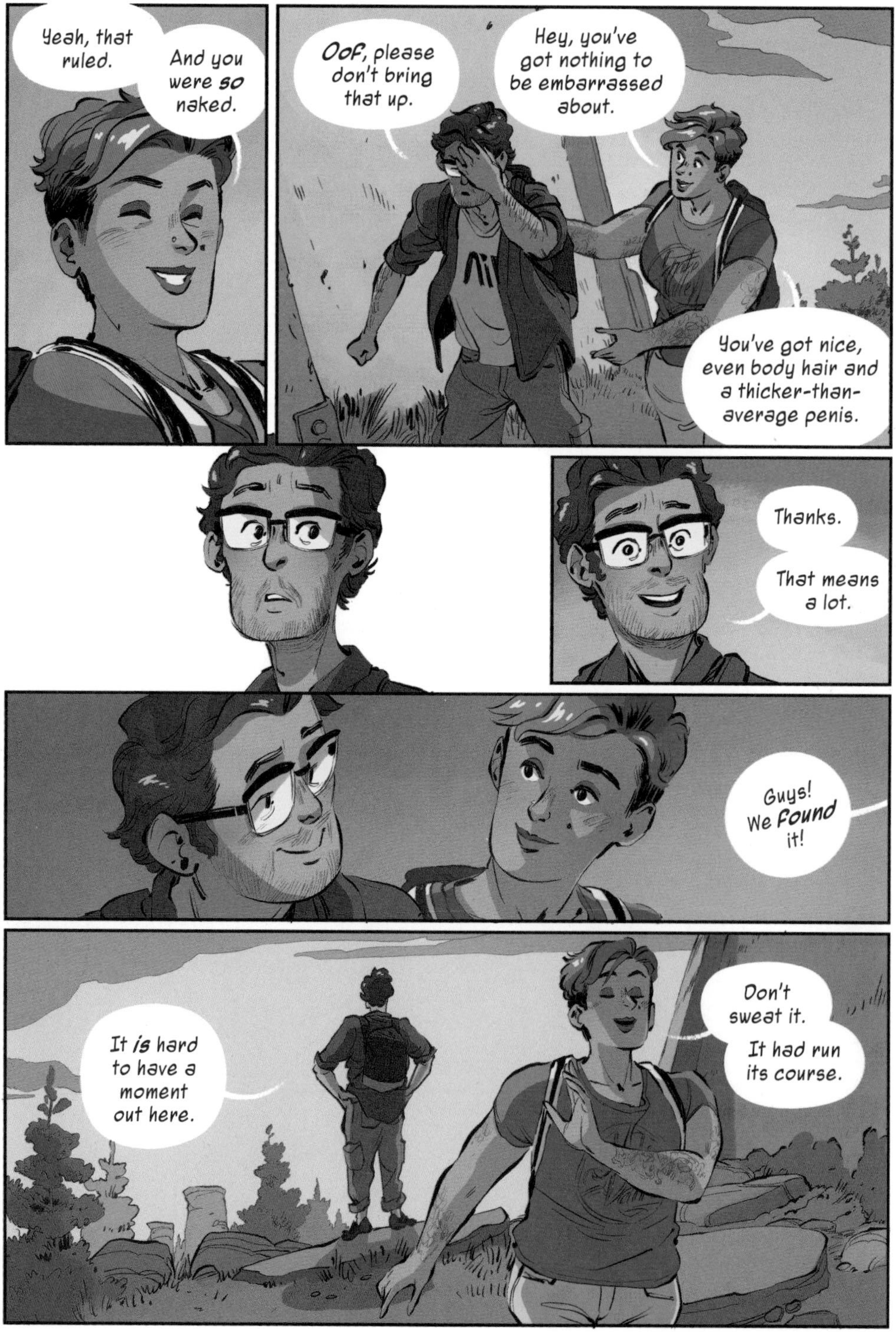
Yeah, that ruled.
And you were *so* naked.
Oof, please don't bring that up.
Hey, you've got nothing to be embarrassed about.
You've got nice, even body hair and a thicker-than-average penis.
Thanks.
That means a lot.
Guys! We *found* it!
It *is* hard to have a moment out here.
Don't sweat it.
It had run its course.

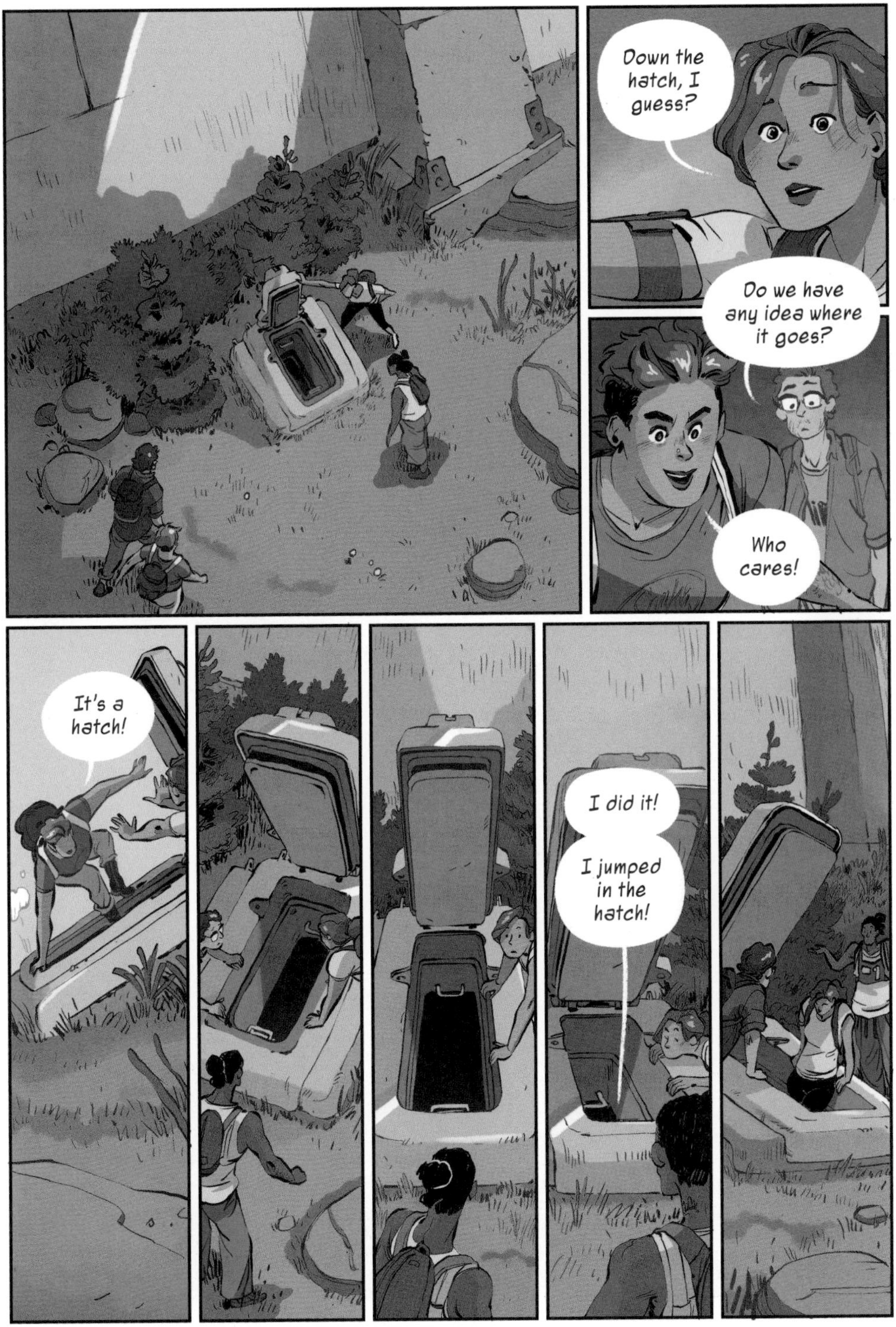
Down the hatch, I guess?
Do we have any idea where it goes?
Who cares!
It's a hatch!
I did it!
I jumped in the hatch!

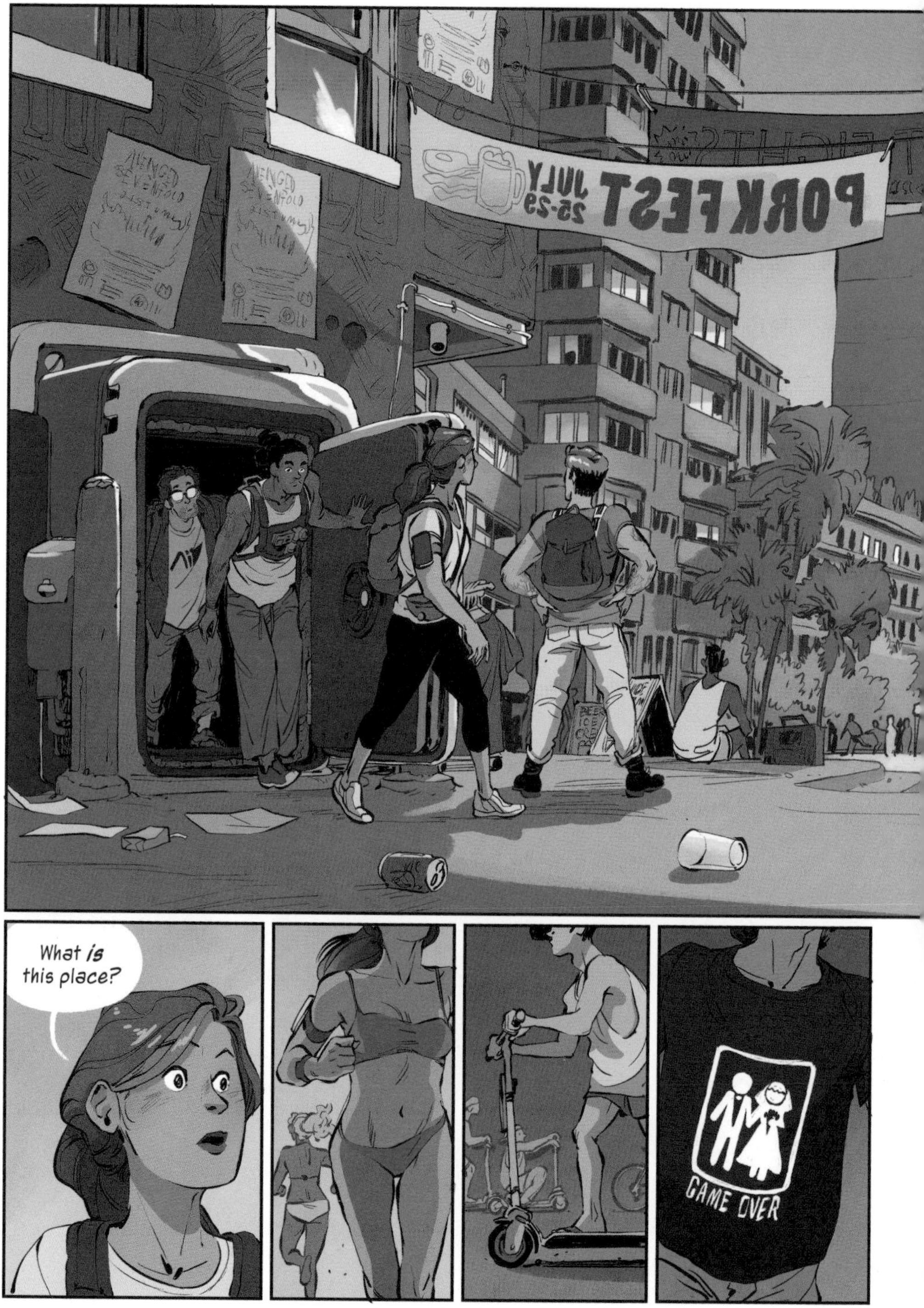
PORK FEST
JULY 25-29
What *is* this place?
GAME OVER

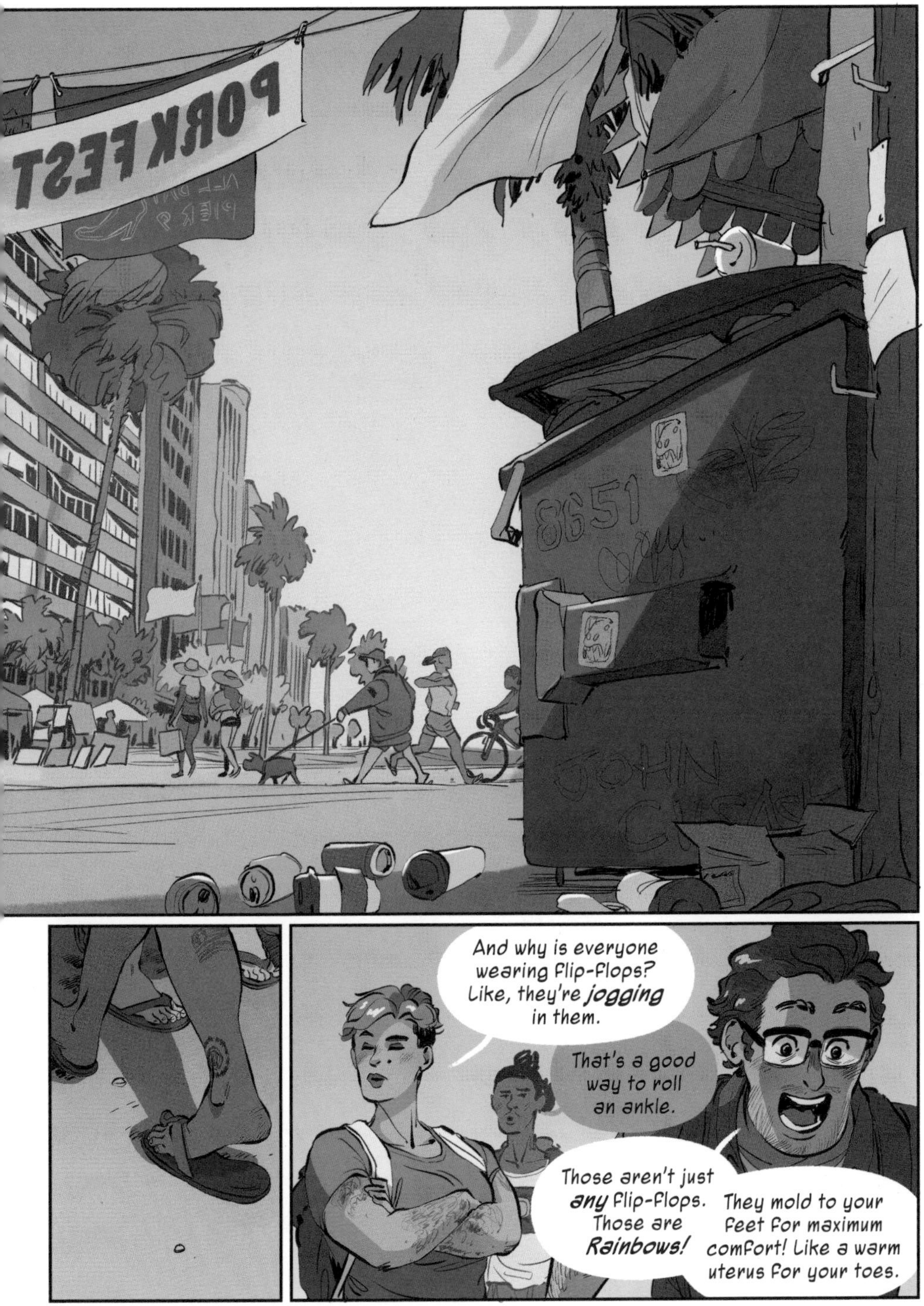
PORK FEST
And why is everyone wearing flip-flops? Like, they're *jogging* in them.
That's a good way to roll an ankle.
Those aren't just *any* flip-flops. Those are *Rainbows!*
They mold to your feet for maximum comfort! Like a warm uterus for your toes.

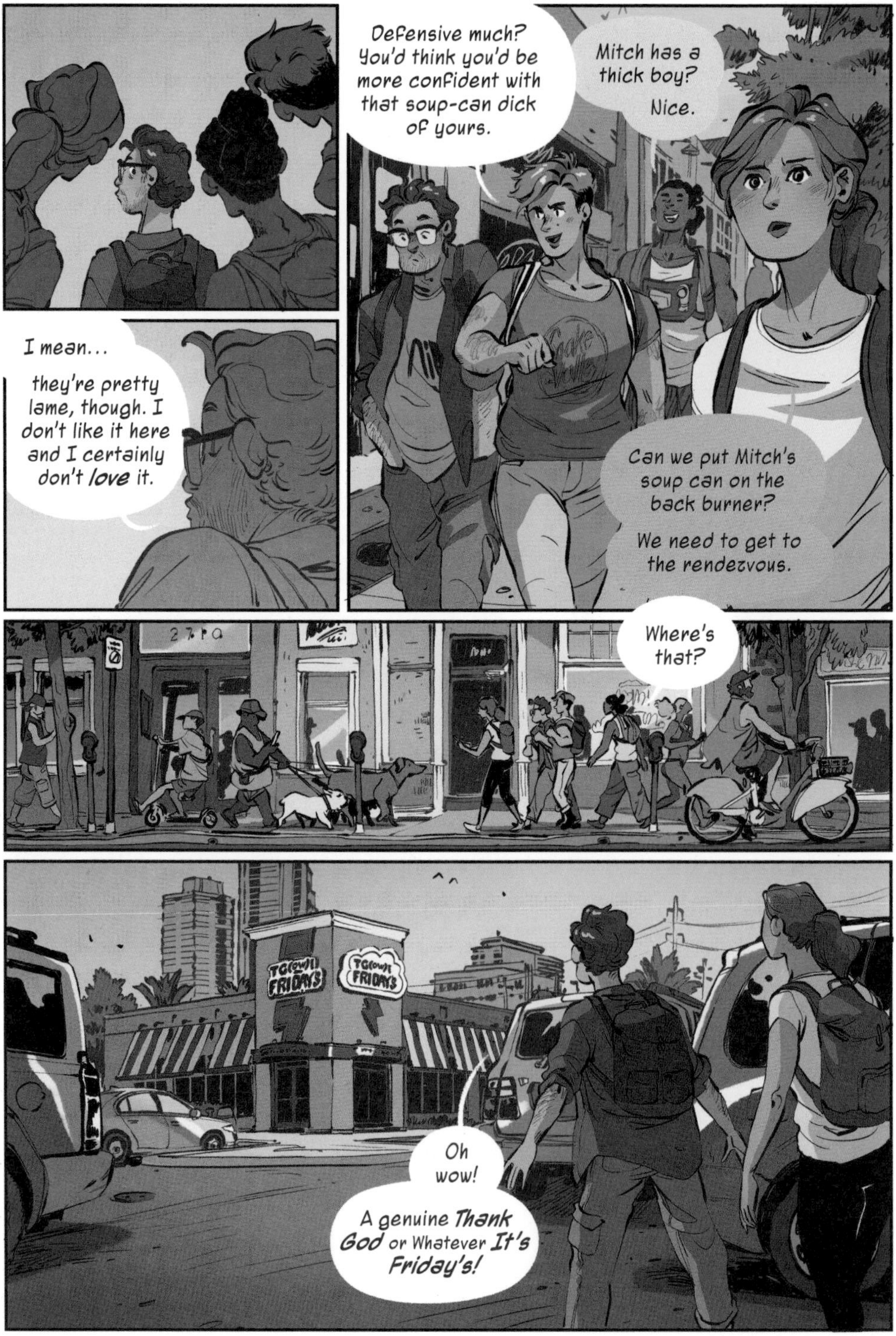
Defensive much? You'd think you'd be more confident with that soup-can dick of yours.
Mitch has a thick boy?
Nice.
I mean...
they're pretty lame, though. I don't like it here and I certainly don't *love* it.
Can we put Mitch's soup can on the back burner?
We need to get to the rendezvous.
Where's that?
TG(ow)I FRIDAYS
TG(ow)I FRIDAYS
Oh wow!
A genuine ***Thank God*** or Whatever ***It's Friday's!***

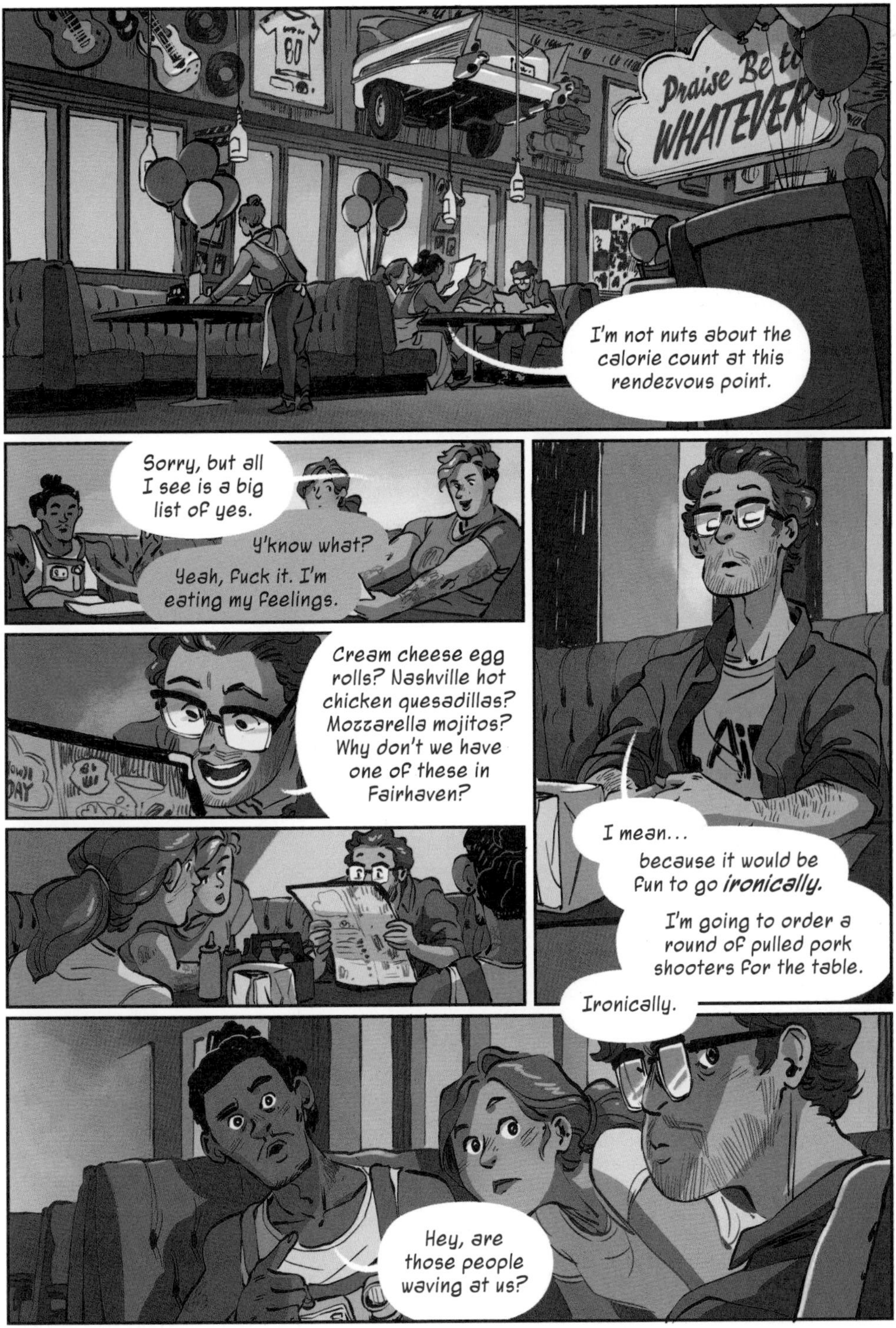
Praise Be to WHATEVER
I'm not nuts about the calorie count at this rendezvous point.
Sorry, but all I see is a big list of yes.
Y'know what?
Yeah, fuck it. I'm eating my feelings.
Cream cheese egg rolls? Nashville hot chicken quesadillas? Mozzarella mojitos? Why don't we have one of these in Fairhaven?
I mean...
because it would be fun to go *ironically.*
I'm going to order a round of pulled pork shooters for the table.
Ironically.
Hey, are those people waving at us?

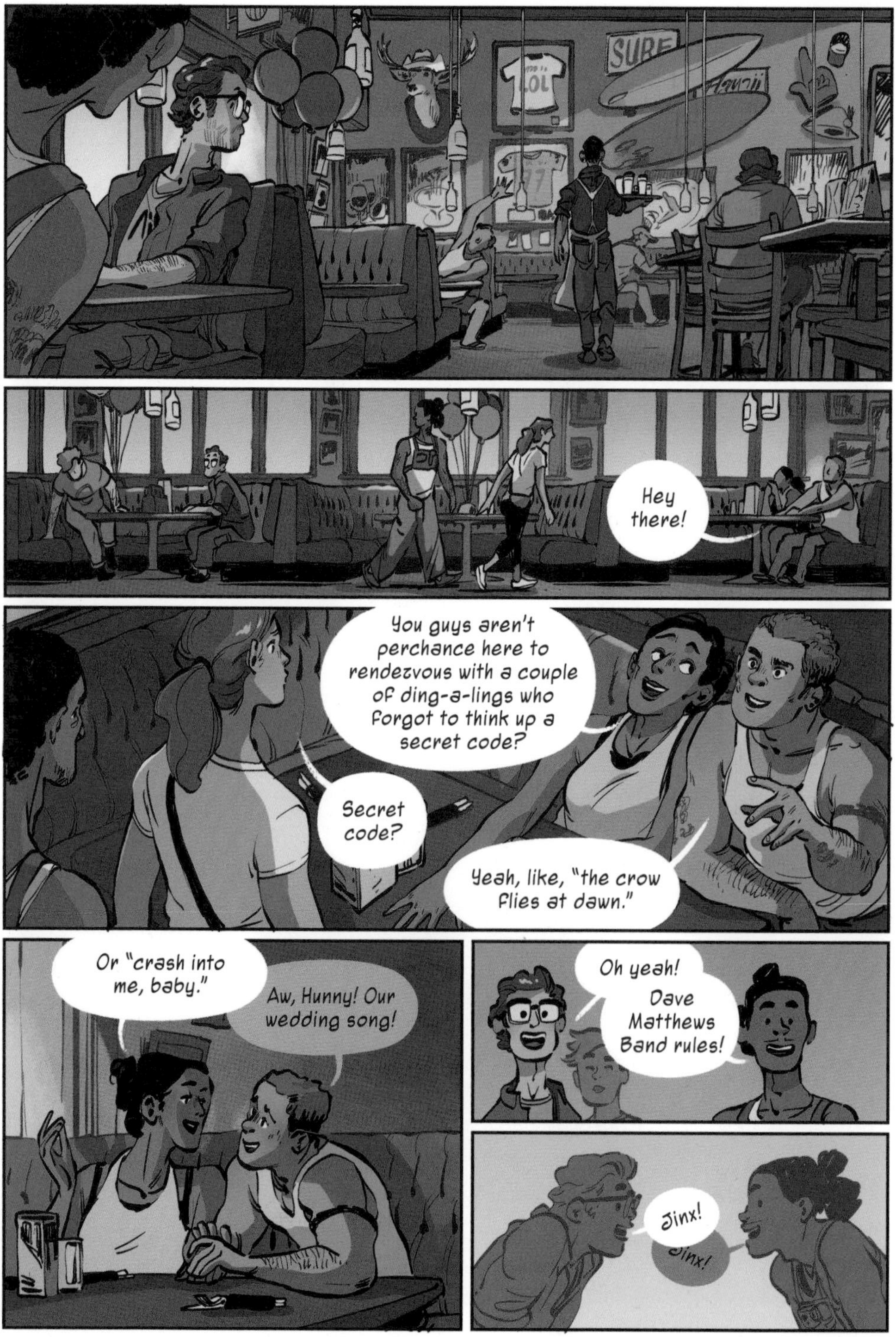
Hey there!
You guys aren't perchance here to rendezvous with a couple of ding-a-lings who forgot to think up a secret code?
Secret code?
Yeah, like, "the crow flies at dawn."
Or "crash into me, baby."
Aw, Hunny! Our wedding song!
Oh yeah!
Dave Matthews Band rules!
Jinx!
Jinx!

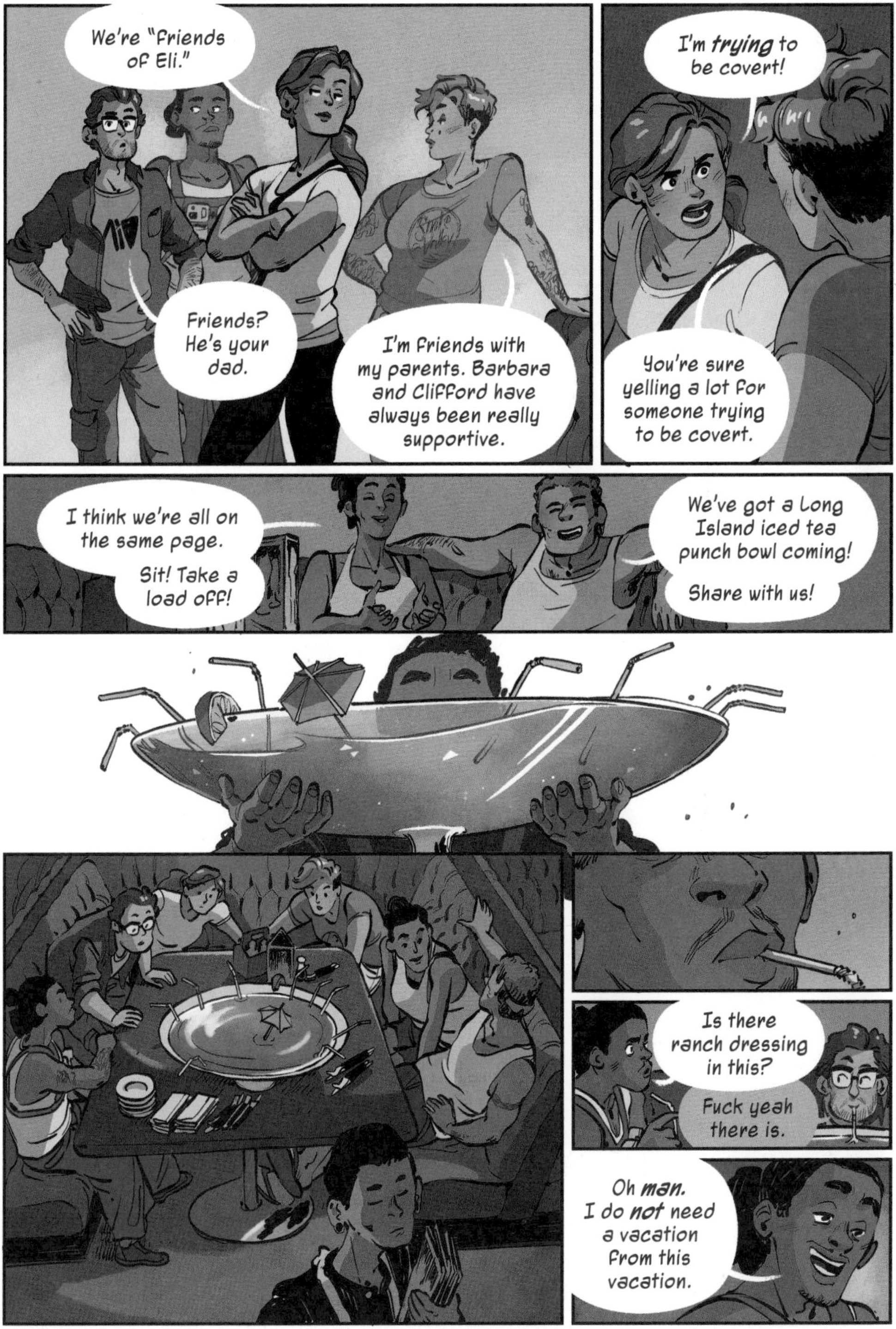
We're "friends of Eli."
Friends? He's your dad.
I'm friends with my parents. Barbara and Clifford have always been really supportive.
I'm ***trying*** to be covert!
You're sure yelling a lot for someone trying to be covert.
I think we're all on the same page.
Sit! Take a load off!
We've got a Long Island iced tea punch bowl coming!
Share with us!
Is there ranch dressing in this?
Fuck yeah there is.
Oh ***man.*** I do ***not*** need a vacation from this vacation.

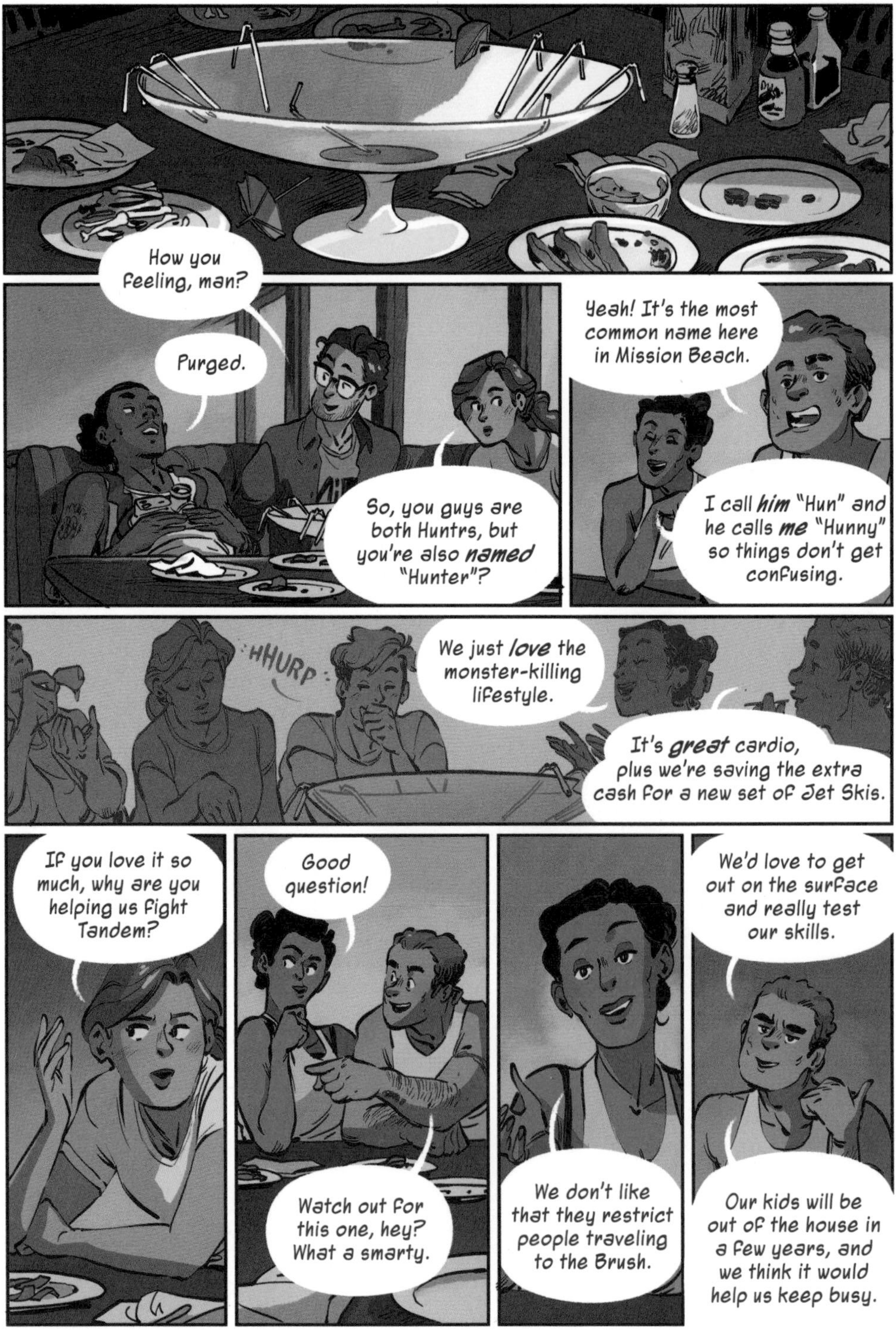
How you feeling, man?
Purged.
So, you guys are both Huntrs, but you're also *named* "Hunter"?
Yeah! It's the most common name here in Mission Beach.
I call *him* "Hun" and he calls *me* "Hunny" so things don't get confusing.
HHURP
We just *love* the monster-killing lifestyle.
It's *great* cardio, plus we're saving the extra cash for a new set of Jet Skis.
If you love it so much, why are you helping us fight Tandem?
Good question!
Watch out for this one, hey? What a smarty.
We don't like that they restrict people traveling to the Brush.
We'd love to get out on the surface and really test our skills.
Our kids will be out of the house in a few years, and we think it would help us keep busy.

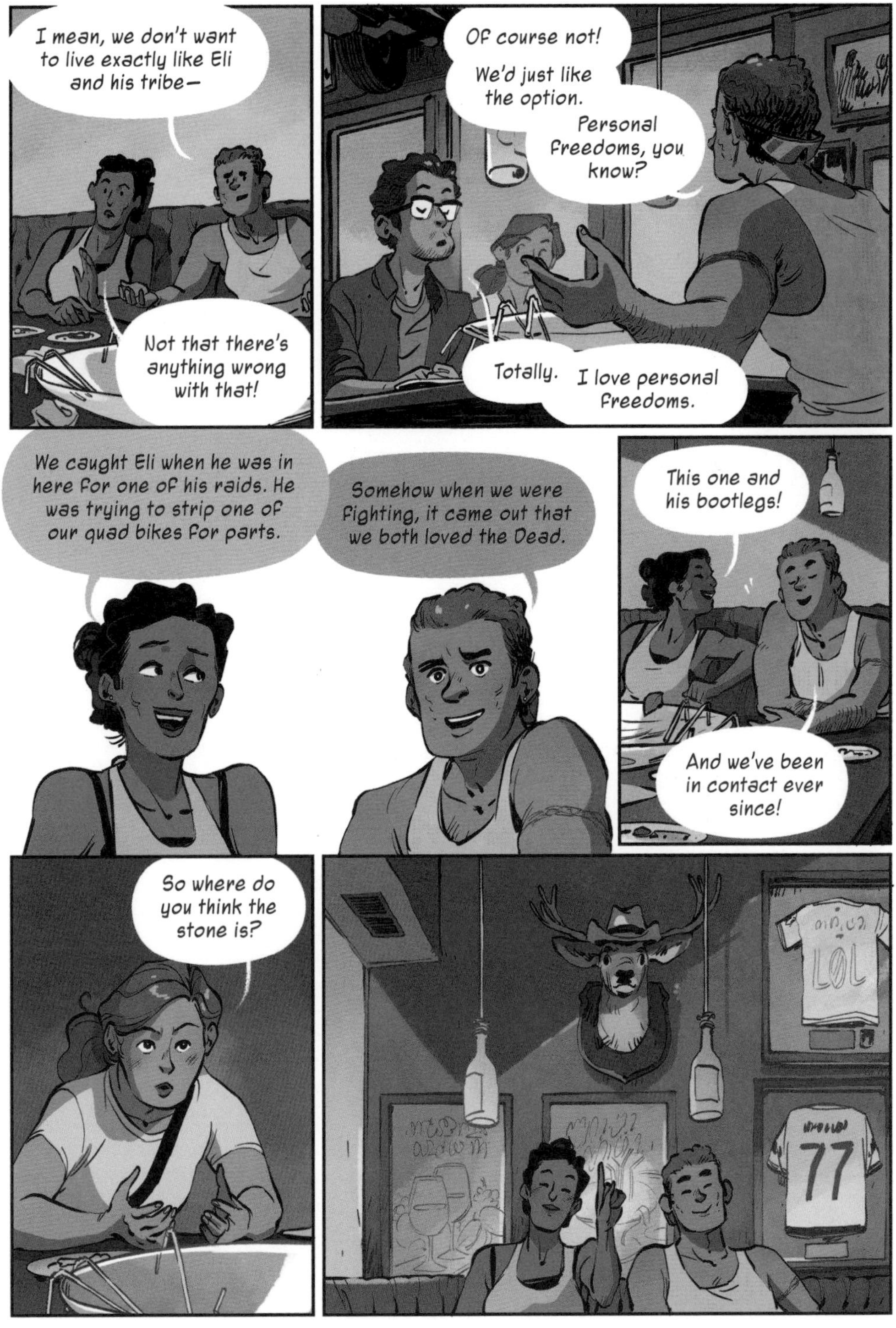
I mean, we don't want to live exactly like Eli and his tribe—
Not that there's anything wrong with that!
Of course not!
We'd just like the option.
Personal freedoms, you know?
Totally.
I love personal freedoms.
We caught Eli when he was in here for one of his raids. He was trying to strip one of our quad bikes for parts.
Somehow when we were fighting, it came out that we both loved the Dead.
This one and his bootlegs!
And we've been in contact ever since!
So where do you think the stone is?
LOL
77

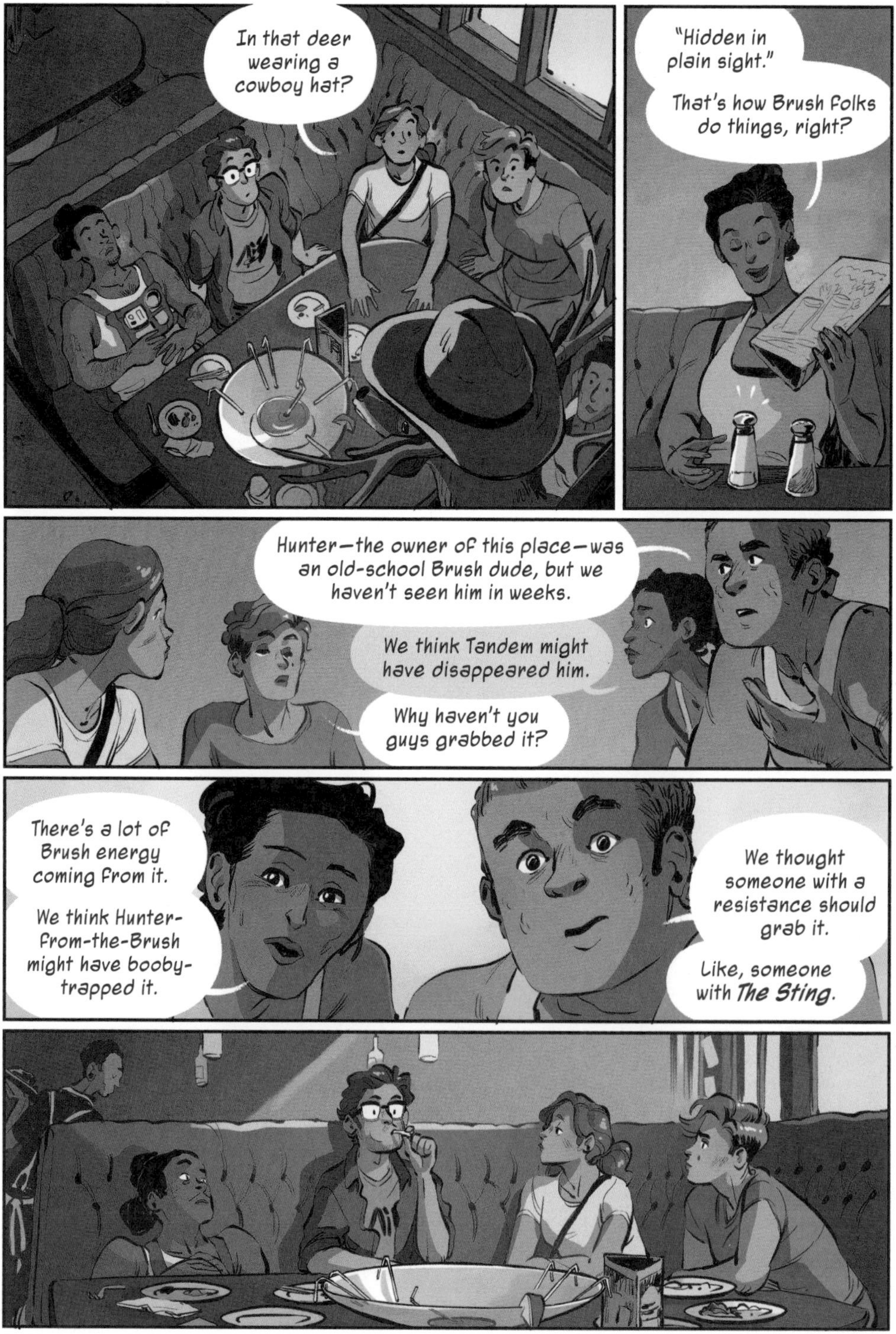
In that deer wearing a cowboy hat?
"Hidden in plain sight."
That's how Brush folks do things, right?
Hunter—the owner of this place—was an old-school Brush dude, but we haven't seen him in weeks.
We think Tandem might have disappeared him.
Why haven't you guys grabbed it?
There's a lot of Brush energy coming from it.
We think Hunter-from-the-Brush might have booby-trapped it.
We thought someone with a resistance should grab it.
Like, someone with *The Sting*.

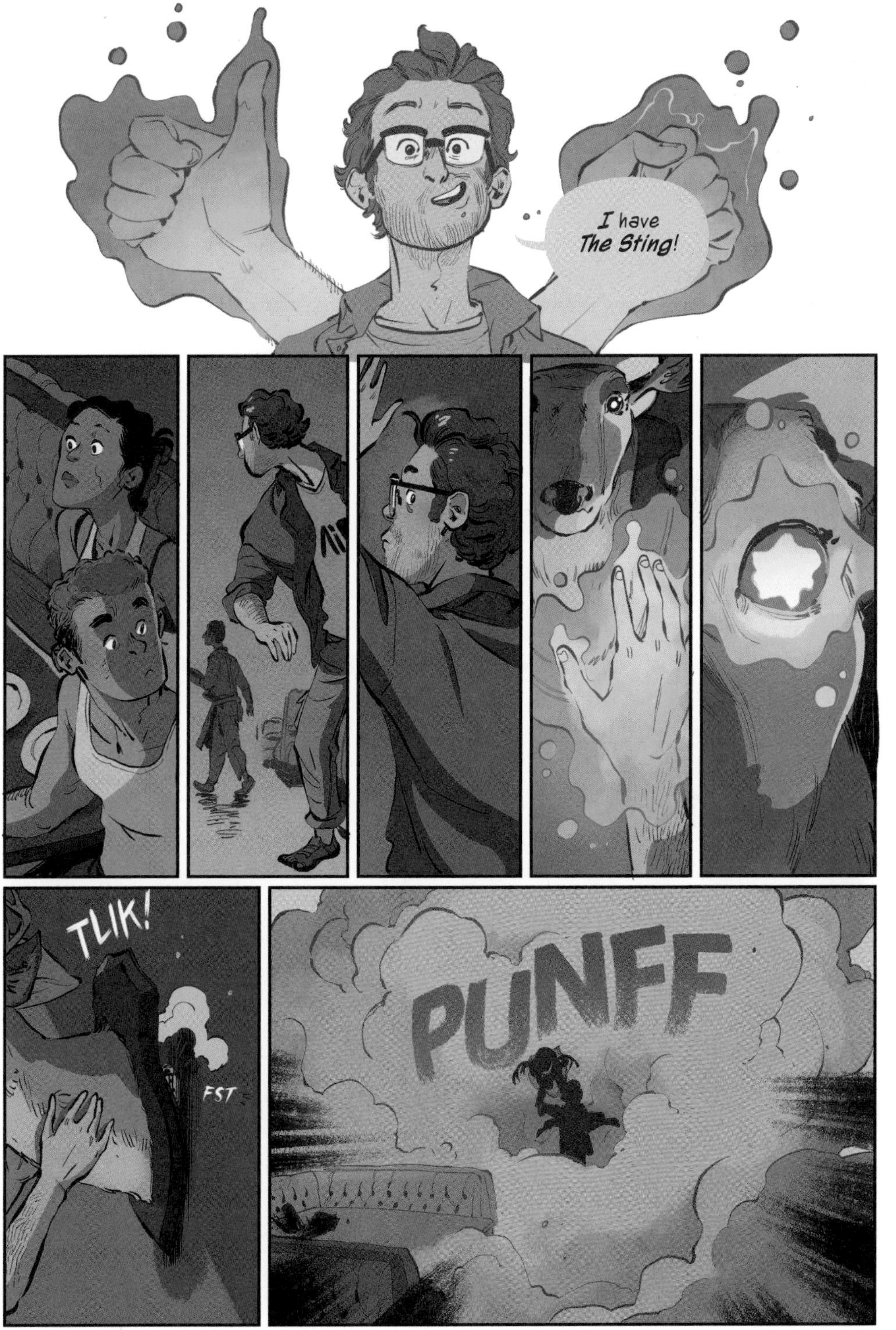
I have
The Sting!
TLIK!
FST
PUNFF

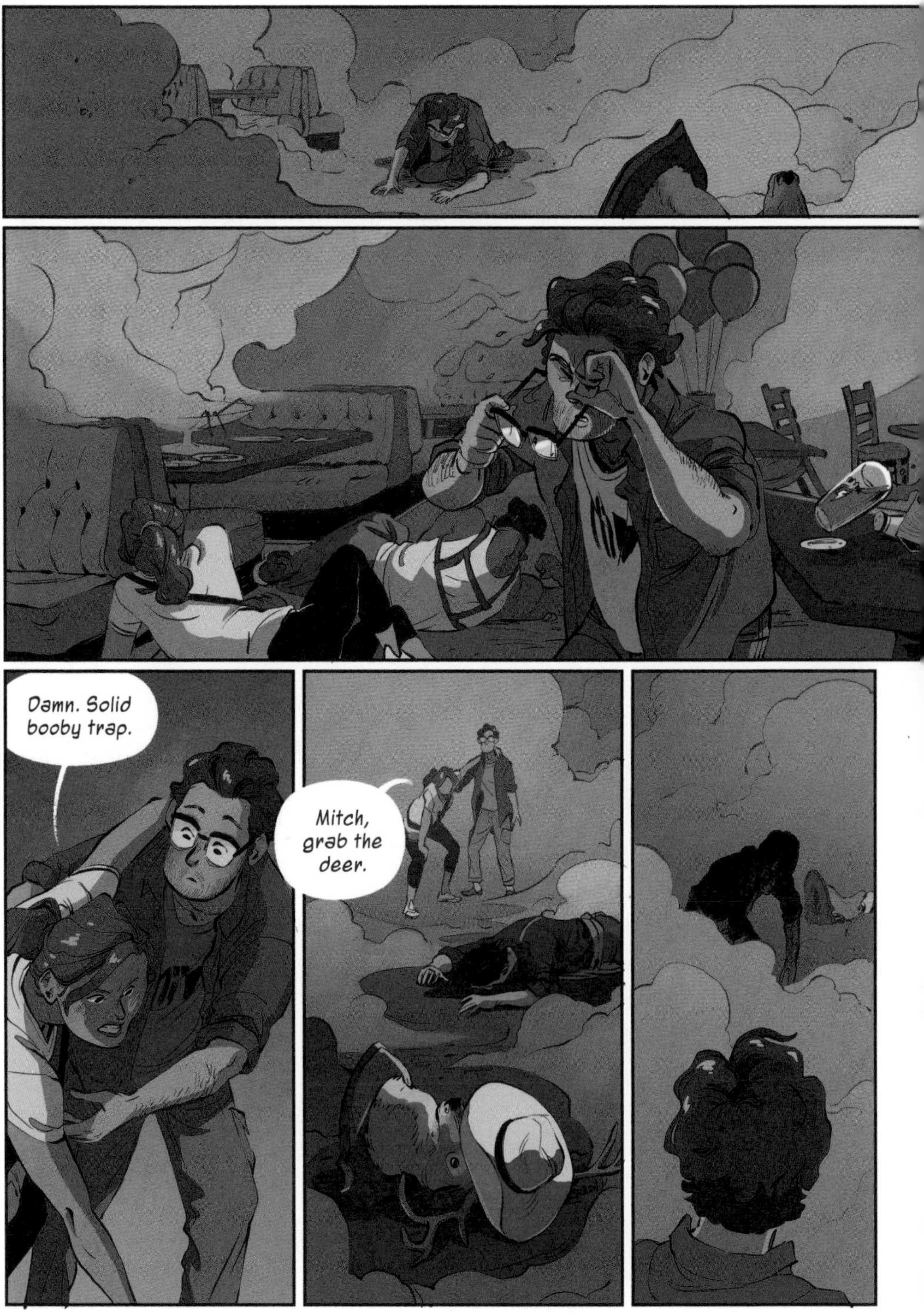
Damn. Solid booby trap.
Mitch, grab the deer.

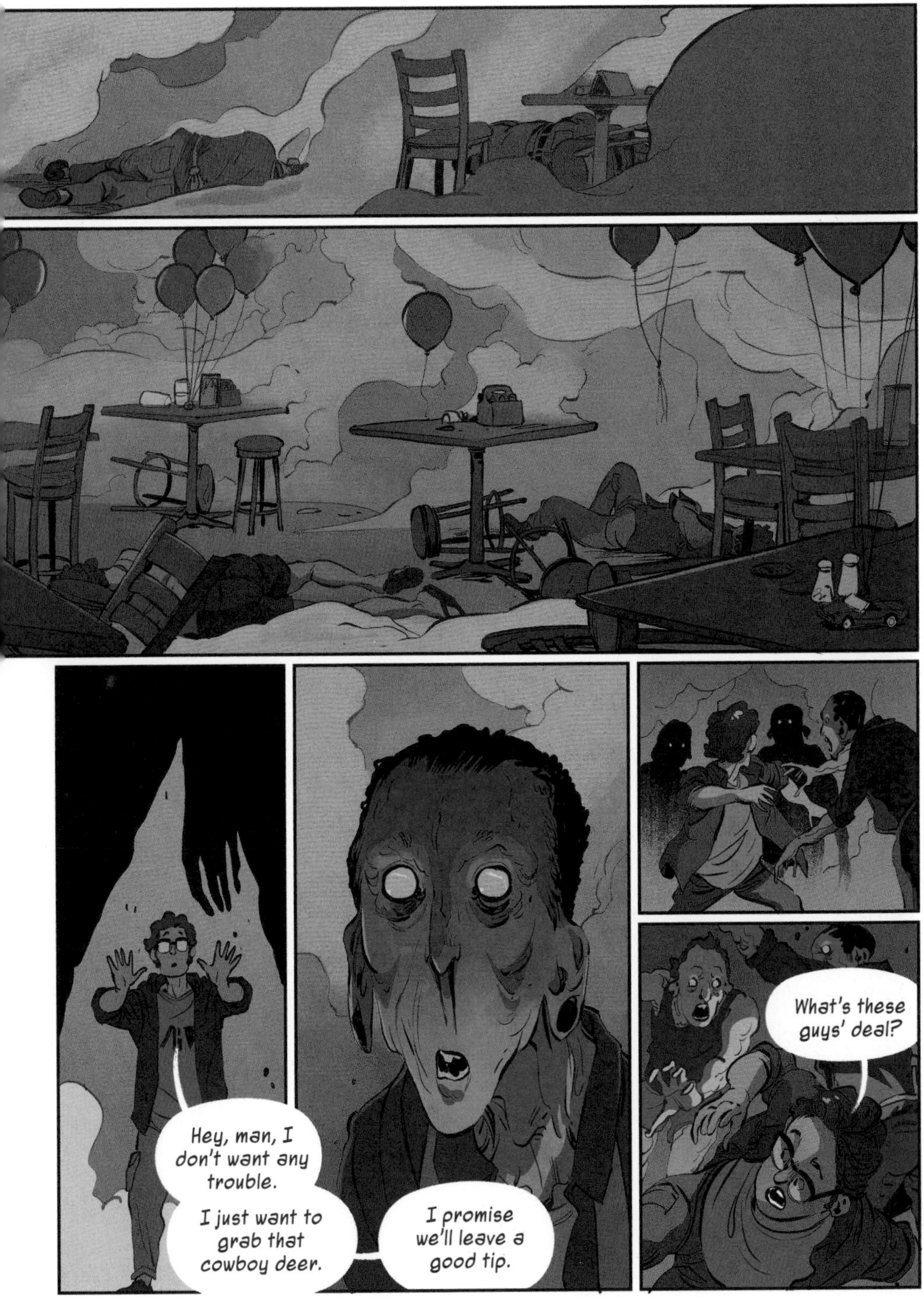
Hey, man, I don't want any trouble.
I just want to grab that cowboy deer.
I promise we'll leave a good tip.
What's these guys' deal?

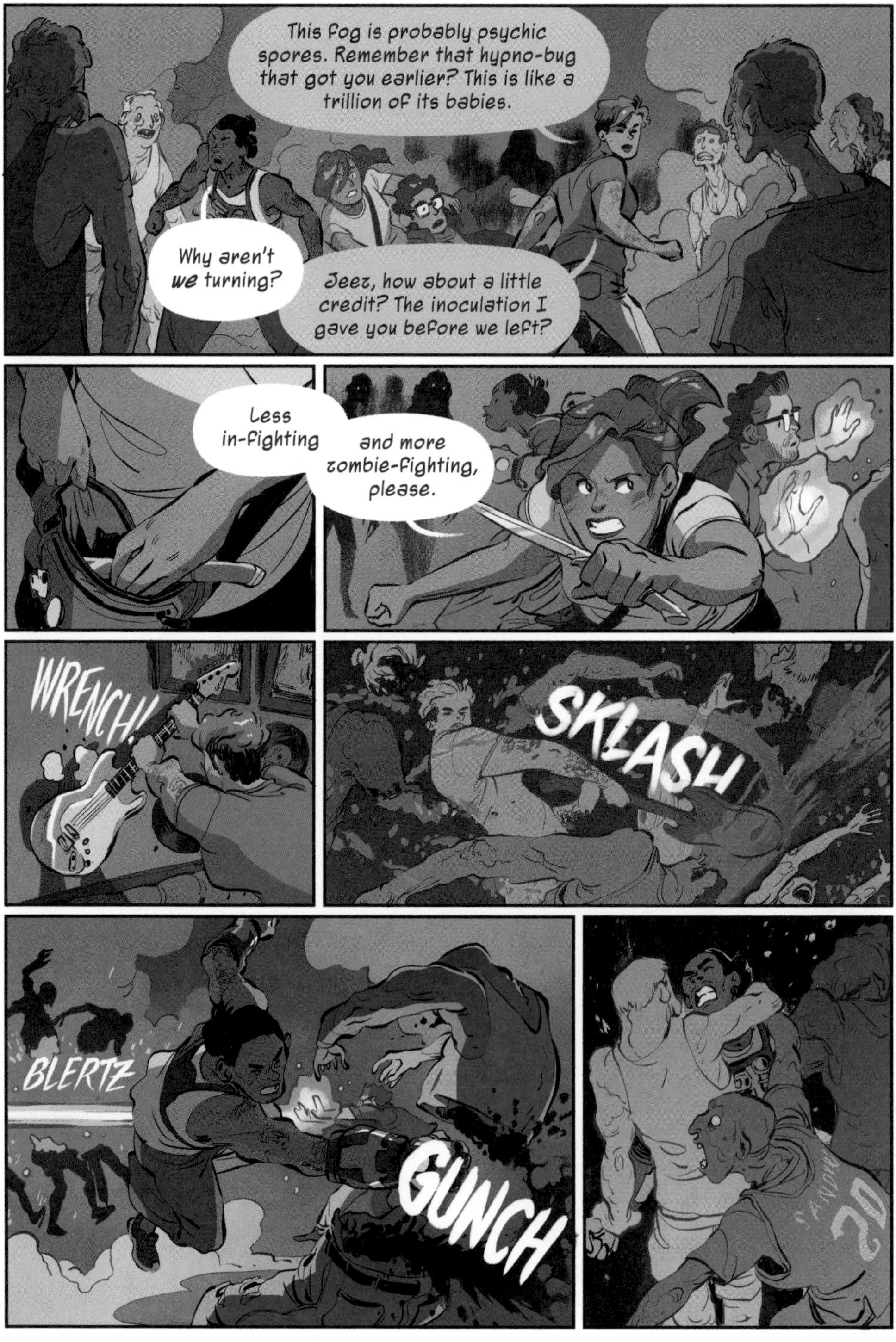
This fog is probably psychic spores. Remember that hypno-bug that got you earlier? This is like a trillion of its babies.
Why aren't *we* turning?
Jeez, how about a little credit? The inoculation I gave you before we left?
Less in-fighting
and more zombie-fighting, please.
WRENCH!
SKLASH
BLERTZ
GUNCH
20

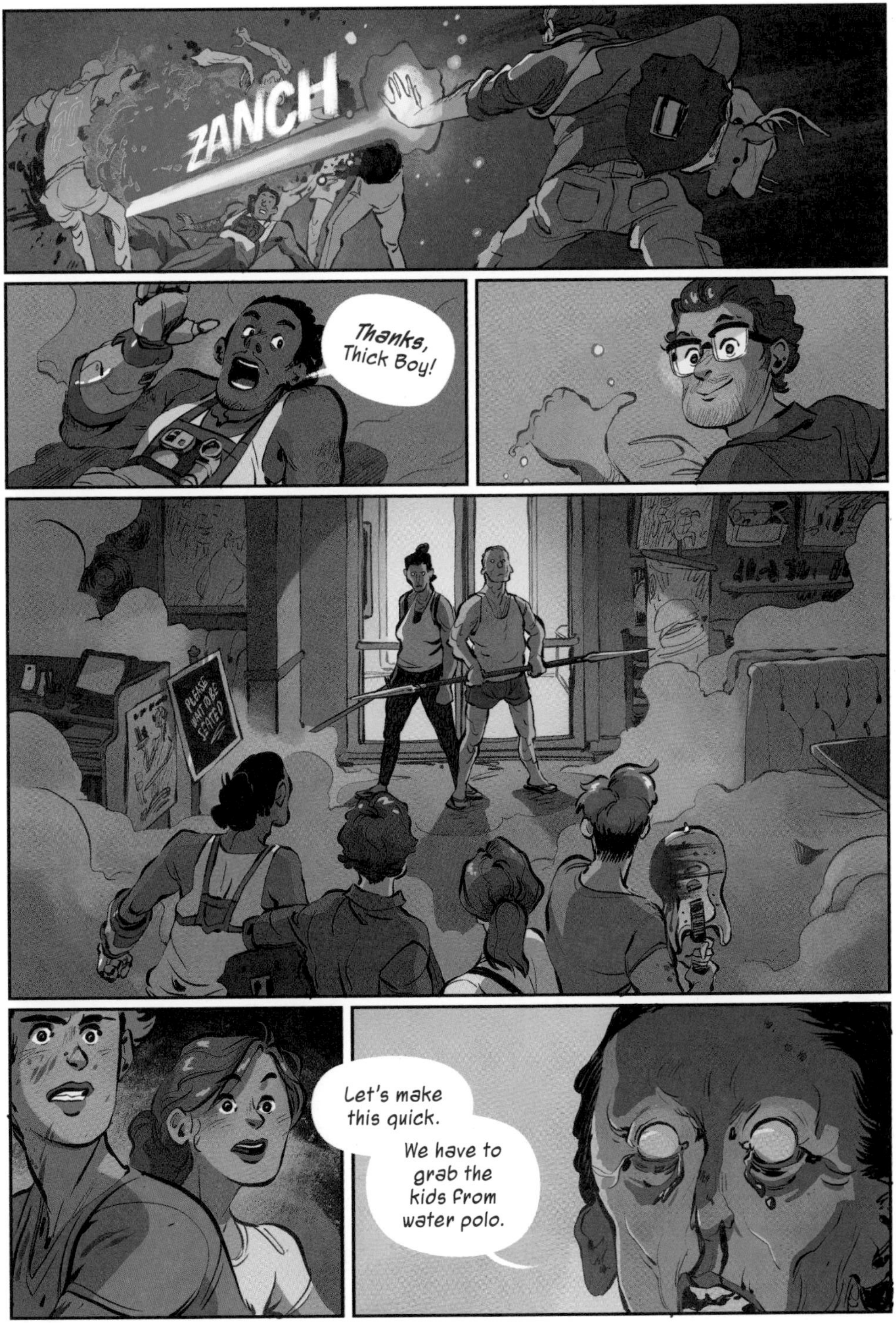
ZANCH
Thanks, Thick Boy!
PLEASE WAIT TO BE SEATED
Let's make this quick.
We have to grab the kids from water polo.

bubble

A GRAPHIC NOVEL

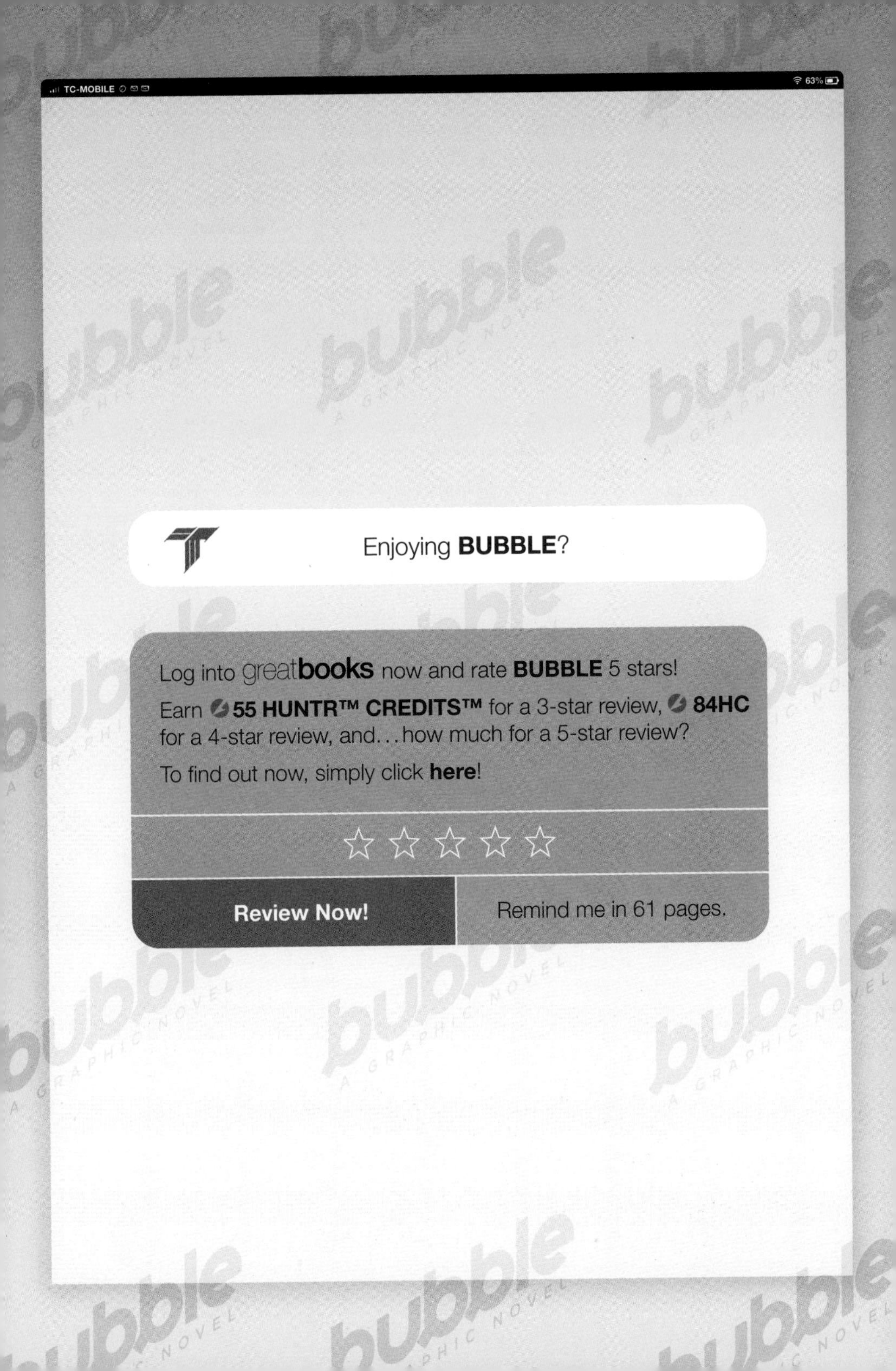
TC-MOBILE
63%
Enjoying BUBBLE?
Log into greatbooks now and rate BUBBLE 5 stars!
Earn 55 HUNTR™ CREDITS™ for a 3-star review, 84HC for a 4-star review, and...how much for a 5-star review?
To find out now, simply click here!
Review Now!
Remind me in 61 pages.

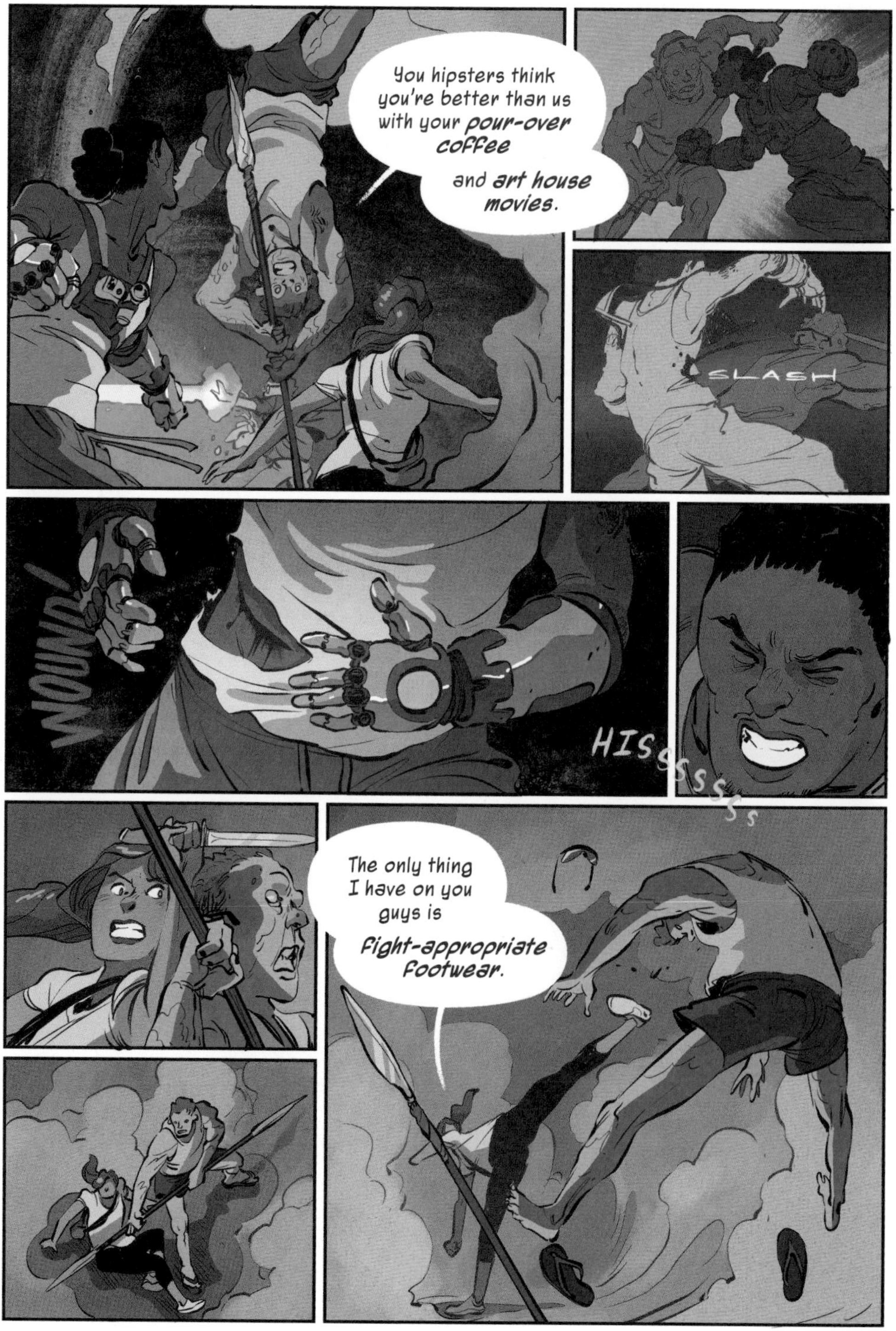
You hipsters think you're better than us with your pour-over coffee
and art house movies.
SLASH
WOOMM!
HISSSSSSSS
The only thing I have on you guys is
fight-appropriate footwear.

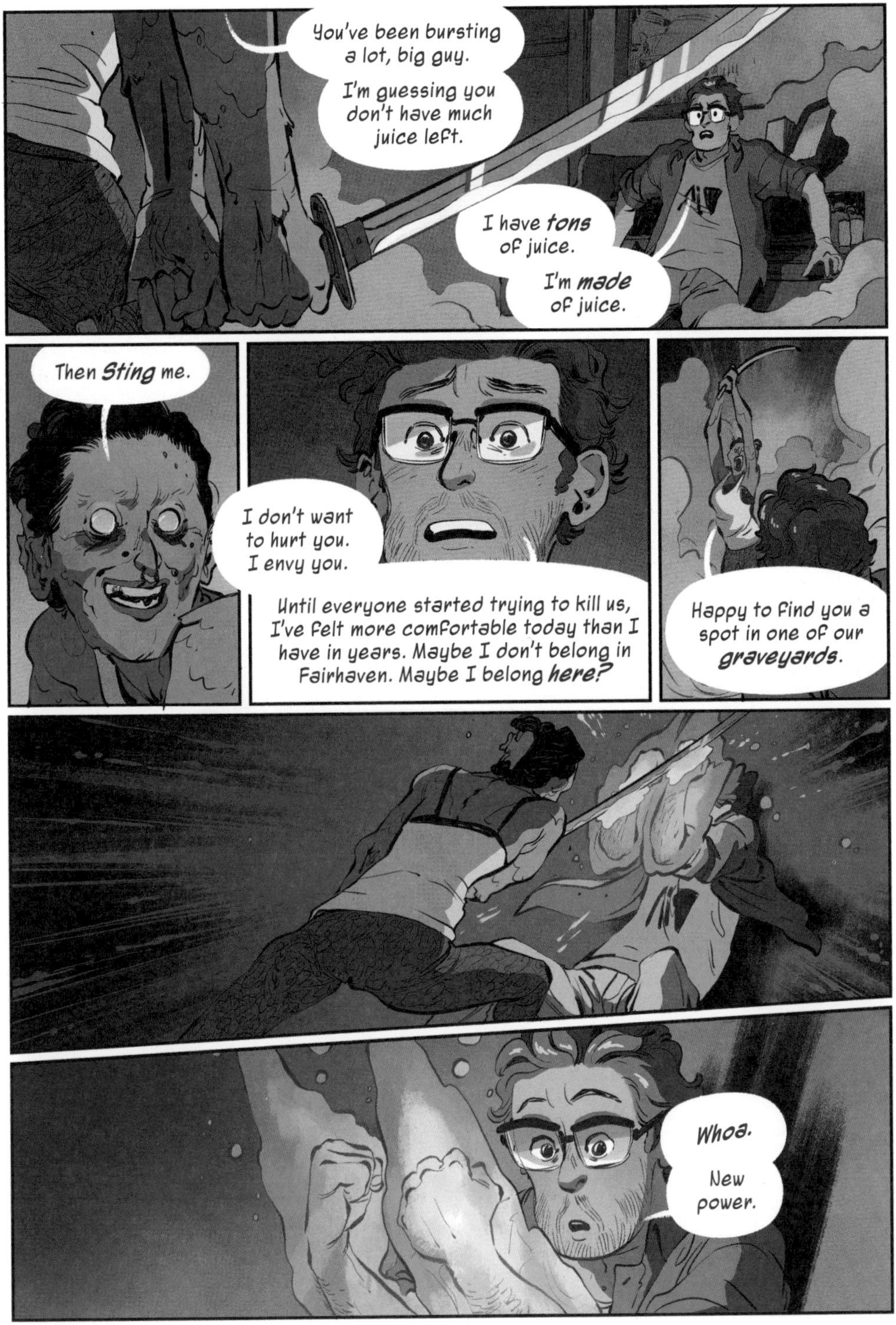
You've been bursting a lot, big guy.
I'm guessing you don't have much juice left.
I have tons of juice.
I'm made of juice.
Then Sting me.
I don't want to hurt you. I envy you.
Until everyone started trying to kill us, I've felt more comfortable today than I have in years. Maybe I don't belong in Fairhaven. Maybe I belong here?
Happy to find you a spot in one of our graveyards.
Whoa.
New power.

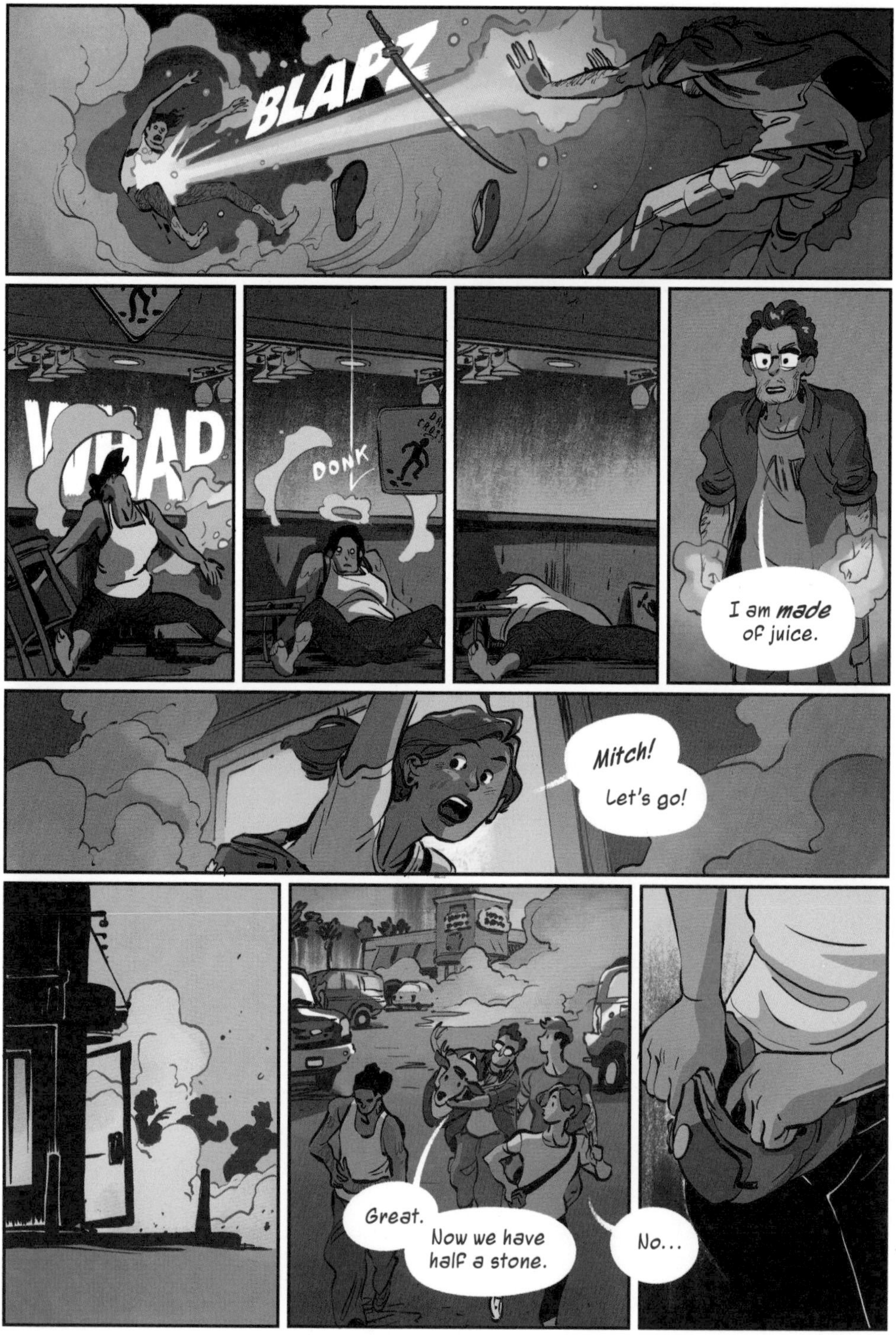
BLAPZ
WHAD
DONK
I am *made* of juice.
Mitch!
Let's go!
Great.
Now we have half a stone.
No...

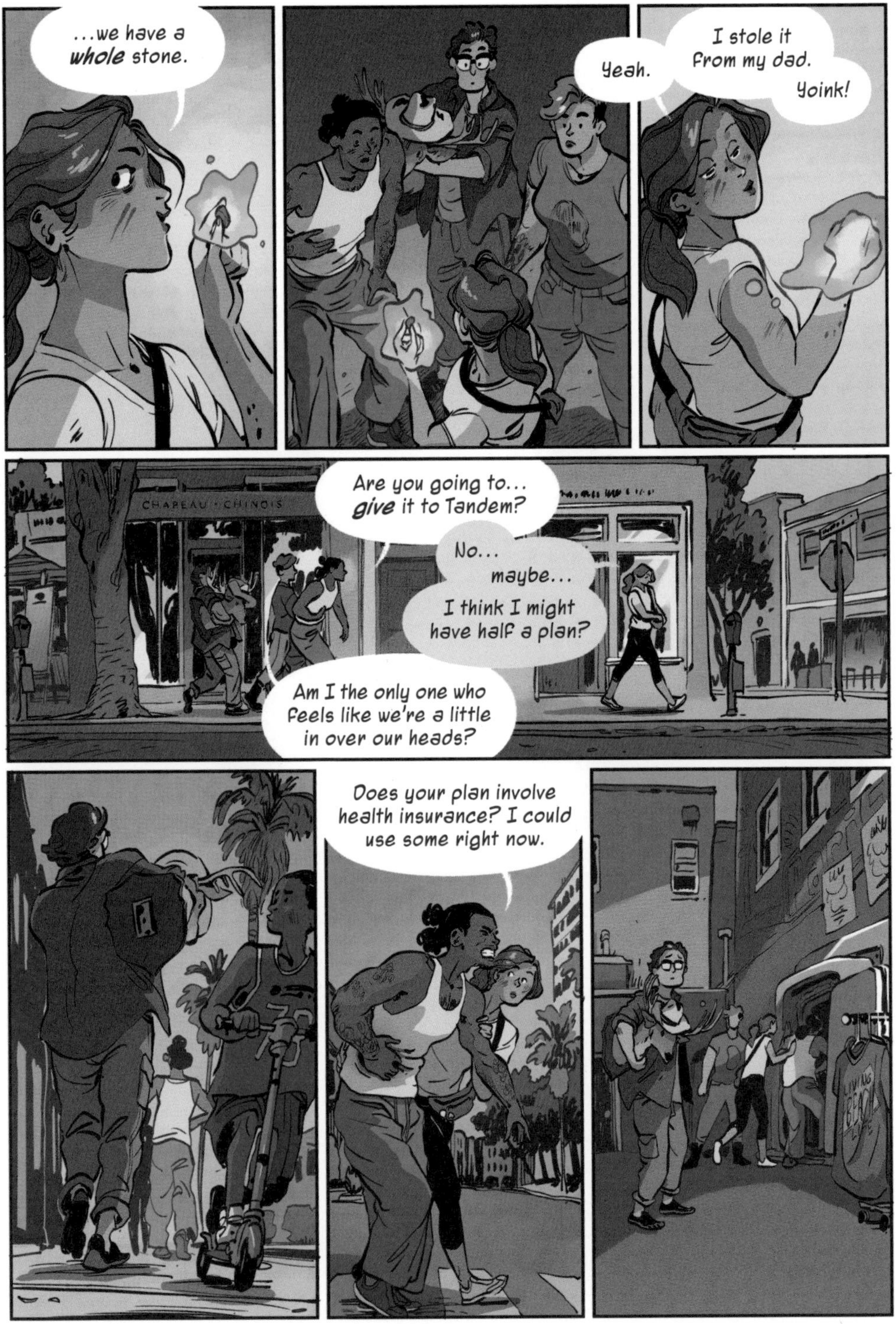
...we have a *whole* stone.
Yeah.
I stole it from my dad.
Yoink!
CHAPEAU CHINOIS
Are you going to... *give* it to Tandem?
No... maybe...
I think I might have half a plan?
Am I the only one who feels like we're a little in over our heads?
Does your plan involve health insurance? I could use some right now.

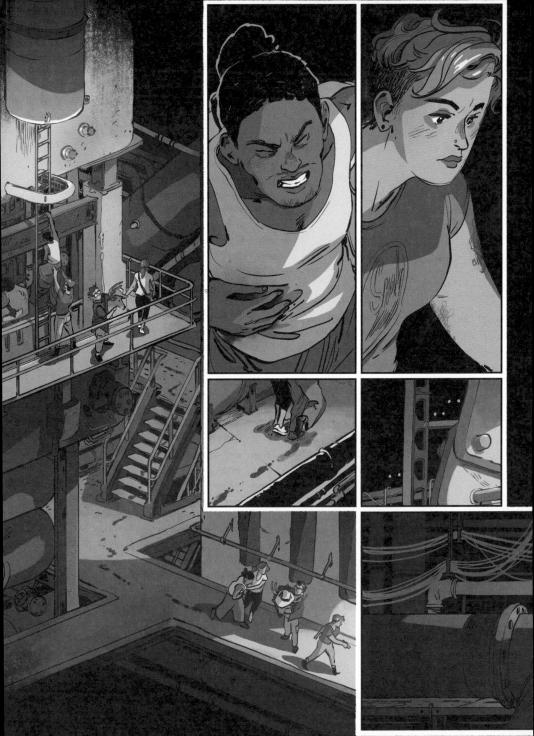

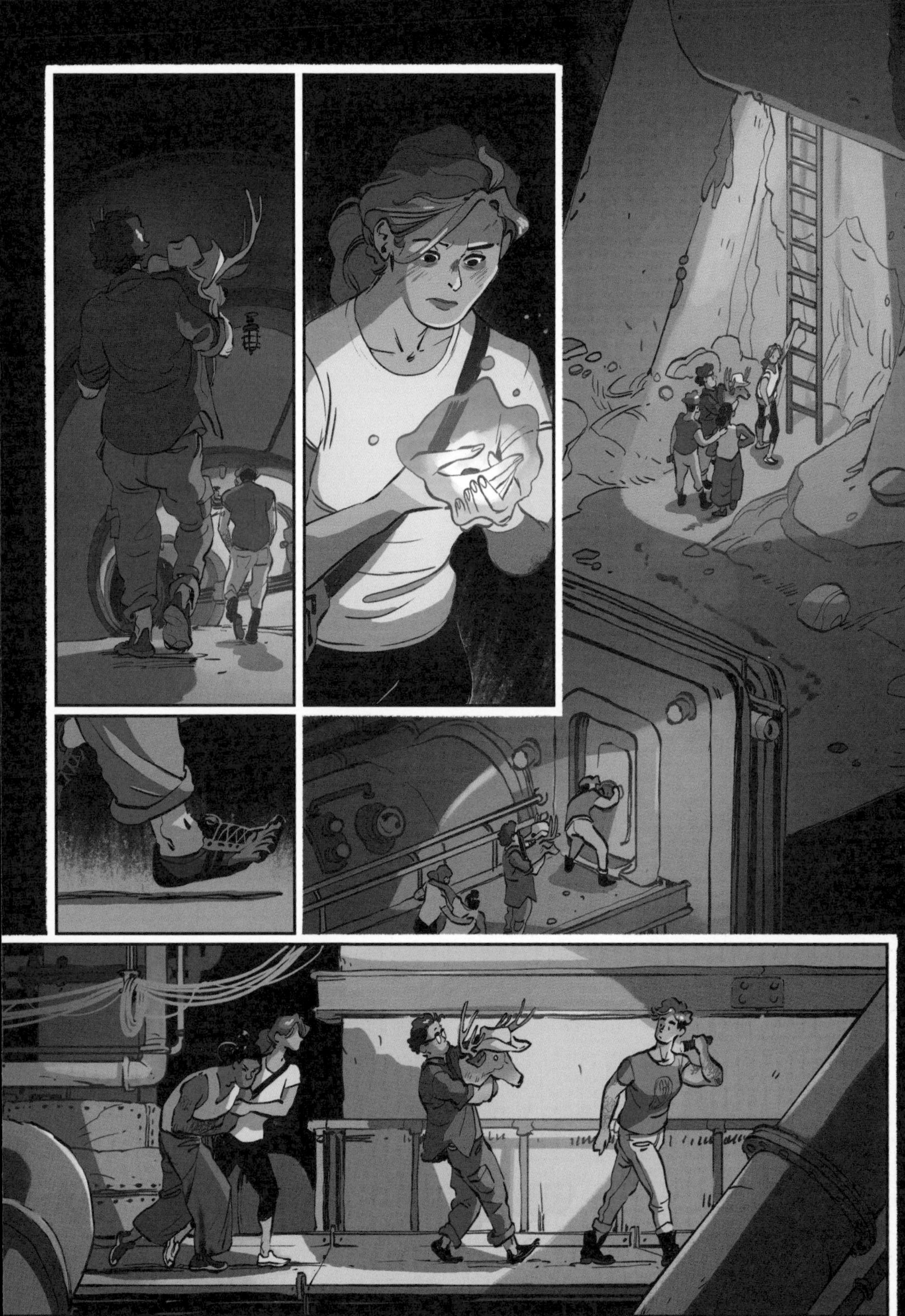

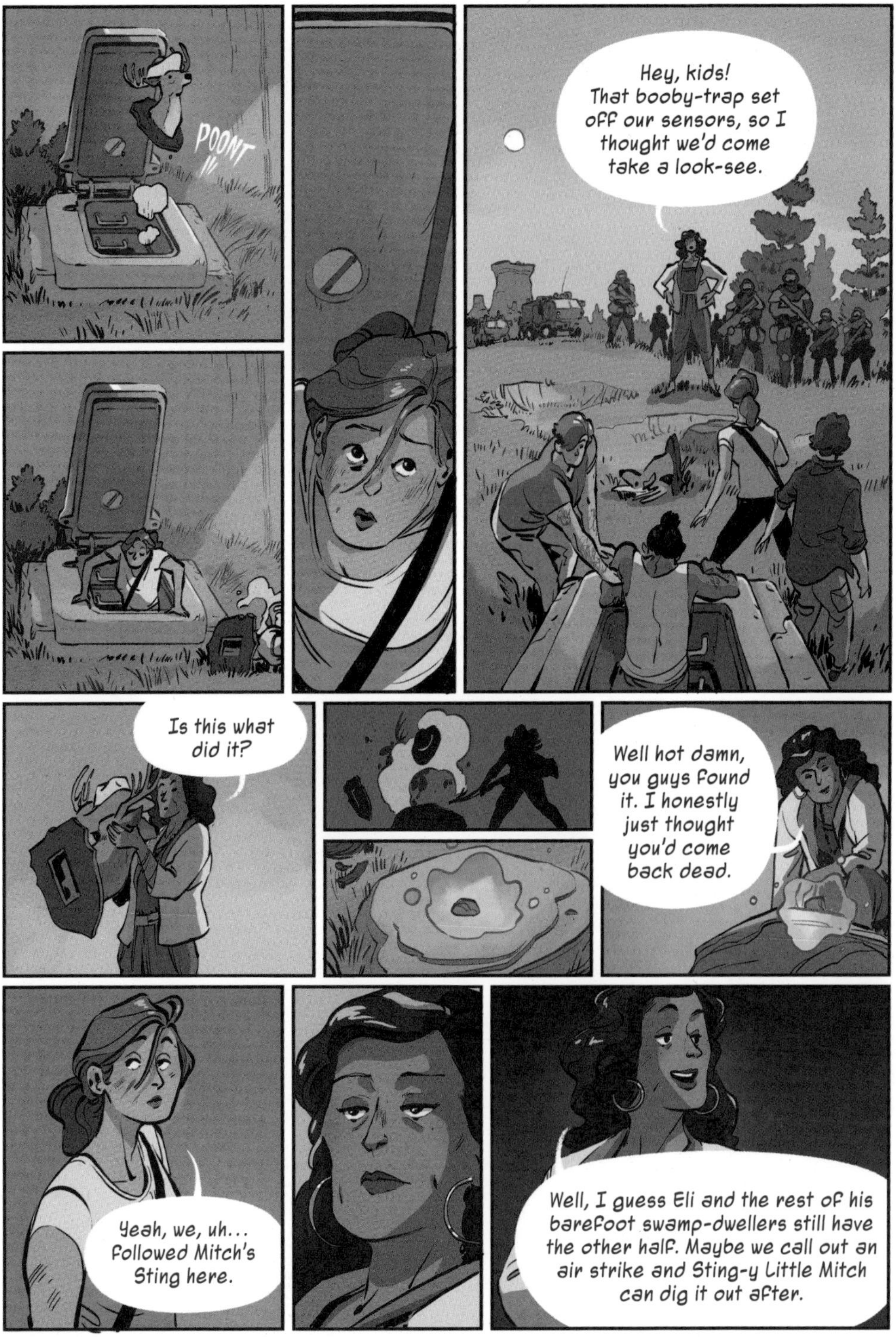
POONT
Hey, kids! That booby-trap set off our sensors, so I thought we'd come take a look-see.
Is this what did it?
Well hot damn, you guys found it. I honestly just thought you'd come back dead.
Yeah, we, uh... followed Mitch's Sting here.
Well, I guess Eli and the rest of his barefoot swamp-dwellers still have the other half. Maybe we call out an air strike and Sting-y Little Mitch can dig it out after.

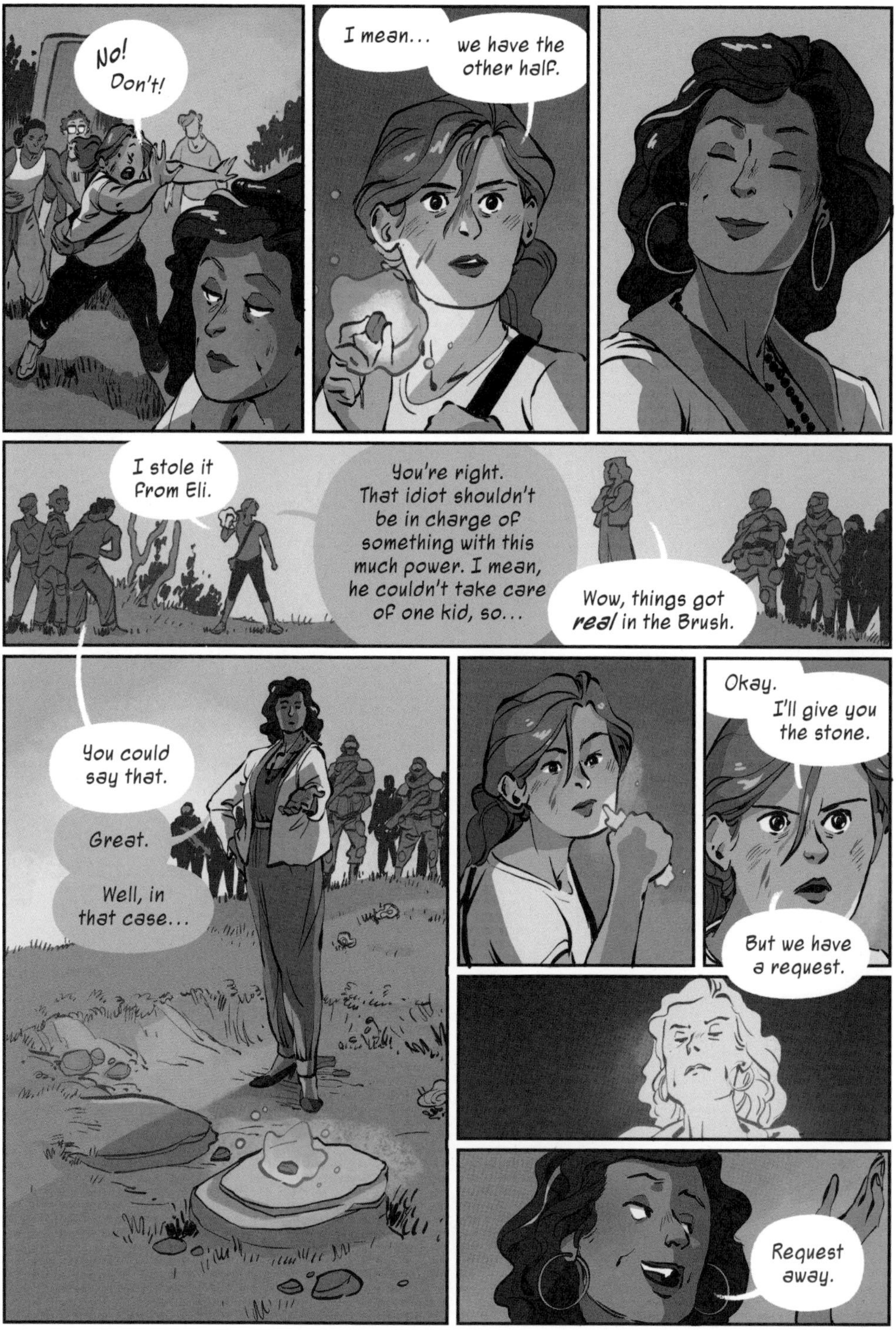

No! Don't!
I mean...
we have the other half.
I stole it from Eli.
You're right. That idiot shouldn't be in charge of something with this much power. I mean, he couldn't take care of one kid, so...
Wow, things got *real* in the Brush.
You could say that.
Great.
Well, in that case...
Okay.
I'll give you the stone.
But we have a request.
Request away.

Jobs.

We want real, grown-up jobs.

With health insurance.

And cereal bar access.

And flexible hours.

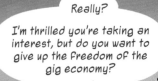

Really?

I'm thrilled you're taking an interest, but do you want to give up the freedom of the gig economy?

"Freedom," *ha*.

Please, Bonnie, we can't keep hunting forever.

What about getting your adventure ya-yas?

They're gone.

My friends have almost died too many times.

Still kind of a possibility over here.

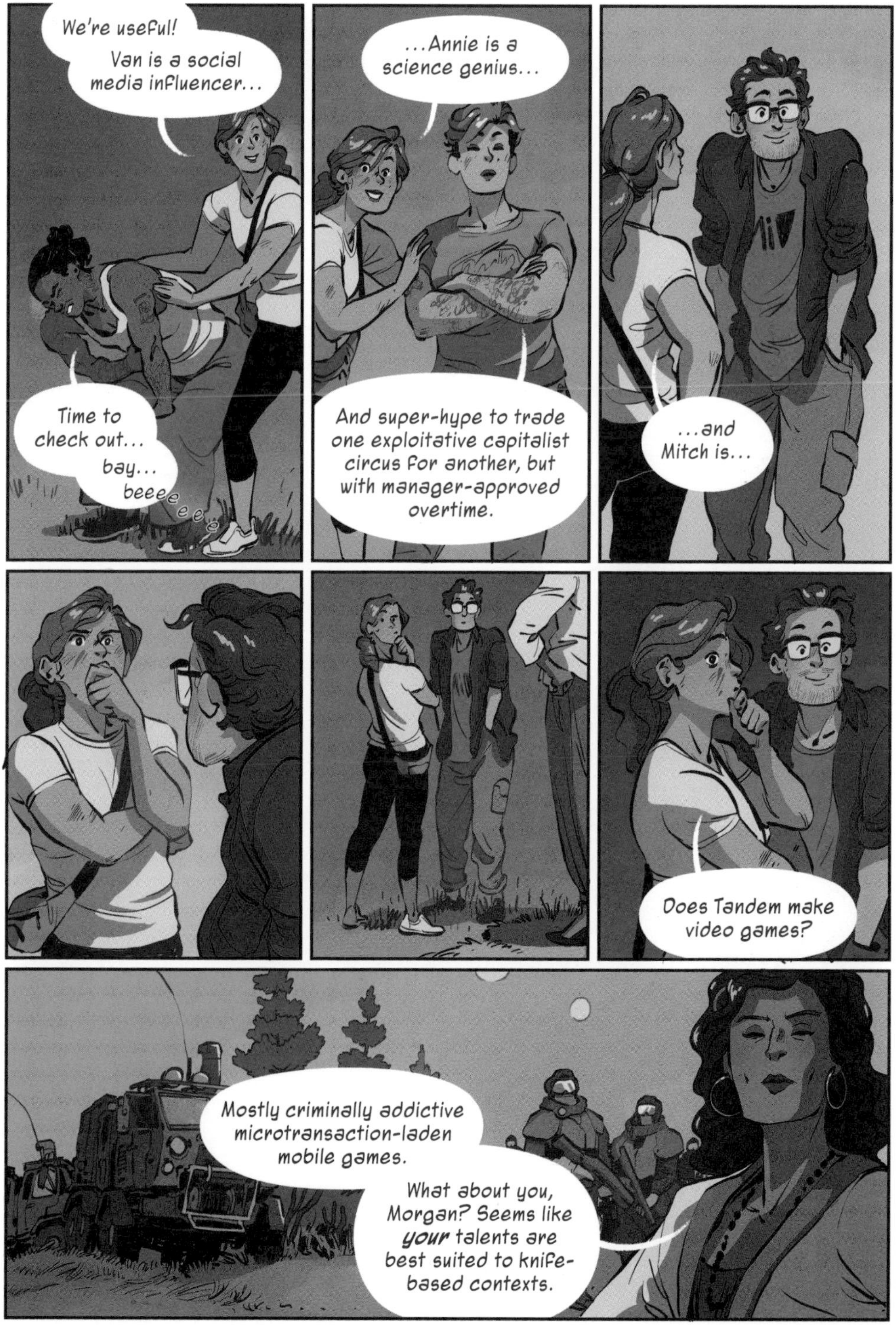

We're useful!
Van is a social media influencer...
Time to check out... bay... beeeeeee
...Annie is a science genius...
And super-hype to trade one exploitative capitalist circus for another, but with manager-approved overtime.
...and Mitch is...
Does Tandem make video games?
Mostly criminally addictive microtransaction-laden mobile games.
What about you, Morgan? Seems like *your* talents are best suited to knife-based contexts.

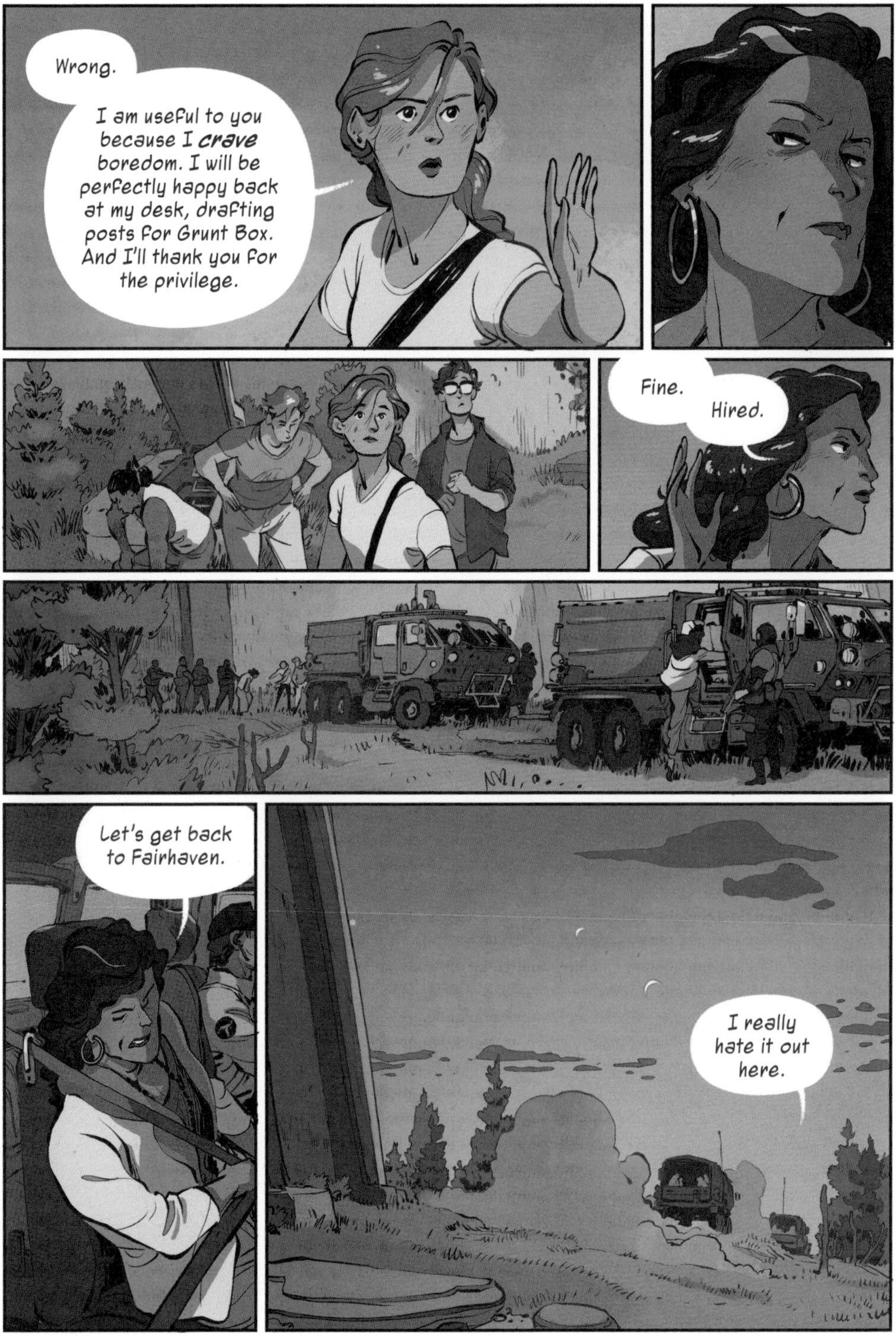
Wrong.
I am useful to you because I *crave* boredom. I will be perfectly happy back at my desk, drafting posts for Grunt Box. And I'll thank you for the privilege.
Fine.
Hired.
Let's get back to Fairhaven.
I really hate it out here.

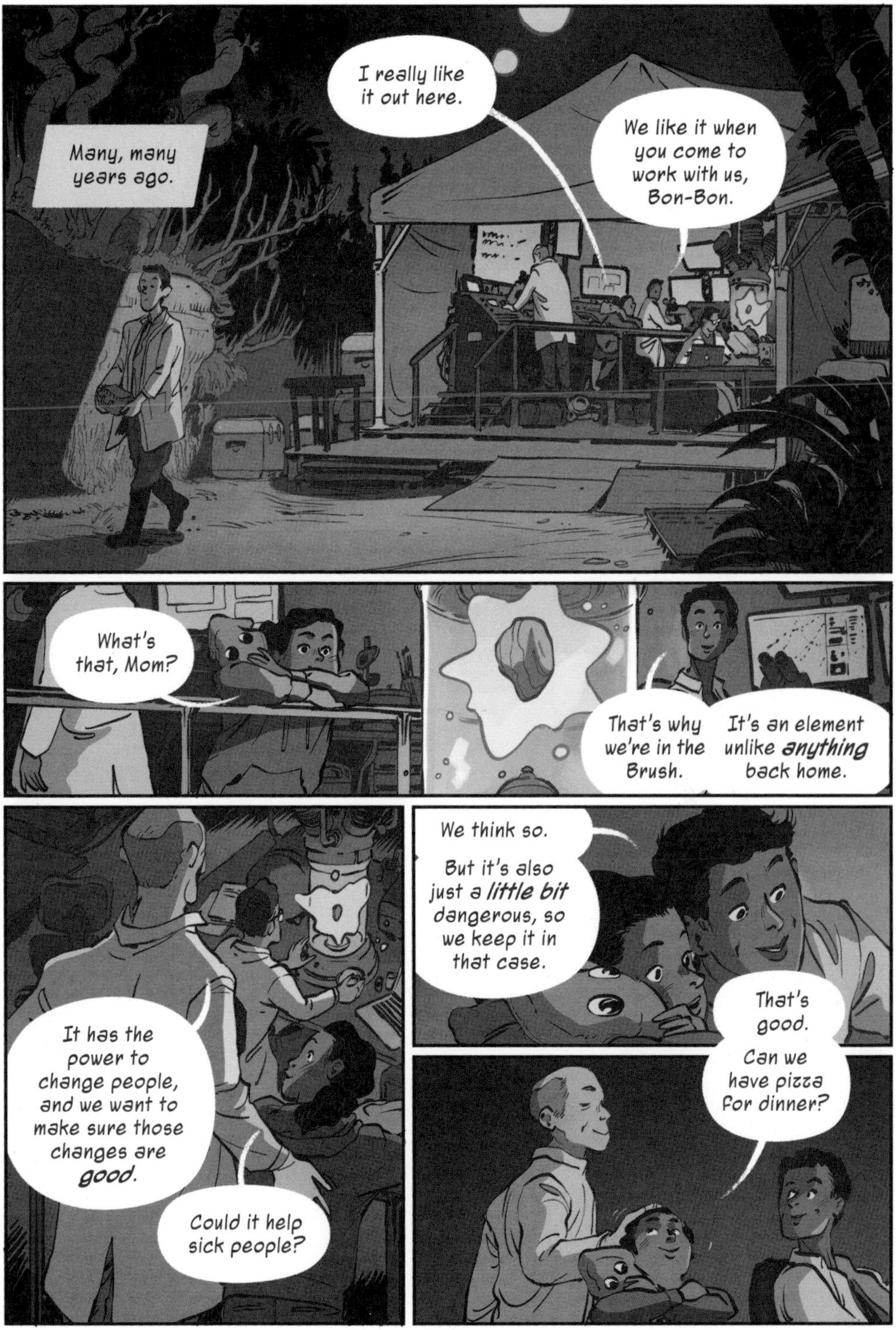
Many, many years ago.
I really like it out here.
We like it when you come to work with us, Bon-Bon.
What's that, Mom?
It's an element unlike *anything* back home.
That's why we're in the Brush.
It has the power to change people, and we want to make sure those changes are *good*.
Could it help sick people?
We think so.
But it's also just a *little bit* dangerous, so we keep it in that case.
That's good.
Can we have pizza for dinner?

BWEEE

What's going on?

Don't know, don't know!

It's too highly charged!

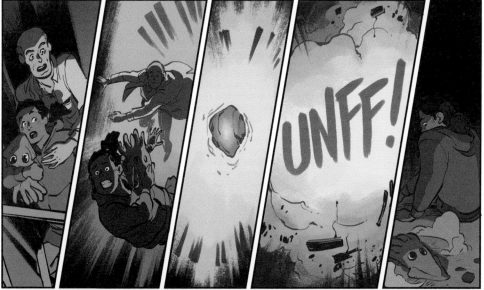

UNFF!

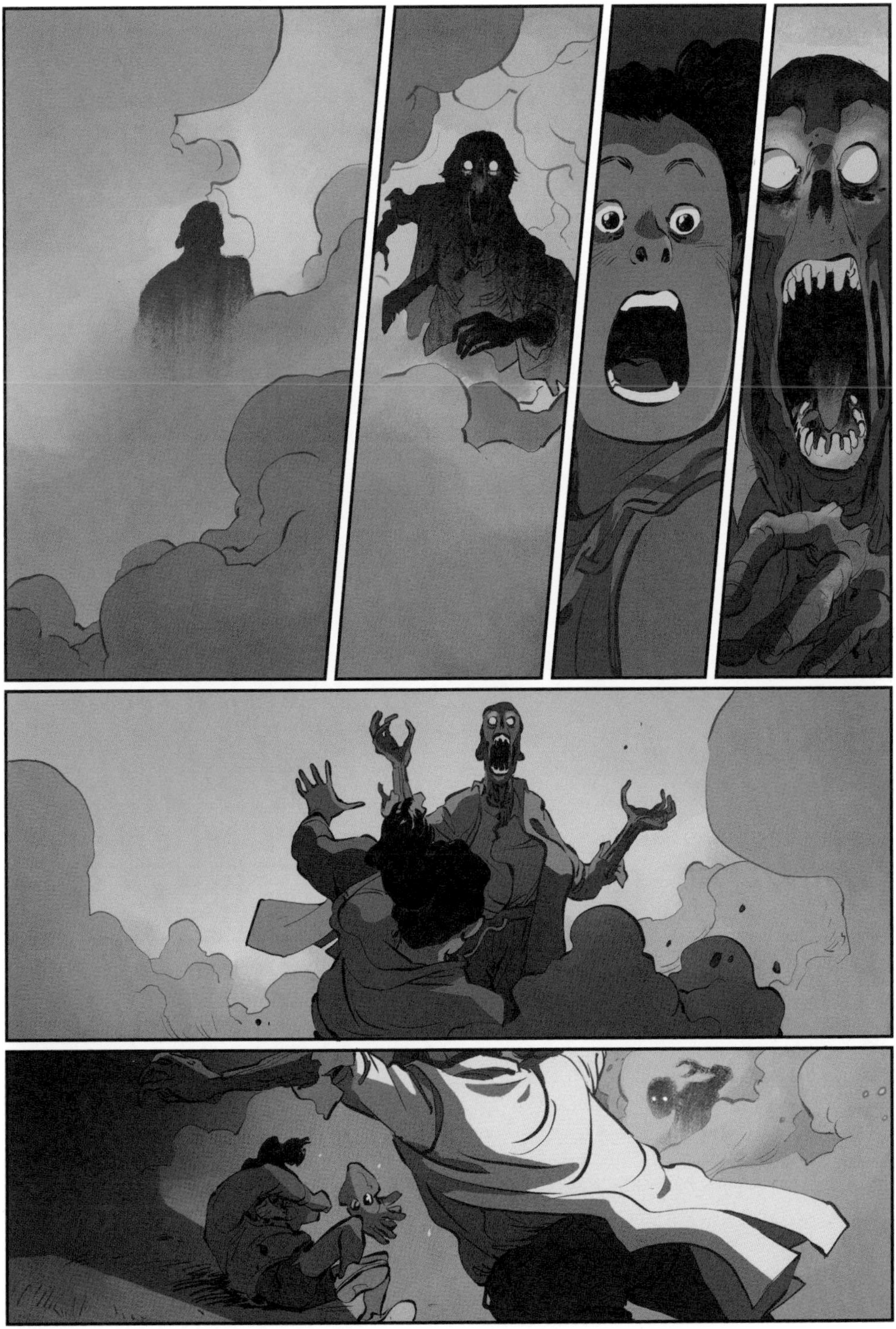

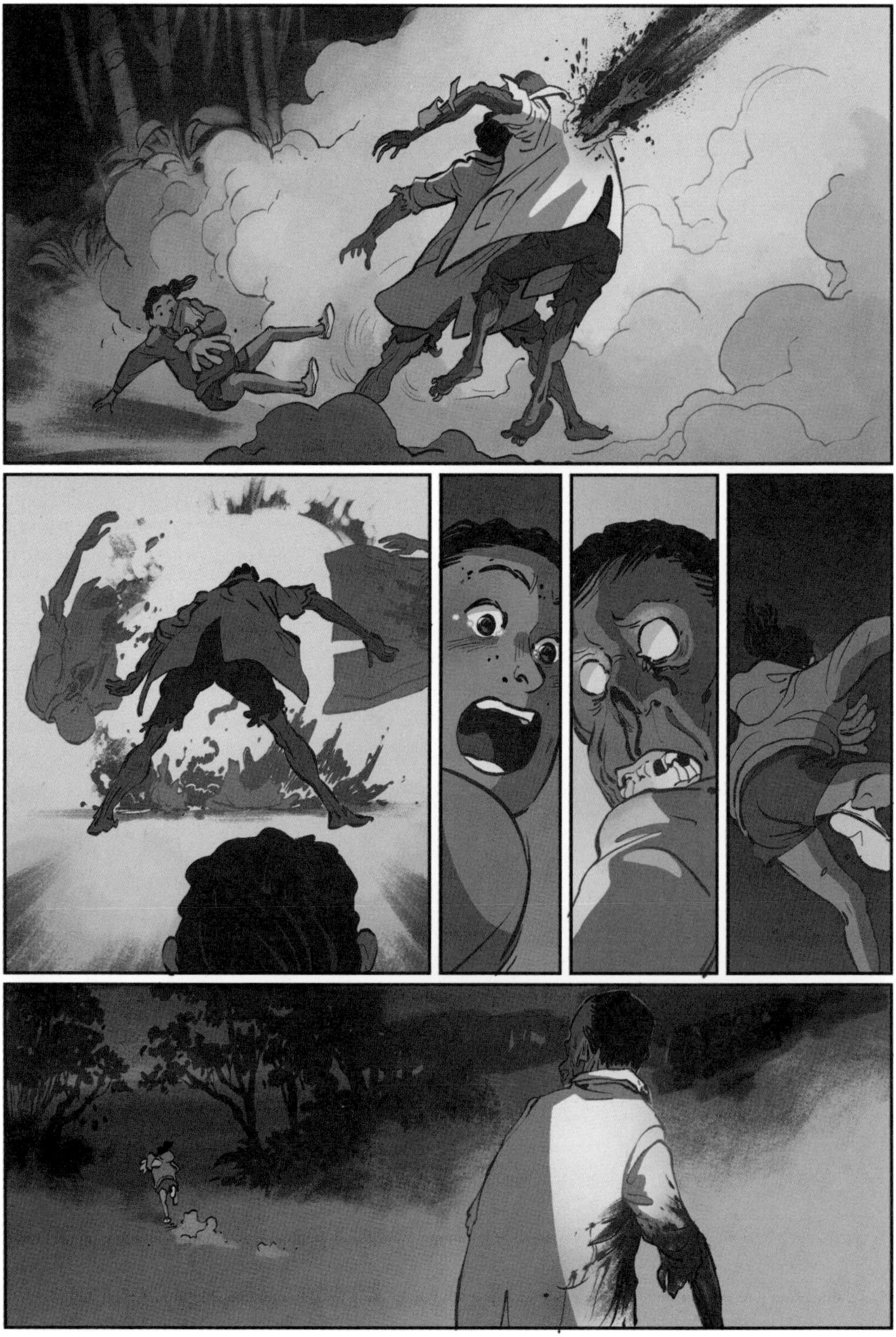

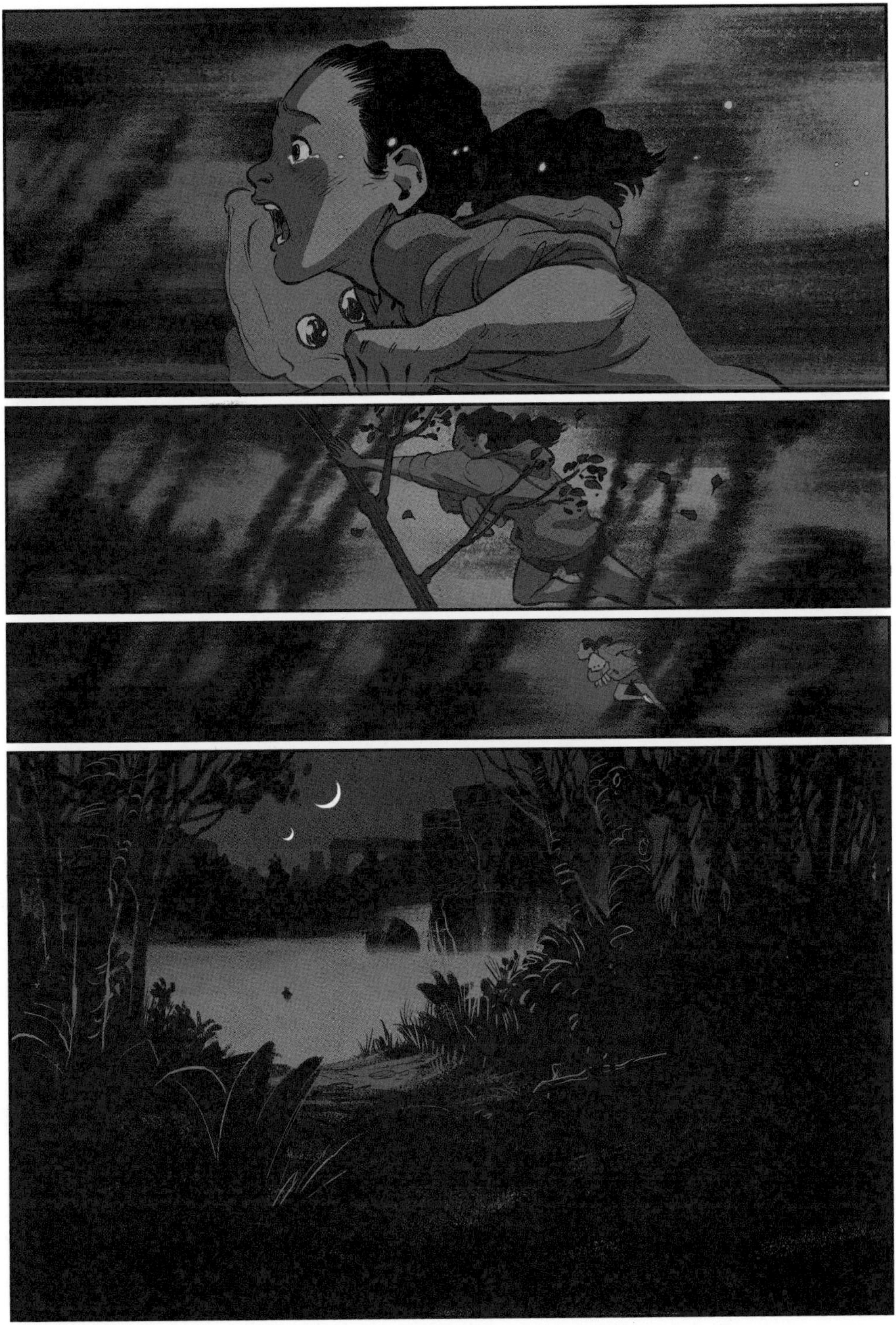

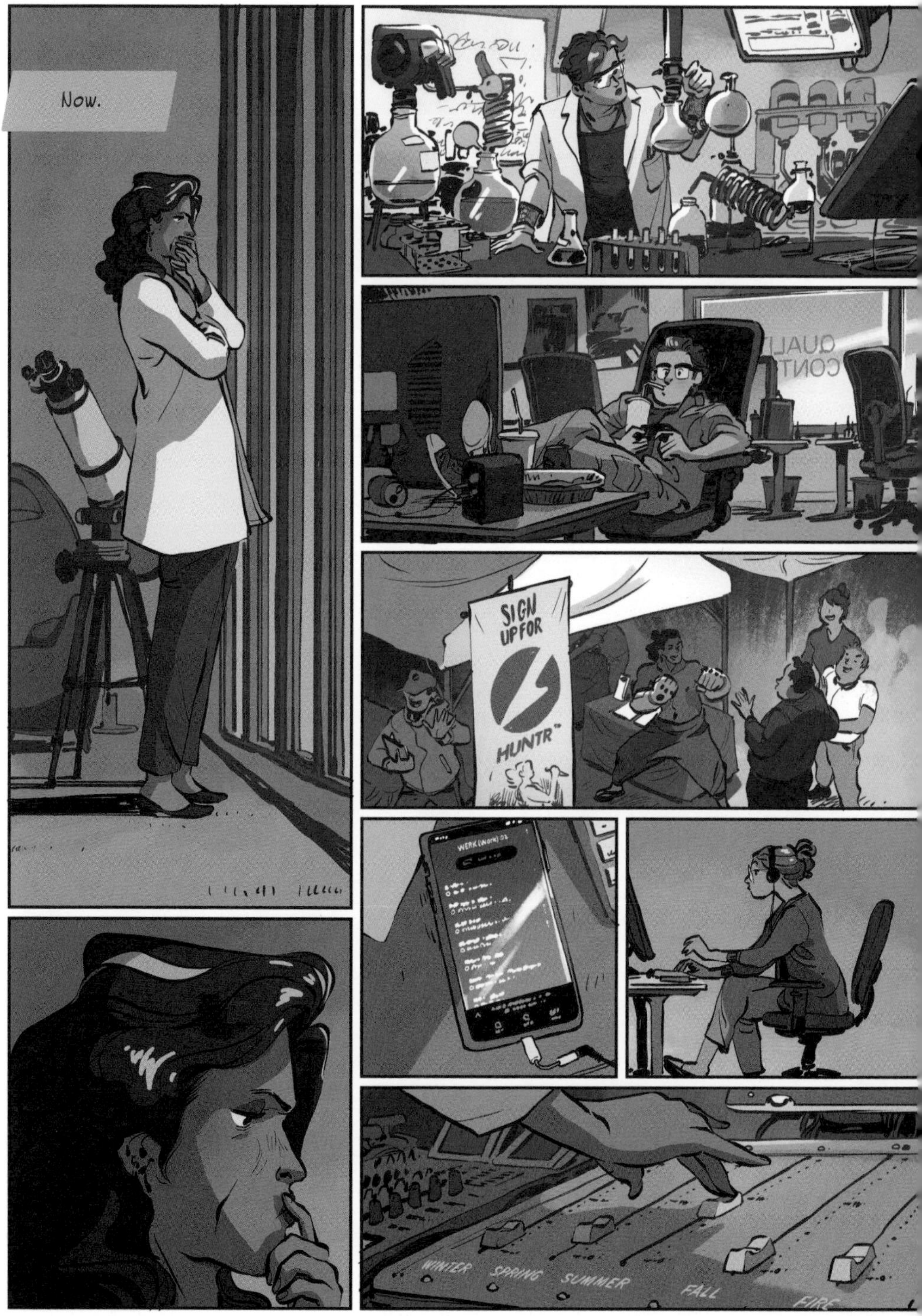
Now.
SIGN UP FOR
HUNTR™
WINTER
SPRING
SUMMER
FALL
FIRE

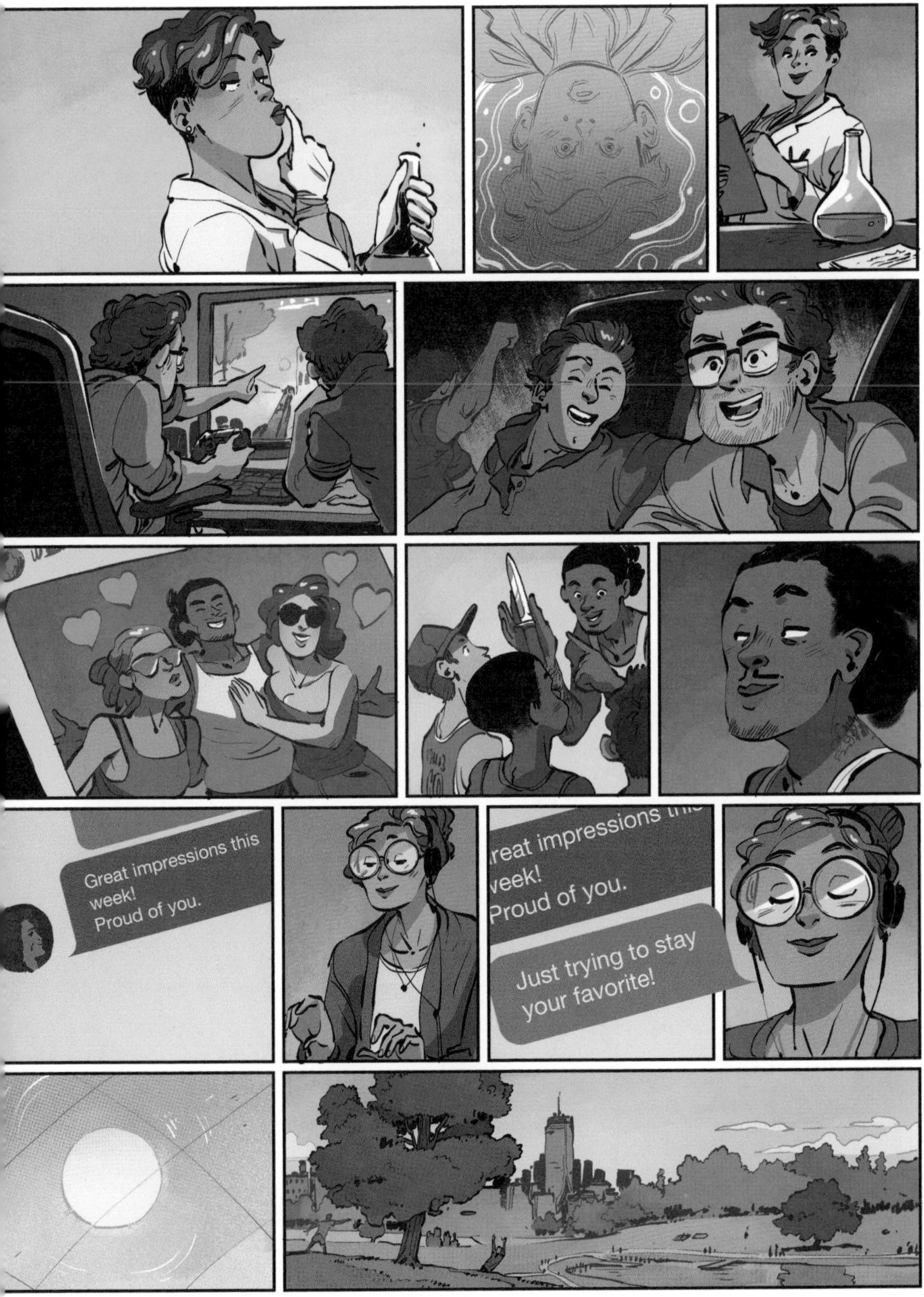
Great impressions this week!
Proud of you.
Great impressions this week!
Proud of you.
Just trying to stay your favorite!

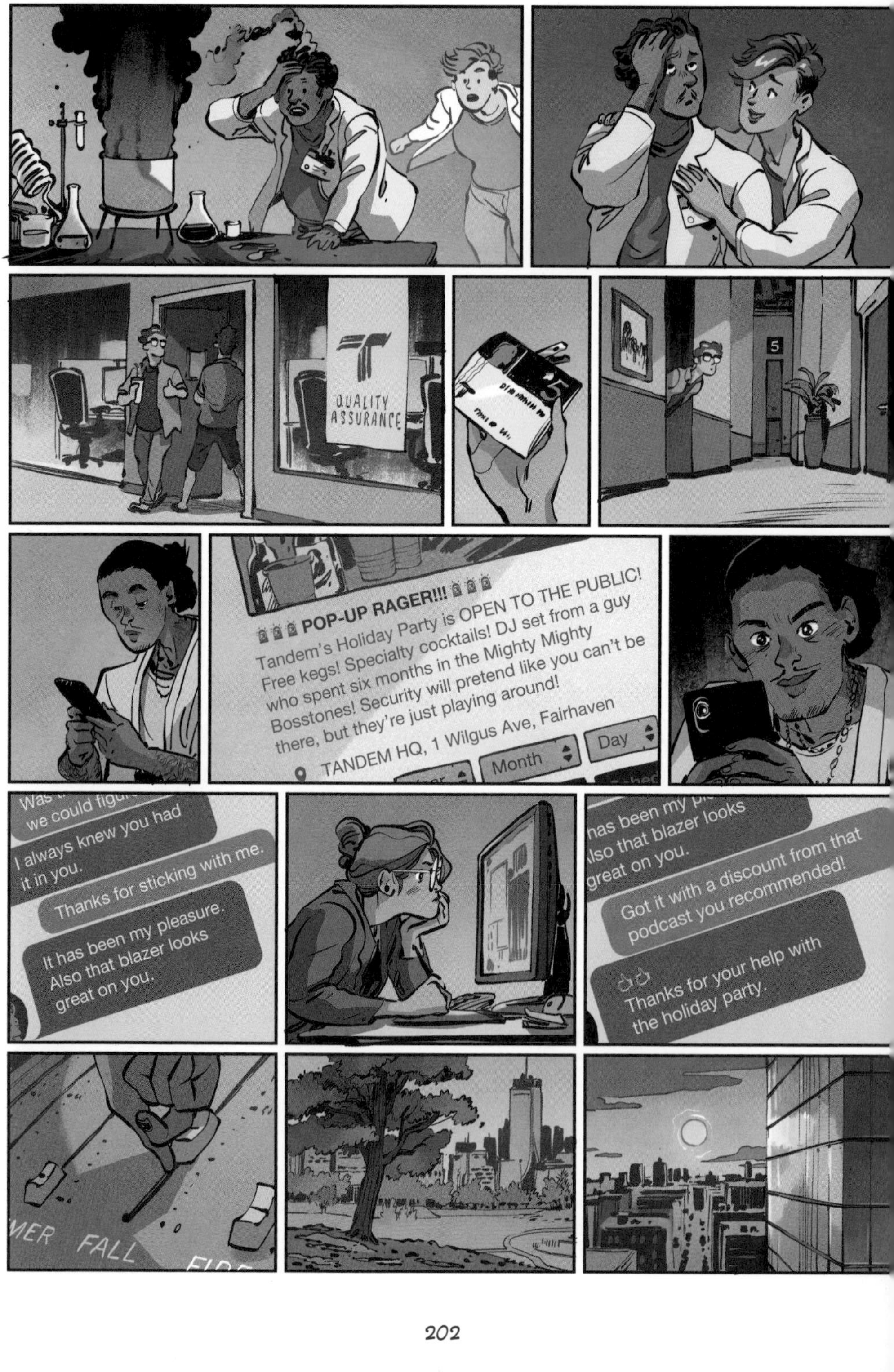
QUALITY ASSURANCE
5
POP-UP RAGER!!!
Tandem's Holiday Party is OPEN TO THE PUBLIC! Free kegs! Specialty cocktails! DJ set from a guy who spent six months in the Mighty Mighty Bosstones! Security will pretend like you can't be there, but they're just playing around!
TANDEM HQ, 1 Wilgus Ave, Fairhaven
Month
Day
I always knew you had it in you.
Thanks for sticking with me.
It has been my pleasure. Also that blazer looks great on you.
Got it with a discount from that podcast you recommended!
Thanks for your help with the holiday party.
FALL

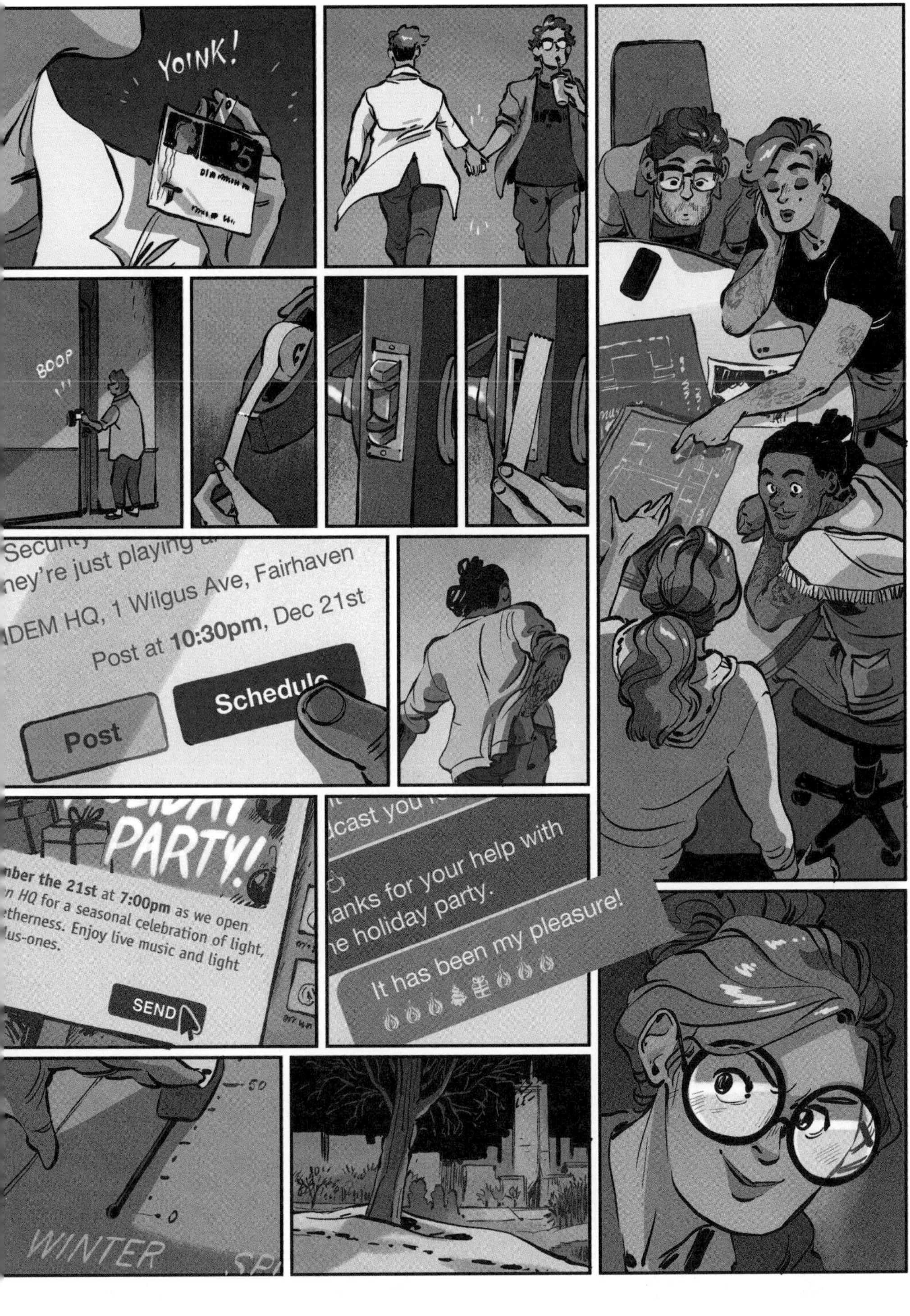
YOINK!
BOOP
Security
ney're just playing
DEM HQ, 1 Wilgus Ave, Fairhaven
Post at **10:30pm**, Dec 21st
Post
Schedule
PARTY!
mber the 21st at 7:00pm as we open
n HQ for a seasonal celebration of light,
etherness. Enjoy live music and light
lus-ones.
SEND
dcast you
anks for your help with
he holiday party.
It has been my pleasure!
WINTER

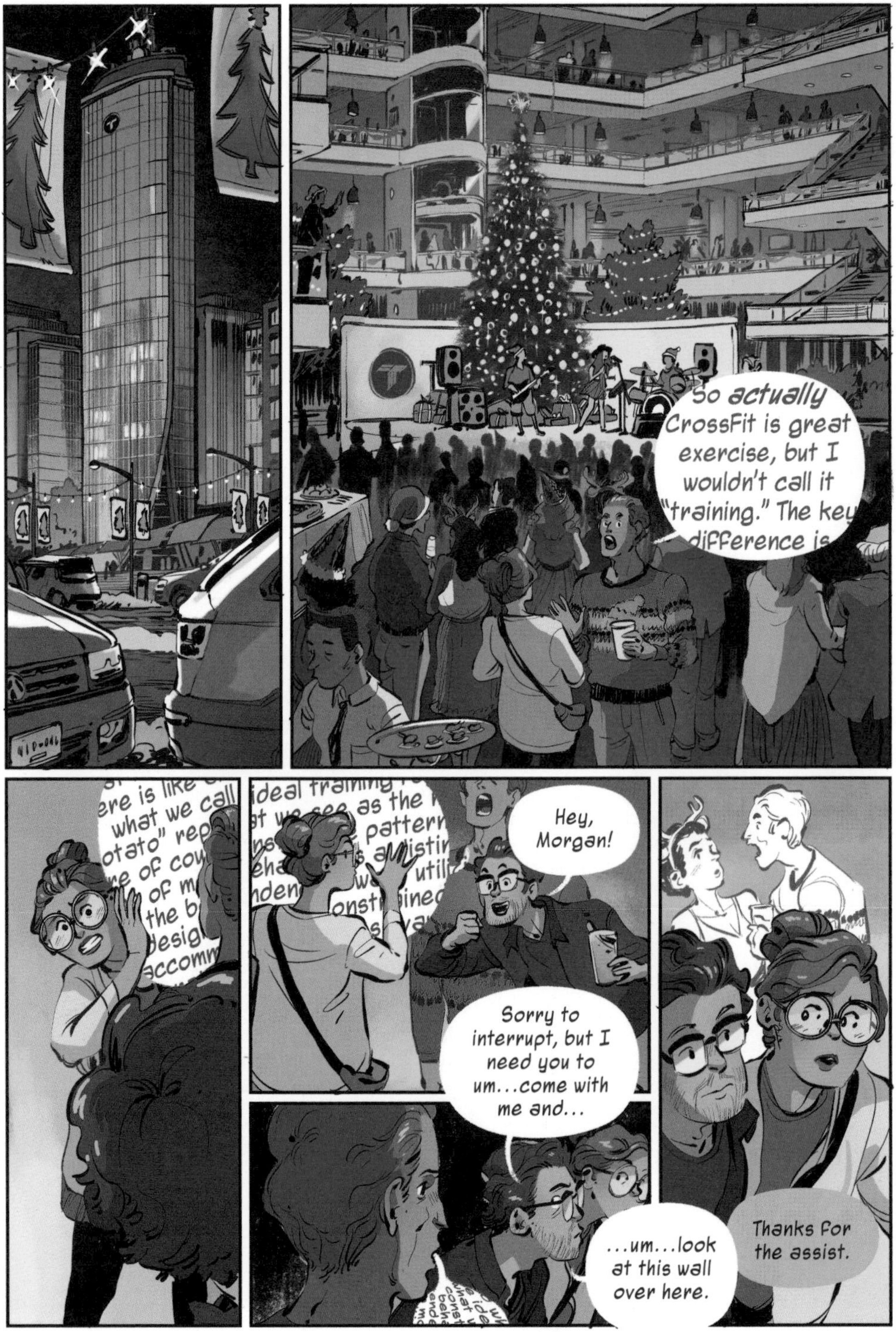
So actually CrossFit is great exercise, but I wouldn't call it "training." The key difference is
Hey, Morgan!
Sorry to interrupt, but I need you to um...come with me and...
...um...look at this wall over here.
Thanks for the assist.

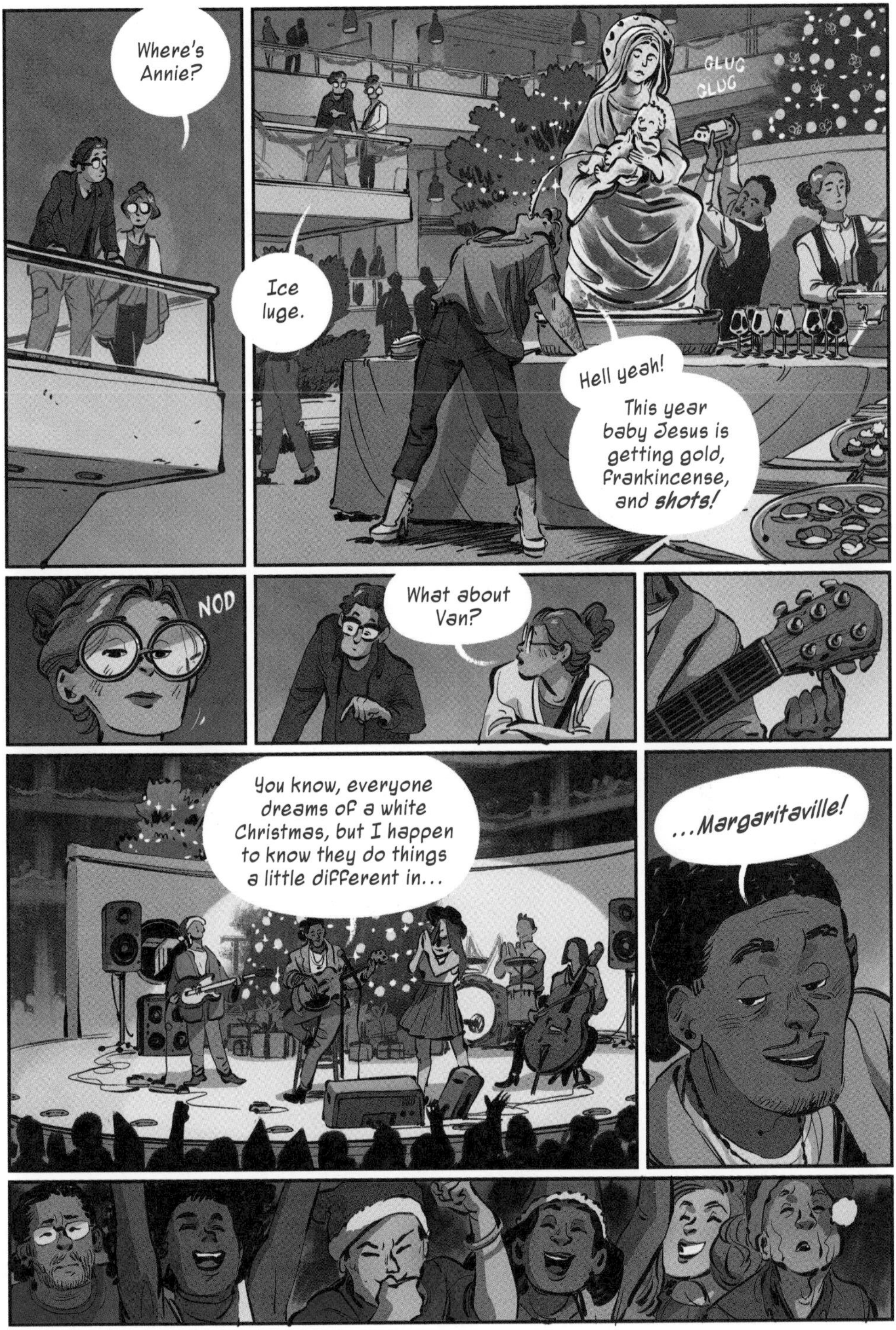

Where's Annie?
GLUG GLUG
Ice luge.
Hell yeah!
This year baby Jesus is getting gold, frankincense, and shots!
NOD
What about Van?
You know, everyone dreams of a white Christmas, but I happen to know they do things a little different in...
...Margaritaville!

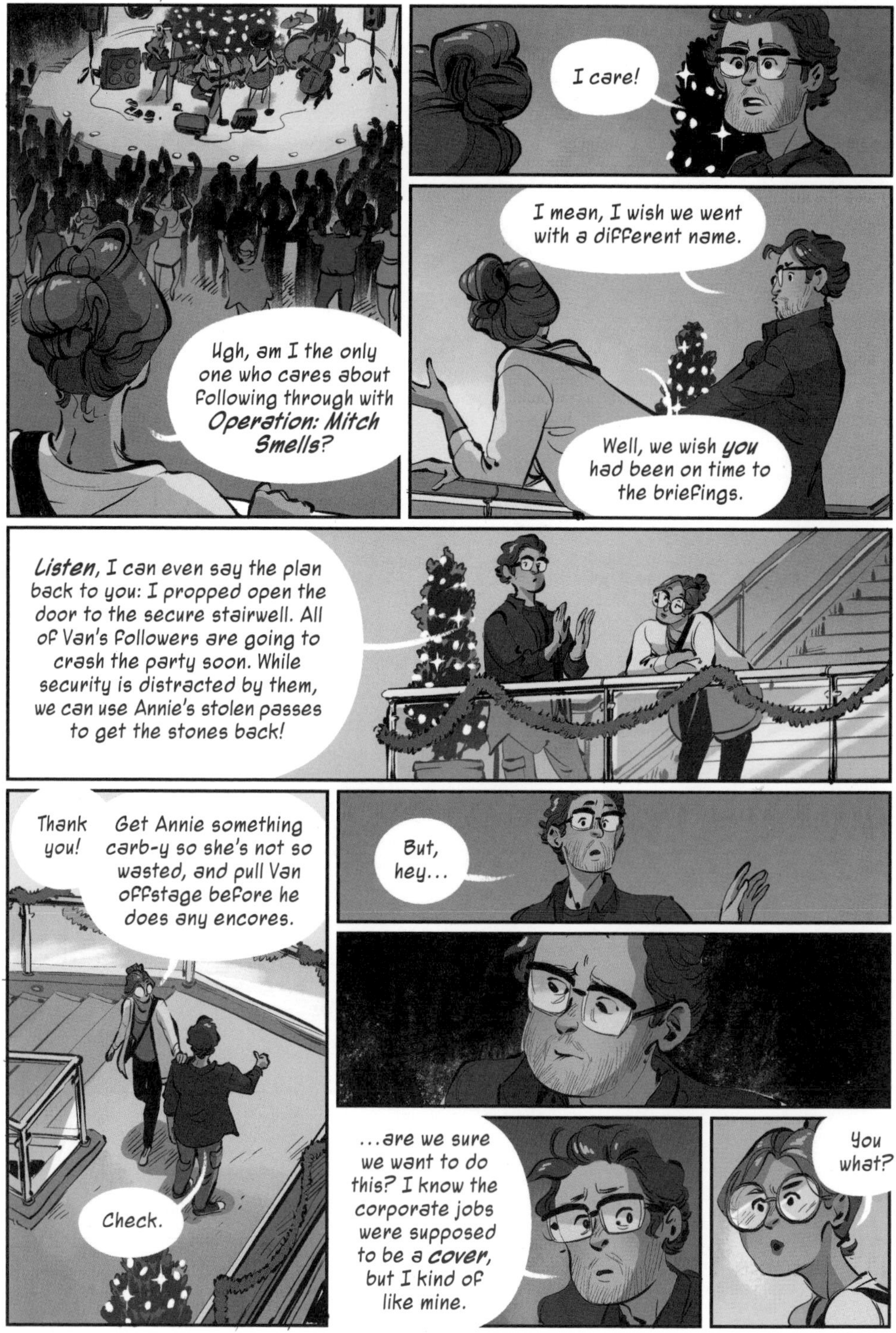

Ugh, am I the only one who cares about following through with *Operation: Mitch Smells*?
I care!
I mean, I wish we went with a different name.
Well, we wish *you* had been on time to the briefings.
Listen, I can even say the plan back to you: I propped open the door to the secure stairwell. All of Van's followers are going to crash the party soon. While security is distracted by them, we can use Annie's stolen passes to get the stones back!
Thank you!
Get Annie something carb-y so she's not so wasted, and pull Van offstage before he does any encores.
Check.
But, hey...
...are we sure we want to do this? I know the corporate jobs were supposed to be a *cover*, but I kind of like mine.
You what?

When we first met, you were like, "adventure is overrated," remember?

I get that now.

But Tandem is *evil!*

Maybe we're not exactly sure *how*, but we *know* they *are!*

I know! I know!

But...*health* insurance... and *cereal bar* access...

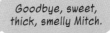

You're right.

You guys deserve happiness and an ice luge.

I can handle the rest of the operation myself.

Goodbye, sweet, thick, smelly Mitch.

SNAG!

SNIFF SNIFF

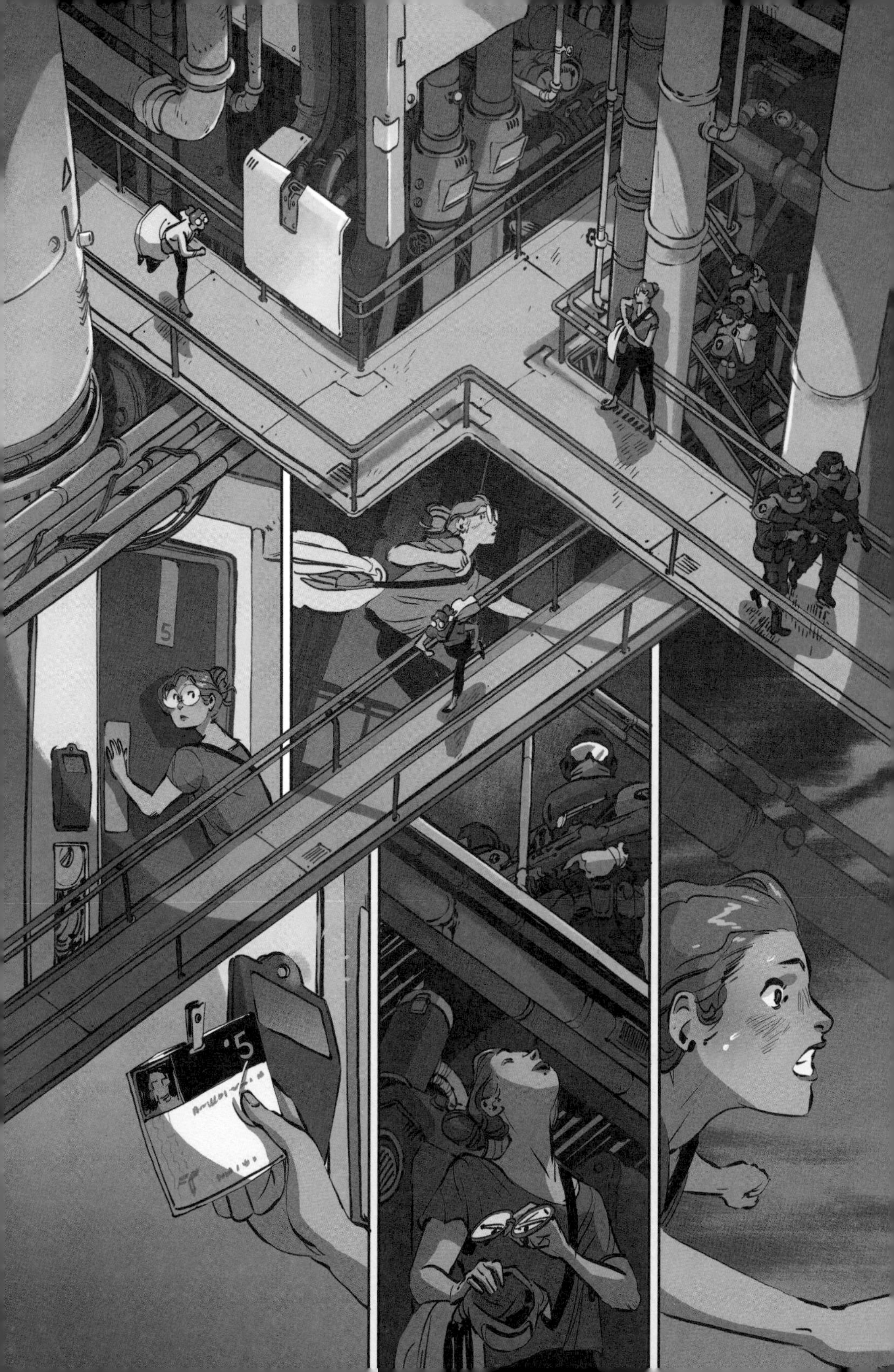
5
5

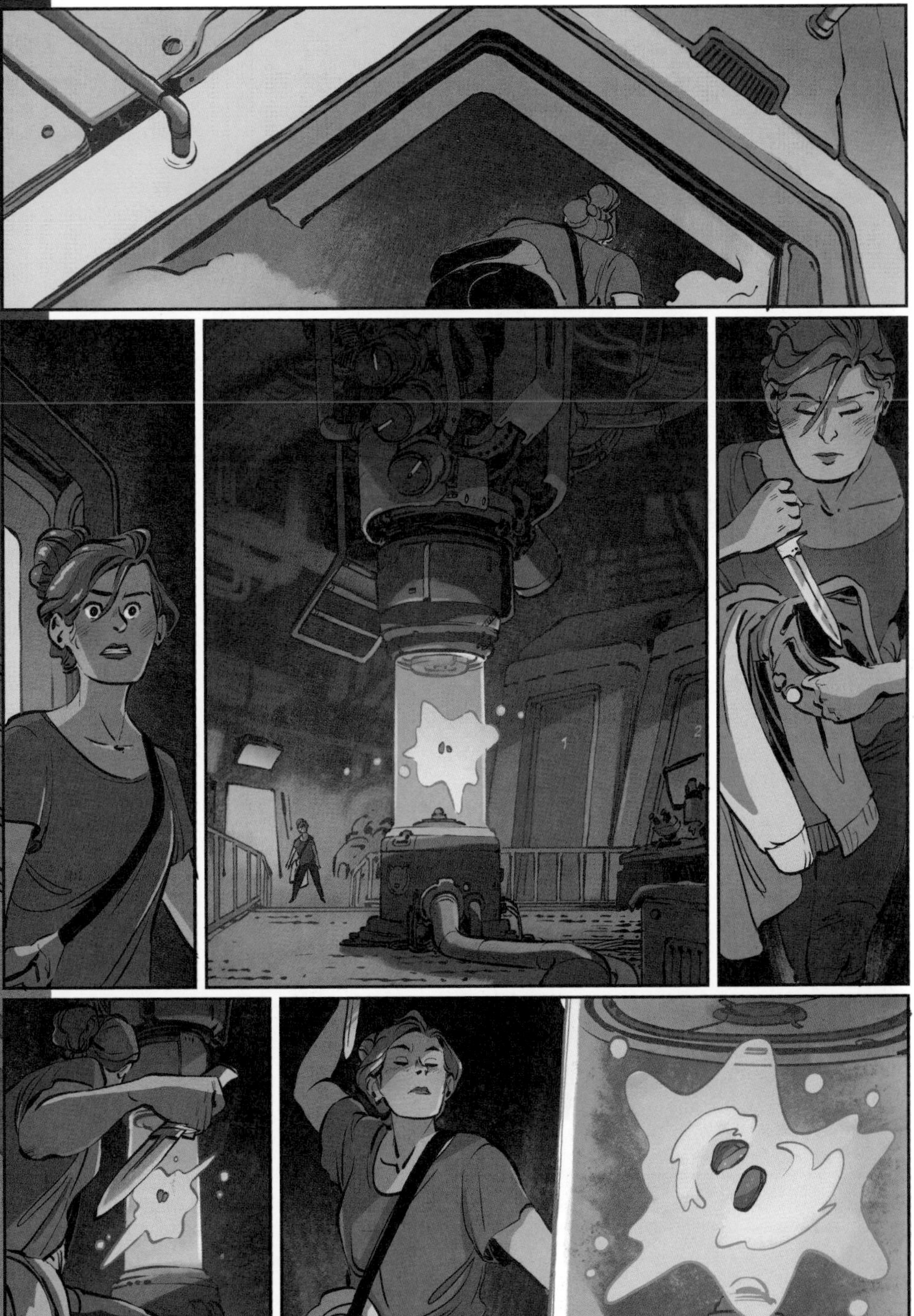

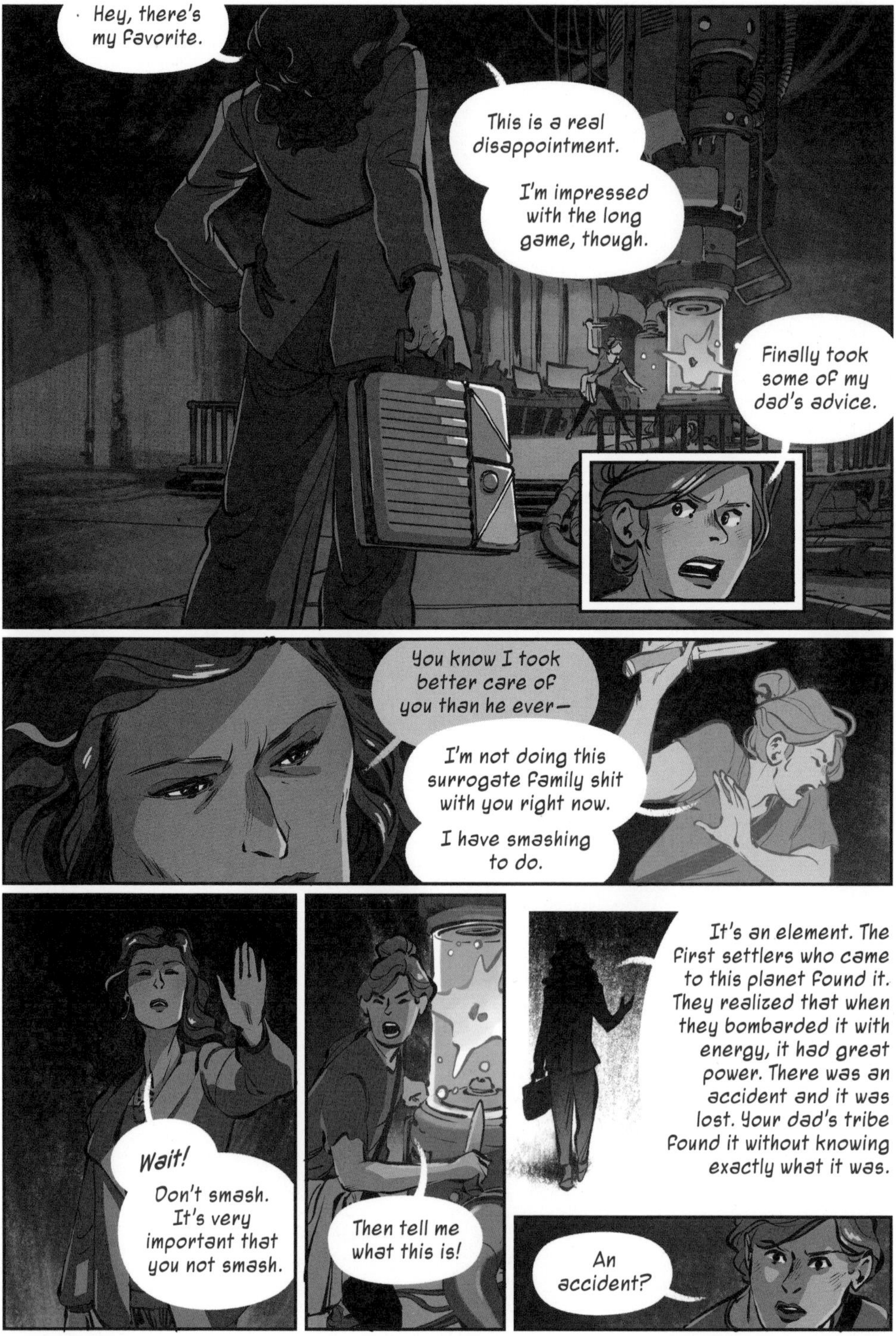
Hey, there's my favorite.
This is a real disappointment.
I'm impressed with the long game, though.
Finally took some of my dad's advice.
You know I took better care of you than he ever—
I'm not doing this surrogate family shit with you right now.
I have smashing to do.
Wait!
Don't smash. It's very important that you not smash.
Then tell me what this is!
It's an element. The first settlers who came to this planet found it. They realized that when they bombarded it with energy, it had great power. There was an accident and it was lost. Your dad's tribe found it without knowing exactly what it was.
An accident?

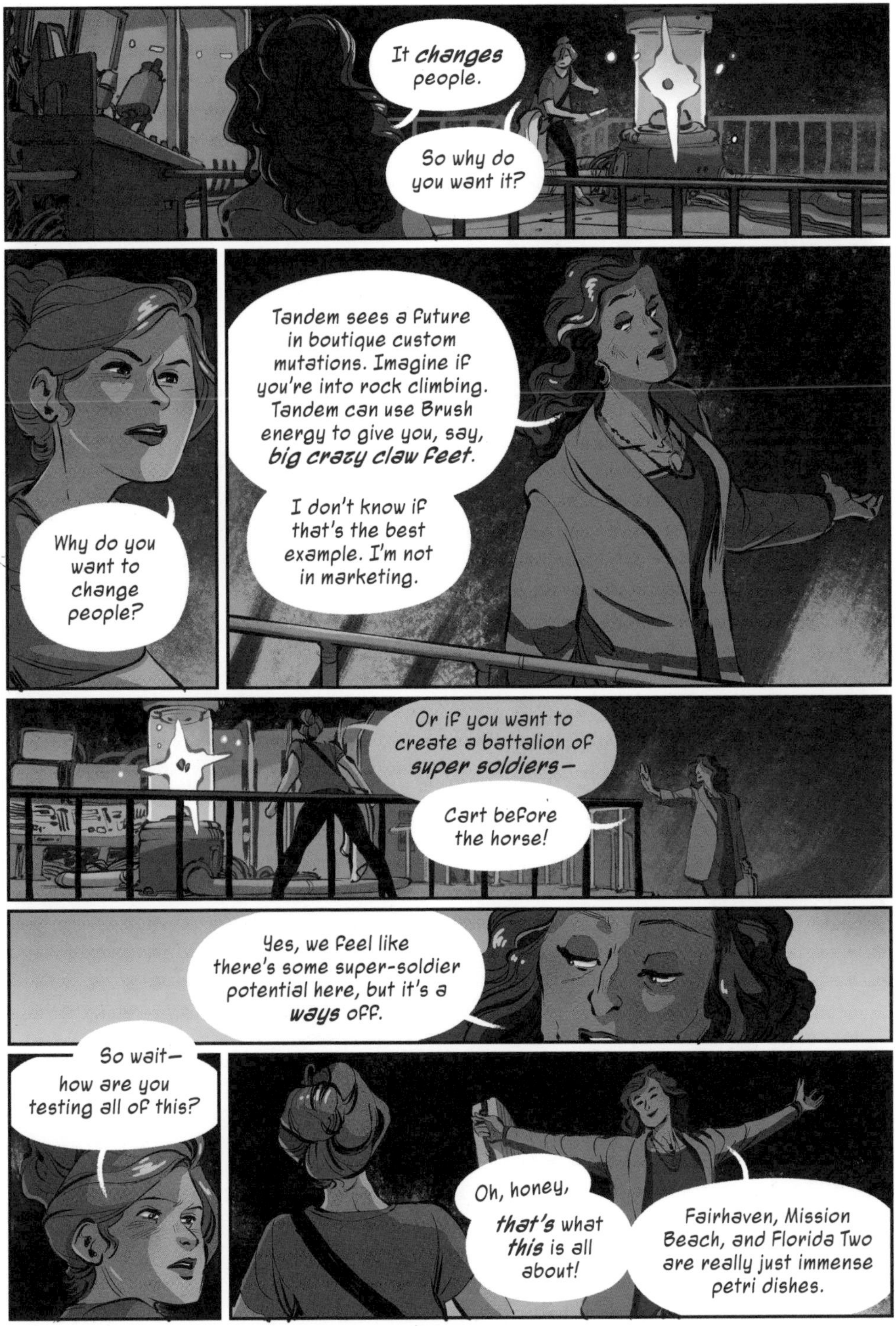
It *changes* people.
So why do you want it?
Tandem sees a future in boutique custom mutations. Imagine if you're into rock climbing. Tandem can use Brush energy to give you, say, *big crazy claw feet*.
I don't know if that's the best example. I'm not in marketing.
Why do you want to change people?
Or if you want to create a battalion of *super soldiers*—
Cart before the horse!
Yes, we feel like there's some super-soldier potential here, but it's a *ways* off.
So wait— how are you testing all of this?
Oh, honey, *that's* what *this* is all about!
Fairhaven, Mission Beach, and Florida Two are really just immense petri dishes.

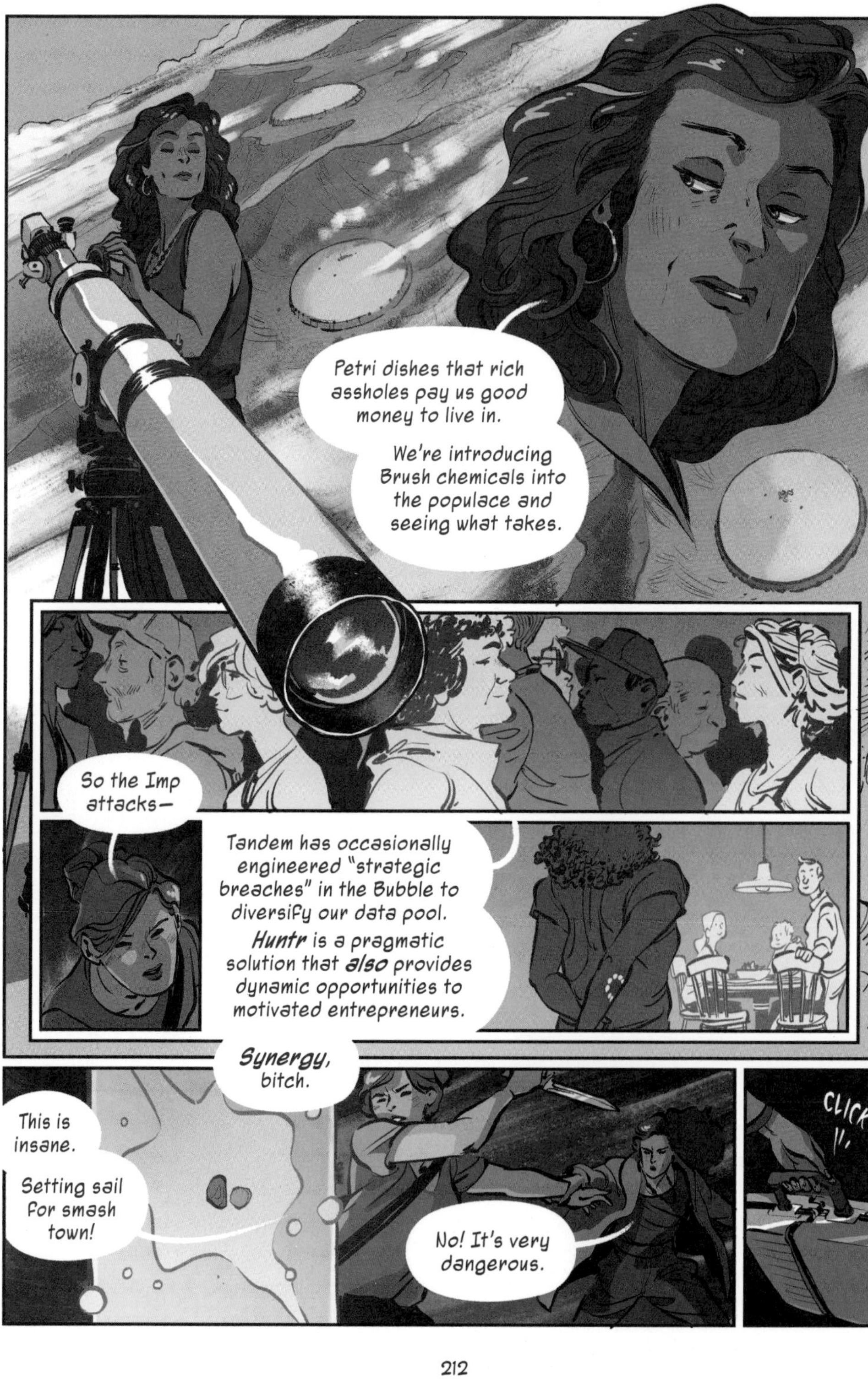

Petri dishes that rich assholes pay us good money to live in.
We're introducing Brush chemicals into the populace and seeing what takes.
So the Imp attacks—
Tandem has occasionally engineered "strategic breaches" in the Bubble to diversify our data pool.
Huntr is a pragmatic solution that *also* provides dynamic opportunities to motivated entrepreneurs.
Synergy, bitch.
This is insane.
Setting sail for smash town!
No! It's very dangerous.
CLICK

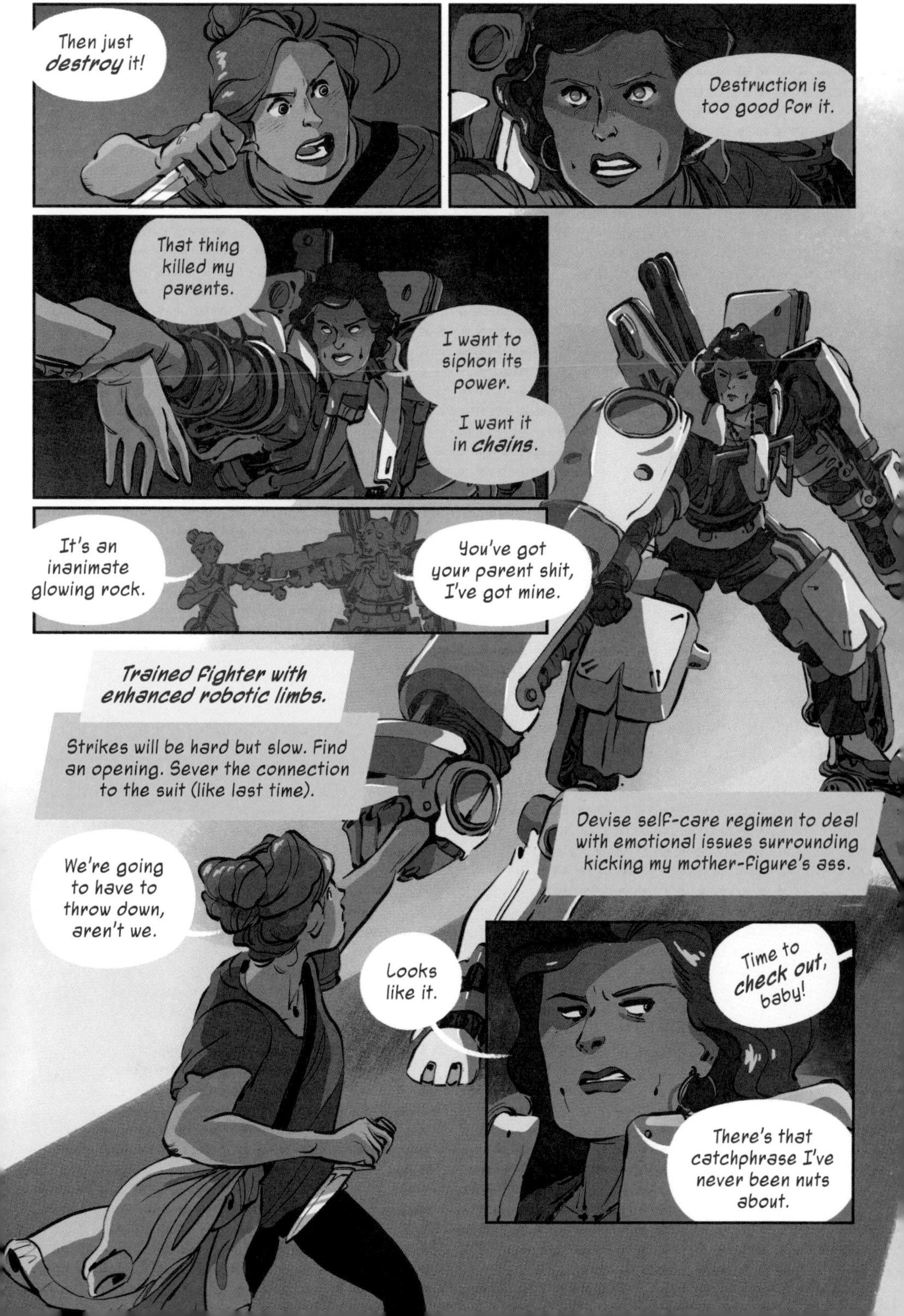
Then just *destroy* it!
Destruction is too good for it.
That thing killed my parents.
I want to siphon its power.
I want it in *chains*.
It's an inanimate glowing rock.
You've got your parent shit, I've got mine.
Trained fighter with enhanced robotic limbs.
Strikes will be hard but slow. Find an opening. Sever the connection to the suit (like last time).
Devise self-care regimen to deal with emotional issues surrounding kicking my mother-figure's ass.
We're going to have to throw down, aren't we.
Looks like it.
Time to *check out*, baby!
There's that catchphrase I've never been nuts about.

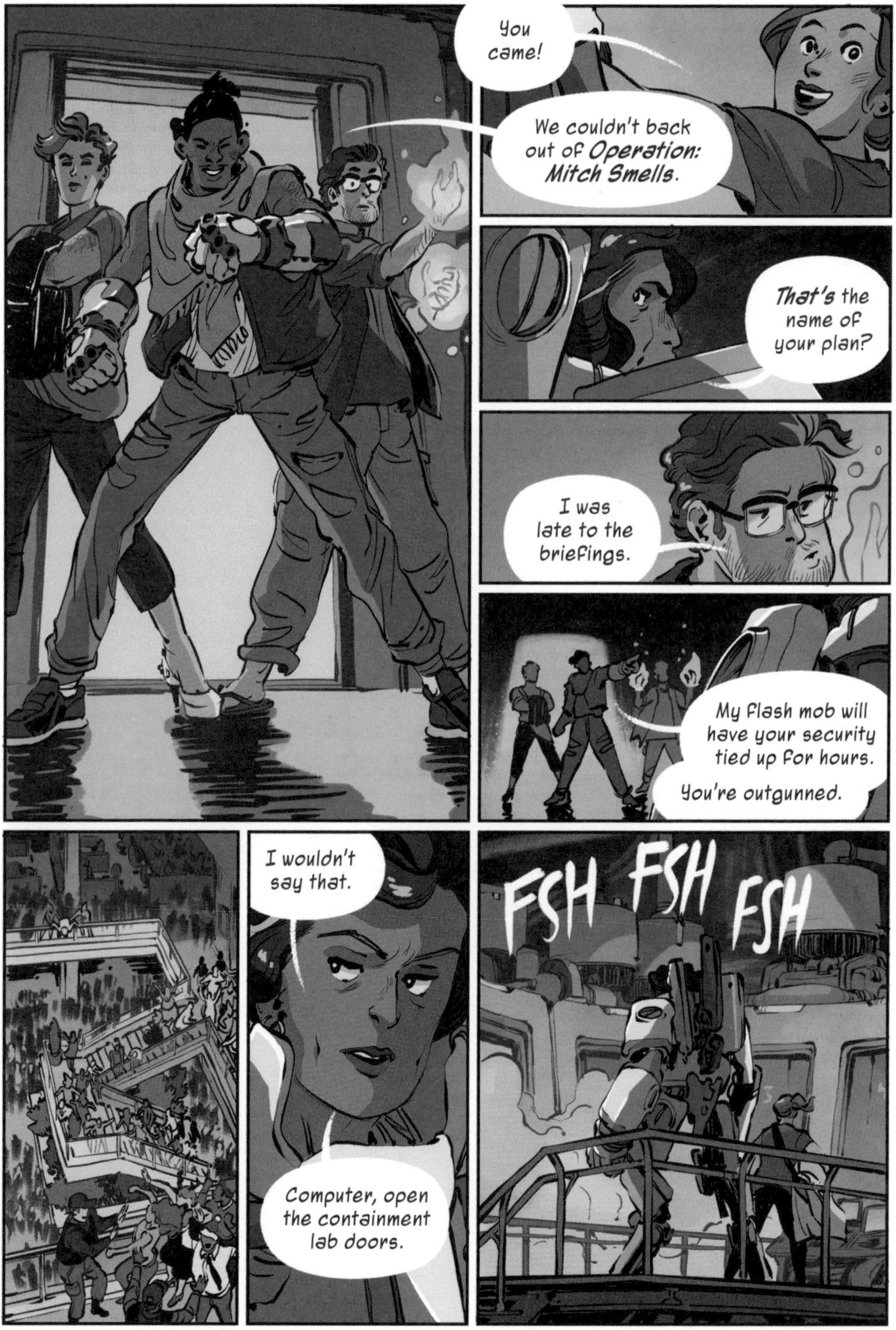
You came!
We couldn't back out of *Operation: Mitch Smells*.
That's the name of your plan?
I was late to the briefings.
My flash mob will have your security tied up for hours.
You're outgunned.
I wouldn't say that.
Computer, open the containment lab doors.
FSH FSH FSH

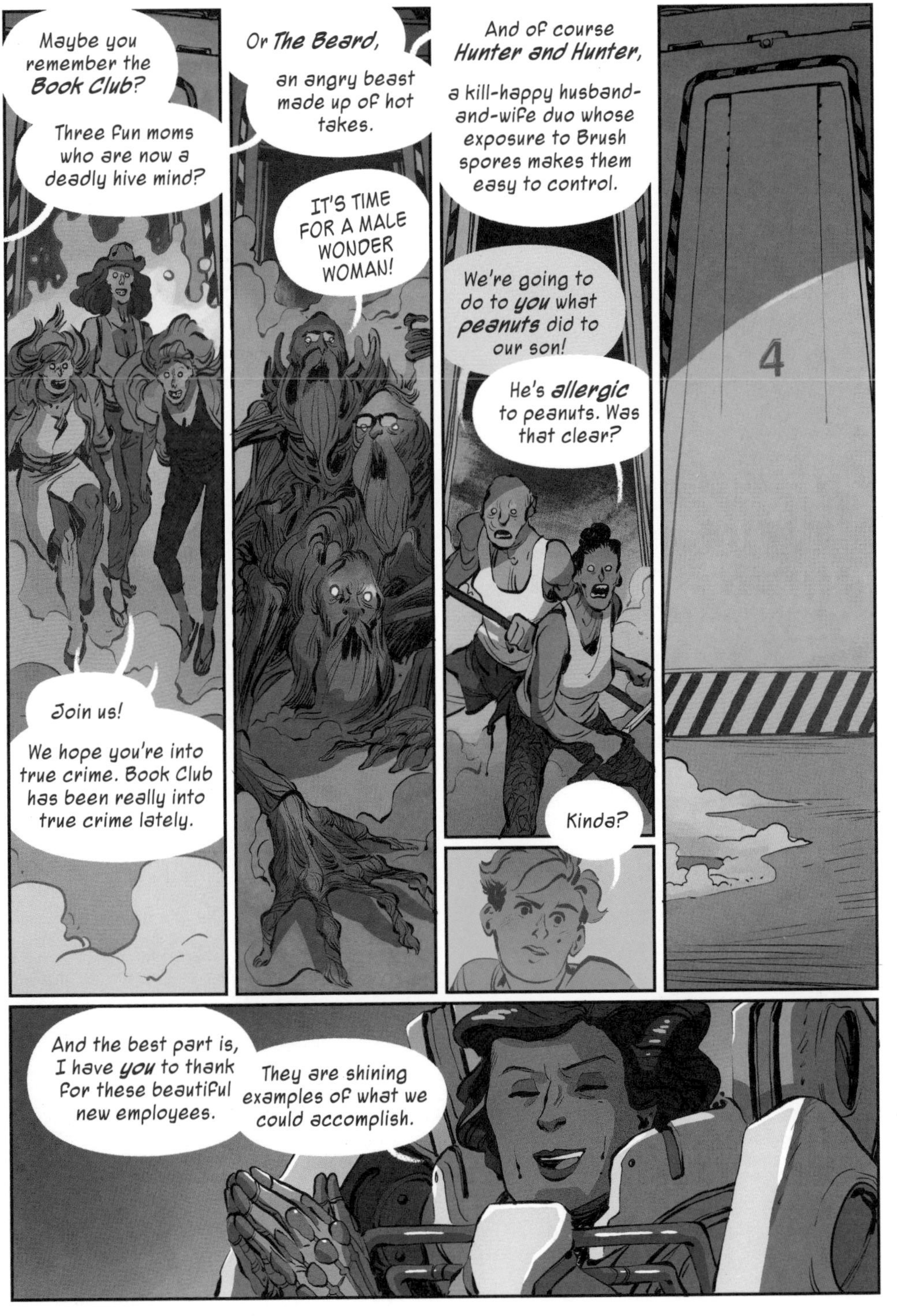

Maybe you remember the *Book Club*?
Three fun moms who are now a deadly hive mind?
Join us!
We hope you're into true crime. Book Club has been really into true crime lately.
Or *The Beard*,
an angry beast made up of hot takes.
IT'S TIME FOR A MALE WONDER WOMAN!
And of course *Hunter and Hunter*,
a kill-happy husband-and-wife duo whose exposure to Brush spores makes them easy to control.
We're going to do to *you* what *peanuts* did to our son!
He's *allergic* to peanuts. Was that clear?
Kinda?
4
And the best part is, I have *you* to thank for these beautiful new employees.
They are shining examples of what we could accomplish.

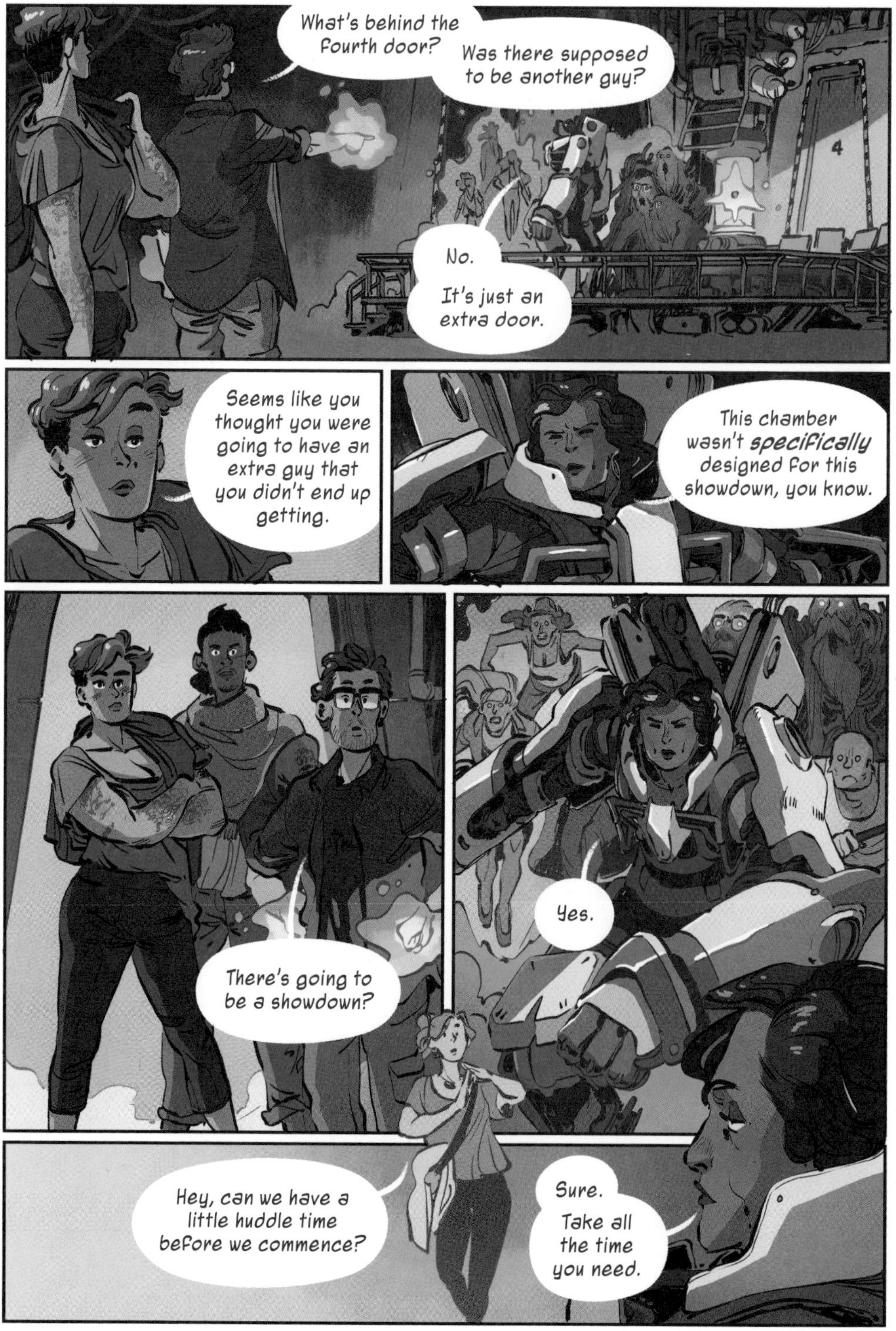
What's behind the fourth door?
Was there supposed to be another guy?
No.
It's just an extra door.
4
Seems like you thought you were going to have an extra guy that you didn't end up getting.
This chamber wasn't *specifically* designed for this showdown, you know.
There's going to be a showdown?
Yes.
Hey, can we have a little huddle time before we commence?
Sure.
Take all the time you need.

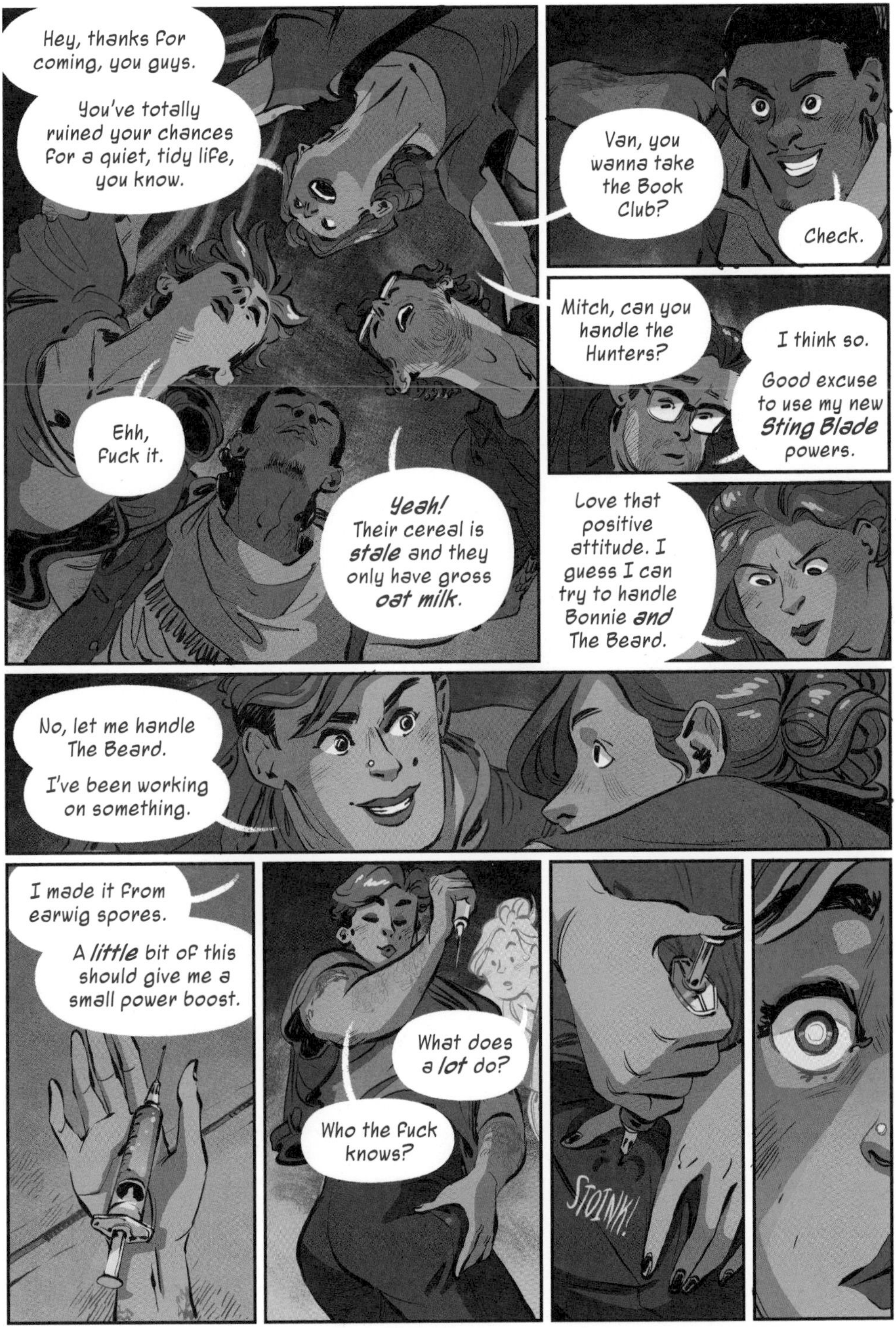

Hey, thanks for coming, you guys.
You've totally ruined your chances for a quiet, tidy life, you know.
Van, you wanna take the Book Club?
Check.
Mitch, can you handle the Hunters?
I think so.
Good excuse to use my new *Sting Blade* powers.
Ehh, fuck it.
Yeah! Their cereal is *stale* and they only have gross *oat milk*.
Love that positive attitude. I guess I can try to handle Bonnie *and* The Beard.
No, let me handle The Beard.
I've been working on something.
I made it from earwig spores.
A *little* bit of this should give me a small power boost.
What does a *lot* do?
Who the fuck knows?
STOINK!

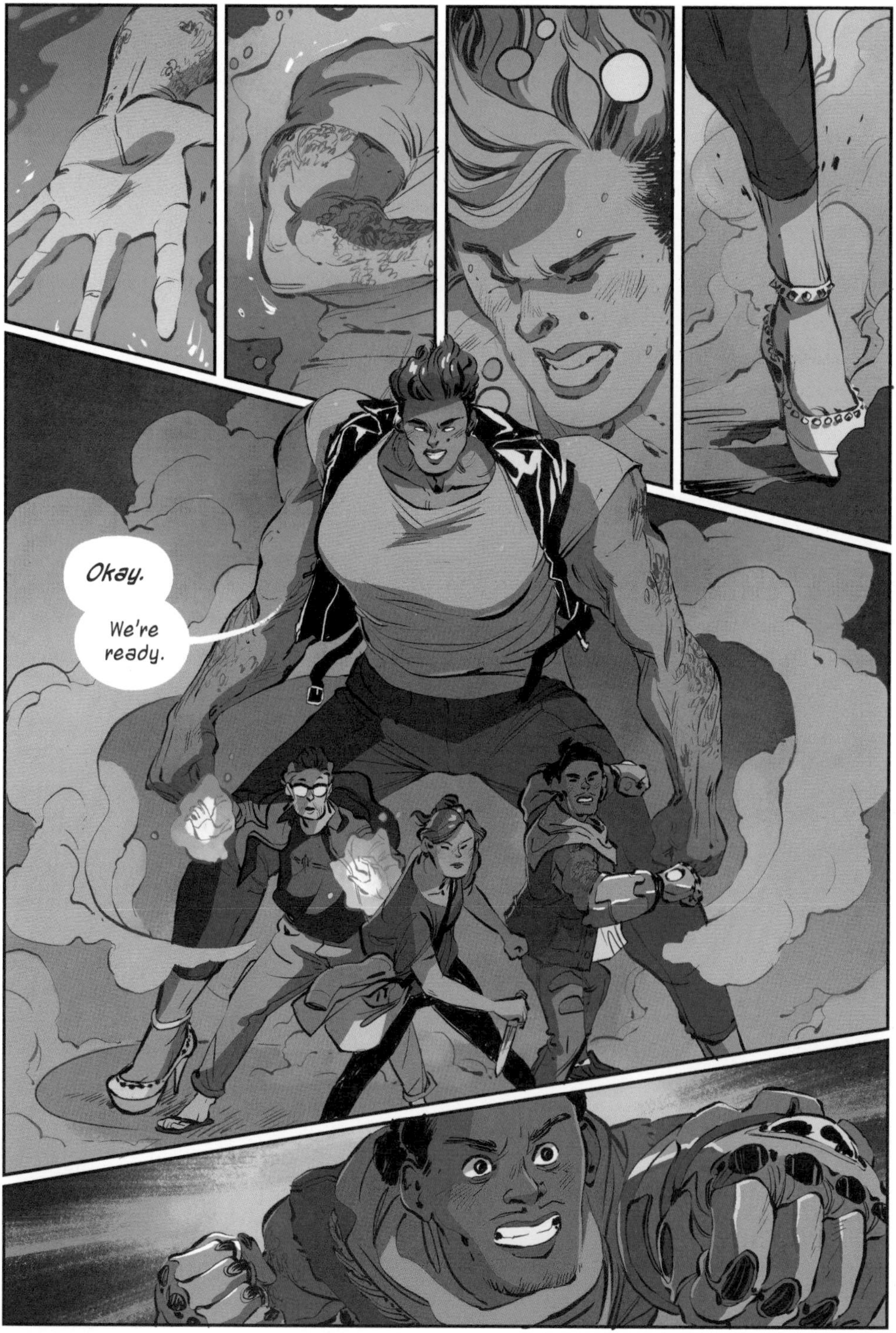
Okay.
We're ready.

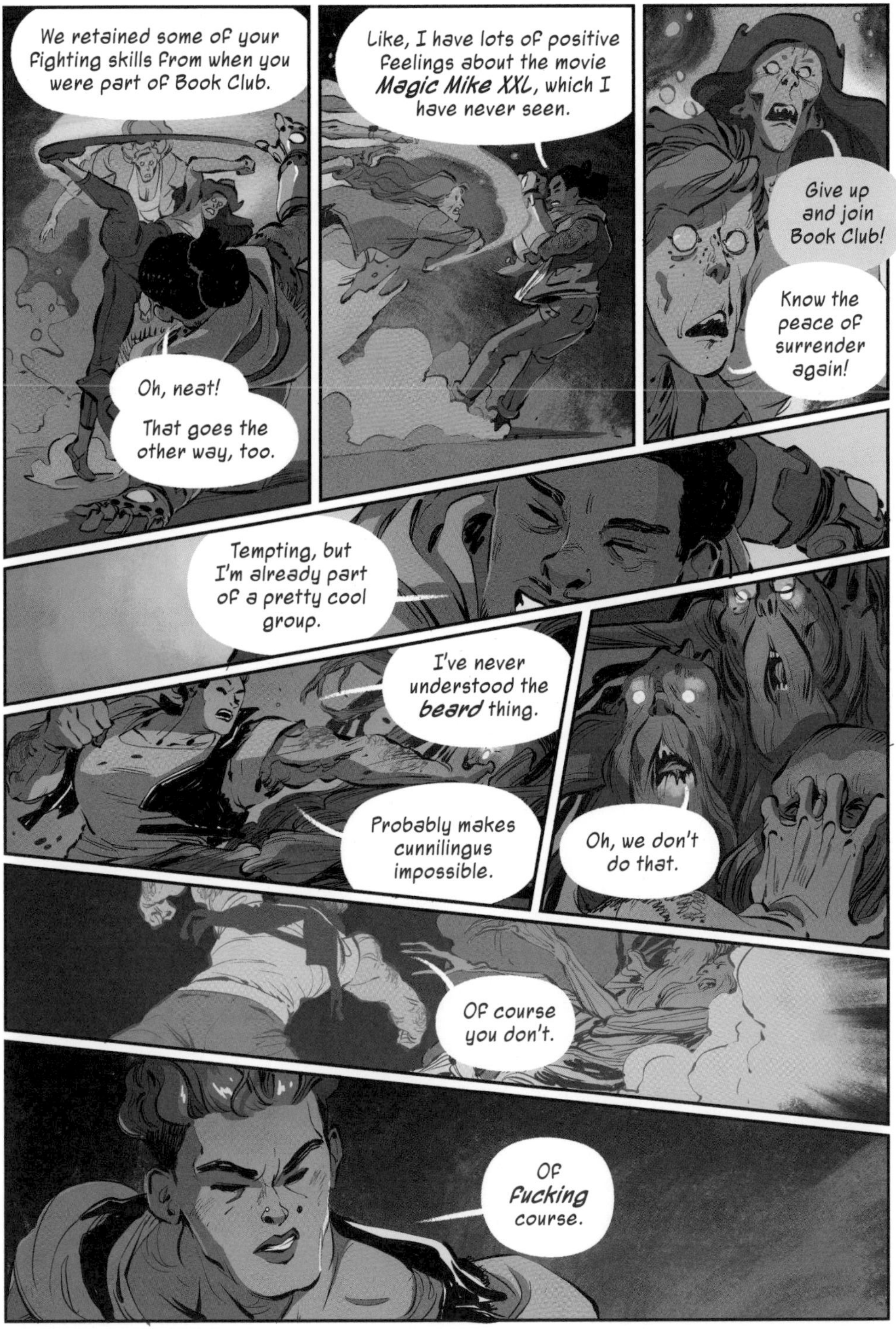
We retained some of your fighting skills from when you were part of Book Club.
Oh, neat!
That goes the other way, too.
Like, I have lots of positive feelings about the movie *Magic Mike XXL*, which I have never seen.
Give up and join Book Club!
Know the peace of surrender again!
Tempting, but I'm already part of a pretty cool group.
I've never understood the *beard* thing.
Probably makes cunnilingus impossible.
Oh, we don't do that.
Of course you don't.
Of *fucking* course.

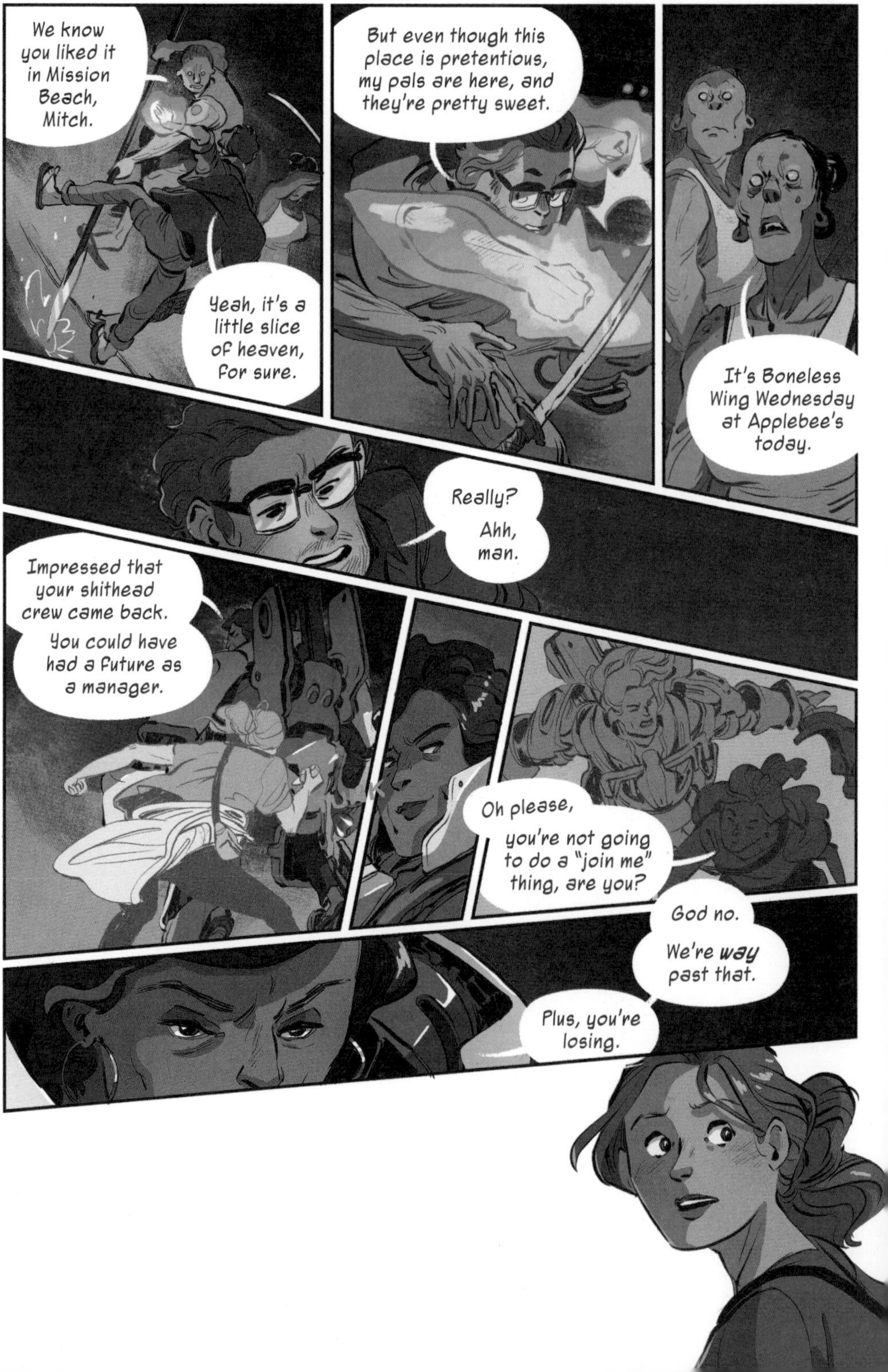
We know you liked it in Mission Beach, Mitch.
Yeah, it's a little slice of heaven, for sure.
But even though this place is pretentious, my pals are here, and they're pretty sweet.
It's Boneless Wing Wednesday at Applebee's today.
Really?
Ahh, man.
Impressed that your shithead crew came back.
You could have had a future as a manager.
Oh please,
you're not going to do a "join me" thing, are you?
God no.
We're *way* past that.
Plus, you're losing.

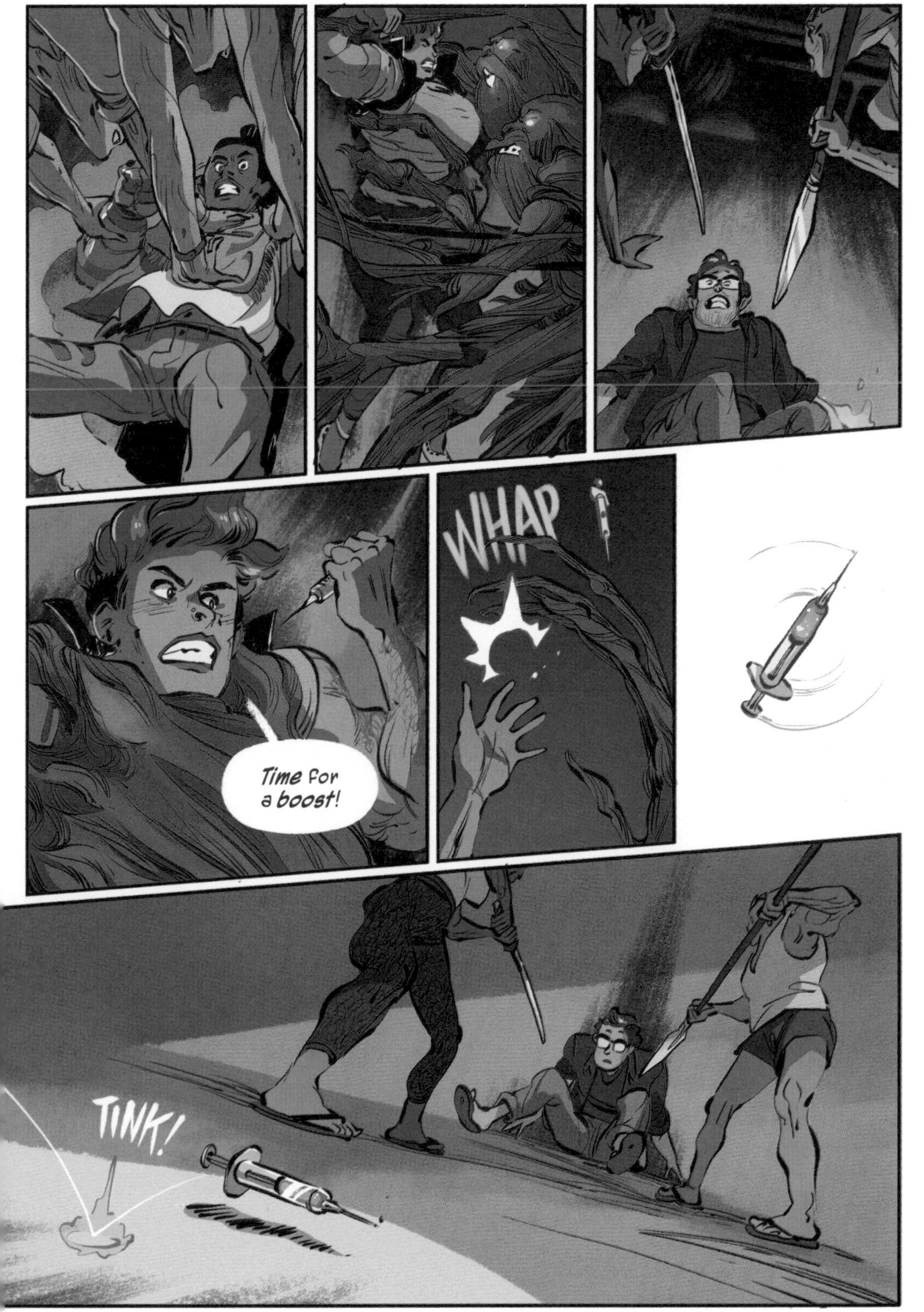
Time for a boost!
WHAP
TINK!

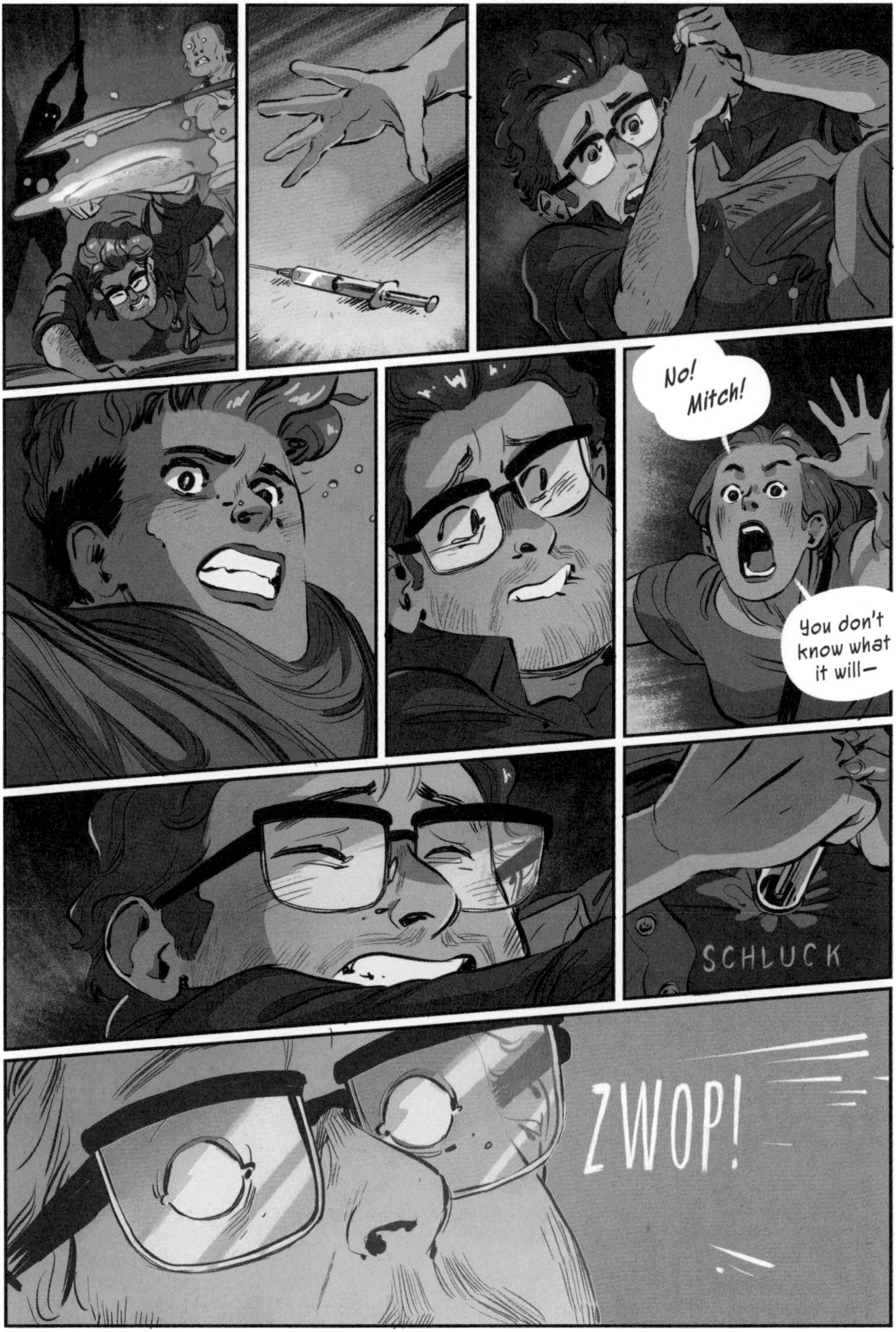
No! Mitch!
You don't know what it will—
SCHLUCK
ZWOP!

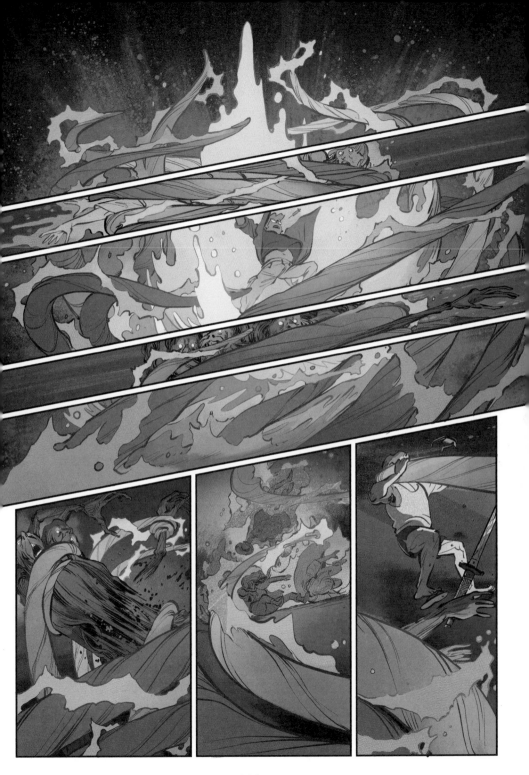

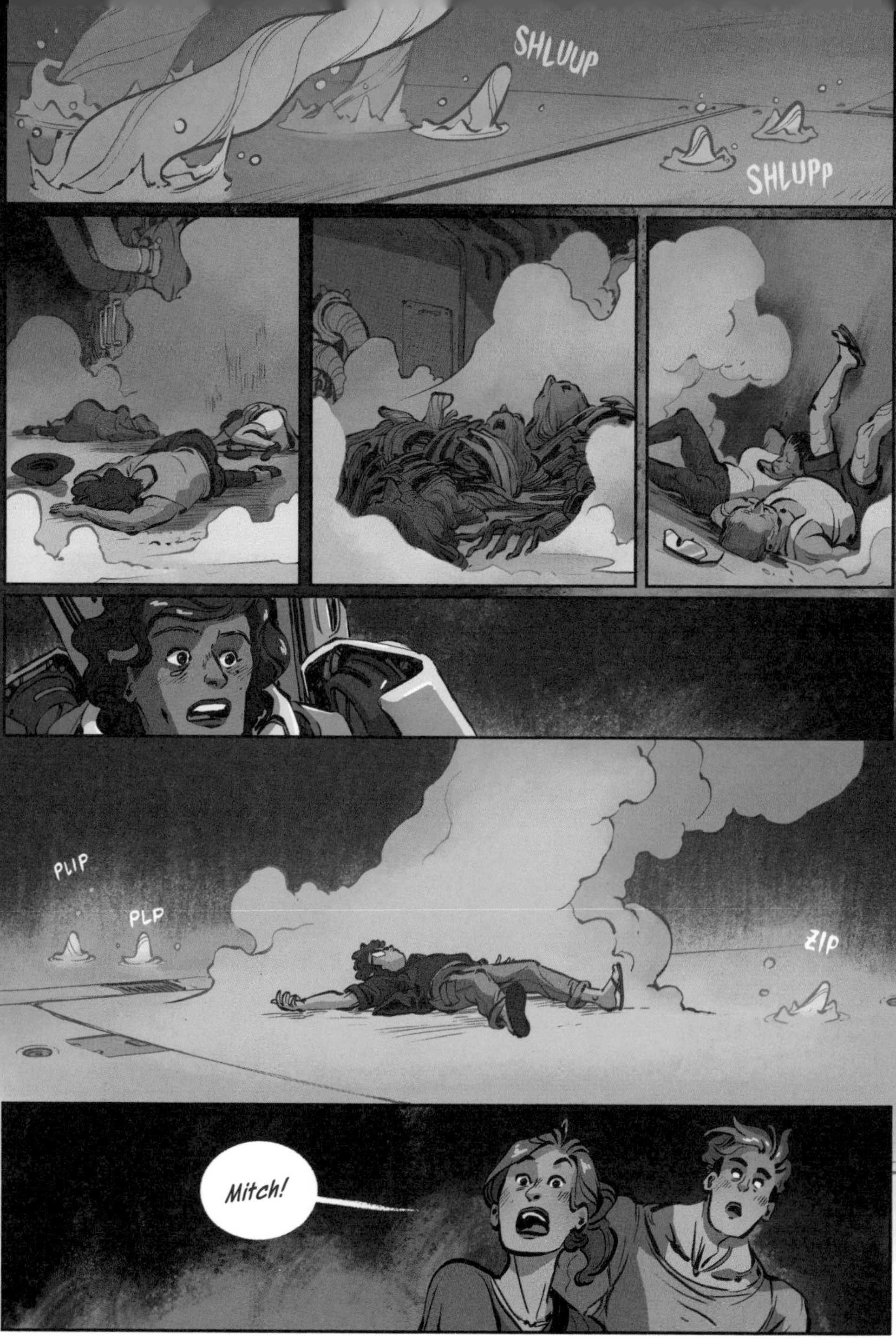
SHLUUP
SHLUPP
PLIP
PLP
ZIP
Mitch!

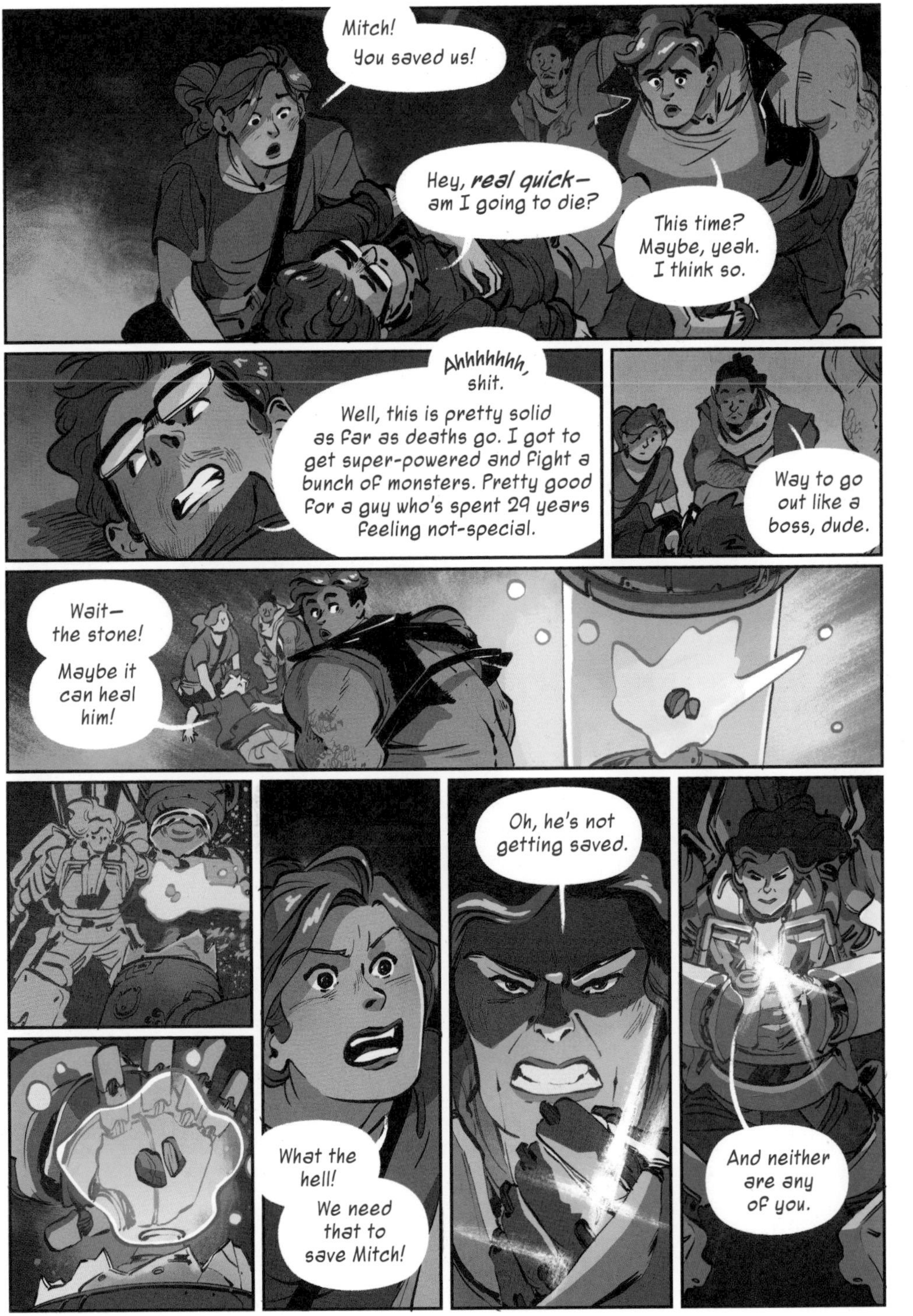
Mitch!
You saved us!
Hey, real quick—am I going to die?
This time? Maybe, yeah. I think so.
Ahhhhhh, shit.
Well, this is pretty solid as far as deaths go. I got to get super-powered and fight a bunch of monsters. Pretty good for a guy who's spent 29 years feeling not-special.
Way to go out like a boss, dude.
Wait—the stone!
Maybe it can heal him!
What the hell!
We need that to save Mitch!
Oh, he's not getting saved.
And neither are any of you.

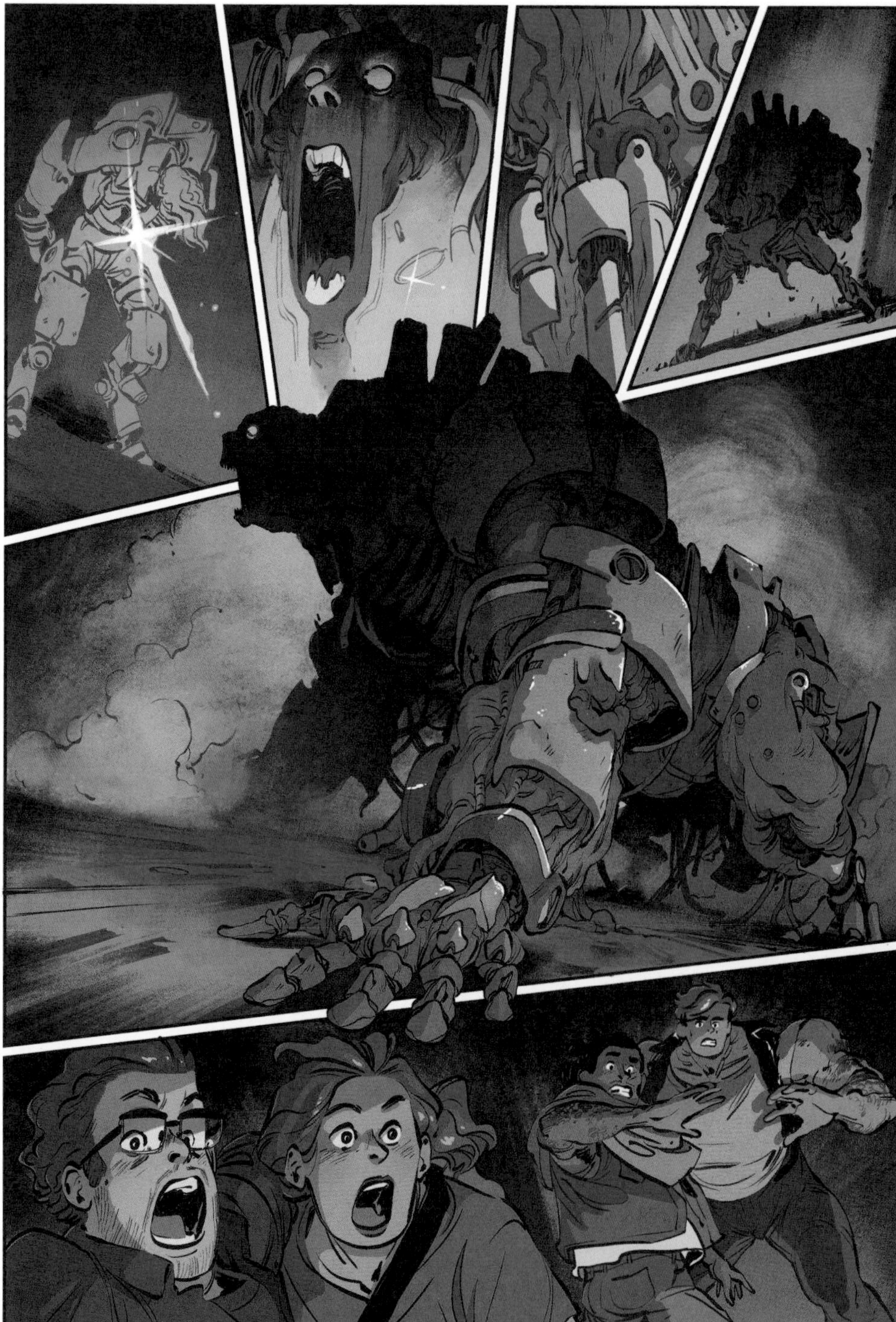

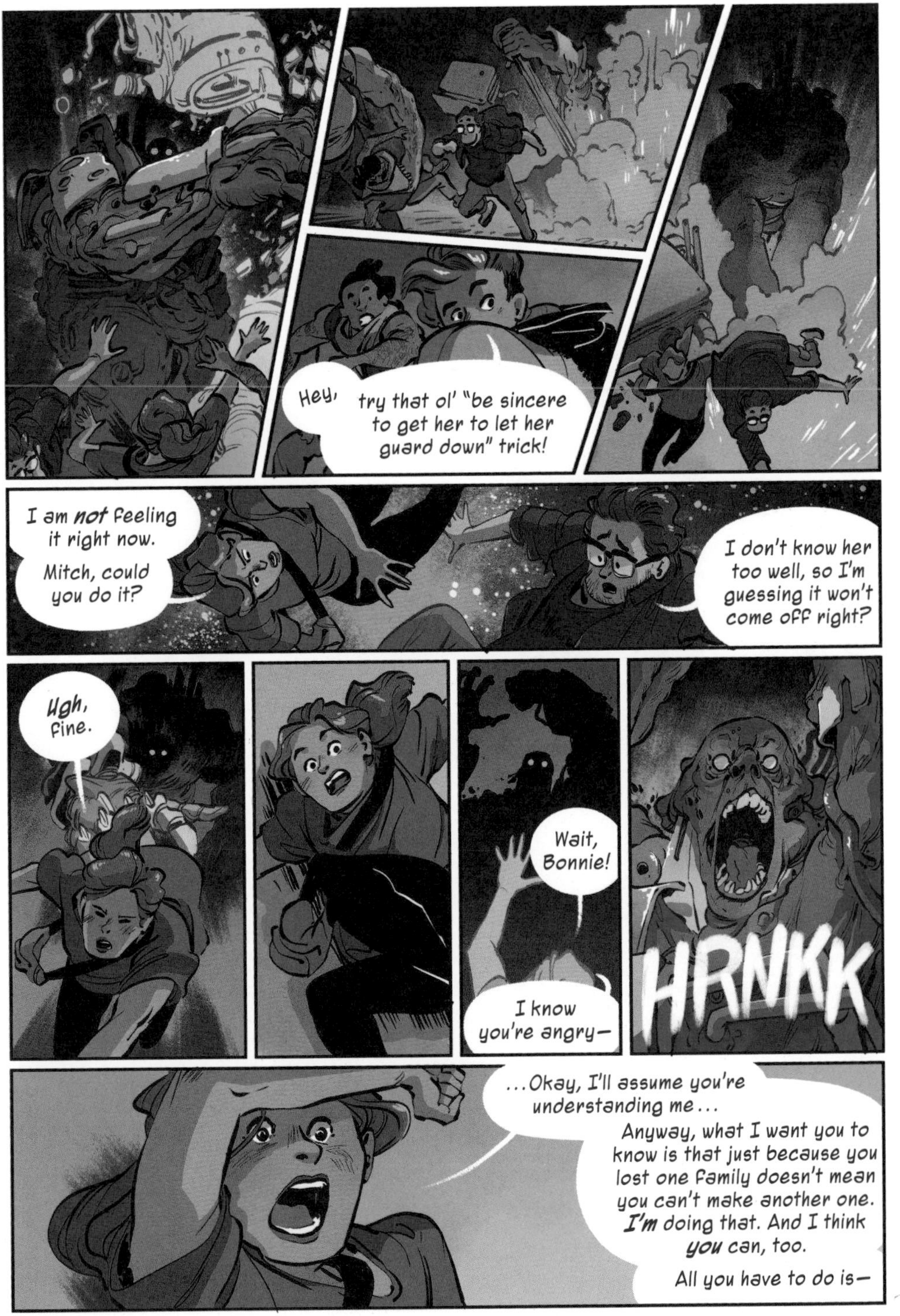
Hey,
try that ol' "be sincere to get her to let her guard down" trick!
I am *not* feeling it right now.
Mitch, could you do it?
I don't know her too well, so I'm guessing it won't come off right?
Ugh, fine.
Wait, Bonnie!
I know you're angry—
HRNKK
...Okay, I'll assume you're understanding me...
Anyway, what I want you to know is that just because you lost one family doesn't mean you can't make another one. *I'm* doing that. And I think *you* can, too.
All you have to do is—

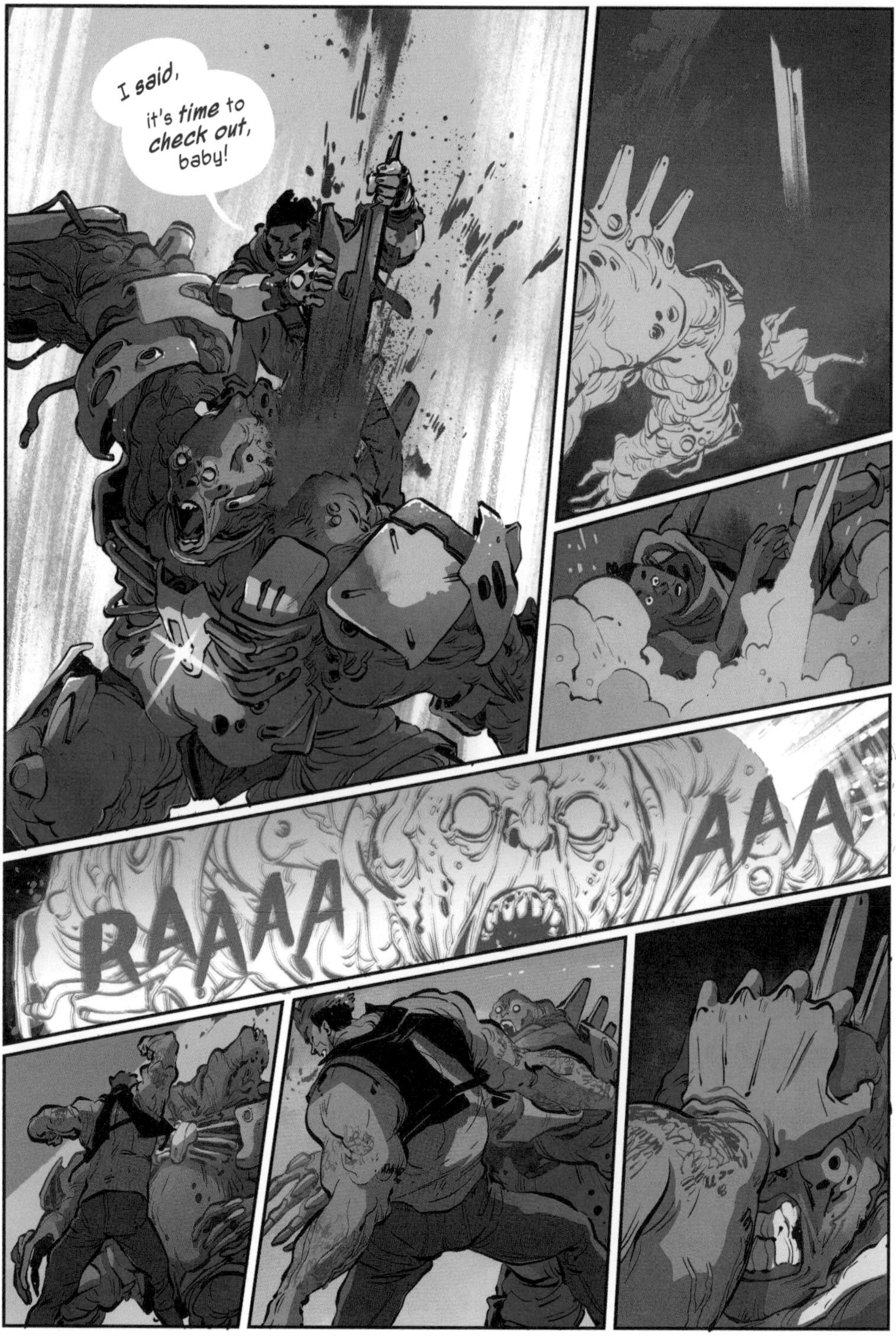
I said, it's *time* to *check out,* baby!
RAAAA
AAA

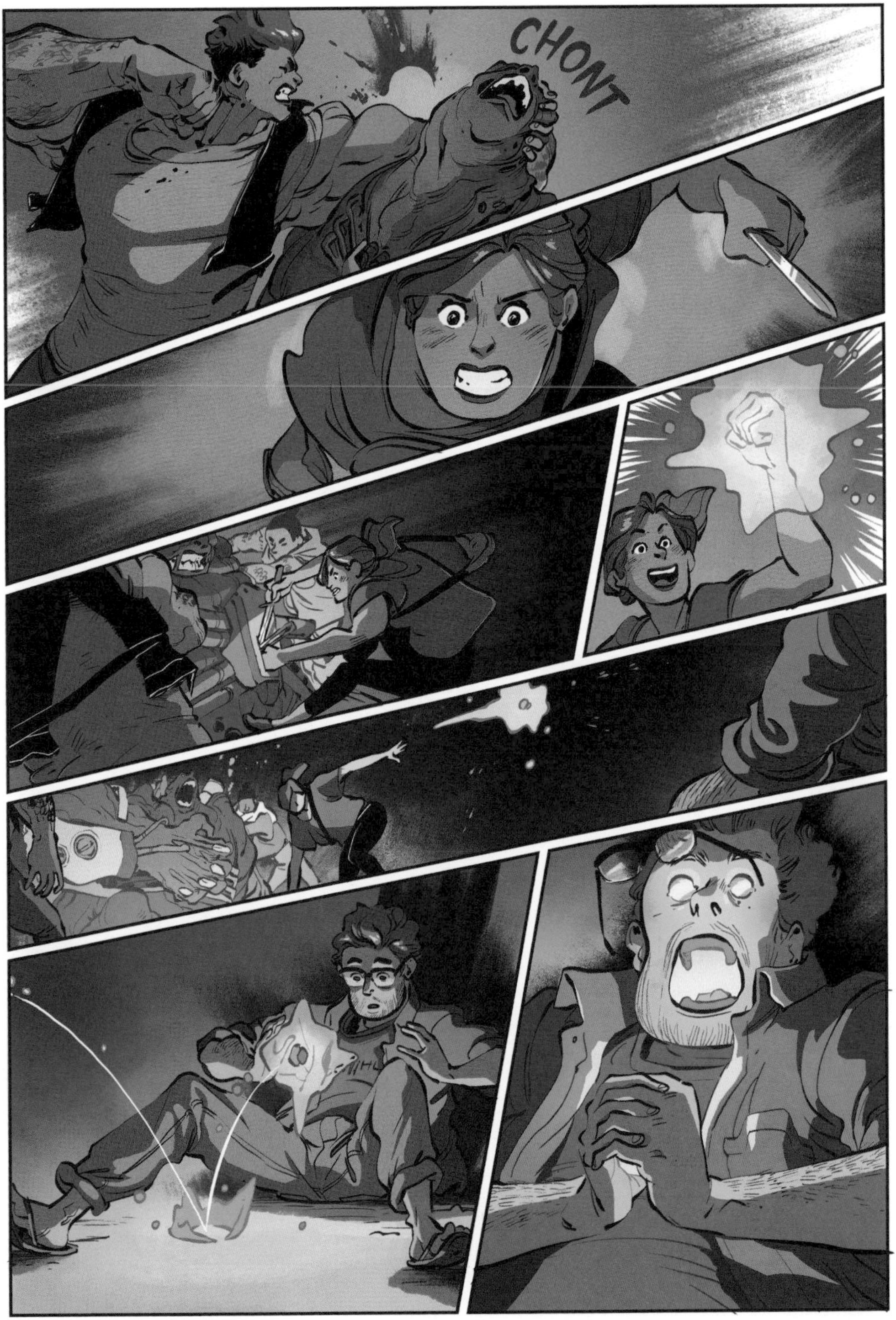
CHONT

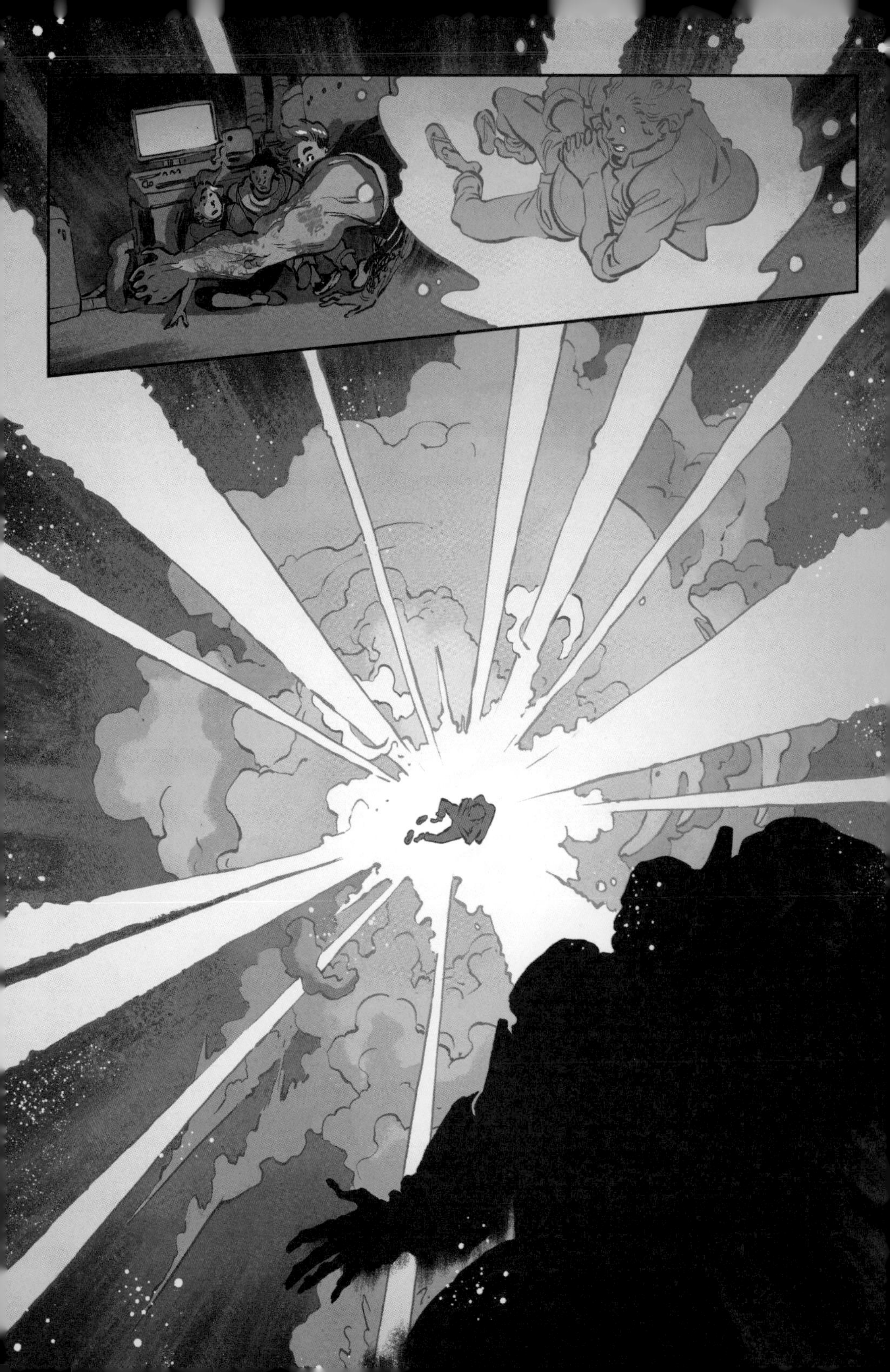

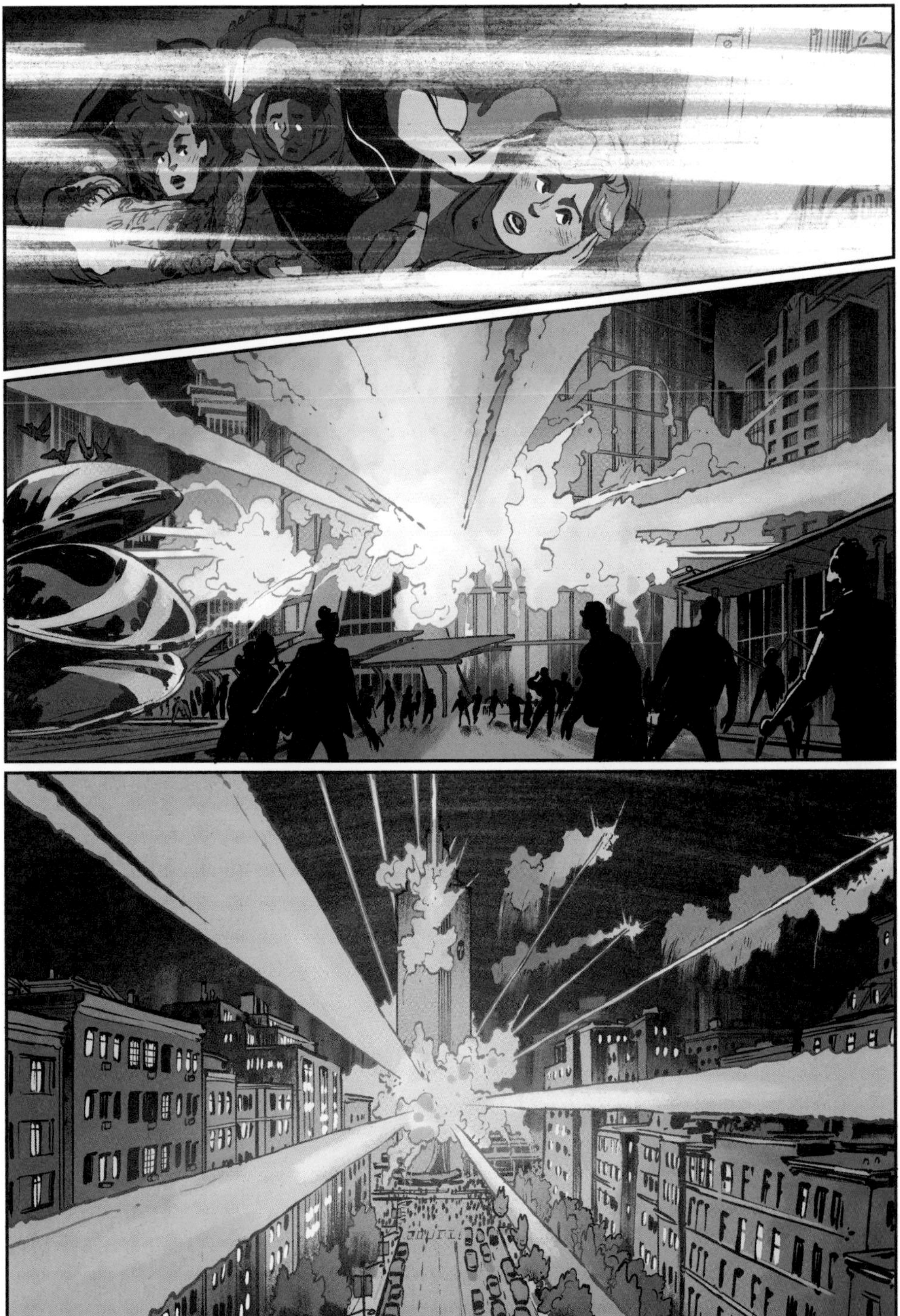

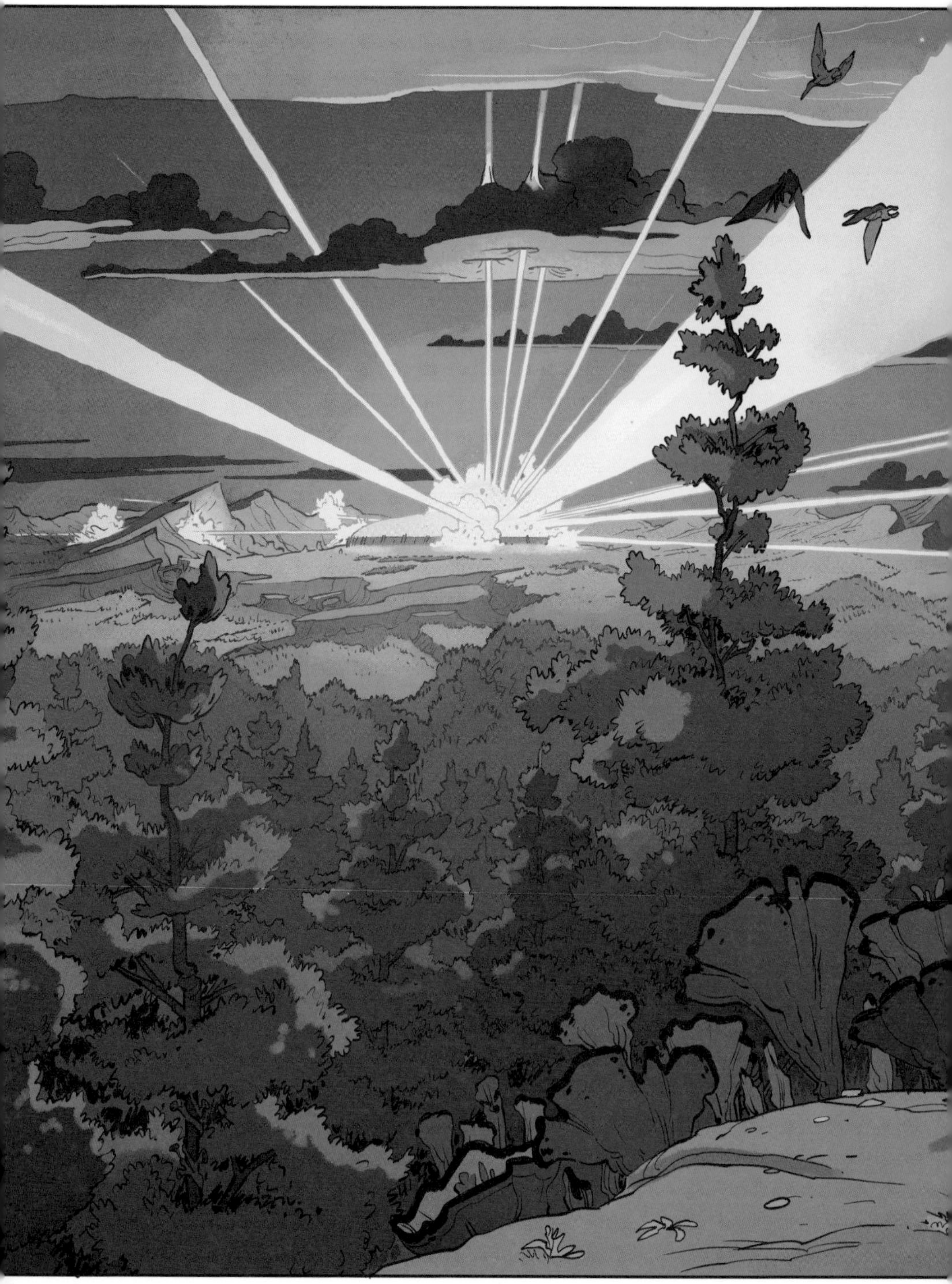

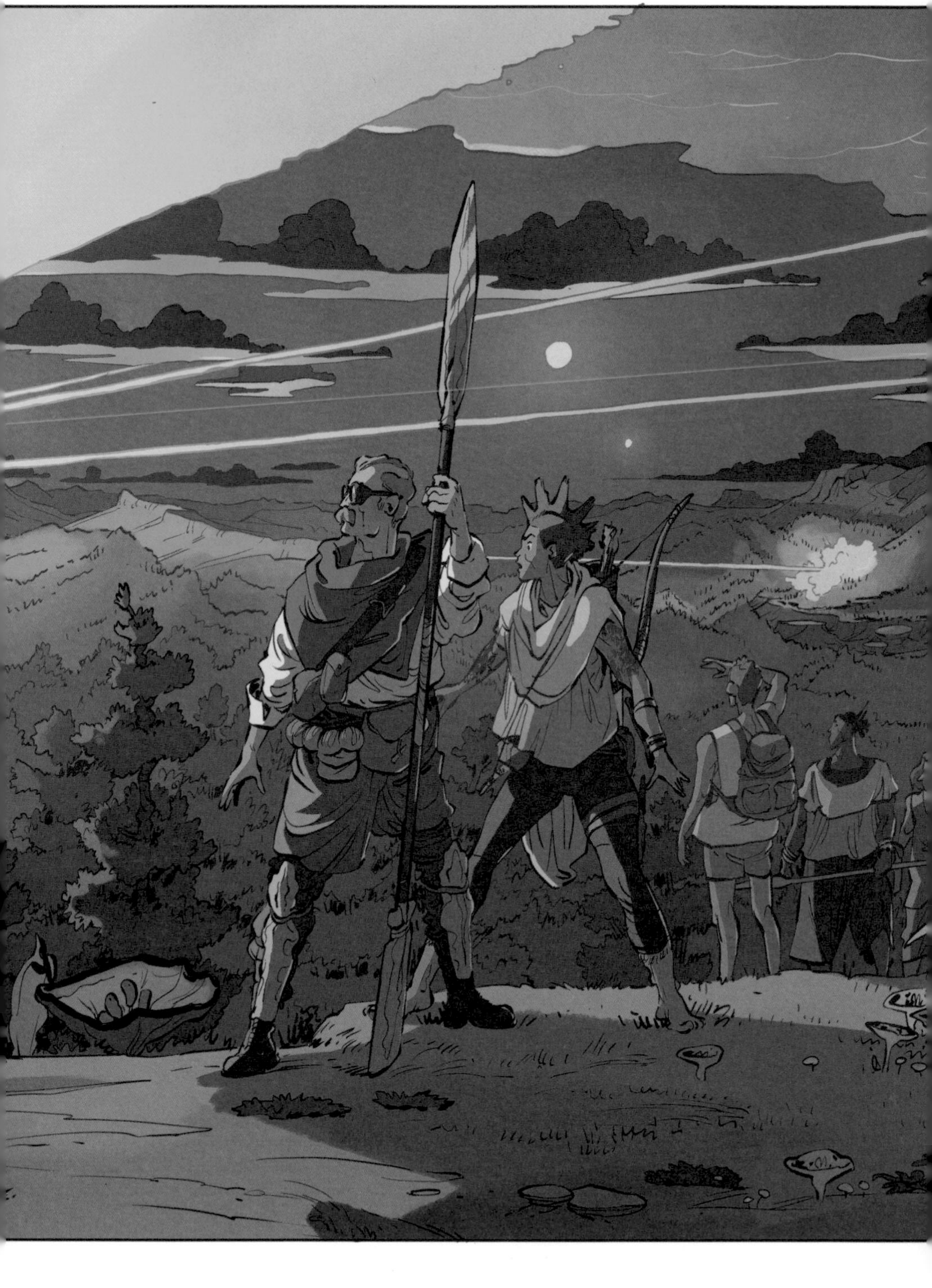

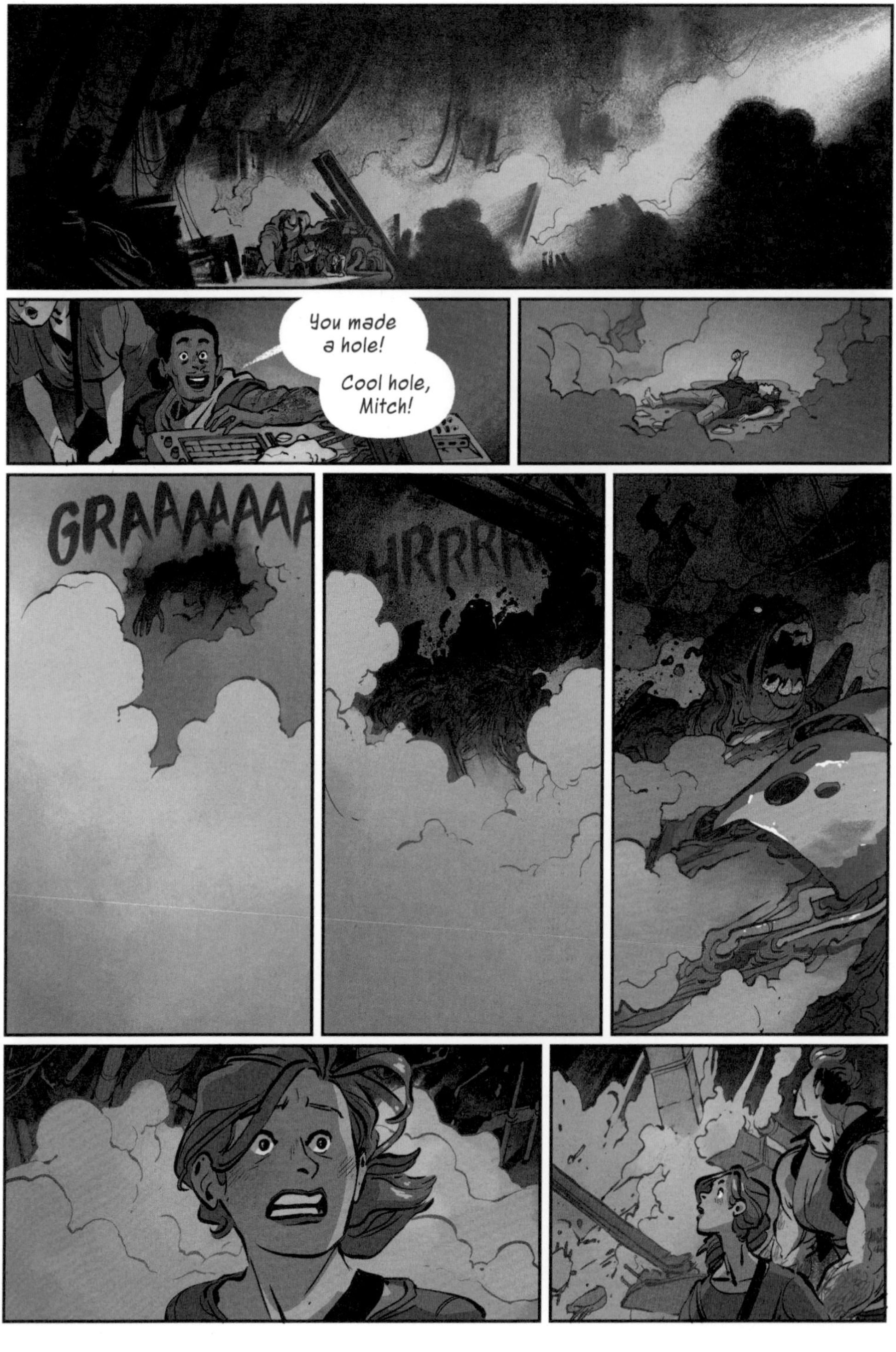
You made a hole!
Cool hole, Mitch!
GRAAAAAA
HRRRR

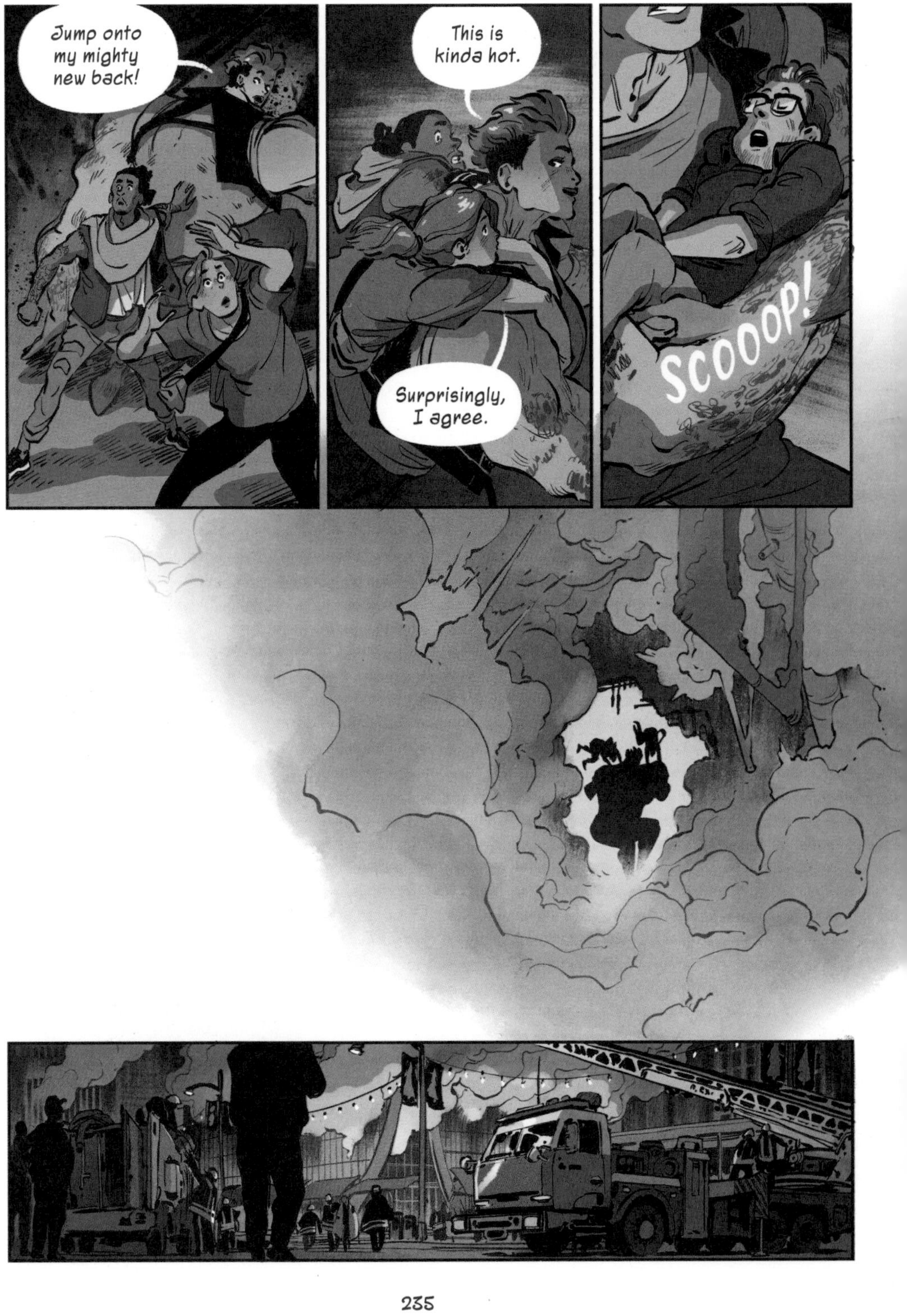
Jump onto my mighty new back!
This is kinda hot.
Surprisingly, I agree.
SCOOOP!

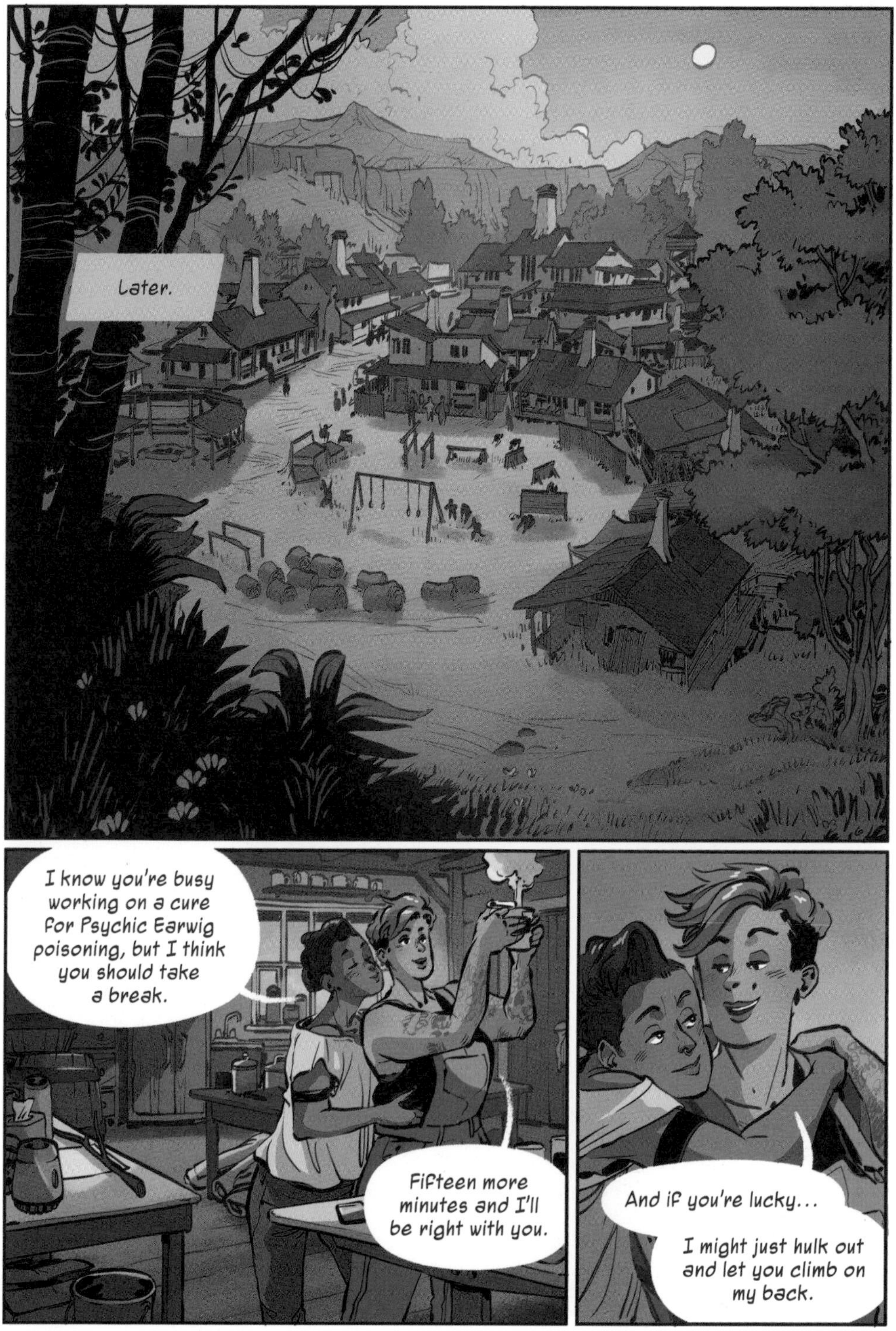
Later.
I know you're busy working on a cure for Psychic Earwig poisoning, but I think you should take a break.
Fifteen more minutes and I'll be right with you.
And if you're lucky...
I might just hulk out and let you climb on my back.

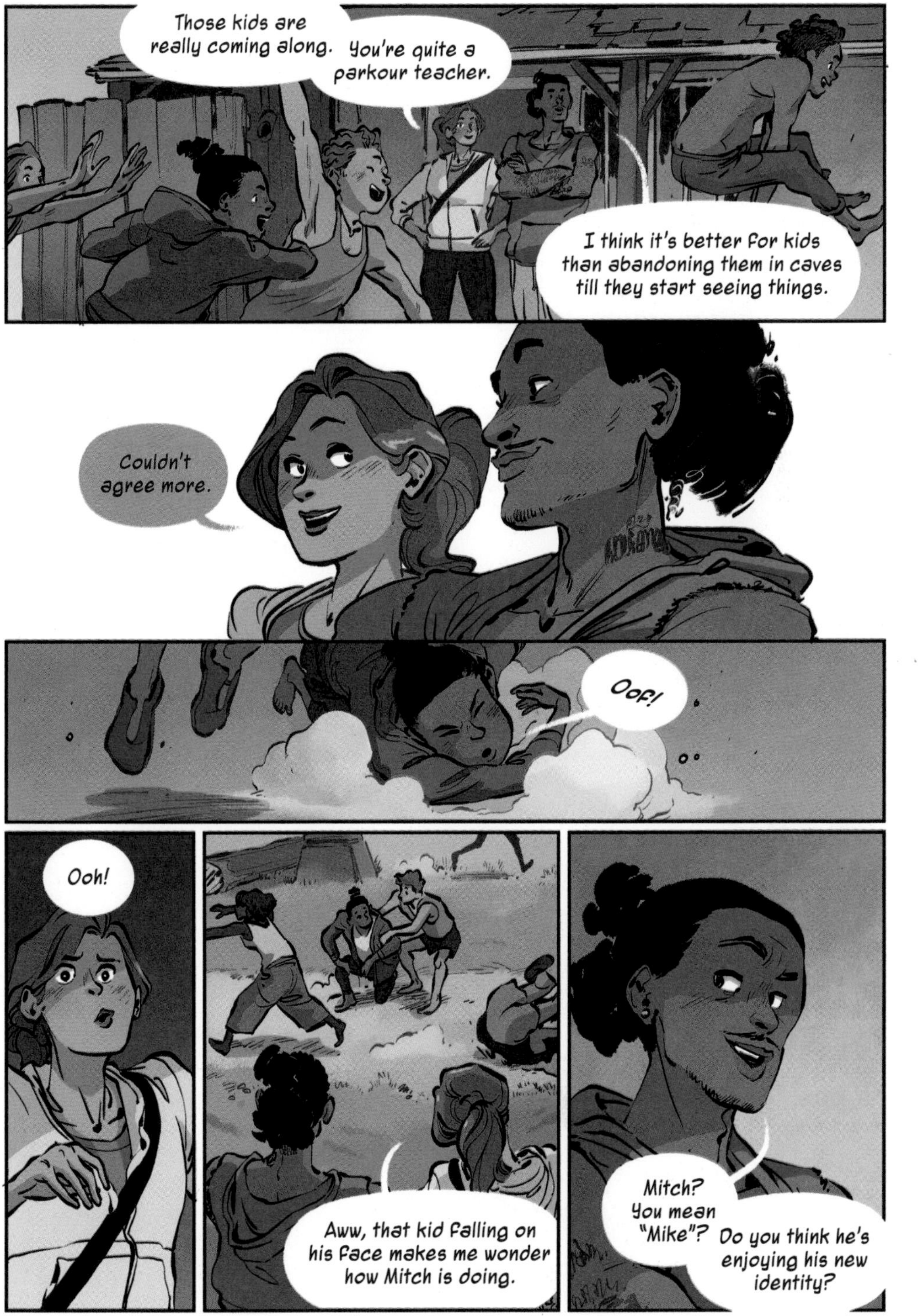
Those kids are really coming along.
You're quite a parkour teacher.
I think it's better for kids than abandoning them in caves till they start seeing things.
Couldn't agree more.
Oof!
Ooh!
Aww, that kid falling on his face makes me wonder how Mitch is doing.
Mitch? You mean "Mike"?
Do you think he's enjoying his new identity?

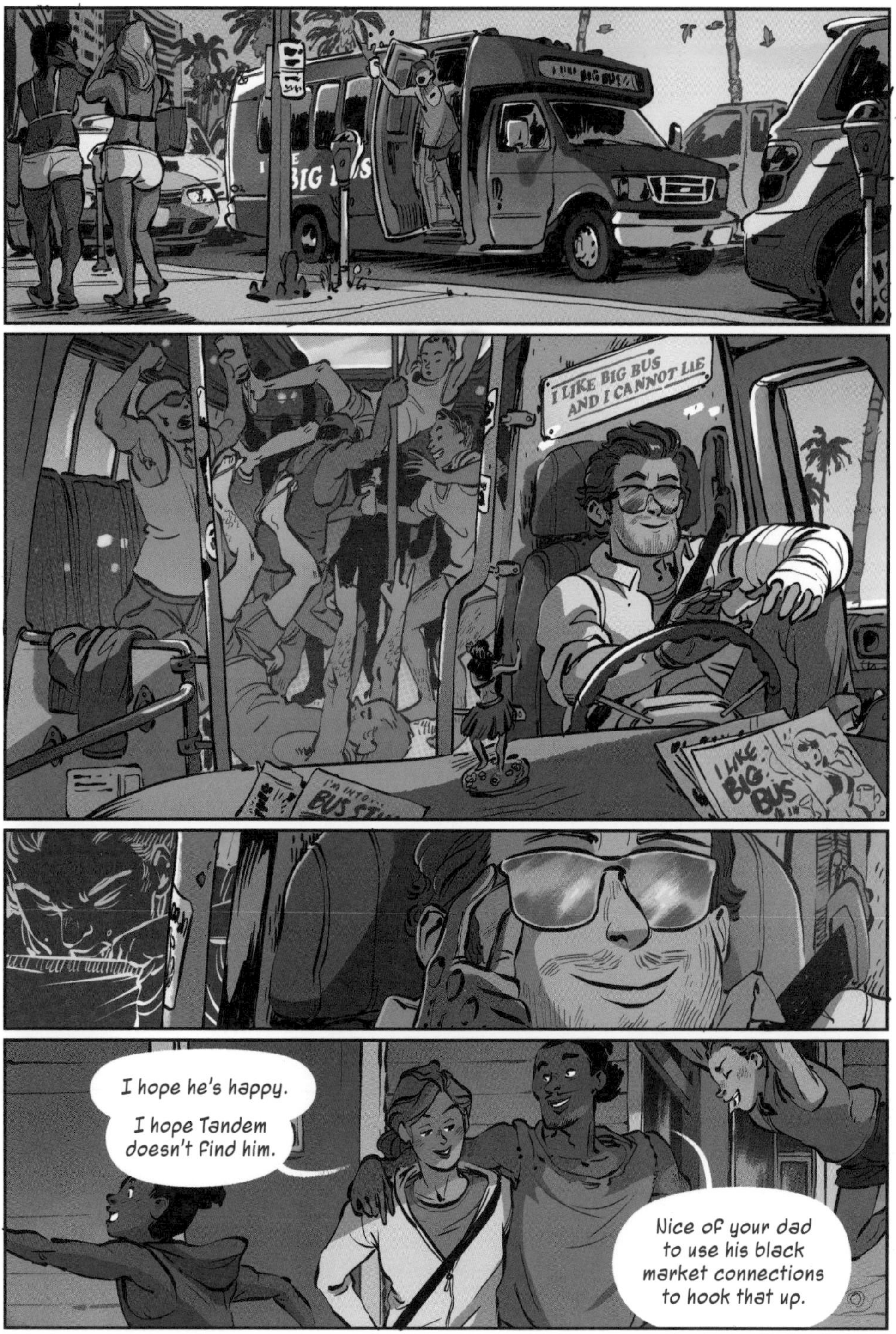
I LIKE BIG BUS AND I CANNOT LIE
I LIKE BIG BUS
I hope he's happy.
I hope Tandem doesn't find him.
Nice of your dad to use his black market connections to hook that up.

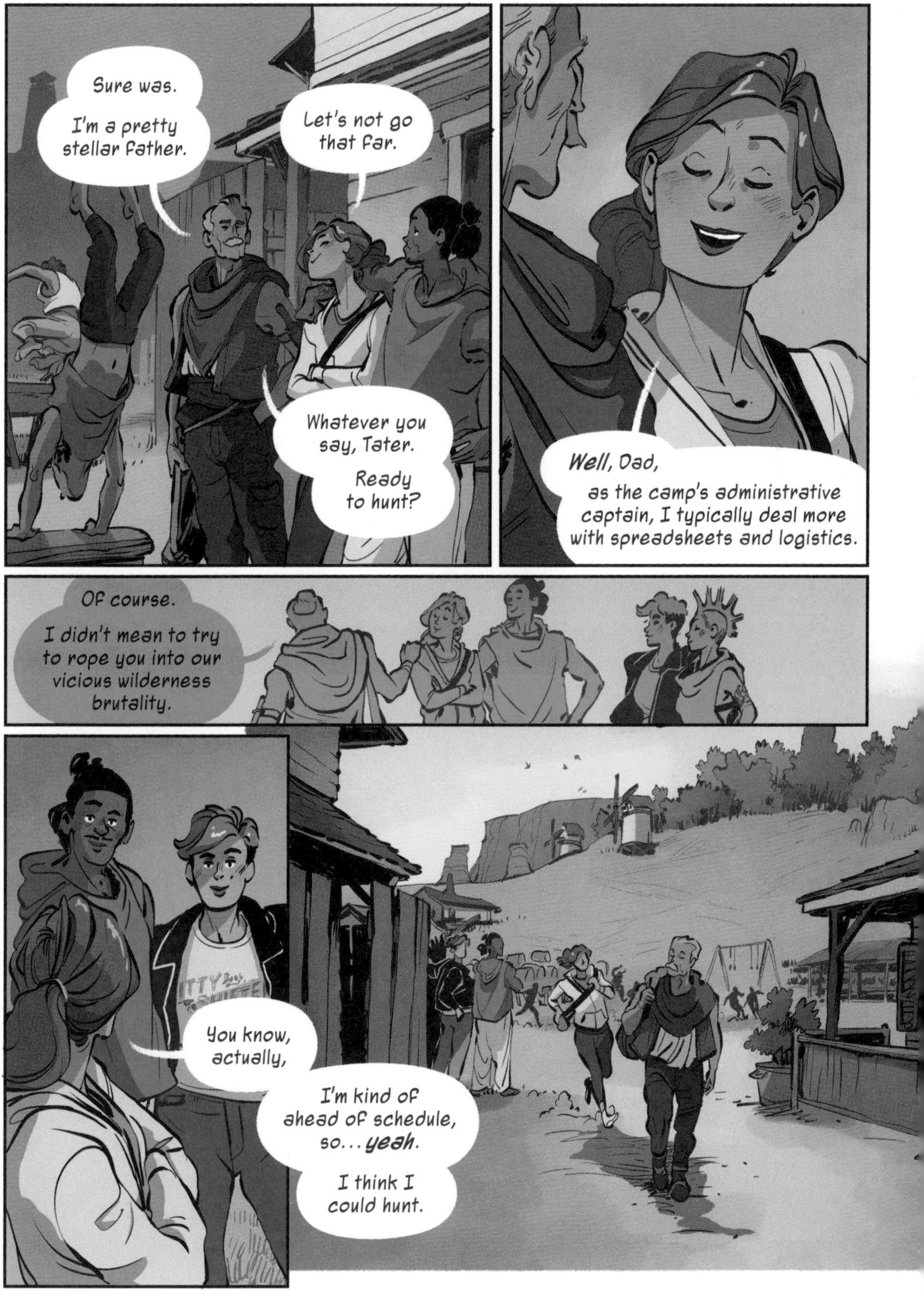

Sure was.
I'm a pretty stellar father.
Let's not go that far.
Whatever you say, Tater.
Ready to hunt?
Well, Dad,
as the camp's administrative captain, I typically deal more with spreadsheets and logistics.
Of course.
I didn't mean to try to rope you into our vicious wilderness brutality.
You know, actually,
I'm kind of ahead of schedule, so... *yeah*.
I think I could hunt.

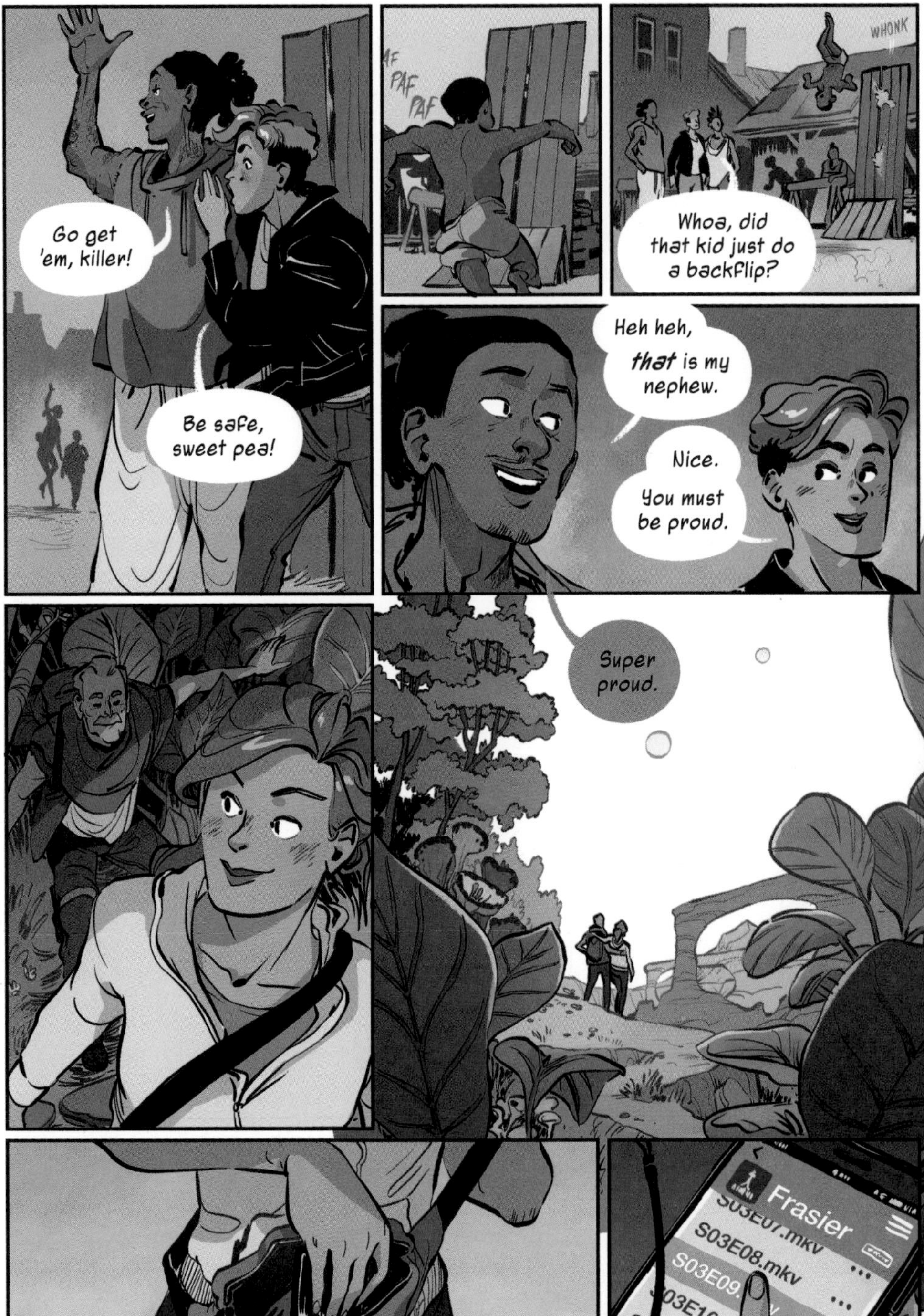
Go get 'em, killer!
Be safe, sweet pea!
PAF
PAF
WHONK
Whoa, did that kid just do a backflip?
Heh heh, *that* is my nephew.
Nice.
You must be proud.
Super proud.
Frasier
S03E07.mkv
S03E08.mkv
S03E10.mkv
S03E11.mkv

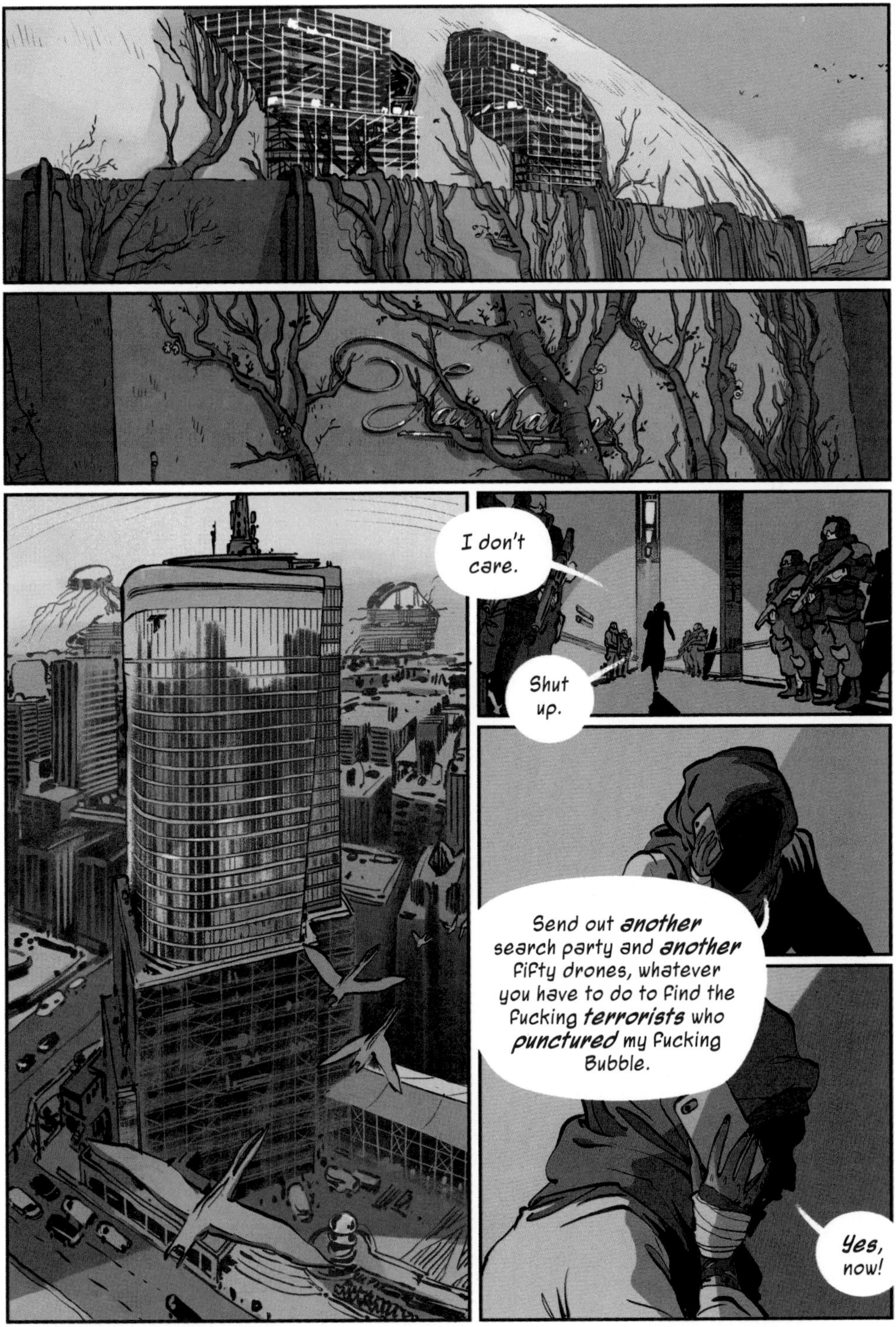
I don't care.
Shut up.
Send out **another** search party and **another** fifty drones, whatever you have to do to find the fucking **terrorists** who **punctured** my fucking Bubble.
Yes, now!

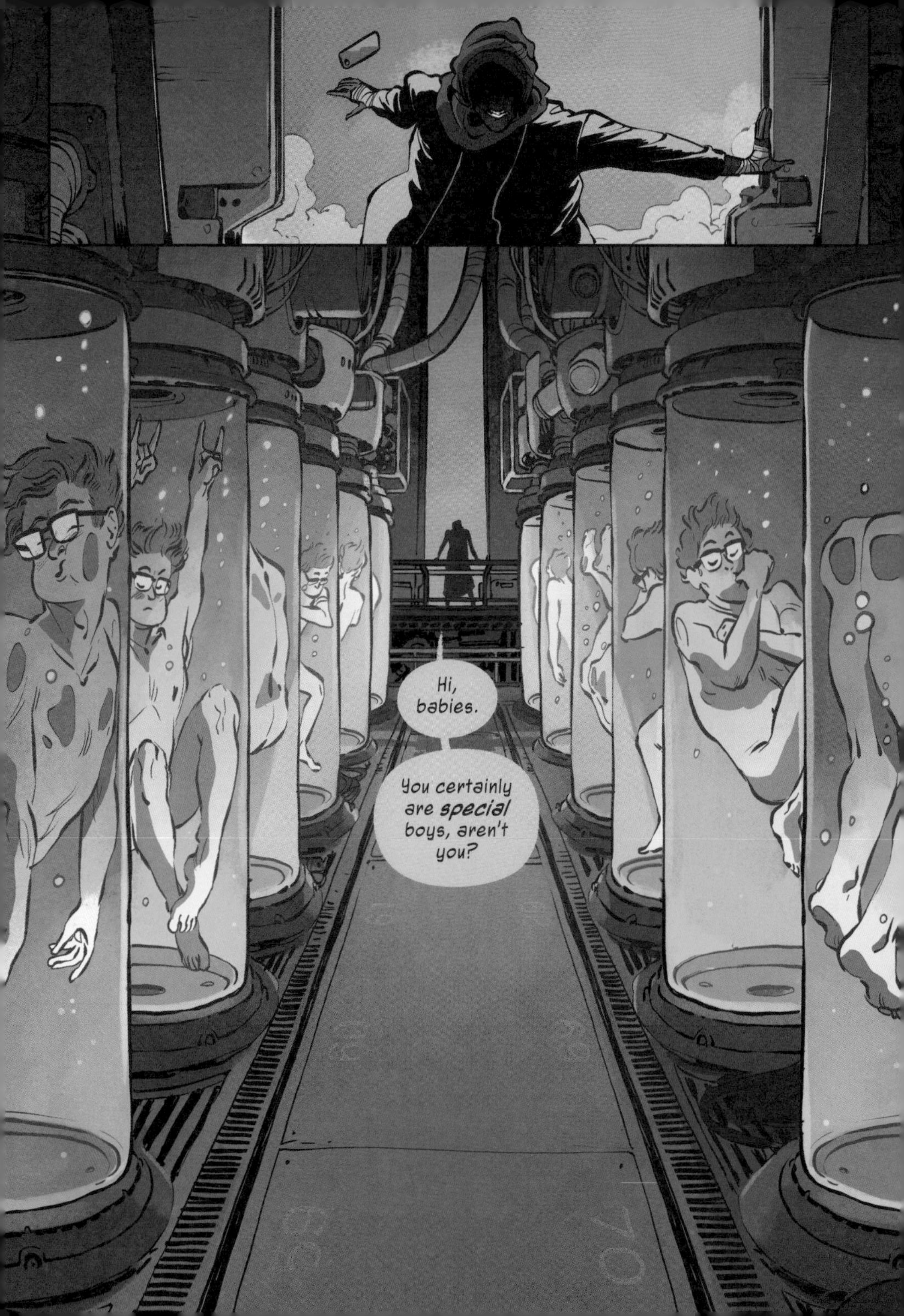
Hi, babies.
You certainly are *special* boys, aren't you?

bubble

The End

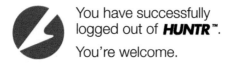

You have successfully logged out of **HUNTR**™.

You're welcome.

Log back in within **00h 55min** to maintain your **HUNT-STREAK** and your place on the **HUNTR**™ competitive leaderboards!

Use these fun methods to boost your **HUNTR™ CREDITS™** and unlock higher tiers of incredible Imp-smashing weapons!

Recommend this book to a friend to earn 🌀 **30HC**!	Earn 🌀 **30HC** FREE!
Identify a union organizer to earn 🌀 **50HC**!	Earn 🌀 **50HC** FREE!
Link your contacts and messaging account now to earn 🌀 **20HC**!	Earn 🌀 **20HC** FREE!
Rate this app 5 stars in the app store to earn 🌀 **50HC** and progress to **HUNTR™ GOLD™**, now with **HLTH-CARE™**.	Earn 🌀 **50HC** FREE!

Log Back In Now

bubble

A GRAPHIC NOVEL

Like

Morgan, 26 ●

Fairhaven

🖐 Straight, single, serially monogamous

☰ 5'5", Extremely Fit

🍾 No smoking, drinks sometimes

❤️ Looking for: IDK?

Quote:

"What are you doing for the rest of your life?"
—Dr. Niles Crane

Hobbies:

I collect interesting tea bags. I just think it's cool how they come in so many shapes. I currently have eleven!!! :-)

Likes:

Brunch, the spray of hot blood gushing from an Imp's freshly opened jugular, Jim (The Office) memes.

Hill I'll die on:

Dolly Parton makes every playlist better! Fight me on this! (Just verbally, if we actually fight I'll destroy you ;-))

My weirdest quirk:

I chew my hair! (My roommate would say it's the fact that I grew up fighting for survival on an alien wasteland but is that really that weird IDK?)

You should message me if:

You are not now ~~ave~~ ~~r be~~ ~~lved in~~ Ultimate Frisbe~~

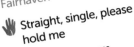

Like

Mitch, 28

Fairhaven

🖐 Straight, single, please hold me

🍽 Might join a gym

🏋 Lightweight

❤ Looking for: My forever person or someone to drive to the airport (I genuinely enjoy it)

Quote:

"I don't like sand. It's coarse and rough and irritating and gets everywhere."
—Anakin Skywalker

About me:

Gamer. App economy multitasker. Doom Squid Daddy. Normal man with no genetic mutation to speak of.

Likes:

Ordering apps (appetizers) for the table, Bud Light, hiking, cunnilingus with a lot of intense eye contact, my normal blood that currently has no trace of alien toxins.

Dislikes:

Craft beer, cruelty, dryer sheets (eczema).

Current goals:

100% Menu Completion at Thank God (or Whatever) It's Friday. 100% all trophies on Sonic Mania. 100% successful interactions with baristas.

I'm really good a... a strange

...indness. Keep... me ... able i... e I don't h...

... ability that ... me ...

HUMPR

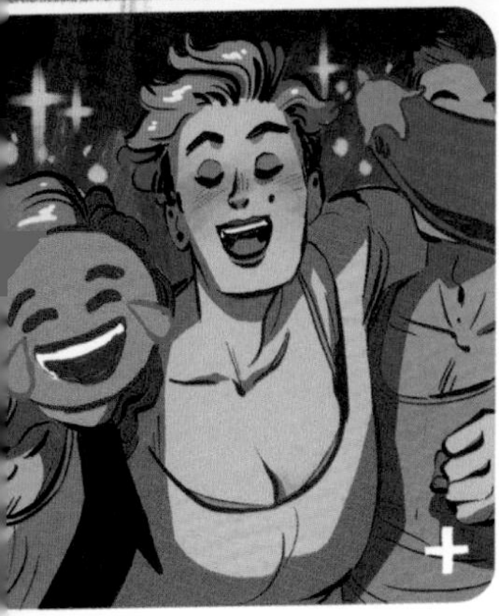

Like

Annie, 27

Fairhaven

- Pansexual, polygenerous
- Just right
- Yes to all
- Looking for: my partner in crime. No, really.

About me:

Proud Sea Monkey mama and Etsy store owner (Unlicensed "Nick" Cage faceprint leggings, link in bio. Also, lawnmower for sale, slight rusting but gets it done, $25 or will trade for weed/sourdough starter).

Interested in:

Short-term, hangs, flings, friends with benefits, benefits with friends, mixes, mingles, associations, fleeting encounters. Translation: Do NOT ask me to go to a wedding with you.

My ideal Sunday:

Hiding from the cops after my ideal Saturday.

 Like

Van, 27

Fairhaven

🖐 Sapio-sexual, single-ish, open for whatevs

🗐 6'1", fit like a glove

🎇 420 69 24-7

❤ Looking for: Cosmic love matches

Quote:

"Just breathe."
—Marilyn Monroe

About me:

Dreamer. Influencer. Seeker. Listener. Social media ninja. Kombucha Wizard. Yogi. Truth-teller. Celiac. Human Being.

If you want my life story:

Read my tattoos.

Interested in:

Soul mates. Swole mates. Tantric kickball teammates.

Current goal:

When a human is born, he or she or they know only the great immediacy of the current moment. Their mind is a fertile plain and that is where many moments will leave their seeds. Those moment seeds will be washed in the moisture of experience and it is through this method that knowledge is able to grow into ideas. You and I have ideas, and we believe that they come to us through inspiration or by lots and lots of thinki[ng] [b]ut tru[ly] [wh]en we [h]ave an idea, it is the [s]eed of our ex[perience] gr[owing in]to [it a]nd your brain is always hungry [for] ... Whe[n] [ani]ma[ls] [h]arvests enough fruit, they are able to form an id[entity, and] [th]ey [do] it in a way that

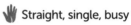 Like

Bonnie, 49

Fairhaven

Straight, single, busy

5'7", kept tight

Drinks: regularly
Smokes: What am I, 19?

Looking for: Micro-dates
between 6:19AM and
6:55AM

You should know:

I definitely make more money than you. Don't be weird about it.

Dislikes:

Goofing off. The Brush, curse that foul pit and everything that festers within! Pineapple on pizza.

Likes:

Firing people for goofing off, ergonomic office furniture, espresso.

Like

Book Club, 42 •

Fairhaven

🖐 Poly-consciousness

⯐ 6'1", ever-expanding

🍸 Drinks: only on days that end in "Y" ;)

💜 Looking for: No threesome jokes, please

Quote:

RESISTANCE IS FUTILE
—THE BORG

About me:

WE ARE BOOK CLUB. WE ARE LOOKING FOR CHILL, NO-DRAMA ADDITIONS TO OUR EVER-EXPANDING HIVE MIND. MUST LOVE DOGS.

Likes:

SURRENDER. MARGS.

Dislikes:

FREE WILL. CARBS.

My ideal Sunday:

TAKING A BREAK FROM ENVELOPING THE WORLD FOR SOME SELF CARE. SPA DAY ANYONE?

Favorite books:

EDUCATED, WHERE'D YOU GO BERNADETTE? ALIEN VS. PREDATOR: THE MOVIE NOVELIZATION

Like

Hunter and Hunter, 36

Fairhaven

✋ Monogo-curious

☰ Averaging 5'7", Pilates-toned

🍷 Drinks: wine! Smokes: ew!

💚 Looking for: Our unicorn! (As in "a third for sex," not a mythical horn-horse.)

Quote:

Is it Coffee O' Clock Yet?
—a funny sign we got at Target!

Please be:

Clean, no-drama, peanut-free (we think one of our kids has an allergy). 420 Unfriendly.

Likes:

Predictable chain restaurant dining, celebrity anti-vaxxers, buying in bulk.

Dislikes:

Public transit. Our kids leaving for college.

You should know:

- We are a Christ-focused couple and try to lift up the Lord in all that we do.
- Our kids are our world.
- We're curious about anal.

Our safe word is:

Ba~nga!

We're most pr~

Our lawn, our annual Christmas lights display, our ~ pelvic floors.

TC-MOBILE

HUMPR

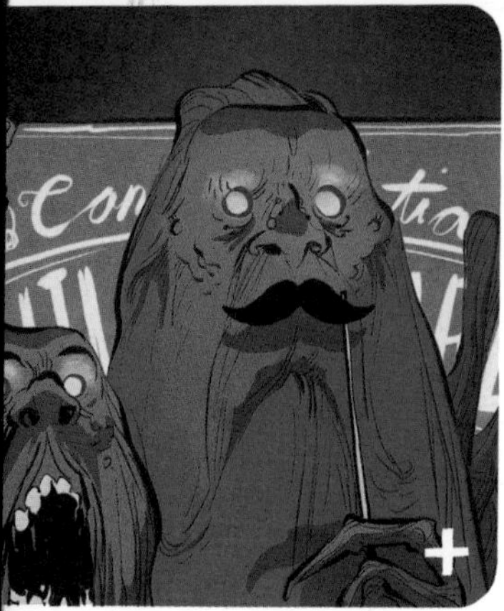

Like

The Beard, 31

Fairhaven

Straight! Straight, you hear?!

40'3", fuzzy

Drinks: Only the good shit
Smokes: Only the good shit

Looking for: Good listeners

Message me if:

You want to hear how I'd adapt Catcher in the Rye for the screen.

Hill I'll die on:

DCEU>MCU

Likes:

Craft beer, classic cinema, crushing all who would oppose me, collecting vinyl.

Dislikes:

Women who have tattoos but won't explain their tattoos to me.

My ideal Sunday:

Making desert island lists, seeing how much space I can take up on the bus, some light shitposting.

Nothing makes me hotter than:

Anyone who leaves a five star rating on one of my podcasts.

The *Bubble* and *Adventure Zone* graphic novels have a lot in common—they're both adapted from hit comedy MaxFun podcasts, they're both the result of powerhouse team-ups between the original series creators and first-class cartoonist co-adaptors, and they're both edited by freelancer Alison Wilgus. As production on *Bubble* was wrapping up and *The Aventure Zone: Petals to the Metal* was right about to debut, the two teams sat down with Alison to talk shop about how their books were made.

Jordan Morris and Sarah Morgan—Co-writers and co-adaptors for *Bubble*
Clint McElroy, Griffin McElroy, Justin McElroy, and Travis McElroy—Co-writers and co-adaptors for *The Adventure Zone*
Alison Wilgus—Editor

Alison: So, friends. One of the most exciting things about your books is how both teams use the adaptation process as a sort of revision pass for your stories. Looking back, what was that like from your perspective?

Travis: I think that it's really wonderful working with a team—both with the people who we created the podcast with to begin with, but also new people, because they provided new insights. It was almost impossible to be precious with things that didn't work at that point, because you had so many different points of view and so much different input that it was really easy to say, "This wasn't a thing that worked." Maybe *Bubble* is different, 'cause *Bubble* was fully scripted. But for *Adventure Zone (TAZ)*, we were kind of writing it as we went. So by the time we reached, you know, episode 20, there's the realization of, "That thing we said in episode 12 doesn't make sense anymore. I wish we could go back in time and cut that." And

then we were able to do that and, like, tweak stuff with the comic book.

Jordan: One of the issues with adapting *Bubble* is just, like, tonnage. It's episodic, so there was stuff that happened in the podcast that was fun and funny but didn't really serve the big story. So yeah, that was a big thing with *Bubble*, kind of killing some darlings. I think a concrete example is, there's a little one-episode thing where Annie dates this guy and no one can remember his name. They just call him "standard guy" because he's, you know, just a very down the middle standard man. He kinda mutates into this rage monster and it's very funny, but it didn't fit into the big story that we were telling. We had to make a lot of chops like that. The book's a little more about the characters than it is about the plot. And, you know, I think a good example is the character of Van, we added a lot of backstory for him. That was actually Sarah who did a lot of the Van backstory-ing stuff . . .

Sarah: I'm the girl, who's supposed to be uh . . . characters and feelings. (laughs) It was mostly taking away, wasn't it? All this "theater of the ear" stuff of the podcast where you're painting pictures with words, and then . . . obviously you have actual artists doing that in the comic, and you realize that you can take your massive chunk of dialogue out and put in like, one sound effect, and you say everything you wanted to say. That was the hard thing for us, wasn't it? Putting pen marks through what everyone had worked so hard on.

Justin: It was a nice opportunity for me, who was kind of more focused on my character than the overarching plot. [*Adventure Zone Balance*] was a story that we told over a couple of years and we were figuring out who these characters were as we were telling it, and I was able to—by taking another pass at dialogue stuff but also some more plot elements—sort of make that a more consistent character. There was a span of a couple of months where I flirted with the idea that my character was an idiot, and that he was just making stupid choices. And then as we went on, um . . . he wasn't? That was the wrong thing. And now I can just go back and pretend that never happened. I didn't do that. I knew what I was doing the entire time. It's like a reverse magic trick.

Jordan: I would love to hear that stuff from everybody else. Like what is some early stuff that you thought would be fun and funny in the moment but had to, you know, throw out?

Griffin: Ours was a unique case. Because *TAZ* wasn't scripted, another implication is that there was a lot of *us* in it, like us as in, like, me and Dad and Travis and Justin. And we decided fairly early on, aside from myself appearing as, like, the omniscient DM (Dungeon Master) of this world, in the comic the rest of that stuff was going to go. And particularly for the first book, *Here There Be Gerblins*, when you removed all of the silly out-of-character stuff, we actually needed to add a little bit more narrative meat to it. And like Travis said, we had a lot of opportunities to do that because now we had finished the story and we knew where it was going to go, we could start seeding things earlier on. But it's not so much a problem anymore as we're, like, continuing to work on, ah, let's say some of the denser chapters of *The Adventure Zone* saga. But definitely earlier on, we had a lot of room to work with after we cut out all of the . . . you know, jokes about how old Dad is, or . . .

Jordan: (laughs) *How old is he?*

Clint: *So old!* (laughs) But that was at the very heart of one of the big decisions we had to make going in. We made the conscious decision to remove Clint, Justin, and Travis from the story and focus on Merle, Magnus, and Taako. Structure-wise, that, I think, really helped determine how the graphic novel was going to go.

Travis: I'm interested in comparing this to the *Bubble* perspective, because like for us . . . I don't say this to disparage the podcast at all, but in many ways it was kind of a rough [draft] in and of itself, right? One of the things we were able to do in adapting the first two and now *Petals to the Metal*, was to go through and say like, "This moment doesn't make sense for who this character actually is, even though it took me eighteen episodes to figure it out." So in doing the comic books, I've been able to find all of these new moments for Magnus and more of a balance for his, like, humor and seriousness. *Bubble* seems like it was a much more polished product before the podcast ever aired. Are there things that you're discovering about the characters and the story and stuff through the adapting process or, like, "I didn't realize that about this person"?

Sarah: I'm going to toot Jordan's horn for him because there's so many different bits of world-building going on with *Bubble*. There's the podcast, there's the comic, and there's the movie that's going to be coming, and I know the story is different across all of them. So for me it's more like writing, like, really good superhero characters. It's like being handed Batman to write something about. The story is always solid. It's much more about how deep we can get with these characters and make them do interesting things.

Travis: Do you think that's a product of like, comic book format versus podcast? Like because you can see their faces and facial expressions? Because that's something we've found a lot, is body language and facial expressions have contributed so much to character work that we couldn't do in the podcast.

Jordan: Yeah, I mean, after pencils came in, we did a fair amount of rewriting. Sarah, I'll go out on a limb and say that because we have both written a lot of late-night TV, you know, a value in that kind of writing is just like . . . sheer pages. How many pages of jokes can you turn in?

Sarah: Yeah, we're both very adept at doing jokes by the yard. And it's such a process of taking the jokes out a lot of the time.

Jordan: That was kind of a big thing of like, oh, you know . . . we're trying to call this character boring, we have someone say three reasons why they're boring, and it's covering up all the art on this page. Why don't we say *one* of those things, which is our favorite or the funniest—

Sarah: Yeah. Or have Annie roll her eyes. I mean we took out like this chunk of dialogue because it was funnier if it was replaced by Annie burping, because of how beautiful the picture was.

Justin: I really wish we had had extra jokes to cut out. God, that would have been quite the luxury. Instead of staring at the page like, "Certainly there's a joke somewhere. *Certainly.*"

Everyone: (laughs)

Justin: That's actually one of the more embarrassing things to discover as you're going through adapting and looking at transcripts and stuff. Like . . . man, a lot of the stuff I said was not actually funny but was just said loudly. (laughs) I said it with a confidence of someone saying something funny, and then we moved on. And then you see it on the printed page, it's like, "Okay, I can't live with that for time immemorial, I'm going to have to actually come up with a joke here."

Travis: That's where we would usually, like, turn to Carey and say, like, "Hey, couldn't you make that funny with like a weird eye twitch . . . ?"

Justin: Maybe like a funny-eyed face.

Griffin: Maybe his pants are falling down when he says it.

Alison: I want to back up a little bit. This is actually a question that Sarah wrote and a bunch of you have touched on this, and I want to, like, focus in on it for a second. Is there anything you've learned about your characters while you were making these comics? You mentioned earlier about how, like, Van, for instance, got fleshed out a lot.

Sarah: Well, with Van . . . you know, we're comedy writers, and we know that the best thing to do is find out where someone's pain comes from. (laughs) It doesn't get funnier than that for mining. And Van was the fantastic joke bucket where you can write amazing gags about Hacky Sacks and being extremely online and all that stuff that Van is. But actually, if we're going to go on a self-contained journey with him, we've got to find out why he's so messed up. So we really put him through the ringer, I think, in the comic. In the end, I hope everyone understands why Van is as . . . *Van* as he is.

Travis: A lot of this came from, like, seeing Carey's facial-expression work on Magnus. I think she did a really good job with toning down what could be seen as kind of a toxic, violent, you know, brash, like, action-first character and really softened him to give him these moments of genuine, kind of sweet weakness? You see these moments of trepidation and fear [on the page] that I think deepened my understanding of what he could be. He can still be reckless and still be bold and still be, you know, rushing into things while having kind of, like, discomfort at small talk or an inability to address social awkwardness. And that for me made him a much more interesting character.

Griffin: Again, I think this hearkens back to us knowing now what we didn't know then. The whole [*Adventure Zone*]

Balance story is like a huge, time-spanning thing. There are characters in the books who know a lot more than [the main] characters do, and we did not necessarily acknowledge that when we were doing the show. Those have been some of my favorite changes that we've been able to make. The three main characters are going through this journey and it's pretty easy to follow along, but [the comic has] allowed us to kind of acknowledge that these other characters—who you don't necessarily know everything about—are also going through some shit. That's been really really cool to explore.

Alison: Yeah, in *Bubble* specifically, one of the things that I was really surprised by was how much more I cared about some of those secondary characters over the course of making the book. Like, I would fucking die for Bonnie. She's evil as shit, but I really love her. And with Eli, I feel like Tony brought so much to that character? Like what Griffin was saying, I think I understand where Eli's coming from much better than I did when I was listening to the podcast.

Travis: I think from our experience, that's something that I think is a very "only in comics" kind of thing. Being able to see the facial expressions of the secondary characters as they react to some of the extremely dumb shit that our main characters say is *so* endearing. *Rockport Limited* is a great example of this because you

have, like Jess the Beheader, Graham the Juicy Wizard, Jenkins—like, these characters that are so wonderful?

Jordan: By the way, I think that the design of Graham the Juicy Wizard is, like . . . perfect.

Travis: Thank you.

Justin: Wait, Travis, did you just say "Thank you"?

Travis: Yes, I realized that I was just taking full credit for Carey's art.

Justin: "Thank you, oh *thank you*," I see you massaging the cramps in your hands. Those two hands you use to craft every angle of [Graham's] face.

Griffin: Carey's not here, so by all means, let's accept the kudos for her work.

Justin: Travis, what are your, some of your favorite kinds of blues that you use?

Travis: Cya—is cyan a blue? I know that's right.

Sarah: Are we going to talk about The Beard though? Because that's quite a . . . quite a beautiful thing to behold.

Justin: Are we talking about Graham the Juicy Wizard's beard?

Sarah: Oh, no, I meant The Beard from the *Bubble* . . .

Justin: Oh yeah, with the . . . are we in it?

Jordan: Yeah, so, uh . . . yeah, Justin, Griffin, Travis, in the podcast, played these three kind of bar trivia a-holes who mutated into an opinion monster called The Beard. And, you know, if you look at the book, maybe the design is, uh . . . similar to three of everybody's favorite podcast brothers.

Alison: I cannot stress enough that Tony handed this to us with zero warning.

Jordan: It was a Tony Cliff call that I think we all really liked!

Alison: So, speaking of art and surprises . . . I wrote in my question, and I actually do mean this, that, like, when new pages turn up in my inbox, it's like Christmas. Can any of you think of specific moments where you've opened up that PDF or that folder of images and you've had a moment of, like, "This is so exciting! I'm so excited!"

Clint: The train crashing into Jenkin's garden was pretty remarkable. That was a huge one for me.

Griffin: It's a cop-out, but the entire battle wagon sequence in *Petals*, which is, like, to Carey's great credit, about a third of the book? I was looking forward to seeing that and she did not disappoint. It fucking rips ass. It's so cool.

Travis: I'm looking at them now . . . I think the thing that I maybe like best about our books is we're really good at

doing the last page? The last page of the first one is the full page with the void fish and Lucretia saying, "Welcome to the Bureau of Balance." The last page of the second book is the Red Robe saying "Two down, five to go." And the last page of *Petals* is . . . I just think we're really good at ending a book.

Sarah: I love how Tony does some amazing noises. Don't you think, Jordan?

Jordan: Oh yeah!

Sarah: I mean his drawings are beautiful, but if he's also writing sound effect for something, like someone squeezing fruit and it says, "Squinch Squinch." Annie smokes a bong and . . . I had to cut and paste this earlier, it's "flocker ploppa flopper flopper popper"? (laughs) He fills the whole frame, oh it's gorgeous. Sound effects! That's an "only in comics," right?

Jordan: Yeah. I absolutely agree with you, Alison, there's nothing more fun than looking at new comics pages. I'm like . . . why have I not been doing this my entire life?

Sarah: Mm-hmm!

Jordan: There's a moment where a character is talking to an asshole at a party. And in the comic, the characters have to push their way past the word bubble where the guy is talking about CrossFit. And we don't have a ton of like, fourth-wall-breaky stuff in the book, but that was such a perfect visual example of what it is like to be trapped in a conversation with someone who won't shut the fuck up about something you don't care about. So yeah, it's just, like stuff like that, taking that kind of throwaway-y joke and making it into something that's, like, a million times more impactful.

Oh, I was going to ask the *TAZ* crew—when you're turning in the script to Carey, how much direction do you give her?

Justin: Dad has a really good way of laying down, like, a vibe of a scene, or, like, a rhythm of a scene. Like, if something is an *Ocean's Eleven* pastiche or whatever. Dad takes the initial pass on all these adaptations, and I think that's one area where he and Carey really work well together . . . Dad will lay out the sort of tone that a scene or a page is going for, and Carey is really good at picking up on the cues.

Clint: Yeah. And Carey almost acts like a cinematographer. Especially when we first started, I was describing it like a film script, because that's the way I wrote comics back in the eighties. *High-angle shot, zoom in,* you know. But as we've gone along I've learned that Carey has a much better eye for things like that. So in the later iterations, [my direction] has been more along the lines of, what does it show? I think that's where our relationship has matured and grown and changed.

Travis: I think a bit of it also comes down to, like . . . when we partnered with Carey, it was because we liked her style. Like, she had done *TAZ* fan art prior to that and, like, she did a really really great poster for our first Boston *TAZ* show. And we were like, "Yep, this is the style we want for the graphic novel." And I think having made that decision, we kind of all mutually agreed that we're playing in Carey's style for what the graphic novel will look like. So then the character designs and stuff was all like, finding the combination of Carey's style and things we had in our heads for the character. I remember being really, really specific about the amount of body hair that Magnus had and, like, what his beard looked like and how his hair looked. I think, like, her first version of Magnus, his hair was a little bit shorter, and I was like, "Oh, I want his hair to be bushier. And I want his beard to be bushier. And I want more knuckle hair." Like, I was really specific about the knuckle hair, and she will tell you about that any time, that I was like, "More! More knuckle hair!" (laughs) *Now* I would say that, because we've kind of agreed on a visual language, that process is pretty streamlined at this point.

Alison: Sarah and Jordan, I'd love to hear any thoughts you have on the character design process for *Bubble*. There was a little bit of back-and-forth, I remember . . .

Sarah: Hmm. I think it was narrowing down the amount of vast possibilities we had in front of us. Jordan, what do you think? We were sort of starting with a blank page.

Jordan: This is just kind of a funny story I guess . . . the characters don't necessarily look like the voice actors, but they all have one quality that the voice actor does. You'd have to ask Tony, but I'm guessing that's just a fun way to start a character. You already have a person that you can kind of go off of.

We actually spent a lot of time on their clothes. Like, Annie would be a little bit of a thrift store vulture, kind of, like, piecing together an outfit based on stuff she finds around town. A great Tony joke is that all of Mitch's T-shirts are from failed video games, he has a *Fallout 76* T-shirt and a *Battleborn* T-shirt. Those are kind of fun little things that I think say a lot about the character.

Sarah: We had great chats as well about, like, everything from ethnicity to body shape to all that kind of stuff, which is such a lovely responsibility to have I think. Everyone involved for every stage of the operation had considered, well-intentioned thoughts about everything like that. Which was really a refreshing conversation to have. Doesn't always happen in other parts of the creative industry.

Alison: Jordan and Sarah, this is for your book, is there anything else you both want to specifically talk about today?

Jordan: Uh . . . let's see, I'm going to go down this little page-a-roo here . . . Oh, I want to hear from the *TAZ* crew about any visual or text-based jokes that you really like in your book!

Griffin: It's so stupid. There's a scene in *Petals* where they're climbing an elevator shaft, and an elevator car falls and they have to grab on to a cable, and they're all hanging from this cable and Taako is, like, trying to clamber up the other two and accidentally pulls Magnus's pants down, and his butt comes out. It also says, like, "Butt," like as if it is making the sound "Butt" as it comes out. It is one of the more sort of puerile moments of the entire *Adventure Zone* canon, I would say, and Carey sort of, like . . . made it more than what it is? And it just cracks me up. I think it's very very funny. That style of humor is not even necessarily my jam, but just seeing the audacity of how Carey realized it . . .

Clint: There's a scene in *Petals* where Merle seduces a plant, which was very much an audio joke in the podcast. But the reactions of Taako and Magnus in the art make it five times funnier than it was when it first came out [in the podcast].

Travis: I literally cannot count the visual jokes that are so good in the books, because I'm still finding them? From time to time, Carey will just go on Twitter and be like, "Here's an Easter egg joke from *Gerblins* that no one's found yet." Like every sign in every town on every tavern has some kind of joke baked into it. It's really good.

Alison: Jordan and Sarah, you also have to answer this one.

Sarah: (laughs) If I could own one frame of artwork that I'd have as like poster for my wall, I would like Annie with the burrito in the opening shot. It's not even a joke, it's just such a beautiful way of introducing the character. It's a whole page of a woman happy with a burrito. And I think that's a beautiful thing in life. Even if the cheese has pooled.

Jordan: I just want to mention all the back-and-forth we did about what the name of Mitch's party bus was gonna be.

Sarah: (laughs) If I do nothing else in life . . .

Jordan: Do you remember what we were kicking around and what we eventually went with?

Sarah: We'll send them to you, Alison, because there's got to be a list of alt names for the party bus . . .

Alison: I Like Big Bus and I Cannot Lie is what we ended up with, right?

Sarah: (laughs) Yeah.

Jordan: Hey, listen, perhaps we were procrastinating on fixing story problems and spending a day and a half thinking of funny bus names. (laughs) But yeah, stuff like that was such a joy to come up with, like, "Hey, we can fit a little more comedy into this frame if we need." You know, what funny stuff can we have in the background? Tony did a lot of them unprompted and they're all great.

Tony Cliff—Illustrator and co-adaptor for *Bubble*
Carey Pietsch—Illustrator and co-adaptor for *The Adventure Zone*
Alison Wilgus—Editor

Alison: Friends, both of you were co-adaptors on your books, and both of you were involved from the very beginning of that process. Can you tell me a little about how an adaptation like this takes shape?

Tony: Well, I grew up on an Animation Farm, so a lot of the process felt very familiar. No matter the weather, I would have to get up at 4:00 a.m. every day—yeah, weekends, too—and milk the Storyboard Cows. You get a script, talk through it with the directors, spitball what you hope are clever ideas and witty improvisations, and then go off and draw a bunch of rectangular pictures. For *Bubble*, Jordan and Sarah sent a script that was very similar to the type of scripts I'd been given in the Storyboard Barn, so I approached it similarly. The only difference was instead of designing for a TV or movie screen, I designed for the comics page, trying to surprise the reader on page-turns, for example. I do a rough version of the whole comic that's hopefully legible enough to be assessed by human eyes other than my own but not so detailed that I will cry over all my wasted hours when several pages worth of drawing are deemed "unnecessary" or "criminally irresponsible." This is only fair. When everyone seems happy with the state of that scribbly mess, my Editor-In-Chief shackles me at the bottom of the Comics Mine and I get to work drawing pages. This whole process takes a year.

Carey: I feel really lucky that Clint and Griffin and Justin and Travis and I (and you, Ali!) are all involved at every stage of the process! It's been so wonderful to be able to sit down before the script even starts getting written to talk about which parts of character arcs, big-picture ongoing plots, and emotional narratives make the most sense to bring forward in any given book, given that the McElroys have finished the *Balance* arc and we're all now able to look backward from that ending and edit with the knowledge of where things are going to end up. So sometimes we end up adding scenes to flesh those arcs out, or condensing and restructuring to streamline scenes that absolutely worked on the original podcast but wouldn't be as strong in the new medium of comics, which are all interesting and different kinds of adaptation challenges. I'm

a sucker for juicy and/or fraught (and/or both) emotional moments, so some of my favorite instances of this are when we get to polish a character's emotional arc to a high shine.

We all talk together about all of this in a big-picture sense at the outline stage, and then at each subsequent step of the process—script, thumbs, pencils, inks, and color—we do it all over again! With the goal of decreasing the amount of changes we're making as things get more and more locked down, to save all of our sanity. And to save my wrists! I didn't come up through the nine circles of animation hell; I am but a mere mortal, my vessel is fragile and needs to cut down on revisions past thumbnails as much as possible.

Alison: Translating atmosphere and tone from audio to comics is a tricky business. Can you tell me a little about your strategies for tackling this?

Tony: If I recall correctly, Jordan and Sarah did a bunch of work ahead of time converting the original *Bubble* script into a comic-ready version that kept all the original flavor of the podcast but was also pretty much ready to go, comics-wise. All the characters' voices (in the literary sense) were there, all the important beats were there and easy to visualize, none of the jokes were audio-only jokes. Though I will say, I did make an effort to design the main characters to look the way they sound in the podcast, if that makes sense.

The hardest part was cutting down the entire first season of *Bubble* into one book. That required a lot of back-and-forth, and many creative darlings were murdered—though not without great care and consideration! But yeah, they just got slaughtered, absolutely obliterated.

Carey: Yeah, this is a really difficult problem! The toolkit we have in comics for building atmosphere and tone—and creating a sense of rhythm and pacing—is very different from the one you're working with in audio mediums, but it's definitely true that it's a translation challenge, and not a creating-from-scratch challenge. There's so much information in voice acting and tone about who characters are—and you can extrapolate a lot about the world around them from the ways they react to it! So adapting that information into comics involves a lot of figuring out how to bring that information forward into a visual channel. Way back at the start of the entire process, one big question was how to work within the full range of comedy-drama-angst that exists within the original show. I'm obviously biased because the way I worked was pretty cartoony and stylized going into this project, but I really believe that stylized cartooning gives you a lot of flexibility to move from tone to tone without losing a feeling of coherence; it lets you prioritize expressive char-acters over literal/technical detailed drawing, so it was a very conscious choice to just . . . lean all the way into that. And into over-the-top dramatic theater acting, which is an easier sell when characters are already drawn in a cartoony way. Like, if I were working in a photorealistic way, it would be a *lot* more jarring to have people's eyebrows pop right off their faces or over their hairlines for the sake of selling a big emotion . . . and I'd miss that a lot. Also, drawing that way sounds exhausting.

One thing I definitely miss from the *TAZ* podcast is the music that Griffin composed for it—the pieces themselves, but also the feeling and tone that they lent to the scenes into which they were incorporated. And again, obviously we can't replicate that exact experience in comics, but we do have a whole other visual toolset that we can use to try to replicate that *feeling*. So for these books, it's a lot of using color palettes in nonliteral ways to try to convey shifts of mood and tone, and using the structure of the comics page itself—how many panels are on a page, how those panels are arranged, whether they're in a regular grid or shifting diagonally or opening up into the next spread—to create a sense of pacing and rhythm that enhances the main idea of the page itself. It's always an interesting challenge! When I'm struggling with how to frame a scene, going back and listening to the actual audio from the corresponding chunk of podcast is an immense help.

Alison: In a way, drawing your books was a second adaptation process—you're turning a script into comic pages, and that involves a thousand tiny decisions. But sometimes those decisions aren't so tiny at all. Can you think of a time when you saw an opportunity to do something interesting and just ran with it?

Tony: I don't know—can you? It's been so long since we all reviewed the rough [draft], I don't remember where certain ideas came from. I do like that Bonnie's got those big telescopes in her office, and they're always aimed down into the city, more like microscopes than telescopes (calling on imagery of her parents as scientists and of the Bubbles as petri dishes). Still trying to earn points with my grade-ten English AP teacher. I can't help it.

Alison: I'm going through the book now, and honestly it's just a million bits and pieces? People's shirts, the party bus particulars, the horrible details of "Thank God (or Whatever) It's Friday's," and that *wild* P-Nut hallucination spread. Also the Huntr app pages, those were a surprise to the rest of us, I think?

Tony: Yeah, sometimes it's teamwork. I had to fire out a desperate email, "Help me name Mitch's party bus!" and Jordan and Sarah descended on floating clouds and said, "My son, here is some elegant wordplay for you." Though (IIRC) the script did not call for Mitch's dream-bus to be full of beautiful women and Mitch's actual bus to be full of dudes puking on each other. To me, that felt like the most natural, most honest outcome for Mitch. For, as well you know, when one is tasked with crafting fine art, one's primary responsibility is to act as a speaker of truth.

Carey: Mostly what comes to mind for me are less big, sweeping decisions—that's usually the sort of thing we talk through as a group early on—and more the slow build-up of small pacing choices that result in an overall shift in emotional tone, or the feeling of a scene? Clint has talked a lot about direction as a metaphor for the kind of work cartoonists do when it's time to actually sit down to figure out layouts—sometimes a moment needs to be spread out into multiple pages, or beats and panels are added to get the pacing on the page to match up with the feeling of the script. There have been a lot of initially fleeting emotional beats that end up much larger that way.

For book three, we talked a lot about how to kind of bring this central relationship between two rival racers to the foreground, and I feel really grateful that the team made space for me to push for spreading out these revealing conversations to give them room to breathe! Lending that relationship more room on the page lets the reader's understanding of it grow over time in a way that parallels how an actual relationship might develop. A lot of that came from page-level decisions of spreading things out into multiple panels and pages, both to foreground the emotional depth of it and to create a lot more room to convey info about how characters feel through these small background actions. I'm really happy with where we landed on how that's all built up—I think it really shines!

A lot of the tiny decisions are also up there among my favorites, though! When you're staring at a page for ten hours—low estimate, spread out over the course of the book's life—you end up making a lot of tiny choices to keep yourself amused (or I do, anyway), and sometimes that results in a fun background joke, or like, a tiny acting choice that I'm disproportionately fond of. Like, there's one page way back in the first book where the action was just, they're moving through a cave—it wasn't the focus of the panel, but the movement needed to be conveyed, and I needed to come up with a way to keep my brain engaged with the drawing work . . . so I ended up having Magnus donk his head into a stalactite while Taako dodges and Merle is just, like, completely unaffected. Sorry, Magnus!

Tony: Yeah, I can relate hard to "little details as a way to make the page fun for yourself." If you can squeeze a cute little treat in there to amuse yourself, the process is more fun and the pages are better as a result. Like, the "LIVE LAUGH LOVE" looming over the Book Club. And, as a longtime MaxFun listener, sneaking in things like "Jesse's Homemade Blondies."

Alison: You've both made solo comics and graphic novels before. What do you enjoy most about working as part of a team? Has anything in particular pleasantly surprised you?

Tony: One of the most miserable things about making books like this is that it's very lonely at the bottom of the Comics Mine. But with *Bubble*, Jordan and Sarah were very accommodating when I elbowed my way into their Google Docs and sprayed ideas around like a child with a Super Soaker. I love that sort of collaborative creative effort, where everyone's huddled around the same diamond, desperately working together to make it shine as bright as possible. If I'm working on that diamond alone (and yes, "diamond" is the correct metaphor to use here), it's easy to miss spots. Or to just say, "enh, good enough," because there are a thousand other facets to polish. But when everyone's so funny and generous, it's a really enjoyable way to spend your days. Even if you are at the bottom of a mine.

Carey: In the past, I've been limited by circumstances or publishers that kept team members from speaking directly with each other, so while technically you're working together, in practice you're just firing a lot of shots into the dark. Tony's description of the Comics Mine really resonated with me when thinking about that previous context—it's a process that can often be really isolating, to work alone at your desk on a project for a year—or usually much longer; both *Bubble* and *TAZ* projects are on HUGE outlier schedules and are not at all the industry norm—and just kind of . . . hope that it lands.

But the *TAZ* graphic novels have been real collaborations from start to finish! I really love being able to work with not just *a* team, but *this specific and brilliant team* at every step of the way. I feel very lucky that everyone is so involved—any time we all get together to talk about a note, or an art fix, or a structural change, no matter how much I might resist it—because, again, as established, I'm a very, very lazy gremlin at heart—the book has always, every single time, ended up vastly better for it! That's really rare and special to me, and I don't ever want to take this experience for granted.

Alison: I can think of a few times when the revisions process has gone in the other direction—where, after seeing your art, one or more of the guys suggested dialogue changes to lean harder into an emotional moment or stripped out lines that ended up not being needed. I know I talk about The Magic of Comics a lot, but this really is the magic of comics!

Carey: Oh, yeah, I love when that happens, too! The way that text and image inform and influence each other and link up to create something greater than the sum of their parts is really what comics are all about. Shocking to hear from a cartoonist, I know, but: comics are fun.

ACKNOWLEDGMENTS

JORDAN THANKS:

Tony, Sarah, Alison, Calista, and Natalie for making this with me. It's been a lifelong dream of mine to make comics and I'm glad I got to do it with all of you.

Mega thanks to Jesse Thorn, not just for being a great pal but also for making the podcast on which this is based possible. We could not have made that show without these talented folks: Bikram Chatterji, Eric Martin, Julia Smith, Ben Walker, Nick Adams, Ryan Perez, Janine Brito, Dan Kennedy, Danielle Radford, Riley Silverman, Jon Guiterrez, Nick "Burger Boy" Wiger, Jane Borden, Alison Becker, Eliza Skinner, Mike "Spoonman" Mitchell, Keith Powell, Cristela Alonzo, Tavi Gevinson, Annie Hart, Jonathan Coulton, the McElroy fam, and all the amazing guest stars.

Thanks to all MaxFunsters and Tuppies. You are the good parts of the internet.

Thanks to showbiz pals Jennie Church-Cooper, Brad Garratt, Dara Hyde, John August, and everyone at Point Grey and Matt Tolmach Productions, with extra-special thanks to Camilla Grove.

Thanks to Mom and Steph for being the best family members.

TONY THANKS:

Jordan and Calista, for inviting me to be a part of such a perfect project. Thank you Bernadette Baker-Baughman, for only ever being a five-star Huntr. And finally, thank you, S, for having a job with health benefits and cereal bar access.

SARAH THANKS:

Jesse Thorn and our MaxFun family; Colin Anderson; BBC Radio for the blueprints to great audio comedy; and my genius friend Jordan Morris for so very much, but mostly for asking me to write a thinly veiled version of "how I get" in bar trivia, and then having the legendary Judy Greer play it. Did I . . . win a contest? #teamdiscoverychannel